Trinitas

A Theological Encyclopedia of the Holy Trinity

Trinitas

A Theological Encyclopedia of the Holy Trinity

by

Michael O'Carroll, C.S.Sp.

Michael Glazier, Inc.
Wilmington, Delaware

Dedication

To the Immaculate Heart of Mary, uniquely interpreted by the convert Jew, Francis Mary Paul Libermann, this book is dedicated. She inspired this work and sustained me in accomplishing it. May she bless it to the glory of the Most Holy Trinity, she who is "the preferred Daughter of the Father, the Mother of God the Son, the Sanctuary of the Holy Spirit" (Vatican II).

First published in 1987 by Michael Glazier, Inc., 1935 West Fourth Street, Wilmington, Delaware 19805.

Distributed in Ireland and Great Britain by Dominican Publications, St. Saviour's, Dublin 1, Ireland.

Library of Congress Card Catalog number: 86-45326.

International Standard Book Number: 0-89453-595-1.

Printed in the United States of America.

Foreword

This book is a contribution to the revival of Trinitarian studies so much in evidence in the last two decades. I have tried to include the dominant themes and the most influential writers. The bibliographies, without any claim to being exhaustive, are deliberately ample to help students engaged in research in this area, the groundwork of all that Christianity claims to be. This is the primordial mystery, the ultimate source of all truth and goodness and beauty. It is the glory of Christians to have it as the centerpiece of their faith. It is the hope of all those anxious, puzzled or tormented by the crises, intellectual, moral, social, of our time. It is the clearly marked starting-point of all ecumenical effort among Christians, the ultimate rendezvous for all those who confess Christ the Son of God, bearer of the Spirit, as their Lord and Saviour.

All work, written or spoken, on such a subject must have an interim, almost fragmentary character. But each must bring to the task of clarifying or furthering knowledge what lies within him to give. All must do so in the hope that the final synthesis will be enlarged and established by the benediction of the Most High.

I wish to thank those who helped me in my labours, especially the librarians at the Bollandistes' library in Brussels, at the Jesuit House of Studies in Chantilly, Trinity College, Dublin and especially, once again, Fr. Dermot Fleury, S.J., librarian to the Institute of Theology, Milltown Park, Dublin; his unfailing efficiency and courtesy I could not over-praise. My warmest thanks too go to Michael Glazier, the publisher.

Michael O'Carroll, C.S.Sp.
Blackrock College,
Feast of Our Lady of Mount Carmel,
16 July, 1986.

v

Abbreviations

AAS	*Acta Apostolicae Sedis*
AB	*Analecta Bollandiana*
ACW	*Ancient Christian Writers*
Altaner	B. Altaner, *Patrologie* ed. 6, A. Stuber, 1966.
ANF	Ante-Nicene Fathers
Bardenhewer	O. Bardenhewer, *Geschichte der altkirchlichen Literatur*, I-V, 1913-1932
BGPM	*Beitrage zur Geschichte der Philosophie des Mittel, Münster*
CBQ	*The Catholic Biblical Quarterly*, Washington, D.C.
CCCM	*Corpus Christianorum Continuatio Medievalis, Turnhout*
CCSG	*Corpus Christianorum, Series Graeca*
CCSL	*Corpus Christianorum, Series Latina*, Turnhout
Congar, The Holy Spirit	Y. M. -J. Congar, O.P., *I believe in the Holy Spirit*, tr, *Je crois en l'Esprit Saint*, 3 vols., Paris, 1979—.
DACL	*Dictionnaire d'Archéologie Chrétienne et de Liturgie*, ed. F. Cabrol, O.S.B. and H. Leclercq, O.S.B., Paris, 1907—.
DCath	La Documentation Catholique, Paris
DGHE	*Dictionnaire d'Histoire et de Géographie Ecclésiastiques*, Paris, 1912—.
DS	*Enchiridion Symbolorum*, Denzinger-Bannwart, ed. 33, A. Schönmetzer, S.J.
DSp	*Dictionnaire de Spiritualité*, Paris, 1937
DTC	*Dictionnaire de Théologie Catholique*, Paris, 1903
EC	*Enciclopedia Cattolica*, 1949-1954
EphLit	*Ephemerides Liturgicae, Rome*
EstBib	*Estudios Biblicos*, Madrid
EstTrin	*Estudios Trinitarios*, Salamanca
ETL	*Ephemerides Theologicae Lovanienses*, Louvain
Fliche Martin	A. Fliche-V. Martin, *Histoire de l'Eglise depuis les origines jusqu'à nos jours*, Paris, 1935—.

ABBREVIATIONS

GCS	*Die griechischen christlichen Schiriftsteller der ersten drei Jahrhunderte,* Leipzig, 1897—; Berlin, 1954—.
Greg	*Gregorianum,* Rome
HE	*Historia Ecclesiastica*
HeyJ	*Heythrop Journal*
HTR	*Harvard Theological Review*
IPQ	*International Philosophical Quarterly*
ITQ	*Irish Theological Quarterly,* Maynooth
JTS	*Journal of Theological Studies,* Oxford
Kelly, Creeds	J.N.D. Kelly, *Early Christian Creeds,* 1958 and later ed.
Kelly, Doctrines	J.N.D. Kelly, *Early Christian Doctrines,* 1958 and later ed.
Lonergan, Nicea	B. Lonergan, S.J., *The Road to Nicea, The Dialectical Development of Trinitarian Theology,* part of *De Deo Trino,* I, tr. C. O'Donovan, 1964
LNPF	*Library of Nicene and Post-Nicene Fathers*
LTK	*Lexikon fur Theologie und Kirche* ed. J. Hofer and K. Rahner, 1957-1968
MGH	*Monumenta Germaniae Historica*
MUS	Muséon
Msi	*Sacrorum Conciliorum Nova et Amplissima Collectio*
MSR	*Mélanges de Science Religieuse,* Lille
NCE	*New Catholic Encyclopaedia,* 1967
NRT	*Nouvelle Revue Théologique,* Louvain
NT	*The New Testament*
OCP	*Orientalia Christiana Periodica,* Rome
PG	*Patrologia Graeca* (Migne)
PL	*Patrologia Latina* (Migne)
OT	*The Old Testament*
OCP	*Orientaliä christiana periodica*
PRE	*Realencyklopädie für protestantische Theologie und Kirche,* 1898-1913
Quasten	J. Quasten, *Patrology,* I, II, III, Washington, D.C., 1950-1960
RAC	*Reallexikon für Antike un Christentum,* Stuttgart, 1950—.
RBen	*Revue Bénedictine,* Maredsous
REA	*Revue des études anciennes*
RHE	*Revue d'histoire ecclésiastique,* Louvain
RSPT	*Revue des Sciences Philosophiques et Theologiques,* Paris
RSR	*Recherches de Science Religieuse,* Paris
RevSR	*Revue des Sciences Religieuses,* Strasbourg

RT	*Revue Thomiste*, Paris
RTAM	*Recherches de Théologie Ancienne et Medievale*, Louvain
SC	*Sources Chretiennes*, Lyons
ScEccl	*Sciences Ecclésiastiques*, Montreal
TDNT	*Theological Dictionary of the New Testament*, ed. G. Kittel
TheolSt	*Theological Studies*, Woodstock, Maryland
TQ	Theologische Quartalschrift
TU	*Texte und Untersuchungen*, Leipzig, 1882—.
VigChr	*Vigiliae Christianae*, Amsterdam
ZKG	*Zeitschrift für Kirchengeschichte*
ZKT	*Zeitschrift für katholische Theologie*, Vienna
ZTK	*Zeitschrift für Theologie und Kirche*
ZNW	*Zeitschrift für Die Neutestamentliche Wissenschaft.*

A

'ABBA

"The complete novelty and uniqueness of 'Abba as an address to God in the prayers of Jesus shows that it expresses the heart of Jesus' relationship to God. He spoke to God as a child to its father: confidently and securely, and yet at the same time reverently and obediently."[1] These words from Joachim Jeremias summarize the research of this biblical scholar on a theme which bears directly on the sonship of Jesus, and therefore on his relationship to God the Father, on his eternal sonship within the Holy Trinity. Jeremias rightly rejects the idea that by using this word Jesus was adopting the language of a tiny child. The fact that in the period before the NT grown-up sons and daughters addressed their fathers as 'Abba rules out any such limitation.

Jeremias also thinks that the form of address 'Abba should not mislead us into "ascribing to Jesus himself in detail the 'Son of God' Christology, e.g., the idea of pre-existence, which developed very early in the primitive church."[2] This is a question of theology on which we can differ from the great Göttingen scholar, who has done so much to establish the importance and NT primacy of the 'Abba form of address on the lips of Jesus: "To his disciples it must have been something quite extraordinary that Jesus addressed God as 'my Father'. Moreover not only do the four Gospels attest that Jesus used this address, but they report unanimously that he did so in all his prayers."[3] The single exception, as the author points out, is the cry from the cross, "My God, my God, why hast thou forsaken me?" (Mk 15:34; Mt 27:46), which is a quotation from Ps 22:1 (see SON OF GOD).

On the theological issue Fr. Schillebeeckx makes the 'Abba experience, the uniqueness and originality of which Jeremias rightly emphasizes (see article Father, God the), the starting-point of Trinitarian theory: "Only in the light of Jesus' life, death and resurrection can we know that the Trinity is the divine mode of God's perfect unity of being. Only on the basis of Jesus of Nazareth, his 'Abba experience—source and soul of his message, ministry and death—and his resurrection, is it possible to say anything meaningful about Father, Son and Spirit. For what matters in the 'Abba experience of Jesus is that this unique turning of Jesus to the Father in absolute priority is 'preceded' and inwardly supported by the unique turning of the Father himself to Jesus. Now early Christian tradition calls this self-communication of the Father—ground and source of Jesus' peculiar 'Abba experience—'the Word'. This implies that the Word of God is the undergirding ground of the whole Jesus phenomenon."[4]

'Abba is an Aramaic word and exegetes wrestle with the question why it is used along with the word Father—hence an apparent tautology.

[1]*New Testament Theology*, London, 1971, 67; cf. *ibid.*, 61–68; *id.*, *Abba*, Göttingen, 1966, 15–67; *id.*, *The Central Message of the New Testament*, London, 1965, 9–30; *id.*, *Abba, Jesus et son Père*, Paris, 1972; [2]*Ibid*; [3]*Ibid*; [4]E. Schillebeeckx, O.P., *Jesus, An Experiment in Christology*, London, 1979, "In Search of Jesus' Abba Experience," "The Heart of His Message," "Life and Death: The Secret of His Life Disclosed," 652–669; See also: J. A. Fitzmyer, S. J., *A Christological Catechism*, New York, 24–25. For Jesus as Son, *ibid.*, 87–91.

ABELARD, PETER (1079–c. 1142)

A's doctrine of the Trinity awaits a definitive review based on painstaking research into texts more fully available in recent times, research supported by impartial interpretation.[1] Apart from his turbulent personal life and tragic suffering, historians and theologians have worked with a traditional story in which condemnation loomed large. He was condemned at Soissons in 1121, allegedly for his work, *De Unitate et Trinitate divina*, which was edited by R. Stolzle in 1891. The critically written edition was given a new title, *Theologia summi boni*, in 1939 by H. Ostlender, nine years after the appearance of some important fragments of A's defence in the subsequent more damaging condemnation at Sens, the *Apologia contra Bernardum*. St. Bernard, briefed on A's writings by William of St. Thierry (*qv*), was the instigator of the charge. This was based on nineteen propositions allegedly extracted from A's writings. These propositions are reproduced in standard collections. They were given to A. at Sens, as they form the object of his reply.[2] Scholars admit to a certain difficulty in finding them in his writings, whatever may be said about the school which formed around him.[3]

Of the nineteen propositions the following relate to Trinitarian theology: 1. "That the Father is complete power, the Son a certain power, the Holy Spirit no power"; 2. "That the Holy Spirit is not of the substance (another version: power) of the Father and the Son"; 3. "That the Holy Spirit is the soul of the world"; 7. "That God is only able to do or to omit those things, either in that manner only or at that time in which he does (them), and in no other"; 8. "That God neither ought nor is he able to prevent evil"; 14. "That to the Father, who is not from another, properly or especially belongs power (full power), not also wisdom and kindness."[4]

A. appealed to Pope Innocent and the council fathers of Sens also stated their case. It was Bernard's influence which was decisive. The Pope, in the course of his letter to Henry, the Bishop of Sens, issued this condemnation: "And so we who though unworthily are observed to reside in the chair of St. Peter, to whom it has been said by the Lord: "And thou being once converted, convert thy brethren" (Lk 22:33), after having taken counsel with our brethren the principal bishops, have condemned by the authority of the sacred canons the chapters sent to us by your discretion and all the teachings of this Peter (Abelard) with their author, and we have imposed upon him as a heretic perpetual silence. We declare also that all the followers and defenders of his error must be separated from the companionship of the faithful and must be bound by the chain of excommunication."[5]

A's conceptualism may have led him into formulations of his thought that would be open to misunderstanding; his dialectical method, based on his determination to bring reason to the service of theology, would not be understood by those rooted in a different method. It would take an Aquinas to accomplish what he intended.

Some characteristic statements of his opinions may be quoted to show the need there is for accurate interpretation of his writings. As J. Cottiaux says or hints, it took a good deal of "interpretation" to discover the condemned theses in his works.[6] "Certainly," he writes, "the mystery of the Incarnation could in no way be grasped from (study of) the visible works of God by human reason, as the power of God, his wisdom and kindness were clearly understood from the things they saw. In these three (attributes) I believe that all distinction in the Trinity consists. God the Father seems to me to express what divine power expresses, generating power that is the Son; and God the Son, just as he is divine wisdom begotten of the Father, and God the Holy Ghost, insofar as he is the love or kindness of the Father proceeding from God the Father and the Son."[7] Later in this same work he speaks of "the unity of God and the Trinity of persons in him."

In the *Apologia contra Bernardum* A. tries, successfully it may be agreed, to harmonize his conceptualist approach with tradition: "When we propose that the wisdom of God is a certain power of his, that is, the ability of knowing all things, and when we say that his love is more his will than his power, we are not thereby obliged to concede that the Son is a certain power of his and the Holy Spirit none. For since the three persons are wholly of the same substance or power, as of the same essence and dignity, wherefore each is said to be omnipotent; and thus we taught in the *Theology* that it is not at all proper to call the Son rather than the Father a certain power and the Holy Spirit none, since each of the three persons is equally powerful and the other two are equally wise and kind, although by the word Father divine power, by the name Son divine wisdom, or by the name Holy Spirit the goodness of divine charity is expressed."[8] Here one feels that A. lacks the idea of appropriation (*qv*) to keep his teaching totally orthodox. He insists elsewhere on the equal power and knowledge of the divine persons. When he comes to the relationship of the incarnate God to the Trinity he is not wholly satisfactory.[9]

A. thought that the Trinity could be known by reason, as is evident from one passage above. St. Augustine (*qv*) saw some *vestigia Trinitatis* in things. The consensus would be that reason cannot know the Trinity.

[1]*Opera Theologica*, ed. E. M. Buytaert, O.F.M., CCCM, XI ff, 1969ff, PL 178; *Ouvrages inédits*, ed. V. Cousin, Paris, 1839; id., *Opera hactenus seorsim inedita*, 2 vols., Paris, 1849, 1859; *De Unitate et Trinitate divina*, ed. R. Stolzle, Freiburg in Br., 1891; *Theologia summi boni*, ed. H. Ostlender, BGPM 35, 2/3; 1939; P. Ruf-M. Grabmann, *Ein Neuaufgefundenes Bruchstück der Apologia Abaelarda* (*Sitzungsberichte der Bayr. Akad. d. Wiss. Philos. - hist. Abtlg.*, 1930, Heft 5); cf. Ph.S. Moore, *Reason in the Theology of Peter Abelard*, Proceedings of the American Catholic Philosophical Association, XII, Washington, 1937, 14–160; esp. J. Cottiaux, "La conception de la théologie chez Abelard," RHE 27(1932), 247–295; 533–51; 788–828; esp. J. Rozycki, *Doctrina Petri Abaelardi de Trinitate*, I, *De cognoscibilitate Dei*; II, *De mysterio Sanctae Trinitatis* (*Studia Gnesnensia*, XVIIa, XVIIb) Poznan, 1938, 39; R. B. Lloyd, *Peter Abelard, the Orthodox Rebel*, London, 1947; J. R. McCallum, *Abelard's Christian Theology*, London, 1948; A. V. Murray, *Abelard and St. Bernard*, Manchester, 1967; D. E. Luscombe, *The School of Peter Abelard*, Cambridge, 1969; R. E. Weingart, *The Logic of Divine Love, A Critical Analysis of the Soteriology of Peter Abailard*, Oxford, 1970; E. Portalie, DTC, 1, 36–55; id., ibid., 15, 1713, 14; E. Vacandard, DHGE, 1, 71–91; [2]Msi, XXI, 568; DS 721–739; cf. PL 178; cf. *Capitula haeresum Petri Abaelardi*, CCCM XII, 473ff; [3]cf. esp. J. Cottiaux, *op.cit.*, 826–28; [4]DS 721–7, 734; [5]Msi XXI 565B; Jaffé Wattenbach 8148; PL 179, 517a; [6]cf. art. j. cit.; [7]*Commentary on Romans*, CCCM XI, 68; [8]*Apologia contra Bernardum*, CCCM XI 365; [9]Ibid. 367.

ACACIUS OF CAESAREA (d. after 365); Acacians

A disciple and successor in the see of Caesarea of Eusebius (*qv*) c. 340, A. shared his master's reservation about the *homoousios*—though the latter, frightened away from Arius, had accepted the creed at Nicaea (*qv*).[1] Nothing is known of A. prior to his episcopal consecration and of his writings only fragments exist of seventeen volumes on Eccl. and other treatises; these included a defence of Asterius (*qv*) against Marcellus of Ancyra. A. enlarged the library at Caesarea. He consecrated St. Cyril (*qv*) bishop of Jerusalem, and later became involved in controversy with him on points of jurisdiction, probably sharpened by differences on the Arian controversy in which Cyril's views are a matter of controversy. He was condemned by the council of Sardica, and became leader of the Homoeans (*qv*). At the council of Seleucia A. put forward the Homoean creed, saw it shortly become the official creed of the empire. He drew up the acts, which are lost, of the Homoean Synod of Constantinople in 360. When the patron of the Homoeans, Constantius, died and his successor, Jovian, supported orthodoxy, A. signed the Nicene creed. He reverted to his own position under Valens, after 364. The Homoiousian synod of Lampsacus condemned A. in 365 but he kept his see until his death.

In a fragment of the work against Marcellus preserved by Epiphanius A. answers the objection that the image of God is not God and the image of the Lord is not the Lord by explaining that he is not thinking of a material image but of a living, perfect image and that the image of essence-itself (*autoousia*) also is essence itself, as the image of will-itself is will-itself. A's followers, Acacians, were influential between the years 357—361. (See ARIANISM).

[1]Sources. St. Jerome, *De Vir. Ill.*, 98; Socrates, H. E., II, 4, St. Epiphanius, *Haer.*, 72, 6–10; Quasten 3:345–46.

ACHARD OF ST. VICTOR (d. c. 1171)

Abbot of St. Victor from 1155 to 1160 when he became bishop of Avranches, A. had Richard of St. Victor (*qv*) as pupil.[1] He may have influenced the latter's Trinitarian doctrine. His own doctrine on the subject is contained in a work *De Trinitate*, which is preserved in a Padua MS. His aim was to make a rational demonstration of the Trinity, following the *Monologion* of St. Anselm (*qv*): to seek the *rationes necessariae*, to join through reason truths which one believes on faith. Though he does refer to Boethius, Plato and Seneca, his avowed authority is St. Augustine (*qv*), whom he quotes frequently, principally the *De Trinitate* and the *Quaestio de ideis* from the *De diversis questionibus*, LXXXIII, q. 46, quoted by A. LXXX. In a second treatise contained in the same MS, *De unitate et pluralitate creaturarum* he approaches Platonism, though he does quote Augustine on the ideas of God, the eternal reasons of things: his theory is not unlike that of John Scotus Eriugena (*qv*).

A's definition of the Trinity is Augustine's: "Unity in the Father, equality in the Son, communion of unity and equality in the Holy Spirit".² He substitutes communion for agreement (*concordia*) in the original. A. exceeds in his use of the concept of plurality. He tries to deduce by *rationes necessariae* from the notion of unity the plurality of divine persons, their relations and their properties. "There is no true plurality in creatures, because there is no true unity; for plurality is nothing but unity multiplied. . . . "³ Between the unity of God and the imperfect plurality of creatures there must be an intermediary. This is the perfect, exemplary plurality of the divine persons: a bold theory of the divine image.

A. emphasizes the concept of personality, with the definition of Boethius as his starting-point: "*Persona est substantia individua rationalis naturae.*" Christ, he thinks, *assumptus homo*, has two natures, each of which could be called a person if they had not been assumed in one by the Word incarnate.⁴ Borrowings, unacknowledged, from Anselm's *Monologion* and *Prosologion* are more easily discernible than from Scotus Eriugena.

---

¹Cf. M. Th. d'Alverny, "Achard de Saint-Victor, De Trinitate, de unitate et pluralitate creaturarum," *RTAM* 21(1954), 299–306; J. Chatillon, *Théologie et spiritualité dans l'oeuvre oratoire d'Achard de Saint-Victor*, Paris, 1969; on textual matters cf. N. M. Haring, "The Eulogium ad Alexandrum papam tertium of John of Cornwall," *MedSt* 13(1951), 267; ²*RTAM*, 303; ³*ibid*, 305; ⁴*ibid.*, 302.

ADOPTIANISM

A heresy which considers Jesus Christ as endowed with a double sonship: as divine he would be the natural Son of God; as man he would be the adopted son. The heresy has been traced to judaizing Christians of the first century and to Paul of Samosata in the third.¹

The most serious manifestation of Adoptianism was in eighth-century Spain. About 785 Elipandus, Archbishop of Toledo, resorted to the theory as a reaction against errors held by one Migetius. His idea was stated thus: "It was not through him who was born of the Virgin that he created the universe, it was by him who was his Son not by adoption but by his origin (*conditione*), not by grace but by nature. And it was by him who is at one and the same time a son of man and Son of God, an adoptive son by his humanity, a non-adoptive Son by his divinity, that he redeemed the world."²

Two monks, Beatus and Etherius, questioned this doctrine and referred the matter to the Pope, Adrian (or Hadrian) I. He immediately sent a letter to Elipandus condemning his teaching. When Elipandus was supported by Felix of Urgel, this prelate was summoned to a council at Ratisbonne in 792 by Charlemagne: Urgel was in his kingdom. There Felix recanted; later in Rome he was obliged by the Pope to sign a profession of faith.

The Spanish bishops next intervened to send a defence of Elipandus to Charlemagne and to the bishops of Gaul. They sought to show the difficulty in the theology of the Incarnation to which Elipandus had offered his solution. Their belief was his: "We confess and believe that God the Son of God before all time born of the Father without beginning, is coeternal, alike and consubstantial not by adoption but in kind (by generation), nor by grace but by nature. We confess and believe that he was born of a woman, born under the law, not being the Son of God in kind (*genere*) but by adoption, not by nature but by grace." "We believe and confess that God the Son of God, light from light, true God from true God is the only-begotten of the Father without adoption; as the firstborn, however, at the end of time, (he is) true man assuming from the Virgin in the adoption of flesh; only-begotten in nature, first-born in adoption and grace."³

The letter to Charlemagne, unfortunately, invoking the parallel of Constantine (*qv*), pointed out that the Roman emperor had fallen in his later years from his earlier greatness. The bishops rebuked Charlemagne for his quasi-tyrannical attitude to his subjects.

The idea of a solemn council had been in the air for some time, to offset the one just held at Nicaea, 787. The letters from Spain prompted an immediate decision. Rome was consulted and agreed. Two bishops, Theophylact and Stephen, represented the Pope at the great assembly which met at Frankfurt in the summer of 794. With Paulinus of Aquileia and Peter of Milan came a host of bishops and abbots from all over Europe save Mozarabic Spain.

Adrian sent a letter to the council. In his earlier letter to the Spanish bishops he had protested against the fact that "certain bishops living there, namely Elipandus and Ascaricus with others agreeing with them, do not blush to confess the Son of God adopted, although no heretical leader, however great, has dared to utter such blasphemy, except that perfidious Nestorius who has declared that the Son of God is pure man."[4]

Now the Pope declared: "among other things which must be rejected was the matter arranged with false arguments giving rise, however, to perfidy concerning the adoption of Jesus Christ the Son of God according to the flesh. This the Catholic Church has never believed, has never taught, has never given assent to those believing wickedly."[5]

The teaching of the council is in the dogmatic definition framed in answer to Charlemagne's question, after his lengthy opening speech—acting in effect as president: "What do you think of the matter? For a year now we have tried to remedy this plague; the ulcer only grows and becomes more poisonous; the error is taking root in a region which is part of our empire; decisions of faith must halt it." The bishops asked for time to reflect; they named a commission to collect opinions. At a later meeting discussion resumed and ended in the following declaration: "The Son of God became the son of man. In true nature he was born of God the Son of God that he who was truly born should from each birth have the name of Son, not adoption, not (mere) designation, that he should be true God and true man strictly one Son from each nature, not adoptive, for it would be impious and blasphemous to say that the only coeternal Son of the eternal Father was adoptive, but he must be believed and preached as the true and only Son from each nature, as has been said above."[6]

The doctrine is amplified in the reply sent by the bishops of Gaul to the Spanish bishops, the synodical letter, the work of Alcuin (qv). The Italian bishops sent a similar document, known as *Libellus sacrosyllabus*, wherein the hand of Paulinus of Aquileia is equally strong. "Certainly," we read in the *synodica*, "the person of the Son remained in the Holy Trinity, to which person human nature was joined so that it was one person, God and man, not man deified and God made human, but God man and man God: on account of the unity of the person, one Son of God and one the same son of man, perfect God, perfect man."[7]

The Word is eternally generated by the Father and whether he is thought of as subsisting eternally in the divine nature, in which he is one with the Father, or subsisting in the human nature which he shares with us, his sonship does not change, is not altered by his assumption of a new nature: "From the moment that he began to be man, this man began to be nothing other than the Son of God . . . so that Christ should be one person, Word and man. Therefore if only one, how could he be adoptive, since there are many adoptive sons? . . . Thus the unity of the person, who is in the Son of God and in the Son of the virgin, eliminates the imputation of adoption."[8]

Christ as man is one of us, like us, a servant like us, adoptive son like us—this was a recurring theme in the Spanish exposition. The *synodica* meets such a view directly: "If he who is born of the Virgin is true God, how then can he be adoptive and a servant? In no way do you dare confess that God is a servant or adoptive. And if the prophet called him a servant, this was not because of a state of servitude, but because of the obedience of humility by which he was made obedient unto death."[9]

The ideas of the *synodica* are supported by Sacred Scripture: St. John tells us that "the Word became flesh and dwelt among us, full of grace and truth; we have beheld his glory, glory as of the only Son from the Father" (1:14). St. Paul says: "He who did not spare his own Son but gave him up for us all . . ." (Rom. 8:32). Pope Adrian quotes also the text in St. Matthew: "You are the Christ, the Son of the living God" (16:16).

A witness to the hold this idea had in tradition is St. Hilary (qv): "We sons of God are many, but this Son is not like us. He is the true and own Son, by origin not adoption, in truth and not (merely) name, by birth and not creation."[10]

The condemnation of Adoptianism was repeated at the council of Friuli, approved by Pope St. Leo III: "Neither was the human and temporal nativity absent from the divine and eternal nativity, but in one person of Christ Jesus true Son of God and true Son of man. Not one Son of man and another of God . . . not the supposed Son of God, but true; not adopted, but his own, because never was he alien from the Father because of the human nature which he assumed. And so in each nature we confess that he is the true and not the adopted Son of God, because unconfusedly and inseparably, man having been assumed, one and the same is the Son of God and the Son of man.

By nature Son to the mother according to humanity, however, true Son to the Father in both natures."[11]

The debate was not, as some later writers tried to maintain, a mere matter of words. It went to the root of Christology (qv) and therefore touched Trinitarian theology. For sonship is related directly to the person and, as St. Thomas says, for those who can think of two persons in Christ, "there is no obstacle to calling Christ the man an adoptive son."[12] Alcuin found himself obliged to compose three apologetic treatises, informative to the abbots and monks of the region, polemical to Felix and to Elipand. In the course of these developments he set forth a highly respectable theology. The capstone on all such arguments would be set by St. Thomas Aquinas: for him adoptive sonship is a participation, whereas in Christ reality gives sonship immediately: "And, therefore, Christ, who is the natural Son of God can, in no way, be called an adoptive son."[13]

Before the theological synthesis of St. Thomas, however, there was another manifestation of adoptianism, or something very like it. The error associated with Abelard (qv) and his school sprang from a misunderstanding of the hypostatic union. They thought of a union which would be one of nature, identifying the components; they could not conceive a personal union, in which each nature retained its proper attributes. They thought that the words "the Word is man, Christ is man" denoted only a purely accidental link between the terms employed. They thought that a substantial union identifying humanity with the person of the Word would introduce into the Trinity a created, temporal, finite person: this might lead to the concept of a created element in the Trinity, even, they feared, a fourth person.

The deficient theory declined into a kind of Christological nihilism; Christ's humanity was but a vesture, which view they tried to support by the text in Phil 2:8: "And being found in human form—*habitu inventus ut homo.*" Texts of St. Augustine (qv), St. Hilary (qv) and Boethius were torn out of context to bolster the theory. Adoptianism was a logical consequence, though it was not always explicitly expressed. The erroneous doctrine went through different phases, in Rome, Germany, France, even in the Orient. Gerhoh of Reichersberg was a champion of orthodoxy.

In 1177 Pope Alexander III in a letter to the Archbishop of Rheims condemned the error:

"Since Christ perfect God is perfect man, it is strange with what temerity anyone dares to say that 'Christ is not anything else but man.' Moreover lest so great an abuse of God be able to spring up in the Church, by our authority through apostolic rescript we bid you, our brother, that having assembled the Masters of Paris and Rheims and other surrounding cities, you should place under anathema, lest anyone dare to say this concerning the other . . . because just as he is true God, so he is true man existing from a rational soul and human flesh."[14]

Controversies arose, in the wake of theories from Scotus (qv) and Durandus, about Christ's possible adoptive sonship of the Trinity, by virtue of sanctifying grace—it being firmly assumed that by the hypostatic union he was the natural Son of God. There were hypotheses on the different meanings that may be attached to the words "as man" in the orthodox statement of faith, "Jesus Christ as man (*ut homo, in quantum homo*) is the natural Son of the Father," for the words must be seen to relate to his divine personality. Arguments on the subject have occasionally been complicated—though with the intention of simplifying them— by suppositions about the Father or the Holy Spirit becoming incarnate.

In conclusion let us note that to say that the eternal Word, as such, is the adoptive Son of the Father is Arianism.

---

[1]Cf. besides the works named in the article, bibliography to article Alcuin; C. W. F. Walch, *Historia Adoptianorum*, Göttingen, 1755; Hefele-Leclerc, III,ii (1910), 1001–1060; E. Amann, "L'Adoptianisme espagnol du VIIIe siècle," *RSR*, 16 (1936), 281–317; *id.*, Fliche-Martin, VI (1937), 129–52; H. Quilliet,*DTC*, 1 (1903), 403–413; *ibid.*, E. Portalie, 413–421; M. Jugie, A. A., *EC*, i (1949), 327–30; *id.*, *DHGE* 1: 586–590; S. J. McKenna, *NCE*, I, 140, 141; [2]*PL* 96, 917; [3]*PL*, 101, 1323, 1325; [4]Msi XII 815D, PL 98 376A; [5]Msi XIII 865D; [6]Apud Amann, 142, 143; [7]Msi XIII, 890C; PL 101, 1337; [8]PL 101, 1340; cf. St. Augustine, *Enchiridion*, 36, PL 40, 250; [9]PL 101, 1340; [10]*De Trinit.*, III, 11, PL 10, 82; [11]Msi XIII, 844, PL 99, 294; [12]III, q. 23, art. 4; [13]*ibid.*; [14]Msi XXI, 1081C; for views of Paulinus of Aquileia cf. *Contra Felicem Urgellitanum episcopum, libri III*, PL 99, 343–468.

ALCUIN (c. 735–804)

A key figure in the Carolingian renaissance, A. made a contribution to the theology of the Incarnation which was at one moment decisive.[1] We have from him *De fide sanctae et individuae Trinitatis, libri III*,[2] largely dependent on St. Augustine (qv). In his *De psalmorum usu liber cum variis formulis ad res quotidianas accomodatis*, VI is entitled *Confessio Patris et Filii et Spiritus Sancti*.[3] A work attributed to A. on the Holy Spirit is not genuine.

A's principal contribution to theology was in the context of the debate on Adoptianism (qv). In addition to the three treatises which bear his name[4] it is recognised that he composed the *synodica* and the letter sent by Charlemagne from the council of Frankfurt. His strength was in his patristic knowledge. Though the essential question is related to the theology of the Incarnation, it bears to some extent on Trinitarian theology also.

A. had drawn on patristic texts in the *synodica* and he had benefitted by other documents such as the letter of Adrian (or Hadrian) to the Spaniards. His research is apparent in the letter to the Abbots and monks: ten Latin authors and ten Greek authors are invoked. In the *synodica* he has laid the central weakness of Adoptianism bare: "It appears that the cause of this heresy in the mind of those in error is that those who assert that Christ was adoptive think that to have assumed is the same thing as to have adopted."[5] For A. this was necessary, as the phrase *homo assumptus* used by St. Augustine was being quoted against him. He showed that it was his saving doctrine. When one speaks of *assumptus* one is speaking of someone who, at no moment of his existence, has had an independent existence, but has been in the very first moment of existence taken by another person. When one speaks of adoption one is speaking of two persons, the one adopted existing already in himself, for himself, retaining his autonomy.

In the treatise to the Abbots and monks A. went still deeper into Augustinian theology. Augustine, though clear in the distinction between Christ, the only true Son of God, and us, God's adoptive sons, nonetheless asserted that Christ's sonship and ours were both a work of grace, and there is a certain analogy between the "grace of union" in Christ and the grace of adoptive sonship in us. A. developed this idea splendidly.

He also dealt with a scandalous excess committed by Felix of Urgel in his return to the fray: the latter used the phrase *Deus nuncupativus* (God in name) of Christ. But other events intervened. Leo III, successor to Adrian I, assembled sixty bishops in Rome, denounced the heresies and blasphemies of Felix, recalled the previous condemnations of his errors and threatened him with

anathema if he did not retract wholly. The next stage was the dispatch of royal *missi* to escort Felix to Aachen, where A. faced him and overwhelmed him with his patristic learning. A text of St. Cyril of Alexandria (qv) against Nestorius apparently clinched the argument. Felix was, nonetheless, kept under discreet surveillance. A. next turned to a refutation of Elipandus, who had reacted sourly to his letter inviting him to lead Felix to submission. He dealt with the arguments adduced by Elipandus—supported by patristic and liturgical, that is, Mozarabic, texts—and expounded the theology of the two natures in Christ. (see LITURGY.)

[1]Works PL 100, 101; Jaffé, ed. W. Wattenbach-E. L. Duemmler, *Monumenta Alcuiniana*, Bibliotheca Rerum Germanicarum, 6 (Berlin, 1873); cf. bibliography to Adoptianism; E. S. Duckett, *Alcuin, Friend of Charlemagne*, New York, 1951; L. Wallach, *Alcuin and Charlemagne, Studies in Carolingian History and Literature* (Cornell Studies in Classical Philology, 32, Ithaca, New York, 1959); [2]PL 101, 11–58; [3]*Ibid*.; [4]PL 101, 87–120; 127–230; 243–300; [5]PL 101, 116.

ALEXANDER OF ALEXANDRIA, ST. (d. 328) A's activity in face of the Arian heresy, first in his own episcopal city and then in the council of Nicaea (qv), is part of the story of Arianism (qv)[1]. His theological opinions are not studied as fully as those of his famous successor, Athanasius (qv). Of the seventy letters by him of which St. Epiphanius speaks, only two survive and these convey his ideas when the Arian crisis had begun. They are the encyclical letter written in 319 or thereabouts against Arius (qv) and the letter to Alexander of Byzantium, taken by most authorities as later in date, about 324. As sources they are supplemented very briefly by a fragment in Syriac and by one sermon, preserved in Syriac and Coptic. Arius, in his letter to Eusebius of Nicomedia, gives a brief insight into A's theology.

Following Origen (qv) and St. Denis of Alexandria, A. asserts that only the Father is unbegotten, wherein he consolidates the Alexandrian tradition: "Therefore to the unbegotten Father, indeed, we ought to preserve his proper dignity, in confessing that no one is the cause of his being; but to the Son must be allotted his fitting honour, in assigning to him, as we have said, a generation from the Father without beginning, and allotting adoration to him, so as only piously and properly to use the words 'he was,' and 'always' and 'before all worlds,' with respect to him; by no means rejecting his godhead, but ascribing to him a similitude which exactly answers in every respect to the image and exemplar of the Father. But we must say to the Father alone belongs the property of being unbegotten, for the Saviour himself said, 'My Father is greater than I' (Jn 14:28)."[2]

As Arius recognised, A. taught that the Son is Son eternally: "Always a God, always a Son; at the same time there is a Father, there is a Son. . . . Not in thought, nor for an instant does God precede the Son. From God himself the Son is."[3] "How, then, is it not impious to say that the wisdom of God once was not, which speaks thus concerning itself: 'I was with him forming all things; I was his delight' (Prov 8:30); or that the power of God once did not exist; or that his Word was at any time mutilated; or that other things were ever wanting from which the Son is known and the Father expressed? For he who denies that the brightness of the glory ever existed, takes away also the primitive light of which it is the brightness. And if the image of God was not always, it is clear also that he was not always, whose image it is. Moreover, in saying that the character of the subsistence of God was not, he also is done away with who is perfectly expressed by it."[4]

The Word, according to A., is the Son of God not by adoption but by nature (see art. Adoptianism): "Hence one may say that the sonship of our Saviour has nothing at all in common with the sonship of the rest. For just as it has been shown that his inexplicable subsistence excels by an incomparable excellence all other things to which he gives existence, so also his sonship, which is according to the nature of the godhead of the Father, transcends, by an ineffable excellence, the sonship of those who have been adopted by him."[5]

"Moreover, in the Psalms the Saviour says: 'The Lord hath said unto me, *Thou art my Son*' (Ps 2:7). Where, showing that he is the true and genuine Son, he signifies that there are no other genuine sons besides himself. And what, too, is the meaning of this: 'From the womb before the dawn (morning) I begot you' (Ps 110:3)? Does he not plainly indicate the natural sonship of paternal bringing forth, which he obtained not by the careful framing of his manners, not by the exercise of an increase in virtue, but by property of nature? Wherefore, the only-begotten Son of the Father, indeed possesses an indefectible sonship; but the adoption of rational sons belongs not to them by nature, but is prepared for them by probity of their lives, and by the free gift of God."[6] The Son is the only-begotten mediator. A. is also, on strict literary evidence, the first to use the title *Theotokos* of Mary.

The Syriac fragment draws on the NT image of Christ the reflection of the Father's glory: "Only the Father is unbegotten and the Son is always near him: in fact he is called the reflection of the light. The light is one thing, the reflection is another, two things indivisible one from the other. The light is cause of the reflection: the Father is likewise of the Son, not as part of him but certainly as cause of the hypostasis of him whom he has begotten by his will."[7]

The sole writer against Arianism prior to Nicaea, A. does not use the *homoousios*. His doctrine is practically identical with it. He says that the Son "was begotten of the Father himself." He is the Father's most perfect, most exact image; to see him was to see the Father.[8]

A. was convinced that Arianism derived from Paul of Samosata (*qv*) and Lucian of Antioch (*qv*). His views on this point and on Arianism itself are considered in that article.

[1]Works: H. G. Opitz, *Athanasius' Werke* III, 1, 19–29; PG 18, 547–572; E. A. W. Budge, *Coptic Homilies in the Dialect of Upper Egypt*, London, 1910, 407–415; 115–132; tr. 417–424, 258–274; on chronology of the letters, V. Hugger, "Wie Sind die Briefe Alexanders von Alexandrien chronologisch zu ordnen?" in *TQ* 91 (1909), 66–86; G. Loeschcke, "Zur Chronologie der beiden grossen antiarianischen Schreiben des Alexander von Alexandrien," in *ZKG* 31(1910), 584–586; O. Seeck, "Die Chronologie der beiden Schreiben des Alexander," *ZKG* 32(1911) 277–281; on the sermon, W. Schneemelcher, "Der Sermo 'De anima et corpore'. Ein Werk Alexanders von Alexandrien," in *Festschrift fur G. Dehn*, Neukirchen, 1957, 113–143; cf. G. Bardy, "St. Alexandre d'Alexandrie a-t-il connu la Thalie d'Arius?" *RevSR*, 6(1926), 527–32; L. Th. Lefort, "Athanase: Sur la Virginité," *Mus* 42 (1929), 256–259; H. Opitz, "Die Zeitfolge des arianischen Streites von den Anfängen bis zum Jahre 328," *ZNW* 33 (1934) 131–159; J. R. Palanque, Fliche-Martin, 3, 69–80; id. et al., *The Church in the Christian Roman Empire*, 2 vols, London, 1953, 1: 73–109; V. C. de Clercq, *Ossius of Cordova*, Washington, 1954, 189–206; esp. M. Simonetti, *Studi sull'Arianesimo*, Rome, 1965, 110–124; id., *La crisi ariana nel IV secolo*, Rome, 1975, 55–60; Quasten, 13–19; X. le Bachelet, *DTC*, I, 1, 764–766; Kelly, *Doctrines*, 224–25; Altaner-Stuber, 269; R. Janin, *DHGE* 2, 187- ; Bardenhewer, 3, 34–41; [2]PG 18, 568; [3]Opitz, *Urkunden*, Iff; [4]Letter to Alexander, 27, PG, 557BC; [5]Letter to Alexander, 28, PG 18, 557C; [6]Ibid., [7]Syriac fragment, Pitra, *Analecta sacra*, IV, 199, 433; Opitz; *Urkunden*, 22 (Greek version); [8]PG 18, 561.

ALEXANDER OF HALES (c. 1185–1245)

A., *Doctor irrefragabilis*, opened the way to Scholasticism by combining philosophical reflection with study of the Fathers; especially he set a new trend in teaching by taking as the basic text of his lectures not the Bible (*qv*) but the *Sentences* of Peter Lombard (*qv*).[1] He treated questions on the Trinity in three of his works: *Glossa in quatuor libros Sententiarum*,[2] a *reportatio* discovered in 1946, which is a *lectio cursoria*, something between a detailed commentary and a set of elaborate questions on the text of Peter Lombard; *Quaestiones disputatae 'antequam esset frater,'*[3] 68 questions of varying length, written between 1220 and 1236; and *Summa theologica*,[4] not all of which is from A. himself.

A. was influenced by Richard of St. Victor (*qv*). He dealt briefly with the Trinity in the *Glossa*, taking a line which he would pursue resolutely: a search for possible harmony between St. Augustine (*qv*) and St. John of Damascus (*qv*). Augustine he saw as dealing with the inner life of God, John with the relationship between God and creatures.

In the *Quaestiones disputatae* he is concerned to justify the names used, the nomenclature of Trinitarian theology. He contrasts the four Greek and Latin words: *ousia, ousiosis, hypostasis, prosopon* and *essentia, subsistentia, substantia, persona*.

In the *Summa Theologica* he has a more extended treatment of questions arising in Trinitarian theology—he does again more than once raise the question of names, even of the very Trinity.

One point which drew A's attention particularly was the solution to the controversy between the Greeks and the Latins about the procession *ab utroque* (see FILIOQUE). He may, in the *Quaestiones* be reporting the results of dialogue.

The Greeks, says A., speak of the Spirit as the Spirit of the Son but they do not say that he proceeds from the Son. The Spirit is the Father's love for the Son and proceeds from the Father to the Son; he does not proceed from the Son to the Father. Neither do they say that he proceeds from the Son to the creature. A. thought that he had achieved the desired concord, stating with Augustine the inner procession of the Spirit from the Son but not to the Father, and with John of Damascus the procession to creatures.[5]

The *Summa Theologica* was continued by his disciple John de la Rochelle. Here he tells us that divine life is a good that is communicated, good being self-diffusive. In the Trinity it takes place in two ways: by mode of nature, the begetting of the Son, and by mode of love or gift, the procession of the Spirit. He attempts to meet the Greek objection: if the Spirit proceeds from the Father and the Son, either he proceeds from the essence (but this he shares) or he proceeds in accordance with the difference between the Father and the Son (but they have no common fund). A. replies that the Spirit does not proceed from the Father and the Son either in accordance with their unity in essence or their difference, but in accordance with the fact that though they are different they are one; as Father and Son they are God.[6]

[1]For general bibliography I Herscher, O. F. M., "A Bibliography of Alexander of Hales," *Franciscan St.*, 26 (1945), 435–454; Works, Quaracchi ed.; cf. E. Bettoni, *Il Problema della Conoscibilità di Dio nella Sculoa Francescana* (Il Pensiero medioevale, Prima Serie, 1, Padua, 1950), 1–106; T. de Régnon, *Etudes*, II, 338–431; Y. M.-J. Congar, O. P., *The Holy Spirit*, III, 108–109; A. Emmen, NCE 1, 296–298; [2]ed. 1951, 135ff; [3]ed. 1960, 1–104; [4]ed. 1924ff; I, 413–751; [5]*Glossa* l.c.; *Quaestiones*, 71ff; [6]452, 602.

ANALOGY

Much research and reasoning have gone into the theory of analogy in recent times, as well as into the theory of participation which is closely linked with it. The justification of our knowledge of God, that which ultimately gives it validity, is analogy. The application of these concepts to the theology of the Trinity calls for much discrimination in thought, much subtlety in formulation. Fortunately this task has been undertaken by a master.[1]

As is well known, analogy is distinguished into analogy of attribution and analogy of proportion, or better worded perhaps, proportionality. Here we are naturally leaving aside anything like analogy in the popular sense. "When metaphysical analysis has intervened, we have (in Trinitarian theology) analogy of strict proportionality, by which we can reach formally divine reality."[2] "For in reality we are not dealing here with a 'psychological' theory, but with a metaphysical doctrine, which, thanks to the analogy of strict proportionality, escapes any reproach of anthropomorphism."[3]

The danger of anthropomorphism (*qv*) is avoided because the mind in its speculation on

God, and in this case on his Trinitarian life, relies on the universality and transcendence of being. When the connection has been established between being and the notions of personality and will, affirmations about the Trinity avoid both univocation and anthropomorphism.

To achieve this full insight with the development it promises, it is necessary to scrutinize basic concepts in Trinitarian theology, purify them of any extraneous ingredients and then elevate their meaning to the highest degree, always assured that thus we shall reach their intrinsic analogical meaning. This is true for the pivotal terms, Father, Son, Word, Spirit, and for the concepts of procession and of subsistent relations.

Analogy does not remove the mystery, does not therefore give us exhaustive knowledge. There are, moreover, problems in effecting a valid synthesis of the elements of revelation, biblical and traditional, and the product of speculative theological reasoning. Those who oppose the validity of analogy in reality reduce divine revelation to metaphor, or leave us in a state of agnosticism. "Would God have spoken to men to tell them that there are processions within him ('x' and 'y'), totally unlike ours, to the point that we cannot form any idea of them, however imperfect? In this case when we speak about the Son of God, about the Word of the Father, we indulge in empty parrot talk, since there is no relationship between these terms when applied to God and the same terms when applied to creatures. The gospel, claiming to give us certain views of the depths of the divinity, would have played on words, to deceive us with the help of homonyms, an effect of pure chance. Even Tyrrell admits that 'revelation is not reducible to mere words; it has a meaning.' For us Catholics this meaning is objective and capable of being thought. On the other hand, if revelation brings us new truths, it does not for all that give us new concepts. We have then to transfer to the heart of the godhead our notions of generation, relation, person and we are bound to admit that these are not just images, mere ways of speaking, but that these terms express, analogically, reality itself."[4]

In other words St. Thomas, by use of analogy, shows that the intuition of St. Augustine on the processions is not merely psychological but metaphysical. The same use of analogy is valid throughout the whole treatise, and it may very well be that theologians of quality whose theories appear to deviate unjustifiably from the consensus of the great Doctors may err through failure to accept this truth or to seek to explore its potentiality.

[1]Cf. *esp.* M. T. L. Penido, *Le rôle de l'analogie en théologie dogmatique*, Fribourg, 1931; critical ed. revised of Thomas de Vio Cajetan, *De Nominum Analogia*, P. H. Hering, O. P., Rome, 1952; id. English tr. E. Bushinski, H. Koren, Pittsburgh, 1953; J. M. Ramirez, O. P., "De analogia secundum doctrinam aristotelico-thomisticam," *La Ciencia Tomista* 24 (1921), 20–40, 195–214, 337–357; 25 (1922), 17–38; I. Le Rohellec, C. S. Sp., "Cognitio nostra analogica de Deo," *DivThP* 30 (1927), 298–319; G. M. Manser, "Die Analoge Erkenntnis Gottes," *DivThF*, 6 (1928), 385–403; G. Phelan, *St. Thomas and Analogy*, Milwaukee, 1941; J. F. Anderson, *The Bond of Being*, St. Louis, 1949; J. Habbel, *Die Analogie zwischen Gott und Welt nach Thomas von Aquin*, Berlin 1949; E. L. Mascall, *Existence and Analogy*, 1949; H. Lyttkens, *The Analogy between God and the World*, Uppsala, 1952; O. A. Varangot, *Analogia de attribución intrinseca y analogia del ente segun Santo Tomas*, Buenos Aires, 1957; H. A. Wolfson, "St. Thomas on Divine Attributes," *Mélanges offerts à E. Gilson*, Toronto, 1959, 673–700; G. P. Klubertanz, *St. Thomas Aquinas on Analogy*, Chicago, 1960; R. M. McInerny, *The Logic of Analogy, An Interpretation of St. Thomas*, The Hague, 1961; J. F. Ross, "Analogy as a Rule of Meaning for Religious Language," *Intern Philos Quart*, 1 (1961) 468–502; B. Montagnes, O. P., *La doctrine de l'analogie de l'être d'après St. Thomas d'Aquin*, Louvain, 1963; W. J. Hill, *Knowing the Unknown God*, New York, 1971; [2]M. T. L. Penido, *op. cit.*, 300; [3]*ibid.*; [4]*ibid.*, 308; E. Przywara, "Die Reichweite der Analogie als katholischer Grundform," *Scholastik*, 15 (1940), 339–362; 508–532; id., "Analogia entis," II–IV, LTK I, 470–73; E. Coreth, "Dialektik und Analogie des Seins. Zum Seinsproblem bei Hegel und in der Scholastik," *Scholastik* 26 (1951) 57–86; id., LTK "Analogia entis," I, 468ff; W. Pannenberg, "Analogie," RGG I, 350–53; id., EKL, I, 113f; J. Track, "Analogie," TRE II, 625–630.

ANGLICANISM

Here we are dealing with the official position of the Church of England as published in the *Book of Common Prayer*, not with the many private theories subsequently expressed. The order of Morning Prayer includes the Apostles' Creed (see Creeds),[1] which is to be replaced by the Athanasian Creed (*qv*) on Trinity Sunday and on thirteen other feasts: Christmas Day, the Epiphany, Easter Day, Ascension Day, Whitsunday and the feasts of these saints: Matthias, John Baptist, James, Bartholomew, Matthew, Simon, Jude, Andrew.[2] Trinity Sunday is pivotal in the liturgical year—the following Sundays being numbered from it until Advent. The Collect for Trinity Sunday is identical with that in the Roman Missal before the changes made after Vatican II (qv). The Epistle is chapter four of Revelation; the Gospel is Jn 3: 1–15.

The faith in the Trinity is explicitly expressed in the first of the Thirty-Nine Articles: "There is but one living and true God, everlasting, without body, parts, or passions; of infinite power, wisdom and goodness; the Maker, and Preserver of all things both visible and invisible. And in unity of this Godhead there be three Persons, of one substance, power, and eternity: the Father, the Son, and the Holy Ghost."[3] Anglicanism, in a word, remained true to the faith of Christendom.

---

[1]Ed. Cambridge University Press, 11, 12;   [2]Ibid., 27–30;   [3]Ibid., 611, 12; for recent Anglican attitudes to the Filioque see article on the subject and that on the Bonn Conference.

ANSELM, ST., DOCTOR OF THE CHURCH (c. 1033–1109)

Because of his use of reason in debating questions of faith A. is styled "Father of Scholasticism;" he did not found a school, but his work marks a turning-point.[1] Well known in the history of theology for the "ontological argument" for the existence of God, A. treats of the Trinity in the Letter to Urban II on the Incarnation of the Word, an answer to the tritheism (qv) of Roscellinus (qv); in the Monologium,[2] wherein he expounds a kind of theodicy; and in the Proslogium[3] in the De processione Spiritus Sancti.[4] In the latter he develops the ideas he had expressed to the Council of Bari, which he attended while in exile, and where he had to defend the western thesis on the Filioque (qv) against the Greeks.

Did A. think that the human reason could attain to knowledge of the Holy Trinity? He did write such words as these: "If anyone will be good enough to read my two small works, namely the Monologium and the Proslogium, which were composed especially (to show) that what we hold on faith about divine nature and its persons, beyond the Incarnation, can be proved by compelling reasons; if, I repeat, anyone reads them, I think that he will find there on this subject what he cannot disprove and will not wish to despise."[5]

Yet his overall principle was the subordination of reason to faith. In his reply to Roscellinus he insists on the distinction between person and nature and with much dialectical skill demolishes the thesis that three persons means three gods. He shows by use of the same distinction that the Incarnation did not disturb the inner life of the Trinity. He wrestles with the problem of essence and person. The Trinity is related to memory, intelligence and love. But A. can write: "What is said in the Word but the essence? And since the essence is unique there is but one reality which is said (the Word). If then there is in the Father and Son only one reality who says (the essence) and only one reality which is said (the essence), unique in effect is the Wisdom who says in them, and unique is the substance which is said. There are not several Words, but only one."[6] There is a danger here of confusing the fatherly origin of the Son and of the Spirit with the essence common to all three.

But A. is saved by his grasp of the importance of the relations. "Since then, when God is born of God or God proceeds from God, the substance cannot lose its singleness, nor the relation its plurality. Consequently there one is three and three one, nor are the three spoken of each other, nor can it be incredible that in a nature which is above all things and is unlike all others there should be that an example of which cannot perfectly be found elsewhere. The Latins call these three persons, the Greeks substances. As we say that in God there are one substance and three persons, they say one person and three substances, meaning by substance what we mean by person, but not differing from us in faith."[7] A. first used the axiomatic formula: "in God all things are one, where the opposition of a relation does not prevent it."[8]

The work on the procession of the Holy Spirit is substantial and an attempt at persuasion. A. takes as his point of departure what is held in common by westerns and Greeks in regard to God and his Tri-unity. His intention is to bring the Greeks to accept a Patre et Filio. The earlier chapters of the book proceed by logical argument; the later chapters seek to extract the doctrine from the biblical texts. Of the Son he uses the word begetting, nascendo, of the Spirit procedendo. The definition of the persons by relationships was already in St. Augustine (qv) and well known to A. and the Greek Fathers. He did not draw on the Fathers in this treatise because the Greeks did not know the Latins and he did not know the Greeks.

A. knows that Augustine had said *principaliter a Patre* but he thinks this idea is absorbed in his theory of the begetting of the Son and the procession of the Spirit understood against the identity of essence and equality of divinity: "The Holy Spirit comes from that in which the Father and the Son are one, that is, from God, not from that in which they differ from each other. Because the Father is neither before nor after the Son, neither greater nor lesser, and because the one is neither more nor less God than the other, the Holy Spirit is not from the Father before (being from) the Son. If then it is said that the Holy Spirit comes from the Father as the principle, nothing more than this is meant: the Son himself, from whom the Spirit comes, has it from the Father that the Spirit comes from him."[9]

A. argues that the meaning of *principaliter* among God's creatures is not the same as within the deity. Equality and identity are inherent to the divinity. Does the teaching contain the traditional idea of the monarchy, or the conceptions of the Greeks? Likewise he did not understand the eastern formula *a Patre per Filium*. He may have learned of this from the bishops whom he met at Bari, but he did not seize its significance and did not see the point of it: "As the Father and the Son do not differ in the unity of the deity and as the Holy Spirit only proceeds from the Father as the deity, if that deity is similarly in the Son, it is not possible to see how the Spirit would proceed from the deity of the Father through the deity of the Son and not (immediately) from that same deity of the Father, but from his fatherhood, and that he proceeds through the sonship of the Son and not through his deity—but that idea is clearly stupid."[10]

A. discusses the image of the source, the river and the lake as representing the three persons. The same image is found in the Greek Fathers, who used it to express their idea of the Spirit coming through the Son, but not from Father and Son conjointly. A. sees that the image will not convey this latter idea if taken too literally: he then says that in the spiritual order things must be different, for we cannot separate the Son from the Father—he is in the Father and is in no way different from him in essence.

To strengthen his case A. devotes some chapters of the book to an analysis of the scriptural texts, Jn 20:22 and 16:13, to which he adds Mt 11:27 and Jn 10:30. In a later chapter he contends that the Son is affirmed in Jn 15:26. He also deals, hastily, with the addition of the *Filioque* clause to the creed.

We may agree with Fr. Congar's summing up: "Anselm was above all a speculative theologian. He did not develop his pneumatology within the framework of the history of salvation; indeed, he did not refer to the latter at all. . . . Even his prayers and meditations are not pneumatological. They do not even mention the Holy Spirit. . . . He is interested in the divine essence and does not take the hypostases as his point of departure. The notion of 'person' seems to have perplexed him. He does not, therefore, make a very clear distinction between their principle *quo*, their nature, and their principle *quod*, the person in the processions. However much we have to admire him, there is always a feeling that there is a need to go beyond his thinking. He would himself have agreed with that sentiment."[11]

---

[1]Works: critical ed. F. S. Schmitt (Seckau, 1938; Edinburgh, 1946–61); Jansens, *De Deo Trino*, Freiburg in Br., 1907, 49, 249, 395, 486, 667, 802, 818; cf. A. Wilmart, O. S. B., "Le premier ouvrage de S. An contre le trithéisme de Roscellin," *RTAM* 3 (1931), 20–36; B. Bouche, *La doctrine du'Filioque' d'après S. Anselme de Cantorbery, Son influence sur S. Albert le Grand et S. Thomas d'Aquin* (dissertation), Rome 1938; C. Vagaggini, *La hantise des 'rationes necessariae' de S. Anselme dans la théologie des processions trinitaires de S. Thomas, Spicilegium Beccense*, I (*Congrès international du IXe centenaire de l'arrivée d'Anselme au Bec*), Le Bec-Hellouin, Paris, 1959, 103–139; R. Perino, *La dottrina trinitaria di S. Anselmo nel quadro del suo metodo teologico e del suo concetto di Dio* (*Studia Anselmiana*, 29), Rome 1952; P. del Prete, *Il concilio di Bari nel 1098*, Bari, 1959; J. Hopkins, *A Companion to the Study of St. Anselm*, Minneapolis, 1972; R. Evans, *Anselm and Talking about God*, Oxford 1978; DTC XV, 1709–1711; F. S. Schmitt, NCE, 1, 581–3; Y. M-J. Congar, *The Holy Spirit*, III, 96–102; [2]Schmitt, II, 5–87; [3]I, 5–87; [4]II, 177–279; [5]I, 6, 20; [6]*Monologium*, 63, I, 73; [7]II, 16, 35; [8]The equivalent, II, 180, 181, 183; for history of the axiom cf. Congar, *op. cit.*, 102, n. 9 (see article Florence, Council); [9]II, 213; [10]II, 202; [11]*op. cit.*, 100, 101.

ANTHROPOLOGY

"Any kind of distinction, then, between Christology and the Trinity is to be avoided in theology and catechetics (*qv*). The mystery of Jesus Christ belongs to the structure of the Trinity. The mystery of the Trinity is Christological. Such a distinction can take on either a neo-scholastic form or a modern form. It was the practice of neo-scholasticism to segregate the consideration of the

Trinity from the whole Christian mystery; nor did it take sufficient account of the Trinity in its understanding of the Incarnation and the deification of man. The Trinity's importance for both the body of the truths of faith and Christian life was repeatedly neglected."[1] Thus the ITC in October 1982—in a report adopted with but one dissentient voice. Later it adds "In the same way anything leading to confusion between the event of Jesus Christ and the Trinity must be avoided."

These general theses must be borne in mind when the later section of the report, *The Relationship between Christology and Anthropology*, is being considered. "Modern Christology," says the report on this subject, "often is based more upon, and developed from an anthropology, as a new principle of understanding, than upon the theology of the triune God. This methodology has its greatest impact on the field of soteriology. The purpose of the redemption is conceived more as a hominisation than as the deification of man. In this process, the crisis in metaphysics, already evident in the field of philosophy, has had great consequences at the very heart of theology. The disjunctive antithesis between "ontological" considerations and merely "functional" considerations (which some hold are closer to the biblical mind) has serious consequences, which are well known in modern theology."

The authors of the text take note of the sign "for us" which marks the announcement of Jesus Christ, the Son of God; they note further that this has led to treating the whole of Christology under the aspect of soteriology, which has given in places a "functional" Christology—"more or less correctly and laudably." Then comes the first advertence to Trinitarian life. "But, conversely, it is likewise true that 'existence for others' means that Jesus Christ cannot be separated from his relationship and intimate communion with the Father, and must for that very reason be rooted in his eternal Sonship. The pro-existence of Jesus Christ, in which God communicates himself to man, presupposes pre-existence. Otherwise the proclamation of Jesus Christ as Saviour would be merely a fiction and an illusion, incapable of defending itself against the modern accusation that it is an ideology."

Having taken as guiding idea the Adam–Christ typology (Rom 5:12–21; 1 Cor 15:45–49), the report links up with the anthropology of Vatican II (*qv*), but with a more explicit Trinitarian awareness: "The Gospel of Jesus Christ not only presupposes man's essence and existence, but brings him to full perfection. This perfection, at least implicitly sought, desired and hoped for by all men, is transcendent and infinite in so far as it can be found only in God. Man's true hominisation, therefore, attains its apex in his divinisation, in his friendship and communion with God, by which man is made the temple of God, enjoying the presence of the Father, Son and Holy Spirit. The adoration and worship of God, especially Eucharistic worship, makes man fully human. Therefore, Jesus Christ, at once God and man, is found to be the eschatological fullness of man, and in him alone is found the 'measure of the stature of the fullness of man' (Eph 4:13). Only in Jesus Christ is man's limitless openness concretely found. It is especially in Jesus Christ that the mystery of man and his exalted vocation are truly shown to us."[2]

To work out this idea in full and to justify a Trinitarian anthropology is to undertake the task left unfinished by St. Augustine. It is undoubtedly true that the only valid basis for any Christian anthropology is the idea of man made in the image of God (*qv*). This Augustine took as the starting point of his theology of the Trinity. The question facing a future Augustine is to elaborate a synthesis on man's relationship with God starting from God as creator, God as Trinity. It must take account of the autonomy recognised in the human person by Vatican II, of the dignity and rights of the person, of the values served by people of different, noble cultures.

In such a synthesis there will be a place for a theory of creation (*qv*) which, while adhering to the traditional doctrine that all three persons of the Trinity act in this work, can accept that they still do so without losing their personal identity and properties. A beginning was discernible in some of the writings of Karl Rahner.[3]

[1]*DocCath* 1983, 121; English tr. ITQ 49 (1982), 285ff; [2]*Ibid.*, cf. GS ch I, especially 22, *Christ as the new Man*; A Gelin, P. S. S., "La doctrine paulinienne du Nouvel Adam," *Bulletin de la Société francaise d'etudes mariales*, 13 (1955), 15–23; M.-J. Nicholas, O.P., "Le Christ, Nouvel Adam dans S. Thomas d'Aquin," *ibid.*, 1–13; H. Rondet, S.J., "Le Christ, Nouvel Adam dans la théologie de S. Augustin," *ibid.*, 25–41; E. Schillebeeckx, *Jesus, An Experiment in Christology*, London, Part IV, section 2, 595ff; [3]cf. esp. *Sacramentum Mundi*, III, 1969, 365–70; *An Encyclopaedia of Theology*, 1975, 887–93; also *Hominisation*, London, 1958; K. Fischer, *Der Mensch als Geheimnis. Die Anthropologie Karl Rahners*, 1974; Rahner's letter, 400–410; Hans Urs von Balthasar,

A Theological Anthropology, London, 1967; F.K. Mayr, "Trinitatstheologie und Theologische Anthropologie," ZTK 68 (1971), 427–477.

ANTHROPOMORPHISM

The attribution to God of human characteristics or activities. This has been prevalent in non-Christian religions, whether primitive or sophisticated as with the Greeks. The latter did not identify men and gods: "One is the race of men, one is the race of gods," said Pindar. Animism sees powers and spirits in all nature.

The Bible, especially in the early chapters of OT, is abundantly anthropomorphic, which is God's pedagogy in the early stages of unfolding revelation. This A. is still very different from that of the ancient religions, wherein gods were fully human in form and were so represented. The God of OT nonetheless has eyes (Am 9:3; Sir 11:12), ears (Dn 9:18) hands (Is 5:25), feet (Gen 3:8, one of the most beautiful uses, "they heard the sound of the Lord walking in the garden in the cool of the day"; Is 63:3); God speaks (Gen 1 passim; Lev 4:1), listens (Gen 16:11), closes the door of Noah's ark (Gen 7:16), whistles (Is 7:18), laughs (Ps 2:4). God is represented as subject to certain emotions: he rejoices (Ps 104:31), is angry (1 Chron 13:10), disgusted (Lev 20:23), regretful (Jer 42:10), revengeful (Is 1:24), jealous (Ex 20:5; Deut 5:9).

OT anthropomorphism is further distinguished from that of the non-Christian religions by explicit warnings: "For I am a God not man, the Holy One in your midst" (Hos 11:9); "Hast thou eyes of flesh? Dost thou see as man sees?" (Job 10:4); "God is not man, that he should lie, or a son of man that he should repent. Has he said and will he not do it? Or has he spoken, and will he not fulfil it?" (Num 23:19). As a further safeguard graven images were forbidden (Deut 4:16; 5:8).

The personal character of Hebrew religion and the power to combine a sense or at least an insinuation of divine transcendence with vivid anthropomorphism is marvellously exemplified in the story of Moses as narrated in Exodus. When anthropomorphism continues in the NT, thought processes and modes of expression are more complex, for God has taken flesh, and the starting-point of anthropomorphism, perceptible reality, is now identified with a divine person incarnate. Another element is added by his choice of metaphor to express his work among men: I am the good Shepherd; I am the Vine, you are the branches. St. Paul further enlarges the use of metaphor by such expressions as Christ's body to represent the faithful united with Christ.

Biblical use of anthropomorphism is generally imaginative. There is a higher form which seeks human terms to give an explanation of divine reality, above merely physical traits or activities. But God's transcendence from what is intelligible as well as what is sensible must be heeded. The theology of the Redemption is particularly vulnerable to the temptation to see in God human motivation.

Spirituality is likewise tempted. Unquestionably some of the noblest mystical poetry, and some striking spiritual treatises, abound in anthropomorphism or in metaphor which is heavily tinged with it: e.g., the *Ascent of Mount Carmel* and *The Pilgrim's Progress*. Dogged by the fear that this, even in rational theology, was inescapable, writers from Maimonides to E. Le Roy have taken refuge in agnosticism. Christians have to give serious attention to the warning that anthropomorphism may enter into their thinking unnoticed: how many think or recall that such a rightly sacred phrase as "seated at the right hand of God" is an anthropomorphism?

The solution to the problems posed is in the doctrine of analogy (*qv*). It has to be used in the strictly dogmatic formulas, in speculative thinking connected with them, and as a corrective in spiritual writing: here the effect of anthropomorphism is seen in the analysis and description of attitudes of soul towards God. For psychological reasons thought and discourse purified of anthropomorphic elements may again lapse into it, in a way which at times is veiled by sophisticated language.

To what extent Christian art fosters or accentuates the trend is a matter for prolonged research. Most admirers of Roublev's Trinity would deny such influence. Certainly Michelangelo's frescoes on the ceiling of the Sistine chapel cannot be easily dismissed. One very powerful protection is the doctrine of the Trinity, fully explained and open to development in thinking and in the existential area.

Cf. A. D. Sertillanges, O.P., *Agnosticisme ou Anthropomorphisme*, Paris 1908; id., same title, *Rev. de Phil.*, 8(1906), 129–165;

E. Le Roy, *Le Problème de Dieu*, Paris, 1922; L. Brunschwicg, *La querelle de l'athéisme*, Bull. de la Soc. franc. de phil., 1928; id., *La raison et la religion*, Paris, 1939; M. T. L. Penido, *Le rôle de l'analogie en théologie dogmatique*, Fribourg, 1931, 346–50; Etienne Gilson, *L'esprit de la philosophie mediévale*, Paris, 1944; H. (Cardinal) de Lubac, S. J., *De la connaissance de Dieu*, Paris, 1946; E. L. Mascall, *He Who Is*, London, 1948; id., *Existence and Analogy*, 1949; *Words and Images: A Study in Theological Discourse*, 1957; B. Lonergan, S. J., *Insight, A Study of Human Understanding*, 1957, ch. 17 and 19; id., *De Deo Trino*, 2nd ed. 1964, I, 15–112; II, 7–64; J. C. Murray, S. J., *The Problem of God*, New Haven, 1964, pt. 2.

APOSTLES' CREED, THE

"I believe in God the Father almighty, creator of heaven and earth; And in Jesus Christ, his only Son, our Lord, who was conceived by the Holy Spirit, born from the Virgin Mary, suffered under Pontius Pilate, was crucified, dead and buried, descended to hell, on the third day rose again from the dead, ascended to heaven, sits at the right hand of God the Father almighty, thence he will come to judge the living and the dead; I believe in the Holy Spirit, the holy Catholic Church, the communion of saints, the remission of sins, the resurrection of the flesh, and eternal life. Amen."[1]

It is fairly generally agreed that this credal formulary (known as T) grew out of the Old Roman Creed (R) which runs as follows:

"I believe in God the Father almighty; and in Christ Jesus his only Son, our Lord, who was born from the Holy Spirit and the Virgin Mary, who under Pontius Pilate was crucified and buried, on the third day rose again from the dead, ascended to heaven, sits at the right hand of the Father, whence he will come to judge the living and the dead; and in the Holy Spirit, the holy Church, the remission of sins, the resurrection of the flesh."[2]

Marcellus of Ancyra delivered to Pope Julius I in Rome in 340 a creed which, as reproduced by Epiphanius, closely resembles R. This text reads thus:

"I believe in God almighty and in Christ Jesus, his only Son, our Lord who was born of the Holy Spirit and the Virgin Mary, who was crucified under Pontius Pilate and was buried and the third day rose from the dead; who ascended into heaven and sitteth on the right hand of the Father, whence he cometh to judge the living and the dead. And in the Holy Spirit, the holy Church, the remission

of sins, the resurrection of the flesh and the life everlasting."[3]

Scholars have to trace the origins, growth and acceptance of these formularies. Towards the middle of the seventeenth century the scholarly archbishop of Armagh, James Ussher, identified the text of Marcellus of Ancyra. The author was in Rome, and to win the Pope's favour and support he pronounced the papal Roman text as his ideal confession of faith.[4] As to the origin of R. one factor in its history is the interrogatory creed which is textually—as a work of restoration—found in the *Apostolic Tradition* of Hippolytus (*qv*):

"Do you believe in God the Father Almighty?"

"Do you believe in Jesus Christ, the Son of God, born by the Holy Spirit of the Virgin Mary, who was crucified under Pontius Pilate and died (and was buried), and rose on the third day, alive from the dead, and ascended into heaven and sat down on the right hand of the Father, who will come to judge the living and the dead?"

"Do you believe in the Holy Spirit, and the holy Church, and the resurrection of the flesh?"

"And he who is being baptized shall say, 'I believe'."[5]

Current expert opinion indicates that before the pontificate of Victor (189–199) a creed in Greek, still the spoken language, was complete. The *Apostolic Tradition* supports the view that a declaratory creed existed which was handed over by the bishop (*traditio*) during the preparatory instruction of catechumens prior to baptism and handed back to him (*redditio*) as an immediate preliminary to the ceremony. Rufinus of Aquileia in his *Commentary on the Apostles' Creed* (404), comparing his local text with R, gave sufficient information on this to enable James Ussher to reconstruct it.[6] His version has been generally accepted. It is also found in Codex E of Acts in the Bodleian Library (Laud gr. 35) and in an eighth century MS in the British Museum (Cotton, 2A XX).

Around the origin of R and T is the legend recalled in the title, Apostles' Creed. The growth of this legend has been traced: The Apostles laid down the content and form of their preaching before they parted to undertake this work; each one, it would be said with the passage of time, contributed an article. St. Ambrose, who gives the title for the first time, may be the author of the *Explanatio symboli ad initiandos*[7] which carries on the tradition, as does the *Apostolic Constitutions*

(6.14). Though the strictly apostolic authorship cannot be demonstrated, "recent (scholarly) work, so far from questioning the apostolic origin of its content, has, on the contrary, established this with much more solidity."[8]

Melchior Hittorp, canon of Cologne, published the text in the *Ordo Romanus antiquus*, the opening section of his *De divinis catholicae ecclesiae officiis et ministeriis*, which appeared in his cathedral city in 1568. The text was, exactly as he published it, in use in medieval times and is first found with Pirminius of Reichenau in his *Scarapsus* (ch. 10; 12; 28), a manual of Christian doctrine, written between 710 and 724. It is also found in the Missal of Bobbio (seventh or eighth century); in the Antiphonary of Bangor, written by Comgall between 680 and 689; and in the *Missale Gallicanum Vetus* of the early eighth century, composed probably in Auxerre, Gaul. Informed opinion locates its place of origin north of the Alps, probably in southwest Gaul. It was to assume considerable importance through the Carolingian territories with the backing of Charlemagne (*qv*). It was incorporated into his program of liturgical uniformity. By the late tenth or early eleventh century it was accepted at Rome; this official recognition meant the decline in the fortunes of the Constantinopolitan creed. Innocent III quoted both in his work on the Eucharist.[9] St. Thomas Aquinas chose T for his commentary on the creed.[10]

The status of T has remained. It has been in universal use in the West for baptismal services. It survived the Reformation in all communions, save that Luther substituted "Christian" for "Catholic." In the present century it is recognised as a rallying central formulary for ecumenical purposes. In 1920 it was put forward by the Lambeth Conference, in an appeal to all Christian peoples, as one of the cardinal points in Christian unity—the three others being the Holy Scriptures, the two dominical sacraments, and the ministry. In 1927 at the World Conference on Faith and Order which met at Lausanne, representatives of East and West recited it together at the opening session and they joined in approving it as a suitable statement of the Christian message.

The formulary, as it now stands, is Trinitarian in an explicit but not very developed fashion. The first article expresses the truth about the Father as creator. Then follows the Christological section, affirming the divine sonship, and recalling the principal events in the life of Christ: the miraculous beginning and end to his earthly career, the virginal conception, his resurrection, his exaltation and his future role as judge of all mankind. The final section contains somewhat disparate elements: the Holy Spirit, without any emphasis on his divinity or function, the Church and the communion of saints, and the eschatological conclusion—eternal life with its prelude, bodily resurrection; the reality of forgiveness of sins is inserted just before that.

Where the creed gains is in its brevity: a great deal is expressed succinctly. Much is assumed, for instance the redemptive or salvific value of the suffering, death and resurrection of Christ, and the sanctifying power of the Spirit. Comparison of the formula with the other creeds will no doubt stir different reactions in different people, though a declaratory creed, never remote from a catechetical context, is not to be compared too closely with a conciliar creed. Each of these was Eastern in origin and would not be expressed in the sober direct language of Rome. For most of its history T was not received in the East; opposition to it has now disappeared.

---

[1] Latin text with this tr. Kelly, *Creeds*, 369; for both R and T cf. J. Pearson, *An Exposition of the Creed*, 1659; J. F. Bethune-Baker, *The Faith of the Apostles' Creed*, 1918; A. E. Burn, *The Apostles' Creed* (Oxford Church Text Books), 1906; F. Kattenbusch, *Das Apostolische Symbolum*, 2 vols, 1894–1900; A. Harnack, *The Apostles' Creed*, 1901; E. Vacandard, "Les Origines du symbole des Apôtres," *RQH*, 67 (1899), 329–77; H. Lietzmann, "Die Anfange des Glaubensbekenntnisses," *Festgabe . . . A. Harnack*, 1921, 226–42; *id.*, "Die Urform des apostolischen Glaubensbekenntnisses," Sb(Berlin) 1919, 269–74; K. Holl, "Zur Auslegung des 2 Artikels des sog. apostolischen Glaubensbekenntnisses," *ibid.*, 2–11; A. Harnack, "Zur Abhandlung des Hrn Holl: Zur Auslegung des 2 Artikels des sog. apostolischen Glaubensbekenntnisses," *ibid.*, 112–16; B. Capelle, O. S. B., "Le symbole romain au second siècle," *RBen* 39 (1927), 33–45; *id.*, "Les origines du symbole romain," *RTAM* 2 (1930), 5–20; *id.*, "L'introduction du Catechuménat à Rome," *RTAM*, 5, (1933); J. Lebreton, *Fliche et Martin*, I, 368–71, *id.*, *RSR*, 1930, 115ff; *id.*, P. Feine, *Die Gestalt des apostolischen Glaubensbekentnisses in der Zeit des neuen Testaments*, 1925; K. Barth, *Credo. Die Hauptprobleme der Dogmatik dargestellt im Anschluss an das Glaubensbekenntniss*, 1935, English tr. 1936; *Histoire du dogme de la Trinité*, II, Paris, 1928, 141–173; O. Cullman, *Les premières Confessions de foi chrétienne*, Paris, 1943; esp. J. de Ghellinck, S. J., *Patristique et moyen-age, I Les Recherches sur les origines du symbole des apôtres*, ed. 2, 1949; J. Crehan, S. J., *Early Christian Baptism and the Creed*, London, 1950, ch. II, "The Christ Creed," cf. III, "The Trinitarian Formula"; P.-T. Camelot, O. P., "Recherches récentes sur le symbole des Apôtres et leur portée théologique," *RSR*, 39 (1952), 323–337; P. Benoit, O. P., "Les origines du symbole des Apôtres dans le Nouveau Testament,"

Exégèse et Théologie, II, Paris, 1960, 193–211; esp. H. (Cardinal) de Lubac, S. J., *La Foi Chrétienne* (a study of the Apostles' creed), Paris, 1969; Kelly, *Creeds*, 368–434, "Apostles Creed," 100–166, "Roman Creed"; Quasten I, 23–28; Altaner, 85–87; F. X. Murphy in *NCE*, 4, 432–38. [2]Latin text with this tr., Kelly, *Creeds*, 102; [3]Tr. Bettenson, *Documents of the Christian Church*, Oxford, 1943, 33; [4]cf. Kelly, *Creeds*, 103; [5]*Traditio Apostolica*, ed. B. Botte, O. S. B., SC, 50, 51; [6]*Ibid.*; [7]PL 17: 1193–96; [8]De Ghellinck, *op.cit.*, 105–106; [9]PL 217, 827f; [10]*Expos. super symb. apost.*

APPROPRIATION

Appropriation is the means of reconciling systematic theology of the Trinity with what readers of the Bible derive by way of knowledge from the sacred text. They do not read of the Trinity as an entity; they read of divine actions or characteristics attributed to one of the named persons. It is sometimes said that appropriation is based on the Bible; without the concept what is said in the Bible would leave us entirely puzzled. In the gospels the references to the Father are vastly more numerous than to God; certain basic texts on Christ (Jn 1:3; Col 1:15–17) as well as the entire Pauline corpus of texts relating to his life-work focus our attention on him as a person. Likewise with the Spirit: the promise of Christ (Jn 14, esp. v. 26; 16, esp. v. 13) and the assertion of Paul (Rom 5:5; 2 Cor 1:22) are directly about him with nothing added.

This direct reference to persons is continued in the early creeds, for example the four best known, the Apostles' (*qv*), Nicene (*qv*), Constantinopolitan (*qv*) and pseudo-Athanasian (*qv*). It entered the liturgy (*qv*) from such texts and especially from Sacred Scripture. Many texts from the Fathers show that they worked with the idea without making the precise analysis which would safeguard all the Trinitarian theology which evolved through the early crises. They used the idea as something in keeping with sound tradition.

It is clear that recent advances in theology will show the need for more than lip service to the doctrine of appropriation.[1] It is needed in a vital sense. The best guide in this renewal is St. Thomas Aquinas (*qv*). "To appropriate," says the Angelic Doctor, "is to apply what is common to that which is proper (*commune trahere ad proprium*)." "What is common to the whole Trinity cannot be applied to the property of any person because it agrees with one more than with another; this would offend their equality of persons, but because what is common has a greater resemblance to the property of one person than to that of another."[2] St. Thomas issued a kind of warning against danger: "When we appropriate essential attributes to individual persons we do not exclude the others, nor do we set up a scale of participation."[3]

St. Thomas illustrates the process of appropriation: "Power implies beginning; it is, therefore, appropriated to the Father who is the beginning without beginning; wisdom is appropriated to the Son, who proceeds as Word; goodness to the Holy Spirit, who proceeds as Love with good for its object. Thus it is the resemblance of the attribute which is appropriated to the property of the Person, which is the objective basis of the appropriation, and this objective basis exists independently of us."[4]

It is not therefore a question of theological method merely, not a question of a device no matter how sophisticated to further our discourse about the triune Godhead. The suitability of the appropriation is within the Trinity. Why this should be, why certain attributes belonging to all three should have this special resemblance, in one case or the other, to a single person, why this should be so eternally, independently of any human thought, is a matter not very fully explored by theologians.

Special problems arise in regard to the Incarnation, to divine grace and to the beatific vision; they are dealt with in the relevant articles.

[1]Cf. De Régnon, I, 317–9, 357–9; III, 305; A. Gardeil, O. P., *La structure de l'âme et l'expérience mystique*, Paris, 1927, 71; id. *Vie Spir.*, Suppl., 32(1932), 7–16; H.-F. Dondaine, *La Trinité*, II, Paris, 1946, 409–423; Enrico di S. Teresa, "Proprietà o appropriazione?" *Ephem Carmel.* 4(1950), 239–290; A. Patfoort, *Bulletin Thomiste*, 8, 864–877; F. Bourassa, "Appropriation ou propriété?" *Sc. Eccl.*, 7(1955), 57–85; A. Chollet, *DTC* 1,2, 1707–8; M. Schmaus, *LTK* 1:773–75; H. Barre, C. S. Sp., *Trinité que j'adore*, Paris 1964, 81–89; J. B. Endres, *NCE*, 1, 708–9; J. G. Page, "L'Appropriation, Jeu de l'Esprit ou Réalisme?" *Laval Théologique Philosophique*, 33(1977), 227–39; Chollet, *DTC*, I,2 1708–1717; [2]*De Ver.*, q.7, a.3; [3]*In I Sent.* q. 1, a. 2, ad 3um; [4]*In I Sent*, D. 31, q. 1, a. 1; q. 2, a. 1, ad 1um; cp. esp. I, q. 39, a. 8.

ARIANISM

The testimony of the first bishop who had to contend with this heresy may serve as a preface: "For since they call in question all pious and apostolic doctrine, after the manner of the Jews, they have constructed a workshop for contending against Christ, denying the godhead of our Saviour, and preaching that he is only the equal of all others. And having collected all the passages which speak of his plan of salvation and his humiliation for our sakes, they endeavour from these to collect the preaching of their impiety, ignoring altogether the passages in which his eternal godhead and unutterable glory with the Father is set forth. Since, therefore, they back up the impious opinion concerning Christ which is held by the Jews and Greeks, in every possible way they strive to gain their approval; busying themselves about all those things which they are wont to deride in us, and daily stirring up against us seditions and persecutions. And we, indeed, though we discovered rather late, on account of their concealment, their manner of life and their unholy attempts, by the common suffrage of all have cast them forth from the congregation of the Church which adores the godhead of Christ."[1]

Thus Alexander of Alexandria (qv). He instructs us also on the origins of the heresy: "For you yourselves are taught of God, nor are you ignorant that this doctrine, which has lately raised its head against the piety of the Church, is that of Ebion and Artemas; nor is it aught else but an imitation of Paul of Samosata (qv), bishop of Antioch, who, by the judgment and the counsel of all the bishops and in every place was separated from the Church. To whom Lucian succeeding, remained for màny years separate from the communion under three bishops."[2]

Possibly the most dangerous heresy in the history of Christian belief, A. had origins, which are obscure, earlier than the man from whom it is named. Arius (qv) precipitated the crisis, but St. Lucian of Antioch (qv) may have been the real starting-point. The essence of the heresy was denial of the full divinity of Jesus Christ.

Setting
The article on Arius narrates the emergence of the heresy through his action in the life of the Church. The Council of Nicaea (qv), the first such assembly in church history, itself showed the dimensions of the problem. The Nicene creed (qv) served the purpose of doctrinal definition and its significance cannot, for this reason, be exaggerated. The faith of Nicaea, the capital word which it canonised, *homoousios* (see article Consubstantial), was the touchstone of orthodoxy. But it did

not prevent expansion of the heresy. Through the activity of Arius, through the concerted efforts of his sympathisers and supporters led by Eusebius of Nicomedia (qv), it spread through the east, indented the west.

One prime factor in this development was the policy of the Roman emperors. Constantine I (qv) had called the Council of Nicaea, presided at its opening session and for a while accepted its teaching. But he came under the influence of Constantia, his sister, and slackened in his support. After his death in 337 his son, Constans, a defender of the Nicene creed, ruled in the west and the other son, Constantius II, in the east. Constans died in 351 and Constantius was then sole ruler.

Constantine had wavered between Athanasius and Eusebius, joining forces with the latter in his last years. He banished Athanasius to faraway Treves and supported the plan to reinstate Arius—a plan thwarted by the heretic's sudden death. He did not tamper with the formulary of the faith.

Nor did Constantius. But if, like his father, he chose to protect the faith, he would choose which faith merited his protection. Unquestionably his influence was decisive in one of the darkest moments in the history of theology and of the Church, the triumph of the radical Arians, the Homoeans (qv), at the councils of Rimini (359), Seleucia (359), and Constantinople (360). At this time St. Jerome made his oft-quoted comment: "The whole world groaned and was astonished to find itself Arian."

Why did the emperor have any such role in church affairs related to doctrine, to the exercise of the teaching authority? Was the imperial power a factor in doctrinal development?

The first question becomes more acute when one remembers that neither Constantine nor Constantius were, at the relevant times, baptized Christians. They were interested in Christianity and seemed to have the intention, which in each case was fulfilled shortly before death, of asking for baptism. But since by the imperial decision the Church had, from about the time of the so-called Edict of Milan (usually dated 313), enjoyed toleration and freedom, it seemed logical to both the ruler himself and the bishops that he would watch over their activity. Things evolved under the impulse of personalities, in response to needs; there was no thought-out theory of Church–state relations.

Many of the bishops who met at Nicaea had just emerged from persecution wherein imperial policy and power were paramount. They did not object to a partnership of religion and politics which at the outset seemed beneficial. With time things worsened: supporters of Athanasius were persecuted bitterly. To secure the compliance of bishops—even a hero like Hosius (or Ossius) of Cordova—and of a Pope, pressure and intimidation were used. Exile was the lot of those who resisted the emperor.

There were, nonetheless, dissidents. Lucifer of Cagliari (qv) opposed Constantius to his face at Milan in 355 and published tracts against him in exile. St. Hilary of Poitiers (qv) published a work *Against Constantius*.

One other general factor in the history of Arianism needs complete elucidation, the role of the faithful. Newman caused something akin to scandal when he published his article in the *Rambler, On Consulting the Faithful in Matters of Doctrine*.[3] In this essay, written largely in reference to the Arian heresy, which he had already studied at length in another work, he contended that the faith of the Church was preserved by the faithful, while the hierarchy generally collapsed.

Thus Newman states his case: "It is not a little remarkable that though, historically speaking, the fourth century is the age of doctors, illustrated as it was by the saints Athanasius, Hilary, the two Gregories, Basil, Chrysostom, Ambrose, Jerome, and Augustine, and all of these saints bishops also, except one, nevertheless in that very day the divine tradition committed to the infallible Church was proclaimed and maintained far more by the faithful than by the episcopate. . . ."

Newman introduces certain nuances which need to be retained: "Here, of course, I must explain: in saying this, then, undoubtedly I am not denying that the great body of the bishops were in their internal belief orthodox; nor that there were numbers of clergy who stood by the laity, and acted as their interpreters and guides; nor that the laity actually received their faith in the first instance from the bishops and clergy; nor that some portions of the laity were ignorant, and others at length corrupted by the Arian teachers, who got possession of the sees and ordained an heretical clergy; but I mean still, that in that time of immense confusion the divine dogma of our Lord's divinity was proclaimed, enforced, maintained, and (humanly speaking) preserved, far more by the 'Ecclesia docta' than by the 'Ecclesia docens'; that the body of the bishops was unfaithful to its commission, while the body of the faithful

was faithful to its baptism; that at one time the Pope, at other times the patriarchal, metropolitan, and other great sees, at other times general councils, said what they should not have said, or did what obscured and compromised revealed truth; while, on the other hand, it was the Christian people who, under Providence, were the Ecclesiastical strength of Athanasius, Hilary, Eusebius of Vercellae, and other great solitary confessors, who would have failed otherwise."[4]

Newman saw "in the Arian history a palmary example of a state of the Church during which, in order to know the tradition of the Apostles, we must have recourse to the faithful." Their voice he thought the voice of tradition. Arianism is therefore instructive for four reasons: it occurred at the beginning of the "*Ecclesia docens*," which in effect began after the age of martyrs; the doctrinal development of the Christian system was momentous; the crisis lasted for sixty years, a long period; and it involved "persecutions, in life, limb, and property to the faithful whose loyal perseverance decided it."[5]

Newman's thesis has been to some extent queried if not modified by a modern patristic scholar, Fr. Jules Lebreton (qv), who concluded that the breach affecting doctrine in the fourth century was between the laity and the theologians, not between the laity and the bishops.[6] His own conclusion that "the history of the dogma of the Trinity in the Ante-Nicene age has much to gain from the study of learned theology and of the common(ly held) faith and of their mutual relations" implies that all the research is not complete—if it can ever be so. One fact seems certain: the faithful played an important part in the defeat of Arianism. The conclusion is not weakened by the fact that the history was set down in part by laymen, Socrates and Sozomen.[7]

Within a few years of Nicaea the exiles whom it had discredited returned and a new phase opened. Arius did not long survive. It was the man who had worked for his return and reinstatement, Eusebius of Nicomedia (qv), who took the lead in resistance to the faith of Nicaea.

The Eusebians

Eusebius, hardened by exile, determined and crafty in character, was bishop of the imperial capital, and increasingly gained power within the imperial circle. With him were associated his namesake, Eusebius of Caesarea, Paulinus of Tyre, and Menophantes of Ephesus. Their tactic was to undermine and drive out the Nicene bishops. Thus they secured the expulsion, by synodical decree, of Eustathius of Antioch—the second city of the east—Marcellus of Ancyra, Asclepas of Gaza, and finally the head and central power of the Nicene party, Athanasius. In place of the exiles Eusebians were everywhere installed: some of the eastern bishops sympathetic to the anti-Nicene faction had felt genuine misgiving if not doubt about the propriety of the word *homoousios*. Eusebius and his associates had never accepted the Nicene faith, professing it only as a tactic (see article Eusebius for consideration of another view).

Their influence was probably enlarged by the quasi-retirement of the papacy for the critical twenty-five years between the council of 313 under Pope Miltiades and the advent of St. Julius I (*qv*) in 338. The change was evident very soon. The new Pope received the eastern exiles in Rome, and at the council held in that city they were vindicated. The Eusebians had asked the Pope to judge between them and Athanasius. When he showed his independence of their previous conciliar decisions, they rebelled against him. This, a side-effect of A., was the first challenge to papal primacy. To the manifesto of revolt the Pope, after the council had held its sessions, replied with a lengthy letter, firm, courteous, and in regard to the matters at issue a model of the just decision and judicial mind.[8]

The Papacy is placed at the center of the Arian debate by Julius: "The Arians who were excommunicated for their impiety by Alexander the late Bishop of Alexandria, of blessed memory, were not only proscribed by the brethren in the several cities, but were also anathematised by the whole body assembled together in the great Council of Nicaea. For theirs was no ordinary offence, neither had they sinned against man, but against our Lord Jesus Christ himself, the Son of the living God. And yet these persons who were proscribed by the whole world, and branded in every church, are said now to have been admitted to communion again; which I think even you ought to hear with indignation. Who then are the parties who dishonour a council? Are not they [those] who have set at nought the votes of the three hundred, and have preferred impiety to godliness? The heresy of the Arian madmen was condemned and proscribed by the whole body of bishops everywhere; but the bishops Athanasius and Marcellus have

many supporters who speak and write in their behalf."[9]

On the reasons for exonerating Athanasius Julius writes thus: "Now when these things were thus represented to us, and so many witnesses appeared in his favour, and so much was advanced by him in his own justification, what did it become us to do? What did the rule of the Church require of us, but that we should not condemn him, but rather receive him and treat him like a bishop, as we have done? Moreover, besides all this he continued here a year and six months, expecting the arrival of yourselves and of whoever chose to come, and by his presence he put everyone to shame, for he would not have been here had he not felt confident in his cause; and he came not of his own accord, but on an invitation by letter from us, in the manner in which we wrote to you."[10]

The Pope was aware of the harsh realities of the heresy. On the intrusion of Gregory into the see of Alexandria: "Dearly beloved, we speak honestly, as in the presence of God, and declare that this proceeding was neither pious, nor lawful, nor ecclesiastical. Moreover, the account which is given of the conduct of Gregory on his entry into the city, plainly shows the character of his appointment. In such peaceful times, as those who came from Alexandria declared them to have been, and as the bishops also represented in their letters, the Church was set on fire; virgins were defiled; monks were trodden under foot; presbyters and many of the people were scourged and suffered violence; bishops were cast into prison; multitudes were dragged about from place to place; the holy Mysteries, about which they accused the presbyter Macarius, were seized upon by heathens and cast upon the ground; and all to constrain certain persons to admit the appointment of Gregory. Such conduct shows plainly who they are that transgress the Canons."[11] The word Canons embraces the traditions governing appointment to office in the Church.

Councils and Creeds

The papal missive did not deter the bishops assembled at Antioch in that same year, 341, for the dedication of the Basilica, from setting themselves up as a council, namely the Dedication Council, *In Encaenis*. A new phase in the Arian struggle was now begun. A set of credal formulae was put forward in open challenge to the Nicene creed. The second of four, going back to Lucian of Antioch (*qv*), was promulgated: it omitted the distinctive phrases of the Nicene creed, "of the essence of the Father" and *homoousios*. "This council, *In Encaenis* of 341," writes Mgr. Philip Hughes, "inaugurates the new strategy of finding synonyms for the technical terms used in conciliar definitions, synonyms designed to betray the truth already decreed and to ensure the condemned heretics their place within the Church."[12]

The council of 341 confirmed Gregory in the see of Alexandria; it condemned the heretics who had failed to make the proper distinction between the Father and the Son: Sabellius, Paul of Samosata and Marcellus of Ancyra, the first two of whom were dead. In that year Eusebius died. Julius began overtures for reconciliation. Through Constans he eventually succeeded in his wish for a council which would effect church unity. The two emperors agreed to call the council, which would meet at Sardica (modern Sofia), near the east but territorially within the western empire. It was a failure, for the eastern bishops refused to sit in an assembly with Athanasius and his fellow exiles. Hosius (or Ossius) of Cordova (*qv*), now an octogenarian, as president rejected the ultimatum of the protesters: it preempted the question to be decided, the status of Athanasius. As the seventy-six departed they left a heated manifesto of dissent. They condemned Athanasius and Marcellus anew, and denied the right of a western council to review a decision taken by an eastern one. They blamed the west for their departure and excommunicated the Pope and Hosius.

The Council of Sardica, without the eastern bishops, judged and approved Athanasius. It reaffirmed the creed of Nicaea and it excommunicated the bishops forced on sees by the emperor; it did likewise for the leaders of the schism from the council. Certain disciplinary canons enacted by the council were intended to save bishops from interference by the civil power and restated the power of the bishop of Rome.

Creeds and personalities were competing for attention in the years thereafter. Constantius II forbade, under pain of death, the bishops rehabilitated by the council to return to their sees, and he sent into exile two bishops from his empire who had supported the council.

The next notable event in the doctrinal history is the Long-lined Creed, an exposition of the faith drawn up for Constantius; it was brought to a meeting at Milan in 345 by four eastern bishops.

It is described by Athanasius as "a faith written at great length and with numerous additions over and above those which have gone before."[13] It is a lengthy formula, many times longer than the Nicene Creed.

Before very long Constantius had a free hand. His brother was assassinated in 350 and though a civil war ensued he was eventually the victor. The strong Pope, Julius, died in 352 and was succeeded by Liberius, a man of less than heroic temper. In 351 the first council of Sirmium took place. The bishop, Photinus, ambiguous in doctrine, was deposed after a theological debate, ordered by the emperor, between him and Basil of Ancyra—a disciple of his old master, Marcellus, also henceforth doctrinally suspect. Sirmium produced another creed, vague but a departure from the Nicene.

The new Pope suggested to Constantius the convening of another council at Aquileia to seek success where Sardica had failed. The assembly took place at Arles, 353. There the bishops of Gaul wished to express their belief in the faith of Nicaea. The emperor was present and blocked this proposal. He demanded the signatures of all present to an edict condemning to exile whoever would not condemn Athanasius. With the exception of Paulinus of Treves, all signed, including the Pope's legates.

Constantius had henceforth a pathological obsession about Athanasius. At Milan, two years later, this abnormal attitude led him, as he coerced the bishops once more to sign a decree against the Alexandrian, to proclaim: "My will is canon law, bishops in Syria make no such objections when I address them. . ." The words were spoken to those who refused to comply—Paulinus of Treves, Lucifer of Cagliari, Eusebius of Vercelli, and Denis of Milan. He threatened them with instant execution, but changed it to exile. Violence was also the means used, in the following year, when another usurper, George of Cappadocia, was thrust into Alexandria in place of Athanasius: under this time-server, bishops, priests and laity were persecuted for their fidelity to their rightful bishop, just as had happened fifty years previously in the persecution of Diocletian and Galerius.

Violence escalated. The Pope was kidnapped in 357 and brought to the imperial court. Constantius gave him three days to decide between signing against Athanasius and going into exile;

he chose the latter. During the dramatic encounter the emperor made a bitter personal attack on Athanasius. The bishop was now in hiding, the Pope in exile, the inflexible champion in the west, Hilary, likewise; the elderly Hosius was detained at the court of Sirmium.

But with the field apparently free of opponents the Arians could not agree on a creed to replace the Nicene formula. Three varieties of opinion had supporters: the Anomoeans, most radical, who thought the Son unlike (*anomoios*) the Father; the Homoeans (*qv*), who thought that he was like (*homoios*) the Father and used this vagueness as a blanket term, covering diverse opinions; and the Homoeousians (*homoiousios*), the moderates, who held that the Son was of like substance to the Father—some of these possibly thought that the word *homoousios* had dangerous implications and embarrassing antecedent use (see CONSUBSTANTIAL).

The Anomoeans had a brief triumph. They drew up a creed at Sirmium in 357 and promulgated it with the support of Constantius. Hilary called it the "blasphemy"; it was Arian and with such language as this expressed blatant heresy: "No one can doubt that the Father is greater than the Son in honour, dignity, splendour, majesty, and in the very name of Father, the Son himself testifying, *He that sent me is greater than I.* . . . The Son is subordinated to the Father, together with all things which the Father has subordinated to him."[14]

The leaders of this extreme faction were Valens and Ursacius in the west and Eudoxius and Eunomius in the east. Their success was the occasion of widespread apprehension in the east and west. The moderates, led by Basil of Ancyra (*qv*) and George of Laodicea, met at Ancyra (spring 358) and at Sirmium (summer 358). They repudiated Anomoeism, and worked for the acceptance of a formula with *homoiousios* as its key word. Basil collected signatures, including that of Liberius, who qualified his approval. Assured of the imperial support Basil planned a general council to meet in the city of Nicomedia. Victory was within the grasp of the Homoeousians when an earthquake forced postponement of the council.

In the interval Basil fell from the imperial favour and the Homoeans led by Acacius of Caesarea (*qv*) seized their opportunity. The fourth creed of Sirmium, dated 25 May 359, was to be signed by all the bishops, from the east and the west. The text was drawn up by Marcus of Arethusa and would be submitted to the bishops at two councils, one for the west at Rimini, the other for the east at Seleucia. This time the word was *homoios*, "like the Father in all things" as the Scriptures declare. The final version of the text did not contain the words "in all things." The creed had been called the *Dated Creed*, because it opens with an elaborate dating, "in the consulate of the most illustrious Flavii, Eusebius and Hypatius, on the eleventh day before the calends of June."

At Rimini more than 400 western bishops assembled. Eighty Arians approved the fourth creed of Sirmium on 12 July, 359; the other bishops rejected it, reaffirmed the faith of Nicaea and excommunicated four bishops attached to the court of the emperor: Valens, Ursacius, Germinius and Gaius. Ten of their own number were sent on a delegation to the emperor. At Nike in Thrace, on 10 October, 359, the delegates were forced to revoke the excommunication and to subscribe to an ambiguously worded creed.

On the return of these delegates to Rimini the orthodox bishops surrendered to the emperor and signed the Homoean formula. At Seleucia in September, 359, there were two parties, Homoeousians and Acacians. Eventually delegates from both councils met in Constantinople. There the final surrender took place. The formula accepted contained the words: "And in the only-begotten Son of God, begotten from God before all ages and before every beginning, by whom all things were made, visible and invisible, and begotten as only-begotten, only from the Father only, God from God like to the Father that begat him according to the Scriptures; whose origin no one knows, except the Father alone who begat him."

The triumph was not to be permanent. Reconciliation was now an apparent necessity to Homoeousians and Homoousians. It became easier through the action of Athanasius at the synod of Alexandria in 362 and with the removal of the essential prop of Homoeism by the death of Constantius in 361. Some years later Homoeism enjoyed the support of Valens, the eastern emperor. Thereafter it died out, deprived of any support by Gratian and Theodoret, champions and supporters of the Nicene faith.

Arianism in its Homoean form infiltrated the Germanic peoples. They were evangelized by

Wulfila, who had been consecrated at the Dedication Council by Eusebius of Nicomedia, and was present in Constantinople in 360. To the Goths whom he converted on the lower Danube he taught a Homoean creed, which they carried with them to the Germanic peoples; these as they moved west to found new kingdoms brought their form of Arianism with them. But there never was an intellectual ferment as in the days of the heresies and the creeds, and gradually the Church succeeded in bringing the new Christians to the faith, which twenty years after the surrender at Constantinople would triumph universally at a general council of the Church in the same city.

[1]Epistle to Alexander of Byzantium, Theodoret, Hist.eccl., 1, 4, ANF, 6; [2]9, ANF, 6; for bibliography since 1955 cf. Bibliographia patristica and bibliographies to Alexander of Alexandria, Anomoeans, Arius, Athanasius, Basil of Ancyra, Constantine, Constantius, Eusebius, Homoeousians, Homoeans, Julius Pope, Liberius Pope, Lucifer of Cagliari, Marcellus of Ancyra, Homoousion, Nicaea, Hosius (or Ossius) of Cordova; Church Histories of the fourth century, H. Lietzmann, Fliche-Martin III, Philip Hughes; J.R. Palanque et al., The Church in the Christian Roman Empire, London, 396–408; H.M. Gwatkin, Studies of Arianism, 2nd ed. 1900; id., The arianischen Streites, Helsingfors, 1904; S. Rogala, Die Anfang des arianischen Streites, 1907; J. Gummerus, Die Homousianische Partei bis zum Tode des Konstantius, 1900; J. Zeiller, Les origines chrétiennes dans les provinces danubiennes, Paris, 1918; A. d'Ales, Le dogme de Nicée, Paris, 1926; G. Bardy, Recherches sur Lucien d'Antioche et son école, Paris, 1936, 246–274; id., in Fliche et Martin III; G. Prestige, God in Patristic Thought, 1935; 2nd ed., 1959; H.G. Opitz, Urkunden zur Geschichte des arianischen Streites, Athanasius Werke, v.3, 1, Berlin, 1934; id., "Zur Kirchengeschichte des 4 Jahrhunderts,"ZNTWiss 34(1935), 129–213; K.D. Schmidt, Die Bekehrung des Germanen zum Christentum, 2 vols, Göttingen, 1939/40; M. Richard, "Saint Athanase et la psychologie du Christ selon les Ariens," MSR 4(1947) 9–54; V. C. De Clercq, Ossius of Cordova, Washington, 1954, 189ff; T.E. Pollard, "The Origins of Arianism," JTS, N S., 9(1958), 103–111, H.A. Wolfson, "Philosophical Implications of Arianism and Apollinarianism," Dumbarton Oaks Papers, 12(1958), 3–28; E. Schwartz, Zur geschichte des Athanasius, Gesammelte Schriften, 3, Berlin 1959; W. Haugaard, "Arius Twice a Heretic," ChHist 29(1960), 251–263; A. Grillmeier, S.J., Christ in the Christian Tradition, London, 1965; M. Simonetti, Studi sull'Arianesimo, Rome, 1965; id., La crisi ariana nel IV secolo, Rome, 1975; M. Meslin, Les Ariens d'Occident, 335–430, Paris, 1967; G.C. Stead, "The Platonism of Arius," JTS 15(1964), 16–31; E. Boularand, L'Hérésie d'Arius et la 'Foi' de Nicée, 2 vols, Paris, 1972ff; id., "Les Débuts d'Arius," Bull.litt.eccl., 75(1964), 175–203; R.C. Gregg–D.E. Groh, Early Arianism, A View of Salvation, 1981; X. le Bachelet, DTC, 1, 1779–1863; Quasten III, 7–13; V.C. De Clercq, NCE, 1, 791–94; Lonergan, Nicaea, 68–87; [3]ed. J. Coulson, London, 1961; [4]Ibid., 76; [5]Ibid., 77; [6]"Le desaccord de la foi populaire et de la théologie savante dans l'Eglise chrétienne du IIIe siècle," RHE 19(1923), 481–506; 20(1924), 357–376; [7]cf. 36; [8]Apud Athanasius, Apologia contra Arianos, 23ff; [9]Ibid., 23; [10]Ibid., 29; [11]Ibid., 30; [12]A History of the Church, I, London, 1948, 2nd ed., 202; [13]Athanasius, De synodis, 26, LNPF, 462; [14]Ibid., 28, 466.

ARIMINUM AND SELEUCIA, SYNODS OF, (359)

The Emperor Constantius (qv) called these two assemblies to end discussion on the Arian question, to end it as he wished.[1] Athanasius devoted a whole work to a narrative of the events and assessment of the findings and teaching.[2] It was the blackest year in the entire history of Arianism, when everything seemed lost and Jerome's comment appeared appropriate. Under pressure from the emperor the orthodox western majority were induced to sign the Creed drawn up at Nice—very Arian in its terms; the poison had been sown by Valens and Ursacius, leaders of the Arian minority at this western synod in Ariminum (Rimini). Acacius and Eudoxius, leaders of the Arians at the eastern synod held in Seleucia in the same year, secured the acceptance of the Creed of Nice also. Into this wilderness of official collapse fell the word of Jerome, "The whole world groaned and wondered to find itself Arian."

[1]Cf. bibliography to article on Arianism, esp. G. Bardy, Fliche Martin III, (1936), 161–69; [2]De Synodis, LNPF, IV, 451–480.

ARIUS (d. 336)

Life

One of the principal heresiarchs of all Church history, A. is not well known to us; his writings are slight in quantity.[1] The heresy which bears his name has roots earlier than his activity, but it was he who gave it the dynamism that kept it going long after his death. Such was its magnitude that a supreme force of grace and nature was needed to overcome it: this force's name was Athanasius (qv and see ARIANISM).

A., who was probably born in Libya, appears first in the circle of disciples gathered around St. Lucian (qv) in the exegetical school founded by this saint at Antioch. He then became head of the exegetical school at Alexandria, the city which was still the intellectual capital of the Roman world. He was in conflict with the Bishop of Alexandria, St. Peter (d. 312), through his membership in the Melitian sect; he was excommunicated. Restored to communion with the Church, he was ordained a priest by Peter's successor, Achillas. Eloquent and ascetic, A. exerted considerable influence. Unfortunately he opposed his Bishop's ideas on a fundamental point of Christian faith, the relationship between God the Father and the Logos, that is, Jesus Christ. The clash was public in the years 319–323. His teaching, a form of Subordinationism (qv), was condemned by a synod at Alexandria in 320 and he was again excommunicated. He continued to spread his teaching and found support among the episcopate.

The emperor Constantine (qv), sole ruler of the Roman world since 324, sent his ecclesiastical advisor, Hosius (Ossius) of Cordova to Alexandria to effect a reconciliation between priest and Bishop. When the attempt failed, the emperor, probably on the advice of Hosius, made a decision which would affect the course of events thereafter: he decided to call a General Council of the Church to deal with the doctrinal question. How this bore on the development of doctrine is dealt with in the section on Arianism. Its effect on the life of A. was twofold: it united him more closely with ecclesiastics with influential access to the emperor, notably his friend, Eusebius of Nicomedia, and it tempted him to look for succour from the civil power in matters strictly theological.

A.'s ideas were condemned first by Bishops meeting under Hosius at Antioch and this condemnation was renewed at Nicaea, (qv) where the General Council met in 325. Already the genius and tenacity of Athanasius (qv) were felt in this assembly, though he was but a Deacon and secretary of Alexander of Alexandria (qv). He influenced the drafting of the conciliar text.

Arius was banished to Illyricum. He was gradually brought back to acceptable status, to the point where a Council held at Jerusalem in 336 decided to reinstate him formally. On the eve of the day fixed by the emperor Constantine for the public ceremony the heretic died suddenly. Alexandria, though its Bishop, Athanasius, was in exile, repudiated any such denouement.

Writings

Arius' extant writings are: a) a letter to Eusebius of Nicomedia, written about 318;[2] b) a profession of faith, in the form of a letter, sent to Bishop Alexander of Alexandria about 320;[3] c) a treatise entitled *Thaleia*, fragments of which survive;[4] d) a profession of faith sent to the Emperor Constantine towards the end of 327;[5] e) some recently discovered texts.[6]

Doctrine

The principal points of Arius' doctrine have been thus summarized: the Son is not eternal; he is created from nothing freely; he is not true God equal and consubstantial with the Father; he is imperfect and changing. Two points less stressed are: in Christ the Logos takes the place of the human soul; the Holy Spirit is not God.

The letters to Eusebius and to Alexander state the views of Arius clearly. Of the second text it has been said that "Orthodox believers refer to it as the most exact expression of the heresy and Arians as the authentic formulary of their belief."[7]

The letter to Eusebius enlightens us on the relations between the two men and on the writer's views; it is less reliable on the Bishop of Alexandria. It reads thus:

"To my most amiable Lord, faithful, orthodox man of God, Eusebius, Arius persecuted unjustly by the pope Alexander, because of truth which triumphs over all, of which you also undertake the defence, greetings in the Lord.

"My father, Ammonios, is going to Nicomedia. It seemed to me opportune and a duty to send you through him my greetings and, at the same time to remind you of the charity and the regard you have for the brothers in God and in Christ. For this Bishop ill treats and persecutes us very much and turns everything against us, going as far as to banish us from the city like atheistic people, because we do not agree with him when he says publicly: 'There is always God, always a Son; there is a Son at the same time as there is a Father; the Son coexists with God without generation, eternally begotten, unbegotten-begotten. Neither by a thought, nor by a moment, does God precede the Son: always God, always the Son. The Son is from God himself.'

"And as Eusebius, your brother, who is at Caesarea, and Theodotus, and Paulinus and Athanasius (of Anazarbe) and Gregory (of Berytes) and Aetius and all the easterns say that the Father exists before the Son, without having a beginning, they are all anathema. Only Philogones, Hellanicos and Macarios are not so, ignorant heretics, some of whom say that the Son is a bursting forth (extruding) or a projection, and others a co-unbegotten. We cannot even listen to such godless things, even if heretics were to threaten us with a thousand deaths. But what do we say, what do we think, what have we taught and what are we teaching? This: that the Son is neither unbegotten nor in any way a part of the unbegotten, and neither was he made from any pre-existing matter; by the will and design (of God) he began to exist before times and ages, full of grace and truth God, the only-begotten Son, unchangeable. Before he was begotten or created or appointed or established he did not exist, for he was not unbegotten. They persecute us because we say: the Son has a beginning, God is without a beginning. This is why they persecute us still, that we say he was drawn from nothing. But we said this in the sense that he is not a part of God, nor was he drawn from pre-existing matter. For that they persecute us, which indeed you know. Remain well with the Lord, remembering our tribulations. This is my wish as a true Lucian colleague, Eusebius."[8]

While the letter faithfully reflects Arius' own views, his understanding of Alexander's opinion is inadequate; he confused the Son's eternity with his relation to the Father, thinking that to be eternal was to be unbegotten. The misrepresentation may have been calculated to belittle Alexander in the eyes of Eusebius.

The profession of faith addressed to Alexander bears the signature of the six priests, six deacons and two Bishops condemned by the council of Alexandria and of a Bishop Pistus whom the Arians had attempted to force on the see of Alexandria. The document is basic and rests on notable testimony. St. Athanasius reproduces it in *De Synodis* and, apart from his reliability in such matters, the critical importance of this text would prompt exactitude.[9] St. Epiphanius reproduces it in his *Panarion*, informing us that it was from Nicomedia that Arius sent it, and that the address was "to Alexandria."[10] Possibly it was meant as an open letter to the faithful. We have a third check on the original. St. Hilary of Poitiers (qv) gives a Latin translation of it in books IV and VI of his *De Trinitate*.[11] This is the text:

"To our blessed father and Bishop Alexander from the priests and deacons, greeting in Christ.

"This is the faith which comes to us from our ancestors, and which we have also learned from you, O blessed father. We acknowledge one only God, who alone is unbegotten, who alone is eternal, who alone is without beginning, who alone is true, who alone holds immortality, who alone is wise, who alone is good, who alone is powerful, judge of all, controller, administrator, unchangeable and unalterable, just and good, God of the Law and of the Prophets and of the New Covenant, who before all time begot his only Son, by whom he made the ages and all things; he begot him not in appearance but in truth, he made him exist by his own will, unchangeable and unalterable, God's perfect creature but not like any other creature, production but not like other beings produced. This offspring of the Father is not, as Valentinus taught, an emission of, neither is he, as Mani taught, a part of the Father, consubstantial with him; neither is he the same person as the Father, as Sabellius said, dividing the unity; nor is it, as Hieracas held, as if there were one torch from another or one lamp with two parts. He did not first exist and was then begotten or constituted a Son, according to the explanation of those whom you, O blessed Father, have often refuted in the midst of the Church and in council.

"But we say that he was created by the will of God before times and the ages, and he received from the Father life and being and glory. For the Father made him subsist with him. The Father, in reality, in giving all things into his possession, did not deprive himself of what he possesses in himself, in an unbegotten way. For he is the source of all things. There are thus three substances (*hypostases*).

"The God who is the cause of all things is absolutely the only one who is without beginning. The Son, born of the Father before time and created and constituted in being before the ages, did not exist before he was begotten: born *outside* of time, generated before all else, he alone received being from the Father, for he is not eternal nor co-eternal, nor is he as the Father is, unbegotten; neither, as some say of things that are related to each other, does he have being simultaneously with the Father. For thus there would be two unbegotten principles. But God, as he is a unity and source of all things, so he exists before all things. That is why he also exists before the Son, as we have learned from you who preached it in the midst of the Church. Inasmuch, then, as the Son has being, glory and life from the Father, in so much is God his source. He is his Lord, as being his God and existing before him.

"If some people understand the phrases *from him, from the womb*, and *I came forth from the Father and I come* as implying that he is a consubstantial part of the Father, or some sort of emission, they make the Father composite, divisible and changeable; indeed God would be a body, if they had their way, and the incorporeal God would be affected in ways in which only bodies can be affected."[12]

A.'s ideas were given versified form in the *Thaleia* ("Banquet"). Extracts are found in the writings of Athanasius, as follows: "According to faith of God's elect, God's prudent ones,/ Holy children, rightly dividing, God's Holy Spirit receiving,/ Have I learned this from the partakers of wisdom,/ Accomplished, divinely taught, and wise in all things,/ Along their track, have I been walking, with like opinions,/ I the very famous, the much suffering for God's glory;/ And taught of God, I have acquired wisdom and knowledge."[13]

Thus Athanasius gives the opening verses of the *Thaleia* and he follows it, in the same work, the first *Oratio contra Arianos*, with this passage: "God was not always a Father; but there was a time when God was alone and when he was not yet a Father, but afterwards he became a Father. The Son was not always; for since all things were made out of nothing, and all are creatures and works, the Word of God himself was made out of nothing, and there was a time when he was not. And he was not before being born, but he also had an origin of creation. For God, he says, was alone, and the Word as yet was not, nor the Wisdom. Then wishing to form us, thereupon he made a certain one and named him Word and Wisdom and Son, that he might form us by means of him."[14]

The next extract is more substantial. It is found in the *De synodis* just before the text of A.'s letter to Alexander. Bardy (*qv*) thinks it a patchwork of quotations, each two or three lines, but each showing an essential aspect of the heresy.[15] E. Boularand argues for continuity, because of the rhythmic character which suggests a poetic whole. Athanasius entitles the passage "Blasphemies of Arius": "God himself then, in his own nature, is ineffable by all men. He alone has no one equal or like him, or one in glory. And ingenerate we call him, because of him who is generate by nature. We praise him as without beginning because of him who has a beginning. And adore him as everlasting, because of him who in time has come to be. The One without beginning made

the Son the beginning of creatures and, after producing him, adopted him as his Son. He has nothing proper to God in the substance which is proper to him. For he is not his equal, nor consubstantial with him. Wise is God, for he is the teacher of wisdom. There is full proof that God is invisible to all beings; both to things which are through the Son and to the Son he is invisible. I will say it expressly, how the Son can see the invisible; it is by that power by which God sees, and in his own measure, it is reserved to the Son to see the Father, as is lawful. The Trinity then is not made of equal glories, nor do their substances intermingle with each other. One is of more glory than another, to infinity. The Father is foreign to the Son in essence, because he is without beginning. Understand then the Monad was; but the Dyad was not, before it was in existence. It follows at once that though the Son was not, the Father was God. Hence the Son not being (for he existed at the will of the Father) is God only-begotten, and he is alien from either. Wisdom existed as wisdom by the will of the wise God. He is conceived in numberless thoughts: Spirit, Power, Wisdom, God's glory, Truth, Image, Word. Understand that he is conceived to be radiance and light. The superior is able to beget one equal to the Son; but not one more excellent, or superior or greater. By the will of God the Son is as great as he is. And when and since he was, from that time he has drawn his existence from God. He, being a strong God, praises in his degree the superior. In a word God is ineffable to his Son. For he is to himself what he is, that is, unspeakable. So that nothing which is called comprehensible does the Son know to speak about; for it is impossible for him to investigate the Father, who is by himself. For the Son does not know his own essence, for, being Son, he really existed, at the will of the Father. What argument then allows, that he who is from the Father should know his own parent by comprehension? For it is clear that one who has a beginning is incapable of conceiving or of grasping in his mode of being one who has no beginning."[16]

There are other fragments of the *Thaleia*, all of which have been located, identified and published by G. Bardy.[17] The principal of them are in these works of Athanasius: the *Oratio I contra Arianos*,[18] the *Epistola ad episcopos Aegypti et Libyae*,[19] the *De sententia Dionysii*,[20] and the *De decretis Nicaenae synodi*.[21] To complete the text of his main extant works we have to include the profession of faith to Constantine. It is found in the works of the two ecclesiastical historians, Socrates and Sozomen.[22] H.-G. Opitz, a critical editor of this and other relevant texts, dates it in 327.[23] E. Boularand argues in favour of 335, for Sozomen links the text with the council of Jerusalem, which in September of that year followed that held at Tyr.[24]

The profession of faith was written by Arius on his own behalf and on behalf of Euzoius, a Deacon excommunicated and exiled with him, how and by whom it is not known. Both were summoned to Constantinople to justify their faith to the emperor. He examined them and, to be fully informed, asked for a written statement. He then sent it to the Bishops assembled in Jerusalem for the dedication of the Anastasis, his magnificent building on Calvary. He urged the bishops to admit the two writers to communion on the basis of their text. It reads as follows:

"To the emperor Constantine, our master, most religious and beloved of God, Arius and Euzoius.

"As your piety, dear to God, O emperor, our master, has ordered us, we set forth our faith and we confess in writing, that we and all those who are with us, believe according to the formula which we submit to you.

"We believe in one only God, the Father, almighty; and in the Lord Jesus Christ, his only-begotten Son, who has been begotten of him before all ages, God the Word, by whom all has been made, both what is in the heavens and what is on earth; who came down and took flesh, suffered and was raised, went up to heaven and will come to judge the living and the dead. And in the Holy Spirit, and in the resurrection of the flesh, and in the life of the world to come, and in one only catholic Church of God, which stretches from one end of the world to the other.

"We have received this faith from the holy gospels from where the Lord said to his disciples: 'Go teach all nations, baptizing them in the name of the Father and the Son and the Holy Spirit.'

"If we do not believe that and if we do not truly receive the Father and the Son and the Holy Spirit, as the whole catholic Church and the Scriptures, according to which we believe everything, teach us, let God be our judge now and hereafter.

"This is why we invoke your piety, O emperor beloved of God, since we are members of the Church and we have the faith and thought of the Church and of the holy Scriptures, that we may be united, thanks to your pacific and religious piety, to our Mother, that is, the Church, once these questions and the superfluous discussions born of them are eliminated, in order that we and the Church may together enjoy peace, and that together we may offer customary prayers for your pacific and religious reign, and all your kindred."[25]

The historian Sozomen commented shrewdly that Arius in composing this draft avoided the novelties he had invented formerly, keeping to the simple language of Scripture. He swore that this was the content of his mind on such subjects.[26] It quite obviously differs from the other documents which reveal his thinking. One text should be quoted to show his inconsistency. In his letter to Alexander he spoke of the Son as unchangeable; likewise in the letter to Eusebius. In the letter of Alexander of Alexandria (qv) to all the Bishops of the Church, about 319, we read: "For the Son is something created, something made." (Alexander is giving the Arian view.) "He is not similar to the Father in respect of substance (ousia); neither is he the true and natural Word of the Father, nor is he the Father's true wisdom, but belongs to the things that have been made and created. He is improperly called the Word and wisdom, since he himself was made through the word of God in the proper sense, and through the wisdom that is in God, in which wisdom God made not only all other things, but him as well. Therefore he is mutable by nature, as all rational creatures are. The Word is outside of God's substance, other than God's substance, apart from God's substance. The Son cannot tell all about the Father; for he cannot see the Father perfectly, and his knowledge of the Father is imperfect and imprecise. Indeed the Son does not even know his own substance, as it is in itself. For it was for our sakes that he was made, so that through his instrumentality, as it were, God might create us; and he would not have existed if God had not wished to bring us into being. To the question, whether it is possible that the Word of God is such that he could be changed in the way that the devil was changed, they did not draw back from answering that it is indeed possible, because, being made and created, he is by nature changeable."[27]

Since little beyond the second creed of Antioch remains of Lucian of Antioch's (qv) work, it remains difficult to decide exactly the genesis of

A.'s thinking, and to trace the stages of his theological development. Was his role principally that of catalyst?

[1]Cf. bibliography to Arianism; H.G. Opitz, ed. *Athanasius' Werke* III, 1, Berlin, 1934, 1–3, 12–13, 36–41, 64; G. Bardy, "S. Lucien d'Antioche," *DTC* 9:1024–31; *id.*, esp. *Recherches sur S. Lucien d'Antioche et son ecole*, Paris, 1936; *id.*, in J. R. Palanque et al., *The Church in the Christian Roman Empire*, tr. E.C. Messenger, vol 1, New York, 1953, 73–132; A. Orbe, *Hacia la primera teologia de la procession del Verbo*, Rome, Gregorian University, 1958; E. Boularand, "Les débuts d'Arius", *Bulletin de littérature eccl.*, 75(1964), 175–203; *id.*, *L'Hérésie d'Arius et la Foi de Nicée*, Paris, 1972; G.C. Stead, "The Platonism of Arius," *JTS*, NS, 15(1964) 16–31; B. Lonergan, S.J., *The Way to Nicaea*, London, 1976, 68–72; Quasten, 3: 7–13; X. le Bachelet, *DTC* 1, 2:1779–1806; R. Aigrain, *DHGE*, 4:208–215; Kirsch, *Enchiridion*, 236–239; [2]H.-G. Opitz, *Athanasius' Werke*, III, 1f; Theodoret, HE 1, 4, PG 82, 909–912; GCS 19, 26–27; [3]Athan., *De synodis*, 16; Epiphanius, *Haer.* 69, 7; Hilary, *De Trinitate*, 4, 12f; 6, 5f; *Athanasius' Werke*, III, 12f; [4]Athanasius, *De synodis*, 15; [5]Socrates, HE 1, 26; Sozomen, HE 2, 27; *Athanasius' Werke*, III, 64; [6]cf. Altaner, 311; [7]Boularand, I, p.48; [8]On details of authenticity cf. P. Nautin, in *AB* 67(1949), 131–141; M. Simonetti, *Sull'Arianesimo*, Rome, 1965, 88–110; [9]Greek text and French tr. Boularand, I, 49–51; [10]*Ibid.*, 48; [11]LNPF, 74, 99; [12]LNPF, 458; Greek and French tr. Boularand, *j. cit.*; [13]LNPF, 308; [14]2, 5, *ibid.*, 309; [15]G. Bardy, *Recherches sur S.Lucien d'Antioche*, 255; Boularand, *op.cit.*, 58; [16]Athanasius, *De synodis* 15, LNPF, 457; Boularand, 58–60; [17]*op.cit.*, 258–274; [18]5, 6, 37 PG 26, 21B, 24C, 88C; [19]12, PG 25, 564B-565C; [20]23, PG 25, 513A-516A; Opitz, III, 2, 62–63; [21]6, 16; PG 25, 433A-B, 452A; [22]references given [23]*op.cit.*, 64; [24]*op.cit.*, 61; [25]Boularand, 62, 63; [26]*Hist.Eccl.* II, 27, PG 67, 1009D; [27]PG 18, 573AB; *Athanasius' Werke*, III,7.

ARTEMAS (3rd century)

A. seems to have been a disciple of Theodotus; he was teaching in Rome c. 235 and was excommunicated for heresy.[1] He taught that Christ was a mere man, though surpassing the prophets. Eusebius of Caesarea (qv) writes of him and his "blasphemous falsehood" and gives extracts from a work written to refute it. The authorship of this work is disputed; Hippolytus of Rome is among those mentioned. "For they say," it reads in Eusebius' version," that all the early teachers and the apostles received and taught what they now declare, and that the truth of the Gospel was preserved until the times of Victor, who was the thirteenth bishop of Rome from Peter, but that from his successor, Zephyrinus, the truth had been corrupted. And what they say might be plausible, if first of all the Divine Scriptures did not contradict them. And there are writings of certain brethren older than the times of Victor, which they wrote in behalf of the truth against the heathen, and against the heresies which existed in their day. I refer to Justin (qv) and Miltiades and Tatian and Clement and many others, in all of whose works Christ is spoken of as God. For who does not know the works of Irenaeus and of Melito and of others which teach that Christ is God and man? And how many psalms and hymns, written by the faithful brethren from the beginning, celebrate Christ the Word of God, speaking of him as divine? How then since the opinion held by the Church has been preached for so many years, can its preaching have been delayed, as they affirm, until the times of Victor? And how is it that they are not ashamed to speak thus falsely of Victor, knowing well that he cut off from communion Theodotus, the cobbler, the leader and father of this God-denying apostasy, and the first to declare that Christ is mere man? For if Victor agreed with their opinions as their slander affirms, how came he to cast out Theodotus, the inventor of this heresy?"[2]

[1]Cf. R.H. Connolly, O.S.B., Eusebius, H.E. V, 28, *JTS* 49(1948), 73–79; [2]H.E. V, 28 LNPF, N.S., I, 246, 247; cf. Epiphanius, *Haer.*, 65, 1, 4; Theodoret, *Haer. Fab.*, II, 4; Photius, *Biblioth.*, 48.

ASTERIUS THE SOPHIST (d. c. 341)

A. was born in Cappadocia and was a pupil of St. Lucian of Antioch (qv).[1] He apostatized during the persecution of Maximinus; for this reason he was not admitted to the ranks of the clergy. A skilled sophist, he travelled considerably, and was allowed to participate in synodal discussions. His precise place in the history of Arianism is difficult to establish, for his *Syntagmation* has survived only in fragments in the writings of Athanasius (qv), our sole informant on his life, and of Marcellus of Ancyra. His *Refutation of Marcellus* is lost. St. Jerome says that he wrote commentaries on the Gospels, the Epistle to the Romans and on the Psalms. A number of his homilies and fragments of the commentary on the Psalms have been discovered since the 1930s by M. Richard and E. Skard. Marcellus refers to a letter by A. in defence of Eusebius of Nicomedia, in particular the latter's letter to Paulinus of Tyr.

On a detailed analysis of the fragments preserved by Athanasius and Marcellus, G. Bardy concluded: "If we are not mistaken, the Cappadocian sophist is an Arian, in the strictest sense of the word, and we ought, without hesitation, to rank him with Arius (qv), Eusebius of Nicomedia (qv), Athanasius of Anazarbe, and George of Laodicea. Of the last two we have but fragments which are too short. We can know the doctrine of Arius and Eusebius better; it does not differ from that of Asterius."[2]

Arius was indebted to A. for his opinions, which fact has prompted some to think of the latter as the first, even the determining Arian writer. Bardy considers him one of a group who were all followers of Lucian, and the latter he considers the originating force in Arianism.

A. made his faith in the Trinity quite clear—he believed in the all-powerful Father, the only-begotten Son of God and the Holy Spirit. But if he even used the word *hypostasis* to signify the distinction of persons and is firmly anti-tritheist, he does hold the superiority of the Father over the Son, that the Son is the result of an act of will on the Father's part, that he was made, and made so that through him the Father might create the world. If God had not wished to create the universe, without doubt he would not have brought forth a Son.

Yet the Son is different from all other products of the Father's will: all other things were made through the mediation of the Son; he came directly from the Father. He was begotten before the ages, the first-born of all creation; he is unique, perfect, king, Lord, God; he is the image of the invisible God, of the substance of the Father. This last assertion by A., though easily paralleled from the writings of Arius, is of course strictly biblical, and shocked the Arian historian Philostorgus;[3] he and the other Anomoeans of the fifth century thought that A. had betrayed the Arian position. But Athanasius and Marcellus of Ancyra would not have taken such pains to refute A. did they not think that he was a genuine Arian. For him all his thinking was in the light of his central thesis that the Son was made by the Father.

A. has a problem with the Johannine texts: "I and the Father are one" (Jn 10:30) and "I am in the Father and the Father in me" (14:10). On the first he writes thus: "If everything that the Father wills, the Son also wills; if he does not oppose him either in his thoughts or in his judgments, but agrees with him in everything, manifesting identity of opinions, teaching a doctrine exactly one

with the teaching of the Father, that is why he and the Father are one."[4] This is but a moral unity; it is not consubstantiality. On the second Johannine text he writes: "It is quite evident that he asserted that he was in the Father and the Father was in him because he declares that even the word which he utters is not his, but the Father's, that his works are not his own works, but the Father's who gave him the power."[5]

On the Incarnation likewise the fragments given by Athanasius and Marcellus tell us practically nothing. There is also little about the Holy Spirit, save that he is truly the Holy Spirit, one of the three *hypostases* of the Trinity. Since it is known that A. was at the council of Antioch in 341, there is some interest in the remarkable similarity between his views and the creed *In Encaenis*, adopted by the council. Did A. then draw up the formulary and put it forward? This seems most unlikely. But he must have professed this creed himself before the council. The explanation is that it derives from Lucian. It was his credal doctrine that the council wished to canonise, as would other later synods, notably that held at Seleucia: one more sign that A. was of the intellectual lineage of Lucian. He was then more a Lucianist than an Arian. His defence against Marcellus was undertaken by Eusebius of Caesarea (qv) in his *Against Marcellus* and *On Ecclesiastical Theology*; Acacius also defended him. Recent scholars, in view of the finds, tend to see A. as a moderate Arian as Epiphanius (qv) seemed to think[6] (cf. Bardy).

[1]Sources: St.Athanasius, *De synodis* 18; Philostorgus, H.E., I, 14–15; Socrates, H.E., I, 36; Sozomen, H.E., II, 33; St.Jerome, *De viris Inlustribus*, 94; cf. E. Skard, "Asterius von Amaseia und Asterios der Sophist," *Symbolae Osloenses*, 20(1940), 86–132; id., "Bemerkungen zu den Asterios Texten," ibid., 27(1949), 54–69; M. Richard, "Le recueil d'homélies grecques d'Asterius le Sophiste," *Symbolae Osloenses*, 29(1951), 24–33; id., "Deux homélies inédites du Sophiste," ibid., 29(1952), 93–96; id., ibid., Commentaries on Psalms and Homilies, Fasc. Supplem. 16(1956); index E. Skard, ibid., 17 (1962); G. Bardy, "Asterius le Sophiste," *RHE* 22(1926), 221–272; id., *Recherches sur S. Lucien d'Antioche et son école*, Paris, 1936, 316–357; [2]*RHE*, 267; [3]H.E., II, 15; [4]Apud Bardy, ibid., 265; [5]Ibid., 266; [6]*Haer.*, 76, 3; Quasten III, 194–197.

ATHANASIAN CREED, THE

"Whoever wishes to be saved, needs above all to hold the Catholic faith; unless each one preserves this whole and inviolate, he will without a doubt perish in eternity. But the Catholic faith is this, that we venerate one God in the Trinity, and the Trinity in oneness; neither confounding the persons, nor dividing the substance; for there is one person of the Father, another of the Son, (and) another of the Holy Spirit; but the divine nature of the Father and of the Son and of the Holy Spirit is one, their glory is equal, their majesty is coeternal. Of such a nature as the Father is, so is the Son, so (also) is the Holy Spirit; the Father is uncreated, the Son is uncreated, (and) the Holy Spirit is uncreated; the Father is immense, the Son is immense, (and) the Holy Spirit is immense; the Father is eternal, the Son is eternal, (and) the Holy Spirit is eternal: and nevertheless there are not three eternals, but one eternal; just as there are not three uncreated beings, nor three infinite beings, but one uncreated, and one infinite; similarly the Father is onmipotent, the Son is omnipotent, (and) the Holy Spirit is omnipotent: and yet there are not three omnipotents, but one omnipotent; thus the Father is God, the Son is God, (and) the Holy Spirit is God; and nevertheless there are not three gods, but there is one God; so the Father is Lord, the Son is Lord, (and) the Holy Spirit is Lord; and yet there are not three lords, but there is one Lord; because just as we are compelled by Christian truth to confess singly each one person as God and (also) Lord, so we are forbidden by the Catholic religion to say there are three gods or lords. The Father was not made nor created, nor begotten by anyone. The Son is from the Father alone, not made nor created, but begotten. The Holy Spirit is from the Father and the Son, not made nor created, nor begotten, but proceeding. There is therefore one Father, not three Fathers; one Son, not three Sons; one Holy Spirit, not three Holy Spirits; and in this Trinity there is nothing first or later, nothing greater or less, but all three persons are coeternal and coequal with one another, so that in every respect, as has already been said above, both unity in Trinity and Trinity in unity must be venerated. Therefore let him who wishes to be saved, think thus concerning the Trinity.

"But it is necessary for eternal salvation that he faithfully believe also the incarnation of our Lord Jesus Christ. Accordingly it is the right faith, that we believe and confess, that our Lord Jesus Christ, the Son of God, is God and man. He is God begotten of the substance of the Father before time,

and he is man born of the substance of his mother in time: perfect God, perfect man, consisting of a rational soul and a human body, equal to the Father according to his godhead, less than the Father according to humanity. Although he is God and man, yet he is not two, but he is one Christ; one, however, not by the conversion of the divinity into a human body, but by the assumption of humanity in the godhead; one absolutely not by confusion of substance, but by unity of person. For just as the rational soul and body are one man, so God and man are one Christ. He suffered for our salvation, descended into hell, on the third day arose again from the dead, ascended to heaven, sits at the right hand of God the Father almighty; thence he shall come to judge the living and the dead; at his coming all men have to arise again with their bodies and will render an account of their own deeds; and those who have done good, will go into life everlasting, but those who have done evil, into eternal fire. This is the Catholic faith; unless everyone believes this faithfully and firmly, he cannot be saved."[1]

This profession of faith, also known as *Quicumque Vult*, differs from the Apostles' (*qv*) and Nicene (*qv*) creeds in the inclusion of anathemas. Each part ends with a warning that acceptance is necessary for salvation. The first part deals with the Trinity, the second with the Incarnation. The movement of ideas indicates a period of doctrinal development coinciding with the age of Chalcedon, 451, though not all are agreed on this interpretation. Some have thought that the heresy attacked was Apollinarianism; J.N.D. Kelly disagreed, thinking that it was Nestorianism, which dates the composition after 428: "One absolutely not by confusion of substance, but by unity of person" seems to echo Chalcedon more than Ephesus.

Since the work of G.J. Voss, *Dissertationes tres de tribus symbolis*, published in 1642, the belief that St. Athanasius (*qv*) was the author has been abandoned. Voss, a Dutch humanist theologian (though born in Germany), showed that the ideas of the creed (or, more accurately, the summary of doctrine) were later than the saint—no early authority attributed it to him, it was evidently composed in Latin, and until recent times it circulated mostly in the west. In Jerusalem, in the ninth century, western monks used the text with the *Filioque* (*qv*) clause against the easterns.

The first appearance of the creed seems to have been in southern Gaul, whence it passed into Spain and then to the Carolingian empire. Authorship must then have been Gallic, and the thesis of H. Brewer, S.J., proposed early in this century, attributing the creed to St. Ambrose, no longer commands much assent. It is first quoted in a sermon by St. Caesarius of Arles (470–542) and the *Excerpta Vincentii Lerinensis* discovered in 1940, dated from 440, appears to be a source for some elements in the composition.

Attempts to trace items in the composition in the writings of churchmen of the fourth to the sixth centuries yield interesting but scarcely conclusive results. Apart from Ambrose, Vincent of Lerins and Caesarius of Arles the investigation has been directed to Augustine, Faustinus of Riez and Fulgentius of Ruspe (*qv*). Other names mentioned have been Nicetas of Remesiana and even Hilary of Poitiers (*qv*). J.N.D. Kelly sums up an informed, thorough inquiry thus: "The connection of the creed with the monastery at Lerins, its dependence on the theology of Augustine, and in the Trinitarian section on his characteristic method of arguing, its much more direct and large-scale indebtedness to Vincent (of Lerins), its acquaintance with and critical attitude towards Nestorianism and its emergence at some time between 440 and the high noon of Caesarius' activity— all these points as well as the creed's original function as an instrument of instruction have been confirmed or established by our studies."[2]

The creed has been widely used in the Christian churches. It is not a recognised standard of faith in the east, but without the *Filioque* clause it has been included in the Greek *Horologium* since 1780 and in Russian service books from the seventeenth century. It was in the old Roman Breviary and was recited on most Sundays. Lutherans regard it as a summary of Christian faith. In the Anglican Book of Common Prayer it replaces the Apostles' Creed on thirteen holydays, these being at equal intervals apart. Attempts to remove it have failed.

---

[1]Text SCD, 15, 16; cf. G.D.W. Ommanney, *A Critical Dissertation on the Athanasian Creed*, 1890; H. Brewer, S.J., *Das sogennante Athansianische Glaubensbekenntnis ein Werk des Hl. Ambrosius*, 1909; G. Morin, O.S.B., "A propos du Quicumque. Extraits d'homelies de S. Caesaire d'Arles sous le nom de S. Athanase," *RBen*, 28 (1911), 417–24; J. Stiglmayr, S.J., "Das Quicumque und Fulgentius von Ruspe," *ZKT* 49 (1925), 341–57; A.E. Burn, "The authorship of the Quicumque Vult," *JTS* 27 (1925–6), 19–28; G. Morin, O.S.B., "L'origine du symbole d'Athanase, temoignage inédit de S. Caesaire d'Arles," *RBen* 44 (1932) 207–219; esp. J.N.D. Kelly, *The Athanasian Creed*, Oxford, 1964; Tixeront, *DTC* 1, 2, 2178–87; Quasten 3, 32–33; Altaner, 319–23; J. Madoz, S.J., E.C., X, 411ff; G. Owens, *NCE*, J. Stiglmayer, *DHGE*, IV, 134–48; [2]*Op. cit.*, 123.

ATHANASIUS, ST., DOCTOR OF THE CHURCH (c. 295–373)

A. had a unique role in the resistance to Arianism (*qv*).[1] The tension of truth versus heresy has scarcely ever been so fully concentrated in one person to the benefit of the whole Church— personality identified with doctrine in struggle and triumph. The saint was proof against every offensive element, sophistry, ecclesiastical conspiracy, political pressure and tyranny; for almost half a century his tenacity held firm, and at times when demoralization was almost universal he seemed to embody the teaching Church. He is deservedly a symbol of orthodoxy.

Born in Alexandria, A. benefited from the excellent classical and biblical schooling then available in the city, as he assimilated its distinctive theological traditions. Ordained a deacon in 318 by Bishop Alexander who chose him as his secretary, he was from the outset totally involved in the anti-Arian struggle. He was present at Nicaea (*qv*) and was named by Alexander to succeed him in office; this he did in 328, with the approval of the Egyptian bishops, despite Arian and Meletian opposition. Before long he was in the wars. In 331 he was called to the court of Constantine I to answer charges laid against him by the Meletians. Then he had to face the campaign mounted by Eusebius of Nicomedia, an Arian sympathizer who had already worked successfully for the deposition of Eustathius of Antioch and other pro-Nicene bishops.

First summoned to the Council of Tyre (335) and seeing that it was packed by bishops opposed to him, A. went to Constantinople to appeal to the emperor. The result, whatever took place in the city, was his first exile: Constantine banished him to Trier in Northern Gaul. When the emperor died (May 337) A. was allowed to return to Alexandria. The Synod of Antioch (337–338), composed of Eusebian bishops, deposed him, putting Pistus and then Gregory in his place. He sent an encyclical letter to all the bishops to protest against this injustice. He went to Rome where he met Marcellus of Ancyra, Asclepas of Gaza and other bishops pursued by the Arians. Pope Julius I (337–352) supported him and convened a synod of 50 bishops (late 340 or early 341) which examined the charges made against him at the council of Tyre and declared him innocent. The verdict was not accepted by the eastern bishops, so A. remained in the west and spent his time promoting monasticism.

He was again vindicated at the council of Sardica—that is, by the western bishops who remained after the departure of the easterns to Philippopolis. In 346, on the death of the usurper Gregory, he was allowed back to Alexandria by Constantius II. He remained for ten years, engaged in effecting reforms and consolidating monasticism. He also added to the corpus of his writings *De decretis* (*On the Decrees of the Nicene Synod*) and *De Sententia Dionysii* (*On the Opinion of Dionysius of Alexandria*).

The enemies of A. did not capitulate; on the death of Constans in 350 they returned to the attack. He was condemned at the Council of Arles in 353 and at the Council of Milan in 355. In the following year he was again forced into exile. He hid in the Libyan desert, relying on the support of his clergy, especially of the monks, eluding capture by changing residence, even visiting Alexandria secretly. An Arian bishop, George of Cappadocia (357–361), had been officially installed in his place.

This was, in the life of A., a period of literary fruitfulness. He composed some of his principal works: the three *Orationes contra Arianos* (*Discourses against the Arians*)—the fourth is now known to be spurious; the *Epistola Encyclica ad Episcopos Aegypti et Libyae* (*Circular Letter to the Bishops of Egypt and Libya*) written after he had been forced to leave Alexandria; *Apologia ad Constantium* (*Defence before Constantius*); the *Life of St. Anthony*; the *History of the Arians*, written at the request of the monks with whom he was staying in 358; the *Apologia de Fuga* (*Defence of his flight*), his answer to the criticisms put into circulation by his enemies because he had gone into hiding; the *Letters to Serapion*, wherein he gives his doctrine on the divinity of the Holy Spirit; and the last great work of the exile, *De synodis* (*On the Councils of Ariminum and Seleucia*).

The Pope, Liberius, and the chief enemy of Arianism in the west, St. Hilary of Poitiers (*qv*)

were also in exile. A. not only maintained contact with his subjects, but learned, through various channels what was happening in the Church at large as *De synodis* shows. After George of Cappadocia had been murdered and the emperor Constantius had died, the exiled bishop was allowed to return by Julian the Apostate.

A. convened a synod, which was to be a milestone in progress towards Church unity. Among the bishops present were Lucius of Cagliari and Eusebius of Vercellae, who had been exiled in Upper Egypt. The *Tomus ad Antiochenos* (*Letter to the Church of Antioch*) contained the directives and teaching of the assembly. While determined to make "a complete renunciation of the abominable heresy of the Arians, to refuse to divide the Holy Trinity or to say that any part of it is a creature," the council document was comprehensive in regard to those who had difficulties in terminology, especially in the use of the word *hypostasis* (subsistence). They had been reassured by those who did use it: "Because they believed in a Holy Trinity, not a Trinity in name only, but existing and subsisting in truth, 'both a Father truly existing and subsisting, and a Son truly substantial and subsisting, and a Holy Spirit subsisting and really existing do we acknowledge,' and that neither had they said there were three Gods or three beginnings, nor would they at all tolerate such as said or held so, but that they acknowledged a Holy Trinity but One Godhead, and one beginning, and that the Son is coessential with the Father, while the Holy Spirit is not a creature, nor external, but proper to and inseparable from the essence of the Father and the Son."

The *Tomus* also taught the true humanity of Jesus Christ and gave firm advice on the way to doctrinal peace: "But while you refuse toleration to those who refuse so to confess and to explain their language, counsel the others also who explain and hold aright, not to enquire further into each other's opinions, nor to fight about words to no useful purpose, nor to go on contending with the above phrases, but agree in the mind of piety. For they who are not thus minded, but only stir up strife with such petty phrases, and seek something beyond what was drawn up at Nicaea, do nothing except 'give their neighbour turbid confusion to drink' (Hab 2:15), like men who grudge peace and love dissensions."[2]

The point of these wise directives was to show sympathy to the Homoeans (*qv*) who had signed under duress and, by allowing for a possible orthodox meaning to the formula of Origen on "three hypostases," to ease the return of the Homoeousians (qv). The sight of growing Christian unity displeased the emperor Julian. From October 362 to June 363 when Julian died, A. was again in exile. After the short reign of Jovian, who died in February 364, Valentinian became emperor. He appointed his brother Valens joint ruler with jurisdiction in the east. Valens was an Arian, a supporter of the Homoean formulary. A. thereon went into exile for the fifth time. Popular discontent, however, forced a change of mind on the emperor and after four months the bishop returned. From 366 to his death in 373 he was in tranquil possession of his office, all his thought and energy directed to restoring peace and strengthening the orthodox.

Writings

A. as a writer was nearly always conscious of Arianism. Most of the works mentioned have a bearing on the contents of the heresy or on its history: even in his life of St. Anthony he refers to the heresy. Many of his works are indispensable as sources—with the caveat that he was occasionally absorbed in polemics. The *Apologia contra Arianos* has been called "the most authentic source of the history of the Church in the first half of the fourth century." It is a collection of papal, imperial and conciliar texts relative to the councils of Sardica and Tyre (the chronological order is inverted); A. provides a connecting, explanatory narrative. The *Ad Afros epistola synodica* (*Synodal Letter To the Bishops of Africa*) was sent by ninety bishops including Athanasius. It aimed at destroying the opinion that the council of Ariminum had by its teaching superseded that of Nicaea; and it warned against the presence of a convinced Arian, Auxentius, in the important see of Milan.

The *Oratio contra Gentes* and the *Oratio de Incarnatione Verbi* are one book, thought—but not by all—to have been written before the Council of Nicaea and before the Arian crisis, to which there is no reference. An important work for Christology and Marian doctrine was written by A. late in his life, the *Epistola ad Epictetum* (*Letter to Epictetus*, about whom nothing is known save that he was bishop of Corinth). The *Epistola ad Adelphum* is on the same theme, and the *Epistola ad Maximum* (the Philosopher) on a kindred topic. A. wrote other personal letters and also festal letters. There is a considerable literature on his writings on virginity;[3] and some controversy on the authenticity of Syriac and Coptic MSS of his sermons—some of the latter have important implications for Marian theology.[4]

Doctrine

A. was a controversialist, but the controversy in which he was engaged was the most important in Christian history: at issue was the divinity of Jesus Christ, the very foundation of the Christian religion. At issue also was the equality of the Son with the Father in the Holy Trinity. If A. did not construct a theological system, it was because he was active in securing the foundation without which Christian theology would be so radically impoverished that any true development would be impossible. He clarified the nature and generation of the *Logos* (qv), surpassing all previous thinkers who had attempted this task. He showed that the essential truth of the Trinity is at the heart of the Church's life and service and he established the Teaching Authority of the Church as God's instrument in the public life of mankind.

So many spiritual factors, distinctive elements and ideas meet in A's person that his greatness eludes our grasp. He rescued the Christian message from a Hellenization which would have nullified it. Yet in the tradition of Origen he pressed the categories of Greek thought into the service of divine revelation. He proved the intrinsic power and primacy of faith without neglecting the valid function of human reason. Philosophy in his hands was truly the handmaid of theology (*ancilla theologiae*). All was ruled by an overriding principle: "the very tradition, teaching, and faith of the Catholic Church from the beginning, which the Lord gave, the Apostles preached, and the Fathers kept."[5] His intellectual mission was vital, not arid, at the heart of the Church where his close bond with monasticism was a source of power, as it nourished his compassion towards those who clung to the truth but who lacked his own indomitable spirit.

Trinity

A. sets forth his idea of the Trinity in this way: "There is then a Triad, holy and complete, confessed to be God in Father, Son and Holy Spirit, having nothing foreign or external mixed with it, not composed of one that creates and one that is originated, but all creative; and it is consistent and in nature indivisible, and its activity is one. The Father does all things through the Word in the Holy Spirit. Thus the unity of the holy Triad is preserved. Thus one God is preached in the Church, 'who is over all (Eph 4:6), and through all, and in all'—'over all' as Father, as beginning, as fountain; 'through all,' through the Word; 'in all,' in the Holy Spirit. It is a Triad not only in name and form of speech, but in truth and actuality. For as the Father is he that is, so also his Word is one that is and God over all. And the Holy Spirit is not without actual existence, but exists and has true being. Less than these (Persons) the Catholic Church does not hold, lest she sink to the level of the modern Jews, imitators of Caiaphas, and to the level of Sabellius. Nor does she add to them by speculation, lest she be carried into the polytheism of the heathen."[6]

A. rejects the Arian opinion that God had first to make and create the Son and Word so that through him all other beings should exist: "If they shall assign the toil of making all things as the reason why God made the Son only, the whole creation will cry out against them as saying unworthy things of God; and Isaiah too who said in Scripture, 'The Everlasting God, the Lord, the Creator of the ends of the earth, fainteth not, neither is weary: there is no searching of his understanding' (Is 40:28). And if God made the Son alone, as not deigning to make the rest, but committed them to the Son as an assistant, this on the other hand is unworthy of God, for in him there is no pride. Nay the Lord reproves the thought, when he says: 'Are not two sparrows sold for a farthing?' and 'one of them shall not fall to the ground without your Father who is in heaven' (Mt 10:29) . . . . If then it be not unworthy of God to exercise his Providence, even down to things so small, a hair of the head, and a sparrow, and the grass of the field, also it was not unworthy of him to make them. For what things are the subjects of his Providence of those he is maker through his proper Word. Nay a worse absurdity lies before the men who thus speak; for they distinguish between the creatures and the framing; and consider the latter the work of the Father, the creatures the work of the Son; whereas either all things must be brought to be by the Father with the Son, or if all that is originate comes to be brought through the Son, we must not call him one of the originated things."[7]

The Son is the offspring of the Father's essence,

not of his will, and can in no way be called a creature of the Father. A. knew his thought was true to Nicaea: "But the Fathers, perceiving their (Eusebius and others') craft and the cunning of their irreligion, were forced to express more distinctly the sense of the words 'from God.' Accordingly they wrote 'from the substance of God,' in order that 'from God' might not be considered common and equal in the Son and in things originate, but that all others might be acknowledged as creatures, and the Word alone as from the Father. For though all things are said to be from God, yet this is not in the sense in which the Son is from him . . . ."[8]

A. insists that the doctrine of the Council was a valid deduction from Scripture: "But the bishops . . . were again compelled on their part to collect the sense of the Scriptures, and to re-say and re-write what they had said before, more distinctly still, namely that the Son is consubstantial with the Father; by way of signifying, that the Son was from the Father, and not merely like, but the same in likeness, and of showing that the Son's likeness and immutability was different from such copy of the same as is ascribed to us, which we acquire from virtue on the ground of observance of the commandments . . . but since the generation of the Son from the Father is not according to the nature of men, and not only like, but also inseparable from the essence of the Father, and he and the Father are one, as he has said himself, and the Word is ever in the Father and the Father in the Word, as the radiance stands towards the light (for this the phrase itself indicates), therefore the Council as understanding this, suitably wrote 'consubstantial,' that they might both defeat the perverseness of the heretics, and show that the Word was other than originated things."[9]

Elsewhere A. develops the image of light and the sun to explain that divine begetting differs from human, since God is indivisible: "Since he is God's Word and own Wisdom, and, being his radiance, is ever with the Father, therefore it is impossible, if the Father bestows grace, that he should not give it in the Son, for the Son is in the Father as the radiance in the light. For, not as if in need, but as a Father in his own wisdom hath God founded the earth, and made all things in the Word which is from him, and in the Son confirms the holy laver. For where the Father is, there is the Son, and where the light there the radiance; and as to what the Father worketh, he worketh through the Son and the Lord himself says, 'What I see the Father do, that I do also'; so also when baptism is given whom the Father baptizes, him the Son baptizes, and whom the Son baptizes, he is consecrated in the Holy Spirit. And again as when the sun shines, one might say that the radiance illuminates, for the light is one and indivisible, nor can it be detached, so where the Father is or is named, there plainly is the Son; and is the Father named in baptism, then must be the Son named with him."[10] "For the Son is in the Father, as it is allowed us to know, because the whole being of the Son is proper to the Father's essence, as radiance from light and stream from fountain; so that whoso sees the Son, sees what is proper to the Father, and knows that the Son's being, because from the Father is therefore in the Father. For the Father is in the Son, since the Son is what is from the Father and proper to him, as in the radiance the sun, and in the word the thought, and in the stream the fountain; for whoso thus contemplates the Son, contemplates what is proper to the Father's essence, and knows that the Father is in the Son."[11]

A. wishes to safeguard the distinction of persons and their identity in the godhead: "For they are one, not as one thing divided into two parts, and these nothing but one, nor as one thing twice named, so that the same becomes at one time Father, at another his own Son, for holding this Sabellius was judged a heretic. But they are two, because the Father is Father and is not also Son, and the Son is Son and not also Father; but the nature (*physis*) is one; (for the offspring is not unlike its parent, for it is his image), and all that is the Father's is the Son's. Wherefore neither is the Son another God, for he was not procured from without, else were there many, if a godhead be procured foreign from the Father's, for if the Son be other as an offspring, still he is the same as God; and he and the Father are one in propriety and peculiarity of nature, and in the identity of the one godhead, as has been said. For the radiance also is light, not second to the sun, nor a different light, nor from the participation of it, but a whole and proper offspring of it. And such an offspring is necessarily one light; and no one would say that there are two lights, but sun and radiance two, yet one, the light from the sun in its radiance enlightening all things. So also the godhead of the Son is the Father's; whence also it is indivisible; and thus there is one God and

none other but he. And so since they are one and the godhead itself one, the same things are said of the Son, which are said of the Father, except his being said to be the Father."[12]

There can be only one Son, as A. thus explains: "The offspring of men are portions of their fathers, since the very nature of bodies is not uncompounded, but in a state of flux, and composed of parts; and men lose their substance in begetting, and again they gain substance from the accession of food. And on this account men in their time become fathers of many children; but God, being without parts, is Father of the Son without partition or passion; for there is neither effluence of the immaterial, or influx from without, as among men; and being uncompounded in nature he is Father of one only Son. This is why he is only-begotten, and alone in the Father's bosom, and alone is acknowledged by the Father to be from him, saying, 'This is my beloved Son, in whom I am well-pleased' (Mt 3:17). And he too is the Father's Word, from which may be understood the impassible and impartitive nature of the Father, in that not even a a human word is begotten with passion or partition, much less the Word of God."[13]

Most of the ante-Nicene writers had not escaped some form of subordinationism (*qv*). The charge has been made against Justin, Tatian, Athenagoras, Theophilus of Antioch, the Letter to Diognetus, Tertullian, Hippolytus, Novatian, Clement of Alexandria (*qqv*).[14] Even Irenaeus (*qv*) was not, according to one commentator, an exception.[15]

A. makes a clean break with this trend: "For only to say 'like according to the essence' (*homoios kat' ousian*) is very far from signifying 'of the essence' (*ek tēs ousias*), by which rather, as they say themselves, the genuineness of the Son to the Father is signified. Thus tin is only like to silver, a wolf to a dog, and gilt brass to the true metal; but tin is not from silver, nor could a wolf be accounted the offspring of a dog. But since they say that he is 'of the essence' and 'like in essence,' what do they signify by these but 'consubstantial'? For, while to say only 'like-in-essence' does not necessarily convey 'of the essence'; on the contrary, to say 'consubstantial' is to signify the meaning of both terms, 'like in essence' and 'of the essence'. And, accordingly, they, the semi-Arians themselves, in controversy with those who say that the Word is a creature, instead of allowing him to be a genuine Son, have taken their proofs against them from human illustrations of son and father, with this exception that God is not as man, nor the generation of the Son as issue of man, but such as may be ascribed to God, and is fit for us to think. Thus they have called the Father the fount of wisdom and life, and the Son the radiance of the eternal light and the offspring from the fountain, as he says, 'I am the life', and 'I wisdom dwell with prudence' (Jn 14:6; Prov 8:12). But the radiance from the light, the offspring from the fountain, and Son from Father, how can these be so fitly expressed as by 'consubstantial'?"[16]

Christology and Soteriology

These questions are not immediately relevant to A.'s trinitarian theology, but his ideas here serve to reinforce his basic position. He is insistent on the unity of Christ: "Being Son of God in truth, he became also Son of Man, and being God's only-begotten Son, he became also at the same time 'first-born among many brethren.' Wherefore neither was there one Son of God before Abraham, another after Abraham: nor was there one that raised up Lazarus, another that asked concerning him; but the same it was that said as man, 'Where does Lazarus lie?' (Jn 11:34), and as God raised him up: the same that as man and in the body spat, but divinely as Son of God opened the eyes of the man blind from his birth; and while, as Peter says, (1 Pet 4:1), in the flesh he suffered, as God he opened the tomb and raised the dead."[17]

A direct consequence of the personal unity of Christ is the true title of Mary, Mother of God. A. used the word *Theotokos* frequently, achieving an insight which Nestorius missed: "Scripture contains a double account of the Saviour; that he was ever God, and is the Son, being the Father's Word and radiance and wisdom; and that afterwards for us he took flesh of a Virgin, Mary, Mother of God."[18]

A. saw clearly that from the Incarnation flowed the possibility of *communicatio idiomatum*. This too Nestorius would miss: "For if the flesh also is in itself a part of the created world, yet it has become God's body. And we neither divide the body, being such, from the Word, and worship it by itself, nor when we wish to worship the Word do we set him far apart from the flesh, but knowing, as we said above, that 'the Word was made flesh,' we recognize him as God also, after having come in the flesh. Who is so senseless as to say to the Lord: 'Leave the body that I may worship thee'?"

All this is a culmination of glory: "For as he was ever worshipped as being the Word and existing in the form of God, so being what he ever was though become man and called Jesus, he nonetheless has the whole creation under foot, and bending their knees to him in this name, and confessing that the Word's becoming flesh, and undergoing death in flesh, has not happened against the glory of his godhead, but to the glory of God the Father. For it is the Father's glory that man, made and then lost, should be found again; and when dead, that he should be made alive, and should become God's temple. For whereas the powers in heaven, both Angels and Archangels, were ever worshipping the Lord, as they are now worshipping him in the name of Jesus, this is our grace and high exaltation, that even when he became man, the Son of God is worshipped, and the heavenly powers will not be astonished at seeing all of us, who are one body with him, introduced into their realms."[19]

It will come as a surprise to students of A. that doubt has been cast on his belief in the soul of Christ. This is not strictly relevant to his trinitarian doctrine; it is mentioned because of A.'s stature in the history of theology. All commentators are not agreed on the opinion. Only an *argumentum a silentio* can be adduced to support it. Nowhere does A. say that Jesus Christ did not have a human soul. Specialists argue that in some sections of his work where he should have mentioned it he does not.[20] They also argue that in his account of the death of Christ where he should have spoken of it he remains silent.

An expert on patristic Christology, A. Grillmeier, S.J., does not accept the passage where, in the *Tomus ad Antiochenos*, A. asserts that the Saviour did not have a "body without a soul," as it is generally translated. Fr. Grillmeier, who has especially studied the Logos-sarx Christology, clearly would have A. among its many exponents, without accusing him of heresy—in this he differed entirely from Arius and Apollinarius. But the learned patrologist nuances his view: "Thus a remark which A. makes in his main work against the Arians is to be regarded as his central Christological formula: '(The Word) became man and did not come into a man.' It should be regarded as the classic formulation of the theology of the 'Logos-flesh' type as opposed to the theology of the 'Logos-man' type. In its extreme form, such as we see with the Arian Eudoxius and with Apollinarius, and as we are still to hear from a monophysitically-inclined bishop even at the Council of Chalcedon, it contains an implicit denial of the soul of Christ. A. does not go so far, and merely rejects the adoptianism (*qv*) of Paul of Samosata without clarifying his formula in the direction of the explicit Logos-sarx Christology of the other group. In A., to 'become' man, to 'become' flesh probably has a special depth of meaning, but he immediately interprets it in the traditional Pauline sense as a 'taking' of the flesh, which is yet so intense that one can and must say that the 'Logos *is* man.'"[21]

Notice, however, that A. says explicitly that in Jn 1:14 "flesh" means "man." 'The Word was made flesh,' St. John tells us, that is, in the language of Holy Scripture, 'was made man.'[22] A. then clearly held more than a Logos-sarx theology; this fact is still clearer from his analysis of the knowledge of Christ, with an important distinction between Christ's knowledge as God and as man.[23] Could such knowledge be attributed to flesh (sarx) only?

The Holy Spirit

A. taught the divinity of the Holy Spirit. The idea is central to this thinking as expressed in the *Letters to Serapion*: if the Spirit were a creature we should have no participation of God in him. "If by participation in the Spirit we are made 'sharers in the divine nature' (2 Pet 1:4) we should be mad to say that the Spirit has a created nature and not the nature of God. For it is on this account that those in whom he is are made divine. If he makes men divine, it is not to be doubted that his nature is of God."[24]

The Holy Spirit is of the Trinity: "It is madness to call him a creature. If he were a creature, he could not be ranked with the Triad. For the whole Triad is one God. It is enough to know that the Spirit is not a creature, nor is he numbered with the things that are made. For nothing foreign is mixed with the Triad; it is indivisible and consistent."[25] The Spirit is, as the Son, consubstantial (*qv*) with the Father. "If the Holy Spirit is one, and the creatures many and angels many—what likeness can there be between the Spirit and things originate? It is obvious that the Spirit does not belong to the many nor is he an angel. But because he is one, and still more, because he is proper to the Word who is one, he is proper to God who is one, and consubstantial with him."[26] "These sayings (of Scripture) concerning the Holy Spirit, by themselves alone, show that in nature and essence

he has nothing in common with or proper to creatures, but is distinct from things originate, proper to and not alien from the godhead and essence of the Son; in virtue of which essence and nature he is one of the holy Triad."[27]

A. bases the divinity of the Spirit on his Christology. In one remarkable passage he speaks of the Spirit possessing the same proper condition precisely towards the Father as does the Son.[28] This led Sergius Bulgakov to assert that A. was dyadic, not triadic in doctrine;[29] but the passages already quoted contradict such a view. Of greater interest is the great Alexandrian's answer to the question: Does the Spirit proceed from the Son? He does say that the Holy Spirit "proceeds from the Father." He does not say explicitly that the Spirit proceeds from the Son, but certain passages leave the impression that the Spirit proceeds from the Son or from the Father through the Son: "For the Son does not merely partake the Spirit, that therefore he too may be in the Father; nor does he receive the Spirit, but rather he supplies it himself to all; and the Spirit does not unite the Word to the Father, but rather the Spirit receives from the Word. He, as has been said, gives to the Spirit, and whatever the Spirit has, he has from the Word."[30] " . . . His gift (the Spirit), who is said to proceed from the Father because through the Son who is confessed from (as coming from) the Father, he is resplendent, and is sent and is given."[31] "For the Father creates all things by the Word in the Spirit, since where the Word is there too is the Spirit, and things created through the mediation of the Word have from the Spirit by the Word the power to be."[32] H.B. Swete thought it impossible to understand the splendour of the Spirit through (*para*) the Son as anything less than essential dependence.[33] This idea A. shared with the Greek Fathers of the fourth and fifth centuries, an idea often hinted or implicit, not expressed in the terms which the *Filioque* (*qv*) controversy of later times would prompt.

[1]Works PG 25–28; critical ed., H.G. Opitz (W. Schneemelcher and M. Tetz), Berlin, 1934 ff.; on the text cf. H.G. Opitz, *Untersuchungen zur Überlieferung der Schriften des Athanasius*, Berlin, 1935 and J. Lebon, *RHE*, 31(1935) 161f., 627f.; for translations cf. Cross, p.102; cf. esp. *De Incarnatione*, critical ed. C. Kannengiesser, SC, 199; *Epp. to Serapion*, J. Lebon SC 15; G. Muller, *Lexicon Athanasianum*, Berlin, 1944–52; X. le Bachelet, *DTC* 1, 2:2143–78; G. Bardy, *DHGE*, 4:1313–40; V.C. De Clercq, *NCE* 1:996–999; J. Quasten, 3:20–79; ClavisG II, 12–60; E. Schwartz, *Zur Geschichte des Athanasius* (Gesammelte Schriften, 3; Berlin, 1959); Doctrine: F. Lauchert, *Die*

Lehre des hl. Athanasius, Leipzig, 1895; A. Gaudel, "La théorie du Logos chez saint Athanase," *RSR* 19(1929) 524–539; 21(1931) 1–26; J. Lebon, "S.Athanase a-t-il employé l'expression Ho curiakos anthropos?" *RHE* 31(1935) 307–329; C. Hauret, *Comment le 'Défenseur de Nicée' a-t-il compris le dogme de Nicée?* Bruges, 1936; J.B. Berchem, *Le rôle du Verbe dans l'oeuvre de la création et de la sanctification d'après saint Athanase*, Ang 15(1938), 201–232; L. Bouyer, *L'incarnation et l'Eglise Corps du Christ dans la théologie de S.Athanase*, Paris, 1943; F.L. Cross, *The Study of St.Athanasius*, Oxford, 1945; G.L. Prestige, *God in Patristic Thought*, London, 1956, 197–218; T.E. Pollard, *Logos and Son in Origen, Arius and Athanasius*: SP 2 (TU 64), Berlin, 1957, 282–87; id., "The exegesis of John 10:30 in Early Trinitarian Controversies," *NTS* 3 (1957), 334–349; G. Florovsky, *The Concept of Creation in Saint Athanasius*, SP 6 (TU 81:1962) 36–57; C. Kannengeisser, S.J., *Athanase d'Alexandrie, Evêque et écrivain. Une Lecture des Traités contre les Ariens*, Paris, 1983; id., "Athanasius of Alexandria and the Holy Spirit," *ITQ* 48(1981) 166–180; J.N.D. Kelly, *Early Christian Creeds*, 235–295; id. *Early Christian Doctrines*, 231–255; G. Bardy, *DHGE*, IV, 1313–1340, s.v.; W.A. Bienert, "The Significance of Athanasius," *ITQ* 48(1981), 181–195; Frances Young, *From Nicaea to Chalcedon*, London, 1983; [2]*Tomus ad Antiochenos*, 5, 8, LNPF 484, 485; [3]For the literature cf. *Theotokos*, M. O'Carroll, C.S.Sp., p.62; [4]*Ibid.*; [5]*Ep. ad Serap.*, 1, 28, SC 15, PG 26 [6]*Ep ad Serap*, 1, 15, 137, C.R.B. Shapland, London, (1951) 134–36; [7]*Or. Arian.*, 2, 25, LNPF 362; [8]*De decretis Nicaen Synod.*, 19, LNPF, 4, 162; [9]*Ibid.*, 20, 163, 4; [10]*Or. Arian.*, 2, 41, LPNF 370; [11]*Or. Arian.*, 3,3, 395; [12]*Ibid.*, 4, 395; [13]*De decretis Nicaen Syn.*, 11, 157; [14]Cf. G. Aeby, *Les missions divines de saint Justin à Origène*, Fribourg (Switzerland), 1958, 14, 15, 23, 68, 97, 106, 130—on Justin, Tatian and Athenagoras, Theophilus of Antioch, the Letter to Diognetus, Tertullian, Hippolytus, Novatian, Clement of Alexandria; [15]Cf. A. Orbe, *Hacia la primera teologia de la procession del Verbo*, Rome, 1958, 114f; [16]*De synod*, 41, LNPF, 472; [17]*Tomus ad Antioch.*, 7, LNPF, 485; [18]*Or. Arian.*, 3, 29, LNPF, 409; [19]*Ep. ad Adelp.*, 3, LNPF 575; *Or. Arian.*, 1, 42, LNPF 330, 31; [20]Cf. A. Grillmeier, *Christ in Christian Tradition*, London, 1965, 193–219; extensive bibliography Quasten, 76: esp. A. Stulcken, *Athanasiana. Literatur- und dogmengeschichliche Untersuchungen*, (TU NF 4,4) Leipzig, 1899; G. Voisin, "La doctrine christologique de saint Athanase," *RHE* 1(1900) 226–248; J. Lebon, "Une ancienne opinion sur la condition du corps du Christ dans la mort," *RHE* 23 (1927) 5–43; 209–241; M. Richard, "Saint Athanase et la psychologie du Christ selon les Ariens," *MSR* 4(1947) 5–54; I. Ortiz de Urbina, S.J., *L'anima umana di Cristo secondo s. Atanasio*, *OCP* 20(1954), 27–43; P. Galtier, "Saint Athanase et l'âme humaine du Christ," *Greg* 36(1955) 553–589; [21]*Op. cit.*, 217; [22]*Or Arian.*, 3, 30, PG 26, 388; cp. *Ep. ad Epict.* 8, LNPF, 573; [23]*Or Arian.*, 3, 32ff; [24]*Ep ad Serap.*, 1, 24, Shapland, 123; [25]*Ibid.*, 1, 17, Shapland, 103; [26]*Ibid.*, 1, 27, Shapland, 133; [27]*Ibid.*, [28]*Ep ad Serap.*, 3, 1; cp. 1, 21; [29]*Le Paraclet*, Paris, 1946, 29–34; [30]*Or. Arian* 3,24, LNPF 406, 7; [31]*Ep. ad Serap.*, 1, 20; [32]*Ibid.*, 3, 5; [33]*The Holy Spirit in the Ancient Church*, London, 1916, 92. LNPF translates "consubstantial" as "coessential."

ATHEISM

Atheism is a complex phenomenon. It presents a challenge on many levels to the Christian faith.[1] In the context of the present work the relevant question would appear to be: How does Trinitarian doctrine confront atheism? How does the believer in the Trinity meet the atheist? First let us take what looks like a simplistic answer, that given by Cardinal Daniélou some twenty years ago: "This is an affirmation massive, enormous, paradoxical. When we make it in the presence of a present-day atheist, his first understandable reaction is to say to us: By what right do you claim to impose on me the duty of believing in the Trinity? But that is exactly what I think. I think that I have the right to ask any atheist today not only to believe in man, not only to believe in God, but to believe in the Trinity, because the Trinity is truth. . . . The Trinity is itself the absolute, the abyss of being, the ultimate depth, which is disclosed to us in Jesus Christ, in such wise that on the day that the opacity of our present existence is dissolved, all, without exception, will meet the Trinity. . . . It is the condition of sincere dialogue with a non-Christian to begin by saying to him: 'I must warn you that one day you will be confronted with the Trinity.'"[2]

To judge, however, by recent literature, such a position, though it may still appear bluntly phrased, would not be lightly dismissed. As we shall see, notable works on the Trinity appear to be oriented directly towards solving the problem of atheism, or atheists. Atheism assumes not necessarily the existence of God, but of believers in his existence: it would be pointless to seek the removal of something which everyone thought non-existent, apart from the fact that it would be unknown, not a subject of thought or discourse. Atheists who achieve a certain intellectual fulfilment in their constructs are, curiously and ironically, indebted to those who have elaborated theologies.

Atheism has in the present century taken concrete form ranged against the concrete embodiment of faith in God, notably of the embodiment of Christian faith which is the Church. Though the League of Atheists, which at one time had a membership of five million inside Russia with an additional one and a half million junior members, has been dissolved for a considerable time, the Russian Constitution recognises and by so doing encourages the thrust of atheistic propaganda. Where the 1936 Constitution guaranteed "freedom to perform religious rites" and "freedom of anti-religious propaganda," the 1977 Constitution alters the phrasing to freedom "to conduct religious worship or atheistic propaganda."[3]

It was consciousness of such hard realities and awareness of widespread systematic atheism which prompted Pius XII's warning in 1949: the Apostolic Exhortation on atheism. "It is of atheism that we speak," wrote the Pope, "or what is worse, of hatred of God. With the utmost impudence the haters of God's name make use of every possible means, that is to say, books, tracts, newspapers, and wireless. Whether in committee, public assembly, private conversation, science or art—they take every opportunity of spreading contempt of all that is sacred. 'And the smoke of the pit arose as the smoke of a great furnace; and the sun and the air were darkened with the smoke of the pit' (Rev 9:2). We think, Venerable Brethren, that, in fact, all this is due to the plotting of the hellish enemy whose aim is to hate God and to hurt mankind."[4]

The Second Vatican Council considered the subject of atheism at length. Some of the council fathers knew that dialectical materialism was providing an intellectual support for atheism, giving it confident pretensions. One council expert, Fr. (now Cardinal) Henri de Lubac, S.J., had written impressively on the subject. A council father, who has since become Pope, Bishop Wojtyla, knew by experience the pressures which officially-sponsored atheism can put on families and individuals. He made the point thus: "It would be appropriate to distinguish in the (conciliar) schema between atheism born of personal conviction and that which is imposed from without by pressures of every kind, physical and moral; especially when it is made impossible to profess one's faith in public or official life, one is practically compelled to profess atheism, and the instruction of children is imbued with it even against the will of their parents."[5]

Vatican II noted that the word atheism is used to signify somewhat different things: it may mean explicit denial of God or an agnostic outlook, or the result of inadequate methodology, or an excessive affirmation of man, or again the rejection of a "God" so fashioned by the atheists themselves that he bears no likeness to the true God. There are also those who feel no religious experience or curiosity and see no point in such things—they seem to be areligious.

As to the causes the Council, without claiming to be exhaustive, mentions the deification of certain human values, and the fact that modern civilization "is engrossed in earthly affairs."[6] Some more particular indications are given as to causal factors; one must include among these the defects of believers: "To the extent that they are careless about their instruction in the faith, or present its teaching falsely, or even fail in their religious, moral or social life, they must be said to conceal rather than to reveal the true nature of God and of religion."[7]

Attention is also given to systematic atheism. Man, such atheists would maintain, achieves thus "freedom to be an end unto himself, the sole artisan and creator of his own history." They claim that this freedom cannot be reconciled with belief in a Lord who is the author and purpose of all things, or at least that this freedom makes such a belief altogether superfluous. "The sense of power which modern technical progress generates in man can give colour to such a doctrine."

Finally there is the form of atheism which claims to achieve the liberation of man "through his economic and social emancipation"; it finds religion with its talk of "hope in a deceptive future life" an obstacle to the construction of the human city, and its proponents, "wherever they gain control of the state, violently attack religion, and in order to spread atheism, especially in the education of the young people, make use of all the means by which the civil authority can bring pressure to bear on its subjects."

The Church is not satisfied, according to the conciliar text, with condemnation. "She tries to seek out the secret motives which lead the atheistic mind to deny God. Well knowing how important are the problems raised by atheism, and urged by her love for all men, she considers that these motives deserve an earnest and thorough scrutiny."

The Council affirms that to acknowledge God is in no way to oppose the dignity of man and states that hope in future things related to the end of time does not "take away from the importance of the duties of this life on earth but rather adds to it by giving new motives for fulfilling those duties." So many problems "of life and death, of guilt and suffering" remain unsolved without God, and despair often sets in.[8]

The Council indirectly touches on the Trinity in sketching a remedy for the evil: "Atheism must be countered both by presenting true teaching in a fitting manner and by the full and complete life of the Church and of her members. For it is the function of the Church to render God the Father and his incarnate Son present and, as it were, visible while ceaselessly renewing and purifying herself under the guidance of the Holy Spirit."

Reaffirming the rights of atheists as persons, the Council "courteously invites them to weigh the merits of the Gospel of Christ with an open mind." Interestingly, in the next part of the Pastoral Constitution on *Christ the New Man* there is a brief existential theology of the Trinity: Christ the new Adam is spoken of as revealing the mystery of the Father and of his love, and the Christian who is conformed to the image of the Son who is the firstborn of many brothers, "receives the 'firstfruits' of the Spirit (Rom 8:23), by which he is able to fulfil the new law of love (cf. Rom 8: 1–11). By this Spirit, who is the 'pledge of our inheritance' (Eph 1:14), the whole man is inwardly renewed, right up to the 'redemption' of the body (Rom 8:23)."[9]

As an organised response to the problem the Church supports the Secretariat for Non-Believers set up by Paul IV. This body was given a wide episcopal framework in 1984. Through a common president, Mgr. Paul Poupard, it is closely associated with the Pontifical Council for Culture. Through a number of publications, notably the review *Dialogue with Non-Believers*, it aims at thorough research into the reality of contemporary atheism, religious indifference and secularisation, and a sympathetic presentation of the Christian message to people of every cultural level. In the instruction issued by the Secretariat in 1968 on dialogue with non-believers it does not deal with the Trinity as a subject of dialogue.

Since then the third general synod of bishops has taken place and one year afterwards Paul VI in *Evangelii Nuntiandi* (8 December, 1975) summarised its findings and recommendations on its chosen theme, evangelization. Atheism is dealt with, more realistically perhaps than in the Council document: "From this a new form of atheism seems to evolve, a man-centered atheism which is not abstract or metaphysical but pragmatic, based on a pre-ordained plan, and militant. Daily and under diverse forms a new consumer society, which is closely connected with secularist atheism, reveals itself. Pleasure is proclaimed as the supreme good; the desire for power and domination; discrimination of every kind. Such are the inhuman propensities of this humanism."[10]

Humanism in the strict sense is not only compatible with Christian faith and practice but should flow from them. Unfortunately the word or its derivatives, particularly among such groups as the Association of Humanists, are being used as if there were rivalry if not hostility between humanism and religion, at least institutional religion.

On the problem of presenting the Trinity to atheists, recent literature is instructive. Two books on the Trinity, *The Christian Experience of God as Trinity* by James Mackey[11] and *Der Gott Jesu Christi* by Walter Kasper,[12] have some reflections on atheism—Mackey's more on secularism, Kasper's as a very lengthy general introduction to, almost a justification for his whole work.[13]

Hans Küng's book, *Does God Exist?* leaves the same impression, though proceeding in the opposite direction. He deals extensively with atheism, its modalities and causes, and with its offspring, nihilism. At the end of an intellectual itinerary through possible systems of thought designed to counter or avert atheism he reaches the final satisfactory answer in the God of Jesus Christ; his exposition of this theme forms a substantial part of his book, and is in fact a study of the biblical elements of the doctrine of the Trinity, with a concise conclusion bringing these elements together.[14] He refers to his treatment of the Trinitarian theme in his other work, *To Be a Christian*.[15]

One general reason why such Trinitarian response is increasingly thought most appropriate to the acute challenge of atheism is that the use of arguments drawn from natural theology does not appear productive, is possibly a hindrance, and leaves the question of valid arguments, that is, proofs, for the existence of God untouched.

Another reason is that man, atheist or believer, bears the image of God. But we know that God is triune. Why then postpone the attempt to discover for each one the reality which he mirrors?

The principal and determining reason for such a choice of theme is that God himself gave us this example. When the decisive moment came for God to reveal himself he did so by sending his Son, one of the sacred eternal three, to be the "mediator and the fulness of this revelation."[16] "His will was," says Vatican II, "that men should have access to the Father through Christ, the Word made flesh, in the Holy Spirit, and thus become sharers in the divine nature (cf. Eph 2:18; 2 Pet 1:4).[17]

To outline such a position summarily does not preclude or dispense with the necessity of important questions of pedagogy, of communication, of levels of intellectual ability—or the illusions thereon occasionally encountered in a society in which the printed word has undue dominance.

---

[1]Cf. *Atheism and Dialogue*, quarterly review, *Secretariat for Non-believers*, Rome; regular bibliographies; P. Roth, *Sowjetische Bücher und Broschuren zum Thema Atheismus, Stimmen der Zeit*, July, 1984, 497–500; *Eléments bibliographiques sur les formes d'incroyance et d'athéisme*, J. Potel, J-F. Six, F. Langendorff, Rome,Vatican, 1969; *L'Eglise devant le défi de l'athéisme contemporain*, Desclée international, Coll. *Athéisme et Dialogue*, Tournai-Paris, 1982; *L'indifferenza religiosa*, Roma, 1978 -French tr. *L'indifférence religieuse*, Paris, 1983; General literature: R. Flint, *Anti-Theistic Theories*, Baird Lecture, 1879; F.A. Lange, *Geschichte des Materialismus und Kritik seiner Bedeutung in der Gegenwart*, 1866, English tr. 3 vols, 1877–81; F. Mauthner, *Der Atheismus und seine Geschichte im Abendland*, (4 vols), 1920–23; A.B. Drachman, *Atheism in Pagan Antiquity*, 1922; J. Laird, Gifford Lectures, I, *Theism and Cosmology*, 1940, II, *Mind and Deity*, 1941 - a defence of atheism; H. (Cardinal) de Lubac, S.J., *The Drama of Atheistic Humanism*, London, 1949; J. Maritain, *The Range of Reason*, London, New York,1952, 103–117; J.S. Collins, *God in Modern Philosophy*, Chicago, 1959; E. Borne, *Atheism*, New York, 1961; I. Lepp, *Atheism in our Times*, New York, 1963; C. Toussaint, *DTC* 1, 2, 2190–2210; M. Schulien, E C., 2, 265–84; C.B. Upton, Hastings (ed.), *Encyclopaedia of Religion and Ethics*, 2, 173–83; J. Murray, S.J., *Catholic Dict.Theol.*, 1, 182–9; G.P. Reed, *NCE*, 1, 1000–10003; M. Schmaus, *Dogma I, God and Revelation*, London, 1968,"Atheism and Scepticism," 70–92; [2]*Mythes païens, mystère chrétien*, Paris, 1966, Ch. VIII, *La Sainte Trinité*, 88,89; [3]Official texts issued by the Russian government; [4]*Catholic Documents*, II, 4f; [5]*Acta Synodalia*, IV,II, 662; [6]*GS* 19; [7]*Ibid.*, [8]*Ibid.*, 21; [9]*Ibid.*, 22. [10]Tr. Vatican Council II, *More post-conciliar Documents*,ed. A. Flannery, O.P., 736; [11]London, SCM Press, 1983; [12]Mainz, 1983; [13]*Op.cit.*, 29–91; [14]English tr. 1980, 667–701; [15]London, 1976, 472–478; [16]*Verbum Dei*, 2; [17]*Ibid.*

ATHENAGORAS (2nd century)

An Apologist who may have been a native of Athens, A. was a Platonist, though he abandoned some Platonic opinions in later life.[1] Philip Sidetes says that he founded a philosophical school at Alexandria, in which he was followed by Pantaenus and Clement (qv). His works are *Embassy for Christians* and *Resurrection of the Dead*. In the first he defended Christians against three charges of atheism, cannibalism and promiscuity. In regard to the first charge he showed that Christians were not polytheists; he thus became the first Christian writer to treat of the Trinity in philosophical terms.

The essential passage is as follows: "I have given sufficient proofs that we are not atheists, but hold God to be one, unbegotten, eternal, invisible, suffering nothing, comprehended by none, circumscribed by none, apprehended by mind and reasoning alone, girt about with light and beauty and spirit and power indescribable, creator of all things by his Word, their embellisher and master. We do indeed think also that God has a Son—please let no one laugh at the idea of God having a Son. This is not a case of the myths of the poets who make the gods out to be no better than men; we have no such ideas about God the Father or the Son. The Son of God is Word of the Father in thought and power. All things were made through him and after his fashion. The Father and the Son are one, the Son being in the Father and the Father in the Son by the powerful union of the Spirit—the Son of God is mind and Word of the Father. Now, if in your exceeding great sagacity, you wish to investigate what is meant by the Son, I will tell you in brief. He is the first-begotten of the Father. He did not indeed come to be, for God was from the beginning being eternal mind and had his Word within himself being from eternity possessed of a Word; but he proceeded to become thought and power over the elements of undifferentiated nature when all the material elements were like a substrate in quiescence and the heavier elements lay mixed with the lighter. The Spirit of prophecy agrees with this account saying, 'The Lord made me in the beginning of his works,' (Prov 8:22). Then again this same holy Spirit that works in those who utter prophecy, we call an outflow from God flowing out and returning like a ray of the sun. Who then would not be amazed hearing those called atheists who call God Father and Son and Holy Spirit, proclaiming their power in unity and in rank their diversity?"[2]

There was much theological development to follow from this synthesis. As a second century statement it cannot but impress.

---

[1]Text PG 6: 887–1024; E. Schwartz TU, iv, 2; P. Ubaldi and M. Pellegrino, *Corona Patrum Salesiana*, Serie Greca 15; English tr. A.N.C.L., 2 1867; Oxford Early English Christian Texts, W.R. Schoedel; ACW, J.H. Crehan, S.J., 23; cf. A. Lucks, *The Philosophy of Athenagoras*, Catholic University of America, Washington, D.C., 1936; M. Pellegrino, *Studi su l'antica apologetica*, 1947, p. 67–105; R.M. Grant, *Athenagoras or Pseudo-Athenagoras*, HTR 47(1954), p.121–9; L.W. Barnard, *Athenagoras, A Study in Second Century Christian Apologetic*, Théologie historique, 18, Paris, 1972; J. Quasten, I, pp. 229–236; [2]PG 6, 908, 9.

AUGUSTINE, ST., DOCTOR OF THE CHURCH (354–430)

A.'s contribution to the theology of the Trinity was so profound and comprehensive that it has influenced thinking in the west down to the present time. He devoted over fifteen years to the composition of his principal work on the subject, *De Trinitate*, in fifteen volumes. But the theme recurs in his writings, notably in *De Doctrina christiana*, *In evangelium Johannis tractatus*, Letters XI and CLXX, *The City of God, Contra sermonem arianorum, Collatio cum Maximino, Contra Maximinum hereticum*.[1]

A. stated his objective in the *De Trinitate*: "to give the justification (*reddere rationem*) of this statement, the Trinity is one, only, true God and it is quite right to say, to believe and to think that the Father, the Son and the Holy Spirit are of one and the same substance or essence."[2] Elsewhere he summarizes his ideas thus: "There is no better word to suit such an exalted being, than the Trinity, one God from whom, through whom and in whom all things are (Rom 11:36). Thus the Father, the Son and the Holy Spirit, each of whom is God and at the same time all are one God; each of these is the full substance and all together are one substance. The Father is not the Son, nor is he the Holy Spirit, the Son is not the Father nor the Holy Spirit, the Holy Spirit is not the Father nor the Son; the Father is only the Father, the Son is only the Son, the Holy Spirit is only the Holy Spirit. All three have the same eternity, immutability, majesty, power. In the Father there is unity, in the Son there is equality, in the Holy Spirit the agreement of unity and equality: and all these three are one because of the Father, equal because of the Son, joined together because of the Holy Spirit."[3]

One important contribution made by A. was to the language of the Trinity. He was so powerful in expression, had such command of Latin, that he provided models for every kind of statement needed about the Trinity. Thus he writes in Letter 170: "And thus if *latria* is due to the Father and the Son and the Holy Spirit and is forthcoming from us, concerning which it has been said 'Thou shalt adore the Lord thy God and him only shalt thou serve,' without any doubt the Lord our God, whom alone we should serve with *latria* is not the Father only, not the Son only, not the Holy Spirit only but the Trinity itself, one only God, Father, Son and Holy Spirit; not that the Father should be he who is the Son, nor that the Holy Spirit should be he who is the Father or the Son, since in the Trinity the Father is of the Son only, but the Holy Spirit is the Spirit of the Father and of the Son; but on account of one and the same nature and inseparable life, the Trinity, as far as is humanly possible, faith leading the way, is understood to be the one Lord our God of whom it is said 'Thou shalt adore the Lord thy God, and him only shalt thou serve,' whom the Apostle preaches saying 'Since from him, and in him and through him are all things: to him be glory forever and ever, Amen' (Rom 11:36).[4]

A. probably knew the previous writings on the Trinity in the west—of Tertullian (*qv*), St. Hilary of Poitiers (*qv*), Marius Victorinus. Through the *De Spiritu Sancto* of St. Ambrose he had access to some of the Greek Fathers, and he may have known others like Origen (*qv*) and Didymus the Blind (*qv*) in translation; he had some acquaintance late in life with St. Basil's writings and those of St. Gregory of Nazianzua (*qv*).

What is implicit in many passages through his works and explicit in the *De Trinitate* is that he changed the whole approach to his subject fundamentally from that of the Greeks: his starting point was the unity of God. In this he was distinctive as he was in giving much more thought to the Trinity as a divine mystery than to the Incarnation, by which the Trinity was made known to man.

Whereas the pre-Augustinian concept brought the Father into prominence as the origin of the persons, A. put the emphasis on the divine nature. Therein he saw the source of identity and equality: "So great is the equality in the Trinity that not only is the Father not greater than the Son in regard to the divinity, but neither are the Father and the Son together greater than the Holy Spirit, nor is any single person of the three anything less than the Trinity itself."[5] "This Trinity is of one only and the same nature and substance: neither less in each than in all, nor more in all than in each; but it is as great in the Father alone or in the Son alone as in the Father and the Son together, and so great in the Holy Spirit alone as in the Father, the Son and the Holy Spirit. Nor did the Father, that he should have a Son from himself, lessen himself, but he so begot from himself another self that he should remain wholly in himself and that he should be in his Son as great as he is in himself alone. Likewise the Holy Spirit is wholly from one still in his wholeness, not going before the one from whom he proceeds, but as great with him as from him; nor does he lessen him by proceeding, nor bring increase by adhering to him. And all are one without confusion, and three without division. Although one they are three and although three they are one. In reality he who gave to the many hearts of his faithful the power to be one heart, all the more ensures that in himself these three separate ones should be God, but together not three gods, but one God. This is our one Lord and God to be served with entire devotion, to whom alone *latria* is due."[6]

A. firmly eliminates the danger of tritheism, far less a threat in his synthesis than in the Greek doctrine. On the other hand it has been pointed out that so much thought of the divinity may tend to make it so separate as to appear almost a fourth person, or again as so dominant that it absorbs the persons; this would be a new kind of Sabellianism.

There are certain consequences that flow from A.'s general position. One is that all divine operations *ad extra* (outside God) are the work of the Trinity. In the *De Trinitate* he considers the theophanies of the Old Testament, from the appearance of God to Adam in the garden of Eden on, many involving the appearance of angels. He asserts that these manifestations are of the whole Trinity, though one of the persons could occasionally be manifested in a special way. A. deals in detail with the questions arising, with a close eye to the biblical texts.

The mystery of the Incarnation is wholly singular. Whereas "the Trinity wrought that human form from the Virgin Mary, yet it is the person of the Son alone; for the invisible Trinity wrought the visible person of the Son alone."[7]

In the initial operation of the Trinity *ad extra*, creation (*qv*), A. sought, after much reflection, for a Trinitarian pattern. His thought—which is highly original here—attributes to the Father the role of principle of existence, to the Son the function of forming and converting what is created to its principle—otherwise having been taken from nothingness it would lapse into nothingness—and to the Holy Spirit the work of unity.[8]

From A.'s general theory about the divine nature operating *ad extra* it also follows that whatever is said in an absolute way about one of the persons is in the singular: the Father is God, he is almighty, as is the Son and the Holy Spirit. But

there are not three Gods, nor three who are good in the plural nor three almightys, but one God, one good, one almighty.[9]

With such emphasis on the unity of the divine nature, how does Augustine explain the distinctions of persons? What are the divine persons? What explains their diversity, which does not affect the unity of substance? A. wrote in the full aftermath of Arianism (*qv*) which had provoked, by way of reaction, an emphasis on the unity and consubstantiality of the three. Previously the distinction of persons had been read in terms of the divine interventions in the economy (see ECONOMIC TRINITY). Already some of the Greek Fathers had based the diversity of persons on relations. This A. consecrated, leaving open the way to the refinements which the Scholastics would formulate in their treatises.

"We do not speak of accidents in God," he writes, "for in him there is nothing changeable; and nevertheless everything that is said of God is not in reference to the substance. In fact there are things which are said in relation to others, thus Father in relation to Son, and Son in relation to Father, which in God is not at all an accident, since one is always Father and the other is always Son; always is not said as from a moment that the Son was born and from the fact that since he never ceases to be Son, the Father would never cease to be Father; but from the fact that he was always born as a Son and never began to be a Son. If there was a moment when he began to be a Son or one when he could cease to be a Son, then he would be called a Son in the context of accident. But if the Father were called Father in regard to himself and not to his Son and the Son were called Son in regard to himself and not to the Father, then one would be called Father and the other Son in reference to the substance. But because the Father is not called Father save in so far as he has a Son, and the Son is not called Son save in so far as he has a Father, these things are not said in reference to the substance. For these things are not said of each in regard to himself, but in regard to the other reciprocally: nor in a context of accident for what is conveyed by Father and by Son is in them eternal and immutable. Wherefore though there is a difference in being Father and Son, there is no difference in the substance, for they are not so named in reference to the substance, but in reference to a relation, which relation is not an accident, since it is not changeable."[10] That the persons are thus constituted does not lessen their separateness and their autonomy.

Nor does A. claim to have emptied the mystery. "If we are asked what are the three, human language labours under great insufficiency. The answer has been "Three persons," not so much to answer as not to refuse an answer."[11]

A. has one difficulty with this theory of relations as constitutive of persons. How can there be a correlative for the Holy Spirit? Father and Son are obviously correlative. But if the Spirit comes from the Father and the Son, being their bond, communion between them, how can the two be the correlative opposite? He is conscious of the difficulty and fixes on the idea of the Spirit as gift. He elaborates his solution thus: "There should be no anxiety, since we have spoken of the Holy Spirit in the context of relation; not the Trinity itself, but he who is in the Trinity, that there is no word corresponding to him as a correlative. We speak of the servant of the master and the master of the servant, the son of the father and the father of the son, for these words are reciprocal, but here we cannot speak thus. We speak of the Holy Spirit of the Father, but not inversely of the Father of the Holy Spirit, lest the Holy Spirit would be taken for his Son. Likewise we speak of the Holy Spirit of the Son, but not of the Son of the Holy Spirit, lest the Holy Spirit should be taken for his father. . . .

"For many things relative it happens that there is no corresponding word to express the correlative. For example what more obviously expresses a relation than "pledge" (*pignus*)? It refers to that of which it is the pledge and a pledge is always a pledge of something. If then we speak of the pledge of the Father and of the Son (2 Cor 5:5; Eph 1:14) can we speak inversely of the Father of the pledge and of the Son of the pledge? . . . When we speak of the gift (*donum*) of the Father and the Son we cannot speak of the Father of the gift or of the Son of the gift, but to have here a reciprocal response we speak of the gift of the giver and the giver of the gift; here we have current language, in the other case not so."[12]

A. gives sufficient place in his synthesis to the visible and invisible missions of the Son and the Spirit, linking them with the eternal processions: the missions reveal a divine person in his eternal origin: "As therefore the Father has begotten, the Son is begotten; thus the Father has sent, the Son was sent. But in the same way as the one who begot and the one begotten are one, so are the one who sent and the one who was sent; for the Father and the Son are one (Jn 10:30). Thus also the Holy Spirit is one with them; for these three are one. For as to be born for the Son is to be of the Father, so for the Son to be sent is to be known in his origin from the Father. And as for the Holy Spirit to be the gift of God is to proceed from the Father, so to be sent is to be known to proceed from the Father. Nor can we say that the Holy Spirit does not proceed from the Son; nor is it vain that we call the same Spirit the Spirit of the Father and of Son. Nor do I see what else he wished to signify when, breathing on the face of the disciples, he said: 'Receive the Holy Spirit' (Jn 20:22)."[13]

A. saw the Spirit as the communion (*communitas*) of the Father and Son. The society of the unity of the Church of God is the work of Spirit, as the Spirit is "in a way the society of the Father and the Son."[14] Continuing, he writes: "The Father is not possessed in common as Father by the Son and the Holy Spirit, for he is not the Father of the two; and the Son is not possessed in common as Son by the Father and the Holy Spirit, for he is not the Son of the two; but the Holy Spirit is possessed in common by the Father and the Son, for he is the only Spirit of the two." Because the Spirit is the substantial communion of the Father and the Son A. can speak of him in a special way as *charitas*.[15]

This is in effect the *Filioque* (*qv*). A. was impressed by the many biblical texts which refer to the Spirit as the Spirit of the Father and the Spirit of the Son. He states quite explicitly that the Holy Spirit is the Spirit of the Father and the Son.[16] A. speaks of the Spirit's proceeding "*principaliter*" (as from a principle): "I have, therefore, added *principaliter* because the Holy Spirit is proved also to proceed from the Son. But this the Father also gave him."[17] A. does use the phrases "*ab utroque*" and "*de utroque*" in regard to the procession by the Spirit: "Wherefore he who can understand the timeless generation of the Son from the Father, should also understand the timeless procession of the Holy Spirit from both (*de utroque*)."[18]

Hence A. can deal with the objection: if the Spirit proceeds from the Father and the Son, why does the Son say that the Spirit "proceeds from the Father" (Jn 15:26)? The Father communicates to the Son all that he is, except that he is Father. Therefore everything that the Son has comes from the Father. When he says that the Spirit proceeds from the Father it is as when he says, "My teaching is not mine but his who sent me" (Jn 7:16); he does not mean that the Spirit does not come from him; there are excellent reasons for thinking that the Spirit comes from him also.

Finally A. contributed to the evolving doctrine of the Trinity an idea which, refined by St. Anselm (qv) and more fully developed by St. Thomas (qv), would enter the theological patrimony of the west. This is the psychological explanation of the processions in God. A. was prone to look for analogies, "*vestigia*" of the Trinity throughout the whole of nature, as he also loved to see things in threes; the assumption was that God, even in his triune existence, is reflected in his handiwork.

God is especially reflected, A. would say, in the highest creature in the visible universe. He saw analogies of the Trinity in the sensory part of man: object seen, external vision, attention of mind; memory, internal vision, will (volition). A's thinking was to prove most stimulating, although it was not literally followed, in his opinion that the image of the Trinity is reflected in the spiritual nature of man. Three triads in particular emerge strongly in his thinking along this line; mind, knowledge, love (*mens, notitia, amor*); memory, understanding, will (*memoria sui, intelligentia, voluntas*); memory (about God), understanding (of God), love (of God), *memoria Dei, intelligentia, amor*. All A's subtlety and dialectical skill are displayed in the elaboration of his thought in these categories. It was a development of the basic biblical and patristic idea that the image (qv) of God is enshrined in man. It enriches the most complete theological synthesis on the Trinity in patristic times.[19]

[1]*De Trinitate*, PL 42; Latin text, tr., notes, *Biblioth. Augustin.*, 15, 1955, M. Mellet and Th. Camelot; 16, 1955, P. Agaesse, J. Moingt; cf. M. Schmaus, *Die Psychologische Trinitätslehre des hl.Augustinus*, Münster, 1927; F. Cavallera, "La doctrine de S. Augustin sur l'Esprit Saint á propos du 'De Trinitate'," *RTAM* 2 (1930), 365–387; 3 (1931) 5–19; I. Chevalier, *S. Augustin et la pensée grecque. Les relations trinitaires*, Fribourg, 1940; id., "La théorie augustinienne des relations trinitaires. Analyse explicative des textes," *Divus Thomas*, Fribourg, 18 (1940), 317–384; F. Cayré, "Le mysticisme et la sagesse dans le Confessions et le De Trinitate de S.Augustin," *Année théolog. augustin.*, 13 (1953) 347–370; G.B. Ladner, "St.Augustine's Conception of the Reformation of Man in the Image of God," *Augustinus Magister*, Paris, 1954, II 867–878; M. Nédoncelle, "L'intersubjectivité humaine est-elle pour S.Augustin une image de la Trinité?," *ibid.*, I, 595–602; E. Portalie, S.J., *A Guide to the Thought of St.Augustine*, tr. R.J. Bastian, S.J., from *DTC* 1,2, 2268–2472; Chicago, London, 1960; J.-L. Maier, *Les Missions divines selon S. Augustin*, Fribourg, 1960; O. du Roy, "L'expérience de l'amour et l'intelligence de la foi trinitaire selon S. Augustin," *Recherches Augustiniennes* 2 (1962) 415–455; id., *L'Intelligence de la foi en la Trinité selon S. Augustine. Génèse de sa théologie trinitaire jusqu'en 391*, Paris, 1966; J.E. Sullivan, O.P., *The Image of God: The Doctrine of St. Augustine and its Influence*, Dubuque, Iowa, 1963, esp. 84–162; P. Verbraken, "Le sermon LII de S. Augustin sur la Trinité et l'analogie des facultés de l'âme," *RBen* 74 (1964) 9–35; F. Bourassa, *Questions de théologie trinitaire*, Rome, 1970; B. de Margerie, S.J., *La Trinité chrétienne dans l'Histoire*, Paris, 1975, 159–172; E.Bailleux, "L'Esprit du Père et du Fils selon S. Augustin," *Rev. Thomiste*, 77 (1977) 5–29; [2]I, 9, 4, PL 42, 822; [3]*De doct. Christ.*, I,5, PL34,21; [4]PL 33, 749; [5]*De Tr.*, VIII, 947; [6]PL 33, 749; [7]*De Tr.*, II, 10, 18 PL 42, 857; [8]*De vera religione*, PL 34, 172; [9]*De Tr*, VIII, PL 42, 947; [10]*De Tr.*, V, 5, 6, 913,14; [11]*De Tr.* V, 9, 10, 918; cp. VII, 4, 8–9, 940, 41; [12]*De Tr.*, V, 12, 13, 919,20; [13]*De Tr.*, IV, 20, 29, 908; [14]Serm 71, PL 38, 463, 4; [15]*De quantitate animae*, 34,77, PL 32, 1077; [16]*De Tr.*, I, 4, 7; 5, 7; 8, 18; PL 42, 824, 832; [17]XV, 17, 29, PL 42, 1081; cf. 26, 47 and *Serm.* 71, 26, PL 38, 459, critical ed. *RBen* 75 (1965) 94; [18]*De Tr.*, XV, 26, 47, 1094; [19]Cf. Y.M-J. Congar, *The Holy Spirit*, III; Portalie, *op.cit.*, 134; O. du Roy, *op. cit.*, 537–40—in each case for lists and tables of triads and images.

B

BAPTISM

The doctrine of the Trinity, at least in a succinct formula, is linked with the sacrament of Christian initiation.[1] Since the sixth century the Constantinopolitan creed (qv) is universally part of the ceremony. This is a manifest case of the relationship between doctrine and liturgy (qv). It is also a means whereby the Sentiment of the Faithful (qv) comes into existence.

On the subject of declaratory creeds J.N.D. Kelly (qv) writes: "This completes our study of the use of creeds in connection with baptism in the first three centuries. The conclusion to which the impressive array of evidence points stares us in the face: declaratory creeds of the ordinary type had no place in the baptismal ritual of the period. If in the fourth century and thereafter their role was, as we saw, secondary, prior to the fourth century they had no role at all. An affirmation of faith was, of course, indispensable, but it took the form of the candidate's response to the officiant's interrogations."[2]

As the author continues, there was no set rule about the mode of response in the Church's early days. One instance was not plenary in Trinitarian terms, but explicit: "I believe that Jesus Christ is the Son of God." Thus the eunuch, minister of Candace, who asking for baptism, was told by Philip, "If you believe with all your heart you may" (Acts 8:36, 37). Mostly it appears that the baptizand's reply was "I believe." "Not only," adds Kelly, "was this the sole profession of faith used at the service, but there is much that goes to suggest that, in conjunction with the triple immersion, it was regarded as the central and operative feature in the whole baptismal action."[3] Liturgical historians think that, at this early stage, the baptismal questions and answers had the role that the baptismal formula ("I baptize thee in the name" . . . "So and so is baptized in the name") would later have. For this formula came later: "Of declaratory creeds, statements of faith in the first person in a more or less fixed form of words, there is no trace at all in the early liturgies."[4]

But the declaratory creeds had a place in the preparation of the candidate for baptism. They belonged to the catechumenate. Thus there was the "tradition" and the "reddition" of the creed:

the bishop "handed out" the creed, article by article, in the later weeks of Lent and the catechumens learned it by heart and "gave it back" on the eve of their baptism, their knowledge of it being the sign of their readiness for the sacrament.

Thereon arises a problem. The command of the Master as reported in Mt 28:19 is to baptize "in the name of the Father and of the Son and of the Holy Spirit." Yet in Acts we read of baptism "in the name of the Lord Jesus" (8:16; 19:5) and "in the name of Jesus Christ" (10:48). We have noted the words used by the Ethiopian eunuch.

One explanation offered for this discrepancy—by Fr. J. Crehan—is that different words were assigned to the candidate for baptism and to the one who baptized him: the latter would have used the Trinitarian formula. This is dismissed by others—by the great liturgist, Fr. J.A. Jungmann for example—as conjecture. He does admit the Trinitarian content in the preliminary interrogation: "Baptism itself, which as early as the second century was connected with Easter, began with a renunciation of Satan ('Dost thou renounce Satan?') and a profession of faith ('Dost thou believe in God the Father Almighty? . . . Dost thou believe in Jesus Christ? . . . Dost thou believe in the Holy Spirit?'). After the separate affirmative answers to each of the three questions about faith the priest poured water over the candidates—three times in honour of the Blessed Trinity."[5]

Jungmann says that "an explicit reference to the Trinitarian formula cannot be found in the first centuries." He dismisses *The Didache*, VII, 1 as it "merely repeats Mt 28:19." It does much more: "1. Concerning baptism, baptize thus: Having first rehearsed all these things, 'baptize, in the Name of the Father and of the Son and of the Holy Spirit,' in running water; 2. but if thou hast no running water, baptize in other water, and if thou canst not in cold, then in warm. 3. But if thou hast neither, pour water three times on the head 'in the Name of the Father, Son and Holy Spirit.'"[6] With this testimony, which may be from the first century, compare the second century St. Irenaeus (*qv*), in the *Proof of the Apostolic Preaching*: "So faith is the cause of salvation, as the presbyters the disciples of the apostles have handed down to us. Above all it exhorts us to remember that we have received baptism for the remission of sins in the Name of God the Father and in the Name of Jesus Christ the Son of God, who became flesh, died and rose again, and by the Holy Spirit of God. This baptism is the seal of eternal life."[7] Again he says: "For this reason the baptism of our new birth takes place under these three headings. There is bestowed upon us God the Father by means of the new birth through his Son, by the Holy Spirit."[8] Does this justify Fr. Crehan's conclusion: "That baptism should take place under the three headings, or be given under the three Names, is quite explicit evidence that the baptizer in the time of Irenaeus used the three Names in the rite"?

We touch ultimately the complicated matter of the evolution of the Creeds (*qv*). A suggestion was made by Lietzmann that two separate Creeds existed: a Christ-Creed for the Eucharist and a Trinitarian Creed for baptism: They would have coalesced almost imperceptibly. Let us end with two quotations: "In the light of the history of the Creed the essential fact is the existence of a short composition, prior to the text of R (see CREEDS), one marked by the absence of the Christological development. Must we believe that at the outset they baptized only simply in the name of Jesus? Are we to think that, under the influence of Mt. 28:19, a baptismal confession comprising only mention of the three persons was soon worked out? We do not know; perhaps in the future this ignorance will disappear."[9]

Fr. Crehan summed up his findings on the subject as follows: "Jesus Christ so occupied the thoughts of early Christians and of the apostles in chief, that to confess him was enough for baptism in the earliest times. The warrant for this in the practice of John the Baptist and in the words of the Lord himself was considered sufficient by such men as John the Apostle. This practice of the early Church led to the grouping together in a short formula of the 'facts about Christ.'"[10] By the time of Ignatius of Antioch (*qv*) the Creed was well diffused. Just before the middle of the second century in face of the danger of Marcionite views some words on God the Father were added. In the next half century a new challenge was met: the Montanists, who questioned the right of the Church to give the Holy Spirit. Thus the "facts about the Holy Spirit" were added—that he hallowed the Church, forgave sins and was the pledge of a blessed immortality.

Through this development or some similar one the Trinitarian formula emerged. It is noteworthy that though it may have taken time, the movement of thought was towards this finished product. Thus in the solemn moment of Christian initiation, the neophyte was instructed on the central importance of the truth about the Trinity and given an inkling about the power of invocation of the triune God. Nor has there ever been any suggestion of changing this practice with its vital implication.

---

[1]Cf. P. de Puniet, O.S.B., *DACL* II,1 (1910), 251–346; C.H. Turner, *The Use of Creeds and Anathemas in the early Church*, London, 2nd ed, 1910; H. Lietzmann, *Symbolstudien*, I–XIV, ZNTW, 1922–1927; id. EB III, 82–84; VI, 656–59; J. Lebreton, S.J. (*qv*), "Les origines du symbole baptismale," *RSR*, 1930, 115ff; id Fliche Martin, I, 368–71; esp. J. Crehan, S.J., *Early Christian Baptism and the Creed*, London, 1948; W.F. Flemington, *The New Testament Doctrine of Baptism*, London, 1948; A. Benoit, *Le baptême chrétien au second siècle, la théologie des Pères*, Paris, 1953; J.A. Jungmann, S.J., *Public Worship*, London, 1957, 73f; id., *NCE*, II, 59–62; J. Quasten, "Baptismal creed and baptismal act in St.Ambrose, 'De Mysteriis' and 'De Sacramentis!'" *Mélanges de Ghellinck*, Gembloux, 1951, I, 223–234; A. W. Wainwright, *The Trinity in the NT*, London, 1975, 3rd.imp., 238f; J.N.D. Kelly, *Creeds*, esp. 48f; V.H. Neufeld, *The Earliest Christian Confessions*, Grand Rapids, 1963, bibl.; [2]*Op.cit.*, 48; [3]*Ibid.*, with added references: R.H. Connolly, *JTS*, 25 (1924), 131ff; H.J. Carpenter, *JTS*, 44 (1943), 1ff; O. Casel and P. de Puniet among the liturgists agreeing with the opinion here; against, J. Brinktine, *EphLit*, 36 (1922), 328ff; [4]*Ibid.*, [5]*Public Worship*, 73; cf. St. Hippolytus (*qv*), *Traditio apostolica*, ed. B. Botte, O.S.B., 50,51; [6]*The Apostolic Fathers*, ed. tr., K. Lake, 318, 320; [7]*Proof of the Apostolic Preaching*, 3, PO 12, 662; [8]*Ibid.*, 7, 758; [9]"Les origines du symbole romain," *RTAM* 2 (1930), 19; [10]J. Crehan, *op. cit.*, 143, 44.

BARDY, GUSTAVE (1881–1955)

Ordained priest in 1906, B., a professor in Besançon, Lille and finally at the University of Dijon, became the outstanding patristic scholar in France of his time.[1] Most of his research and published work was in the area of third and fourth century history and theology: cf. his early biographies *Didyme l'Aveugle* and *Athanase*. The first edition of his monograph on Paul of Samosata (*qv*), 1923, was delated to Rome and he had to revise it, 1929; the anti-Modernist climate was hampering. Rigorously scientific, he was author of some thirty books and a very large number of scholarly articles, many of these contributions to the great collections under way or initiated in the post-war years, *DTC*, *DSp*, Fliche-Martin, *DHGE*. His work

on Lucian of Antioch (*qv*) and his school is authoritative. To Fliche-Martin III he contributed "the best general account of Arianism—a critical and well documented statement";[2] To *DTC* he contributed many articles, e.g. *Monarchianisme* (*qv*) and the lengthy, scriptural and patristic sections on the Trinity.[3] He translated and edited Eusebius's "Ecclesiastical History" for SC, 31, 41, 55, 73; he had edited the works of Theophilus of Antioch (*qv*).

---

[1]Cf. J. Lebon, *RHE* 51 (1956), 348,49; "Mémorial Gustave Bardy," *REA* 2 (1956), 1–37; G. Jacquemet, *Catholicisme*, I, 1247, with over twenty titles of books; F. X. Murphy in *Catholic Authors* II, s.v.; [2]P. Hughes, *A History of the Church*, I, 314; [3]XV, 2 (1950), 1545–1702.

BARTH, KARL (1886–1968)

B's eminence in the world of theology has drawn considerable attention to his theory of the Trinity. He felt obliged to rethink the doctrine in the light of his general theological principles.[1] Thus he opens the long section of volume one in the *Church Dogmatics* where he treats of the subject with this statement: "God's Word is God himself in his revelation. For God reveals himself as the Lord and that according to Scripture signifies for the concept of revelation that God himself in unimpaired unity yet also in unimpaired difference is Revealer, Revelation and Revealedness."[2]

When B. comes to explain this more fully he proposes his theory of the modes of existence: "By the doctrine of the Trinity we understand the Church doctrine concerning the oneness of God in the three modes of existence of Father, Son and Holy Spirit or concerning the threefold otherness of the one God in the modes of existence of Father, Son and Holy Spirit. All that had, and still needs to be expounded here in detail could and can only be an exposition of the oneness in threeness and the threeness in oneness of God. As such this doctrine is not to be found in the texts of the Old and New Testament witness to God's revelation. It did not arise out of the historical situations to which these texts belong. It is the exegesis of these texts in the language, which means also the light of the questions arising out of a later situation. It belongs to the Church. It is a theologoumenon. It is a dogma. We have inquired into its root, that is, into the possibility on the basis of which it could become dogma in a Church which wished to regulate by the biblical witness. And we saw that its possibility consists in the fact that in the Bible revelation signifies the self-unveiling imparted to men of a God who according to his essence cannot be unveiled to man. This content, according to the biblical witness, is of such a nature that in view of the three elements of veiling, unveiling and impartation of God we have cause to speak of a three fold otherness of the one God who according to the witness of the Bible has revealed himself. The biblical witness to God's revelation faces us with the possibility of interpreting the one proposition 'God reveals himself as Lord three times' in a different sense. This possibility is the biblical root of the doctrine of the Trinity. But in the Bible it remains on the level of possibility."[3]

How B. applies this idea of God seen in revelation to each person (though he rejects the word) of the Holy Trinity is interesting. On the Father: "The one God reveals himself according to Scripture as the Creator, that is, as the Lord of our existence. As such he is God our Father, because as the Father of God the Son he is so."[4] On the Son: "The one God reveals himself according to Scripture as the Reconciler, that is, as the Lord amidst our enmity towards him. As such he is the Son come to us, or the Word spoken to us, because he is so antecedently in himself as the Son or Word of the Father."[5] On the Holy Spirit: "The one God reveals himself according to Scripture as the Redeemer, that is, as the Lord who sets us free. As such he is the Holy Spirit by receiving whom we become the children of God, because as the Spirit of the love of God the Father and God the Son he is so previously in himself."[6]

By binding the idea of the Trinity so closely to God, the event of revelation, B. has incurred questioning if not criticism on divine transcendence; by his use of the term "modes" he is bound to awaken memories of the early Modalism. Of this he seems free, as perusal of the lengthy exposition of the Father, Son and Spirit will make clear.

It can scarcely be said that his theory gained widespread adherence. But it has the merit of rooting the doctrine of the Trinity, by means of exegesis, in the Bible.

[1]Extensive bibliographies in reference works e.g. Cross and Livingstone, *The Oxford Dictionary of the Christian Church*, 137; on the Trinity, J. Moltmann, *The Trinity and the Kingdom*, London, 1981; R. Roberts, "Karl Barth," in *One God in Trinity*, ed. P. Toon, J.D. Spiceland, Westchester, 1980, 78–93; W.J. Hill, *The Three-Personed God*, Washington, 1982, "The Trinity as Modes of Divine Self-Manifestation," 113–124; [2]*Church Dogmatics*, tr. G.J. Thomson, I, 339; [3]*Op. Cit.*, 441; [5]*Op. Cit.*, 457; [6]*Op. Cit.*, 513.

BASIL, "THE GREAT", ST., DOCTOR OF THE CHURCH (c. 330–379)

Closely attached to St. Athanasius (qv), and an ardent defender of the faith of Nicaea (qv), B. had a very influential role in the final defeat of Arianism, which he met in the person of an extremist, Eunomius (qv); he also resisted the Pneumatomachians (qv), who denied the divinity of the Holy Spirit.[1] He strove to effect reconciliation between the Homoeousians, who held that the Son was "like in substance" to the Father and those who held the Nicene doctrine of the *Homoousios* ("of one substance") (qv). B.'s Trinitarian doctrine is found especially in his *Adversus Eunomium*, *De Spiritu Sancto* and certain of the dogmatic letters.

B. furthered doctrine by clarifying the meaning of *ousia* and *hypostasis*, substance and person, as they would be known from the Latin equivalents. His terminology would eventually be consecrated at Chalcedon.

St. Athanasius had not distinguished between *ousia* and *hypostasis*, stating that "Hypostasis is *ousia* and means nothing else but simply being." The council of Alexandria in 362, over which he presided, admitted either one *hypostasis* or three *hypostases*. B., on the contrary, was explicit on the distinction: "If you ask me," he writes, "to state shortly my own view I shall state that *ousia* has the same relation to *hypostasis* as the common has to the particular. Every one of us both shares in existence by the common term of essence (*ousia*), and by his own properties in such a one and such a one. In the same manner, in the matter in question, the term *ousia* is common, like goodness, or godhead, or any similar attribute; while *hypostasis* is contemplated in fatherhood, sonship or the power to sanctify.... (He wishes) that the principle of the *homoousion* may be preserved in the unity of the godhead, and that the doctrine preached may be the recognition of true religion, of Father, Son and Holy Spirit, in the perfect and complete hypostasis of each of the persons named."[2] "It is indispensable," he says elsewhere, "to have clear understanding that, as he who fails to confess the community of the essence or substance falls into polytheism, so he who refuses to grant the distinction of the *hypostases* is carried away into Judaism."[3] "Wherefore, in the case of the godhead, we confess one essence or substance so as not to give a variant definition of existence, but we confess a particular hypostasis, in order that our conception of Father, Son and Holy Spirit may be without confusion and clear. If we have no distinct perception of the separate characteristics, namely fatherhood, sonship and sanctification, but form our idea of God from the general idea of existence, we cannot possibly give a sound account of our faith."[4]

Zahn, Loofs and especially Harnack maintained that B. had altered the sense of the *homoousion*, while retaining the word; Harnack distinguished thus "old Nicenes"—the West, Alexandria and notably St. Athanasius—and "new Nicenes," the Cappadocians, who would have diluted the meaning of the basic word of Nicaea to approximate to a view like that of Basil of Ancyra (*qv*). Harnack does not prove his assertion. What must be noted is that the Cappadocians, especially B., insisted on the three *hypostases*, whereas Athanasius concentrated on the consubstantiality.

B.'s teaching on the Holy Spirit has likewise been questioned. In his treatise on the subject he never once says that the Holy Spirit is God. But the whole thrust of the work and the direct implication of the truth in certain sections leaves no doubt about his belief. St. Gregory of Nazianzus (*qv*) defends B. on this matter. "The enemies were on the watch for the unqualified statement 'the Spirit is God,' which, although it is true, they and the wicked patron of their impiety imagined to be impious; so that they might banish him and his power of theological instruction from the city and themselves be able to seize upon the Church, and make it the starting-point and citadel from which they could overrun with their evil doctrine the rest of the world. Accordingly by the use of other terms, and by statements which unmistakably had the same meaning, and by arguments necessarily leading to this conclusion, he so overpowered his antagonists, that they were left without reply, and involved in their own admissions—the greatest proof possible of dialectical skill. . . . That he, no less than any other, acknowledged that the Spirit is God, is plain from his often having publicly preached this truth, whenever opportunity offered, and eagerly confessed it when questioned in private."[5]

Gregory further said that in his presence B. called "upon himself that most terrible fate of separation from the Spirit, if he did not adore the Spirit as consubstantial and coequal with the Father and the Son." He allowed Gregory full freedom of speech on the subject, he himself practising the kind of restraint described so that by their combined efforts "the gospel might be firmly established."[6] (see DOXOLOGY.)

B.'s words do imply the belief: "Such is, as nearly as possible the meaning of these words—the Spirit was borne: let us understand, that is, prepared the nature of water to produce living beings: a sufficient proof for those who ask if the Holy Spirit took an active part in the creation of the world."[7] B. is commenting on Gen 1:2; he had previously written in the same passage of "the Holy Spirit, the Spirit who completes the divine and blessed Trinity." "Ever be spoken among us with boldness that famous dogma of the Fathers, which destroys the ill-famed heresy of Arius, and builds up the Churches in the sound doctrine wherein the Son is confessed to be of one substance with the Father, and the Holy Ghost is ranked and worshipped as of equal honour, to the end that through your prayers and co-operation the Lord may grant to us that same boldness for the truth and glorying in the confession of the divine and saving Trinity which he has given you."[8]

"As then baptism has been given us by the Saviour, in the name of the Father and of the Son and of the Holy Spirit, so in accordance with our baptism, we make the confession of the creed, and our doxology in accordance with our creed. We glorify the Holy Spirit together with the Father and the Son, from the conviction that he is not separated from the divine nature; for that which is foreign by nature does not share in the same honours. All who call the Holy Spirit a creature we pity, on the ground that, by this utterance, they are falling into the unpardonable sin of blasphemy against him."[9] "One, moreover, is the Holy Spirit, and we speak of him singly, conjoined as he is to the one Father through the one Son and through himself completing the adorable and blessed Trinity. Of him the intimate relationship to the Father and the Son is sufficiently declared by the fact of his not being ranked in the plurality of the creation, but being spoken of singly; for he is not one of many, but One. For as there is one Father and one Son, so there is one Holy Spirit. He is consequently as far removed from created nature as reason requires the singular to be removed from compound and plural bodies; and he is in such wise united to the Father and to the Son as unit has affinity with unit."[10] "Shall we not then highly exalt him who is in his nature divine, in his greatness infinite, in his operations powerful, in the blessings he confers, good?"[11]

B. also considers the sanctifying work of the Spirit in the soul, wherein he seems dependent on Origen and on Plotinus. There remains the question which still draws so much comment: Why did B. not say explicitly that the Holy Spirit was God and why did he not say that he was consubstantial with the Father and the Son?[12] Different reasons have been advanced to explain the "silence", his "economy" on the subject. Was Athanasius right in saying that he "became weak to the weak to gain the weak"?[13] Bishops, B. must have known, criticised him for the silence. Gregory of Nazianzus urged him to make good the omission. He was, after all, defending the true doctrine against the Pneumatomachians (qv). Gregory himself showed complete freedom from inhibition in the matter. Why can a recent commentator write: "The striking and puzzling thing about all this is that Basil, though prepared to make such immense claims for the Holy Spirit, is not prepared to make the final one that he is God and consubstantial."?[14] Was it that he felt bound to the strict text of Nicaea, which did not deal with the Spirit as the Constantinopolitan creed would do? Or is B. Pruche's reminder of the distinction between *dogma* and *kerygma* as then understood to be borne in mind? Pruche and J.N.D. Kelly find B. entirely orthodox as does P. Piuslampe.

---

[1]Works PG 29–32; crit. ed. *De Spiritu Sancto*, C.F. Johnson, Oxford, 1892 and (with introduction and notes) B. Pruche, O.P., SC 17bis (1968); T. Schermann, *Die Gottheit des Heiligen Geistes nach den griech. Vätern des vierten Jahr.*, Freiburg, 1901, ch.IV, 89–145; F. Nager, *Die Trinitätslehre des Hl. Basilius des Grossen*, Paderborn, 1912; A. Grandsire, "Nature et Hypostases divines en S.Basile," *RSR* 13 (1923), 130–153; M. Richard, "L-introduction du mot Hypostase dans la théologie de l'Incarnation," *Mél. Sc. Rel.*, 2 (1945), 5–32, 243–270; M. Lot-Borodine, "La doctrine de la déification dans l'Eglise grecque jusqu'au XIe Siecle," *Rev. de l'Histoire des Religions*, 1932, 1–43, 525–574; Y.M-J. Congar, O.P., "La déification dans la tradition spirituelle de l'Orient," *VieSp* 43 (1935), 91–107; I.Chevalier, *S.Augustin et la pensée grecque; les relations trinitaires*, Fribourg en Suisse, 1940; G.L. Prestige, *God in Patristic Thought*, London, 1952 (reprint); J. Lebon, "Le sort du consubstantiel nicéen: II, S. Basile et le consubstantiel nicéen," *RHE* 48 (1953), 632–683; H. Dorries, *De Spiritu Sancto. Der Beitrag des Basilius zum Abschluss des trinitärischen Dogmas*, Göttingen, 1956; B. Capelle, O.S.B., "La procession du Saint-Esprit d'après la liturgie grecque de S.Basile," *Or. Syr.*, 7 (1962), 69–76; B. Pruche, O.P., "L'originalité du Traité de S.Basile sur le S.Esprit," *RSPT*, 32 (1948) 207–224; id., "Autour du Traité sur le S.Esprit de Basile de Césarée," *RSR* 52 (1964) 204–232; articles in *Verbum Caro* 89, 1968: B. Bobrinskoy, "Liturgie et ecclésiologie trinitaire de S. Basile,"1–32; J.-M.Hornus, "La divinité du S.Esprit comme condition de salut personnel selon Basile," 33–62; T.-F. Torrance, "Spiritus Creator," 63–85; P.C. Christou, "L'enseignement de S.Basile sur le S.Esprit," 86–99; J. Gribomont, O.S.B., "Intransigence and Irenicism, Word and Spirit," 1979—reprint from *Estudios Trinitarios*, 9 (1975); P. Piuslampe, *Spiritus Vivificans: Grundzuege einer Theologie des Heiligen Geistes nach Basilius von Caeserea*, Münster, 1981; A. Meredith, "The Pneumatology of the Cappadocian Fathers," *Irish TheolQuart.*, 48 (1981), *Basil the Great*, 198–205; H. Denhard, *Das Problem der Abhaengigkeit des Basilius von Plotin*, Berlin 1964; Quasten, III, 228–33; Kelly, *Doctrines*, 263–269; [2]*Ep.* 214, 4, LNPF 254; [3]*Ep.* 210, 5, LNPF 251; [4]Ep. 236, 6, LNPF, 278; [5]*In Laudem Basilii Magni*, Or 43, 10, PG 36, 587A; [6]*Ibid.*; [7]*Hexaemeron, Hom* 2, 6 LNPF, 63; [8]*Ep.* 90, 2, 176; [9]Ep. 159, 2, 212; [10]*De Sp. Sancto*, 45, 28; [11]*De Sp.*, 23, 54, 34; [12]Cf. Kelly, *Creeds*, 342; B. Pruche, SC 17bis, 82–93; [13]63, LNPF 4, 580; A. Meredith, *op.cit.*, 200; cf. *Contra Eunomium*, 3, 2; [14]A. Meredith, *l.cit.*

BASIL OF ANCYRA (d. c 364)

B., a physician, was elected in 336 to succeed Marcellus of Ancyra, who had been deposed by the synod of Constantinople because of statements against Asterius (qv). Basil was a leader of the moderate party among the Arians.[1] Deposed by the Council of Sardica in 343, he was reinstated in 348 by Constantius. He was present at the synods of Sirmium (351), and Ancyra (358) and Seleucia (359); he presided at Ancyra, where the extreme Arian views and the Nicene *homoousios* were rejected, and those who denied the essential likeness of the Son to the Father were anathematized—especially those who misinterpreted the words of Christ to think him "unlike" (*anomoios*) the Father. In reference to B.'s letter to all bishops after the synod of Ancyra, St. Athanasius wrote: "Those who deny the Council (of Nicaea) altogether, are sufficiently exposed by these brief remarks. Those, however, who accept everything else that was defined at Nicaea, and doubt only about the 'consubstantial' (*homoousios*), must not be treated as enemies; nor do we here attack them as Ariomaniacs, nor as opponents of the Fathers, but we discuss the matter with them as brothers with brothers, who mean what we mean and dispute only about the word. For, confessing that the Son is from the essence of the Father, and not from other subsistence, and that he is not a creature nor work, but his genuine and natural offspring, and that he is eternally one with the Father as being his Word and Wisdom, they are not far from accepting even the phrase 'consubstantial.' Now such is Basil who wrote from Ancyra concerning the faith."[2]

Recognised as leader of the Semi-Arians or Homoiousians, B. went with Eustathius of Sebaste and Eleusius of Cyzicus to Sirmium, to obtain from the imperial court acceptance of the so-called Sirmian formula, the creed of the Homoiousians. He was successful and the emperor gave him the task of preparing a general council which would make peace between the different Arian parties. But the Anomoeans gained his ear before the event and he adopted their plan for two synods, one for the westerns at Ariminum and another for the easterns at Seleucia. A conference was held at Sirmium, under the presidency of Constantius, to draft a creed to be presented to the two assemblies. On 22 May, 359, the fourth Sirmian formula appeared: *ousia* was dropped as being non-biblical; "like in all respects" (*homoios kata panta*) was to bring all moderates together. Basil signed, hoping for peace. But he composed a text in self-justification, which is a summary of Homoiousian theology, not far removed from that of St. Athanasius (*qv*). For B. "like in all things" comprised not only the will, but the hypostasis and essence also. He showed that though the word *ousia* does not occur in the Old or New Testament, its sense is everywhere.[3]

The western synod met at Ariminum. The dated creed was not accepted; *kata panta* was dropped and only *homoios* accepted. The eastern creed ended in a split. Basil and the same companions went once again to the emperor. On 31 December, 359 he obtained their signatures to the formula of Ariminum. The Homoeans were in the ascendancy. Acacius (*qv*), their leader, at Constantinople in 360 deposed and banished the trio who had sought to save the day. B. died c. 364, having revoked his consent to the formula of Ariminum.

Besides the Trinitarian treatise St. Jerome attributes to B. a work, *Against Marcellus*, which is lost. Epiphanius of Constantia judged him harshly. Athanasius tried to see the good in him. So apparently did St. Hilary: "There was nothing whatever suspicious in the document which some of you with the assent of certain Orientals took on your embassy to Sirmium to be there subscribed. But some misunderstanding has arisen in reference to certain statements at the beginning which I believe you, my holy brethren, Basil, Eustathius

and Eleusius, omitted to mention lest they should give offense. If it was right to draw them up, it was wrong to bury them in silence. But if they are now unmentioned because they were wrong we must beware lest they should be repeated at some future time."[4]

---

[1]Cf. J. Schladerach, *Basilius von Ancyra. Eine historisch-philosophische Studie*, Leipzig, 1898 (Dissertation); J. Gummerus, *Die homousianische Partei bis zum Tode des Konstantius*, Leipzig, 1900, 121f; R. Janin, *DHGE*, sv. 6, 1104–1107; E. Schwartz, "Zur Kirchengeschichte des vierten Jahrhunderts," *ZNW* 34 (1935), 149–158; O. Perler, *LThK*, 2 (1958), 31–32; H. Musurillo, *NCE* 2, 147–8; Quasten, III, 201, 203; [2]*De Synodis*, 41, LNPF, 472; but cf. *Ad episcopos Aegypti*, I, 7, 226 and *Apologia contra Arianos*, 3, 49, 126; [3]Text Epiphanius, *Haer.*, 73, 12–22; PG 42, 425–444; [4]*De Synodis*, 90 LNPF, IX, 28.

BIBLE, THE
Old Testament

Revelation of the Trinity in OT was certainly not explicit; it would be excessive too to say that it was implicit save in the sense that OT was a preparation for it, provided an intellectual climate within which it would one day be acceptable, and gradually fashioned language which could, without too much distortion, be used to express it (see FATHER, and SPIRIT).[1] OT gives us an overwhelming sense of God, the one who reveals himself, who takes the initiative in this self-disclosure. The whole fabric of relationships between God and man follows on divine choice and design: choice of moments when God intervenes, design of human conduct whereby a relationship with God is assured, of prayers which are received by God, appointment of spokesmen heard by God, bearers of his authentic message. Those receptive to this whole divine living fabric, as we know that the *Anawim* (the Poor of Yahweh) were at the approach of NT times, would be open to further self-communication by God.

There are four moments in OT times when the plural is used about God; at one time they were taken as at least hints of the Trinity. They are: "Then God said, 'let *us* make man in our image, after our likeness'" (Gen 1:26); "Then the Lord God said, 'Behold, the man has become like one of us, knowing good and evil'" (Gen 3:22); "Come, let us go down, and there confuse their language, that they may not understand one another's speech" (Gen 11:7); "And I heard the voice of the

Lord saying, 'Whom shall I send and who will go for us?'" (Is 6:8).

These texts do not, modern scholars generally agree, suggest the Trinity. The moments in salvation history when the words were spoken were decisive: the creation of man, his sin and its consequence, exclusion from Trinitarian life, man's failure in his first attempt to organise the world independently of its Maker, the choice of the great messianic prophet. What is insinuated, in such epoch-making moments, is a certain interior divine richness, a plenitude, infinite resource and inventiveness. The ancient Jewish mind could not interpret this in terms of personal existence, as such concepts were as yet unformed. God, in his personal intimate life, his self-communication or communion, was not the object of Old Testament speculation. It was his choice of the Jews, his works among them, all the wonderful tapestry of their relations with him, that seized their attention. The very institution of prophecy, so characteristic of the OT world, was God's means of manifesting to them his care, his compassion, his demands and his power. The prophets told the Jews what God desired from them, what they must do to please him, what would be the consequences of disobedience on their part. They did not open up to speculation the inexhaustible treasures of the Godhead.

That general context enables us also to situate in OT theology the set of special concepts linked with the idea of God, angel, word, wisdom, spirit. They are personifications requiring, at times, careful interpretation; they are not divine persons.

New Testament

Two scholars offer conflicting opinions about the basic idea. O. Cullmann maintains that it is Christological, but J.N.D. Kelly (qv) opts for a Trinitarian pattern as "already part and parcel of the Christian tradition of doctrine." The position is nuanced on one side and the other. Cullmann distinguishes between professions of faith and liturgical formulae: the latter, he concedes, are triadic, the former not. Kelly admits that Trinitarian creeds are rare. Both authors are dealing with a mentality rather than a precise revelation.

When we turn to detailed analysis what we get in the literature on the subject is exhaustive, confident treatment of the biblical teaching on each of the Three, and some hesitancy, if not outright scepticism, on the direct Trinitarian content, taking this as a single concept. The texts in NT on Father and Son, and on the Holy Spirit are endlessly discussed. But is there in NT any text which unequivocally proclaims the truth of the Trinity? At once Mt 28:19 is invoked: "Go, therefore, and make disciples of all the nations, baptizing them in the name of the Father and of the Son and of the Holy Spirit, teaching them to observe all that I have commanded you; and lo, I am with you always, to the close of the age." Or again, 2 Cor 13:13: "The grace of the Lord Jesus Christ and the love of God and the fellowship of the Holy Spirit be with you all."

The authenticity of the Matthaean text has been challenged on textual, literary and historical grounds. "Many scholars suppose that the saying reflects the teaching of the Church of the late first century and is not an utterance of Jesus himself."[2] The textual arguments are not sufficient to eliminate the text. The literary argument is that no parallels are found in the synoptic gospels or elsewhere. Mk 16:15–17 has: "And he said to them: 'Go into all the world and preach the gospel to the whole creation. He who believes and is baptized will be saved; but he who does not believe will be condemned. And these signs will accompany those who believe; *in my name* they will cast out demons; they will speak in new tongues." We rely therefore entirely on Matthew for the threefold formula.

The historical argument is still stronger, as is made clear in the article on Baptism (qv); why, if the injunction of the Master was so clear, is there no recorded instance of obedience to it in NT? Perhaps we should accept the judgment of A.W. Wainright: "The conclusion to which this discussion leads is that the threefold formula is part of the original text of Mt 28:19 but unlikely to have been uttered by Jesus himself. It is probably a formula which was developed in the early Church and was later ascribed to Jesus. A formula of this nature may have been in use for some time before it was included in the gospel tradition."[3] He thinks that it was in the tradition by about 80 A.D. and may have been in use ten or twenty years earlier, but concludes, "It cannot, however, be brought forward as evidence about the teaching either of Jesus or of the earliest Jerusalem church."[4]

How Paul reached the formulation of the second passage quoted is a matter of conjecture. Has he expanded another formula which he was accustomed to use: "The grace of our Lord Jesus

Christ be with you" (Rom 16:24; 1 Cor 16:23; 1 Thess 5:28; 2 Thess 3:18), and if so why? In a less sharply phrased way Paul uses other triadic formulas: "And because you are sons, God has sent the Spirit of his Son into our hearts, crying: 'Abba! Father!'" (Gal 4:6); "But it is God who establishes us with you in Christ, and has commissioned us; he has put his seal upon us and given us his Spirit in our hearts as a guarantee" (2 Cor 1:21–22); "and to show that you are a letter from Christ delivered by us, written not with ink but with the Spirit of the living God," . . . (2 Cor 3:3).

If we assume with Karl Rahner (*qv*) that when Paul speaks of God in these texts he is thinking of the Father, there is evidence that he thought much about the Trinity—as A.W. Wainright says, "there is material for the development of a doctrine." Consider the following: "But we are bound to give thanks to God always for you, brethren beloved by the Lord, because God chose you from the beginning to be saved, through sanctification by the Spirit and belief in the truth" (2 Thess 2:13,14). "There is one body and one Spirit, just as you were called to the one hope that belongs to your call, one Lord, one faith, one baptism, one God and Father of us all, who is above all and through all and in all" (Eph 4:4–6). "I appeal to you, brethren, by our Lord Jesus Christ and by the love of the Spirit to strive together with me in your prayers to God on my behalf" (Rom 15:30). "Now there are varieties of gifts, but the same Spirit; and there are varieties of working, but it is the same God who inspires them all in every one" (1 Cor 12:4–6).

Those who expect a full-blown theory of the Trinity in NT may be disappointed in these texts. Such a sentiment, even if given an appearance of reason, springs from the groundless assumption that the mentality, ideas, and mental categories of NT readers had undergone a radical transformation from the OT situation. It is to assume that there had been an overwhelming break with the traditional mentality and the neophytes were ready to accept and assimilate a whole new world of ideas, a theology which we know, in fact, developed within the Church, under the inspiration of the Spirit, over centuries. If we were given in NT dress a fully articulated theory of the Trinity, we should have grave reason to question its bona fides.

What effected the necessary change was the Christ event. It was in his message, his person, his challenge to the mind and heart that he was the "mediator and the fullness of all revelation" in regard to this mystery as to others. He loosened OT intellectual fabric, not to break or nullify it, but to release and detach elements for a new and permanent synthesis, elements in it precious because they needed him for meaning and enrichment. He is the key to biblical understanding, global and particular.

Two extremes are to be avoided in studying this witness: on the one hand to reduce the Bible to a mere adjunct, a collection of texts from which items are chosen to support theses drawn up independently of biblical revelation; on the other, to refuse acceptance of any idea or term which is not found in the sacred text. Writers of the theological manuals have to beware of the first pitfall; opponents of the *homoousion* (see CONSUBSTANTIAL) were sometimes caught in the second. They refused to accept a key word which they did not find in the Bible.

The literature on the Trinity shows that more abstract words are used here than in any other single theological concern. Such words are so easily divorced from biblical contexts that the entire discourse of which they are part may appear alien to Sacred Scripture. For the language (*qv*) of Scripture is concrete, factual, existential.

A theme prominent in some recent Trinitarian literature, the identity of the "economic" (*qv*) with the "immanent" Trinity, may also diverge from the testimony of Scripture. Thus it becomes increasingly a subject of pure dialectics.

[1]Cf. J. Lebreton (*qv*), *Les origines du dogme de la Trinité*, vol. I, Livre II, Ch. 1, *L'Ancien Testament*; F. Prat, S.J., *The Theology of St. Paul*, II, *Trinitarian Texts*, Note S, 431–34; O. Cullmann, *Les premières confessions de foi chrétienne*, Paris, 1943; A.R. Johnson, *The One and the Many in Ancient Israel*; G.A.F. Knight, *The Biblical Doctrine of the Trinity*; J. Isaac, O.P., *La Révélation progressive des Personnes divines*, Paris, 1960; R.G. Crawford, "Is the Doctrine of the Trinity Scriptural?" *Scottish Journal of Theology*, 20 (1967), 282–94; A.W. Wainwright, *The Trinity in the New Testament*, London, 1962, 2nd impr., 1969, 3rd impr., 1975; A. Lopez, O.SS.T., "Ya en el Antiguo Testamento apuntes de la Trinidad," *Estudios Trinitarios*, IV, 1970, 3–26; B. de Margerie, S.J., *La Trinité chrétienne dans l'histoire*, Paris, 1974, 11–89; [2]A.W. Wainwright, *op cit.*, 238; [3]*Ibid.*, 240; [4]*Ibid.*

BIBLIOGRAPHY

Most theological reviews will list or comment on works dealing with Trinitarian subjects under the general rubric of "God" or "Theology" or some similar title. There are occasionally notices or reviews of books or articles related to the Trinity in the "Bulletins" carried by well-known reviews, and studies of one kind or another in the domain of Patrology may bear on the development of Trinitarian doctrine. Bibliographies of the Fathers or Doctors who wrote specifically on the Trinity will have relevant items. The one specialized review on our subject, *Estudios Trinitarios*, carries in each issue reviews or notices of books under the specific Trinitarian rubric; it also carries reviews of general theological interest. One special issue of the review was devoted almost entirely to bibliography;[1] the issue is very much larger than the normal size. A lengthy section deals with works on the NT;[2] a shorter one on Patrology,[3] another on Catholic theology,[4] a section on the Orthodox[5] and an article on recent Protestant Trinitarian theology, which includes bibliographical references.[6] This is the most complete bibliography on the subject to appear so far. Works dealing with the subject may give bibliographies by chapters, as does W. Kasper's *Der Gott Jesu Christi*,[7] or generally, as B. de Margerie's *La Trinité Chrétienne dans l'histoire*[8] and W. J. Hill's *The Three-Personed God*.[9] The Oxford Dictionary of the Christian Church, ed. F. L. Cross, 2nd ed, E. A. Livingstone, contains very many entries relevant to Trinitarian theology. The bibliographies, as throughout the valuable work, are excellent

[1]*EstTrin.*, 11 (1977) "Numero extraordinario: Bibliografia," 132–524; [2]X Pikaza, "Bibliografia trinitaria del Nuevo Testamento," 138–305; [3]A. Hamman, 307–331; [4]J.R. Garcia-Marca, "Bibliografia teologico-catolica," 333–367; [5]M.M. Garijo Guembre, 369–442; [6]A.L.G.E. Joos, *Lineas sobresalientes del itinerario trinitario en la Teologïa Protestante de los ultimos decennios*, 443–507; [7]Mainz, 1983; e g on "Jesus Christus-Gottes Sohn," 209; on "Grundlegung der Trinitätslehre," 285; [8]Paris, 1975, 5–9; [9]Washington, 1982, 315–326.

BLONDEL, MAURICE (1861–1949)

The importance of B. in twentieth-century philosophy gives some point to his treatment of the doctrine of the Trinity.[1] There are controverted passages in his work on the question whether reason can attain to knowledge of the Trinity. In *La Philosophie de l'Esprit chrétien* he states explicitly that the Trinitarian dogma in its depth escapes our modes of thinking: "it cannot be the object of philosophical demonstration." But in *La Pensée*

he speaks of certain "*convenances*" which seem to imply that the doctrine could be naturally perceived. This tendency to believe that to be personal God is triune is, a at worst, a vague ambivalence. B. had a lofty theory of the centrality of the Trinity in Christian outlook: "the Trinitarian life is for us and our destiny the principle, the paradigm, the notion and the supreme purpose of our vocation."

[1]For bibliography cf. standard reference works, *The Oxford Dictionary* or *NCE*; cf. *esp.*, A. Minon, "La Sainte Trinité selon M. Blondel," *ETL*, 23 (1947).

BOETHIUS (480–524)

Readers of St. Thomas Aquinas (*qv*) may be surprised to see so many references to B. in the treatise on the Trinity.[1] His treatment of the subject is in two opuscula, now generally accepted as genuine: *Quomodo Trinitas unus Deus*[2] and *Utrum Pater et Verbum et Spiritus Sanctus de divinitate substantiali praedicentur*.[3] The first is in six sections: *Sententia catholica de Trinitate et unitate Dei; Substantia divine forma est; In divina substantia non est numerus; Quomodo Deus sit in praedicamentis; Quomodo Deus sit in relatione; Quomodo unitas et Trinitas sit in Deo*. The very phrasing here reveals the Aristotelian and logician who so influenced later generations. In the brief exposition B. was an incipient Scholastic. His definition of person remained classic: *rationalis naturae individua substantia*. In certain points St. Thomas finds it necessary to correct him. Gilbert de la Porrée (*qv*), in the lengthy commentaries which he wrote on B's opuscula, expressed the views which occasioned so much controversy but apparently no formal condemnation. A telling sentence of B.: "*Trinitas quidem in pluralitate personarum consistit, unitas vero in simplicitate substantiae.*"[4]

[1]On Boethius cf. H. Chadwick, *Boethius*, Cambridge, 1980; M. Gibson (ed), *Boethius, His Life, Thought and Influence*, Oxford, 1981; [2]PL 64, 1247–1256; followed by commentaries of Gilbert de la Porrée; [3]PL 64, 1299–1302; followed by commentaries of Gilbert de la Porrée; [4]1302.

BOLOTOV, BASIL, (1855–1900)

This Russian historian was appointed with A. L. Kalansky in 1892 to prepare a report on the *Filioque* (*qv*) in Russian Orthodox history.[1] After the Bonn conference, 1875 (*qv*), between Orthodox,

Anglicans and Old Catholics, the Russian Holy Synod appointed a commission to continue the work and to strengthen the relationship with the Old Catholic Church; a report from historians was thought necessary.

B. distinguished three levels of theological affirmation—the level of dogma in the creeds and ecumenical councils, that of individual theologies, and that of the theologoumena, expressions of faith framed by one or more Fathers when the Church was still undivided, and accepted by that undivided Church. B. appended to his thorough study twenty seven theses, of which the following are particularly important:

"The Russian Orthodox Church regards as a dogma that has to be believed only the following truth: the Holy Spirit proceeds from the Father and is consubstantial (qv) with the Father and the Son. The other aspects, insofar as they do not have the same meaning, should be regarded as theologoumena.

"The fact that the idea that the Holy Spirit proceeds, comes or shines from (*ekporeuetai, pro-eisi, eklampei*) the Father through the Son is frequently found in patristic texts, its occurrence in the treatise on *Orthodox Faith* by John Damascene, above all its introduction into the synodicon of Tarasius of Constantinople, the orthodoxy of which has been confirmed not only by the East, but also by the orthodox West in the person of the Roman pontiff Hadrian, (or Adrian) and even by the Seventh Ecumenical Council, gives to this idea of procession such importance that theologians cannot simply regard it as the private opinion of a Father of the Church, but are bound to accord it the value of an ecumenical theologoumenon, so to speak, with authority everywhere in the orthodox East.

"The opinion that the expression *dia tou Huiou* implies nothing but a temporal mission of the Holy Spirit in the world leads to violent distortions of some patristic texts.

"At least we cannot find fault with this interpretation, according to which the expressions frequently found in the teaching of the Fathers of the Church of the Holy Spirit's coming through the Son and his shining or manifestation from the Father through the Son contain an indication of a mysterious aspect in the activity, the life and the eternal relationships of the Holy Spirit with the Father and the Son, an aspect that is also known as the Holy Spirit's dwelling and remaining in the Son (*meson, anapauomenon*).

"This aspect is the imaginative expression of the identity of nature (*sumphues*) between the Spirit and the other two Persons and of that incomprehensible truth, revealed in the gospel, that the Holy Spirit is the third and the Son is the second Person of the Holy Trinity.

"This doctrine is not identical in meaning with that which is revealed in the words *ek tou Patros ekporeuetai*, if these words are interpreted in the strict sense of the technical terms *ekporeutos* and *ekporeuetai*.

"As a result of this, the Holy Spirit proceeds from the Father alone, in the strict sense of the word *ekporeutos*. This thesis, however, is not a dogma, but only a theologoumenon.

"The formula *ex Patre et Filio*, as found in the writings of St. Augustine, is not identical in its terminology, nor even in its meaning, with the teaching of the Eastern Fathers.

"The difference in opinions between Western and Eastern Christians is not so much in the words *ex Patre Filioque* as in the Augustinian idea that is connected with it, namely of a single spiration by the Father and the Son, according to which both form the single principle of the Holy Spirit. This idea is unknown to the Eastern Fathers; as we know, none of them ever said that the Son was *spirans* or *sumproboleus*.

"Even as a private opinion we cannot recognize the Western *Filioque* as equivalent to the Eastern *di'Huiou*.

"Within God's unfathomable plan, however, no protest was made by the Eastern Church at the time of St. Augustine against the view suggested by him.

"Many Western Christians who preached the *Filioque* to their flocks lived and died in communion with the Eastern Church, and no objection was raised on either side.

"The Eastern Church honours the Fathers of the early Western Church as it honours its own Fathers. It is therefore quite natural that the West should regard the individual opinions of those Fathers as holy.

"Photius and those who followed him remained in communion with the Western Church without obtaining from that Church an explicit and conciliar denial of the *Filioque*, even, as far as we know, without asking for it.

"It was therefore not the question of the *Filioque* which caused the division in the Church.

"The *Filioque*, as an individual theological opinion, ought therefore not to constitute an *impedimentum dirimens* for the re-establishment of communion between the Eastern Orthodox and the Old Catholic Churches."

The German text of B's report was published in the Old Catholic *Revue internationale de Théologie*[2] and appeared in French translation recently in the ecumenical publication *Istina*;[3] the extract from it here reproduced had appeared almost seventy years earlier in *Etudes*.[4] Two Russian Orthodox theologians, Sergey Bulgakov[5] and Paul Evdokimov[6] accepted B's theses, despite the heated controversy they caused during the author's life; Vladimir Lossky (*qv*) was acid in his refusal to accept them.[7]

The theses brought to light after a period of oblivion deserve serious attention from ecumenists and historians of Orthodox theology.

---

[1]Cf. *Istina*, 17 (1973), 261–467, several articles on *Filioque*; Y. M.-J. Congar, O.P., *The Holy Spirit*, III, 193f; A. Palmieri, *DTC*, V, 2331–2342; M. Jugie, A.A., *Theologia dogmatica Christianorum Orient. ab Eccl. cath. diss.*, II, Paris, 1933, 467–478; [2]6 (1898), 681–712; [3]17 (1973), 261–289; [4]101 (1904), Fr. Malvy (using the pseudonym Valmy), *Bulletin de théologie russe*, 856–879, esp. 866–67; [5]*Le Paraclet*, Paris, 1944, 99f; 116,137; [6]*L'Esprit Saint dans la tradition orthodoxe*, Paris, 1969; 74–75; [7]*In the Image and Likeness of God*, London, 1975, 72.

BONAVENTURE, ST., DOCTOR OF THE CHURCH (c. 1217–1274)

The great Franciscan doctor was influenced in his Trinitarian doctrine by Richard of St. Victor (*qv*), and in a fundamental point by Pseudo-Denis.[1] B. summarizes his theory in a passage in the *Itinerarium mentis ad Deum* written in 1259. Goodness is self-diffusing, as Pseudo-Denis would have it. From Richard B. borrows the idea of "dilectus condignus" and "condilectus", the distinction between love that is entirely free and love that is owed or received, and the mixture of the two. B. adds the idea of communication or emanation by nature or by will. This idea linked with that of "condilectus" allows B. to justify as necessary the existence of the third person. In all this theory one must not lose sight of the fact that B., eager to construct a system, feels rigorously obliged to

do so within the data of the faith: "you can see that through the sovereign communicability of good it is necessary that there be the Trinity of Father, Son and Holy Spirit. Because of supreme goodness, there must be in them supreme communicability, and because of the supreme communicability, a sovereign consubstantiality, and by the force of the sovereign consubstantiality, a sovereign configurability and in virtue of all that a sovereign coequality, and thereby, a sovereign coeternity, and as a consequence of all that a sovereign cointimacy, by virtue of which one is necessarily in the other by a sovereign circumincession; one operates with the other by the total indivision of substance, of power and operation of the blessed Trinity itself."[2]

For B. the Spirit is Love and Gift. He shows how love exists in God and how from love that is mutual between Father and Son the Spirit comes.[3] He insists at length on the primacy of the Father, and he cherishes the notion of hierarchy and of primacy in other areas of thought. "The Father," he writes, "is the principle of the whole divinity, because he comes from no one." He argues this position at great length.[4]

B. is in the line of St. Augustine (*qv*), both by his doctrine of the Spirit as the bond of love between Father and Son, and by his psychological analysis of the image of God in the *mens*. This, however, which he noted in Peter Lombard's (*qv*) *Sentences*, did not become the dominant idea in his synthesis. Through Richard, St. John of Damascus and Alexander of Hales, he approximates to the insights of the Greeks. His mode of presentation does remain Scholastic, but his key notions are Greek. He emphasizes the "monarchy" of the Father, with words like *primitas*, *innascibilis*, fruitfulness, (*fontalis plenitudo*)—St. Thomas thought that the Father's *innascibilitas* is merely negative, but B. proceeds from it as a positive attribute. He defines person as "the suppositum of a reasonable nature, owing its distinctness to a property." This property is a relation, but B. does not exploit the principle of which Anselm was aware, "in God all is one, save where the opposition of relation does not interfere." Persons arise through their distinctive property, which is identical with their origin, therefore with the relation; they cannot be distinguished by absolute properties. In affirming the unity of substance B. gives special place to the communication of life from person to person. He has the sense of mystery, which leads him, the first perhaps in the West, to include circumincession (qv) (spelled thus) in his synthesis.[5] This is consonant with Trinitarian life as life of persons.

---

[1]Works, Quaracchi ed.; cf. J.G. Bougerol, O.F.M., *Introduction a l'étude de S.Bonaventure*, Paris, 1961; A. Gerken, O.F.M., *Theologie des Wortes, Das Verhältnis von Schöpfung und Inkarnation bei Bonaventura*, 1963; R.Guardini, *Systembildene Elemente in der Theologie Bonaventuras*, Leiden, 1960; De Régnon, II; J.-F.Bonnefoy, O.F.M., *Le Saint Esprit et ses dons selon S.Bonaventure*, Paris 1929; Y.M-J.Congar, O.P., The Holy Spirit, III, 109–115; E. Longpre, O.F.M., *DHGE*, 9, 741–788; id. *DSp*, 1 (1937), 1768–1843, both with bibliographies;   [2]*Itinerarium*, VI, 2,Quaracchi, V, 311;   [3]*In I Sent.*, d.13, a.unic. q. 1, no.4, Quaracchi, V, 202;   [4]*In I Sent.*, d.27, q1, a.1, q.1 ad 3, 485;   [5]cf. n.2.

BONN CONFERENCE, THE, (1875)

A conference held in Cologne and Bonn, 1874–1875, was attended by twenty-two bishops and priests of the Orthodox Church, by American and English representatives of the Anglican Church and by some Old Catholics, who in view of their recent break from Rome had an interest in links with other Christian bodies. The theologian Dr. Döllinger, though objecting to the title "Old Catholic," was present: there were 120 in all.[1] A principal subject of discussion was the *Filioque* (qv). The Old Catholics and Anglicans agreed that the addition to the creed had been made in an illicit way and without the agreement of an ecumenical council. Among the conclusions reached by the participants were the following: "We agree totally that we should accept ecumenical creeds and decisions made by the early, undivided Church in matters of faith. We agree totally that we should recognize that the addition of the *Filioque* was not made in a way that was in conformity with the rules of the Church. We are in agreement with all the aspects of the representation of the teaching about the Holy Spirit suggested by the Fathers of the undivided Church. We reject every representation or mode of expression containing any acceptance of the idea of two principles, *archai* or *aitiai* in the Trinity." The conference went on to add a summary of the teaching of St. John Damascene" (qv) in the sense of the teaching of the early, undivided Church."[2]

---

[1]Cf. A. Palmieri, *DTC* V, "Filioque," 2331–2342; H. Reusch, *Bericht über die vom 10 bis 16 August 1875 zu Bonn gehaltenen Unionskonferenz*, Bonn, 1875; E.B. Pusey, *On the Clause 'And the Son' in regard to the Eastern Church and the Bonn Conference*, Oxford, 1876; E. Michaud, "L'état de la question du'Filioque' après la Conference de Bonn de 1875," *Rev. Internat.de Théologie*, 5 (1897), 89–99 (Old Catholic publication); cf. *ibid.*, 1897, 1 and 2; Y. M.-J.Congar, O.P., *The Holy Spirit*, III, 192–97;   [2]Apud Y. M.-J. Congar, *op.cit.*, 192.

BREASTPLATE OF ST. PATRICK

This outstanding example of the *Lorica*, or protection prayer, attributed to St. Patrick (qv), but composed by an eighth-century Irish monk, is noteworthy for its prologue and epilogue centred on the Trinity, as it is for a much-quoted Christocentric passage in the final part of the body of the prayer.[1] The prologue: "I arise to-day: in vast might, invocation of the Trinity; belief in a threeness, confession of a oneness; towards the Creator." Epilogue: "I arise to-day; in vast might, invocation of the Trinity; belief in a threeness; confession of oneness; meeting in the Creator; salvation is of the Lord, salvation is of the Lord, salvation is of Christ; may your salvation, Lord, be always with us." The example of prayer thus phrased to the Trinity has been powerful where St. Patrick is venerated.

---

[1]Bibliography art. *Lorica*, M. O'Carroll, C.S.Sp., *DSp*. IX, 1007–1111.

C

CALVIN, JOHN (1509–1564)—See Reformation, The

CATECHETICS

Modern Catechetics has nobly served the truth entrusted to the Church. There is no need here to trace its history or to analyse its innovations in the field of religious pedagogy, nor to investigate the reasons why it was chosen as a theme for the 1977 Episcopal Synod, the recommendations of which were to form the basis of John Paul II's Apostolic Exhortation *Catechesi Tradendae.* Previously Paul VI had approved the General Catechetical Directory (18 March, 1971), addressed the participants in the First International Catechetical Congress (25 September, 1971) and established the International Council for Catechesis (1975); he dealt with the subject in his Apostolic Exhortation *Evangelii Nuntiandi* (8 December, 1975); Vatican II (*qv*) had done likewise.[1]

What concerns us is the attention given in different ages to the doctrine of the Trinity by those who drew up official instructions for catechists or indicated the content of catechesis. Before the modern catechetical movement two catechisms would be taken as characteristic of Catholic ideals and practice: the *Catechism of the Council of Trent*[2] and the *Catholic Catechism* by Cardinal Gasparri.[3] They deal with the mystery of the Trinity at the beginning of their treatment of Christian themes.

The *Catholic Catechism*, issued in Germany in 1957, made a change. The Father, Son, and Holy Spirit were treated first and then, well on in the book, came the section on the Trinity, a brief but accurate summary.[4] This composition was considered a landmark in the catechetical movement.

The *General Catechetical Directory* gives a very large place to the Trinity. Having laid down the principle in its treatment of the "Christian Message" that "catechesis must necessarily be christocentric" since Christ is "the centre of the Gospel message within salvation," the Directory takes up the Trinitarian theme: "Just as Christ is the centre of the history of salvation, so the mystery of God is the centre from which this history takes its origin and to which it is ordered as to its last end. The crucified and risen Christ leads men to the Father by sending the Holy Spirit upon the People of God. For this reason the structure of the whole content of catechesis must be theocentric and trinitarian: through Christ, to the Father, in the Spirit."

"*Through Christ*: The entire economy of salvation receives its meaning from the incarnate Word. It prepared his coming; it manifests and extends his kingdom on earth from the time of his death and resurrection up to his second glorious coming, which will complete the work of God. So it is that the mystery of Christ illumines the whole content of catechesis. The diverse elements—biblical, evangelical, ecclesial, human, and even cosmic—which catechetical education must take up and expound are all to be referred to the incarnate Son of God."

"*To the Father*: The supreme purpose of the incarnation of the Word and of the whole economy of salvation consists in this: that all men be led to the Father. Catechesis, therefore, since it must help to an ever-deeper understanding of this plan of love of the heavenly Father, must take care to show that the supreme meaning of human life is this: to acknowledge God and to glorify him by doing his will, as Christ taught us by his words and the example of his life, and thus to come to eternal life."

"*In the Spirit*: The knowledge of the mystery of Christ and the way to the Father are realized in the Holy Spirit. . . . Therefore, catechesis, when expounding the content of the Christian message, must always put in clear light this presence of the Holy Spirit, by which men are continually moved to have communion with God and men and to fulfil their duties."

"If catechesis lacks these three elements or neglects their close relationship, the Christian message can certainly lose its proper character."[5]

The Directory tells us: "On all levels catechesis should take account of the hierarchy of the truths of Faith.

"These truths may be grouped under four basic heads: the mystery of God the Father, the Son, and the Holy Spirit, Creator of all things. . . ." There follows among the basic truths mention of the mystery of Christ, the mystery of the Holy Spirit and the mystery of the Church. This idea of the hierarchy of truths originated in the Decree on Ecumenism of Vatican II; it has not yet been expounded and applied to the satisfaction of all theologians."

Later in dealing with "the more outstanding elements of the Christian message" the Directory begins with this statement: "The history of salvation is identical with the history of the way and plan by which God, true and one, the Father, the Son, the Holy Spirit, reveals himself to men, and reconciles and unites with himself those turned away from sin.

"The Old Testament (see BIBLE) while clearly affirming the unity of God in a polytheistic world, already gives some foreshadowings of the mystery of the Trinity. These are completely unfolded in the person, in the works and, in the words of Jesus Christ. For when he reveals himself as the Son of God, he also reveals the Father and the Holy Spirit. An intimate knowledge of the true God pervades the entire soul of the divine

Master. He shares it with his disciples, calling them to become sons of God through the gift of his filial Spirit which he bestows on them (cf. Jn 1:12; Rom 8:15).

"In catechesis, therefore, the meeting with the Triune God occurs first and foremost when the Father, the Son, and the Spirit are acknowledged as the authors of the plan of salvation that has its culmination in the death and resurrection of Jesus (cf. S. Irenaeus, *Proof of the Apostolic Preaching*, n.6). In this way the growing awareness of the faithful responds to the revelation of the mystery transmitted by the Church; for the faithful understand through faith that their life, beginning at baptism, consists in acquiring a more intimate familiarity with the three divine Persons, inasmuch as the faithful are called to share in their divine nature. Finally, Christians, through the gift of the Holy Spirit, can already now contemplate with eyes of faith and cherish with filial love the Most Holy Trinity of Persons, as it is from eternity in God's intimate life."[6]

The *Dutch Catechism*, "the Catholic Faith for Adults," had appeared before the *Catechetical Directory*. Apart from a fleeting reference to the "mystery of God, one in three persons; the Father who sends, the Son who is sent, the Spirit whom the two give," nothing is said about the Trinity until the last pages of the book. Then we read this passage:

"When we try to penetrate this revelation prayerfully, we begin to realize that our whole life is in the hands of an eternal love. Being brought to the Father by Jesus and filled with their holy Spirit, we are perpetually involved in a mystery of love. Since we are privileged to be the family of God, the most magnificent glory is revealed to us.

"This is something which we shrink from summing up briefly, since it is the mystery of the Father, the Son and the Spirit. We shrink from the task, because we know that in order to know God, we must not leave the ground where his revelation has brought us—our ordinary life, the world of men. We must not ascend to dizzy heights, because our imagination might at once be captured by some such figure as three interlocking circles. Or our thought might be preoccupied at once by combinations of the numerals one and three, and thus miss the riches of this revelation as given in the Bible. The Bible does not use the word 'three' to speak of the mystery, any more than do the twelve articles of the Apostles' Creed, or the Nicene Creed. But it is a warning not to begin too readily with a brief formula in an attempt to proclaim the mystery which is so utterly comprehensive. In the religious instruction now given to children, attention is first fixed on the Son and on how he speaks of the Father and how he loves the Father. At Whitsuntide, the Spirit whom they send is spoken of, but it is only years later that the term Holy Trinity is used. . . . After a whole volume in which everything spoke of the Father, the Son and the Holy Spirit, a 'treatment' in a few pages would be to set the mystery too much apart . . . . The message of Scripture proclaims so vigorously both the distinct properties of the Father, the Son and the Holy Spirit, and their divine oneness, that we cannot but confess one God in three persons. We live all this out, by trying to be with Christ. When we try to live with him, through the Spirit which comes from him and the Father, we realize that the humble obscurity, as it would seem, of our existence, flows with him from the Father and to the Father. . . . Hence it is to the triune love that we must look for a hint which may point to the answer to the question: why does the world exist? All things have been created because in God this Spirit of love of the first-born is breathed forth. 'In him all things hold together' (Col 1:17), in the Son. 'All things were created through him and for him.'"[7]

A Commission of Cardinals examined the text of the Catechism. On this section they made this recommendation: "A more suitable way of speaking should be used with regard to the three adorable persons in God, whom Christians rightly contemplate with the eyes of faith and reverence with childlike love, not merely as they appear in the economy of salvation but also as they exist from eternity in their immanent life, the vision of which we await."[8]

A rewritten text was published in the *Supplement to a New Catechism*.[9] Significant passages are: "We must always contemplate God in the light of this world and the history of salvation in which he has given us a place. But we have received the Spirit, St. Paul tells us, who 'searches everything, even the depths of God' (1 Cor 2:10). And it is well that we should gaze with the eyes of faith at the Father of our Lord Jesus Christ, at Jesus the Son, born of God before all ages, descending on earth to reveal to us the heart of God, and at the Holy Spirit who lives in the Church and with the Father and the Son is the guest of our souls. It is

well to gaze at the one God in three persons, since in this fundamental mystery we are confronting an eternal exchange of love, and can hear the summons to unity in faith and love. 'That they may be one even as we are one' was the prayer of Jesus to his Father (Jn 17:22f). All our Christian life, from baptism (*qv*) on is under the sign of the Father, Son and Holy Spirit. When we make the sign of the cross, we confess that we belong to the three divine persons. And we walk in faith until we one day may contemplate the one God in three persons and abide for eternity in his love."[10]

"The message of Scripture brings so clearly to our minds both the special attributes of the Father, the Son and the Holy Spirit, and at the same time their adorable unity, that the Church makes us confess in the Creed; I believe in God, the Father almighty . . . and in Jesus Christ his only-begotten Son . . . and in the Holy Spirit who is Lord and gives life."[11]

It will be well to compare the Dutch Catechism which uses mostly biblical, pre-Nicene language, with the treatment of the Trinitarian theme in Vatican II (*qv*) and in the *Credo of the People of God*, published by Paul VI (*qv*) on 30 June, 1968, and with such teaching on the Holy Trinity as occurs in the pronouncements of John Paul II, notably in *Catechesi Tradendae*. Let it be noted that the Dutch text implies an experiential approach to the doctrine of the Trinity, as it also closely links creation (*qv*) to the theme.

Recent Catechisms in the English language give space to the theme of the Trinity.[12]

[1]Bibliographies on Catechetics are readily available, e.g. G.S. Sloyan, *NCE*, 3, 220–25; [2]Tr. D. Donovan, Dublin, 1966, 32; [3]English ed., 1932, 71–73; [4]English tr., 112–114 and cf 423–425; [5]41; cf. *More Post Conciliar Documents*, ed. A. Flannery, O.P., 552–53; [6]47, 48, *ibid.*, 556, 57; [7]*A New Catechism*, English tr., London 1967, 498, 99; [8]Text of the declaration, *AAS* 60 (1968), 690f; [9]English tr. of work by Edouard Dhanis, S.J., and Jan Visser, London, 1970; [10]47; [11]*Ibid.*; [12]*The Catholic Catechism*, A. Hardon, S.J., 1974, "The Trinity: Mystery and Meaning," 63–67; *The Teaching of Christ*, ed. R. Lawlor, D. Wuerl, T.C. Lawlor, "The Holy Trinity," 174–85; esp. E. Hill, *The Mystery of the Trinity*, London, 1985.

CATHERINE OF SIENA, ST., DOCTOR OF THE CHURCH (1347–1380)

One of the great charismatic figures of all time, C. in her sublime work, *The Dialogue*,[1] returns frequently to the idea of the Trinity. All her profound mystical insight is concentrated in the prayer which is directed to the Trinity and ends her work: "O eternal Trinity! O Godhead! That Godhead, your divine nature, gave the price of your Son's blood its value. You eternal Trinity, are a deep sea: The more I enter you, the more I discover, and the more I discover, the more I seek you. You are insatiable, you in whose depth the soul is sated yet remains always hungry for you, thirsty for you, eternal Trinity, longing to see you with the light in your light. Just as the deer longs for the fountain of living water, so does my soul long to escape from the prison of my darksome body and see you in truth. O how long will you hide your face from my eyes?

"O eternal Trinity, fire and abyss of charity, dissolve this very day the cloud of my body! I am driven to desire, in the knowledge of yourself that you have given me in your truth, to leave behind the weight of this body of mine and give my life for the glory and praise of your name. For by the light of understanding within your light I have tasted and seen your depth, eternal Trinity, and the beauty of your creation. Then when I considered myself in you, I saw that I am your image. You have gifted me with power from yourself, eternal Father, and my understanding with your wisdom—such wisdom as is proper to your only-begotten Son; and the Holy Spirit, who proceeds from you and from your Son, has given me a will, and so I am able to love.

"You, eternal Trinity, are the craftsman; and I your handiwork have come to know that you are in love with the beauty of what you have made, since you made of me a new creation in the blood of your Son.

"O abyss! O eternal Godhead! O deep sea! What more could you have given me than the gift of your very self?

"You are a fire always burning but never consuming; you are a fire consuming in your heat all the soul's selfish love; you are a fire lifting all chill and giving light. In your light you have made me know your truth: You are that light beyond all light who gives the mind's eye supernatural light in such fullness and perfection that you bring clarity even to the light of faith. In that faith I see that my soul has life, and in that light receives you who are Light.

"In the light of faith I gain wisdom in the wisdom of the Word your Son; in the light of faith I am strong, constant, persevering; in the light of faith I have hope: It does not let me faint along

the way. This light teaches me the way, and without this light I would be walking in the dark. This is why I asked you, eternal Father, to enlighten me with the light of most holy faith.

Truly this light is a sea, for it nourishes the soul in you, peaceful sea, eternal Trinity. Its water is not sluggish; so the soul is not afraid because she knows the truth. It distills, revealing hidden things, so that here, where the most abundant light of your faith abounds, the soul has, as it were, a guarantee of what she believes. This water is a mirror in which you, eternal Trinity, grant me knowledge; for when I look into this mirror, holding it in the hand of love, it shows me myself, as your creation, in you, and you in me through the union you have brought about of the Godhead with our humanity.

"This light shows you to me, and in this light I know you, highest and infinite Good: Good above every good, joyous Good, Good beyond measure and understanding! Beauty above all beauty; Wisdom above all wisdom—indeed you are wisdom itself! You who are the angels' food are given to humans with burning love. You, garment who cover all nakedness, pasture the starving within your sweetness, for you are sweet without a trace of bitterness.

"O eternal Trinity, when I received with the light of most holy faith your light that you gave me, I came to know therein the way of great perfection, made smooth for me by so many wonderful explanations. Thus I may serve you in the light, not in the dark; and I may be a mirror of a good and holy life; and I may rouse myself from my wretched life in which, always through my own fault, I have served you in darkness. I did not know your truth, and so I did not love it. Why did I not know you? Because I did not see you with the glorious light of most holy faith, since the cloud of selfish love darkened the eye of my understanding. Then with your light, eternal Trinity, you dispelled the darkness.

"But who could reach to your height to thank you for so immeasurable a gift, for such generous favours, for the teaching of truth that you have given me? A special grace, this, beyond the common grace you give to other creatures. You willed to bend down to my need and that of others who might see themselves mirrored here.

"You responded, Lord; you yourself have given and you yourself answered and satisfied me by flooding me with a gracious light, so that with that light I may return thanks to you. Clothe, clothe me with yourself, eternal Truth, so that I may run the course of this mortal life in true obedience and in the light of most holy faith. With that light I sense my soul once again becoming drunk! Thanks be to God! Amen."[2]

This beautiful prayer transcribes a mystical experience pure, sublime, creative as it confronts us with a Trinitarian doctrine at once soundly structured and daringly existential. Let scholars debate what one of the greatest of them has called Catherine's "academic pedigree,"[3] her sources, totally assimilated in this passage of exalted writing.

---

[1]*The Dialogue*, tr. Suzanne Noffke, O.P., (*The Classics of Western Spirituality*); bibl. 367–70; [2]364–66; [3]Professor Giuliana Cavallini, *op.cit.*, 10.

CHARISMATIC MOVEMENT, THE

The charismatic movement focuses attention on the Spirit and in its spontaneous prayers praises the Lord.[1] Evidently the Trinity is implied, but a profound theology of the Spirit would make the Trinitarian background more explicit, with ensuing benefit. The task is to relate the characteristic practices of the movement, its aspirations and its gains, to the comprehensive doctrine. The root of all spiritual benefit is the adoptive sonship which we hold in Christ. Therein we are directly related to the Father, who adopts us in his eternal Son. Therefrom come the gifts, the theological virtues and the graces freely given, the charisms. The Spirit as the sanctifier is eternally one with the Father and Son, in his being and in his operation.

The experiential factor appears at times to figure prominently in the charismatic renewal movement. Experience of the Trinity is elusive, scarcely within the reach of all but highly favoured Christians, and not necessarily lasting. But the intrinsic reality of the Trinitarian indwelling (qv) transcends any such element. Thereto all activity in the context of the Spirit's action on the soul is inseparably related.

The revival of awareness of the Spirit's presence and action in the lives of the faithful and in the life of the Church, the positive advertence to the reality of charisms in the Church at all times, the harmony at the deepest level fashioned between such spiritual impulses and true devotion to Our Lady have undoubtedly enriched many lives and fostered genuine Christian hope. It is but seeking to see explicit what is in reality implicit in all this supernatural ferment that one may hope for recognition, within the charismatic movement, of the Trinitarian dimension of Christian life at its most dynamic.

---

[1]Cf. E.D. O'Connor, CSC, *The Pentecostal Movement in the Catholic Church*, Ave Maria Press, Notre Dame, 1971, Bibl. 295–301; *id.*, *Pope Paul and the Spirit*, Notre Dame, 1978 (address to Charismatic Congress, Pentecost 1975, Rome, 228–230; *id.*, *Pentecost in the Modern World, The Charismatic Renewal Compared With Other Trends in the Church and the World Today*, Notre Dame, 1971; esp. R. Laurentin, *Catholic Pentecostalism*, London, 1977; bibl. 204–212; Y.-M.J. Congar, O.P., *The Holy Spirit*, II, 245–212.

CHARLEMAGNE (c. 742–814)

The great emperor's contribution to theology was understandably indirect; it was at certain moments important.[1] His role in the crisis of Adoptianism (qv) was to coordinate the intellectual forces opposed to it and ensure them a wide audience; he called the Council of Frankfurt, the greatest thus far seen in the west. We may thus see him as an ally of the teaching authority as Constantine had been, more consistently as the problem was more swiftly solved. Alcuin (qv) was here as in other matters his enlightened spokesman and speech-writer. He especially supported the emperor in promoting liturgical uniformity.

C. took action that was decisive in establishing the *textus receptus* of the Apostles' Creed (see article Creeds) as the one official version throughout his dominions. He aimed at purity of faith, as the *Admonitio Generalis* of 23 March, 789 makes clear. The vital moment was between 811 and 813 when C. wrote to all the metropolitans in his empire— he was now the Roman emperor crowned by the Pope—asking for information about the baptismal rites and the creed used in conferring the sacrament. Thus to Odilbert of Milan he wrote: "After that, what you tell them about the other parts of the service in order—as regards the scrutiny, what the scrutiny is; as regards the symbol, what the term means according to the Latins; as regards belief (*de credulitate*), after what fashion they are supposed to believe in God the Father almighty, and in Jesus Christ his Son, who was born and suffered, and in the Holy Spirit, the holy Catholic Church, and the other items which follow in the same creed. . . ."[2]

C. also took an active part in promoting the addition of the *Filioque* (*qv*) to the Constantinopolitan creed (*qv*). Pippin, king of France, C's father, had been present at the council of Gentilly. For the son the *Filioque* became a sacred cause. He had the addition made to the Creed recited in his chapel at Aachen, saw that it was taken up in his realms. In 794 he sent a letter of protest to Hadrian I over the latter's acceptance at the Council of Nicaea in 787 of the confession drawn up by Tarasius, Patriarch of Constantinople (*qv*), "who professes that the Holy Spirit proceeds not from the Father and the Son, according to the faith of the Nicene symbol, but from the Father through the Son."[3] The Pope did not accept C's opinion, but defended Tarasius; he did not share the Patriarch's opinion personally, but thought it had support in the teaching of many of the Fathers and in the practice of the Roman church.

In the year of this correspondence the council of Frankfurt took place. In the *Libellus* of the Italian bishops, thought to be the work of St. Paulinus of Aquileia, the idea of the double procession was explicitly affirmed. It was so too in the creed appended to C's letter to Elipandus and the Spanish bishops, probably the work of Alcuin.

In 808 some Frankish monks settled on Mount Olivet near Jerusalem. They chanted the Constantinopolitan Creed at Mass with addition of the *Filioque*, for which their Orthodox neighbours treated them as heretics and threatened them with expulsion. They appealed to the Pope who informed C. The latter now became protector of the Christians in the Holy Land. He commissioned Theodolphus of Orleans to compose his treatise *De Spiritu Sancto* and assembled a council at Aachen in 809–10. Theodolphus's book was approved and endorsed by the members, who also declared for the *Filioque*, possibly ordering its inclusion in the creed.

C. next sent an embassy to Leo III to urge him to approve the findings of the council. While conceding that the *Filioque* was essential to orthodoxy, Leo did not think that all essential truths should be included in the creed. His approval of the singing of the creed in the Frankish territories had not been intended to cover an amended version of it. He thought it would be better to drop the creed from the Mass altogether, beginning with the royal chapel. Leo III himself placed two shields with the creed in St. Peter's basilica: one in Greek,

the other in Latin. The third article read *proceeding from the Father*. Rome held out for a long while thereafter, despite the widespread use of the *Filioque*, despite the fact that the theory of the double procession was universally held in the West. Eventually it appears that the addition was made in the days of the emperor Henry II, in the pontificate of Benedict VIII.

---

[1]European and Church histories for the time give abundant material. Cf. L. Halphen, *Etudes critiques sur l'histoire de Charlemagne*, Paris, 1921; id., *Charlemagne et l'empire carolingien*, Paris, 1947; esp. R. Folz, *Etudes sur le culte liturgique de Charlemagne dans les eglises de l'empire*, Strasbourg, 1951; D.A. Bullough, "Charlemagne and his Achievement in the light of recent scholarship," *English Historical Rev.*, 85 (1970), 59–105; P.F. Palumbo, *EC* III (1950), 866–82; A.P. Frutaz, *ibid.*, 882–6, each with bibliog.; A. Dumas, *DHGE*, XII 424–441; esp., J.N.D. Kelly, *Creeds*, 420–426, "Charlemagne and the Creed;"[2]A. Boretius, *Capitularia Regum Francorum* (MGH, Legg.II) 1, 25 (No.3), 246f; cf. C. de Clercq, *La législation religieuse Franque*, Louvain, Paris, 1936, 216; [3]*Mon. Germ. Hist.*, Epp, v, 7ff.

CHRISTOLOGY

In the second part of an essay on Christology, the International Theological Commission dealt with the relation between Christology and Trinitarian theology: the statement was adopted unanimously in October, 1982.[1] Those pursuing this subject have to consider this illuminating document which will repay extensive study. The relevant passages are:

"*The relationship between Theocentrism and Christocentrism*:

"(1) In the recent history of western theology (and so leaving medieval theology out of consideration) the question treated so far can be discussed from different perspectives, namely 'Theocentrism' and 'Christocentrism'. The question these terms pose is whether the proper object of Christology is immediately God or Jesus Christ. We consider this problem by addressing, formally and logically, the relationship between Theocentrism and Christocentrism.

"(1.1) In fact the question rests on a false foundation if the Theocentrism which one opposes to Christocentrism is not a Christian Theism (that is, revealed and trinitarian) but is in some sense a 'natural' Theism, which places in doubt either the possibility or the fact of revelation. The question immediately vanishes because, in the first place, there is lacking in theism a purely 'natural' reason which could contradict Christocentrism; in the second place, Christian Theocentrism and Christocentrism are in fact one and the same.

"(1.2) Christian Theism consists properly in the triune God, and he is known uniquely in the revelation to us in Jesus Christ. Thus, on the one hand, knowledge of Jesus Christ leads to a knowledge of the Trinity and attains its plenitude in the knowledge of the Trinity; on the other hand, there is no knowledge of the triune God except in knowledge of Jesus Christ himself. It follows that there is no distinction between Theocentrism and Christocentrism; the two terms denote the same reality.

"(1.3) Leaving aside less suitable interpretations, Christocentrism properly connotes the Christology of Jesus of Nazareth, which, taken in its own more profound sense, expresses the 'singularity' of Jesus Christ. But this singularity of Jesus Christ properly accords with the revelation of the Trinity when it is defined on the one hand by the singular relationship of Jesus himself with the Father and the Holy Spirit, that is, with God; and, in consequence, on the other hand, by the singular condition according to which Jesus exists with and for men.

"(2) Christian Theism does not exclude natural Theism, but on the contrary presupposes it in its own way. For Christian Theism takes its origin from God revealing himself according to a most free intention of his will; while natural Theism pertains intrinsically to human reason, as the first Vatican Council teaches (cf. DS 3004, 3026).

"(3) *Natural Theism* is not the same as, and therefore is not to be confused with, either the Theism/monotheism of the Old Testament or historical Theism, that is, Theism which non-Christians have professed in various ways in their religions. The monotheism of the Old Testament has its origins in a supernatural revelation, and therefore retains an intrinsic relation to—indeed, demands—the trinitarian revelation. Historical theisms do not arise from a 'pure nature' but from a nature subject to sin, objectively redeemed by Jesus Christ and elevated to a supernatural destiny.

"(C) *Christology and the Revelation of the Trinity*

"(1) The economy of Jesus Christ reveals the triune God. Jesus Christ, however, is recognised in his mission only if the unique presence of God in him is properly understood. For this reason

Theocentrism and Christocentrism illustrate and need each other. Still, there remains the question of the relationship of Christology to the revelation of the triune God.

"(1.1) According to the testimony of the New Testament, the tradition of the primitive Church has always held with certainty that through the event of Jesus Christ and the gift of the Holy Spirit, God has revealed himself to us as he is, while remaining hidden in his essence. In himself he is such as he appeared to us: 'Philip, he who sees me, sees the Father' (Jn 14:9).

"(1.2) Consequently such are the three divine names which intervene in the economy of salvation, such they are also in 'theology', that is to say, as the Greek Fathers understood things, in our knowledge of the eternal life of God. For us this economy of salvation is the only definitive source of all knowledge of the mystery of the Trinity. The elaboration of the doctrine of the Trinity had its beginnings in the economy of salvation. Again an eternal and immanent Trinity is of necessity presupposed by the economic (*qv*) Trinity. Theology and catechetics (*qv*) must both take into account this datum of the primitive faith.

"(2) Therefore a fundamental axiom of modern theology is very correctly put in the following terms: the Trinity which manifests itself in the economy of salvation is the immanent Trinity: it is the immanent Trinity which gives itself freely and graciously in the economy of salvation.

"(2.1) Any kind of partition, then, is to be avoided between Christology and the Trinity in theology and catechetics. The mystery of Jesus Christ belongs to the structure of the Trinity. The mystery of the Trinity is Christological. The partition which we reject may take on either a neo-scholastic form or a modern form. Certain representatives of what is called neo-scholasticism isolate consideration of the Trinity from the whole Christian mystery, and do not take sufficient account of it in its understanding of the Incarnation or of the deification of man. The importance of the Trinity for the entire body of the truths of the faith and for the Christian life was at times completely neglected.

"The partition in question, in its modern form, puts a veil between men and the eternal Trinity, as if Christian revelation did not invite man to know the triune God and to participate in his life. As far as the eternal Trinity is concerned this leads to a certain 'agnosticism' which can in no way be accepted. For if God is above all that we can know of him, Christian revelation asserts that this 'extra' is always of a trinitarian nature.

"(2.2) In the same way anything leading to confusion between the event of Jesus Christ and the Trinity must be avoided. It is not true that the Trinity was brought about only in salvation history by the Incarnation, the cross and Resurrection of Jesus Christ, as though an historical process were necessary for God to emerge as trinitarian. Therefore the distinction must be maintained between, on the one hand, the immanent Trinity, wherein liberty and necessity are the same thing in the eternal essence of God, and the Trinitarian economy of salvation, where God exercises his liberty absolutely, with no suggestion of his being forced to it.

"(3) The distinction between the 'immanent Trinity' and the 'economic Trinity' is in harmony with the real identity between them. It is not to be used to justify new modes of separation, but is to be understood according to the triple way of affirmation, negation and eminence. God is beyond all divisions we might attribute to him. In the economy of salvation we see the Eternal Son take on in his own life the 'kenotic' event of birth, of human life, and of death on the cross. This event, in which God reveals and communicates himself absolutely and definitively, affects in some way the being proper to God the Father, in so far as he is God who accomplishes these mysteries and lives them as his own in union with the Son and Holy Spirit. In reality not only in the mystery of Christ does the Father reveal and communicate himself to us freely and gratuitously by the Son in the Holy Spirit, but even the Father, with the Son and Holy Spirit, leads the Trinitarian life in a very profound and—according to our way of thinking—some kind of new way in so far as the relationship of the Father with the incarnate Son in the consummation of the gift of the Spirit is identically the constitutive relation of the Trinity. In the intimate life of the Trinitarian God there exists the possible condition for these events, which reach us in the salvation history of the Lord Jesus Christ. In this way the great events of the life of Jesus translate clearly for us and endow with new efficiency to our advantage the dialogue of the eternal generation in which the Father says to the Son: 'You are my Son; this day I have begotten you' (Ps 2:7; cf. Ac 13:33; He 1:5; 5:5 and also Lk 3:22)."[2]

This lengthy statement summarizes much speculation on aspects of Christology which will recur (see ECONOMIC TRINITY). It is pointless to survey here the many Christologies which have been published in recent decades. We are concerned with the work of those who, facing all the demands of the strictest methodology, recognise that "the profession of faith of the ancient Councils in Jesus true God and true man is by no means outmoded. On the contrary the task of future Christology will consist in deepening the spirit of these declarations." At present we should applaud especially the attempt being made by W. Casper and others who wish to establish a Christology on a Trinitarian Basis. These theologians see Jesus in his relation with the Father, as they see the doctrine of Christ as linked with the doctrine of the Holy Spirit and finally achieve an insight into the very deity, evoking that proclaimed by the early councils.

It is presumably here that the best in the Christologies "from above" and those "from below" meet. Therein when methodology is strict and every important element in revelation is included in the final synthesis, Trinitarian theology cannot but gain immensely. But to judge from the conflicting viewpoints and conclusions, there is yet much research and reflection to be done.

---

[1]Text of the statement *ITQ* 49 (1982), 285ff; A. Rodenas, "Cristo revelador del Padre y del Espiritu en los Sinópticos," *EstTrin*, VI, (1972) 23–82; [2]*ITQ* q.c., 287–90.

THE CHURCH

Is a 670 page book on the "Church of the Triune God" justified?[1] Is the theme one which has inner logical coherence or is it an example of artificial synthesis, vaguely valid through the principles which govern all reflection on God's revelation? We are encouraged to answer favourably by the teaching of Vatican II (*qv*). Among the many relevant statements let us note that in the Decree on Ecumenism: "This is the sacred mystery of the unity of the Church, in Christ and through Christ, with the Holy Spirit energizing its various functions. The highest exemplar of this mystery is the unity, in the Trinity of Persons, of one God, the Father and the Son in the Holy Spirit."[2] There is a parallel passage in the Pastoral Constitution on the Church in Modern World: "Furthermore, the Lord Jesus, when praying to the Father 'that they may all be one . . . even as we are one' (Jn 17:21–22), has opened up new horizons closed to human reason by implying that there is a certain parallel between the union existing among the divine Persons and the union of the sons of God in truth and love. It follows, then, that if man is the only creature on earth that God has wanted for his own sake, man can truly discover his true self only in a sincere giving of himself."[3]

It is, however, in the basic text of the Council, the Constitution on the Church, that the fullest teaching on this important subject is given. The opening chapter on the "Mystery of the Church" outlines the part played by each Person of the Trinity in the origin of the Church: "The eternal Father, in accordance with the utterly gratuitous and mysterious design of his wisdom and goodness, created the whole universe, and chose to raise up men to share in his own divine life; and when they had fallen in Adam he did not abandon them, but at all times held out to them the means of salvation, bestowed in consideration of Christ, the Redeemer, 'who is the image of the invisible God, the first-born of every creature' and predestined before time began 'to become conformed to the image of his Son, that he should be the first-born among many brethren' (Rom 8:29). He determined to call together in a holy Church those who should believe in Christ. Already present in figure at the beginning of the world, this Church was prepared in marvellous fashion in the history of the people of Israel and in the old Alliance . . . . The Son, accordingly, came, sent by the Father who, before the foundation of the world, chose us and predestined us in him for adoptive sonship. For it is in him that it pleased the Father to restore all things (cf. Eph 1,4–5 and 10). To carry out the will of the Father Christ inaugurated the kingdom of heaven on earth and revealed to us his mystery; by his obedience he brought about our redemption. The Church—that is, the kingdom of Christ—already present in mystery, grows visibly through the power of God in the world . . . . When the work which the Father gave the Son to do on earth (cf. Jn 17:4) was accomplished, the Holy Spirit was sent on the day of Pentecost in order that he might continually sanctify the Church, and that, consequently, those who believe might have access through Christ in one Spirit to the Father (cf. Eph 2:18). He is the Spirit of life, the fountain of water springing up to eternal life (cf. Jn 4:47; 7:38–39). To men, dead in sin, the Father gives life through him, until the day when in Christ he raises to life their mortal bodies (cf. Rom 8:10–11) . . . . Hence the universal Church is seen to be a 'people brought into unity from the unity of the Father, the Son and the Holy Spirit.'"[4] The last conciliar text ends with a quotation from St. Cyprian. The annotation refers to two other patristic passages.

But some other Trinitarian references merit attention: "As he had been sent by the Father, the Son himself sent the apostles (cf. Jn 20:21) saying, 'Go, therefore and make disciples of all nations, baptizing them in the name of the Father, and of the Son, and of the Holy Spirit, teaching them to observe all that I have commanded you; and behold I am with you always, even to the consummation of the world' (Mt 28:18–20). The Church has received this solemn command of Christ from the apostles, and she must fulfil it to the very ends of the earth (cf. Acts 1:18).[5] "Taking part in this movement which is called ecumenical, are those who invoke the Triune God and confess Jesus as Lord and Saviour."[6] "The Church on earth is by its very nature missionary since, according to the plan of the Father, it has its origin in the mission of the Son and the Holy Spirit. As the principle without principle from whom the Son is generated and from whom the Holy Spirit proceeds through the Son, God in his great and merciful kindness freely creates us and, moreover, graciously calls us to share in his life and glory."[7] "Proceeding from the love of the eternal Father, the Church was founded by Christ . . . and gathered into one by the Holy Spirit."[8]

It is noteworthy that the advance in ecclesiology in the present century—the gradual shift from an institutional approach which need not be abandoned entirely, to a spiritual, Johannine and Pauline concept, searching deep into the mystical constitution of the entity which prolongs Christ through the ages—should reach in these products of Vatican II a new, somewhat unexplored area: the Trinity as the origin and exemplar of the Church.

The revival of interest, devotional and scholarly, in the Mystical Body of Christ—which description did not please all the fathers of Vatican I—had its fruit and the ratification of its orientation in the Encyclical of Pius XII, *Mystici Corporis Christi*. Vatican II, which chose ecclesiology as its principal subject, added a new dimension by putting some emphasis on another Pauline idea, the Church as the People of God. But almost by instinct, spiritual instinct of course, it seems in the extracts quoted from the Council Documents to feel its way towards a Trinitarian ecclesiology.

Much remains to be explored. The patristic references added in the Church Constitution are to St. Augustine (*qv*) and St. John of Damascus (*qv*). St. Augustine says: "But as we have said more than once already, the remission of sins whereby the kingdom of the spirit who is divided against himself is overthrown and ejected, the achievement of the unity of the Church of God, outside which there is no remission of sins, is as it were the proper work of the Holy Spirit, the Father and the Son certainly cooperating, because the Holy Spirit is in a certain manner the bond of the Father and Son. For the Father is not generally held to be the Father by the Son and the Holy Spirit; for he is not the Father of both. And the Son is not generally held to be the Son by the Father and the Holy Spirit; for he is not the Son of both. But the Holy Spirit is held to be by the Father and the Son, for he is one from both."[9]

St. John of Damascus says: "We believe therefore in the one holy Catholic and apostolic Church of God, in which we have been trained and schooled. We also know the Father, the Son and the Holy Spirit and we are baptized in the name of the Father and the Son and the Holy Spirit and we communicate in the saying 'body and blood of the Son of God who for us by the goodwill of the Father was made man and who died for us.'"[10]

To return to the work first mentioned. The author reviews the development of ecclesiology in the Catholic, Orthodox and Protestant communions since Vatican I, where the institutional concept deriving from Bellarmine prevailed—the "metaphor," "abstract, mystical" language of the Mystical Body abandoned. But a current of thought stemming from Johann Adam Möhler (d.1838) turned to the interior aspect of the Church and in the present century a whole spate of writing on the Mystical Body altered the perspective considerably.[11] Interestingly a quotation given by the author from an Orthodox theologian convinced of this interior, mysterious reality points to the Trinity as its ultimate explanation: "The Church is the Mystical Body of Christ, the continuation of Pentecost on earth, it is the image of the Trinity, the absolute Church of the three divine persons."[12]

The bulk of the book, which is richly erudite all through, considers separately "The Church of the Father," "The Church of the Word Incarnate" and "The Church of the Holy Spirit." It is easier to analyse and set out the relationship between the Church and each single Person than to show how the Church is related to the whole Trinity. But the author has some helpful suggestions here too—relying on the indications given by the Council—not that here too one does not find the tendency to treat of the Persons singly.

The Trinity is the origin of the Church. The Trinity is the exemplar of the Church, especially in the attribute of unity. The Trinity is the cause of unity in the Church. The Trinity is the ultimate goal of the Church. To elaborate these principles and make the necessary deductions from them is the task of those in search of a Trinitarian ecclesiology.

[1]V.Mondello,*La Chiesa del Dio Trino*, Naples, 1978; exhaustive bibl.; R. Aubert, *'L'Ecclesiologia nel Concilio Vaticano I*, Il Concilio e i Concili, Ed.Paoline, 1961, 345–397; A.de Bovis, *L'Eglise et son mystère*, Paris, 1961; Y. M.-J. Congar, O.P., *Ecclesia de Trinitate*, Irenikon,1937; id.*L'Eglise,sacrament universel du salut, L'Eglise aujourdhui*, symposium, Desclée, Paris, 1967, 5–30; id., *Chronique de trente ans d'études, Sainte Eglise, études et approches ecclesiologiques*, Paris, 1963, 449–689; L.Cerfaux, *La théologie de l'Eglise suivant S.Paul*, Paris, 1948, 303–376; J.Alfaro,S.J., "Cristo Sacramento de Dios Padre; La Iglesia, Sacramento de Cristo glorificado," *Greg.*, 1967, 6–27; G.Philips, *L'Eglise et son mystère au IIe Concile du Vatican*, 2 Vols., Paris,Tournai,1967, 1968; H.U.von Balthasar, *Sponsa Verbi*, 1969; L.Sartori, "La Chiesa, sacramento di unità," *Ut unum sint*, 27(1970) 5–15; articles in *La Chiesa del Vaticano II*, esp. M.Philipon, "La SS Trinità e la Chiesa," 329–350; C. Journet, "Il carattere teandrico della Chiesa fonte di tensione permanente," 351–362; articles in "L'Ecclesiologia dal Vat.I al Vat.II," *La Scuola*, 1973, esp. A.Anton, "Lo sviluppo della dottrina sulla Chiesa nella teologia dal Vat. I al Vat II," 27–86; *ibid.*, J.Defaifve, "L'Ecclesiologia del Concilio Vaticano II," 87–98; esp. A.A. Ortega, C.M.F., "La Iglesia y el Mistero Trinitario," *Est.Trinit.* I, 81–138; R.Sears, "Trinitarian Love as Ground of the Church," *ThSt*, 37 (1976) 679; H deLubac, S.J., *The Motherhood of the Church*, San Francisco, 1982, pp. 113–139; E. Mersch, S.J. *La Theologie du Corps Mystique*, Louvain, 1955, pp. 9–160; [2]art. 2; [3]art. 24; [4]art. 2, 34; [5]*Constitution on the Church*, art. 17; [6]*Decree on Ecumenism*, art. 1; [7]*Decree on the Missionary Activity of the Church*, art. 2; [8]*Pastoral Constitution on the Church in the Modern World*, art. 40; *ibid.*, 21.6, 20, 33 ; [9]*Serm* 71, PL 38, 463f; [10]*Adv. Iconocl.* 12, PG 96, 1358D; text of St. Cyprian, *De Orat. Domin.* 23; PL 4, 553; [11]R. Aubert, *op. cit.*; [12]P. Evdokimov, *L'Orthodoxie*, apud V.Mondello, 24.

CIRCUMINCESSION

The word denotes the mutual immanence of the three divine persons, their reciprocal interiority, their ceaseless vital presence to each other, interpenetration. *Circuminsession* emphasizes the abiding reality; *circumincession* the dynamic circulation of Trinitarian life from each to the others. The first appeals more to the Latin mind which thinks first of the divine essence, the second to the Greek which begins from the persons, borne to each other eternally, irresistibly, by their very identity as subsistent relations. It is infinitely more than community or participation as understood in human existence.

The Johannine texts on which the idea rests are: "If I am not doing the works of my Father, then do not believe in me; but if I do them, even though you do not believe me, believe the works, that you may know and understand that the Father is in me and I am in the Father" (Jn 10:37, 38); "Have I been with you so long and yet you do not know me, Philip? He who has seen me has seen the Father; how can you say, 'Show us the Father'? Do you not believe that I am in the Father and the Father in me? The words that I say to you I do not speak on my own authority; but the Father who dwells in me does his works. Believe me that I am in the Father and the Father in me; or else believe me for the sake of the works themselves" (Jn 14:9–11); "I do not pray for these only, but also for those who believe in me through their word, that they may all be one; even as thou, Father, art in me, and I in thee, that they also may be in us, so that the world may believe that thou hast sent me" (Jn 17:20, 21). To show the circumincession of the Spirit in the Father and Son, appeal is sometimes made to 1 Cor 2:10f: "For the Spirit searches everything, even the depths of God. For what person knows a man's thoughts except the spirit of the man which is in him? So also no one comprehends the thoughts of God except the Spirit of God." The doctrine is implied here, but scarcely explicit.[1]

The idea grew among the Fathers. It is implicit in a letter of St. Basil (*qv*): "For all things that are the Father's are beheld in the Son, and all things that are the Son's are the Father's; because the whole Son is in the Father and has all the Father in himself. Thus the hypostasis of the Son becomes as it were form and face of the knowledge of the Father, and the hypostasis of the Father is known in the form of the Son, while the proper quality which is contemplated therein remains for the plain distinction of the hypostases."[2]

St. John of Damascus is more explicit: "For, as we said, they are made one not so as to commingle, but so as to cleave to each other without any coalescence or commingling. Nor do the Son and the Spirit stand apart, nor are they sundered in essence according to the diaeresis of Arius. For the deity is undivided amongst things divided, to put it concisely; and it is just like three suns cleaving to each other without separation and giving out light mingled and conjoined into one."[3]

St. Thomas (*qv*) treated the subject analytically: "I answer that three things have to be considered in the Father and the Son: namely essence, relation and origin, and according to each of these the Son is in the Father and reciprocally. 1. For according to essence the Father is in the Son, because the Father is his essence and communicates his essence to the Son, not through any change in himself. Whence it follows that since the essence of the Father is in the Son, the Father is in the Son. And likewise as the Son is his essence, it follows that he is in the Father, in whom his essence is . . . . 2. According also to relations it is clear that relatively one of opposites is in the other, as we understand things. 3. According to origin also it is clear that the procession of the intelligible Word is not something outside, but remains in the One speaking. What is spoken in the Word is contained in the Word. And the same is valid for the Holy Spirit."[4]

The eleventh Council of Toledo (*qv*) expresses the doctrine thus: "We must not, however, consider these three persons separable, since we believe that no one before the other, no one after the other, no one without the other ever existed or did anything. For, they are found inseparable both in that which they are, and in that which they do, because between the generating Father and the generated Son and the proceeding Holy Spirit we believe that there was no interval of time in which either the begetter at any time preceded the begotten, or the begotten was lacking to the begetter, or the proceeding Holy Spirit appeared after the Father or the Son. Therefore, for this reason we proclaim and believe that this Trinity is inseparable and unconfused."[5]

---

[1] Cf. George Bull, *Defensio Fidei Nicaenae*, 1685, Bk IV, ch iv, secs.13,14; T. de Regnon, *Etudes*, I, 409–420; A. Deneffe, "Perichoresis Circumincessio, Circuminsessio, Eine terminologische Untersuchung," *ZKT*, 47 (1923), 497–532; L. Prestige, "Perichoreo, Perichoresis in the Fathers," *JTS*, 29 (1928), 242–252; A. Chollet, *DTC* II, 2,2527–32; M. Schmaus, *LTK*, VIII, 274–6; E. Bailleux, "La Réciprocité dans la Trinité," *Rev.Th.*,

74 (1974), 356–390; B. Hebblethwaite, "Perichoresis- Reflections on the Doctrine of the Trinity," *Theology*, 80 (1977), 255–61; [2]Letter 38, 8, PG32, 340, LNPF, VIII, 141; but cf. Kelly, *Doctrines*, 264, n.1, for possible authorship by Gregory of Nyssa; [3]*De Fide Orthodoxa*, I, 8, PG 94,829; LNPF, IX, 11; [4]I, 42, 5; Cp.Cyril of Alexandria (*qv*), *In Jo.*, 1, 5, PG 73, 81; [5]DS 532.

CLEMENT OF ALEXANDRIA, ST. (c. 150–c. 215)

Successor to Pantaenus in 190 A.D. as head of the Catechetical School of Alexandria, in an age of Gnosticism (*qv*), C. thought that gnosis was the most important element in Christian perfection. But it must be gnosis based on the faith, nourished by divine revelation.[1] He was also convinced, in opposition to Irenaeus, Hippolytus and Epiphanius, that Greek philosophy was not a source of errors, but, in a certain sense a gift of God: "So it appears that the liberal arts of the Greeks, along with philosophy itself, came to man from God. Not that God is the immediate source of the liberal arts and of philosophy so that all of their products should be attributed directly to him—think rather of the rain, which pours down not only on good earth, but also on dung, and on people's dwellings . . . . By philosophy I mean not the Stoic or Platonic or Epicurean or Aristotelian school, but a selection from them of what was correctly said and taught, justice along with pious knowledge. The other elements, which are adulterated fruit of human reasoning, these I would never call divine."[2]

The concept of the omnipotent one is central to C's thinking on the godhead: "If then, abstracting from all the qualities of bodies, and of the things we call incorporeal, we cast ourselves into the magnitude of Christ, and thence in holiness advance into his immensity, we reach some slight understanding of the omnipotent; not that we understand what it is, but rather what it is not."[3] "Therefore, he is without shape, and he cannot be named. If at times we do—in an applied sense— name him, calling him one, or good, or mind, or that-itself-which-is, or Father, or God, or Creator, or Lord, we do so not as giving out his proper name; we use these other beautiful names in order to focus our thought on them, and prevent it from going astray. For although these names taken singly do not signify God, taken all together they suggest the power of the Omnipotent. For names

denote either the accidental qualities or the relationships of things, and nothing of this sort can be said of God; for such knowledge proceeds from what is prior and better known, but there is nothing before the unbegotten. It remains, therefore, certainly, that it is by the grace of God, and only through his Word, that we come to understand the unknown God himself. This is the meaning of Paul's 'To the unknown God' recalled by Luke in the Acts of the Apostles."[4]

Here is evident too the immense importance which C. attached to the Logos (*qv*). He saw in this concept the key to understanding the whole religious meaning of the world. The Logos is the creator of the world. He showed forth God in the Law of OT, in the philosophy of the Greeks and in the fullness of time in the Incarnation. He is the teacher and lawgiver of mankind. Through Christ, the incarnate Logos is God and man and through him we have a new life which begins with faith, advances to knowledge and contemplation, and brings us through love and charity to immortality and deification.

We do not get a developed theology of the Trinity from C. What he makes clear, as he expounds his essential doctrine of Logos, is his *faith* in the blessed Three: "O wonderful mystery! There is but one Father of the universe, there is but one Logos of the universe, and the Holy Spirit likewise is one and the same everywhere. And there is but one Virgin Mother, for so I love to call the Church. This mother alone is without milk, for she is not a woman, but a virgin as well as a mother, pure as a virgin, loving as a mother; she calls her children and feeds with a holy milk the Logos made child."[5] "By night, by day, awaiting the perfect day, let us sing a hymn of thanksgiving to the one Father and to the Son, to the Son and to the Father, to the Son teacher and master with the Holy Spirit."[6] "We are ignorant of the treasure which we carry in vessels of clay, a treasure which has been entrusted to us by the power of God the Father, by the blood of God the Son, by the dew of the Holy Spirit."[7] "Every word stands which is confirmed by two or three witnesses; these are the witnesses and the helpers who oblige us to keep the stated epistles."[8]

Not only does C. give us his faith, but one has the feeling that he believes it is the faith of the Church. We know that he was esteemed by Alexander of Jerusalem, Jerome, Cyril of Alexandria (*qv*), Maximus the Confessor (*qv*).

[1]Works PG 8, 9; GCS 1–4; cf. R.P. Casey, "Clement and the Two Divine Logoi," *JTS* 25 (1923), 43–56; *id.* "Clement of Alexandria and the Beginnings of Christian Platonism," *HTR* 18 (1925) 39–101; G.Bardy (*qv*), *Clément d'Alexandrie*, Paris, 1926; Th. Camelot, "Clément d'Alexandrie et l'utilisation de la philosophie grecque," *RSR* 21 (1931) 541–569; *id. Foi et gnose. Introduction a l'etude de la connaissance mystique chez Clément d'Alexandrie*, Paris 1945; J.D. Frangoulis, *Der Begriff des Geistes bei Clemens Alexandrinus*, Leipzig, 1936; B. Pade, *Logos Theos. Untersuchungen zur Logos-Christologie des Titus Flavius Clemens von Alexandrien*, Rome, 1939; P.J. Schmidt, *Clemens von Alexandria in seinem Verhälinis zur griechischen Religion und Philosophie*, Dissert., Vienna, 1939; C. Mondesert, *Clément d'Alexandrie. Introduction à l'etude de sa pensée religieuse à partir de l'Ecriture*, Paris, 1944; J. Moingt, "La gnose de Clément d'Alexandrie dans ses rapports avec la foi et la philosophie," *RSR*, 37 (1950) 195–251; J. Lebreton (*qv*), *DSp*, II, 950–961; *id.*, *Fliche et Martin*, III, ch XXIII, 2, English tr. 733–755; *id.* esp. "La Théologie de la Trinité chez Clément d'Alexandrie," *RSR*, 34 (1947) 55–76; 142–179; W. Volker, *Der wahre Gnostiker nach Clemens Alexandrinus*, with bibl. TU, 57, 1952; S.R.C. Lilla, *Clement of Alexandria, A Study in Christian Platonism*, Oxford, 1971; Altaner, 190–97; Quasten II, 5–36; A. de la Barre, *DTC* III, (1908) 137–99; G. Bekes, *EC* III (1950) 1842–57; M. Spanneut, *NCE* III, 943–44; G. Bardy, *ibid.*, XV, 1638f; [2]*Strom.*, I, 7, 37, 6; [3]*Ibid.*, V, 11, PG 9, 108; [4]*Ibid.*, V, 12, PG 9; [5]*Paed.* I, 6, 42; [6]*Ibid.*, III, 12, 101; [7]*Ibid.*, *Quis dives*, 34; [8]*Eclog. proph.* 13.

CONSTANTINE THE GREAT (c. 280–337)

Proclaimed emperor at York on the death of Constantius Chlorus his father, C. became senior ruler of the empire after his defeat of Maxentius at the Milvian bridge in 312. He took as his standard thereafter the *Labarum* and instituted an era of freedom and imperial support for Christianity, whether the historicity of the Edict of Milan is accepted or not. His first effect therefore on Christian teaching was to provide a climate favourable to open exercise of the office at the highest level. This was at a time when Trinitarian controversy was at its most acute in the history of the Church.[1]

Trained at the court of Diocletian, he was imbued with the Byzantine idea of absolute power, in contrast to the old Roman concept of the principate. Since he was the key factor in maintaining public order and communications needed by church leaders in the new movement of councils and creeds which followed the restrictions of the previous phase of persecution, and since he was the guarantor of such free association, he was tempted to encroach on ecclesiastical affairs. Though in the judgment of most historians a convinced Christian, he claimed a singular call and did not consider the catechumenate. He thought himself the equal of the bishops, a colleague, and in cases beyond their power sought a kind of jurisdiction. Unfortunately, he found among the bishops a willing acceptance and, in one case—that of Eusebius of Nicomedia (*qv*)—positive connivance in such a policy. Fortunately at the outset of a church-state relationship which was to last for centuries and leave disparate effects in differing cultures, C. met a formidable champion of Christian doctrinal integrity and independence: Athanasius of Alexandria (*qv*).

C's most influential moment was undoubtedly Nicaea (*qv*). He took the initiative in calling the first general council of the Church. His adviser then was Hosius (or Ossius) of Cordova (*qv*), and C. sent him to act as intermediary between Alexander (*qv*) and Arius (*qv*). It was probably Hosius who gave him the idea of a general council. He facilitated the arrangements by providing the imperial transport and housing the bishops in Nicaea. At the first assembly C. addressed the bishops as he would have done the Roman senate. We cannot follow his participation thereafter since there are now no acts of the council, if they ever existed. Eusebius of Caesarea (*qv*), who was to become an uncritical admirer of C., writes that he commended his own creed—read, it is thought, to clear Eusebius: "Our most pious emperor, before anyone else, testified that it comprised most orthodox statements. He confessed moreover that such were his own sentiments, and he advised all present to agree to it, and to subscribe to its articles and to assent to them, with the insertion of the single word *homoousios*, which moreover he interpreted as not in the sense of the affections of bodies, nor as if the Son subsisted from the Father in the way of division, or any severance; for that the immaterial, and intellectual, and incorporeal nature could not be the subject of any corporeal affection, but that it became us to conceive of such things in a divine and ineffable manner. And such were the theological remarks of our most wise and religious emperor."[2]

Later Eusebius tells us that "our most religious emperor did, at the time, prove, in a speech, that he (the Son) was in being even according to his own divine generation which is before all ages, since even before he was generated in energy, he was in virtue with the Father ingenerately, the Father being always Father, as King always, and Saviour always, being all things in virtue, and being always in the same respects and in the same way."[3]

In the letters of promulgation C. spoke of himself as "one of you Christians who took part in the deliberations"; he thought that the bishops' decision was a judgment of God. After the council he banished Eusebius of Nicomedia (qv) and Theognis of Nicaea. He quickly acquired the habit of banishing or recalling bishops, almost as if they were subordinate officials in a system where church and state made one entity. In 327 he pardoned Eusebius and Arius (qv); in the following year he exiled Marcellus of Ancyra and Eustathius of Antioch.

Informed that the Melitians were attacking Athanasius, the emperor called a synod at Caesarea; Athanasius refused to attend. The bishop was then, in 335, summoned to a synod in Tyre. He found the atmosphere hostile and fled to the imperial court. In the following year he was driven into exile to Trier, at the instigation of the Eusebian faction. C. informed the bishops assembled in Jerusalem for the dedication of the Basilica that he had restored Arius to communion with the Church. An important item in the heretic's writings is his letter to C. preliminary to this decision. Eusebius baptized the emperor a short time before his death.

A legend grew up around him which led to his being, in places, honoured as a saint as was his mother Helena, who inspired some of his church-building. She had been abandoned by his father for a political marriage, but C. exalted her. The encomiums of Eusebius, in his life of the emperor, favoured the legend. Disinterested authors also praised C.: "of sacred memory"—Hilary of Poitiers; "most pious" and "of blessed memory"—Athanasius; "most religious and of ever-blessed memory"—Epiphanius. He stands in the history of the Church and of its doctrine as an intriguing figure whose role has not been fully explained.

[1]Abundant material in church and general histories; Cf. P. Battifol, *La Paix Constantinienne et le Catholicisme*, 3 ed., Paris 1914, Ch 1 and 3; E. Schwartz, *Kaiser Konstantin und die Christliche Kirche*, ed. 2, 1936; esp. N.H. Baynes,"Constantine the Great and the Christian Church," *The Proceedings of the British Academy*, XV (1929), 341–442; A. Piganiol, *L'Empereur Constantin*, 1932; H. Berkhof, *Kirche und Kaiser, Eine Untersuchung Entstehung des byzantinischen und des theokratischen Staatsauffassung im vierten Jahrhundert*, German tr. Zurich, 1947 (Dutch original 1946); J. Vogt, *Constantin der Grosse und sein Jahrhundert*, Munich, 1949; H. Dorries, *Das Selbstzeugnis Kaiser Konstantins*, Göttingen, 1954; H.Kraft, *Kaiser Konstantins religiöse Entwicklung* (Beiträge zur historischen Theologie, 20, 1955); R. McMullen, *Constantine*, New York, 1969, London, 1970; *Dumbarton Oaks Papers*, 21 (1967); G. Bardy (qv), "La politique religieuse de Constantin après le Concile de Nicée," *Rev.SR*, J.R. Palanque, *DHGE*, XIII, 593–608; [2]LNPF IV, 75; [3]*Ibid.*, 76.

CONSTANTINOPLE, FIRST COUNCIL OF (381)

Arianism was well nigh dead by the last quarter of the fourth century. As emperors had played lively and inconsistent roles through its different phases, Theodosius I, the greatest ruler between Constantine (qv) and Justinian, baptised from the inception of his reign and a convinced practising Catholic, wished to preside at the official burial of the heresy. Through laws enacted seven times he had deprived heretics of their churches, which were given to the orthodox Christians, forbade them to make wills or inherit property. Civil Law defined the faith which the Roman church has received from the apostle Peter as that of Pope Damasus and Peter, bishop of Alexandria—the Pope and bishop at the time. Anomoeans, Arians, Apollinarians, and Macedonians were named as the heretics.

The event which would seal this policy was the council called at Constantinople in 381. It would be eventually accepted as a General Council of the Church, but it did not have this status at once. A mighty figure in the last phase of the Arian struggle, Basil the Great (qv), had died two years earlier, but his close friend, St. Gregory of Nazianzus (qv), one of the greatest preachers of all time, took part, as did the third of the great Cappadocians, St. Gregory of Nyssa (qv), and another luminary of the age, St. Cyril of Jerusalem (qv).

The participants in the council numbered one hundred and fifty. Rome and the West were not represented. Only half the bishops came from Thrace and Asia, while almost one half were from the vast civil diocese called the East (*Oriens*). Since Antioch was the principal see in this area, Melitius, its bishop, presided at the council. He died before there was much time to act and was succeeded by St. Gregory of Nazianzus, who was also recognised as bishop of Constantinople (the bishop in office, an Arian, having withdrawn). When the bishop of Alexandria, Timothy, arrived, he made a bitter attack on Gregory because he had accepted the appointment in Constantinople. Thereon Gregory resigned see and presidency.

The choice for his successor fell upon Nectarius, a retired Roman imperial official who was not baptized; he was at once baptized and ordained. The council, having begun in May, ended its sessions on 9 July. It enacted four canons. Three do not concern theology directly: the second limited the activities of bishops to their civil dioceses; the third declared: "The bishop of Constantinople shall have primacy of honour after the bishop of Rome, because Constantinople is new Rome"; the fourth condemned Maximus the Cynic.

The first canon is of theological interest: "The faith of the three hundred and eighteen fathers who assembled at Nicaea in Bithynia is not to be disregarded; but it remains authoritative, and all heresy is to be anathematized: and especially that of the Eunomians or of the Anomians, and that of the Arians, or that of the Eudoxians, and that of the Macedonians, that is to say, of those opposing the Spirit, and that of the Sabellians, of the Marcellians and that of the Photinians and that of the Apollinarians."[2]

Did the council draw up and approve a creed? This question is dealt with in the article on the Constantinopolitan creed.

[1]Mansi III, 521-600; Hefele-Leclercq, II, 1, 1–48; I. Ortiz de Urbina, S.J., *Nicée et Constantinople*, 139–242, Paris, 1963; M.A. Chevallier, "El Concilio de Constantinople y el Espíritu Santo," *EstTrin* XVII (1983), 3–23; N. King, *Theodosius and the Establishment of Christianity*, London, Philadelphia, 1961; A.M. Ritter, *Das Konzil von Konstantinopel und sein Symbol*, Göttingen, 1965; B. Schultze, *Die Pneumatologie des Symbols von Konstantinopel*, OCP, 47 (1981), 5–54; N.Q. King, "The 150 Holy Fathers of the Council of Constantinople 381 A.D.," *Studia Patristica* I (TU, 63, 1957); C. Bardy (qv), *DDC* IV, 424-28; id. with J.R. Palanque, Fliche-Martin, III, (1936) 285–92; J. Bois, *DTC* III 1227–31; R. Janin, *DHGE* XIII, 629–740; G.L. Dossetti, *Il simbolo di Nicea e di Constantinopoli*, 1967: esp. special issue (9 contributors) of *ITQ*, 48 (1981), 3 and 4, for 16th centenary of the Council; also the pronouncements of John Paul II for the centenary celebrations; [2]DS 151.

CONSTANTINOPLE, SECOND COUNCIL OF (553)

Though called by the Emperor Justinian to settle the controversy over the "Three Chapters," especially to decide whether Theodore of Mopsuestia, Theodoret of Cyprus and Ibas of Edessa should be condemned as tainted with Nestorianism, or whether, in the spirit of Chalcedon, they should be spared, this council opened its anathemas by a succinct statement of Trinitarian doctrine: "If anyone does not confess that (there is) one nature or substance of the Father and of the Son and of the Holy Spirit, and one power and one might, and that the Trinity is consubstantial, one godhead being worshipped in three subsistences, or persons, let such a one be anathema. For there is one God and Father, from whom are all things, and one Lord Jesus Christ, through whom are all things, and one Holy Spirit, in whom are all things.

"If anyone does not confess that there are two generations of the Word of God, the one from the Father before the ages, without time and incorporeally, the other in the last days, when the same came down from heaven, and was incarnate of the holy and glorious Mother of God and ever Virgin Mary, and was born of her, let such a one be anathema."[1]

[1]DS 421, 2; on the council cf. C. Moeller, "Le Cinquième Concile oecuménique et le magistère ordinaire au VIe siècle," *RSPT*, 35 (1951), 413–23; Hefele-Leclercq III, 2, 1–156; Mansi IX 157–658; L. Bréhier, Fliche-Martin IV (1937) 472–487; J. Bois, *DTC* III 1231-59; R. Janin, *DHGE* XIII 757–760.

CONSTANTINOPOLITAN CREED, THE (C)

"We believe in one God, the Father almighty, maker of heaven and earth, of all things visible and invisible; and in one Lord Jesus Christ, the only begotten Son of God, begotten from the Father before all ages, light from light, true God from true God, begotten not made, of one substance with the Father, through whom all things came into existence; who because of our salvation, came down from heaven and was incarnate from the Holy Spirit and the Virgin Mary and became man, and was crucified for us under Pontius Pilate, and suffered and was buried and rose again on the third day according to the Scriptures and ascended to heaven, and sits on the right hand of the Father, and will come again with glory to judge living and dead, of whose kingdom there will be no end; and in the Holy Spirit, the Lord and life-giver who proceeds from the Father, who with the Father and the Son is together worshipped and together glorified, who spoke through the prophets; and in one, holy Catholic and apostolic Church. We confess one baptism to the remission of sins; we look forward to the resurrection of the dead, and in the life of the world to come. Amen."[1]

A comparison of this text with that of the Nicene creed (*qv*) will show a series of differences. Besides the anathemas at the end, C omits "that is from the substance of the Father," "God from God," "things in heaven and things on earth"; but it adds to the text of N "maker of heaven and earth" in the first article, "before all ages" with "begotten" in the second, "from heaven" with "came down," "from the Holy Spirit and the Virgin Mary" with "was incarnate," "was crucified for us under Pontius Pilate" with "suffered," "according to the Scriptures" after "rose again on the third day," "and sits on the right hand of the Father" after "ascended," "with glory" before "to judge living and dead" and "of whose kingdom there will be no end" immediately after it.

These additions make the section on Christ much longer than in the Nicene creed. But there is also a final passage on the Holy Spirit, entirely new, to which is appended mention of the Church, Baptism, the remission of sins, the resurrection of the dead and the life hereafter.

The origin of this creed is a problem much discussed. A mere summary can be given here. The formulary was traditionally described as the "symbol of the Council of Constantinople." But for some time this traditional view has not been thought credible. There is no reference to the creed in the Acts of the Council, nor in the letter sent to Theodosius who had convened it. Historians of the period are silent on it and there is silence in the years 381 to 451 in official records of synods in the East or West or in the writings of theologians, orthodox or heterodox.

It would be understandable that the creed would have limited support, for the delegates at the Council of Constantinople came exclusively from sees in Thrace, Asia Minor and Syria. But "the obscurity in which C is wrapped extends not only to the West and to Egypt, where it is perhaps explicable, but to the East as well, and even to Constantinople itself."[2]

More damaging still to the genuineness of C was the fact that the text was in existence for some time before the Council. It appears (emphasize this word) to have been recommended in 374 by St. Epiphanius as a baptismal formula to the presbyters of Syedra in Pamphylia; he reproduces it in his *Ancoratus*.[3] If it existed at this date it could not have been drafted at Constantinople in 381, though it could have been adopted there, which is not thought probable.

Questions remain to tease the curiosity of scholars. If the creed was not drawn up at Constantinople, what was its origin? One theory, proposed by F.J.A. Hort, is that it was fashioned from the Jerusalem creed, which may be extracted from St. Cyril of Jerusalem's *Cathechetical Lectures*; in this view, Cyril himself did the redrafting which is a Nicene sense.

There still remains the question how the creed was associated with Constantinople. Again Hort had a reply: Cyril recited the revised creed at the Council to allay any suspicions about his own orthodoxy, since he was not always a zealous supporter of the Nicene party—to which was added the fact that Meletius of Antioch, first president of the Council, was highly suspect in the west.

Against this theory stands that of J. Kunze, backed by E. Molland. C was used at the baptism and ordination of Nectarius, the retired Roman official, as yet unbaptized, chosen as bishop of Constantinople.

Yet not all scholars have abandoned the traditional view, despite the fact that N seems to have been the only official creed affirmed by the council and that C may have been in existence a decade before it. A number of conservative historians, foremost and most influential among them E. Schwartz, mounted a counter-attack. The identity of the Jerusalem creed and C was anything but substantial; nor was there any reason to suppose that the 150 council fathers needed to see Cyril of Jerusalem justify himself—his orthodoxy had not been questioned for some time. The conjecture about Nectarius has also been treated lightly: if the creed were used at his baptism and ordination, would not that rather indicate that the council already approved of it?

But it is the history of Chalcedon which tends essentially to nullify the criticism and the plausible conjectures. The imperial commissioners, at the close of the first session, spoke of the emperor's beliefs being "in accord with the *ekthesis* (exposition) of the 318 holy fathers at Nicaea and the *ekthesis* of the 150 who met subsequently." The 150 are, of course, the fathers of Constantinople. The commissioners, at the opening of the second session, again asserted that, along with the emperor, they "adhered loyally to the orthodox faith delivered by the 318 and by the 150 and by the other holy and illustrious fathers." The bishops were asked to draw up a new creed, but this they refused to do, the speakers appealing to N but not to C, in justification of their view that the teaching of the fathers should prevail. On the motion of Cecropius of Sevastopol, N was read out and received with immense applause. The commissioners ordered the "*ekthesis* of the 150" to be read out also. This was done to less applause. But no one objected or expressed dissent. The fathers then may not have been as informed on C as on N, but they had no reason to reject it.

There still remains another apparently grave objection to Constantinopolitan parentage of C. Did it not already exist before the council, as Epiphanius testifies? Here too research has progressed; at least it has achieved a question-mark. Critical study of the Epiphanius text suggests strongly that it was not C which he reproduced but N. Still another objection to the traditional view may also have been met: that which said that no surviving records indicate that the council of Constantinople did compose its own creed. Suffice it to say that there are in contemporary documents brief passages susceptible of interpretation as such evidence. As Schwartz, the great defender of C's status, also contended, the silence between the council of Constantinople and Chalcedon could be explained, not only by the very fact that there was delay in recognising the council of Constantinople as ecumenical, but through a certain rivalry between Rome and the "new Rome," wherein Alexandria would have been on Rome's side. On this view the giant of Alexandria in the period between Constantinople and Chalcedon, St. Cyril, would have spread the idea, in Ephesus as elsewhere, that no creed could rank with N.

Canon J.N.D. Kelly has advanced some considerations which merit attention. The council could be said to propose the Nicene creed, for the word was used without strict reference to the phrasing of N. It would have been the text of N with such additions as were deemed necessary, especially in regard to the Holy Spirit. This particular section was drafted carefully without calling the Spirit "God" or "consubstantial," in an eirenical spirit, as a gesture to win over the Macedonians (*qv*) or Pneumatomachians (*qv*). There were, on this subject, many discussions. Eventually they failed in their objective; the Macedonians departed. But the formula worked out would have been retained. Again Canon Kelly invokes the decrees of Chalcedon in support: "This in fact we have accomplished," the fathers state in the prologue to the Definition, "having by a unanimous vote driven

away misleading doctrines, and having renewed the unerring faith of the fathers, proclaiming to all the creed of the 318, and in addition accepting as our fathers those who received this statement of orthodoxy, the 150 fathers who subsequently met together in great Constantinople and set their seal to the same faith."[4]

Later in the Definition the fathers of Chalcedon declared that the council, "proclaiming the creed of the 318 holy fathers inviolate on account of those who contend against the Holy Spirit, ratifies the teaching subsequently set forth by the 150 holy fathers assembled in the royal city concerning the essence of the Spirit, not as adducing anything left lacking by their predecessors, but making distinct by Scriptural testimonies their conception concerning the Holy Spirit against those who were trying to set aside his sovereignty."

Kelly concludes: "It seems clear that the council's primary object was to restore and promote the Nicene faith in terms which would take account of the further development of doctrine, especially with regard to the Holy Spirit, which had taken place since Nicaea. This it did in its first canon and also, more circumstantially and without any attempts at eirenical compromise (there was no need for that now), in the dogmatic *tomos* which, according to the synodal letter of 382, it published. Nevertheless, at a critical juncture in its proceedings it had adopted C and used it as a negotiating instrument. In consequence C could with some justification claim to be the creed of the 150 fathers, and all the more so as they had promulgated no others."[5]

[1]F.J.A. Hort, *Two Dissertations*, 1876, 73 150, "On the Constantinopolitan Creed and other Eastern Creeds of the fourth century"; J. Kunze, *Das nicänisch-konstantinopolitanische Symbol*, 1898; E.C. Gibson, *The Three Creeds*, Oxford, 1908; A.M. Ritter, *Das Konzil von Konstantinopel und sein Symbol, Forschungen zur Kirchen-und Dogmengeschichte*, XV, 1965, 133–208; B. Capelle, O.S.B., "L'introduction du symbole à la Messe," *Mélanges Joseph de Ghellinck*, Louvain, 1951, 1003–27; J. Jungmann, Mass of the Roman Rite, I, 461–474; [2]Kelly, *Creeds*, 310; [3]118, Holl, I, 146ff; [4]Kelly, *Creeds*, 330; [5]*Ibid.*, 331.

CONSTANTIUS II (Emperor 337–361)

A short time before C. died St. Jerome made a remark that has become classic: "The whole world groaned and wondered to find itself Arian."[1] If this disastrous situation were an achievement, one man could claim it: the emperor Constantius, son of Constantine the Great (*qv*) who had taken effective measures to arrest Arianism in its first poisonous moments. Ruler of the eastern empire from 337, sole emperor from 351, C. directed his energy to destroying paganism on the one hand and to imposing Arianism on the other. Influenced in his first ruling years by Eusebius of Nicomedia (*qv*), assuming fully the power which had quickly been vested in his office of summoning bishops to meet in council, he exploited every resource to impose his will. He not only detained the most venerable bishop in the Church, Hosius of Cordova (*qv*), a martyr or "Confessor of the faith," but he also bent a Pope to his will (see LIBERIUS). Through a tough group of "politicals," bishops that is, he dictated procedure and eventually the formulation of doctrine by the bishops assembled in council, moving gradually but surely to the final triumph of Seleucia, Rimini and Constantinople (360). Against the dissident church rulers his weapon was exile. A few great figures—Hilary (*qv*), Denis of Milan, Lucifer of Cagliari (*qv*), Eusebius of Vercelli (*qv*)—stand out in the record as unbreakable by such a weapon. C. first pursued Athanasius, then eased off for a while, and eventually was devoured by the passion to destroy him. In this he failed.

In the whole story of darkness and gloom there are, through these heroic figures and others, a few moments of light that foretold the eventual triumph of truth: the letters of Athanasius and of Lucifer, the tract of Hilary against C., the dialogue between Liberius and C. preserved by the historian Theodoret, the letter of Hosius written in freedom (not long afterwards, in his very last year, he was forcibly detained and overcome). It is tempting to interpret the career of C. as spiritual drama, a Christian "Greek" tragedy with himself cast in the role of angel of darkness and Athanasius an angel of light. Certainly there are here imponderables beyond our grasp and it would be idle to deny it.

[1]Cf.Bibliography to Arianism and Athanasius; Church histories give abundant material, e.g., A. Piganol, *L'empire chrétien*, Paris, 1947; "Constance II, Athanase et l'édit d'Arles" in K. M. Girardet, *Politique et Théologie*, Paris, 1974, 63–83.

CONSUBSTANTIAL

The word *homoousios*, translated consubstantial in English, is the focus of the anti-Arian resistance from the Council of Nicaea on. The history of the word is varied. The pre-Nicene vicissitudes in its use do something to explain the hesitancy which some felt during and after the Council.[1]

We first meet the word in a second-century writing, *The Letter to Flora* by the Gnostic Ptolemy, but therein the meaning is not that of Nicaea. "Since," writes Ptolemy," as we believe and profess, the Source of all things is one, ungenerated and incorruptible, and also good; since, further, the good by its very nature generates and produces what is most like itself, and of the same nature as itself (*homoousia*); you may wonder how both of these natures can exist, namely, that which is corruptible and that which is in a kind of middle state, since they are different in nature from (*anomoousia*) what is incorruptible. Do not let this problem disturb you."[2]

After the *Letter to Flora* the word *homoousios* occurs often in Gnostic writings. St. Irenaeus, who called his *Adversus Hareses* in an early draft *Denunciation and refutation of false gnosis*, gives sure evidence of this as does Hippolytus of Rome. St. Clement of Alexandria also refers to *homoousios* in the course of a work entitled *Extracts from Theodotus*, a Valentinian gnostic; the work is attributed by recent editors to Clement himself.[3] Valentinus taught between 140 and 160.

The word is also found in *Poimandres*, the first volume of the esoteric *Corpus Hermeticum* of Hermes Trismegistus; the ideas and mental categories resemble Gnosticism strongly. Certain points may then be made: the fact that the word *homoousios* had been in such widespread use by Gnostic and esoteric teachers left the impression that it had been first used by heretics; in addition, even within any one system the word was given a variety of meanings, which made it appear unsuitable to Christian thinking; finally, the wide meaning given the word did not meet the demand for precision inherent in Trinitarian theology.[4]

But in due course the word was taken into Christian literature. Here the leaders were the giants of the great school of Alexandria, Clement and Origen, conscious of the use made of the word by the Gnostics but seeking to purify it and baptize it. Clement cautious as a beginner uses the word to establish negatives: "unless someone dares to say that we are a part of him and of the same substance as God," or again if it is being asserted that others, not Christ, have conquered death he adds, "unless you say that he is of the same substance as they."[5]

Origen, not a convert from Hellenism as was Clement, and not from a background where acquaintance with esoteric systems was normal, was impelled by his universal curiosity to investigate these strange currents of thought. It was in the writings of Heracleon, a disciple of Valentinus, that he met the word *homoousios*. Heracleon used it in his commentary on St. John, but not in a Trinitarian context.[6] Origen, moreover, objects to the exegesis which contains the word.

Clearly the word was in frequent use towards the end of the second and beginning of the third centuries. The passage to Christian literature and particularly to Trinitarian writing was almost assured. What word could more accurately express the truth that the Son is God since, in his generation, he received the very substance of the Father?

Origen provides the first texts, though one is of doubtful authenticity. A fragment on Matthew in an exegetical chain applies the word in a strictly Trinitarian sense to the Son: "He who saves is unique, salvation is unique, the living one, Father, Son and Holy Spirit, is unique. But not through the fusion of the three; but there is a unique essence in the three hypostases, which are perfect in everything, which are related to one another. It is according to the nature that the Father has begotten. Therefore the one begotten is consubstantial (*homoousios*)."[7] The passage is thought to be by Severus of Antioch (c. 465–538); it reads like a post-Nicene writing.

Another passage in Origen is genuine. It is from his commentary on the Epistle to the Hebrews, and is preserved in a work by Pamphilus, *Apologia pro Origene*, only the first volume of which, in a translation by Rufinus, survives. "Light without brightness is unthinkable," says the great exegete. "If that is true, there never was a time when the Son was not the Son. He will be . . . as it were . . . the splendour of the unbegotten light. Thus Wisdom, too, since it proceeds from God, is generated out of the divine substance itself. Under the figure of a bodily outflow, nevertheless, it too is thus called a sort of clean and pure outflow of omnipotent glory (Wis 7:25). Both these similes manifestly show the community of substance between Son and Father. For an outflow seems *homoousios*, that is, of one substance with that body of which it is the outflow or exhalation."[8]

Pamphilus concludes: "It has been shown openly, I think, and with much clarity that Origen has said that the Son of God was born of the very substance of God, that is, that he was *homoousios*, of the same substance as the Father, and not a creature, nor an adopted Son but a true Son by nature, begotten by the Father himself."[9]

Between Origen and Nicaea there are two episodes which bring the word to prominence. About 262 Denis, bishop of Alexandria, was denounced to Rome, where his namesake, St. Denis, was Pope, for having said that the "Son is a creature and that he is not consubstantial with the Father."[10] A later bishop of Alexandria, the world-famous Athanasius (*qv*) would defend Denis in the course of a work specially written on his role in the antecedents of the controversy about to break: he maintained that Denis in the first part of the accusation ("the Son is a creature") was thinking of the sacred humanity only. As to the word *homoousios* Denis offered his own defence to the Pope: he had not found the word in Sacred Scripture and had not used it. He proposed a number of similes, not all of them happy, to show that he did think of the Father and Son as having one nature. Among the more acceptable of these similes are those of children and parents, plant and seed, river and source. The Pope had to bear in mind that those who denounced his namesake in Alexandria had incurred a just condemnation by the latter for Sabellian heresy.

About the same time, though the word was common, it is remarkable that the Pope did not use it in the synodal letter he sent to Alexandria to remind the faithful of the true doctrine of the Trinity. We should possibly expect it in such passages as these: "But nonetheless they should be blamed who think that the Son is a work, and that the Lord was made just as one of those things which were actually created; since divine statements bear witness that he was begotten, as is proper and fitting, not created or made . . . . Neither therefore ought the admirable and divine unity be separated into three godheads, nor ought the dignity and supreme magnitude of the Lord be lessened by the designation of making; but we must believe in God the Father Almighty, and in Christ Jesus his Son, and in the Holy Spirit, that the Word, moreover, is united to the God of all. For he said: 'I and the Father are one' (Jn 10:30), and: 'I am in the Father, and the Father in me' (Jn 14:10). Thus it is evident that the divine Trinity and the holy proclamation of the monarchy will be preserved intact."[11]

Eight years after the question of the two bishops named Denis, *homoousios* was at the centre of another debate, when the issue was more clear-cut. The word was condemned by the council of Antioch in the sense which Paul of Samosata (*qv*) adopted in using it. We do not possess sufficient information on the precise meaning which the word had for the heretic.

But the word was rejected: "The second reason that you added," says St. Hilary in *De synodis*, "was that our fathers, when Paul of Samosata was pronounced a heretic, also rejected the word *homoousion*, on the ground that by attributing this title to God he had taught that he was single and undifferentiated, and at once Father and Son to himself. Wherefore the Church still regards it as most profane to exclude the different personal qualities, and, under the mask of the aforesaid expressions, to revive the error of confounding the persons and denying the personal distinctions in the godhead."[12] The saint was replying to supporters of the *homoiousios*, answering the reasons they had for rejecting the *homoousios*. The document has perished, but Hilary had it before him.

Athanasius refers to the same difficulty: "This is to show that the meaning of the beloved ones is not far from the 'Consubstantial.' But since, as they allege (for I have not the Epistle in question), the bishops who condemned the Samosatene have said in writing that the Son is not consubstantial with the Father, and so it comes to pass that they, for caution and honour towards those who have so said, thus feel about that expression, it will be to the purpose cautiously to argue with them this point also."[13]

Another testimony deserves attention. St. Basil the Great (*qv*) dealt with the problem of Paul of Samosata in a letter written at the beginning of his episcopate. Speaking of the "Fathers who once at Nicaea promulgated their great decree concerning the faith," he goes on: "Of this, some portions are universally accepted without cavil, but the term *homoousion*, ill received in certain quarters, is still rejected by some. These objectors we may very properly blame, and yet on the contrary deem them worthy of pardon. To refuse to follow the Fathers, not holding their declaration of more authority than one's own opinion, is conduct worthy of blame, as being brimful of self-sufficiency. On the other hand, the fact that they view with suspicion a phrase which is misrepresented by an opposite party does seem to a small extent to relieve them from blame. Moreover, as a matter of fact, the members of the synods which met to discuss the case of Paul of Samosata did find fault with the term as an unfortunate one "[14] (see PAUL OF SAMOSATA).

All three Doctors, Athanasius, Hilary and Basil, are agreed that the *homoousion* was not condemned at Antioch with the same meaning that it had at Nicaea; fifty-seven years separated the two councils, a time during which Arius achieved most of his career. In that interval no clash occurred about the word. It is found in a work by Methodus of Olympus, in one of the fragments preserved of his treatise on the Resurrection; and it occurs too in a formula of belief, of anonymous authorship, transmitted by Adamantius. In the second instance it has some kinship with Nicaea.

[1]Cf. J.F. Bethune-Baker, *The Meaning of Homoousios in the 'Constantinopolitan' Creed*, Texts and Studies, VII, 1, Cambridge, 1901; G.L. Prestige, *God in Patristic Thought*, London, 1936, 197–241; C. Hauret, *Comment le 'Défenseur de Nicée' a-t-il compris le dogme de Nicée?*, Bruges, 1936; I. Ortiz de Urbina, S.J., "L' 'Homoousios preniceno'," OCP, 8 (1942), 194–209; id., *El simbolo Niceno*, Madrid, 1947; E. Boularand, S.J., *L'Hérésie d'Arius et la 'foi' de Nicée*, Paris, 1972, I, 337–353; B. Lonergan, S.J., *The Way to Nicaea*, London, 1976, 88–104; J.N.D. Kelly; A. Mendizabal, *El Homoousios Preniceno Extraeclesiastico*, Madrid, 1956; [2]*Epistula Ptolemaei ad Floram*, Epiphanius,*Haer.*, 33,7; PG 41, 567B; K. Holl I (GCS 25), p.457, 8–12; G. Quispel, SC 24, 66ff; Mendizabal, l.c., 36ff; [3]cf. R.P. Casey, *The Excerpta ex Theodoto of Clement of Alexandria*, London, 1934, 14; F. Sagnard, *Clément d'Alexandrie, Extraits de Theodote*, Paris, 1948, SC 23, 12f; [4]cf. Boularand, 339, and n. 242; [5]*Stromata*, II, 16, 74, PG 8, 1013A; SC 38, 92; GCS 15, .152, 10; *Stromata*, IV, 13, 91; PG 8, 1300A, GCS 15, 288,14; [6]cf. Boularand, 341,42; [7]Origen, Matthaüserklärung, *Katenen-fragmente*, 572, on Mt 28:18–20; GCS 12, 235; PG 17, 309CD (corrupt text); [8]PG 14, 1308CD; cf. Prestige, *op.cit.*, 200; [9]PG 17, 580C–581C; [10]cf. article Denis of Alexandria; [11]DS 109–115; [12]81, LNPF 25, 26; [13]*De synodis*, 43, LNPF, 473; [14]*Epist. ad Canonicas*, 1, LNPF, 155.

COUNCILS

Trinitarian doctrine has been taught in local councils, (Alexandria, 362; Friuli, 796; Rome, 382; Frankfurt, 794; Rheims, 1148; Sens, 1190; Toledo XI, 675) and in Ecumenical or General Councils (Chalcedon, 451; Constantinople I, 381; Constantinople II, 553; Florence, 1439; Lateran IV, 1215; Lyons II, 1274; Nicaea, 325; Trent, 1545ff; and Vatican I, 1870 (chiefly repetition); Vatican II,

1962–65). The principal doctrinal matters are dealt with in the relevant articles; here another question arises: what is the value of the conciliar statements made since the disruption of Christendom in the eleventh and sixteenth centuries? Paul VI in a letter to Cardinal Willebrands (5 October, 1974) on the seventh centenary of Lyons II, spoke of it as a general council (*synodus generalis*); he did not use the word "ecumenical." Some recent writers question the ecumenical character of these councils, in the plenary sense; this without denying the infallible character of their teaching. One has but to recall the considerable effect of an article at the time of Vatican II by N. Nissiotis (see article Spirit, the Holy). Nissiotis, an Orthodox theologian, regrets what has been missed by the absence of the eastern Churches from full participation in general councils.[1]

---

[1]Cf. V. Peri, *I Concili e le Chiese*, Rome, 1965; Y.M-J. Congar, O.P.,"1274–1974: structures ecclésiales et conciles dans les relations entre Orient et Occident" *RSPT* 58 (1974), 378ff, with bibl.; L. Bouyer, C. Orat., *L'Eglise de Dieu et Temple de l'Esprit*; Paris, 1970, Excursus II, 678, 79; B. Margerie, S.J., *La Trinité chrétienne dans l'histoire*, Paris, 1974, 204, 269,70.

CREATION

In the Church's teaching on the creation of the world by God there is at times an explicit reference to the Trinity. The first affirmation of God as creator is in the creeds (*qv*). The first anathema pronounced against those who say or believe "that this world and all its furnishings were not made by God almighty"[1] was by the provincial council of Toledo in 400 A.D. The statement was: "We believe in one true God, Father, and Son and Holy Spirit, maker of the visible and invisible, by whom were created all things in heaven and on earth."[2] The ecumenical Fourth Lateran Council, in 1215, has a more developed doctrine: "Firmly we believe and we confess simply that the true God is one alone, eternal, immense, and unchangeable, incomprehensible, omnipotent and ineffable, Father and Son and Holy Spirit; indeed three persons but one essence, substance or nature entirely simple. The Father from no one, the Son from the Father only, and the Holy Spirit equally from both; without beginning, always and without end; the Father generating, the Son being born, and the Holy Spirit proceeding; consubstantial and coequal and omnipotent and coeternal; one unique principle of all things, creator of all things,

visible and invisible, the spiritual and the physical, who by his almighty power has from the beginning of time made out of nothing both sorts of creature, the spiritual and the physical, namely the angelic and earthly kinds; and finally the human, which is as it were joined together out of spirit and body."[3] The First Vatican Council, in its teaching on creation, was content to repeat the concluding words "from the beginning of time . . ." of the previous statement. It made no explicit reference to the Trinity. Vatican II (*qv*) related creation to God the Father, evoking the principle of appropriation (*qv*): "The eternal Father, in accordance with the utterly gratuitous and mysterious design of his wisdom and goodness, created the whole universe, and chose to raise up men to share in his own divine life."[4]

Theologians following the lead of St. Augustine (*qv*) generally relate the creation of the world to the Trinity: "It must be admitted that the Father and the Son are one God and, as far as concerns creation, a single Creator and a single Lord, so are they a single principle as far as the Holy Spirit is concerned. But with regard to creation the Father, the Son and the Holy Spirit form a single principle, just as they form a single Creator and a single Lord."[5]

St. Thomas accepted this idea, but developed it considerably: "To create belongs to God according to his existence, which is his essence, and this is common to the three persons. Therefore to create is not proper to any person, but common to the whole Trinity. Nevertheless the divine persons, according to the meaning of the procession in each case, exercise causality in the creation of things. As has already been shown, when there was question of the knowledge and will of God, God is the cause of things by his intellect and will, as the artist is of works of art. But the artist works through the word (or thought) conceived in his mind and through the love (or inclination) of his will directed towards something in particular. Therefore God the Father worked on creation through his word which is his Son, and through his love which is the Holy Spirit. And in this way the processions of the persons are the basis of creative activity, in so far as they comprise essential attributes, that is, knowledge and will."[6]

St. Thomas amplified his opinion, almost as if to forestall a modern objection that insistence on the Trinity in this context would nullify the centrality of Christ in creation: "As the divine nature, though common to the three persons, nonetheless is suited to each in a certain order, in so far as the Son receives the divine nature from the Father and the Holy Spirit from both, in the same way the power of creating, though common to the three persons, nonetheless belongs to each in a certain order. For the Son has it from the Father and the Holy Spirit from both. Therefore to be creator is appropriated to the Father, as to one who has not the power of creating from another. Of the Son it is, however, said 'Through whom all things were made' (Jn 1:3), in so far as he has the same power but from another. For this preposition 'through' generally signifies an intermediate cause, or a beginning from (another) beginning. To the Holy Spirit, who has the same power from both, is attributed that he should rule and vivify what are created by the Father through the Son. The common ground for this attribution can be taken from the appropriation of essential attributes. For as has been said, power is attributed and appropriated to the Father and this is especially evident in creation; accordingly to be creator is attributed to the Father. Wisdom is appropriated to the Son, and through this one acting operates through his intellect; accordingly of the Son it is said 'Through whom all things were made.' Goodness is appropriated to the Holy Spirit and to that pertains government which leads things to their proper outcome and life-giving power. For life consists in a certain interior movement; but the first mover is the end or outcome in view and goodness."[7]

This ample explanation of the Trinitarian aspect of creation shows that due consideration of the primacy and centrality of Christ in creation is by no means compromised. As the Fourth Lateran Council declared, "the only begotten Son of God, Jesus Christ, incarnate by the whole Trinity in common, conceived of Mary ever Virgin with the Holy Spirit cooperating, made true man, formed of a rational soul and human flesh, one person in two natures, clearly pointed out the way to life."[8] On 5 March, 1986, John Paul II spoke in public of creation as the work of the Triune God.[9]

---

[1]The subject is dealt with in most works of dogmatic theology. Cf. St.Thomas (qv), Cont.Gentes, II, qq. 6–38; Summa Theol., I, qq. 44–46; F. Suarez, S.J., De opere sex dierum, 2 vols, Lyons, 1621; D. Petavius, Theol. Dogm., III, Paris, 1644, 220–285; K.Barth, Church Dogmatics, 3.1, 1958; J. Brinktine, Die Lehre von der Schöpfung; L. Scheffczyk, Schöpfung und Vorsehung (Handbuch der Dogmengeschichte, ed. M. Schmaus—A. Grill-

meier, S.J., II, fasc 2a, 1963, Eng. tr., 1970), with bibl.; M. Flick—Z. Alszeghy, Il creatore: l'inizio della salvezza, 2nd ed. Florence, 1961; R. Guelluy, La création, Paris, 1963; P. Gisel, La création, Geneva, 1980; H. Pinard, DTC 3.2, 2034–2201; J. Ratzinger, LTK 9, 460–466; K. Rahner, ibid., 470–74; C. Boyer, S.J., EC IV (1950), 814–25; esp., B. de Margerie, La Trinité chrétienne, Création et Trinité, 254–262; E. Bailleux, "La création, oeuvre de la Trinité, selon S.Thomas," Rev.thom., 62 (1962), 27–50; D.J. Ehr, NCE IV, 419–425; P. Schoonenberg, Covenant and Creation, London, 1968; [2]DS 188; [3]DS 800; [4]Constitution on the Church, 2; [5]De Trinitate, V,14, PL 42, 921; cp. De Gen. ad litt. III, 1, 2, PL 221; Contra Admim., I, 8, PL 29ff; [6]I, 45, 6; [7]Ibid., ad 2um; [8]DS 801; [9]Osservatore Romano, 6 March 1986.

CREEDS

The four creeds, Apostles', Nicene, Constantinopolitan and Athanasian, are dealt with in separate articles (qqv). We are not concerned here with the problems which have been raised in regard to the formation and growth of the early Christian creeds.[1] Certain facts are established. Though creeds were associated with the sacrament of Baptism, these were not in the first three centuries declaratory; such statements of faith as were necessary were in response to the minister's interrogation. The old Roman creed (R) was at the origin of several others, notably the Apostles' creed. Scholars debate how the later Trinitarian formulas grew up when there is so much early evidence, from the New Testament times, of Christ creeds, embryonic and developed. This question is connected with the debate polarised in the names of O. Cullmann and J.N.D. Kelly (qv) on whether the central divine truth in the New Testament (qv) is Christological or Trinitarian.

---

[1]Bibliographies to separate articles.

CYRIL OF ALEXANDRIA, ST., DOCTOR OF THE CHURCH (d. 444)

Renowned for his decisive role in the Theotokos controversy, rightly called Sigillus Patrum because of his excellence in patristic science, a worthy exponent of the great Alexandrian theological tradition, C. put into two works the essence of Trinitarian theology developed in that school: Thesaurus de sancta et consubstantiali Trinitate and De sancta et consubstantiali Trinitate dialogi, both written before 428.[1] Here is the intact patristic legacy, orthodox and sure. One point recurs in regard to C. Did he teach the *Filioque*? He was rebuked for doing so by Theodoret. His name is generally listed with those who support the double procession. G. Bardy (*qv*) rejected the view. He was prepared to admit that for C. the Son possesses the Spirit as proper, that the Spirit is of him and substantially in him, that he is substantially of the Father and the Son, essentially of one and the other.[2] But he did not think that C. taught that the Spirit proceeds from the Father and the Son. He would presumably interpret the much-quoted text in the sense of the "economy," not the immanent life of the Trinity: "Since the Holy Spirit is sent into us that he should make us like God, and since he proceeds from the Father and the Son, it is clear that he is of the divine substance, is substantially in it and proceeding from it."[3] It is easily seen, however, why not all commentators agree with the great French patrologist.

---

[1]Works PG 75; cf. H. du Manoir de Juaye, S.J., *Dogme et spiritualité chez S.Cyrille d'Alexandrie*, Paris, 1944; N. Charlier, C.SS.R., "Le Thesaurus de Trinitate de S.Cyrille d'Alexandrie," *RHE* 14 (1950) 25–81; [2]*DTC* XV; [3]*Thesaurus* PG 75, 585.

CYRIL OF JERUSALEM, ST., DOCTOR OF THE CHURCH (c. 313–387)

C. assumes importance in the history of Arianism (*qv*) through the prestige of his see and through his own interest and achievement in doctrine, manifest in the *Catecheses*.[1] Though a boy when the crisis broke, he lived to take an active part in the events which followed Nicaea (*qv*). He has been the victim of summary judgments, largely because he was for a long time reluctant to use the word *homoousios*: possibly through the bad memory of Paul of Samosata (*qv*), or through fear of the danger of Sabellianism, or because he thought it ambiguous and disliked a word not found in Sacred Scripture. A monograph by a prestigious patrologist, Mgr. Joseph Lebon, concludes that all that C. lacked was the word and his orthodoxy was not in any way in doubt.[2] A more recent writer, A. Grillmeier, S.J., another great patrologist, though admitting C.'s unqualified belief in the divinity of the Son, expressed some reticence on the saint's idea of the Father-Son relationship in the Trinity,[3] thinking that subordinationism lingered.

C. was unfortunate in his proximity to a persistent troublemaker, a gifted one, Acacius of Caesarea (*qv*). He had been ordained priest by Maximus and witnessed the demonstration of loyalty by Maximus with sixteen bishops to Athanasius in 346. In a moment of controversy over the succession to Maximus (who had in vain consecrated an anti-Arian, Heraclius, for the see) Cyril accepted consecration from Acacius, even consenting to reordination, c. 349.

If C. was compromised by the circumstances and persons favouring his appointment, he was no tool of Acacius, who turned against him, arraigned him, 355 and had him deposed by the council of Antioch, 357–358. Exiled in Tarsus he joined forces with the Homoeousians, Basil of Ancyra, George of Laodicea, Eustathius of Caesarea and Sylvanus of Tarsus. They were rigidly opposed to the Anomoeans (*qv*). They thought that if the word *homoiousios* were properly interpreted it could be acceptable.

At the council of Seleucia these ideas were accepted. The assembly adopted the second creed of the Dedication Council of 341, which was moderate. A delegation was due to await the emperor to win him to their view. But the Acacians were there first. The Homoean council of Antioch, 360, deposed Basil, Eustathius, Sylvan and Cyril.

St. Athanasius sought, at this time, to make contact with C. and his associates. His words are revealing: "Those who received all the decisions of the Council of Nicaea and who have no scruple save for the *homoousion*, are not to be treated as enemies. We do not attack them as Ariomanites or as enemies of the Fathers but we discuss with them as brothers with brothers, who think like us and differ only in what concerns a word."[4]

The question remains: When did C. accept the *homoousios*? The historians Socrates and Sozomen think only at the Council of Constantinople, 361. Others think that it was when at the instigation of the emperor Theodosius in 379 he signed the Nicene creed. L. de Tillemont and F. Hort suggest that C. and Meletius of Antioch agreed in 363 to submit to the Nicene terminology.

Those who defend C.'s orthodoxy generally invoke such passages as are found in the *Catecheses* XI: "Since the Father is very God he begot the Son like to himself, very God. Therefore the Son is very God, having the Father in himself, not changed into the Father. Let us not, thinking to honour the Son, call him Father, nor thinking to honour the Father suppose the Son to be but one of his creatures. But let one Father be worshipped through the one Son and let not their worship be separated. Let one Son be proclaimed sitting at the right hand of the Father before all ages, not having received this dignity in time by advancement after the Passion but possessing it eternally."[5]

To these add such words as these: "He who has seen the Son has seen the Father, for the Son is like in all things to him who begot him, begotten Life of Life, Power of Power, God of God. The characteristics of godhead in the Son are unchangeable and he who is deigned worthy to behold the godhead of the Son comes to the enjoyment of the Father. Let us neither separate nor confuse Father and Son . . . . Perfect is he who begot, perfect that which was begotten. He who begot is God, God he was begotten, God indeed of all things but calling the Father his own God; for he is not ashamed to say: 'I ascend to my Father and your Father, to my God and your God' (Jn 20:17)."[6] From these texts one can scarcely justify the charge of subordinationism (qv).

C. is clear on the distinct personality of the Holy Spirit: "He who speaks and sends is living and subsisting and operating."[7] He is expansive on the subject: "It is established that there are various appelations, but one and the same Spirit—the Holy Spirit—living and personally subsisting and always present together with the Father and the Son; not as being spoken or breathed forth from the mouth and lips of the Father and the Son, or diffused into the air; but as a personally existing being, himself speaking and operating and exercising his dispensation and hallowing, since it is certain that the dispensation of salvation in regard to us which proceeds from the Father and Son and Holy Spirit is indivisible and concordant and one."[8]

C's succinct affirmation of his belief in the Trinity: "Undivided is our faith, inseparable our reverence. We neither separate the Holy Trinity, nor do we make confusion as Sabellius does."[9]

---

[1]Works: Maurists, 1720, in PG 33, 33–1180, improved by W.K. Reischl and J. Rupp, 2 vols, Munich, 1848, 1860, repr. Hildesheim, 1967. French tr. J. Bouvet, *Cyrillus Hierosolymitanus, Cathechéses baptismales et mystagogiques*, Namur, 1962; Eng. tr. E. Telfer, *Cyril of Jerusalem and Nemesius of Emesa*, London, 1955; esp. L. McCauley and A. A. Stephenson, *The Works of St. Cyril of Jerusalem*, 2 vols., Washington, 1969, 1970; cf. J. Mader, *Der Heilige Cyrillus, Bischop von Jerusalem in seinem Leben und seinem Schriften*, Einsiedeln, 1891; M. Niederberger, *Die Logoslehre des hl. Cyril von Jerusalem*, Paderborn, 1923; esp., J. Lebon, "La position de St. Cyrille de Jérusalem dans les luttes provoquées par l'arianisme," *RHE* 20 (1924), 181–210, 357–386; A. Grillmeier, S.J., *Christ in Christian Tradition*, London, 1964, 256; A. Paulin, *Saint Cyrille de Jérusalem, Catéchète*, Paris, 1959; T. Schermann, *Die Gottheit des Heiligen Geistes nach den griechischen Vätern des vierten Jahrhunderts*, Freiburg i.B., 1901, 17–47; H. Leclercq, *DACL*, VII, 2, 2374–2392; X. Le Bachelet, *DTC* III (1908), 2527–2577; M. Jugie, A.A., (qv) *EC* III (1950), 1725–1728; P. Galtier, *Le Saint-Esprit en nous d'après les Pères grecs*, Rome, 1946, 105–115; [2]*Op.cit.*, esp. 384–6; [3]*Op.cit.*; [4]*De synodis*, 41; [5]Tr. McCauley and Stephenson, XI, 17, p.220f; [6]*Ibid.*; [7]*Cat.* 17, 9,28, 33, 34; [8]17, 11; [9]16,4.

D

DE RÉGNON, THEODORE (1831–1893)
Author of the first substantial work on the history of Trinitarian doctrine, *Etudes de théologie positive sur la Sainte Trinité*, in four volumes, a quarry for students ever since.[1] The first volume dealt with the dogma, the second with scholastic theories; the second and third volumes, published after the author's death, dealt with Greek theories.

De R. first planned a work on Mary, Mother of grace; he thought it more expedient to work on other subjects, began with *Banes et Molina*, went on to *La metaphysique des causes*, then embarked on his major project, a study of the Trinity in the history of theology. From a study of the Greek and Latin authors he came to the conclusion that the western and eastern Church share the same faith, but have approached the mystery from different vantage points: "The Latins regarded the personality as the way in which nature was expressed, while the Greeks thought of nature as the content of the person. These are contrary ways of viewing things, throwing two concepts of the same reality on to different grounds . . . . The Latin theologian therefore says: 'three persons in God', whereas the Greek says: 'one God in three persons.' In both cases, the faith and the dogma are the same, but the mystery is presented in two different forms . . . . If we think first of the concept of nature and the concept of personality is then added to it, the concrete reality has to be defined as a 'nature personalised.' This is seeing nature *in recto* and the person *in obliquo*. If, on the other hand, we think first of the concept of the person and the concept of nature comes later, then the concrete reality must be defined as a 'person possessing a nature.' This is seeing the person *in recto* and nature *in obliquo*. The two *definitions* are true and complete and both are adequate to the object in mind, but they are the result of two different views, and that is why the logical deductions from them follow opposite paths.

The Scholastic theology of the Latin Church followed one of these ways, while the dogmatic theology of the Greek Church continued on the other path. The consequence is that the two theologies express the same truth, just as two symmetrical triangles may be equal, but cannot be placed one on top of the other."[2]

It is well known that De R. throughout the four volumes of his work tends on occasion to invoke or even assume this thesis on the difference between East and West. Sometimes he does so with scant justice to great western ideas or writers. His research stands nonetheless massive and generally helpful, allowing for the scholarly conditions of his time. The last two volumes were not finally revised by him. The western reader will be surprised to note little attention to St. Augustine (*qv*). "His insights," says Fr. Congar, "sometimes hardened to the point of caricature."[3]

[1]Cf. A. d'Alès, S.J., *DTC* XII, 2, 2121–34; Congar, *The Holy Spirit*, III, xvi–xvii; as an example of a writer influenced by De R., cf. H. Barré, C.S.Sp., *'Trinité que j'adore'*, Paris, 1964, ch I, "Grecs et Latins," 21–54; [2]*Etudes de théologie positive sur la Sainte Trinité*, 4 vols, Paris, I and II, 1892, III and IV, 1898; I, 433–434; 251–252; [3]*Op.cit.*, xvii.

DEHELLENIZATION OF DOGMA

Professor Leslie Dewart in his book, *The Future of Belief, Theism in a World Come of Age*,[1] raised "the problem of integrating Christian theistic belief with the everyday experience of contemporary man"; "the integration of Christian belief with the post-medieval stage of human development." Can "one, while complying with the demand that human personality, character and experience be inwardly integrated, at one and the same time profess the Christian religion *and* perceive human nature and everyday reality as contemporary man typically does?"[2] The language is identifiably that of the age of Pope John XXIII, the movement of thought from a Catholicism allegedly withdrawn from the world to a new thinking which would seek to discern the values, insights, achievement of the world. John recommended attention to the signs of the times. If he did not cherish the notion of a Catholic self-imposed ghetto, he certainly had sufficient realism to see that the contemporary world, and contemporary human consciousness and striving, if they are to be saved, need conversion to Christ as did men of past ages. Those who misinterpreted John took to dismantling Catholic institutions, traditions, conventions, modes of thought and mental categories.

Professor Dewart struck at what he thought the outmoded Hellenic mould of Catholic theology. He thought that the "integration of theism with today's everyday experience requires not merely the *demythologization of Scripture* but the more comprehensive *dehellenization of dogma*, and specifically that of the Christian doctrine of God."[3] Behind this demand is the fear that Greek thought took over Christian teaching. But history shows the exact opposite: it was Christian theology that took over Greek ideas and words and adapted them to its own needs. A test case in the development of Trinitarian dogma is the *homoousion*, which was taken up and admirably adapted to the need of the time; a Hellenic technique was used to deal with a Christian problem and give it Christian

content: "This technique pertains not to the limitations of Hellenism antiquated by modern culture but to the achievements of Hellenism that still survive in modern culture and, indeed, form part of it."[4] There is then no need to fear the crypto-theism of which Dewart speaks.

[1]New York, 1966; cf. B. Lonergan (*qv*), "The Dehellenization of Dogma," *TheolSt*, 28 (1967), 336–351; repr. *A Second Collection*, Papers by B. Lonergan, ed. W. F. J. Ryan, S. J. and B. J. Tyrrell, S. J., 1974; [2]*op.cit.*, 19; [3]49; [4]B. Lonergan, *op.cit.*, 24.

DEVELOPMENT OF DOGMA

"In the first place, within the ante-Nicene movement we have to recognise two distinct, though related developments. There is no doubt that those early Christian centuries produced a development in trinitarian and christological doctrine, but this doctrinal development contained within it another, more profound development: the development of the very notion of dogma."[1] Thus Fr. B. Lonergan analyses the problem of development in its relevance to ante-Nicene theology of the Trinity. As he continues, there must be a clear transition from obscurity to clarity and from one kind of clarity to another. "The emergence of the very notion of dogma, grounded in the word of God as true, was a movement from obscurity to clarity; on the other hand, the doctrine of the Christian Church concerning Jesus Christ advanced not from obscurity to clarity, but from one kind of clarity to another."[2] What Mark, Paul and John thought about Christ, though not obscure, was clarified by the definition of Nicaea. "But further dogmas had to follow, and then the historical investigation of dogmas, before the fact and nature of dogmatic development itself could be clearly established."[3]

It is for the experts in such matters to show that though the formulation of conciliar decrees on the Trinity—which is what concerns us—differs from the language of the gospels, though each mode of expression retains its specific function in God's dealing with man, though each reflects the action of God's spirit, there is no place for rivalry in appealing to the human spirit, and—the nub of the question—there is not only continuity, but identity in God's self-communication, that is, in his revelation.

As the same author explains, this is a vast, complex subject which must be explored from four aspects: objective, subjective, evaluative and hermeneutical. Consideration of these separate aspects eliminates the fear that the dogmas lack continuity with the gospels and that they lack religious significance. Such manifold reflection will also act as a corrective against the tendency to separate, not in any inferior department, dogmatic theology on the Trinity from the carefully garnered yield of biblical and traditional data.

The words of Vatican II are here relevant: "The Tradition that comes from the apostles makes progress in the Church, with the help of the Holy Spirit. There is a growth in insight into the realities and words that are being passed on. This comes about in various ways. It comes through the contemplation and study of believers who ponder these things in their hearts (cf. Lk 2:19, 51). It comes from the intimate sense of spiritual realities which they experience. And it comes from the preaching of those who have received, along with the right of succession in the episcopate, the sure charism of truth. Thus, as the centuries go by, the Church is always advancing towards the plenitude of divine truth, until eventually the words of God are fulfilled in her . . . . And the Holy Spirit, through whom the living voice of the Gospel rings out in the Church—and through her in the world—leads believers to the full truth, and makes the word of God Christ dwell in them in all its richness" (cf. Col 3:16).[4]

Having expounded the unity and interdependence of Scripture and Tradition, the Council Constitution points to the role of the Teaching Authority in deciding what is authentic development: "But the task of giving an authentic interpretation of the Word of God, whether in its written form or in the form of Tradition, has been entrusted to the living teaching office of the Church alone. Its authority in this matter is exercised in the name of Jesus Christ. Yet this Magisterium is not superior to the Word of God, but is its servant. It teaches only what has been handed on to it. At the divine command and with the help of the Holy Spirit, it listens to this devotedly, guards it with dedication and expounds it faithfully. All that it proposes for belief as being divinely revealed is drawn from this single deposit of faith."[5]

Thus, as the Council concludes, God has so arranged that sacred Tradition, sacred Scripture and the Magisterium of the Church "are so connected and associated that one of them cannot stand without the others." It is within the three-fold protective frame that development of doctrine takes place, organically continuous, responding, within the life of the Church which it is designed to nourish, to those factors of growth within the body, the questionings thrown up by one generation after another, the challenge of heresy, the impact of mighty intellects imbued with faith, the thirst unquenchable in man for the fullness of saving truth.

---

[1]Cf. K. Rahner (qv), "The Development of Dogma," with bibl., *Theological Investigations*, I, 2nd ed., 1965, 39–77; B. Lonergan (qv), *The Way to Nicea, Dogmatic Development*, 1–17; here quoted, 13; [2]B. Lonergan, *op.cit.*, 13; [3]*Ibid.*; [4]*Constitution on Divine Revelation*, 8; [5]*Ibid.*, 10.

DEVOTION

Devotion has had different meanings through the centuries.[1] To what extent personal attitudes and prayerful response was absorbed in liturgical acts is for the historian of the early centuries to investigate. From the outset the Christian community centered on the liturgy. When the sacrament of initiation implied a profession of faith in the Trinity (see BAPTISM). here surely was an act of devotion, personal and ecclesial. Later doxologies (qv) of one kind or another channel a spiritual impulse towards the Blessed Three; they are found as early as St. Justin (qv), and St. Clement of Alexandria (qv). St. Basil (qv) says that Christians were wont, from antiquity, to recite this prayer when lighting evening lamps: "We praise the Father, the Son and the Holy Spirit."[2] The hymns composed to the Trinity by Marius Victorinus (qv) were probably intended to serve as prayers. The first lengthy prayer, enlightened and noble, to the Holy Trinity is found in the last book of St. Hilary's (qv) *De Trinitate*. It ends thus: "Keep, I pray thee, this my pious faith undefiled, and even till my spirit departs, grant that this may be the utterance of my convictions; so that I may ever hold fast that which I professed in the creed of my regeneration, when I was baptized in the Father, and the Son, and the Holy Spirit. Let me in short adore thee our Father, and thy Son together with thee; let me win the favour of thy Holy Spirit, who is from thee, through thy Only-begotten. For I have a convincing witness to my faith, who says, *Father, all mine are thine and thine are mine*, even my Lord

Jesus Christ, abiding in thee, and from thee, and with thee, forever God: who is blessed forever and ever. Amen."[2] The last words of St. Augustine's treatise on the Trinity are also a prayer.

Nor must we forget, before leaving the early centuries, the eloquent witness of St. Cecilia who, after her martyrdom, was found with outstretched hand—her fingers, thumb, index and second, open to signify that she died for her faith in the triune God. Devotion sublime.

In the eighth century forms of piety centered on the Trinity are found in the monasteries of Aniane and Tours. St. Benedict of Aniane made them part of his monastic reform; he dedicated his abbey church to the Trinity in 872. With the foundation of the Order of the Most Holy Trinity a stable foundation was provided in places for the practice of devotion to the Trinity. With time striking figures publish their original insights—witness Catherine of Siena (qv).

The revival of a Trinitarian doctrine of grace (qv), with consequent awareness of the divine indwelling (qv) must contribute to a deepening of such spiritual attitudes. The way is open for an authentic Trinitarian spirituality. Teachers and preachers must still bend their efforts to making the essence of the dogma accessible to the faithful, meaningful in the fullest sense.

When the spirituality of St. Thérèse of Lisieux was given approval and encouragement by the Church, interest was awakened in the fatherhood of God. This facilitates the approach to God the Father. Christian reflection was further oriented this way by the achievement of Dom Columba Marmion in teaching convincingly the truth of our adoptive sonship. Therein certainly the Trinitarian dimension to Christian holiness has its warrant and sure recommendation.

The teaching of Vatican II (qv) must with time add its measure to a revival of this true Christian piety—in the sense that revival is always possible. So, undoubtedly, will the example and spiritual doctrine of the newly beatified Elizabeth of the Trinity (qv).

Finally there is the question as to what place intellectual activity and writing or speaking the results on a religious topic has in the totality of Christian commitment. Who can think of Didymus the Blind or Novatian or Hilary or Marius Victorinus or Augustine or Richard of St. Victor (qqv) labouring on their treatises on the Trinity without interior dedication to the Blessed Three? And what of the greatest of them all, Athanasius?

[1]Ph. Ferlat, *Prêcher la Trinité,* Francheville, 1973; C. Spicg, O.P., *Vie morale et Trinité selon S. Paul,* Paris, 1962; see bibl. to articles on Father, God the, Spirit, the Holy; Son of God, Charismatic Movement, Vatican II; Liturgy; [2]*De Spiritu Sancto,* ch. 29, 73; LNPF VIII, 46; [3]Bk XII, 57; LNPF, N.S. IX, 233; cp St. Augustine's concluding prayer, *De Trinit.,* XV, ch. 28, PG 42, 1007, 8.

DIDYMUS THE BLIND (c. 313–398)

D., blind since his infancy, was appointed head of the Catechetical School of Alexandria by Athanasius (qv); here he had among his pupils Gregory of Nazianzus, (qv), Jerome, Rufinus and Palladius. D's immense learning was known to his contemporaries and his asceticism admired.[1] Of his many writings much has perished, due to the suspicion attached to his name during the controversy on Origenism; a find of 6th or 7th century papyrus codices in 1941 has no bearing on the works which interest us. These are the *De Trinitate* and *De Spiritu Sancto* and *De dogmatibus et contra Arianos.* The first survives in three books; the second is extant in a translation by St. Jerome—it was used by St. Ambrose for his work with the same title and Jerome accused the Latin Doctor of plagiarism; the third is partially preserved in the fourth and fifth books of the *Contra Eunomium* attributed to St. Basil (qv) since the fifth century but spurious as to his authorship.[2] The text, though abridged, matches the fourteen references to the work made by D. in the *De Trinitate.*; book IV deals with biblical texts invoked by the Arians, book V with the Holy Spirit. A short work *Adversus Arium et Sabellium* found among the works of Gregory of Nyssa (qv) is of disputed authorship. K. Holl, supported by J. Leipoldt, thought it was from D. but G. Bardy (qv) disagreed.

D's Trinitarian doctrine is Nicene. In the first book of the *De Trinitate* he deals with the Son, in the second with the Holy Spirit, and in the third he summarizes the two and faces objections taken by opponents from Scripture. For him all three persons are consubstantial and he rejects any subordinationism; D's knowledge of Scripture was massive, his interpretation not always true.

The Trinity was at the centre of his thinking: his key phrase, showing how he stands between Athanasius and the Cappadocians, was "one substance (*Ousia*), three hypostases." The formula is found for the first time in the *Discourse against Arius and Sabellius.* As there is but one substance in the Trinity there can be but one operation: "It is proved that in all things there is one same operation of the Father, the Son and the Holy Spirit. There is but one operation where there is but one substance, because whatever are *homoousia* with the same substance, have likewise the same operations."[3] Again from unity of operation he argues to unity of nature: "Since, therefore, these *homoousia* are worthy of the same honour and have the same operation, they have the same nature, and do not differ from one another in divinity or in operation; they alone can exist together, be placed together in the same grade of dignity, and be everywhere understood with him who is one."[4] All three Persons share in Divine Providence. D. is imbued with the sense of mystery in which all this is necessarily enveloped: "It is impossible to grasp even this, how the Trinity has one will, and speaks and grants favours in such a way that this speech and granting of favours is common to all the Persons."[5]

In the *De Spiritu Sancto* D. elaborates the same ideas: "Whoever communicates with the Holy Spirit communicates immediately with the Father and the Son. And whoever shares in the glory of the Father has this glory from the Son, contributed through the Holy Spirit. So it is proved that in everything there is one same operation for the Father, the Son and the Holy Spirit."[6] Quoting 2 Cor 13:13, D. comments: "From these words is shown one assumption of the Trinity; since whoever receives the grace of Christ has it as much through the administration of the Father as through the distribution of the Holy Spirit. For this grace is given by God the Father and by Jesus Christ according to the words: 'Grace be with you and peace from God the Father and from our Lord Jesus Christ'; the Father does not give one kind of grace, and the Son another. But St. Paul describes this grace as being given by the Father and by our Lord Jesus Christ and completed by the communication of the Holy Spirit."[7] "For when anyone has received the grace of the Holy Spirit he will have it as a gift from the Father and our Lord Jesus Christ. By one same grace, however, which is from the Father and the Son, completed by the operation of the Holy Spirit, is proved the Trinity of one substance."[8] This is a remarkable statement of the Trinitarian dimension of grace (*qv*).

Whatever may be said about Athanasius (*qv*), there can be no doubt that D. explicitly opposes the Arian opinion that Jesus had no soul. Jesus as a perfect man is subject to the human condition in all save sin; the sacred humanity was sanctified through its union with the Logos. On the Holy Spirit his doctrine is plenary and wholly satisfying: "It has been proved that the Holy Spirit is not only God, but also equal and similar to the Father, because in an equal and similar way man is a temple of the three persons; and likewise whoever is the dwelling-place of the Father has the Son also dwelling within him, as well as the Spirit of God; just as in turn, whoever has the dignity of having the Holy Spirit or the Son, has the Father also."[9]

What of the *Filioque*? In the *De Trinitate* he states that the Holy Spirit "proceeds from the Father and remains divinely in the Son."[10] The Holy Spirit is the image of the Son, as the Son is the image of the Father; he is the Spirit of the Son, of the Logos, of the Saviour. In the *De Spiritu Sancto*, if we can follow Jerome's translation, D. uses language like "he is inseparable from my and the Father's will, because he is not from himself but from the Father and from me; because he is produced from the Son, that is, proceeding from the truth, a consoler coming from a consoler, God from God, proceeding as the Spirit of truth; Nor is the Son anything save those things which are given him by the Father, nor is there any substance of the Holy Spirit beyond what is given him by the Son."[11]

D. sees the work of sanctification as peculiar to the Spirit. He is the first gift because he is Love and this is the origin of all other gifts: "In the substance of the Holy Spirit is understood the plenitude of all gifts."[12] Characteristically Greek thinking.

[1]Works PG 39, 131–1818, *De Trinitate*, 269–992; *De Spiritu Sancto* PL 39, 1031–1086; *Contra Eunomium* (inter opera S.Basil), IV and V; cf. T. Schermann, *Die Gottheit des Heiligen Geistes nach den griechischen Vätern des vierten Jahrhunderts*, Freiburg i.B., 1901, 189–223; E. Stolz, "Didymus, Ambrosius, Hieronymus," *ThQ* 87 (1905), 371–401; J. Leipoldt, *Didymus der Blinde von Alexandrien*, TU 29 Hft 3, 1905; G. Bardy, *Didyme l'Aveugle*, Paris, 1910; E.L. Heston, *The Spiritual Life and the Role of the Holy Ghost in the Sanctification of the Soul as Described in the Works of Didymus of Alexandria*, Notre Dame (Indiana), 1938; P. Galtier, B. Altaner, "Augustinus und Didymus der Blinde, Eine quellenkritische Untersuchung," *VCh* 5 (1951), 116–120; A Quattrone, "La pneumatologia nel trattato De Spiritu Sancto di Didimo Allessandrino," *Regnum Dei* 8 (1952) 82–88; 140–152; 9 (1953) 81–88; L. Doutreleau, "Le De Trinitate est-il l'oeuvre de Didyme l'Aveugle?," *RSR* 45 (1957), 514–557; L. Beranger, "Sur deux enigmes du De Trinitate de Didyme l'Aveugle," *RSR*, 51 (1963), 255–280; Altaner, 280f; M. Pellegrino, *EC* IV, 1567f; A. Van Roey, *DHGE*, 14, 416–27; G. Bardy, *DSp* III, 868–71; Quasten III, 85–98; [2]Cf. F.X. Funk, "Die zwei letzten Bücher der Schrift Basilius des Gr. gegen Eunomius:"

DIONYSIUS THE GREAT

Kirchengeschichtliche Abhandlungen und Untersuchungen 2, Paderborn, 1899, 291–329 and, in reply to J. Leipoldt, *Kirchengeschichtl. Abhand. und Unters.* 3, 311–323; G. Bardy, *op.cit.*, 23–27 and esp. J. Lebon, "Le Pseudo-Basile (Adv.Eunom. IV-V) est bien Didyme d'Alexandre," *Mus.* 50 (1937) 61–83; [3]*De Spiritu Sancto*, 17; [4]*De Trinitate*, 2; [5]*De Trinitate*, 2, 5, 1; [6]17; [7]6; [8]16; [9]*De Trin.* 2, 10; [10]1, 31; [11]34, 36, 37; [12]De Spir. S., 28.

DIONYSIUS THE GREAT (d. c. 264)

A pupil of Origen (*qv*), D. succeeded Heraclas as head of the famous catechetical school at Alexandria and in 247 followed him as Bishop of Alexandria.[1] To the vicissitudes of the Decian persecution was added a doctrinal crisis, which brought D. into conflict with his namesake, St. Dionysius (*qv*), the Pope. About 250 Sabellianism began to appear in Pentapolis, possibly spread by Sabellius himself. D. felt bound to intervene as the area was in his jurisdiction, and did so by a letter wherein he seems to have overreacted. We have a prime document on the matter, the defence of D. written by his famous successor in the see of Alexandria, Athanasius (*qv*), *De Sententia Dionysii*. The Arians in the time of Athanasius were trying to justify themselves from the writings of D.

Athanasius thus sets the scene: "At that time certain of the bishops in Pentapolis, Upper Libya, held with Sabellius. And they were so successful with their opinions that the Son of God was scarcely any longer preached in the churches. D. having heard of this, as he had the charge of those churches, sent men to counsel the guilty ones to cease from their error, but as they did not cease, but waxed more shameless in their impiety, he was compelled to meet their shameless conduct by writing the said letter, and to expound from the Gospels the human nature of the Saviour, in order that since those men waxed bolder in denying the Son, and in ascribing his human actions to the Father, he accordingly by demonstrating that it was the Son and not the Father that was made man for us, might persuade the ignorant persons that the Father is not a Son, and so by degrees lead them up to the true Godhead of the Son, and the knowledge of the Father."[2]

Eusebius mentions several letters sent by D. to bishops now unknown (H.E., VII, 26). We have no text of any of these. What is certain is that about 260 the Pope was informed that the writing of his Alexandrine namesake contained doctrinal errors: he separated and divided the Son from the Father; he denied the eternal fatherhood of God and the eternal existence of the Son; he did not say that Christ was consubstantial with God; he made the Son out to be the adoptive son of God and used images to express their relationship which shocked—the Father was the vinedresser, the Son the vine, the Father was the carpenter, the Son the boat.

The Pope published a lengthy letter clearing up points at issue with Sabellius and the charges laid against Dionysius. The latter sent at once a *Refutation and Defence*. All we have of this document are extracts quoted by Athanasius in the course of his enthusiastic defence of D. For instance on the charge that he had separated the Father from the Son: "Each of the names I have mentioned is inseparable and indivisible from that next to it. I spoke of the Father, and before referring to the Son I designated him too in the Father. I referred to the Son—and even if I did not also expressly mention the Father, certainly he was to be understood beforehand in the Son. I added the Holy Spirit, but at the same time I further added both whence and through whom he proceeded. But they are ignorant that neither is the Father *qua* Father separated from the Son—for the name carries that relationship with it—nor is the Son expatriated from the Father . . . . Thus then we extend the Monad indivisibly into the Triad, and conversely gather together the Triad without diminution into the Monad."[3]

On the charge that he did not support the consubstantial, D. wrote thus: "I showed also that the charge they allege against me is untrue, namely that I denied Christ to be of one essence with God. For even if I argue that I have not found this word (*homoousion*) nor read it anywhere in the Holy Scriptures, yet my subsequent reasonings, which they have suppressed, do not discord with its meaning."[4] Athanasius was convinced that to compare D. and Arius would be madness; he thought all the accusations could be answered and that consideration of D.'s other works would be reassuring.

St. Basil (*qv*) was not so happy with the ideas of D.: "I do not admire everything that is written; indeed of some things I totally disapprove. For it may be, that of the impiety of which we are now hearing so much, I mean the Anomoeans, (*qv*) it is he, as far as I know, who first gave men the seeds.

I do not trace his so doing to any mental depravity, but only to his earnest desire to resist Sabellius .... In his writings he exhibits a miscellaneous inconsistency, and is at one time to be found disloyal to the *homoousion*, because of his opponent who made a bad use of it to the destruction of the hypostases, and at another admitting it in his Apology to his namesake."[5]

The great patrologist, G. Bardy (*qv*) was severe on D. "These (complaints) are serious, and the whole of Arianism is contained, more than in germ, in the formulas of the Bishop of Alexandria. One may well ask where he borrowed his theories: we can easily see that they are in the line of Origenist thought, but much more daring since Origen never seems to have taught that the Son of God was a creature and that there was a time when he did not exist. The demands, true or supposed, of the controversy, probably carried D. much further than was needed. Besides, we must not forget that we have not the complete text of the letter to Ammonius and Euphranor, but only the most suspect passages, those quoted by opponents."[6]

[1]PG 10, 1233–1344; crit. ed. C. L. Feltoe, Cambridge Patristic Texts, 1904; Eng. tr. by C. L. Feltoe, SPCK 1918; F. Dittrich, *Dionysius der Grosse von Alexandrien*, 1867; P. Nautin, *Lettres et écrivains des IIe et IIIe siecles*, Paris, 1961; 151–165; Marta Sordi, "Dionigi d'Alessandria, Commodiano ed alcuni problemi della storia del III sccolo," *Atti dello Pontificia Accademia Romana di Archeologia, Serie III, Rendiconti*, 35 (1963), 123–46; W. A. Bienert, *Dionysius von Alexandrien* (Patristsche Texte und Studien, 21), 1978; Altaner-Stuiber,(1966) 20f; 210f; Quasten, II, 101–9; A. van Roey, *DHGE* XIV, 248–53; [2]*De sententia Dionysii*, 5, LNPF IV, 177f; [3]*Ibid.* 17, 182; [4]*Ibid.* 18, 183; [5]*Letter* IX, LNPF VIII, 122; [6]*DTC* XV, 2, 1647.

DIONYSIUS, POPE (d.268)

D. figured in one episode of a doctrinal kind which resulted in a document of great importance. When Dionysius the Great (*qv*) had been delated to him he published a letter on Trinitarian errors: "Next, I may reasonably turn to those who divide and cut to pieces and destroy that most sacred doctrine of the Church of God, the divine Monarchy, making it as it were three powers and partitive subsistences and godheads three. I am told that some among you who are catechists and teachers of the divine Word, take the lead in this tenet, who are diametrically opposed, so to speak, to Sabellius's opinions; for he blasphemously says that the Son is the Father, and the Father the Son, but they in some sort preach three Gods, as dividing the sacred Monad into three subsistences foreign to each other and utterly separate.

"For it must needs be that with the God of the universe, the divine Word is united, and the Holy Spirit must repose and abide in God; thus in one as in a summit, I mean the God of the universe, must the divine Triad be gathered up and brought together. For it is the doctrine of the presumptuous Marcion, to sever and divide the divine Monarchy into three origins—a devil's teaching, not that of Christ's true disciples and lovers of the Saviour's lessons. For they know well that a Triad is preached by divine Scripture, but that neither Old Testament nor New preaches three Gods.

"Equally one must censure those who hold the Son to be a work, and consider that the Lord has come into being, as one of things which really come to be; whereas the divine oracles witness to a generation, suitable to him and becoming, but not to any fashioning or making. A blasphemy then it is, not ordinary, but even the highest, to say that the Lord is in any sort a handiwork. For if he came to be Son, once he was not; but he was always, if (that is) he be in the Father, as he says himself, and if the Christ be Word and Wisdom and Power (which as you know, divine Scripture says), and these attributes be powers of God. If then the Son came into being, once these attributes were not; consequently there was a time, when God was without them; which is most absurd. And why say more on these points to you, men full of the Spirit and well aware of the absurdities which come to view from saying that the Son is a work?

"Not attending, as I consider, to this circumstance, the authors of this opinion have entirely missed the truth, in explaining, contrary to the sense of divine and prophetic Scripture in the passage, the words, 'The Lord created me a beginning of his ways unto his works.' For the sense of 'He created,' as you know, is not one, for we must understand 'He created' in this place, as 'He set over the works made by him,' that is, 'made by the Son himself.' And 'He created' here must not be taken for 'made,' for creating differs from making. 'Is not he thy Father that hath bought thee? hath he not made thee and created thee?' says Moses in his great song in Deuteronomy. And one may say to them, O reckless men, is he a work who is 'the First-born of every creature, who is born from the womb before the morning-star,' who said, as Wisdom, 'Before the hills he begets me?' And in many passages of the divine oracles is the Son said to have been generated, but nowhere to have come into being; which manifestly convicts those of misconception about the Lord's generation, who presume to call his divine and ineffable generation a making. Neither then may we divide into three godheads the wonderful and divine Monad; nor disparage with the name of 'work' the dignity and exceeding majesty of the Lord; but we must believe in God the Father Almighty, and in Christ Jesus his Son, and in the Holy Spirit, and hold that to the God of the universe the Word is united. For 'I' says he 'and the Father are one;' and 'I in the Father and the Father in me.' For thus both the divine Triad and the holy preaching of the Monarchy will be preserved."[1]

This is the first extensive pronouncement by a Pope on the Trinity; and what is known to us is but part of the whole statement. Popes Zephyrinus and Callistus had already made contributions to the doctrine, by way of reproof and not with such firm and lengthy argumentation. D. distrusted the word *hypostasis*, subsistence, which had not yet been clarified and refined in this context; in the fragment preserved, here reproduced entirely, he does not use the word *homoousios*: scholars differ on why he may have made the omission.[2] Bardy (*qv*) thought it current at the time, Tixeront something of a novelty (see article Paul of Samosata). An interesting circumstance recalled by Bardy is that with the exception of Irenaeus (*qv*) the prominent theologians of the Trinity thus far, Justin, Tertullian, Hippolytus, Novatian and Origen (*qqv*) were not bishops.

---

[1]Cf.Athanasius, *De Sententia Dionysii* and *De Decretis*; for the little known works of D. cf. Bardenhewer II, 664f; B. Botte, O.S.B., *DHGE*, XIV (1967) 247f; B. de Margerie, S.J., *La Trinité chrétienne dans l'histoire*, Paris, 1974, 127–129; [2]*De Decretis*, LNPF, IV, 167, 68; DS112–115.

DOXOLOGY

A formula intended to give glory to God by its terms and in the recitation of it.[1] The greater Doxology is the *Gloria in excelsis*; the lesser Doxology is the *Gloria Patri*. Doxology was an integral part of Jewish prayer. NT hymns of praise are directed to God as Father and to Christ as God.

There is no direct Doxology to the Holy Spirit. There are Doxologies in the writings of the Apostolic Fathers to the Father and Son. Thus in St. Clement's epistle to the Corinthians: "The grace of our Lord Jesus Christ be with you and with all, in every place, who have been called by God through him, through whom be to him glory, honour, power and greatness and eternal dominion, from eternity to eternity. Amen."[2] Likewise in *The Didache*: "deliver us from the evil one, for thine is the power and the glory for ever."[3] *The Martyrdom of Polycarp*: "And to him who is able to bring us all in his grace and bounty, to his heavenly kingdom, by his only-begotten Child, Jesus Christ, be glory, honour, might, and majesty forever." Already here from the same writer we have a Trinitarian form of Doxology: "For this reason I also praise thee for all things, I bless thee, I glorify thee through the everlasting and heavenly high Priest, Jesus Christ, thy beloved Child, through whom be glory to thee with him and the Holy Spirit, both now and for the ages that are to come. Amen."[4]

As the Doxology took the Trinitarian form it assumed a very large place in the Church's worship, and, as two episodes show, it was, in the manner of formulation, the test case of orthodoxy, with all the passion that opposing views might stir. It may be recalled that the Greek Fathers used the Doxology much more frequently than was the custom in the west—witness particularly St. John Chrysostom and St. Cyril of Alexandria, who particularly favoured end doxologies.

In Antioch the Catholic bishop Eustathius was banished in 330. The Arians were in control and the resistance came from two laymen, Diodorus of Tarsus and Flavian. The Arians, to signify their triumph, used the Doxology, "Glory to the Father *through* the Son *in* the Holy Spirit"; the Catholics used "Glory to the Father and to the Son and to the Holy Spirit." The two formulae were the passwords of the two parties. Bishop Leontius (344–358), sympathetic to the Arians but not willing to rouse the Catholics, would not recite the Doxology aloud; not even those standing near him knew which he spoke.[5]

In Caesarea the incident had more dramatic and permanent results. St. Basil the Great (*qv*) one day began to recite "to the God and Father *with* the Son *together with* the Holy Spirit" alongside the other "*through* the Son *in* the Holy Spirit." There was stormy protest against the fact that Basil had used formulae not only different but, seen by his critics, who therein showed their hand, as opposed to each other.

In his book *De Spiritu Sancto* Basil dealt with the subject at length. He was thus preparing for the final overthrow of the Pneumatomachi (*qv*) at Constantinople, 381 (see SPIRIT, THE HOLY). Before him the tradition had taken root. St. Clement of Alexandria (*qv*) at the end of the *Paedogogus* invites us to join in a prayer to the *Logos* (*qv*), and we are to give "grateful praise to the one Father and Son, to the Son and Father, the Son leader and teacher, and with the Holy Spirit."[6] Origen (*qv*) ending *Hom 37 in Luc* wrote thus: "Let us speak and praise God the Father, Son and Holy Spirit, to whom is glory and empire for ever and ever."[7] St. Cyril of Jerusalem (*qv*) often uses an end Doxology to his catecheses: "In the palace of the Father, to whom be glory with the Only-begotten and Saviour, Jesus Christ, with the holy and life-giving Spirit."[8] St. Athanasius (*qv*) ends the *De decretis* thus: "to God the Father is due the glory, honour and worship with his co-existent Son and Word, together with the all-holy and life-giving Spirit, now and unto endless ages of ages. Amen."[9]

The *Gloria Patri* was henceforth part of Church prayer, established at some cost. It customarily ends psalms, as it does the decades of the Rosary, and is linked with the *Our Father* and *Hail Mary* in intercessory prayers of different kinds.

One notable Trinitarian Doxology occurs at the end of the Eucharistic Prayer during Mass. Oriental liturgies abound in such formulae, the Byzantine for example: "For thou art a kind and loving God and we offer up praise to thee, the Father, the Son and the Holy Spirit, now and always and unto all eternity."[10]

The present form in the Roman Missal is *Per ipsum et cum ipso et in ipso est tibi Deo Patri omnipotenti in unitate Spiritus Sancti omnis honor et gloria per omnia saecula saeculorum*. This formula is similar to that which ends the *Eucharistia* in the *Apostolic Tradition* of Hippolytus; it runs as follows: *Per quem tibi gloria et honor Patri et Filio cum Sancto Spiritu in sancta Ecclesia tua et nunc et in saecula saeculorum*.[11] The sacred names are expressed together in Hippolytus; the Roman formula makes an adjustment which outlines a whole theology of salvation. The unique mediation of Christ is stated, but with it is subtly recalled the communion of all the elect redeemed by him, constituted by this fact members of his Mystical Body: he is the High Priest of all mankind who are "*in ipso et cum ipso*" "In truth they are in him, taken up into the living union of his Body and therefore drawn into the fervent glow of his prayer, so that they are really in a position to worship the Father 'in spirit and in truth'."[12]

Hippolytus has *in sancta Ecclesia tua* where the Roman Canon has *in unitate Spiritus Sancti*. The association of the Trinity with the Church (*qv*) is an ancient idea. As Fr. Jungmann says, these different phrases reflect different aspects of the same reality. The Church derives its unity and is set in communion by the Holy Spirit. "'In him' and 'in the communion of the Holy Spirit' therefore designate one and the same all-encompassing wellspring whence arises the glorification of the Father. It may be considered in relation to Christ since the redeemed comprise his Mystical Body, or in relation to the Spirit whose breath inspires them."[13]

As the same author points out, the Doxology is not in the form of a wish, but is an affirmation of reality. In the sacrifice here offered by its very existence glory is given to the triune God and the prophecy of Malachi is fulfilled: "For from the rising of the sun to its setting my name is great among the nations, and in every place incense is offered to my name, and a pure offering; for my name is great among the nations, says the Lord of hosts (1:11)."

The author of the *Gloria in excelsis* is unknown. It is in three parts: the song of the angels at the birth of Jesus; praise of God the Father; an invocation of Christ with an allusion to the Holy Spirit. It was adopted in the Roman Mass for Christmas from early in the sixth century, then extended to Sundays and feasts of martyrs, and was taken up widely by late eighth century.

The *Te Deum* is not the work of either St. Ambrose of St. Augustine, possibly of Niceta of Remesiana. The lengthy hymn of praise displays the participation of the whole heavenly court and of all the saints in this worship. Inset is a Trinitarian statement: "Father whose majesty is boundless, your true and only Son, who is to be adored, the Holy Spirit sent to be our Advocate." The section following this assertion is strongly Christological, and then the hymn reverts to the prayer of petition which is addressed to the Lord.

A short Trinitarian acclamation must be mentioned, the *Te decet laus*. St. Benedict ordered it to be said (*Reg. Monast.*, c.11), but it is no longer found in the Roman liturgy.

[1]Cf. F.H. Chase, *The Lord's Prayer in the Early Church* (Texts and Studies, I, 3) Cambridge, 1891, 168–76; J.A. Jungmann, S.J., *The Mass of the Roman Rite*, London, 1959, 455–461; *id.*, *The Place of Christ in Liturgical Prayer*, London, 1965, 172–190; *id.*, *Doxologie*, LTK III (1959), 534–36; J. Lebreton, *Les origines du dogme de la Trinité*, 330; H. Leclercq, O.S.B., *DACL*, IV, 2, 1525–36; H.R.E. Masterman, *NCE*, IV, 1029–30; E.J. Gratsch, *ibid.*, 1030; [2]LXV, 2, tr. K. Lake, *The Apostolic Fathers*, London, 1912, I, 121; [3]*The Didache*, VIII, 2, tr. K. Lake, *ibid.*, 331; cf. *ibid.*, IX, 2, 323; [4]XX, 2, *The Apostolic Fathers*, II, 339; *ibid.*, XIV, 3, 333; cf. XXI, 341; [5]J.A. Jungmann, *op.cit.*, 175; for St. Basil, 176f; [6]III, c.12, GCS, *Clem. Al.*, I, 291; 1–12, Stählin; [7]St. Jerome's tr., PG 13, 1896; [8]*Cat.*, 7, Reischl, I, 226; [9]LNPF IV, 172; [10]Apud Jungmann, *op.cit.*, 457; [11]*Traditio apostolica*, 6, ed. B. Botte, O.S.B., SC. 18; 33; [12]*Ibid.*, 458; [13]*Ibid.*

DUNS SCOTUS, JOHN (c. 1265–1308)

The *Doctor Subtilis* introduced some subtleties into the theology of the Trinity without departing from the thought patterns already established.[1] He conceived the processions as productions of the persons; he thought that the generation (*qv*) of the Word was in a second intellectual act *dictio* coming after *intellectio* and likewise for the procession of the Holy Spirit, *spiratio* in *via voluntatis*, second in a twofold act of love. He was convinced that the Incarnation would have taken place even if Adam had not sinned, could not think of the Incarnate Word as a *bonum occasionatum*, an after-thought.

From such a conception would logically arise a close connection between the Incarnation and the creative act of God. Scotus died too young to bring this intuition of genius to all its logical conclusions.

S. preferred Richard of St. Victor's definition of person: *divinae naturae incommunicabilis existentia* to that of Boethius, by now traditional: *rationalis naturae individua substantia*. He insisted on the incommunicability as the distinguishing mark. He saw Christian perfection in terms of the primacy of love and the will, eternal happiness with the Holy Trinity in like terms. On the *Filioque* S. thought that there were different modes of expression, without any real disagreement. But since the Catholic Church had declared it as having to be held as faith he thought it necessary to maintain that the Holy Spirit proceeds *ab utroque*. He also thought that pluralism should extend to thinking whether "the Persons are constituted by relationships or by their mode of being."[2]

[1]Works: Vives ed., Paris, 1891–95, critic. ed. C. Balič, O.F.M., 1950ff; cf. esp., P. Raymond, *DTC*, IV, 1882, 83; P. Minger, O.F.M., "Zur Trinitätslehre des Duns Scotus," *Franc.Studien*, 1919 24ff; Congar, *The Holy Spirit*, III, *180f*; R. Seeberg, *Die Theologie des Johannes Duns Scotus*, Leipzig, 1900, "Die Lehre von der Trinität," 182–211; P. Parthenius Minges, O.F.M, *Johannis Duns Scoti Doctrina Philosophica et Theologica*, Quaracchi, 1930 II, ch. 2, "De Deo Trino in Personis," 189–254; M. Schmaus, *Der Liber Propugnatorius des Thomae Anglicus und die Lehrunterschiede zwischen Thomas von Aquin und Duns Scotus*. II: *Die Trinitärischen lehrunter schiede*, Aschendorff, 1930; [2]*In I Sent.*, d.XI, q. 1, *Opera omnia*, Paris, 1893, IX, 325; crit. ed. V, 2–3; crit. ed., Vatican, XVI, 166, 67; 328ff.

E

ECKHART, O.P. (c. 1260–1327)

An important figure in the history of mysticism, E. made a clouded entry into history.[1] Exercising the functions of superior, reformer, teacher, and especially, at Cologne, preacher, he was the victim of delation, faced a trial on grounds of alleged heresy, and appealed from the verdict of the lower court to the Pope then at Avignon. He died before the decision. The indictment was on statements extracted from his works, which leaves much room for research: context has its value.

Posthumously, E. has suffered from sponsors of dubious theological competence, the Romantic poets, as he has had to endure specious, wholly arbitrary allegations of influence on people like Luther, Kant, Hegel, even the Nazi Rosenberg. A great historian, H. Denifle, O.P, has rescued him from this disturbing association; already his effect on the teaching of Tauler and Henry Suso was a warrant of wholesome things. His defect was in the use of language and he does seem to have chosen daring formulas.

The student of his thought must, with some regret at the loss of part of his writing and at the failure, through want of time, to complete his comprehensive work, *Opus Tripartitum*, note fully his role in promoting a mysticism Trinitarian in its distinctive quality—though here he was not a pioneer. Account must also be taken of the selected propositions condemned by Pope John XXII. Those relevant to the present work are:

(3) "Likewise at the same time and once, when God was, when he begot the Son coeternal with himself, through all things coequal God, he also created the world." (11) "Whatever God the Father gave to his only begotten Son in human nature, all this he has given to me; here I except nothing, neither union, nor sanctity, but he has given all to me as to himself." (13) "Whatever is proper to divine nature, all this is proper to the just and divine man; because of this that man operates whatever God operates, and together with God he created heaven and earth, and he is the generator of the eternal Word, and God without such a man does not know how to do anything." (20) "A good man is the only begotten Son of God." (21) "A noble man is that only begotten Son of God whom the Father has begotten from eternity." (22) "The Father begot me his Son and the same Son. Whatever God does, this is one; because of this he himself begot me with his Son without any distinction."[2]

E. thought that it is the whole soul living the Trinitarian life which is in the image (qv) of God. The three theological virtues faith, hope and charity unite the soul to God, matching the powers of the soul, of knowing, of willing and of passion. He gives a primacy to knowledge, knowledge purified entirely.

[1]Ample bibl. in esp. R.-L. Oechslin, *DSp*, IV, 93–116; id., F. Vernet, *DTC*, IV (1911), 2057–81; F. Vandenbroucke, O.S.B.,

DHGE, XIV (1960), 1385–1403; id., *NCE*, V, 38–40; cf. esp. Oeschlin, "La question de l'orthodoxie d'Eckhart," *op.cit.*, 112–113; exhaustive bibl. from H. Denifle on, *ibid.*, 115–116; [2]DS 951–978.

ECONOMIC TRINITY, THE

The phrase is now so much used that it appears to be theological currency; it is open to confusion because the word economic has other fixed meanings.[1] In Trinitarian theology it means the Trinity as it is manifest in the economy of salvation, in the saving acts of God. Fr. Karl Rahner (*qv*), very eager to keep the theology of the Trinity in the forefront of research and reflection, has been insistent in his many writings on the subject on the truth, which for him is almost an axion, that the economic Trinity is the same as the immanent Trinity. One characteristic passage among many gives his view: "The methodical principle is the identity of the economy of salvation and the immanent Trinity. The identity does not of course mean that one denies that the 'economic' Trinity, one with the immanent Trinity, only exists by virtue of the free decree of God to communicate himself (supernaturally). But by virtue of this free decree, the gift in which God imparts himself to the world is precisely God as the triune God, and not something produced by him through efficient causality, something that represents him. And because he is the triune God, this 'trinitarian character' also affects the gift and makes it triune. And conversely it is therefore also true that the trinitarian character of this divine self-communication, the economic Trinity, makes the immanent Trinity known, *quoad nos*, because they are the same."[2]

Later in the same essay Fr. Rahner makes a deduction from this principle relevant to the organisation of the matter of the theology of the Trinity, the question of structure: "We propose, therefore, as the basic principle in question, for the organisation of the matter and presentation, the identity of the immanent Trinity and of the Trinity of the economy of salvation. Our proposition would be that the economic Trinity is (already) the immanent Trinity, because the basic event of the whole economy of salvation is the self-communication of God to the world, and because all that God (the Father) is to us in Jesus Christ the Son and the Holy Spirit would not really be the self-communication of God, if the two-fold missions were not intrinsic to him, as processions bringing with them the distinction of the three persons."[3]

Karl Rahner's general Trinitarian doctrine is considered in the article under his name. There is a measure of agreement with his thesis, but not a universal consensus. The Trinity as a mystery has been revealed to us and this implies identity of the kind suggested. The "mission" intrinsic to the Incarnation certainly coincides with the reality of God the Son made man. As Karl Rahner emphasizes, the history of salvation is not only the history of God's revelation but of his communication of himself. This gift would not be complete if it were not in the Son and the Spirit, identical with what he is in himself.

Certain reservations must be made, however, to the Rahner thesis. As an example of what may be deduced from a literal acceptance of the *grundaxiom* we may take Piet Schoonenberg's conclusions. He leans unduly on the side of the "economy": "The fact remains that Jesus Christ and the Father personally face each other and that the Holy Spirit prays to the Father in us and calls to the Son and therefore also personally faces them. According to Scripture, then, the Father, the Son and the Holy Spirit face each other as persons *in* the history of salvation. It follows from thesis 23 that this is possible only *through* the history of salvation. The immanent Trinity is a Trinity of persons through the fact that it is an economic Trinity."[4]

What saves this opinion from doctrinal deviation is that Schoonenberg is using the word person in its modern sense—connoting separate consciousness, freedom and interpersonal relationships—and also by the fact that he considers our knowledge limited by the economy of salvation, which for him leaves the mystery of the immanent Trinity open, but unknown and unknowable. "The immanent Trinity, vice versa, is the economic Trinity. It is accessible for us only as the economic Trinity. The fact that God is, apart from his communication of himself in the history of salvation, Trinitarian, can neither be presupposed as a matter of course nor denied."[5] He thinks that in God himself the Father, Son and Holy Spirit are only modes of the godhead; there are persons or personal relationships only in the economy. For us God is three-personal only in the economy. "Through the history of salvation there is a Trinity in God himself; through his own saving action, God himself becomes three-personal, that is, three persons."[6] One may ask the question whether this theory is wholly orthodox.

For certain reservations must be made to the Rahner *grundaxiom*. As Fr. Congar says: "The first half of the statement by Rahner ("The economic Trinity is the immanent Trinity") is beyond dispute, but the second half ("and vice versa," (*umgekehrt*) has to be clarified. Can the free mystery of the economy and the necessary mystery of the Tri-unity of God be identified? As the Fathers who fought against Arianism said, even if God's creatures did not exist, God would still be a Trinity of Father, Son and Spirit, since creation is an act of free will, whereas the procession of the persons takes place in accordance with nature *kata phusin*. In addition to this, is it true to say that God commits the whole of his mystery to and reveals it in his communication of himself?"[7]

The second reservation made by Fr. Congar is put thus: "God's communication of himself, as Father, Son and Holy Spirit, will not be a full self-communication until the end of time, in what we call the beatific vision. Thomas Aquinas' thesis on this matter is well known—he describes it as a vision without created *species*, that is, God himself as the objective form of our understanding. This is, however, an heroic, an almost untenable thesis, and it has been widely disputed."[8] Leaving aside the differences arising in this matter between east and west, the author goes on to develop his thought: "Here, however, we are above all concerned with the perception that God's communication of himself will be complete only in the eschatological era. This self-communication takes place in the economy in accordance with a rule of 'condescendence,' humiliation, ministry and 'kenosis.' We have therefore to recognize that there is a distance between the economic, revealed Trinity and the eternal Trinity. The Trinity is the same in each case and God is really communicated, but this takes place in a mode that is not connatural with the being of the divine persons. The Father is 'omnipotent,' but what are we to think of him in a world filled with the scandal of evil? The Son who is 'shining with his glory and the likeness of his substance,' is the Wisdom of God, but he is above all the wisdom of the cross and so difficult to recognize that blasphemy against him will be pardoned. Finally, the Spirit has no face and has often been called the unknown one."[9]

It may help to conclude with the measured judgment of the International Theological Commission (*qv*): "The Trinity was not simply brought about in the history of salvation by means of the Cross and Resurrection of Jesus Christ, as though an historical process were necessary for God to emerge as trinitarian. Therefore, the distinction must be maintained between the immanent Trinity, where liberty and necessity are the same thing in the eternal essence of God, and the Trinity of the economy of salvation, where God exercises his liberty absolutely, with no necessity arising from his nature. The distinction between the 'immanent' Trinity and the 'economic' Trinity is intrinsic to their real identity. It is not to be used as justifying new modes of separation, but is to be understood according to the way of affirmation, negation and eminence. God is beyond all divisions one might attribute to him. In the economy of salvation we see the eternal Son take on in his own life the 'kenotic' event of birth, of human life, and of the death on the cross. This event in which God reveals himself absolutely and definitively, affects in some way the being proper to God the Father, insofar as he is the kind of God who accomplishes these mysteries and really shares them as belonging to himself, together with the Son and the Holy Spirit. For not alone in the mystery of Jesus Christ does God the Father reveal and communicate himself to us freely and graciously through the Son and in the Holy Spirit; but also, the Father leads a trinitarian life with the Son and the Holy Spirit in a manner most profound and almost new, according to our way of speaking, insofar as the Father's relationship to the incarnate Son, in the communication of the gift of the Spirit, is the very relationship which constitutes the Trinity. In the intimate life of the triune God the very potential exists for the realization of these events, which, through the inexplicable freedom of God, take place for us in the history of salvation brought by our Lord Jesus Christ. These great events in the life of Jesus clearly make applicable to us, and make efficacious in a new way, the eternal word of generation, in which the Father says to the Son: 'You are my Son; this day I have begotten you' (Ps 2:7; cf. Acts 13:33; Heb 1:5; 5:5; Lk 3:22)".[10]

[1]Cf. bibliography to article Rahner, Karl; H. (Cardinal) de Lubac, S.J., "Trinité economique," in *La Foi chrétienne*, Paris, 1969, 55–83; P. Schoonenberg, "Trinität- der vollendete Bund. Thesen zur Lehre vom dreipersönlichen Gott," *Orientierung*, 37 (Zurich, 1973, 31 May), 115–117—sequel to *The Christ*, London, 1972; *id.*, "Continuïteit en herinterpretatie in de Drieëeheidsleer," *Tijdschrift voor Theologie*, 14, 1, 1974, 54–72; Mario de Franca Miranda, *O Misterio de Deus em nossa vida*, San Paolo, 1975; *ibid.*, preface by K. Rahner, 7–13; E. Jungel, "Das

Verhältnis von 'okonomischer' und 'immanenter' Trinität," *ZTK*, 72 (1975), 353–64; esp., G. Lafont, *Peut on connaître Dieu en Jésus Christ?*, Paris, 1969, 220–226; B. Rey, *RSPT*, (1970), 645; esp. Congar, *The Holy Spirit*, III, 11–18; W.J. Hill, *The Three-Personed God*, Washington, 1982, 178ff; H.U. von Balthasar, *Theodramatik* III, Einsiedeln, 1980, 297ff; W. Kasper, *Der Gott Jesu Christi*, Mainz, 1982, 333–336; R.A. Markus, "Trinitarian Theology and the Economy," *JTS* 9 (1958), 89–102; [2]*Encyclopaedia of Theology*, London, 1975, 1758; [3]*Ibid.*, 1766; [4]*Orientierung*, j.c., cp. *The Christ*, 85–86, n.16; [5]*Ibid.*; [6]*Ibid.*; [7]*The Holy Spirit*, III, 13; [8]*Ibid.*, 15; [9]*Ibid.*; [10]*DocCath* 1983, 121; *ITQ* 49(1982), 289, 90; see article International Theological Commission.

ECUMENISM

The ecumenical movement will gain from time to time by reflecting on what is commonly held in faith by all the Christian communions[1]—primarily the central mystery of the Christian faith, one God in three Persons. This belief is now integrated into the charter document of the World Council of Churches (*qv*).

Another striking demonstration of the unifying power of the Trinitarian doctrine was given at the third ecumenical encounter between the Council of European Bishops' Conferences and the Conference of European Churches at Trent in 1984. This time the theme was "Our Creed, Source of Hope." The position paper was a commentary on the Constantinopolitan Creed (*qv*). "We are able to make common confession of our faith in the triune God. Our risen Lord empowers us to do so in his commission: 'Go . . . and make disciples of all nations, baptizing them in the name of the Father and of the Son and of the Holy Spirit' (Mt 28:19). The Creed of Constantinople, in which we confess our faith in the triune God, itself goes back to the baptismal liturgy of the early Church. It was accepted by the whole Church in the year 451 at the ecumenical synod of Chalcedon, and is still in liturgical use today, if with varying frequency, in all the Orthodox churches, in the Roman Catholic Church, in the Anglican Communion and in the Churches of the Reformation. In this creed we confess our faith in God. We are seeking a common understanding of this creed. It is a bond uniting the divided Churches. These Churches which all confess the gospel to which the New Testament bears witness, are also able to recite the Creed of Constantinople together. Their enduring conviction that they are able to do this places upon them the forceful obligation to overcome those differences in their understanding of it which separate the Churches. These differences continue to the present day and are among the reasons for the continuing division between the Churches."

Noting that "the very antiquity" of the creed represents a "unique opportunity," the statement asserts that abandonment of "the tradition of the whole Church in an attempt to reformulate the Christian creed could threaten the basic and indispensable unity and coherence of the Christian faith at all times and in all places." "A reformulation of the universal creed on the basis of the apostolic faith" could be done only by a Council in which all the Churches would again take part—only such a body would have the right to do it. It is also noted that from ancient times the creed has been intimately connected with the sources of Christian unity "with baptism (*qv*) and with the eucharistic community"[2] (see EUCHARIST).

The statement enlarges on the subject of baptism: "Historically and materially, the one confession of faith in the triune God is rooted in the liturgy of the one *baptism*, which we celebrate in all our Churches and which unites us at a profound level, especially since we are united in our mutual recognition of it across all confessional boundaries. In baptism, God incorporates those baptized into the one body of Christ and in this way delivers them 'from the dominion of darkness and transfers us to the kingdom of his beloved Son, in whom we have redemption, the forgiveness of sins' (Col 1:13f). Baptism and the faith which issues in the confession of faith belong together. When we recite the creed, alone or in common worship, we renew our acceptance of baptism, encourage our sisters and brothers to enter into the faith and to join in its confession, and affirm the message which will shape our life and be the standard by which it is measured."[3]

The text of the creed chosen for commentary is the original one which did not have the *Filioque*, "who proceeds from the Father; with the Father and the Son he is worshipped and glorified." This is a reminder that the *Filioque* (*qv*) still stands as an obstacle to reunion between the Orthodox (*qv*) and the Catholic Church. A reading of recent Orthodox writing will show that the differences between their attitude to the Trinity and that of the western Christian communions demand serious consideration.[4] These differences are outlined forcibly in a paper read at a seminar on

Orthodox theology by Metropolitan Emilianos of Silibria, of the Ecumenical Patriarchate in Geneva: the seminar was held in the spring of 1983. He spoke of "the simplification of the doctrine of grace and the Holy Spirit by the equation of these two terms," thought that Latin thinking on the Redemption had been unduly influenced by juridical ideas, that the Latin attitude to the "world"—bearing with it," "traversing it" was a departure from the patristic ideal of *transfiguring* it, man acting as God's steward, invested with this potential because of God's *philanthropia*.

Such an opinion need not discourage ecumenists. It does show that the work of reconciliation in every sense of the term must proceed at the deepest level.

---

[1]Cf. T.F. Torrance, "Towards an Ecumenical Consensus on the Trinity," *Th. Zeitschrift* (Basel), 31 (1975), 337–350; J. Thompson, "The Holy Spirit and the Trinity in Ecumenical Perspective," *ITQ* 47 (1980) 272–285; [2]Text in *One in Christ*, 21 (1985), 83–96; separate issue, Ladywell Press, Godalming, Surrey; 86; [3]*Ibid.*, 95; [4]*One in Christ*, 21 (1985), 1–18.

ELIZABETH OF THE TRINITY, BLESSED
(1880–1906)

The young Carmelite of Dijon had a profound intuition on the relationship between her and the Trinity.[1] The focus of her attention was the indwelling (*qv*). Her reflections have theological substance as has her well-known prayer. Her beatification on 25 November, 1984 will have an effect on theologians as on the faithful, prompting an increase in the gathering effort to renew the theology of the Trinity.

E.'s ascent to the mystical heights was swift. At 14 she took a vow of virginity; at 19 she was reading—influenced in this by her mother—*The Way of Perfection* by St. Teresa of Avila; she entered Carmel 2 August, 1901 and was professed on 11 January, 1903 (the solemnity of the Epiphany). On 21 November, 1904 she felt during her renewal of her vows an irresistible movement of grace raising her to the Trinity. Returning to her cell, she wrote her prayer without a single correction. In the autumn of 1905 she found in St. Paul's writings her ultimate vocation of "the praise of the glory of the Trinity." She died 9 November, 1906.

From St. Teresa E. received a strong sense of God's presence within her. From Fr. G. Vallée, O.P. (1841–1927) came the conviction that this presence was Trinitarian. Then in the *Spiritual Canticle* and *The Living Flame of Love* of St. John of the Cross E. learned of the transformation of the soul into the three divine persons. She also realised in her short life the meaning of the "dark night." Though strongly attached to the magnificent passage on the Trinity which ends St. Catherine of Siena's (*qv*) *Dialogue*, she knew that she herself must "compose a more personal prayer"; she hoped she would be inspired to do so. This then happened and here is her prayer:

"O my God, Trinity whom I adore! Help me to become wholly forgetful of self, that I may be immovably rooted in you, as changeless and calm as though my soul were already in eternity. May nothing disturb my peace or draw me forth from you, but may I, at every moment, penetrate more deeply into the depths of your mystery!

"Establish my soul in peace; make it your heaven, your cherished abode, and the place of your rest. Let me never leave you alone, but remain wholly absorbed in you, in living faith, plunged in adoration, and wholly yielded up to your creative action.

"O my Christ whom I love! Crucified for love! Would that I might be the bride of your heart! Would that I might cover you with glory and love you even until I die of love. Yet I realize my weakness and beseech you to clothe me with yourself; possess me wholly; substitute yourself for me, that my life may be but a radiance of your life. Enter my soul as Adorer, as Restorer, as Saviour!

"O eternal Word, utterance of my God! I long to spend my life in listening to you; to become wholly teachable, that I may learn all from you! Through all darkness, all privations, all helplessness, I yearn to keep my eyes ever upon you and to dwell beneath your great light, O my beloved Star! So fascinate me that I may be unable to withdraw myself from your rays.

"O consuming fire, Spirit of love! Come down into me and reproduce in me, as it were, an incarnation of the Word that I may be to him a super-added humanity, wherein he may renew all his mystery! And you, O Father, bend down towards your poor little creature and overshadow her, beholding in her none other than your beloved Son in whom you are well pleased.

"O my Three, my All, my Beatitude, infinite Solitude, Immensity wherein I lose myself! I yield myself to you as your prey. Immerse yourself in me that I may be immersed in you, until I depart to contemplate in your light the abyss of your greatness."[2]

The personal papers of E., letters, retreat notes and similar material, have had a very wide audience. Coming in the wake of the worldwide interest and cult aroused by the personality of the other young French Carmelite, St. Thérèse of Lisieux, the Carmelite from Dijon while true to the tradition of the Order made a distinctive contribution to spirituality; this must be enhanced by her Beatification.

What we have in her slight but very precious corpus of writing is an existential highly persuasive statement of basic truths related to the life of grace (qv). She truly excels in the right proportions which her presentation of these ideas retains. The indwelling of the Holy Trinity was all-important: "The whole Blessed Trinity dwells in us, the whole of that mystery which will be our vision in heaven. Let it be our cloister. You tell me that your life is passed there. So is mine. I am 'Elizabeth of the Trinity,' that is: Elizabeth disappearing, losing herself, allowing herself to be invaded by the Three."[3]

Steeped in the writings of St. Paul, to whom she refers again and again, her Trinitarian outlook was matched by very strong Christocentrism: "Go on ordering your lives in Christ Jesus. I think this means to forsake self, forget about self, renounce self in order to enter more deeply into him with every passing minute; so to enter into him as to be rooted in him, and be able to challenge everything that happens with this proud boast: Who will separate us from the love of Christ? When the soul is thus deeply established in him, thus deeply rooted in him, the divine sap floods into her, and all that is imperfect, commonplace and natural in her life is destroyed. Then says the Apostle: 'Our mortal nature is swallowed up in life.' The soul thus stripped of self and clothed in Christ need no longer fear external contacts, nor interior difficulties, for, far from being an obstacle, they only root her more securely in love for her Master. No matter what happens, come what may, she continues to adore him for his own sake, because she is free, liberated from self and detached from everything."[4]

The passage gives an idea of the pure mystical sense of the writer; this is the voice of an authentic contemplative, one who was imbued with a conviction on the apostolic dimension to Carmelite spirituality. An apostolate wherein her spiritual advice would lead souls to God through interior silence and advertence to his presence: "It seems to me that in heaven my mission will be to attract souls by helping them to go out of themselves, in order to cling to God with a very simple and loving movement, and to keep them in the great interior silence which allows God to imprint himself on them, to transform them into himself."[5]

---

[1]Cf. M.M.Philipon, O.P. *DSp* 4, 590–94,; id., *La doctrine spirituelle de S. Elizabeth de la Trinité*, Paris, many editions, 11th 1955; English, *Sister Elizabeth of the Trinity, Spiritual Writings*, ed. M.M. Philipon, London, 1962; *Reminiscences*, tr. A Benedictine of Stanbrook Abbey, Cork, 1951; E. Vandeur, *O mon Dieu, Trinité que j'adore, Elevations*, many editions and translations; Hans Urs von Balthasar, *Elizabeth of Dijon*, London, 1956; *À la Trinité par l'Hostie, Elévations*, Maredsous, 1946; further bibliography *Carmelus*, Rome, 1955, n. 194–208, p. 327–28; *Revista di Vita spirituale*, 10 (1956), Rome, *Saggio bibliografico*, 135–168; [2]Translations by Carmelite Sisters; [3]*Spiritual Writings*, 54; [4]*Op. cit.*, 173; [5]*Op. cit.*, 122.

EPICLESIS

The word means "invocation" and is generally used for the invocation to obtain the sending of the Holy Spirit during the celebration of the Eucharist.[1] In its widest sense it can refer to any invoking of a divine name, such as is made in the sacraments of Baptism, Confirmation and Ordination, even at the blessing of a font. In the Eucharistic context it has four different purposes: a simple invocation; an invocation that God the Father send his Holy Spirit; an invocation that the Holy Spirit transform the bread and wine into the body and blood of Christ; an invocation that the Holy Spirit apply to the faithful the sanctifying effects of the Eucharist.

Different opinions are expressed about the reality of the epiclesis in the traditional Latin liturgy: there is no epiclesis; the *Quam oblationem* is an epiclesis; the *Supplices te rogamus* is an epiclesis; the laying on of hands is a silent epiclesis.

Epiclesis in the east has for a long time been considered vital and its force is, since the days of Nicholas Cabasilas, a subject of acute controversy. A recent Orthodox theologian, Paul Evdokimov, writes thus: "It would seem that, in the ecumenical dialogue, the question of the epiclesis is as important as that of the *Filioque* since it is above all in the light of the epiclesis that the *Filioque* can be correctly resituated within the whole problem."[2]

The eastern emphasis on the epiclesis springs from a different liturgical outlook, more Trinitarian than Christological as is the western; in the latter there is emphasis, at the moment of consecration, on the fact that the priest acts *in persona Christi*, and makes this his *intention*. Such a view meets this kind of response from an Orthodox theologian: "For the Latins, the *verba substantialia* of the consecration, the institutional words of Christ, are pronounced by the priest *in persona Christi*, which bestows on them a value that is immediately consecratory. For the Greeks, however, a similar definition of the priestly action—*in persona Christi*—which identifies the priest with Christ is absolutely unknown. Indeed, it is quite unthinkable. For them, the priest invokes the Holy Spirit precisely in order that the words of Christ, *reproduced and cited* by the priest, acquire all the effectiveness of the speech-act of God."[3]

Yet Fr. Congar, who quotes these words, has been able to align a number of quotations from easterns, beginning with John Chrysostom and Severus of Antioch and ending with Anthony Bloom, Mgr. Meletios and the agreed text of the Anglican-Orthodox Doctrinal Commission meeting in Moscow, 1976, all saying either verbally or equivalently that the priest acts *in persona Christi*. The great French Dominican suggests that the use of phrases like *sacerdos alter Christus* should not be careless: they refer to a functional, not an ontological or juridical reality.

Though for the easterns the coming of the Spirit determines the efficacy of the words spoken, this does not mean that the conversion of bread and wine into the body and blood of Christ only happens after the epiclesis has been spoken. It is important also to consider the anaphora as a totality, which is the eastern manner.

The General Instruction which introduced the reformed Roman Missal deals with the epiclesis as one of the elements of the Eucharistic Prayer, describing it thus: "In special invocations the Church calls on God's power and asks that the gifts offered by men may be consecrated, that is, become the body and blood of Jesus Christ and that the victim may become a source of salvation for those who are to share in communion."

Practical effect was given to this idea in drafting the three new Eucharistic Prayers. The words used before and after the Consecration are:

"II. Let your Spirit come upon these gifts to make them holy so that they may become for us the body and blood of Our Lord Jesus Christ . . . . May all of us who share in the body and blood of Christ be brought together in unity by the Holy Spirit.

"III. And so we bring you these gifts. We ask you to make them holy by the power of your Spirit that they may become the body and blood of your Son, Our Lord Jesus Christ, at whose command we celebrate this eucharist . . . . Grant that we who are nourished by his body and blood may be filled with his Holy Spirit and become one body, one spirit in Christ.

"IV. Father, may this Holy Spirit sanctify these offerings. Let them become the body and blood of Jesus Christ Our Lord, as we celebrate the great mystery which he left us as an everlasting covenant . . . . Lord, look upon this sacrifice which you have given to your Church, and by your Holy Spirit gather all who share this one bread and cup into the one body of Christ, a living sacrifice of praise."

Of these epicleses one may perhaps say that though praying for the coming of the Spirit, they are in composition markedly Trinitarian.

[1]Cf. J. Brinktine, *De Epiclesis Eucharistiae Origine*, Rome, 1923; J.W.Tyrer, "The Meaning of Epiklesis," *JTS* 25 (1923–24), 139–150; O. Casel, O.S.B., "Neuere Beitrage zur Epiklesenfrage," *Jahrbuch für Liturgiewissenschaft* 4 (1924), 173; E.G.C.F. Atchley, *On the Epiclesis in the Eucharistic Liturgy and in the Consecration of the Font*, Alcuin Club Collections, 31, 1935; M. Jugie, A.A., *De Forma Eucharistiae. De Epiclesibus Eucharisticis*, Rome, 1943; G. Dix, *The Shape of the Liturgy*, London, 1945; B. Botte, O.S.B., "L'Epiclèse de l'Anaphore d'Hippolyte," *RTAM* 14 (1947) 241–251; *id.* "L'Epiclèse dans les liturgies syriennes orientales," *Sacris Erudiri*, 6 (1954) 46–72; B. Capelle, O.S.B., "L'Anaphore de Serapion. Essai d'exégèse Muséon," 59 (1946), 425–443; =*Travaux liturgiques*, II, Louvain, 1962, 344–58; C. Kern, "En marge de l'epiclèse," 24 (1951) 166–94; G.S. Smit, "Epiclèse et théologie de l'anaphore selon les Pères de l'école d'Antioche," *L'Orient syrien*, 6 (1961), 385–412; J.M.R. Tillard, O.P., "L'Eucharistie et le Saint Esprit," *NRT* 90 (1968), 363–387; L. Bouyer, Cong. Or., *Eucharist: Theology and Spirituality of the Eucharistic Prayer*, Notre Dame, Ind., London, 1968; J.H. McKenna, C.M., *Eucharist and the Holy Spirit*, Alcuin Club Collections 57, 1976; W. Schneemelcher, *Die Epiklese bei den griechischen Vätern, Die Aufrufung des Heiligen Geistes im Abendmahl* (Beiheft zu ökumenischen Rundschau, 31, Frankfurt, 1977; D. Lallement, "Le Saint Esprit dans les prières eucharistiques nouvelles," in *Bienfaits spirituels de la nouvelle liturgie romaine de la Messe*, Paris, 1979, 35–46; P.-M. Gy, "Les paroles de la consécration et l'unité de la Prière eucharistique selon les théologiens de Pierre Lombard à S.Thomas d'Aquin," *Mélanges C.Vagaggini*, Rome, 1980, 189–201; esp. Congar, *The Holy Spirit*, III, 228–249; esp. S. Salaville, A.A., *DTC* V (1913), 194–300; F. Cabrol, O.S.B., *DACL* V, 1 (1922), 142–184, bibliography, 181–84; M. Jugie, A.A., *EC* V (1951), 409–413; J. Laager,

RAC V (1962), 583–599; ²*L'Esprit Saint dans la tradition ortho-doxe*, Paris, 1969, 101; ³Id., *L'Orthodoxie*, Paris, 1959, 250; ⁴*Op.cit.*, 237.

EUCHARIST, THE

"But the other sacraments, and indeed all ecclesiastical ministries and works of the apostolate are bound up with the Eucharist and are directed towards it. For in the blessed Eucharist is contained the whole spiritual good of the Church, namely Christ himself our Pasch and the living bread which gives life to men through his flesh—that flesh which is given life and gives life through the Holy Spirit."[1] At this centre of supernatural life, the soul meets the Holy Trinity in the most profound way. The encounter is not a pious figment. It takes its meaning from the full reality of the God-man and the import of his incarnation for revelation, for the redemption and renewal of mankind, in every phase of existence, personal and collective.

In the Eucharist as sacrifice much attention has been given to the Trinity in the official texts of the Church (see article Liturgy). There is need too for a fuller appreciation of the Trinitarian dimension of the Eucharist as sacrament. One important aspect of this subject is related to the *Epiclesis* (*qv*). All others arise out of the essential reality: Jesus Christ, the incarnate Son of God, is really present in the Sacrament of the Altar. The present author has prepared a large work in which this question is dealt with in every aspect.

[1]Vatican II, *Decree on the Ministry and Life of Priests*, art. 5; cf.

heresy, and exile at the hands of the emperors all made E's life difficult.

He is really known for the treatises written against him by two of the Cappadocians, Basil (*qv*) and Gregory of Nyssa (*qv*); in answer to his *Apology*, 360, Basil composed his *Adversus Eunomium* and to E's reply, in three books, Gregory answered with his *Contra Eunomium*. When E. addressed a Profession of Faith (*Ekthesis Pisteos*) to Emperor Theodosius, Gregory met it with his *Refutatio Confessionis Eunomii*. Most of E's works disappeared; the emperor Arcadius ordered them to be burned in 398.

E. was Anomoean in his theories: one single supreme Substance without any conceivable distinction of properties or attributes; the Son was not generated by the Father but produced; the Holy Spirit was the first creature made by the Son with the creative power he had received from the Father.

E. exemplifies the law of heresy: it is fatally but logically drawn to the extreme of self-destruction. The Anomoean extreme speaks of a Son unlike God the Father, which is to borrow the technique of analogy while rejecting its very meaning.[1]

[1]Works, PG XXX 835–68, fragments of the second reply in Gregory of Nyssa's *Contra Eunomium* in crit. ed. W. Jaeger, *Gregorii Nysseni Opera*, I–II, Leyden, 1960; *Ekthesis Pisteos*, PG 67, 587–90; cf. J. (Cardinal) Daniélou, S.J., "Eunome l'Arien et l'exégèse neo-platonicienne du Cratyle," *Rev. des Et. Grecq.*, 69 (1956), 412–32; A. Benito y Durán, "El nominalismo arriano y la filosofia cristiana: Eunomio y San Basilio," *Augustinus*, 5 (1960), 207–26; M. Spanneut, *DHGE* XV, 1399–1405; X. le Bachelet, *DTC* V, 2, 1501–14; L. Abramowski, *RAC* VI (1966), 936–47; Quasten III, 306–9, bibl.; V. de Clercq, *NCE* V, 631.

EUNOMIUS (d. 394)

Born in Cappadocia, E. became at Alexandria a pupil and secretary of Aetius, the extreme Arian leader. With Aetius he went to Antioch, where he was ordained deacon. Basil of Ancyra, in favour with Constantius (*qv*), denounced E. together with Aetius and Eudoxius—sponsor of an Arian Synod in Antioch—for conspiracy. They were sent into exile, but on the fall of Basil Eudoxius returned as Bishop of Constantinople and E. was made Bishop of Cyzicus, which office he accepted on condition that Aetius be rehabilitated. An early resignation due to clerical opposition, delation for

EUSEBIUS OF CAESAREA (c. 260–c.340)

The father of church history, Bishop of Caesarea from 315, E. had theological interests without genius, was entangled in different phases of the Arian crisis.[1] He was of the intellectual lineage of Origen (*qv*). An example of his thinking before Nicaea (*qv*): "The Son was begotten, but not in the sense that at first he did not exist, and then came into existence: he existed before all time, proceeding from, and always present to the Father. He is not unbegotten, but begotten, the only-begotten Son of the unbegotten Father. He is from God, is God's Word, and is himself God. He was produced not by any kind of division of the Father's substance; but from all the aeons of eternity, or rather, before all the aeons of eternity, he was born, in a manner which is beyond the power of words to express or of thought to conceive, of the ineffable and incomprehensible will and power of the Father."[2]

In a letter to a certain Euphratio written about 318, E., drawing on Johannine texts, speaks of the Father as distinct from the Son but greater than him (14:28), the only true God (17:3), though the Son is also God (1:1). He adds the Pauline ideas of the Son as the image of the one true God (Col 1:15), as one mediator between God and man (1 Tim 2:5). The Father and the Son are not then, he thinks, strictly simultaneous; the Father exists before the Son—this he thinks must be if the Father is to be Father and first, unbegotten. If they were simultaneous, they would both be unbegotten or begotten.

E. was present at the synod of Antioch in 325; he was censured as suspect of heresy and warned. He was present at the Council of Nicaea and deals with the event in his *Life of Constantine*, which is generally an uncritical eulogy. He speaks of a bishop, presumably himself, who rose to address the emperor and make a short speech "in a strain of thanksgiving to Almighty God on his behalf."[3] He had described the emperor as "like some heavenly messenger of God," adding a string of superlatives. He reproduces the text of the emperor's opening speech.[4]

A more important point is E's contribution, if any, to the creed of Nicaea. In his letter after the Council, written to his flock to explain why he had accepted the council creed, he says that he felt "obliged to transmit to you, first, the formula of faith presented by ourselves, and next, the second, which (the Fathers) put forth with some additions to our words." What he read out was the creed of Caesarea and he notes that it was well received, especially by the emperor: "He confessed, moreover that such were his own sentiments, and he advised all present to agree with it, and to subscribe its articles and to assent to them, with the insertion of the single word, *homoousios*, which moreover he interpreted as not in the sense of the affections of bodies, nor as if the Son subsisted from the Father in the way of division, or any severance."[5]

The creed which E. read was: "We believe in one God, the Father Almighty, the Maker of all things visible and invisible. And in one Lord Jesus Christ, the Word of God, God from God, Light from Light, Life from Life, Son only-begotten, first-born of every creature, before all ages, begotten from the Father, by whom all things were made; who for our salvation was made flesh, and lived among men, and suffered, and rose again the third day, and ascended to the Father, and will come again in glory to judge the quick and dead. And we believe also in one Holy Ghost."[6]

A further passage of belief was added to this formula. Why did E. read it out? Was it to clear himself of the kind of suspicion raised at Antioch? Or as a basis for possible agreement? He accepted the Nicene creed, but scarcely through conviction. He was then involved in the post-Nicene quarrels: accused by Eusthatius of Antioch of opposition to it he countered with an allegation that Eusthatius was Sabellian, though his main grievance may have been that his critic was anti-Origen—he did more than connive at the expulsion of his opponent from Antioch, though he refused to replace him there, a decision which won the emperor's praise. Next E. had a running battle with Athanasius (*qv*). The latter refused an imperial invitation to a council at Caesarea, for he distrusted E. The latter was still his judge when the council met at Tyre. E. was here taunted for his conduct under persecution. Athanasius went to Constantinople to appeal directly to the emperor in 335. He was exiled, as was Marcellus of Ancyra. Against the latter E. then wrote two works, *Contra Marcellum*, two parts, and *De Ecclesiastica theologia*, three parts. In the first he defends the Arian leaders, chiefly Asterius and Eusebius of Nicomedia, from the attacks of Marcellus and by quotations from the latter's own works tries to convict him of Sabellianism. In the second he puts forward a *Logos* (*qv*) doctrine which amounts to subordinationism (*qv*).

The Son of God is not, he thought, of the essence of the Father; he is born of his free will. The Holy Spirit is no more than a creation of the Son. He feared that to recognise the true divinity of the Son would compromise the oneness of the divinity. In a passage like the following he reveals the influence of Origen: "We are constrained to acknowledge a single divine reality transcending all things, which is ineffable, good, simple, not composite, and one in form. This is God-himself, mind-itself, word-itself, wisdom-itself, light-itself, life-itself, the beautiful-itself, the good-itself, and whatever else anyone might think of, greater than these things, and indeed away beyond the power of any mind to conceive or words to express. We acknowledge also his Son, his only begotten, born of the Father as the Father's image, in all things most like to him who begot him.[7] Though he declares the Son God he does not say he is consubstantial with the Father. Nowhere in the two works does the word occur.

---

[1]Works, PG 19–24; GCS 1902ff—9 vols; Eng. tr., Eccl. Hist., K. Lake, J.E.L. Oulton, Loeb, 2 vols, 1926–32; of GCS ed. H.J. Lawlor, J.E.L. Oulton, 2 vols, 1927, 28; R.J. Ferrari, *Fathers of the Church*, Washington, 19, 29, 1953, 1955; French tr. G. Bardy (*qv*), SC 31, 41, 55, 73; cf. J. Stevenson, *Studies in Eusebius*, 1929; id., *NCE* V, (1967) 633–636; H. Berkhof, *Die Theologie des Eusebius von Caesarea*, Amsterdam, 1929; M. Weis, *Die Stellung des Eusebius von Caesarea im arianischen Streit*, 1920; H.G. Opitz, "Eusebius von Caesarea als Theolog," *ZNTW*, 34 (1935), 1–19; J.N.D. Kelly, *Doctrines*; J.R. Laurin, *Orientations maîtresses des Apologistes chrétiens de 270 à 361*, Rome, 1954, 94–145, 344–401; K.M. Setton, *Christian Attitudes towards the Emperor in the fourth century*, New York, 1941; D.S. Wallace-Hadril, *Eusebius of Caesarea*, London, 1960; C. Luibheid, *Eusebius of Caesarea and the Arian Crisis*, Dublin, 1981; J. Moreau *DHGE* XV (1963), 1437–60; [2]*Demonstratio evangelii*, IV, PG 22, 257; [3]*H.E.*, III, 11, LNPF, N.S., I, 522; [4]*H.E.*, III, 10, *ibid.*; [5]LNPF, IV, 75; [6]*Ibid.*; [7]De Eccl. Theol. II, 14, PG 24, 928.

EUSEBIUS OF NICOMEDIA (d. c. 342)

The principal, most influential supporter of Arius (*qv*) and opponent of Athanasius (*qv*), E. presents an instructive example, the earliest, of a bishop drawing on the civil power to further his theological opinions, hoping even to achieve their triumph over the Church's official teaching.[1] One man defeated the combined forces, Athanasius.

With Arius E. had been a student under St. Lucian of Antioch (*qv*). He was appointed bishop of Berytus in Phoenicia, and was later promoted to the capital city Nicomedia. He enjoyed the favour of the emperor Licinius and his wife Constantia, sister of Constantine. When the latter, having defeated Licinius, entered Nicomedia in 324, E. was spared in the reprisals through the influence of Constantia. Soon he had Constantine's ear and the letter sent to Alexander of Alexandria (*qv*) and Arius by the emperor may have been inspired by E.

When Arius was condemned by Alexander he was welcomed by E., who in a synod held in Bithynia tried to nullify the decision of the synod of Alexandria. He sent many letters to his fellow bishops defending Arius.

At the council of Nicaea E. caused dismay by the formulary he put forward. But he signed the Nicene creed, at Constantine's request or possibly also on the advice of Constantia; he withdrew his assent three months later and was sent into exile. But about 328 he had satisfied Constantine on his opinion and returned.

E. now set to work to undo Nicaea by a different means. He aimed at unseating from their bishoprics the principal supporters of the doctrine. The first victim was Eustathius of Antioch. He was deposed by a council in 331—there was a strong pro-Arian faction in the city used by E. to secure his objective. Opposition was silenced by the exile of Eustathius. Paulinus of Tyre, one of the few bishops who at Nicaea had openly defended Arius, was elected bishop. He died within months and then something ominous happened: the new bishop, for the first time in history, was a nominee of the emperor, E. aiding and abetting.

E. then attacked the citadel of orthodoxy directly. He wrote to Athanasius, inviting him to open his church to the friends of Arius. Athanasius explained that this was impossible, since they were under the anathema of Nicaea. Then came a letter from the emperor himself, threatening to depose the bishop of Alexandria if he did not comply. Athanasius resisted the pressure and some time later, events being complicated by another dispute at Alexandria—the Meletian schism—he had to appear before the emperor and then before his brother to answer grossly slanderous charges; he defended himself successfully, clearing himself of the charge that he had murdered a bishop by producing the bishop in person.

E., on imperial orders, had to postpone a council at Caesaraea. He then instigated one at Tyre (335) and there Athanasius was condemned and deposed. Despite an appeal to Constantine E. was able to sway the course of justice and Athanasius was banished to the end of the world, Treves.

The triumph of E. and his followers, Eusebians, was to be sealed by the reception of Arius back into the Church. This was done by the bishops meeting under the presidency of E. in Jerusalem, where they had gone from Tyre to mark the consecration of the Constantinian basilica built on the site of the Lord's tomb. For the official, ceremonial reception, Constantinople was chosen for tactical reasons—Alexandria was rioting against the heretic. This he still was despite the letter sent to the emperor professing his faith, a cunning document (see ARIUS). The imperial city was in upheaval too, with Catholics besieging heaven to avert the calamity. On the eve of the proposed ceremony there was an unexpected denouement as Athanasius relates (attributing the story to an eye-witness): "When he (Arius) thus came forth from the presence of the emperor, Eusebius and his fellows, with their accustomed violence, desired to bring him into the Church. But Alexander, the bishop of Constantinople of blessed memory, resisted them, saying that the inventor of the heresy ought not to be admitted to communion; whereupon Eusebius and his fellows threatened, declaring, 'As we have caused him to be invited by the Emperor, in opposition to your wishes, so to-morrow, though it be contrary to your desire, Arius shall have communion with us in this Church.' It was the Sabbath when he said this. When the Bishop Alexander heard this, he was greatly distressed, and entering the church, he stretched forth his hands unto God, and bewailed himself; and casting himself upon his face in the chancel, he prayed lying upon the pavement. Macarius also was present, and prayed with him, and heard his words. And he besought these two things, saying, 'If Arius is brought to communion to-morrow, let me thy servant depart, and destroy not the pious with the impious; but if thou wilt spare thy Church (and I know thou wilt spare) look upon the words of Eusebius and his fellows, and give not thine inheritance to destruction and reproach, and take off Arius, lest if he enter into the Church, the heresy also may seem to enter with him, and henceforth impiety be accounted for piety.'"[2]

The account closes with the sudden death of Arius, that is, before he could be received back into the Church. It is a striking instance of what strange circumstances marked the struggle for truth in Trinitarian theology. Constantine died the following year, 337, having been baptized by Eusebius some days before his death. In that year too a strong man, St. Julius, became Pope. E. had himself transferred to Constantinople. He presided at the Dedication Council in Antioch, 341. He died the following year.

E's career as thus completed has been a subject of condemnation by adherents of orthodoxy from St. Alexander of Alexandria and St. Athanasius down to every present-day writer on the history of theology. Has he been the victim of apologetics? Was he in truth an Arian? Examples of what Alexander wrote about him are: "But seeing that Eusebius, now of Nicomedia, who thinks that the government of the Church rests with him, because retribution has not come upon him for his desertion of Berytus, when he had cast an eye of desire on the Church of the Nicomedians, begins to support these apostates and has taken upon himself to write letters everywhere in their behalf, if by any means he may draw in certain ignorant persons to this most base and antichristian heresy; I am therefore constrained, knowing what is written in the law, no longer to hold my peace but to make it known to you all; that you may understand who the apostates are, and the cavils which their heresy has adopted, and that, should Eusebius write to you, you may pay no attention to him, for he now desires by means of these men to exhibit anew his old malevolence, which has so long been concealed, pretending to write in their favour while in truth it clearly appears that he does it to forward his own interests."[3] "And we have made known this to your piety, dearly beloved and most honoured fellow-ministers, in order that should any of them have the boldness to come unto you, you may not receive them, nor comply with the desire of Eusebius, or any other person writing in their behalf. For it becomes us who are Christians to turn away from all who speak or think anything against Christ, as being enemies of God and destroyers of souls;"[4]

Athanasius suffered much from E. Is his testimony for that reason to be dismissed or taken lightly? E. did not scruple to use the imperial power against his brother bishop. Examples of the latter's opinion of E: "Upon learning this (the emergence of the Meletians again), Eusebius who had the lead in the Arian heresy sends and buys the Meletians with large promises, becomes their secret friend, and arranges with them for their assistance on any occasion when he might wish for it. At first he sent to me, urging me to admit Arius and his fellows to communion, and threatened me in his verbal communications, while in his letters he (merely) made a request. And when I refused, declaring that it was not right that those who had invented heresy contrary to the truth and had been anathematized by the Ecumenical Council should be admitted to communion, he caused the Emperor also, Constantine of blessed memory, to write to me, threatening me, in case I should not receive Arius and his fellows, with those afflictions which I have before undergone, and which I am still suffering. The following is part of his letter. Syncletius and Gaudentius, officers of the palace, were the bearers of it. 'Having therefore knowledge of my will, grant free admission to all who wish to enter into the Church. For if I learn that you have hindered or excluded any who claim to be admitted into communion with the Church, I will immediately send some one who shall depose you by my command, and shall remove you from your place."[5]

On the Council of Sardica Athanasius writes thus: "For what the heretical party of Eusebius and heirs of Arius have maintained and spread abroad, all the bishops who assembled have pronounced false and fictitious."[6] An excerpt on E's influence: "Men who have been promoted by E. and his fellows for advocating this Antichristian heresy, venture to define articles of faith, and while they ought to be brought to judgment as criminals, like Caiaphas, they take upon themselves to judge. They compose a Thalia, and would have it received as a standard of faith, while they are not yet determined what they believe."[7]

As to E's theological opinion, the text invoked to reveal it is his letter to Paulinus of Tyre: "We have never heard that there are two unbegotten beings, nor one divided in two. We have never learned nor believed, master, that this being experienced anything corporeal. Rather there is one who is unbegotten and one brought to being by him, not, however, from his own substance. He (i.e. the begotten one) is entirely without share in the unbegotten or its substance. He has come to being as one entirely distinct in nature and power. In character and power he is completely like the one who made him. We believe that his beginning is not only inexpressible but is incomprehensible to the intelligence of man as much as of every superior to man. We say this, not by advancing our own process of reasoning, but as things we have learned from holy scripture. We have learned that he was created, established and begotten in respect of his being but of immutable and unspeakable nature like the one who made him. As the Lord himself said 'God created me, the beginning of his ways. Before time he established me. Before the hills he begot me.' He would not have been described as created or established if he were from him, that is, if he were from him by way of being a part of him or an effluence of

his being. You yourself, my lord, are not unaware of this. For that which proceeds from the unbegotten would neither be created nor established either by him or by another, since he would come forth as one who was unbegotten from the beginning.

"But if the description of him as begotten gives some grounds for saying that he came to be from the being of his father and has thereby the same nature, we recognise that scripture does not speak of him alone as begotten but also of things entirely dissimilar to by nature. Of man it is said: 'I have begotten and brought up sons and they have rebelled against me' and 'You have forgotten God who begot you' and elsewhere 'Who begot the drops of dew?' This is not the description of a nature derived from the divine nature but rather of the fact that everything was formed according to his will. There is nothing which is formed from his substance. Each and everything, in coming into being, has done so by his will. He is God, and as for the likeness to him all things would be so through a logos, and all would come to be by his will. All things were made by God through the Son."[8]

The ideas here would correspond broadly with those of Arianism (qv). Whether their force may be attenuated by circumstances, by the need to nourish a continuing debate, or by anxiety felt about the word homoousios (qv) is problematic. What is clear is that we have no text showing that Eusebius ever fully rallied to the teaching of Nicaea, nor any hint that such a statement of acceptance ever existed.

[1]Works: *Athanasius Werke*, III, 1, 15–17, 65–66; cf. A. Lichtenstein, *Eusebius von Nikomedien*, Halle, 1903; G. Bardy, *Recherches sur S.Lucien d'Antioche et sur son école*, Paris, 1936, 296–315; G. Bareille, *DTC* 5,2, 1539–51; M. Spannent *DHGE* 15, 1466–71; Quasten 3, 190–93; V.C. De Clercq, *NCE*, 5, 636; C. Luibheid, "The Arianism of Eusebius of Nicomedia," *I.TheolQuart.*, 43 (1976), 3–23; [2]Athanasius, *Letter to Serapion*, NPNF IV, 565; [3]Encyclical Letter of Alexander, *ibid.*, 69, 70; [4]*ibid.*, 71; [5]Athanasius, *Apologia contra Arianos*, 59, *ibid.*, 131,2; [6]Athanasius, *Letter to the Church of Alexandria, ibid.*, 555; [7]Athanasius, *Ad episcopos Aegypti*, 7, *ibid.*, 226; [8]Theodoret, HE, I, 5; PG 82, 914; *Athanasius Werke*, III, 16, tr. C. Luibheid, *op.cit.*

EUSEBIUS OF VERCELLI (d. 371)
E., anti-Arian, born in Sardinia, bishop from 340, was a representative of Pope Liberius to Constantius, 354, defended Athanasius (qv) at the Synod

of Milan, 355, and was exiled in consequence (see article Lucifer of Cagliari).[1] He benefitted by the general release in the reign of Julian, 362. E. is the author of three extant letters and his editor, V. Bulhart, thinks that he is also the author of a *De Trinitate* in seven books entitled as follows: I. *De unitate Trinitatis*; II. *De propriis personis et de unito nomine divinitates*; III. *De assumptione hominis*; IV. *Adversus novellas hereses Potent*; V. *De unita ac sempiterna substantia Trinitatis hic contradicentis persona est arriomanitarum*: VI. *De beatitudine Fidei et de praescriptione sectae pessimae*; VII. *De professione regulae catholicae cum increpatione hereticae*.

This work was for long attributed to Athanasius (*qv*). The attribution to E. has not been universally accepted.

---

[1]Crit. ed. V. Bulhart, CCSL IX, 1957; cf. C.H. Turner, "On Eusebius of Vercelli," *JTS* 1 (1899–1900), 126–28; E. Dekkers, O.S.B., *Clavis Patrum Latinorum*, ed 2, 24f (Nos 105–111), Altaner-Stuiber, 1966, 366f; V.C. de Clercq, *DHGE* XV (1963), 1477–83 bibl.

EXPERIENCE OF THE TRINITY

There are distinct aspects to the problem of experience in regard to the Trinity, granted the reality of the divine indwelling.[1] One is the possibility of experience and the identification of its happening; the other is the ability to describe what has taken place at the level of experience. Possibly some who have deep direct awareness of the reality either have not the literary skill or the wish to disclose what they have passed through to others. Certain truths are agreed. The indwelling is primarily a matter of faith. The capacity to register it with a sense of personal awareness, and this beyond reasonable doubt, does not appear to follow immediately and certainly from the reality. There is not a fixed moment when the experience would be known. There are for adults certain moments of an identifiably religious kind, for example conversion to a religious faith, recovery of lost faith. It is practically impossible to pass through such change without knowing at the level of experience what one has been through. With entry on the state of grace (*qv*) the soul becomes the temple of God, who comes to abide in it, but without marking his presence in a way open to the soul's direct perception.

What mystical literature does show is that those who have advanced notably on the way of mysticism (*qv*), passing through the classic ordeals, purifying phases, dark night of the senses, of the spirit, may then be the recipients of a direct experiential knowledge. It is a special grace, God's free gift. It was clearly given to St. Teresa of Avila and to Blessed Mary of the Incarnation; very probably also enjoyed by Blessed Elizabeth of the Trinity. But if this direct experience is not universally shared, there are indirect manifestations of God's presence more widely known. Of these the principal is true interior peace.

---

[1]Cf. *DSp*, "Expérience mystique de l'inhabitation," 7, 1757–1767 (Guy-M. Bertrand); *Connaissance mystique de Dieu, ibid.*, 3, 915–920; A. Garcia Evangelista, "La experiencia mistica de la inhabitación," *Archivo teologico granadino*, 16 (1953), 63–326; Ermanno del SS Sacramento, "Le settime mansioni," in *Santa Teresa, maestra di orazione*, Rome, 1963, coll. *Fiamma viva* 4, 221–242; H. Cuzin, *Du Christ à la Trinité d'après l'expérience mystique de Marie de l'Incarnation*, Lyons, 1936; N. Molloy, O.P., "The Trinitarian Mysticism of St. Thomas," *Angelicum*, 58 (1981), 373–388.

F

FAITH OF CHRIST, THE?

The suggestion that Jesus Christ possessed the theological virtue of faith will appear a surprising novelty to many, not only those who have completed their theology for some decades.[1] Yet the idea which appeared in some brief isolation towards the end of the last century, being eventually traced to the early eighteenth, has been revived, and so is the subject of an essay by Hans Urs Von Balthasar. J. Haussleiter maintained that the NT phrase *the faith of Jesus Christ* must, at least in the Epistle to the Romans, mean the faith of Jesus Christ: it must be taken in its subjective meaning. He adduced these reasons: when Paul spoke of *the faith of Jesus* (Rom 3:22) the early Christians would not have understood this as faith *in* Jesus, for they believed that he had become Christ and Lord only after his resurrection; the parallel expression in Rom 4:16, *the faith of Abraham* must be given the subjective sense; Paul deliberately uses *the faith of Jesus* to show the faith which Jesus had during his mortal life—still putting Jesus before Christ when he used the two words, Rom 3:22.[2]

Haussleiter sought to reinforce his thesis in a second article; he used a dissertation which he had discovered in the University of Greifswald, 29 August, 1704, by a certain Ritter who as his title shows defended the idea of Christ's subjective faith, *De fide Christi, sive utrum Christus habuerit*

fidem?; he appealed to four Protestant theologians in support of his thesis.

Haussleiter met criticism.[3] G. Kittel alone shared his view, at least thought his opinion probable. The general consensus of scholars, irrespective of religious affiliation, disagreed. The reasons for rejecting the opinion are solid: the NT never uses the verb "to believe" of Christ—Heb 12:2, "the pioneer (*archegos*) and perfecter of our faith does not imply subjective faith; many texts present Christ as an object of faith (Gal 2:16; Col 2:5; Philem 5); Jesus is also an object of faith (Rom 10:9; 1 Cor 12:3; 2 Cor 4:5, 14); elsewhere in the NT faith of Christ means faith *in* Christ (James 2:1; Rev 2:13; 14:12), as faith of God is faith *in* God in Mk 11:22 and also in Philo and the Talmud. When Paul speaks of faith in the gospel (Phil 1:27), in the truth (2 Thess 2:13), in the power of God (Col 2:12), he uses the genitive "of" in each case.

Hans Urs Von Balthasar widens the whole concept of faith to escape the rigid conclusion of St. Thomas, which he recalls: since Christ had the beatific vision from the first moment of his existence, since he saw what was divine, he could not believe in it.[4] Von Balthasar thinks of the faith of the Old Testament, the faith at the heart of the ancient covenant, *fidelitas Dei*, as evoking a similar response. After a long development he can write that "when the Word of God becomes man the *fides Dei*, God's faithfulness to mankind, is embodied in him." "He answers God with a faith which gathers together the whole faith of mankind, exalting it to establish it at its source so as to become the incarnate covenant of mankind with God."[5]

This is an interesting perspective, but is beyond the context and meaning which for most people "faith of Christ" would have. The subject is relevant to Trinitarian theology for the question arises: Did Christ reveal the Trinity? Did he believe in it and, if he did, on what authority? From whom did he learn it? The debate about his faith is thus confronted with a problem, a set of problems, which are not often mentioned. One is forced back to consider the content of his faith, the motive of credibility, the sources of divine revelation in his case, the grounds on which he based his right to teach others without reservation or reliance on others. So, many epistemological questions are not considered and not answered by those who maintain that he was a man of faith: and there are many others.

---

[1]F. Prat, S.J., *The Theology of St. Paul*, London, 1945, Detached Notes V, "Faith" in St. Paul, 448–455; H. Urs von Balthasar, *La Foi du Christ*, Paris, 1968; J. Sobrino, S.J., *Christology at the Crossroads*, London, 1976, 79–139; [2]J. Haussleiter, "Der Glaube Jesu Christi und der Christ. Glaube; ein Beitrag zur Erklärung des Römerbriefs, *Neue Kirchl. Zeitschrift*, 2 (1891) 109–145, 205–230; "Eine theol. Disputation über den Glauben Jesu," *Neue Kirchl. Zeitschrift*, 2 (1891), 507–520; [3]Hilgenfeld, *Zeitschrift für wissensch. Theol.* 35, 391; cf. G. Kittel in *Stud. und Krit.*, 79 (1906), 419–436; [4]St. Thomas, III, q.7, a.3; [5]*Op.cit.*, 77.

FATHER, GOD THE

In Christian tradition the name of the first person of the Trinity.[1] How did the idea emerge? The mythology of the ancient Near East fostered the notion that the deity is the father of men or of certain categories of men. A divine ancestor is often found at the origin of tribes, families, peoples. The king, as representative of the people, gathers the privilege to his person. "Father" in this world especially denotes authority, authority unchallenged. Texts from Sumerian-Accadian and Sumerian-Babylonian sources testify to the belief. God holds authority and exercises mercy.

Thus too he is seen in the OT. The word "Father" is found only fourteen times in all, but each time with some significance. He is Creator: "Is he not your father, who created you, who made you and established you?" (Deut. 32:6). "Have we not all one father? Has not one God created us?" (Mal 2:10). He is merciful too: "As a father pities his children, so the Lord pities those who fear him. For he knows our frame; he remembers that we are dust" (Ps 103:13f).

There are important differences in the OT from the Near Eastern mythologies. There is never reference to God as a direct physical ancestor, one who begets. The divine fatherhood is, moreover, towards Israel as God's special elect: "For you are a people holy to the Lord your God, and the Lord has chosen you to be a people for his own possession, out of all the peoples that are on the face of the earth" (Deut 14:2). "And you shall say to Pharaoh. 'Thus says the Lord, Israel is my first-born son, and I say to you, "Let my son go that he may serve me'; if you refuse to let him go, behold I will slay your first-born son'" (Ex 4:22, 23). "I am a father to Israel, and Ephraim is my first-born " (Jer 31:9).

What is entirely distinctive is the unique saving act of God on which Israel's sonship is based, the exodus from Egypt. All subsequent history is conditioned by this event. The sonship arising out of it recalls an experience of the divine.

A recurring theme in the prophetic literature is Israel's ingratitude (Jer 3:4; 19; Mal 1:6; 2:10). She answers the call to repentance with a cry for mercy and forgiveness, very poignant in Third Isaiah (Is 63:15,16; 64:8,9). God's answer is pardon (Hos 11:3,8; Jer 3:22; 31:19,20). But always it is fatherly compassion to the community, the corporate entity of Israel, God's people.

The restriction in the idea of fatherhood to the people is strong in attitudes of prayer. "To date," says J. Jeremias, "nobody has produced a single instance in Palestinian Judaism where God is addressed as 'my Father' by an individual person." Two verses in Sirach 23 seem to be exceptions to this generalization: "O Lord, Father and Ruler of my life, do not abandon me to their council and let me not fall because of them." "O Lord, Father and God of my life, do not give me haughty eyes, and remove from me evil desire." (23:1,4). The verses are extant in Greek only and in the present century a Hebrew paraphrase was found which reads differently, "O God of my father"; this was most probably the original form, and may have derived from Ex 15:2, "The Lord is my strength and my song, and he has become my salvation; this is my God and I will praise him, my Father's

God and I will exalt him." This kind of designation is found elsewhere. Jeremias concludes: "This means that there is no evidence so far that in Palestinian Judaism of the first millennium anyone addressed God as 'my Father'."[2]

The advent of God's Son on earth would change entirely the focus of the word and idea of Father. NT unfolds the mystery steadily and fully. Jesus speaks constantly of the Father, not often of God. In Matthew alone he speaks of "my Father" six times (15:13; 16:17; 18:10,19,35; 20:23). In Mt 11:25–27 = Lk:10:21f, he emphasizes the difference between the Father's self-revelation to him and to others: these cannot receive it. In the many references to his Father in John he affirms his exclusive share in the Father's love (3:35; 5:20; 10:17) and his uniquely privileged knowledge of him (1:18; 6:46; 10:15). He and the Father are one (10:30); to know and to see him is to see the Father (14:7–9); he is in the Father and the Father is in him (10:38; 14:10). God the Father is invoked in the exordium of each of the 13 epistles attributed to St. Paul. The Father is the Father of our Lord Jesus Christ (2 Co 1:3; Gal 1:1; Eph 1:3; Col 1:3).

This plenary revelation was the basis of all the theological speculation which followed, especially from second century preoccupation with the *Logos* (*qv*) and subsequent controversy over the consubstantial (*qv*) Son and the coequal Spirit, on to the Trinitarian systems outlined in the east, formally articulated in the west.

We still await a fully satisfying synthesis which will combine creatively all the insights of early times on the Monarchia, all manifold fruits of Christian experience of God the Father. K. Rahner was searching for the deepest insight into NT witness when he proposed that "God" means Father.

---

[1]Cf. bibl to articles Logos, Missions, Properties, and Son of God; also articles in biblical dictionaries s.v. Father. M.-J. Le Guillou, *Le Mystère du Père*, Paris, 1973; A. de Villamonte, *El Padre plenitud fontal de la deidad, S.Bonaventura 1274–1974*, Grottaferrata, Rome, 1974; K. Rahner, "Theos in the New Testament," Theological Investigations I, 79–148; L. Bouyer, *Le Père Invisible*, Paris, 1976; Y.M.-J. Congar, O.P., *The Father, the Absolute Source of Divinity, The Holy Spirit* III, 133–143; [2]*The Central Message of the New Testament*, London, 1965, 16ff with reference to J. Marcus, "A fifth century MS of Ben Sira," *Jewish Quarterly Review* 21 (1930), 238.

FILIOQUE ("And from the Son")
These words, added to the Constantinopolitan creed (*qv*) after "proceeding from the Father" in the Latin church and the communions dependent on it, have become, with the passage of time, a focus of bitter dissension and controversy.[1] The subject is in the forefront of dialogue in the ecumenical climate which followed Vatican II (*qv*). With the papacy and the epiclesis (*qv*) it is a point where views diverge between Catholics and Orthodox.

Theology
Once the concept of procession (*qv*) is introduced to Trinitarian theology, the question is how one of the three proceeds from another. Theological reflection is agreed that the Son and the Spirit proceed; the Father does not. The Son proceeds from the Father by generation (*qv*), as his only begotten; the Spirit also proceeds from the Father. Only from the Father or conjointly from the Father and the Son? This is the question of Double Procession.

The biblical evidence is slight, mostly from St. John: "But when the Counsellor comes, whom I shall send to you from the Father, even the Spirit of truth, who proceeds from the Father, he will bear witness to me" (15:26). "He (the Spirit of truth) will glorify me, for he will take what is mine and declare it to you" (16:14). In the first of these texts it is clear that the Spirit proceeds from the Father, as it is clear that he is sent by the Son. In the second text a very close relationship between the Spirit and the Son is described. That he proceeds from the Father and the Son is not stated explicitly; but what is said is in harmony with this truth.

"I and the Father are one," said Jesus (Jn 10:30). If to this is added the word in Jn 20:22 the *Filioque* may seem to be implied: "And when he had said this, he breathed on them, and said to them: 'Receive the Holy Spirit.'"

The Spirit is named third, equal to the others in the baptismal formula in Mt 28:19; but there is no hint there of procession. Some other texts are mentioned as possibly suggesting the double procession: "And because you are sons, God has sent the spirit of his Son into our hearts crying, 'Abba, Father!'" (Gal 4:6); "But you are not in the flesh, you are in the Spirit, if in fact the Spirit of God dwells in you. And any one who does not have the Spirit of Christ does not belong to him" (Rom 8:9). Since in the second text God probably means Father, the conjunction of "Spirit of God" and "Spirit of Christ" is important.[2] There is reference also to the "Spirit of Jesus Christ" in Phil 1:19.

The Fathers

The doctrine of the *Filioque* was to become a distinctive element of western Trinitarian theology. The first hint is in Tertullian (*qv*): "I think of the Spirit as only from the Father through the Son."[3] Marius Victorinus (*qv*) was feeling his way towards it: "Therefore the Spirit receives from Christ, Christ himself from the Father, and accordingly the Spirit from the Father. All are thus one, but from the Father."[4] A text from Hilary that the Spirit was *Patre et Filio auctoribus confitendus* refers more to witness borne by the Father and the Son. But he did think that *de meo accipiet* (Jn 16:14) could possibly be interpreted in the sense of receiving and therefore proceeding from the Father.[5] Ambrose, in 381, the year of the First Council of Constantinople (*qv*), wrote, "the Holy Spirit, since he proceeds from the Father and the Son" but commentators agree that here he was speaking of the temporal mission of the Holy Spirit; he did possibly think that *de meo accipiet* could refer to the communication of the divine life itself.[6]

Augustine was clearcut and emphatic: "And we cannot say that the Holy Spirit does not also proceed from the Son; for it is not in vain that the same Spirit is called the Spirit of the Father and the Spirit of the Son. Nor do I see what else he wished to express when breathing on the face of the disciples he said: *Receive the Holy Spirit* (Jn 20:22). Nor was that physical breath proceeding from the body with the meaning of bodily contact, the substance of the Holy Spirit, but the proof by appropriate expression that the Holy Spirit proceeds not only from the Father but from the Son. For who is mad enough to say that the Spirit he gave when he breathed is different from the one he sent after his ascension (Acts 1:1–4)? For there is one Spirit of God, the Spirit of the Father and of the Son, the Holy Spirit who works all things in all."[7] "It must be confessed that the Father and Son are one principle, not two, of the Holy Spirit; but as the Father and Son are one God, and in regard to the creature, one Creator and one Lord, thus in regard to the Holy Spirit (they are) one principle." "If therefore I say that the Holy Spirit proceeds from the Father and the Son, why does the Son say, 'He proceeds from the Father?' (Jn 15:26) Why, do you think, except that that he is accustomed to refer to him from whom he himself is, whatever is his own?"[8]

That was the pattern of thought set; none in the west tried to change it. It was immediately reinforced by Fulgentius of Ruspe (*qv*), soon after by Leo the Great and a number of fifth and sixth century writers. The twelfth and thirteenth century doctors gave it increasingly systematic demonstration.

What of the eastern Fathers? At the Council of Florence (*qv*) a text from St. Basil's (*qv*) work on the Holy spirit was contested, each party having its version. St. Epiphanius did appear to countenance the idea. St. Cyril of Alexandria (*qv*) is most frequently cited in evidence of an eastern Father who accepts the *Filioque*. He did write as follows: "Jesus breathed on his disciples, saying, 'Receive the Holy Spirit', so that we shall be formed again in the first image and shall appear conformed to the Creator through participating in the Spirit. Thus, as the Spirit who is sent to us makes us conformed to God and as he proceeds from the Father and the Son, it is clear that he is of the divine *ousia*, proceeding essentially in it and from it."[9] Many other texts must be considered.[10]

St. John of Damascus (*qv*) summed up eastern Trinitarian theology and as to the relation between the Son and Spirit was content to adhere to *per Filium*, not *Filioque*: "The Holy Spirit is the power of the Father making the secrets of the deity known and proceeding from the Father through the Son in a way that he knows, but which is not begetting."[11] For John the Father was the source of the Son and of the Holy Spirit; the Spirit is not Son of the Father, he is the Spirit of the Father, as proceeding from him. He is also Spirit of the Son, not as proceeding from him, but proceeding through him from the Father. Only the Father is cause. Tarasius, Patriarch of Constantinople (*qv*), also used the formula "through the Son" in a confession of faith which was recited at the second Council of Nicaea (787).[12]

With Photius (*qv*) the eastern position hardened. From 867 he declared his opposition many times to the *Filioque* and insisted on the idea of the procession from the Father alone, *ek monou tou Patros*.[13] He sadly misread the Latin doctrine of the Trinity, which allows for perfect consubstantiality of the persons and their distinction on the basis of relationship and the opposition of relationship, this being of origin and procession.

Church Authority

The Papacy was slow to pronounce on the question of including the *Filioque* in the creed, or to put the idea on any synodal agenda. St. Gregory the Great (d. 604) taught the procession from the

Son but towards the end of that century Pope St. Agatho (d. 681), approved a profession of faith in the name of a Roman synod which did not contain the *Filioque*. Spain was the home of early pronouncements. As to the first council of Toledo (*qv*) the reader must be referred to the expert monographs which attempt to trace the origin of official documents around that time: the so-called creed of Damascus which contains the words "proceeding from the Father and the Son," the creed with twelve anathemas (possibly, thought Dom Morin, the long-lost *Libellus in modum symboli* of Pastor, bishop of Gallicia) which also had the words "proceeds from the Father and the Son."[14]

It is sometimes thought that the reason why so many Spanish creeds of the time contained the *Filioque* was the need to oppose Priscillianism (*qv*). But this is not so. Priscillianism called for much more by way of Trinitarian theology than the single word *Filioque*. Which brings us to the first indisputable conciliar pronouncement, Toledo, 589. At this assembly king Reccared renounced Arianism (*qv*) and proposed to publicize the true faith. He recited a statement of his faith which had this passage: "In equal degree must the Holy Spirit be confessed by us, and we must preach that he proceeds from the Father and the Son and is of one substance with the Father and the Son: moreover, that the person of the Holy Spirit is the third in the Trinity but that he nevertheless shares fully in the divine essence with the Father and the Son."[15] The third anathema of the council, instigated by Reccared, read as follows: "Whoever does not believe in the Holy Spirit, or does not believe that he proceeds from the Father and the Son, and denies that he is coeternal and coequal with the Father and the Son, let him be anathema."[16] Study of manuscript evidence, however, appears to show that the official creed recited at Toledo was the Constantinopolitan without the *Filioque*. Manuscripts of the centuries thereafter show that as the doctrine had been accepted it found its way into creeds. The creed with the addition was introduced into the Mozarabic Mass before the *Pater Noster* about the time of the council.

Almost a century later, in 680, a synod at Hatfield which was to be a doctrinal shield against Eutychian tendencies of Monothelism, professed adherence to the first five ecumenical councils and Pope Martin's Rome synod of 649. This was its profession of faith: "We acknowledge and glorify our Lord Jesus Christ as they (i.e. the fathers of the general councils) glorified him, neither adding nor subtracting anything, and we anathematize with heart and voice those whom they anathematized, and we acknowledge those whom they acknowledged glorifying God the Father without beginning, and his only-begotten Son, begotten of the Father before all ages, and the Holy Spirit proceeding in an inexpressible manner from the Father and the Son, as those holy apostles and prophets and doctors taught whom we have mentioned."[17] The president, archbishop Theodore, had been a monk at Tarsus and knew the original text of the creed.

From Spain the doctrine passed into Gaul. Things came to a head at the council of Gentilly, where east and west met. On the agenda were the worship of images and the return of territories in Italy which Constantinople claimed. But the question of the Trinity was raised between Greeks and Romans, "and whether the Holy Spirit proceeds from the Son in the same way as he proceeds from the Father." The affirmative answer was defended. In 796 or 797 St. Paulinus of Aquileia summoned a synod to Cividale in Italy; here the creed with the *Filioque* was set forth and the addition defended by St. Paulinus in his opening address to the council; he thought those who held that the Holy Spirit was of the Father alone were "heretics."

At the same time Charlemagne (*qv*), seeking to rival the Byzantine emperors, was assuming a role in matters liturgical and doctrinal; he sought to influence Leo III towards a public stand on the *Filioque*, without success. The formula was now adopted very widely, though as late as 1240 it was omitted in Paris. By then Charlemagne's successor, Henry II, had achieved the support of the papacy.

St. Anselm (*qv*) was present at the Council of Bari in October 1098; he there defended the *Filioque* against Greek monks and we have his thinking in the *De processione Spiritus Sancti* which was the outcome of his intervention in the council debate. He was critical of a *Patre per Filium*. He wished to lead the Greeks to confess the procession of the Spirit *a Patre Filioque tanquam ab uno principio*; he invoked NT texts in his favour.

The *Filioque* is included in the synthesis of St. Thomas Aquinas (*qv*). In the year of his death the Council of Lyons met and was attended by delegates of Michael VIII Palaeologus; during the Mass, at which St. Bonaventure preached, the

Greeks repeated the *Filioque* three times. The doctrine was defined. It was rejected, however, by the people and clergy of Constantinople despite severe pressure from the emperor. The east eventually reverted to its ancient opposition and by the end of the fourteenth century abjuration of the *Filioque* was required of converts. The next attempt to secure agreement, the Council of Florence (*qv*), did not have lasting success.

Attempts have been made in modern times to heal the division caused by the *Filioque*. In 1875 a conference was held in Bonn to discuss the matter; it was attended by twenty-two bishops and priests of the Orthodox Church, by American and English representatives of the Anglican Church, by a number of Old Catholics, and by Döllinger (who would not be described as Old Catholic). Among the conclusions reached were the following: "We agree totally that we should accept ecumenical creeds and decisions made by the early, undivided Church in matters of faith. We agree totally that we should recognize that the addition of the *Filioque* was not made in a way that was in conformity with the rules of the Church . . . . We reject every representation or mode of expression containing any acceptance of the ideas of two principles, *archai* or *aitiai* in the Trinity."

In addition the conference accepted a number of theses taken from the writings of St. John Damascene; they are reproduced in the article on him: included are the statements that the Holy Spirit does not come from the Son, but that he does come from the Father through the Son.

As a result of the Bonn Conference there was further intellectual activity. The Russian Holy Synod, however, appointed a commission to continue the work begun at Bonn and to seek closer relations with the Old Catholics. Two historians were named to prepare a report: A. L. Katansky, who contended "from the Father alone," and B. Bolotov, whose findings are dealt with in the article on him. The Old Catholics also set up a commission, which expressed the embarrassing opinion that the Son was a "secondary cause" of the Spirit.

Recent developments may be noted. In 1966 at Belgrade, representatives of the Orthodox Church complained to the Old Catholics that a promise made in 1931 and 1932 to withdraw the *Filioque* from the creed had not been fully kept: individual Old Catholics were still allowed to hold the opinion privately. The Greeks in particular asked for total repudiation of the Latin theory. The International Conference of Old Catholic Bishops, which comprises the pastors of the Churches belonging to the Union of Utrecht, officially deleted the *Filioque* from the creed in 1969, on the grounds that the insertion had not been made canonically, that it lacked a theological basis and had been a cause of disunity. A conference held at Chambesy in August 1975 adopted the Orthodox position. Anglicanism (*qv*) and the *Filioque* are considered in a separate article.

[1]Cf. P. de Meester, O.S.B., "Etudes sur la théologie orthodoxe, IV 'Le Filioque'," *RevBen* 24 (1907), 86–103; A.E. Burn, "Some Spanish MSS of the Constantinopolitan Creed," *JTS* 9 (1908), 301–303; V. Grumel, A.A., "St. Thomas et la doctrine des Grecs sur la procession du S. Esprit," *Echos d'orient*, 25 (1926), 257–280; M. Jugie, A.A., *Theologia Dogmatica Christianorum Orientalium ab Ecclesia Catholica Dissidentium*, Paris, I, 1926, 286–311, II, 1933, 296–535; id., *De Processione Spiritus Sancti ex Fontibus Revelationis et secundum Orientales Dissidentes*, Rome, 1936; id., "Origine de la controverse sur l'addition du Filioque au symbole," *RSPT* 28 (1939), 369–85; V. Lossky, "The Procession of the Holy Spirit in the Orthodox Triadology," *East. Churches Quart.*, 7 (1948), supplem. 2, 31–53; *Istina*, 1950 special articles, cf. esp., J. Meyerndorff, "La procession du S. Esprit d'après la triadologie orthodoxe," 197–209; A.M. Dubarle, O.P., "Les fondements bibliques du 'Filioque'," 229–244; M. Gordillo, *Compendium theologiae orientalis*, 3rd. ed., Rome, 1950; B. Capelle, O.S.B., "Le Pape Léon III et le 'Filioque'," 1054–1954, *L'Eglise et les églises*, offered to Dom Lambert Beaudouin, Chevetogne, 1954, 309–322; repr. *Travaux liturgiques*, III (1967), 35–46; *Istina*, 1972, special articles— esp. J.-M. Garrigues, "Procession et ekporese du S. Esprit," 345–366; "Theses sur le 'Filioque' par un théologien russe" by Basil Bolotov, now known (*qv*); J.-M. Garrigues, "Le sens de la procession du S. Esprit dans la tradition latine du premier millenaire," *Contacts*, 3 (1971), 283–309; A. de Halleux, "Pour un accord oecuménique sur la procession du S. Esprit et l'addition du 'Filioque' au symbole," *Irenikon*, 51 (1978), 451–469; ed. L. Vischer, *La theologie du Saint Esprit dans le dialogue entre l'Orient et l'Occident*, 12 essays on the *Filioque* from different aspects (L. Vischer, M.A. Orphanos, D. Ritschl, A. de Halleux, D. Allchin, K. Stalder, A. Heron, H. Aldenhoven, B. Bobrinskoy, J.-M. Garrigues, J. Moltmann, D. Stanisloaf); *Faith and Order Document* 103, Paris, 1981; Congar, *The Holy Spirit*, III, 49–60, 60, 174–214; A. Palmieri, *DTC*, V (1913), 2309–43; J. Gill, *NCE* V, 913f; (and see articles, Florence Council, Bonn Conference, Bolotov, Basil). [2]Cf. K. Rahner, "Theos in the New Testament," *Theological Investigations* I, p. 141; [3]*Adversus Praxean*, 4, CSEL 47, 232; PL 2, 159, cp. 8, 238, 163; [4]*Adversus Arium*, Lib. I, c.13, PL 8, 1048; [5]*De Trin.*, II 29 PL 10, 69; *ibid.*, VIII, 20, PL 10 250–251; [6]*De Spir. Sanct.* I, 11, PL 16 762; [7]*De Trin.* IV, 20, 29, PL 42, 908; [8]*De Trin.*, V, 14,15, PL 42 921; *Tract. 99 in Joannem*, 8, PL 35, 1890; [9]*Thesaurus* etc., PG 75, 585; [10]*DTC* III, 2505; [11]*De Fide orthod.*. I, 12, PG 94, 849; [12]Mansi XII, 1122; [13]PG 102, 721–741; [14]DS 71; Mansi III, 1003; *RevB* 10 (1893) 385f; [15]Mansi IX, 977ff; [16]Mansi IX, 985; [17]Bede, *Hist. eccl.* 4, 17, PL 95, 199.

FLORENCE, COUNCIL OF (1439)

The great reunion Council, held under the shadow of the impending collapse of Constantinople to the Turks, had on its agenda the questions of theology and church jurisdiction which divided east and west. What concerns Trinitarian theology is the continuing debate on the *Filioque*; it eventually led to the Decree for the Greeks, *Laetentur Coeli*, July 6, 1439. The Greek contingent, composed of the Emperor John VIII Palaeologus and his brother, Demetrius, the Patriarch of Constantinople, Gregory, the Emperor's confessor, 20 metropolitans (five of whom acted as procurators of the patriarchates of Alexandria, Antioch and Jerusalem, and a large group of lesser clerics and officials, numbered in all about 700; 118 Latin prelates assisted at the solemn inauguration, which took place on 9 April, 1438 in Ferrara; Isidore, Metropolitan of Kiev and all Russia, came in the month of August.

A delay of some months was sought by the Emperor, who desired to see representatives of the western kings participating in the Council; he hoped for military aid from them against the Turkish menace. After some inconclusive discussion between committees on purgatory, the Council reached the crucial doctrinal problem in October. After an opening address by Cardinal Bessarion of Nicaea, Mark Eugenicus, Metropolitan of Ephesus, opened the debate on the *Filioque*: had the Latins the right to add it to the Nicene creed? He spoke in eleven sessions held at Ferrara, Bessarion having spoken in the first two. The Greek case was that any addition to the creed had been forbidden by the Council of Ephesus, irrespective of whether the word or words added were true or not. The Latins replied that this prohibition referred to the faith expressed, not the verbal formulation: the principal Latin speakers were Andrew of Rhodes, O.P., Aloysius of Forli, O.F.M., and Cardinal Cesarini. There was no agreement and the Greeks wished to return home. They yielded, however, to the plea of Eugene IV, the Pope of the Council, that they should assemble with the Latin conciliar fathers in Florence, there to discuss the *Filioque*. Mark Eugenicus continued as sole representative of the Greeks, while John of Montenero spoke for the Latins. Five sessions were taken up with debates on patristic texts, especially a crucial passage in St. Basil's (*qv*) *Adversus Eunomium*, III.

The version of this text upheld by the Latins read as follows: "Even if the Holy Spirit is third in dignity and order, why need he be third also in nature? For that he is second to the Son, *having his being from him and receiving from him and announcing to us and being completely dependent on him*, pious tradition recounts; but that his nature is third we are not taught by the Saints nor can we conclude logically from what has been said."

The Greeks proposed the following version: "Even if the Holy spirit is third in dignity and order, why need he be third in nature? For that he is second pious tradition *perhaps* recounts; but that his nature is third we are not taught by Scripture nor can we conclude from what has been said."[1]

Three further sessions were spent on arguments in which both sides appealed to Scriptures, the Fathers and the Councils to support their theses. Committee meetings could not produce agreement on a text which would be acceptable. The Pope intervened in May to urge a new joint effort. One way out of the deadlock was the Greek belief that every saint, because he was a saint, was inspired by the Holy Spirit and could not err in faith. Latin saints held that the Holy Spirit "proceeds from Father and Son"; Montenero and Bessarion had copiously shown that Greek fathers had said that the Spirit "comes forth from," "issues from," "springs from," "the Father," "the Father and the Son," "from both," "from the Father through the Son." Tarasius, Patriarch of Constantinople, had said "proceeds from the Father through the Son." When the Greeks, hindered by ignorance of Latin, finally understood that the Latin Fathers had written *Filioque*, they were satisfied that the Greek fathers meant the same thing. On 3 June they thought that it was not only possible but a duty to affirm a common faith; their synod accepted the cedula of the Latins on the procession. It is incorporated into the Bull "*Laetentur coeli*," 6 July 1439:

"In the name of the Holy Trinity, of the Father, and of the Son, and of the Holy Spirit, with the approbation of this holy general Council of Florence we define that this truth of faith be believed and accepted by all Christians, and that all likewise profess that the Holy Spirit is eternally from the Father and the Son, and has his essence and his subsistent being both from the Father and the Son, and proceeds from both eternally as from one principle and one spiration; we declare that what the holy Doctors and Fathers say, namely, that the Holy Spirit proceeds from the Father through the Son, tends to this meaning, that by this it is signified that the Son also is the cause, according to the Greeks, and according to the Latins, the principle of the subsistence of the Holy Spirit, as is the Father also. And that all things, which are the Father's, the Father himself has given in begetting his only begotten Son; without being Father, the Son himself possesses this from the Father, that the Holy Spirit proceeds from the Son from whom he was moreover eternally begotten. We define, in addition, that the explanation of the word 'Filioque,' for the sake of declaring the truth and also because of imminent necessity, has been lawfully and reasonably added to the Creed."[2]

This statement recognised *Filioque* and *per Filium* as possibly equivalent: this was done later at Brest in 1596. Fr. Congar rightly sums up the achievement of Florence, despite the immediate failure in the East as: "1. the intention to recognize that the two formulae were compatible and even equivalent—I would willingly say that they are complementary; 2. the principle on the basis of which this intention was pursued, namely that the Fathers of the Church, inspired by the Holy Spirit, held in communion both formulae. Any new attempt to approach this question should take this as a point of departure and as a basis for discussion."[3]

[1]Sources: Hardouin, IX, 1–1080; Mansi XXXI (1798), 459–1120; supplement to vol XXXI (1801), 1121–1998; crit. ed., *Concilium Florentinum: Documenta et Scriptores*, Rome, Pontifical Oriental Institute, 1940–1971; further documents ed. L. Petit, PO, 17, 307–524; cf. G. Hofmann, *Papato, Conciliarismo, Patriarcato*, 1438–1439, Rome, Gregorian University, 1940; esp. J. Gill, S.J., *The Council of Florence*, Cambridge, 1959; id., *Personalities of the Council of Florence*, Oxford, 1964; id., *Constance et Bâle-Florence (Les conciles oecuméniques)*, Paris, 1965, id. NCE, J. Descarreaux, *Les Grecs au Concile de l'union Ferrare-Florence*, (1438–1439), Paris, 1970; A. Leidl, *Die Einheit der Kirchen auf den spätmittelalterlichen Konzilien von Konstanz bis Florenz*, Paderborn, 1966; H. Mühlen, "Das Konzil von Florenz (1439) als vorläufiges Modell eines kommenden Unionskonzils," *Theol. und Glaube*, 63 (1973), 184–197; J. Marx, *Filioque und Verbot eines anderen Glaubens auf dem Florentinum. Zum Pluralismus in dogmatischen Formeln*, Steyl, 1977; Congar, *The Holy Spirit* III, 184–190; [2]DS 1300–1302; [3]*Op.cit.*, 188.

FULGENTIUS OF RUSPE, ST. (468–533 or c. 462–527)

F., at one time a Roman public official, then a monk, was Bishop of Ruspe in North Africa, c.507 (or 502).[1] In theology he was an ardent Augustinian. He suffered much, including forced exile twice, from the Arian king Thrasamund. To the latter one of his works is addressed. He deals with the Trinity in the *De Trinitate ad Felicem*, in the *De Fide*, in the *Responsiones ad dicta Regis Trasamundi*, and occasionally in his other works. In the *De Trinitate* he summarizes orthodox doctrine thus: "There is not a different essence of the Father, the Son and the Holy Spirit. For if there were the Son would not be truly begotten from the Father, nor would the Holy Spirit proceed from the Father and the Son. But since he is true Son, that is, begotten from the essence of the Father, the Holy Spirit is true proceeding from the Father and the Son. But if the Son or the Holy Spirit is of a different kind to the Father, the Son is not truly of the Father, for the different essence makes him a stranger, nor likewise could the Holy Spirit proceed from the Father and the Son. But it is irrational to say such a thing, for holy Scripture makes clear in a true account that the Son is begotten of the Father and that the Holy Spirit proceeds from him. There are therefore three coeternal, consubstantial (*qv*), coessential. But when the question was put to the Fathers: What three?, they did not dare to speak of essences or substances or natures, lest it should be believed that there was a diversity of essences or natures or substances, but they spoke of three persons, one essence, as one essence would declare God to be one, three persons would show the Trinity. Nor do we say this as if only the Trinity was God and not each person. For the Father by himself is God, and the Son by himself is God and the Holy Spirit by himself is God."[2]

At the time he wrote F. was not very original, but he did have some impressive sayings: "The whole Trinity is found in each person"; "Man is made in the image of the Trinity, the creator of all things"; "We are the temple of the Trinity"; "Even if only the Father's name is mentioned, what is offered is to the whole Trinity"; "throughout the whole world the holy Church continuously offers the sacrifice of bread and wine to the Father and Son and Holy Spirit."

In his reply to the remarks of Thrasamund he dealt with the question of the *homoousion* and also with the indwelling (*qv*) of the Trinity.

[1]Works PL 65, 103–1020; CCSL 91, 91A, J. Fraipont; cf. H.J. Diesner, *Fulgentius von Ruspe, als Theologe und Kirchenpolitiker*, Stuttgart, 1966; J.J. Gavigan, "Fulgentius of Ruspe on Baptism," *Traditio* 5 (1947), 313–22; M. Jugie, A.A., "Considérations génerales sur la question de l'epiclese," *Echos d'Orient*, 1936, 324–330; S. Salaville, "L'epiclèse africaine," *Echos d'Orient*, 39 (1941–1942), 268–282; J. Stiglmayr, S.J., "Das Quicunque und Fulgentius", ZKT 49 (1924), 341–357—on F's authorship? [2]*De Trinitate ad Felicem*, II, 3, CCSL, 91A, 635.

G

GENERATION

When the unexampled Christ event took place and when he was revealed to be the Son of God in a unique way, a reality conveyed by the Latin translation *unigenitus*, though not so fully by the Greek word it translates, *monogenes* (Jn 1:14, 18; 3:16; 18; 1 Jn 4:9) was explained on the analogy of human nature by the word generation: thus his very meaning within the godhead was explained, and thus his origin was revealed. Immediately there is a relationship with another who must be God the Father; the language of the Bible pointed that way. But to attain complete clarity and avoid the pitfalls, much reflection, much challenge and resolute resistance was needed. It must be made manifest that here there was no question of dependence in a creaturely manner. The Son generated from the Father whose attribute was *agennesia* (not being begotten) must be seen and expressed in accessible language, as seen to be equal to the Father. That is the history of Arianism (*qv*) and the answer given by the enlightened Church.[1]

---

[1] Cf. St.Thomas I, 27, ii; M.J. Scheeben, *The Mysteries of Christianity*, ch. IV, 16, ; B. Lonergan, *De Deo Trino*, II, 66ff; B. de Margeries, S.J., *La Trinité chrétienne dans l'histoire*, 212–222.

GILBERT DE LA PORRÉE (c. 1080–1154)

G. was born in Poitiers, a student of Bernard of Chartres, Anselm of Laon and the Paris masters. He taught in his native town and in Chartres and Paris before being named bishop of Poitiers, 1142.[1] He was delated to Pope Eugene III for his views on the Trinity by Calon of Thouais and Arnold of Brioux. A first hearing proved inconclusive so the Pope referred the matter to the Council of Rheims, 1148. It is for experts to settle controverted questions on those of G's opinions singled out as erroneous. The sources are John of Salisbury's *Historia Pontificalis*, Otto of Freising's *Gesta Friderici*, and the *Libellus* written against G. by Geoffrey of Auxerre, secretary of St. Bernard, which is a somewhat clumsy document. From one or another of these sources we learn that G. held: that the divine essence is not God; that God is not the divinity; that the divine nature was not made flesh, did not assume human nature; that no divine person can be made the predicate of a sentence. Bernard set forth a set of passages against G's theories, which the latter accepted. On promising the Pope that he would correct his writings, G. was acquitted. He made no change in these writings.

G. was the author of commentaries on the Psalms and on the Pauline epistles, as well as of lengthy commentaries on the opuscula of Boethius on the Trinity. These latter are the quarry for his critics. He had an ambition ahead of his time, and possibly of his ability: to apply a theory of speculative grammar to Trinitarian theology. The results were tentative, though this was not realised even by himself, and could not be reconciled with accepted beliefs and formulations. The gain to Trinitarian theology was in the teaching of the Council of Rheims (*qv*).

[1]Works: PL 54, 1255–1412; crit. ed. N.M. Haring, S.A.C., *Studies and Texts* 13, Pontifical Institute of Medieval Studies, Toronto, 1966; M.E. Williams, *The Teaching of Gilbert Porreta on the Trinity as found in his commentaries on Boethius*, Analecta Gregoriana 56 (1951); H.C. van Elswijk, O.P., *Gilbert Porreta, Sa vie, son oeuvre, sa pensée*, Louvain, 1966.

GNOSTICS

Gnosticism had a peak moment in the second century when theological reflection on the mystery of the Trinity was accelerating.[1] Mental categories and nomenclature which would be significant in this reflection are found among the writings of the Gnostics: the psychological analogy, the notion of procession, and the word which was to prove with the passage of a century intellectually explosive, *homoousios* (see CONSUBSTANTIAL). The links are a haphazard borrowing if not largely fortuitous, despite the opinion popular since Harnack that the Gnostics were the first Christian theologians.

[1]For general bibliographies on Gnosticism cf. standard reference works, e.g. Cross, 574; esp. B. Lonergan (*qv*), *Nicaea*, 28–35.

GRACE

The subject is intertwined with doctrine on the divine image (*qv*) in man, and on the divine indwelling (*qv*) in man.[1] Here we are concerned with the interactions between a theory of grace and Trinitarian theology. A cursory look at a work which aims at renewing theology on the subject, *The New Life of Grace* by Peter Fransen, S.J., will convince the reader that it is in the proper understanding of Trinitarian life that we shall grasp the meaning of grace. Fransen can write in summary of his position: "Essentially, grace consists in this: that God, the Blessed Trinity, loves us. The Trinitarian love consists in the union of the Father, Son and Spirit with us; or better, their drawing us into the intimacy of their own Trinitarian life by uniting us with themselves."[2]

Therein, however, are veiled a number of questions debated in recent times. There has been the question of "nature and grace" opened to discussion by Fr. (now Cardinal) H. de Lubac, S.J.,[3] who wished to dispense with the concept of "pure nature," that is, of human nature oriented to a purely natural end, and to force an admission that man as a created spirit was possessed of a fundamental inclination, aspiration or, in the philosophical sense, desire for the infinite, that is, for the eternal vision of God. Karl Rahner (*qv*) differed from de Lubac on the philosophical support for his idea, deeming that the concept of "pure nature" should be retained as a possible hypothesis, but granting that every human being, believer or not, is oriented to a supernatural destiny. The mark of the supernatural is on him, but not as essential, rather as a factual supernatural existential. All Catholic theorists assume that grace when given and received is entirely gratuitous.

Rahner, preferring to speak of "man" rather than "nature", writes thus: "God wishes to communicate himself, to pour forth the love which he himself is. That is the first and last of his real plans and hence of his real world too. Everything else exists so that this one thing might be: the miracle of infinite love. And so God makes a creature whom he can love: he creates man. He creates him in such a way that he can receive this love which is God himself, and that he can and must at the same time accept it for what it is: the very astounding wonder, the unexpected, unexacted gift." Whence follow some important theological conclusions: "Man should be *able* to receive this love which is God himself; he must have a congeniality for it. He must be able to accept it (and hence grace, the beatific vision) as one who has room and scope, understanding and desire for it. Thus he must have a real 'potency' for it. He must have it *always*. He is indeed someone always addressed and claimed by this love. For, as he now in fact is, he is created for it; he is thought and called into being so that love might bestow itself. To this extent this 'potency' is what is inmost and most authentic in him, the centre and root of what he is absolutely . . . . The real man as God's real partner should be able to receive this love as what it necessarily is: as free gift. But that means that this central, abiding existential, consisting in the ordination to the threefold God of grace and eternal life, is itself to be characterized as unexacted, as supernatural . . . . For that nature should remain nature for the sake of grace and yet always be grasped by the Christian as an intrinsic element in the single object willed by God when he willed man as his beloved in his Son—to bring this about is a task of the Christian life, and so a serious question for theology."[4]

It is clear that Rahner's theory leads on to a personalist doctrine of grace. He found himself obliged to discuss also the scholastic concept of uncreated grace. From this in recent times created grace had been very much separated, with unhappy results in the contexts of doctrine and spirituality. The eastern church knows nothing of the distinction between created and uncreated grace; nor did the west know much of a formulation on the subject until the eleventh century. Now it is assumed that the terms are correlative; one cannot be considered apart from the other. Previously, thinking had been influenced by the Aristotelian idea of causality. Grace, created grace that is, was an effect. This was attributed to God, not to God as Trinity, but as one in nature. Thereon followed the attribution of the indwelling to grace as an effect.

There has been growing dissent from this rigidly systematic view. Grace will always be considered as God's gift justifying, elevating, empowering the soul for a new life and equipping it for truly supernatural activities. The essential question is whether God as three persons in one nature, uncreated grace, first comes to the soul and causes therein the new life, or whether grace is first infused and then God comes. The view held here is that of Rahner thus expressed: "It would have to be proved in the strictest possible way that it was impossible for there to be this kind of communication of the divine Persons each in his own particularity, and hence a non-appropriated relation to the three Persons. There is no way of producing such a proof. Consequently there can be absolutely no objection to maintaining on the basis of the positive data of revelation that the attribution of determinate relations of the recipient of grace to the three divine Persons is not merely a matter of appropriation, but is intended to give expression to a proper relationship in each case. In Scripture it is the Father in the Trinity who is our Father, and not the threefold God. The Spirit dwells in us in a particular and proper way. These and like statements of Scripture and Tradition are first of all 'in possessione'. It would be necessary to prove that they may be merely appropriated, on the grounds that they can be understood merely as such and that the contrary is impossible; it cannot be presupposed. So long as this has not been

achieved, we must take Scripture and the expressions it uses in as exact a sense as we possibly can."[5]

Rahner adds another point. As he says, the doctrine of "bare appropriation" (qv) has not only attenuated the "Trinity in the economy of salvation" into a kind of pre-Christian monotheism; logically it endangers the interior or immanent Trinity to the benefit of a rationalistic monotheism; in this conception the three divine names would only be for us three aspects of the one divine essence.

Again to quote Fr. Fransen: "Such is the image of God imprinted on us when through grace we are united with the Son, encounter him in the Church and in the sacraments and thus share in his filial life. The immediate union with the Son brings with it a union with the Father and with the Holy Spirit; both these unions are likewise immediate, and both bear the mark of the characteristic property of the respective divine persons. The origin of all grace can be traced to the election by the Father. To him belongs the initiative in granting grace. And as the prime cause he is also the ultimate end: we are called to the Father as the final goal of all grace."[6]

This is rather explicit, anticipates somewhat the question of the divine indwelling. It is understandable as a reaction against the closed systems, the hard partitions, the impersonal ideas of times now fortunately past.

[1]Cf. J. Auer, *Die Entwicklung der Gnadenlehre in her Hochscholastik, I. II*, Freiburg, 1942, 51; id., "Um den Begriff der Gnade, Grundsätzliches zur Frage nach der Methode, mit der Übernatur als Gnade etc.," *ZKT* 70 (1948) 341–68; H. Bouillard, *Conversion et grâce chez S.Thomas d'Aquin*, Paris, 1944; id., "Le théologie de la grâce au XIIIe siècle," *RSR*, 35 (1948) 469–480; H. de Lubac, S.J., *Le surnaturel*, Paris, 1946; id., "Le mystère du surnaturel," *RSR* 36 (1949); id., *Le mystère du surnaturel*, Paris, 1965 (English tr. 1967); H. Rondet, S.J., "Le problème de la nature pure et la théologie au XVIe siècle," *RSR* 35 (1948), 481–521; id., *Gratia Christi, Essai d'histoire du dogme et de théologie dogmatique*, Paris, 1948; id., "La divinisation du chrétien," *NRT*, 71 (1949), 449–476, 561–588; G. de Broglie, "De gratitudine ordinis supernaturalis," *Greg* 29 (1948), 435–463; S. Dockx, *Fils de Dieu par grâce*, Paris, 1948; P.J. Donnelly, "Discussions on the supernatural order," *ThSt* 9 (1948), 213–249; id., "The Gratuity of the Beatific Vision and the Possibility of a Natural Destiny," *ThSt* 11 (1950), 374–404; J. Alfaro, S.J., *Lo Natural y lo Sobrenatural, estudio histórico desde santo Tomas hasta Cayetanó*, 1274–1534, Madrid, 1952; L. Malevez, "La gratuité du surnaturel," *NRT* 75 (1953), 561–86; 673–89; J. Daujat, *The Theology of Grace*, New York, 1959; C. Baumgartner, *La grâce du Christ*, Tournai, 1963; R. W. Gleason, *Grace*, New York, 1962; esp. K. Rahner, S.U., *Theological Investigations*, I, 1961, "Concerning the Relationship between Nature and

Grace," 297–318; "Some Implications of the Scholastic Concept of Uncreated Grace," 319–346; M. Flick- A. Allzeghy, *Il Vangelo della grazia*, Florence, 1964; J. Van der Meersch, *DTC* 6 (1920), 1554–1687; *LTK* 4: 977–1016 (K. Rahner et al.); *Catholicisme*, 5:135–172 (J. Guillet et al.); esp. *DSp* 6 (1967), 701–50 with bibliographies (G. Baumgartner-P. Tihon); [2]P. Fransen, S.J., *The New Life of Grace*, London, 1969, 55; cf. also "Created and Uncreated Grace," *ibid.*, 86–106; [3]Cf. *Le Surnaturel*; [4]*Op.cit.*, 310ff; [5]*Ibid.*, 345; [6]*Op.cit.*, 56.

GREGORY OF NAZIANZUS, ST.

Cappadocian, close friend of St. Basil the Great (*qv*), Bishop of Nazianzus, G. was incessantly concerned to defend the doctrine of the Trinity; he returns to the subject in almost every discourse.[1] His preaching in the church of the Anastasis in 379 was an invaluable preliminary to the Council of Constantinople (*qv*). Here he was president and was elected bishop of the see, but withdrew to promote peace. Especially important are the *Five Theological Orations*, in the fifth of which he deals with the Holy Spirit.

As with Basil and Gregory of Nyssa (*qv*) "the essence of their doctrine is that one godhead exists simultaneously in three modes of being, or hypostases." He faced the essential problem of reconciling strict monotheism with the trinity of persons: "For us there is only one God because there is only one divinity and because those who proceed are related to the one from whom they proceed, while being three according to faith. For one is not more God, the other is not less God; one is not before, the other after. They are not divided in will or separated in power; there is nothing to suggest division. To put it all in one word, the divinity is undivided in those who are divided. As in three suns which interpenetrate, the mixture of light would be unitary. Thus when we regard the divinity, first cause, the monarchy, it is one that appears to us; and when we regard those in whom the divinity exists, and those who proceed from the first principle in the same eternity and glory, we adore the three."[2]

G. dissociates himself tactfully from the opinion of his colleague, Gregory of Nyssa (*qv*). Pagans speak of divinity, but believe in several gods; they speak of humanity and speak of several men. Men are not one in their humanity save in the mind, he tells us. But things are different in God. Each person is as much one with the other as with itself, because of the identity of substance and of power.

The persons only differ in their character of origin: "The Son is not the Father, for there is only one Father; but he is what the Father is; the Spirit is not the Son, because he proceeds from God, for there is only one unique Son; but he is what the Son is. One are the three in divinity; three are the one in those characters which are particular to them. It is not then the one of the Sabellians, nor the three of current heresy."[3]

Or again, "One sole divinity and one power, found in the three in unity, and comprising the three separately, not unequal in substances or natures, neither increased nor diminished by addition or subtraction, in every respect one and the same; just as the beauty and greatness of the heavens is one; the infinite conjunction of three infinite ones, each being God as considered apart, as the Father so the Son, as the Son so the Holy Spirit, each being distinct by his personal property (*idiotes*, *proprietas*), the three one God when contemplated together; each God because of the consubstantiality (*homoousiotes*), one God because of the monarchy (*monarchia*)."[4]

G. wished to avoid the heresy of Arius (*qv*) as well as that of Sabellius: "Three in individualities or *hypostases*, if any prefer to call them, or persons (*prosopon*), for we will not quarrel about names so long as the syllables amount to the same meaning; but one in respect of the substance—that is the godhead. For they are divided without division, if I may say so; and they are united in division. For the godhead is one in three, and the three are one, in whom the godhead is, or to speak more accurately, who are the godhead. Excesses and defects we will omit, neither making the unity a confusion, nor the division a separation. We would keep equally far from the confusion of Sabellius and from the division of Arius, which are evils diametrically opposed, yet equal in their wickedness. For what need is there heretically to fuse God together, or to cut him up into inequality?"[5]

The unity of the Trinity is guaranteed for G. by the fact that in the Trinity there is but one principle: the Son and the Holy Spirit (*qv*) are not understood save through the Father, in whom the entire Trinity is summed up: "If to honour the Son and the Spirit we were to suppose them without origin or to relate them to a foreign principle, we should fear to dishonor God or to set something in opposition to him. But, no matter to what height I raise the Son and the Spirit, if I do not place them above the Father and do not separate them from their principle, if I place at that height a sublime generation and an admirable procession, let us see, Arian, I ask you, which of us two dishonours God? Is it not you, who recognise him as the principle of creatures, but who will not have him as principle of his equals in nature and in glory, as we confess him to be? . . . As for me, in asserting that the principle of the divinity is beyond time, division or definition, I honour first the principle and in the same degree those who proceed from the principle: the former because he is the principle of such realities, the latter because of what they are and proceed in such a manner from such a principle, without being separated from it neither by time, nor nature, nor honour. They are one while remaining (mutually) distinct, and distinct while being united, though that seems a paradoxical thing to say; they are to be adored not less in their reciprocal relations than each one considered in himself."[6]

G. insists, on the one hand, on the one sovereignty of God, and on the other, on clearly defining the divine relations. G. is at the origin of the doctrine of relations elaborated by the Scholastics; the dictum which summarizes the teaching of the Council of Florence (qv), *in Deo omnia sunt unum, ubi non obviat relationis oppositio* (in God all things are one where no opposition of the relation interferes), is equivalently found in G's writings. There is complete identity among the divine persons, except for the relations of origin.[7] For him the three persons have each a property of relations; their properties are relations of origin. On this doctrine G. bases his defence of the coeternity of the persons and their identity of substance. Whereas Basil considers the property of relation in regard to the Son (qv), G. discussed it in regard to the Holy Spirit also (see SPIRIT, HOLY).

G. clarified the notions which are involved in the origin and mutual opposition of the divine persons, achieving for the first time a definition of the distinctive characters of the three. Here he is in advance of Basil: he sees the distinctive character of the Holy Spirit as *procession*—to him this idea is due: "The Father is Father and is unoriginate, for he is of no one, the Son is Son, and is not unoriginate, for he is of the Father. But if you take the word 'origin' in a temporal sense he too is unoriginate, for he is the maker of time, and is not subject to time. The Holy Spirit is truly Spirit, coming forth from the Father indeed but not after the manner of the Son, for it is not by generation but by procession *since I must coin a word for the sake of clearness*; for neither did the Father cease to be unbegotten because of his begetting something, nor the Son to be begotten because he is of the unbegotten, nor is the Spirit changed into Father or Son because he proceeds, or because he is God—though the ungodly do not believe it."[8]

G. was more explicit also than Basil in his doctrine of the Holy Spirit: "How long shall we hide the lamp under the bushel, and withhold from others the full knowledge of the divinity (of the Holy Spirit)? The lamp should rather be placed on the candlestick that it may give light to all churches and souls and to the whole fullness of the world, no longer by means of metaphors, or intellectual sketches, but by distinct declaration."[9] He argues for the consubstantiality of the Spirit because he is God: "Is the Spirit God? Most certainly. Well then is he consubstantial? Yes, if he is God."[10] "The Old Testament proclaimed the Father clearly, but the Son more darkly; the New Testament plainly revealed the Son, but only indicated the deity of the Spirit. Now the Holy Spirit lives among us and makes the manifestation of himself more certain to us; for it was not safe, as long as the divinity of the Father was still unrecognised, to proclaim openly that of the Son and so long as this was still not accepted, to impose the burden of the Spirit, if so bold a phrase may be allowed."[11]

G. did admit that he could not fully explain wherein the procession of the Spirit differed from the generation of the Son, but he had set the mode of thinking on the theme. He notably advanced the development of Trinitarian theology.

[1]Cf. J. Hergenrother, *Die Lehre von der göttlichen Dreieinigkeit nach dem hl. Gregor von Nazianz, dem Theologen*, Regensburg, 1850; T. Schermann, *Die Gottheit des Heiligen Geistes nach den griechischen Vätern des vierten Jahrhunderts*, Freiburg i.B., 1901, 143–167; K. Holl, *Amphilochius von Ikonium in seinem Verhältnis zu den grossen Kappadoziern*, Tübingen, 1904, 158–196; J. Draseke, "Neuplatonisches in des Gregorios von Nazianz Trinitatslehre," *BZ* 15 (1906) 141–160; P. Galtier, *Le Saint Esprit en nous d'après les Pères grecs*, Rome, 1946, 175–180; J.N.D. Kelly, *Doctrines*, 264–268; [2]*Orat.5, On the Holy Spirit*, 14; [3]*Ibid.*, 9; [4]*Orat*, 40, *On Holy Baptism*, 41, LNPF VII, 375; [5]*Oration 30, 11, On the Holy Lights*, ibid., 355, 56; [6]*Orat.* 23, 7–8; PG 35, 1157ff; [7]cf. preceding n.; [8]*Orat.* 39, LNPF 356; [9]*Orat* 12, 6, LNPF 247; [10]*Fifth Orat., De Spiritu Sancto*, 10, LNPF, 321; [11]*Orat.* 5, 36, LNPF 326.

GREGORY OF NYSSA, ST., DOCTOR OF THE CHURCH (331–392)

The mystical theologian of the Cappadocian Fathers, G., a monk, became Bishop of Nyssa in 371.[1] Like his fellow Cappadocians he championed the faith of Nicaea (qv). Removed from his bishopric by the Arians in 376, he went into exile, returned on the death of Valens in 378. He attended the Council of Antioch in 379 and at the Council of Constantinople (qv) in 381 warmly defended the faith of Nicaea.

G.'s ideas about the Trinity are found through his many works; principally relevant are the polemical treatises against Eunomius (qv), and the *Quod non sunt tres dii*, with the part of the "Catechetical Oration" which deals with the Trinity. He would be included under the general summary of Cappadocian doctrine that "the essence of their doctrine is that the one Godhead exists in three modes of being, or hypostases."[2] The influence of Plato is seen in his reply to the crucial question how to reconcile the Trinity with the oneness of God. Platonic realism is implicit in his view: "We say then to begin with that the practice of calling those who are not divided by nature by the very name of their common nature in the plural and saying they are 'many men' is a customary abuse of language, and that it would be much the same thing to say there are 'many human natures.'"[3] The term man, he holds, expresses nature, not the individual: "there are many who have shared in the same nature—many disciples, say, or apostles, or martyrs—but the man in them all is one; since, as has been said, the term man does not belong to the nature of the individual as such, but to that which is common".[4]

"The principle of hypostasis," G. affirms, "by identifying individual properties in each case, determines the sharing and by arrangement introduces number. As for the nature it is one. It is the same, united to itself, absolutely indivisible and unique, not increasing by addition, not decreasing by subtraction, always remaining one, undivided though it is manifest in multiplicity, continuous, integral, and not suffering the division of its participants. We say one people, one tribe, one army, one assembly, though the idea of such things comprises multiplicity. In the same way, to be accurate, we should say absolutely: one only man, though those found with this nature make a multitude."[5]

G. thinks it would be better to change usage, but recognises the difficulty: "Since the correction of the habit is impracticable, we are not so far wrong in not going contrary to the prevailing habit in the case of the lower nature, since no harm results from the mistaken use of the name: but in the case of the statements concerning the divine nature the various use of terms is no longer free from danger: for that which is of small account is in these subjects no longer a small matter. Therefore we must confess one God, according to the testimony of Scripture, 'Hear, O Israel, the Lord thy God is one Lord,' even though the name of the godhead extends through the holy Trinity."[6]

The difficulty here is that the concept of divinity may become a pure abstraction. Elsewhere G. seeks an issue in the mystery of the divine name: "Many say," he says, "that the word divinity has been applied strictly to name the supreme divine nature. But we, in conformity to the teachings of Scripture, know that this nature is ineffable and beyond naming and that every name, whether taken from human things, or given by Scripture, expresses some one thing which we can conceive about the divine nature, but does not contain the meaning of the nature itself."[7]

G. is a staunch Trinitarian, even if his attempt to marry belief with philosophy may not always satisfy. On the mutual relations of the persons he writes: "While we confess the invariable character of the nature we do not deny the difference in respect of cause, and that which is caused, by which alone we apprehend that one person is distinguished from another; namely, by our belief, that one is the cause and another is of the cause. Again in that which is of the cause we recognise yet another distinction. For one is directly from the first cause, and another only mediately and through that which is directly from the first cause; so that the character of being only-begotten abides without doubt in the Son, and the mediation of the Son, while it guards his character of being only-begotten, does not exclude the Spirit from his natural relation to the Father."[8]

Activity *ad extra* is to be attributed to all three persons: "Since among men the action of each in the same pursuits is discriminated, they are properly called many, since each of them is separated from the others within his own environment, according to the special character of his operation. But in the case of the divine nature we do not similarly learn that the Father does anything by himself in which the Son does not work conjointly, or again that the Son has any special operation apart from the Holy Spirit; but every operation extends from God to the creation, and is named accordingly to our variable conceptions of it, has its origin from the Father, and proceeds through the Son, and is perfected in the Holy Spirit. Since then the holy Trinity fulfils every operation in a manner similar to that of which I have spoken not by separate action according to the number of the persons, but so that there is one motion and disposition of the good will, which is communicated from the Father through the Son to the Spirit, so neither can be called those who exercise this divine and superintending power and operation towards ourselves and all creation, conjointly and inseparably, by their mutual action, three gods."[9]

G. was clear on the divinity and consubstantiality of the Holy Spirit. It also appears that he thought that the Spirit proceeded from the Father through the Son, immediately from the Son, mediately from the Father. So much is clear from the text quoted here. Elsewhere G. compares the Father, Son and Holy Spirit to three torches; the first imparts its light to the second and through the second to the third.

---

[1]Cf. for ample bibliographies M. Canevet, *DSp*, 6, 971–1011; K. Holl, *Amphilochius von Ikonium in seinem Verhältnis zu den grossen Kappadoziern*, Tübingen, 1904, 196–235; G. Isaye, "L'unité de l'opération divine dans les écrits trinitaires de S.Grégoire de Nysse," *RSR* 27 (1937) 422–439; S. Gonzales, "El simbolo de S.Gregorio de Nisa y su posición entre los simbolos de Cappadocia," *Greg* 19 (1938) 130–134; *id.* "La identidad de operación en las obras exteriores y la unidad de la naturaleza divina en la teologia trinitaria de S.Gregorio de Nisa," *Greg.* 19 (1938) 280–301; M. Gomes de Castro, *Die Trinitätslehre des hl. Gregor von Nyssa*, Freiburg i.B., 1938; J.N.D. Kelly, 264–269; G. Lafont, *Peut-on connaître Dieu en Jésus Christ*, Paris, 1969, 39–68; J. Quasten, III, 285–287; *DTC*, 1675–1677; [2]Kelly, *Doctrines*, 264; [3]*Quod non sint tres Dii*, LNPF V, 332; [4]*Ibid.*; [5]Ibid., [6]*Quod non sint tres Dii*, LNPF, 332; [7]*Ibid.*, 332; [8]*Quod non sint tres Dii*, 336; [9]*Quod non sint tres Dii*, LNPF, V, 334.

GÜNTHER, ANTON (1783–1863)

An Austrian priest who had the ambition to interpret certain truths of the Catholic faith in terms of the philosophic systems of Schelling and Hegel (*qv*); he did not accept Hegel's ideas. G. was eventually condemned by name by Pius IX.[1] His ideas on the distinction between natural and supernatural were erroneous; so was his notion that theological dogmas were subject to revision, with advancing knowledge. He thought that, with the aid of a kind of ontological argument, the existence of God could be discovered from an analysis of self-consciousness.

Turning to Trinitarian theology G. defined the person as consciousness of self. God does not have consciousness of himself through his essence, for this would be to see in him one sole person. If God knows himself, it can only be through the persons in him by opposing himself to himself as subject to object, while at the same time affirming the equality of this subject and this object. The self-conscious subject is the first person; the self-conscious object is the second person; the third is the consciousness of equality between subject and object, that is, between Father and Son. This Trinity, which is necessary, is bound with a creation which is necessary. Each person, distinguishing himself from another, denies that he is another, and it is this denial of something infinite and absolute which causes God to think of what is finite and relative. God's goodness demands that he give existence to these beings possible but not divine. Thus necessary creation follows the necessary Trinity—which, if it needs to be said, G. thought could be deduced from reason alone.

Definition of personality as consciousness of self would imply many errors: it would expose personality to the partial or permanent loss of consciousness. In divine reality, G. unwittingly fell into tritheism (*qv*). He left himself open to the charge of rationalism. His books were banned in February, 1857 and he submitted edifyingly. When his followers, because his errors had not been itemized, thought it lawful to adhere to them, Pius IX, in a letter to Cardinal de Geissel, Archbishop of Cologne, was specific: "Not without sorrow are We especially aware that in these books that erroneous and most dangerous system of rationalism, often condemned by this Apostolic See, is particularly dominant; and likewise we know that in the same books these items among others are found, which are not a little at variance with the Catholic Faith and with the true explanation of the unity of the divine substance in three distinct eternal Persons. Likewise, we have found that neither better nor more accurate are the statements made about the mystery of the Incarnate Word, and about the unity of the divine Person of the Word in two natures, divine and human."[2]

[1]Cf. esp. L. Orban, *Theologia Guntheriana et Concilium Vaticanum. Inquisitio historico-dogmatica de re Guntheriana juxta vota inedita consultoris J. Schwetz actaque Concilii Vaticani exarata* (Anal. Greg. 28, 50) 1942, 1949; [2]DS 2826.

H

HEGEL, G.W.F., (1770–1831)

The German philosopher's entry into theological speculation led him to formulate a theory about the Trinity.[1] It is not a contribution to doctrine on the subject, and is of interest merely because of the author's place in the development of German philosophy. His views are found principally in *Die Phänomenologie des Geistes*, in *Die Encyclopaedie der philosophischen Wissenschaften im Grundrisse*, in the *Vorlesungen über die Philosophie der Religion*. The reader is referred to a number of attempts to summarize H's Trinitarian theory.[2] In the following passage he appears to do so himself. "What we have said above about the nature of spirit is to be demonstrated and has been demonstrated through philosophy alone, needing no confirmation by means of ordinary consciousness. Still, to the extent that our non-philosophical thinking requires, for its part, that the developed concept of spirit should be more representational, we can remind ourselves that Christian theology too conceives of God, i.e., the truth, as spirit, and it regards spirit not as a quiescence, a persistence in empty uniformity, but as necessarily entering into the process of differentiating itself from itself, of positing its other, and as first coming to itself not through relinquishment but through the preserving supersession of this other. As is well known theology expresses this process in the following representational manner: God the Father (this simple universal being-in-itself), putting aside his solitariness, creates nature (that which is external to himself, self-externality), begets a Son (his other ego), but by virtue of his infinite love, beholds himself in this other, recognises his image therein, and returns in this image to unity with himself. This unity is no longer abstract or immediate, but concrete, being mediated through difference in that it is the Holy Spirit proceeding from the Father and the Son, and attaining perfect actuality and truth in the Christian community. Thus must God be grasped in his absolute truth as the actual being-in-and-for-self of the Idea. It is thus that he has to be known, not simply in the form of the mere concept, of abstract being-for-itself, or in the equally untrue form of an individual actuality in non-agreement with the universality of its concept, but in the full agreement of his Concept with his actuality."[3]

"Thus," says a commentator, "the rational exposition of Trinitarian theology is the highest task of philosophy. This exposition identifies the Persons of the Trinity with the three phases of the speculative Idea: God the Father is the Absolute Thought—the Idea of philosophy expounded in Metaphysics. God the Son is the divine Life of the finite 'Universe', expounded in the philosophy of nature (including *Sittlichkeit*). God the Spirit is the totality of Speculation, the conceptual motion through which the life of the world receives its rational explanation."[4]

Understandably H. has been suspected of pantheism—his theory on the relationship of God and the world leaves him open to this charge, which some have attenuated to panentheism. Yet he continues to attract exponents of his difficult theory, some of whom will not hear of pantheism.

[1]For general bibliography cf. standard reference works, e.g., Cross-Livingstone, *The Oxford Dictionary of the Christian Church*, 628; on H's Trinitarian ideas cf. J. Hessen, *Hegel's Trinitätslehre*, Freiburg in B., 1922; H. Rondet, S.J., "Divinisation du chrétien," *NRT* 71 (1949), 564–576; *id.*, *Hegelianisme et Christianisme*, Paris, 1965; C. Bruaire, *Logique et religion chrétienne dans la philosophie de Hegel*, Paris, 1964; V.J. Splett, *Die Trinitätslehre G.W.F. Hegels*, Freiburg, Munich, 1965; A. Chapelle, *Hegel et la religion*, Paris, 1967, esp., II, 53–109; L. Oeing-Hanhoff, "Hegels Trinitätslehre," *Theol.Phil.*, 52, (1977), 378–407; *id.*, same title, *Theol.Quartal.*, 159 (1979), 287–303; add items in n.2, infra; Washington, 1982, 150–55;   [2]B. Margerie, S.J., *La Trinité*, 345–351; H. Küng, *Does God Exist?*, London, 1980, 157f; W.J. Hill, *The Three-Personed God*; Q. Lauer, S.J., *Hegel's Concept of God*, New York, 1982, 300, 305–306; W. Casper, *Der Gott Jesu Christi*, Mainz, 1982, 322–25; H.S. Harries, *Hegel's Development*, *Night Thoughts* (1801–06), Oxford, 1983, 155ff;   [3]*Die Encyclopaedie*, 381 Zusatz, *Werke*;   [4]H.S. Harries, *op.cit.*, 155.

HILARY OF POITIERS, ST., DOCTOR OF THE CHURCH (c. 315–367)

Bishop of Poitiers in the age of Arianism, H. became the principal defender of orthodoxy in the west; thereto he brought the theology of the east.[1] His treatise on the Trinity is the first complete work to appear on the subject in the west. The *De Synodis* was a letter written to western bishops during the exile forced on him after his defence of St. Athanasius (*qv*) at the synod of Beziers, 356; his main literary activity during the four year absence from his see was the *De Trinitate*. Though banished from his diocese he took part in the synod of Seleucia, 359—he had refused to go to the Arian synod of Milan in 355.

His Trinitarian theology is contained in the twelve books of the treatise which is so entitled. Consideration must also be given to the *De Synodis*, the first part historical, dealing with the creeds of the east, with initial emphasis on the "blasphemy" of Sirmium (9–65, 1–8 being the preamble), the second part (66–91) dogmatic, being a statement of his own belief. He offers an explanation of the *homoousion* and tries to convince the defenders of the *homoiousios* that their sole means of orthodoxy was to see in it the sense of the *homoousion*: "I pray you, brethren, remove all suspicion and leave no occasion for it. To approve of *homoiousion*, we need not disapprove of *homoousion* . . . . Brethren, forgive my anguish; it is an impious act that you are attempting. I cannot endure to hear the man anathematized who says *homoousion* and says it in the right sense. No fault can be found with a word which does no harm to the meaning of religion. I do not know the word *homoiousion*, or understand it, unless it confesses a similarity of essence. I call the God of heaven and earth to witness, that when I had heard neither word, my belief was always such that I should have interpreted *homoiousion* by *homoousion*. That is I believed that nothing could be similar according to nature unless it was of the same nature. Though long ago regenerate in baptism, and for some time a bishop, I never heard of the Nicene creed until I was going into exile, but the gospels and epistles suggested to me the meaning of *homoousion* and *homoiousion*. Our desire is sacred. Let us not condemn the fathers, let us not encourage heretics, lest while we drive one heresy away we nurture another. After the Council of Nicaea our fathers interpreted the meaning of *homoousion* with scrupulous care; the books are extant, the facts are fresh in men's minds: if anything has to be added to the interpretation, let us consult together. Between us we can thoroughly establish the faith, so that what has been well settled need not be disturbed and what has been misunderstood may be removed."[2]

For a total picture of the mind of H. on the Trinitarian question one must take account of the *Liber adversus Valentem et Ursacium*, of which fragments remain; it was composed after the synod of Milan, designed to expose the intrigues of the Arians; of some relevance too are the *Contra Auxentium*, that is, the Arian bishop of Milan, predecessor of St. Ambrose, and H.'s hymns. Lucifer of Cagliari (*qv*), a hard-line anti-Arian, took exception to the conciliatory approach of the *De Synodis* and H. replied with *Apologetica ad reprehensores libri de synodis responsa*, mere fragments of which remain.[3]

It is in the *De Trinitate*, however, that we shall seek the full doctrine of H. on our subject. Since the first three books seem to be a separate entity, a kind of treatise *De Fide*, it was thought that H. had completed them before his exile; the opening words of book four seemed to lend support for the opinion: "The earlier books of this treatise, written some time ago, contain, I think, an invincible proof that we hold and profess the faith in Father, Son and Holy Spirit, which is taught by the evangelists and apostles, and that no commerce is possible between us and the heretics, inasmuch as they deny unconditionally, irrationally and recklessly, the divinity of our Lord Jesus Christ."[4] Recent critical research shows that all twelve books were composed in the east, during the exile. In book one, chapters 20–36, which give an analysis of the books that follow, were presumably added later than the composition of the rest of the book. Further details as to the phases of H's work, the arrangement of the books in their present order, the date of composition of the separate books, have been worked out by patient scholarly study.[5]

As to the contents, book one begins with an autobiographical account of H's conversion to the faith, then outlines the treatment of the main theme as it will be developed in the subsequent books. Book two from the starting point of Mt 28:19 ("Go therefore and make disciples of all nations, baptizing them in the name of the Father and of the Son and of the Holy Spirit"), deals first with heresies against its meaning: "Thus do they destroy the consistency and completeness of the mystery of faith. They break up the absolute unity of God by assigning differences of nature where all is clearly common to each; they deny the Father by robbing the Son of his true sonship; they deny the Holy Spirit in their blindness to the facts that we possess him and that Christ gave him." On each divine person H. then sets forth the context of the ancient Latin catechesis. The key text in book three is Jn 14:11: "I am in the Father and the Father in me." H. first recalls his teaching on the Father already set forth in the previous book, then deals with the eternal birth of the Son, much in the line of Novatian, then, proceeding from Jn 17:1–6, outlines a theology of the Incarnation. He expresses a stimulating idea of the Son as image (*qv*) of the Father: "For the Son has received all things from the Father; he is the likeness of God, the image of his substance. The words *the image of his substance* discriminate between Christ and him from whom he is, but only to establish their distinct existence, not to teach a difference of nature; and the meaning of *Father in Son and Son in Father* is that there is the perfect fullness of the godhead in both. The Father is not impaired by the Son's existence, nor is the Son a mutilated fragment of the Father. An image implies its original; likeness is a relative term. Now nothing can be like God unless it have its source in him; a perfect likeness can be reflected only from that which it represents; an accurate resemblance forbids the assumption of any element of difference."[6]

H. ends the book with 1 Cor: 1:17–25, culminating in Paul's rich phrase, "Christ the power and the wisdom of God." The approach changes in the next three books, four, five and six. Here he undertakes refutation of the Arian theses, "in order to make our assurance of the faith even more certain by exposure of every one of their falsehoods and blasphemies."[7] H. incorporates in the text of book four the letter of Arius (*qv*) to Alexander (*qv*). In the three books H. is abundantly biblical, drawing enthusiastically on the theophanies and prophecies of OT, lining up gospel texts and assertions of the apostles against the Arians—this especially in book six.

Book seven, loaded with biblical texts, not too clearly ordered, serves as a link with books eight, nine and ten, where H. shows his skill as a controversialist. In book eight he rebuts the Arian perversion of the Johannine text, "That they all may be one, as thou Father in me and I in thee, that they also may be in us" (Jn 17:21); the argument is reinforced by many NT texts which point to the unity of substance between Father and Son, those for instance which attribute to each the same relations with the Holy Spirit. In book nine the array of NT texts and H.'s unravelling of their meaning continue—this time texts which seem to show Christ turning aside from himself divine powers and attributes, Mt 9:18, 13:32, or again which seem to indicate inferiority of nature in regard to the Father, Jn 11:9, 14:28. In book ten H. comes to grips with the effects of Christ's self-emptying, the sentiments manifest in the gospel record, fear, anxiety, suffering, weakness. "How could Jesus Christ, the Son of God, have been born of Mary, except by the Word becoming flesh: that is, by the Son of God, though in the form of God, taking the form of a slave? When he who was in the form of God took the form of a slave, two contraries were brought together. Thus it was just as true that he received the form of a slave, as that he remained in the form of God." With that principle fixed he can go on to deal with the particular instances, many of which are raised almost with a sense of novelty by modern proponents of a reductionist Christology (*qv*), a Christology from below in more senses than one, the sufferings of the Passion, the prayer in Gethsemani, the cry to the Father from the cross "why hast thou forsaken me?", all the words and episodes which reveal true humanity: H's text is heavily laced with biblical quotations.

In book eleven H. deals with the post-Resurrection texts, wrestling especially with 1 Cor 15:21–28, ending with the mysterious phrase "when the Son himself will also be subjected to him who put all things under him." In book twelve it is Proverbs 8:22, "The Lord created me at the beginning of his work, the first of his acts of old," a text used by the Arians to show that the Son of God had a beginning in time, to which H. turns his lively attention. A number of other points are dealt with in a not too closely connected fashion and the book ends with a beautiful prayer to the Trinity. The final passage is: "Keep, I pray thee, this my pious faith undefiled, and even till my spirit departs, grant that this may be the utterance of my convictions; so that I may ever hold fast that which I professed in the creed of my regeneration, when I was baptized in the Father, and the Son, and the Holy Spirit. Let me, in short, adore thee our Father, and thy Son together with thee; let me win the favour of thy Holy Spirit who is from thee, through thy Only-begotten. For I have a convincing witness to my faith, who says, *Father, all mine are thine, and thine are mine,* even my Lord Jesus Christ, abiding in thee, and from thee, and with thee, forever God: who is blessed for ever and ever. Amen."[8]

There has been much discussion of H's Trinitarian theology, on his understanding of the *homoousion*, and on certain points of resemblance with the teaching of the Homoeousians, for example that the generation of the Son was not from the nature but the will of the Father. He has not the precision and vast perspective of St. Augustine (*qv*), nor the systematic coherence of St. Thomas Aquinas. But he was first in the west to see the need for a large treatment and synthesis, within which, in the terms of theology in his time, he was fully orthodox, a champion of orthodoxy.

What of his doctrine on the Holy Spirit? He never says that the Holy Spirit is God, or consubstantial with the Father and the Son; he is not explicit on the personality.[9] One can say that everything he says in the passages on the Holy Spirit is utterly consistent with sound doctrine: for example: "And when the Spirit of Christ dwells in us, this indwelling means not that any other Spirit dwells in us than the Spirit of God. But if it is understood that Christ dwells in us through the Holy Spirit, we must yet recognise this Spirit of God as also the Spirit of Christ. And since the nature dwells in us as the nature of one substantive being, we must regard the nature of the Son as identical with that of the Father, since the Holy Spirit who is both the Spirit of Christ and the Spirit of God is proved to be a being of one nature. I ask now, therefore, how can they fail to be one by nature? The Spirit of truth proceeds from the Father, he is sent by the Son and receives from the Son. But all things that the Father hath are the Son's, and for this cause he who receives from him is the Spirit of God, but at the same time the Spirit of Christ. The Spirit is a being of the nature of the Son, but the same being is of the nature of the Father. He is the Spirit of him who raised Christ from the dead; but this is no other than the Spirit of Christ who was so raised. The nature of Christ and of God must differ in some respect so as not to be the same, if it can be shown that the Spirit which is of God is not the Spirit of Christ also."[10]

H. expresses the equivalent of a theory of the circumincession (*qv*) of the Father and Son; in the passage quoted he comes near to doing so for the Spirit also. If he does not teach the *Filioque* he uses a phrase "he must be confessed as from the Father and the Son," but the Latin "*qui Patre et Filio auctoribus confitendus est*" is susceptible of another rendering, "confess him on the evidence of the Father and the Son." Elsewhere H. deduces a procession (*qv*) from Jn 16:14, "he will take what is mine"; "for the Spirit of truth proceeds from the Father and is sent from the Father by the Son."[11]

[1]Works: PL 9, 10; CSEL 22, 65; Eng. tr. of *De Trinitate*, S. McKenna, Fathers of the Church, Washington, 1954; for complete bibliography cf. C. Kannengeisser, S.J., *DSp*, VII 466–499; on Trinitarian theology, A. Viehhauser, *Hilarius Pictaviensis geschildert in seinem Kampfe gegen den Arianismus* Klagenfurt, 1860; J.P. Baltzer, *Die Theologie des hl.Hilarius von Poitiers*, Rottwell, 1879. Th. Froster, "Zur Theologie des Hilarius," *Theologische Studien und Kritiken*, vol 61, 1888, 645–686; A.

Beck, *Die Trinitätslehre des hl. Hilarius*, Mainz, 1903; G. Rasneur, "L'homoiousianisme dans ses rapports avec l'orthodoxie," *RHE* 4 (1903), 189–206, 411–431; S. Palumbo, *Unità e distinzione in Dio secondo S.Ilario*, Capua, 1940; esp. P. Smulders, *La doctrine trinitaire de S.Hilaire de Poitiers*, Rome,1944; cf. review of last-named work by J. Lebon, *RSR*, 33 (1946), 484–89; A. Verrasto, *Il fondamento ultimo della perfetta consustanzialità del Figlio al Padre nel De Trinitate di S.Ilario*, Potenza, 1948; A. Segovia, "La clausula 'Sine differentia discretionis sentimus' del prefacio trinitario, y sus precedentes patristicos," *Mélanges J.de Ghellinck*, I, Gembloux, 1951, 375–386; M. Simonetti, "La processione dello Spirito Santo nei Padri latini," *Maia*, 7 (1955), 308–24; P. Galtier, "Saint Hilaire, trait d'union entre l'Occident et l'Orient," *Greg*, 40 (1959), 609–623; P. Loeffler, "Die Trinitätslehre des Bischofs Hilarius von Poitiers zwischen Ost und West, Zeitschrift für Kirchengeschichte," 71 (1960), 26–36; J. Moingt, *La théologie trinitaire de St. Hilaire* in *Hilaire et so temps*, Actes du Colloque de Poitiers, 1968, *Etudes Augustiniennes*, Paris, 1968. [2]*De synodis* 91 LNPF, IX, 28, 29; [3]Cf. LNPF Introduction, xxxviii; [4]LNPF 70; [5]Cf. C. Kannengeisser, *op.cit.*, following M. Simonetti, *Note sulla struttura e la cronologia del De Trinitate di Ilario*, Studi Urbinati, 39, 1965; [6]LNPF 53, 69; [7]LNPF 70; [8]LNPF 233; [9]cf. P. Smulders, *op.cit.*, 275; [10]VIII, 26, LNPF 144, 5; [11]see article *Filioque*.

HIPPOLYTUS OF ROME, ST. (c. 170–c. 236)

H., who wrote in Greek, suffered posthumously by the Latinization of theology in the West.[1] His writings were listed by Eusebius of Caesarea (*qv*) and Jerome, and he would have been highly valued in his time. Though some light was shed on his literary output by a statue discovered in 1551, it is only in the nineteenth and twentieth centuries that his works have become known, with inevitable controversies over authenticity. There is a paucity of firm continuous fact on his personality and career, on his entanglements with Popes and his possible phase as an anti-Pope.

H's Trinitarian doctrine has to be rescued from such works as survive, most in fragments, some of dubious or suspect authenticity: the *Syntagma against all the heresies*, the *Refutation of all heresies* (sometimes called the *Philosophumena*), the *Traditio Apostolica*, which has a multiple manuscript tradition,[2] commentaries on Scripture and quotations in other works.

H., in his Trinitarian theology, is more satisfactory on the Father and the Son than on the Holy Spirit, whom he nonetheless names frequently. He was, in his lifetime, accused by Callistus, a deacon who later became Pope, of "ditheism"; his rebuttal was acid and on the personal level inflamed. But the point at issue was the eternal generation of the Word prior to all things, central to H's system, not acceptable to Callistus.

It has also been maintained that H. was subordinationist (*qv*) or leaned in that direction.[3] Nowhere does he say that the Word is inferior to the Father, and he asserts frequently, without the slightest reservation, the divinity of Christ. Again, as a result of the false attribution of the *Contra Noetum*, still quoted by scholarly people as a work of H. though it is not so, the opinion was expressed in certain quarters that he thought that the Word did not become Son, or at least perfect Son, of God save through the Incarnation. All that survives of his work flatly contradicts such an interpretation.

Photius (*qv*) who had read the *De universo* of H., a work now lost, says of his doctrine on the generation (*qv*) of the Son: "On the subject of Christ, our true God, he expounds ideas rigorously exact; he attributes to him formally even the name of Christ and he gives an impeccable explanation of his ineffable procession from the Father."[4] On the divinity of the Son we have an explicit passage: "The Father, having then put all things under his own Son, things in heaven, on earth and under the earth, has shown everywhere that he was first-born in all: the first-born of God, so that it should be evident that he is second after the Father, Son of God; first-born before the angels, so that he should appear Lord of the angels; first-born of a Virgin so that he should be seen recreating in himself the first created Adam; first-born of the dead, so that he should become the first-fruits of our resurrection."[5] For H. it is the Son of God who chastises the Egyptians and drowns them in the Red Sea; it was the Son of God who gave the law to Moses on Sinai; it was the Son of God who was seen and confessed by Nebuchadnezzar.

On the generation of the Son H. writes as follows: "Therefore this one God, who is above all things, first, by thinking, brought forth the Word; not a word like that which comes from the mouth of man, but rather an interior word, expressing his understanding of all things. He, the Word, is the only being generated by God; for the Father himself is the being from whom came that which was generated. The Word was the cause of things which exist, bearing in himself the will of his begetter, not ignorant of the fatherly thought. For as soon as he proceeded from his begetter, having become his first-born voice, he holds within him the ideas thought out by the Father; wherefore as the Father ordered the world to be made, the Word completed all things pleasing God. His Word is the only thing that comes out of him; therefore he too is God, since he is God's substance. The world, however, came from nothing; therefore it is not God."[6]

Irenaeus (qv) and Theophilus of Antioch (qv) thought that the Wisdom of God was the Holy Spirit. Judging from the *Contra Noetum* commentators have attributed the same idea to H. But he is the one who perhaps best developed the idea of the Logos as Wisdom of God.[7] What is his doctrine of the Holy Spirit? His role in important moments is mentioned, in prophecy, in the birth and baptism of Christ, in the baptism and life of the Christian, in the renewal of the world at the end of time. His doctrine was really Trinitarian.

Did he use Trinitarian formulas? This raises the vexed question of the *Traditio Apostolica*. In practically all the sources we have for this document there is, or is assumed to be—in the case of defective MSS—a Trinitarian creed.[8]

---

[1]Cf. esp. M. Richard, *DSp*, VII, 531–571 with exhaustive bibl.; Works PG 10, 261–962; *Contra Noetum*, ed. P. Nautin, Paris, 1949; id. *Hippolyte et Josipe*, Paris, 1947, attributing the *Philosophumena* to a certain Josephus, a view rejected generally—on which cf. M. Richard, *op.cit.*, 533; id. P. Nautin, *Lettres et écrivains chrétiens des 2e et 3e siècles*, Paris, 1961, 177–190, same thesis; for doctrine cf. A. d'Ales, *La théologie de saint Hippolyte*, Paris, 1906; G. Bardy, *La vie spirituelle d'après les Pères de trois premiers siècles*, ed. 2, A. Hamman, Tournai-Paris, II, 177–191; B. Capelle, O.S.B., "Le Logos Fils de Dieu dans la théologie d'Hippolyte," *RTAM* 9 (1937), 109–124; J. Barbel, *Christos Angelos, Die Anschauung von christus als Bote und Engel in der gelehrten und volkümlichen Literatur des Christlichen Altertums*, Bonn, 1964, 68–70; A. Orbe, *Hacia la primera teología de la procesión del Verbo*, Analecta Gregoriana, 99–100, Rome, 1958; G. Aeby, *Les missions divines de S.Justin à Origene*, Fribourg, Suisse, 1958, 88–102; P. Beskow, *Rex Gloriae, The Kingship of Christ in the early Church*, Uppsala, 1962; A. Grillmeier, S.J., *Christ in Christian Tradition*, London, 1964, 134–139; J.M. Hanssens, S.J., *La Liturgie d'Hippolyte*, Orientalia Christiana Analecta, 1965; Altaner-Stuiber, 1966, 164–69; E. Amann, *DTC* VI (1920), 2487–2511; T. Camelot, *Catholicisme*, V (1958), 755–60; Quasten II, 163–210; [2]Cf. J. Crehan, S.J., *Early Christian Baptism and the Creed*, London, 1948, 159ff; J.M. Hanssens, *op.cit.*; [3]G. Aeby, *op.cit.*; [4]Apud M. Richard, *op.cit.*, 546; [5]*In Dan.* IV, 11, 5, *ibid.*, 548; [6]*Philosophumena*, 10, 33, PG 163, 3447; [7]M. Richard, *op.cit.*, 549; [8]J. Crehan, *op.cit.*, 112–114.

HOMOEANS

Identified with and led by Acacius of Caesarea (qv), the H. sought to evade the dominant parties, those who based their thinking on the *Homoousion* (see Consubstantial) and the *Homoiousion* (qv) by making their basic principle that the Son was like (*Homoios*) the Father.[1] The possibility of establishing this view did exist for a short while, 357–360, with dissatisfaction at the Anomoean formula (see article Eunomius). But the sponsorship of the emperor, then decisive in rallying voting support in a council, regardless of personal conviction and the "Sentiment of the Faithful" (qv), was not theirs. It went for a time to Basil of Ancyra (qv).

---

[1]Cf. bibl. to article Arianism.

HOMOIOUSION

"Of like substance": this was a word used by moderate Arians, those who did not feel authorized by Sacred Scripture to use the *Homoousion*.[1] Some whose orthodoxy was not in doubt, like St. Cyril of Jerusalem (qv), found themselves faced with this difficulty. Some were driven to use the word when they realised the extremes to which the Arian heresy was going. Such was Basil of Ancyra (qv) of whom Athanasius wrote thus: "Those who deny the Council altogether, are sufficiently exposed by these brief remarks; those, however, who accept everything else that was defined at Nicaea, and doubt only about the Consubstantial (qv), must not be treated as enemies; nor do we here attack them as Ariomaniacs, nor as opponents of the Fathers, but we discuss the matter with them as brothers with brothers, who mean what we mean, and dispute only about the word. For confessing that the Son is from the substance of the Father, and not from other subsistence, and that he is not a creature or work, but his genuine and natural offspring, and that he is eternally with the Father as being his Word and Wisdom, they are not far from accepting even the phrase "Consubstantial." Now such is Basil, who wrote from Ancyra concerning the faith."[2]

---

[1]Cf. Bibl. to article Arianism; [2]*De synodis*, 41, LNPF, 472.

HOSIUS OF CORDOVA (c. 257–357)

Hosius (or Ossius) exemplifies dramatically at the outset of his episcopal career and again at its end the problems of churchmen in the first phase of

Christian freedom within the Roman empire.[1] Selected as ecclesiastical adviser by the first Christian emperor, Constantine, under whose father he had suffered for the faith, he played a key role in the first ecumenical council which was called by the emperor; in his last year, a centenarian, he was a victim of Caesaro-papism: Constantius II, son of his early patron, not only chose what interpretation of the faith he would protect, but used the civil power to coerce the teaching authority. He was defied by a few bishops, principally one who for a while carried the Church on his back. Nor must we forget Newman's considered judgment: it was the laity, along with Athanasius, who saved the day.

With the exception of the one fatal lapse in his last year H. was throughout on the side of orthodoxy. A bishop since 295, counsellor to Constantine from 312, he was sent to Alexandria to disentangle the conflict between Arius (qv) and Alexander (qv) in 324. He presided at a synod at Antioch in the spring of 325; there the errors of Arius were condemned. It probably was he who suggested a council to Constantine (qv); after the emperor's opening speech he presided at the assembly. He may also have suggested, personally or through Constantine, the key word of the council, *homoousios* (see CONSUBSTANTIAL).

H. certainly presided at the Council of Sardica. He is probably the author of the Canons and of the three synodical letters: these are reproduced by Athanasius;[2] they are addressed to the Church of Alexandria, to the Bishops of Egypt and Libya, and to all the bishops.

While Constans ruled the west, H. was safe. When Constantius became sole emperor, he was in danger. As the campaign to destroy Athanasius reached its climax, pressure was put on H. to disown him. He steadily refused. Finally the emperor brought him to Sirmium for a whole year and with violence and threats forced him to submit; "at last broken by suffering, he was brought, though hardly, to hold communion with Valens Ursacius and their fellows, though he would not subscribe against Athanasius."[3] Returning home he withdrew his assent and died in the faith of Nicaea.

The one text which we can be sure is from his pen is his letter to Constantius in the course of his tribulation. He was old enough, he pointed out, to be the emperor's grandfather! He warned him about some of the Arians in his entourage,

pointed to the example of his brother, Constans, and rebuked him thus: "Cease these proceedings, I beseech you, and remember you are a mortal man. Be afraid of the day of judgment, and keep yourself pure thereunto. Intrude not yourself into ecclesiastical matters, neither give commands unto us concerning them; but learn them from us. God has put into your hands the kingdom; to us he has entrusted the affairs of his Church; and as he who would steal the empire from you would resist the ordinance of God, so likewise fear on your part lest by taking upon yourself the government of the Church, you become guilty of a great offence. It is written, 'Render unto Caesar the things that are Caesar's, and unto God the things that are God's.' Neither therefore is it permitted unto us to exercise an earthly rule, nor have you, Sire, any authority to burn incense. These things I write unto you out of a concern for your salvation. With regard to the subject of your letters, this is my determination; I will not unite myself to the Arians; I anathematize their heresy. Neither will I subscribe against Athanasius, whom both we and the church of the Romans and the whole council pronounced to be guiltless. And you yourself also, when you understood this, sent for the man, and gave him permission to return with honour to his country and his Church. What reason then can there be for so great a change in your conduct? The same persons who were his enemies before, are so now also; and the things they now whisper to his prejudice (for they do not declare them openly in his presence) the same they spoke against him before you sent for him; the same they spread abroad concerning him when they come to the Council. And when I required them to come forward, as I have before said, they were unable to produce their proofs; had they possessed any, they would not have fled so disgracefully."[4]

---

[1]Cf. Athanasius, *History of the Arians*, 42–45 LNPF IV, 285–87; *Apologia contra Arianos*, 8 89, *ibid.*, 147; *Apologia de fuga*, 5, *ibid.* 256; Hilary, Fragmenta 2, 6; *De synodis*, 10f, LNPF, IX, 6f; Socrates H.E., II, 31; esp. V.C. De Clercq, *Ossius of Cordova*, Washington, 1954; id., *NCE* VII, 153, 54; id., *Ossius of Cordova and the Origins of Priscillianism* SP (K. Aland and F.L. Cross, Berlin, 1957), I: 601–608—all with bibl.; ed. J.M.F. Manque, *Leaders of Iberian Christianity*, Boston, 1962; H. Chadwick, "Ossius of Cordova and the presidency of the Council of Antioch, 325," *JTS* 9 (1958), 292–304; U. Dominguez del Val, O.S.A., "Osio de Córdoba," *Revista Española de Teologia*, 18 (1958), 141–165; 261–281; [2]*Apologia contra Arianos*, 36f; 119ff; C. Kirch, Enchiridion, 504f; [3]*History of the Arians*, 45, *op. cit*, 287; [4]*Op.cit.*, 286.

I

ICONOGRAPHY

Andrei Rublev's (c. 1410) icon on the Trinity, used as the frontispiece of this work, is a supreme example of its genre; rivalled only for excellence by the icon of Our Lady of Vladimir. It captivates by its daring and power and at the same time raises the problem about artistic representation of the Trinity: how to depict in elements or symbols taken from what is material the transcendent, pure spirit. Art historians plot the course of attempts made thus far.[1]

Early Christian architecture symbolized the Trinity by the *ecclesia triplex*, three churches which were within one complex or under a single roof. This tendency is found in medieval times.

In the mosaics on the arch of St. Mary Major there is a peculiar version of the Trinity theme: the *etimasia*, the empty throne, the book on a cushion and a purple veil, the dove and the *crux gemmata*, which is surrounded by the *aurun coronarium*.

Iconography has been influenced by the OT episode when Abraham had a vision by the oaks of Mamre: "And the Lord appeared to him by the oaks of Mamre, as he sat at the door of his tent in the heat of the day. He lifted up his eyes and looked, and behold three men stood in front of him. When he saw them, he ran from the tent door to meet them, and bowed himself to the earth, and said, 'My Lord, if I have found favour in your sight, do not pass by your servant . . . .'"

(Gen 18:1–3); after they had accepted a meal, "They said to him, 'Where is Sarah your wife?' And he said, 'She is in the tent.' The Lord said, 'I will surely return to you in the spring, and Sarah your wife shall have a son'" (18: 9, 10).

St. Ambrose[2] and St. Augustine (*qv*)[3] saw an allusion to the Trinity in the passage; Augustine, considering the change from the plural to the singular used a pithy phrase," *et ipse Abraham tres vidit, unum adoravit.*" This representation of three individuals is found on a mosaic of the nave of St. Mary Major and in mosaics in St. Vitale, Ravenna, sixth century, and in Sicily, Monreale, late twelfth century. From illuminated Greek manuscripts it was taken up by icon makers, given a place of honour in the iconostasis.

Rublev chose to show a double theme, the Eucharist (*qv*) and the Trinity. Specialists differ on the precise interpretation of the three figures. V. Lossky (*qv*), L. Ouspensky, Daniel Ange, and J. Klinger think that the angel on the left represents the Father, as do the art historians V. Lazarev and M. V. Alpatov; P. Evdokimov, an Orthodox theologian of the beautiful in the icon medium, thought that the angel in the centre represented the Father.

Orthodox theologians often elaborate their theology from the icons—witness S. Bulgakov's giant synthesis from the icon of Our Lady of Novgorod. M. Wojciechowski has sought to build a theory on the procession of the Holy Spirit from a detailed analysis of Rublev's famous icon. Discussing three possible formulae, *ex Patre, ex Patre Filioque* (qv), *ex Patre per Filium*, he writes: "The monarchy, (qv) (that is for the writer *ex Patre*) the generation and the *per Filium* are visibly manifest. What of the *Filioque*? Could it have raised an echo in Rublev's mind? In principle it is not impossible. At the beginning of the fifteenth century, an Orthodox painter, sufficiently cultured to be abreast of contemporary theological discussions and to know Italian art, could have intended to include the content of this formula in his work. It would besides be subordinate to the others more clearly expressed. Another explanation appears more probable. "The Trinity" of Rublev expressed Trinitarian theology in such an inspired, plenary and perfect manner that all aspects of the procession of the Spirit are to be found in it, even one of which the painter was not conscious."

This author thinks that so profound and complete is the vision of the Trinity conveyed by Rublev that the third formula, *ex Patre Filioque* appears therein as the logical complement of the others, an integral element in the synthesis which unites all three. "That would confirm the opinion that 'The Trinity' has exceptional value and is timeless. It would contain in harmonious unity truths of which the comprehension and mutual agreement still meet obstacles. The *lex orandi*, or which the icon is part, precedes the *lex credendi*."[4]

Byzantine influence penetrated western religious art through German illuminators. A different form of the threefold figure, that is, the same divine Person three times repeated, with a cruciform nimbus is found in tenth century pen drawings. A new idea would be added before long, that of the Trinity creating the world, particularly man made in the semblance of God; thus Herrad of Landsberg's *Hortus Deliciarum* shows it.

In the later Middle Ages the Trinitarian theme was presented in the *Synthronos*, on which the three Persons were seated. Inspired by the final scene in the *Drama of the Virtues*, Jean Fouquet (c. 1450) depicted the three Persons, white and alike, on a sedilia with three canopies, Jesus enthroned at his Father's right; to the right of the Trinity Our Lady occupied another throne.

What is probably the oldest illustration of the feast of the Trinity is an Anglo-Saxon drawing between 1023 and 1035 showing the Virgin *Theotokos*, holding the Word Incarnate and crowned by the dove, with God the Father and the Son.

The *Theotokos* of the *Sedes Sapientiae* is replaced by the Ancient of Days. Thus Daniel writes of this figure: "As I looked, thrones were placed and one that was ancient of days took his seat; his raiment was white as snow, and the hair of his head like pure wool; his throne was fiery flames, its wheels were burning fire .... I saw in the night visions and behold, with the clouds of heaven there came one like the Son of man and he came to the Ancient of Days and was presented before him ... until the Ancient of Days came, and judgment was given for the saints of the Most High, and the time came when the saints received the kingdom" (7:9, 13, 22). The change from the *Theotokos* is made with God the Father holding in his lap the Logos, Emmanuel; the dove is in the lap of Christ. Another variant of the *Sedes Sapientiae* in which the Virgin holds Emmanuel in a shield was also adopted to represent the Ancient of Days.

In time elements of the Passion of Christ were integrated into symbols of the Trinity: Christ crucified is beneath God the Father, who is surrounded with a cruciform halo, the two linked by the dove; or again God supports the cross in the *mandorla* and his lips are joined to those of the crucified One by the dove: an image of the spiration of the third Person by Father and Son. There are variations on this theme which would probably appeal to Jürgen Moltmann; the most striking is probably that from the Franciscan church at Torun, Poland, now housed in the National Museum, Warsaw.

[1]Cf. A.N. Didron, *Iconographie chrétienne, Histoire de Dieu*, Paris, 1844; A. Hackel, *Die Trinität in der Kunst*, Berlin, 1931; A. Heimann, *L'Iconographie de la Trinité et son développement en Occident, L'art Chrétien*, 1 (1934); "Trinitas Crator Mundi," *Journal of the Warburg and Courtauld Institutes*, 2 (1938), 42–52; W. Braunfels, *Die Heilige Dreifaltigkeit*, Düsseldorf, 1954; *La Trinité*, Coll. *Prière et Art*, Paris, 1955, Introd. H. Schipperges; T. Dormzeniecki, "The Torun Quinity in the National Museum in Warsaw," *ArtBull* 46 (1964); P. Evdokimov, *L'Art de l'Icône, Théologie de la beauté*, Paris, 1972; *The Icon of the Trinity of Andrei Rublev*, 231–243; L. Ouspensky, V. Lossky (qv), *The Meaning of Icons*, London, 1983; L. Ouspensky, *The Holy Trinity*, 200–205; M. Wojciechowski, "Trois formules sur l'origine du Saint-Esprit; ex Patre, ex Patre Filioque, ex Patre per Filium," *Nova et Vetera*, Fribourg, 1982/83, 189–200; [2]*De Abraham*, PL 14, 435; [3]*Contra Maximinum Arianum Episcopum*, PL 42, 809; [4]*Op.cit.*, 197.

IGNATIUS OF ANTIOCH, ST. (c. 35–c. 107)

Totally consumed with love of Christ and eager to shed his blood for this love, I. in the seven letters now accepted as genuine, does not do the work of a speculative theologian.[1] His purpose was to encourage the different communities to which he wrote to adhere to the traditions that had been received from the apostles: he is therefore primarily a witness to the facts, the realities of the Christ event—against Docetism—and the demands of the Christian vocation against Judaism.

I's reference to the three divine persons in his letter to the Ephesians is very much in the context of the "economy": "You consider yourselves stones of the Father's temple, prepared for the edifice of God the Father, to be taken aloft by the hoisting engine of Jesus Christ, that is, the Cross, while the Holy Spirit serves you as a rope; your faith is your spiritual windlass and your love the road which leads up to God. And thus you are all travellers together, God-bearers and temple-bearers, Christ-bearers and bearers of holiness, with the commandments of Jesus Christ for festal attire."[2]

The context to the passage in the letter to the Magnesians is somewhat different, loyalty to the traditions, to authority, and to belief in life with the Three: "Be zealous, therefore, to stand squarely on the decrees of the Lord and the Apostles, *that in all things whatsoever you may prosper*, in body and in soul, in faith and in love, in the Son and the Father and the Spirit, in the beginning and the end, together with your most reverend bishop and with your presbytery—that fittingly woven spiritual crown!—and with your deacons, men of God. Submit to the bishop and to each other's rights, just as did Jesus Christ in the flesh to the Father, and as the Apostles did to Christ and the Father and the Spirit, so that there may be oneness both of flesh and of spirit."[3]

[1]For the controversy on authenticity cf. J.B. Lightfoot, *The Apostolic Fathers*, Part II (3 vols) critical text, Eng. tr., London, 1885; critical ed. F.X. Funk, revised K. Bilmeyer, *Die Apostolischen Väters*, 1 Teil, Tübingen, 1924; Eng. tr., J.H. Strawley, *The Epistles of St.Ignatius*, London, 1935; P.T. Camelot, SC 10, 1944, 2nd ed., 1951; id. esp., *DSp* VII, 1250–56; J.A. Kleist, ACW, 1946, Eng. tr. used here; cf. J.H. (Cardinal) Newman, *The Theology of St. Ignatius, Essays Critical and Historical*, ed. 5, 1881, 222–262; J. Lebreton, S.J. (*qv*), "La théologie de la Trinité dans saint Ignace d'Antioche," *RSR* 15 (1925), 97–126; 393–419; L.W. Barnard, "The Background of St.Ignatius of Antioch," *VigChr* 17 (1963), 193–206; Altaner 47–50; G. Bareille, *DTC* VII, 1, (1922), 685–713; F.X. Murphy, *NCE* VII, 353–54; Quasten I, 63–76; C. Ollivier, *Catholicisme*, V, 1190–92; [2]ACW, 63–64; [3]ACW, 73.

IMAGE OF GOD

The International Theological Commission in a report adopted unanimously in October 1982—with one dissenting vote—dealt with a number of problems relevant to our general subject.[1] On the "Image of God" they wrote as follows: "'The Word of God became man so that man should become God'.[2] We see this axiom of the soteriology of the Fathers, especially of the Greek Fathers, denied in our time for different reasons. Some maintain that 'divinization' is a typically Hellenistic notion of salvation, that it incites us to escape from the human condition and that it moves towards a denial of man. In their eyes divinization eliminates the distance between God and man and implies fusion without distinction. To the patristic maxim they oppose another which they claim is better suited to our time: 'God became man to make man more human.' Assuredly the words 'divinization,' 'theosis,' 'theopoiesis,' 'homoiosis theo', etc. carry a certain ambiguity. We must, therefore, explain briefly the real, Christian meaning of 'divinization', this by distinguishing its chief aspects.

"2. It is a fact that certain trends of Greek philosophy and religion have recognised a natural kinship between the human spirit and the divine spirit. Biblical revelation, on the other hand, treats man firmly as a creature who tends towards God by contemplation and love. It is not man's intellectual capacity but conversion of heart, a new obedience, and moral action which bring man closest to God. This is impossible without God's grace. Man can become what God is only by grace.

"3. Stronger arguments arise from Christian preaching. Created in the image and likeness of God, man is called to a sharing of life with God who alone can fulfil the deepest desires of the human heart. The idea of deification reaches its summit by virtue of the incarnation of Jesus Christ. The Word assumes our mortal nature so that we can be freed from death and sin and can share in the divine life. Through Jesus Christ we are partakers in the divine nature (2 Pet 1:4). Deification consists in the very grace which frees us from the death of sin and communicates to us the divine life itself. We are sons in the Son.

"4. The Christian meaning of our proposition is made much more profound through the mystery of Jesus Christ. Just as the Incarnation of the Word does not change the divine nature, in the same way the divinity of Jesus Christ does not change or dissolve human nature, but rather makes it more itself and perfects it in its original condition of creaturehood. Redemption does not, in a general way, simply convert human nature into something divine, but renews human nature along the lines of the human nature of Jesus Christ.

"According to Maximus the Confessor, this idea is further determined through the final experiences of Jesus Christ, namely, his passion, and his abandonment by God. The more deeply Jesus Christ participates in human mystery, the more man participates in the divine life.

"In this sense deification properly understood can make man perfectly human; deification is the truest and ultimate hominisation of man.

"5. The process whereby man is deified does not take place without the grace of Jesus Christ, which comes especially through the sacraments in the Church. These sacraments unite us efficaciously to the deiform grace of the Saviour, in visible fashion, and under symbols borrowed from our earthly life (cf. LG 7). More than that, this deification is not communicated to the individual as such but as a member of the Communion of Saints. Moreover, the invitation given by divine grace in the Holy Spirit is open to the whole human race. Christians therefore should realise the holiness they have achieved in their way of life (LG 39–42). The fullness of deification belongs to the beatific vision of the triune God which comprises beatitude in the Communion of Saints."

With roots in Plato and Philo, the doctrine of the image traverses the writings of the early Fathers with recurring discussion of the relationship of "image" and "likeness" affirmed in Gen 1:26; LXX, followed by the Fathers, translated "to our image and likeness," while the Hebrew has "to our image after our likeness." Thus Clement of Alexandria (qv): "Is it not thus, according to the interpretation of some of our (teachers) that man, immediately at birth, received the 'image' and will later, in the degree to which he becomes perfect, welcome to himself the likeness."[3]

To be "in the image of God" and to be "the image of God" are not synonymous: Genesis read in the light of St. Paul makes this clear. Philo thought that only the *Logos* (qv) was the genuine image and that man could aspire to be but an "image of the image." Irenaeus (qv) advances thinking on the subject. The Word made flesh confirmed the image and the likeness: "he proved the truth of the image, himself becoming what his image had been, and he ensured the solidity of the likeness, making man like the invisible Father, thanks to the visible Word."[4]

Origen (qv) expresses the same idea: "Then Celsus failed to see the difference between what is 'in the image of God' and his image. He did not realize that the image of God is the firstborn of all creation, the very Logos and truth, and further, the very wisdom himself, being 'the image of his goodness', whereas man was made 'in the image of God', and, furthermore, every man of whom Christ is head is God's image and glory."[5] Athanasius (qv) follows on the same line: "Thus the Word of God himself came, so that being the image of the Father, he could recreate man in the image. Further, that could not be done without the destruction of death and corruption; thus it was proper that he should take a mortal body, to be able to destroy death in himself and renew men in the image. To that end none other would do but the image of the Father."[6]

The progress of the idea was not without difficulty and it was not until Maximus the Confessor (qv) that a true harmony was achieved by basing the idea on the person of Christ and his saving mission. Cyril of Alexandria (qv) raised the question of a Trinitarian aspect to the relationship between the creature and the Word incarnate, reaching much the same conclusion as Gregory of Nyssa (qv): to be in the image of God is to be in the image of the *consubstantial* Trinity, though our divine sonship is the imprint of the Son in us; Gregory held that we participate in the divine virtues, but not in the divine persons. The Greek fathers did not have on this question a systematic doctrine of the kind elaborated by Augustine (qv). Though they express from time to time very relevant ideas, a coherent persisting system is lacking. They do see the divine persons acting on us in diverse fashion.

The Latin fathers before Augustine in the course of their reflection on the biblical texts occasionally see or hint at a Trinitarian dimension to the concept of man made in the image of God. Thus Tertullian (qv) speaks of Gen 1:26 "let us make" as spoken "by the Father to the Son who was to take on man and to the Spirit who was to sanctify him."[7] Marius Victorinus (qv) worked out a triadic scheme for the soul, *being, life, thought*, and in the corresponding activity he saw the soul as the "image of the Triad above".[8] Augustine, in the *De Trinitate*, develops at length the thesis that man, in his *mens*, with its faculties and acts, is the image of the whole Trinity.

St. Thomas Aquinas (qv) in his earlier work, *In Sententias*, retained the Augustinian triadic approach, *memoria, intelligentia, voluntas* and *mens, notitia, amor.* Already in the *De Veritate* he was showing the influence of Aristotle, who did not consider memory a purely intellectual faculty. In the *Summa* he abandoned the Augustinian idea and based the image of the Trinity in the purely intellectual nature of man. In later centuries Eckhart's (*qv*) theory of the image suffers from his complicated Trinitarian ideas. Tauler revived the Augustinian conception. Vatican II (*qv*) outlined an idea of the image linked with an existential Trinitarian theory: "He who is the 'image of the invisible God' (Col 1:15) is himself the perfect man who has restored in the children of Adam that likeness to God which had been disfigured ever since the first sin . . . . Conformed to the image of the Son who is the firstborn of many brothers, the Christian man receives the 'first fruits of the Spirit' (Rom 8:23) by which he is able to fulfil the new law of love."[9]

Modern analyses of the concept of the image, wherein there is increasing confessional agreement, accept a natural image, as in the design of God, and a supernatural image, the latter conferred by grace in Christ. Add to this the emphasis on a teleological and eschatological dimension and one can see how valid is the conclusion that "the ultimate determination of the unique image of God in man, natural and supernatural, which sends us back to the mystery of the Trinity"[10] is reached through spiritual reflection on Christ, the image of God by his essence. As the same writer says, to conceive man as a being in dialogue with God is to recall the intra-divine dialogue which is the very life of the Trinity: "Thus the Trinity, as the archetype of the dialogue image in man, helps the believer to recognise how deep is man's participation in the life of God through Christ but at the same time to read the signs of the ontological distance which separates him from it. Thus appears the final meaning of the image of God in man; there is question of a participation, as exalted as possible in the divine community by imitating the union of the Son with the Father in the power of the Spirit."[11]

---

[1]Cf. biblical passages: Gen 1:26–27; Wis 7:24–28; Rom 8:29; 2 Cor 4:4; Col 1:15; Heb 1:3; 1 Jn 3:2; esp., "Image et Ressemblance," *DSp* 7, 1402–1472 (Scripture, P. Lamarche Fathers, A. Solignac; 11th and 12th centuries, R. Javelet; 13th century Scholastics, A. Solignac; Rhineland mystics and Reformed Carmel, R-L. Oeschlin; present day theology and spirituality, L. Scheffczyk); Grecque (Eglise), *DSp*, 6, *Image et Ressemblance*, J. Kirchmeyer (Greek Fathers), 813–822; ample

bibliographies in each article; J. Gross, *La divinisation du chrétien d'après les Pe'agres grecs*, Paris, 1938; E. Peterson, "L'immagine di Dio in S.Ireneo," *La Scuola Cattolica*, 69 (1911), 46–54 (French tr. VS 1959, 584–594); H. Rahner, "Das Menschenbild des Origenes," *Eranos-Jahrbuch*, 15 (1947), 197–248; P.T. Wild, *The Divinization of Man according to St. Hilary of Poitiers*, Mundelein, 1950; R. Leys, *L'image de Dieu chez S. Grégoire de Nysse*, Brussels-Paris, 1951; I. Hislop, "Man, the Image of Trinity according to St. Thomas," *Dominican St.*, 3 (1950), 1–9; J.J. Meany, *The Image of God in Man according to the Doctrine of St.John Damascene*, Manila, 1954; St. Otto, *Gottes Ebenbild und Geschlechtlichkeit*, Paderborn, 1954; *id.*, "Der Mensch als Bild Gottes bei Tertullian," in *Münchener theol. Zeitschr.*, 10 (1959), 276–282; T. Szabo, *De SS Trinitate in creaturis refulgente doctrina S. Bonaventurae*, Rome, 1955; M.J. de Beaurecueil, "L'homme image de Dieu selon S.Thomas d'Aquin, Etudes et Recherches," *Cahiers de théologie et de philosophie* (Ottawa), 8 (1952), 45–82; 9 (1955), 37–96; H. Crouzel, *Théologie de l'image chez Origène*, Paris 1956; *id.*, "L'image de Dieu dans la théologie d'Origène," TU 64, Berlin, 1957, 194–201; W.J. Burghardt, *The Image of God in Man according to St. Cyril of Alexandria*, Woodstock, Maryland, 1957; G.A. McCool, "The Ambrosian Origin of St. Augustine's Theology of the Image of God in Man," *TheolSt.* 20 (1959), 62–81; M. Nedoncelle, "L'intersubjectivité humaine est-elle pour S.Augustin une image de la Trinité?" in *Augustinus Magister*, I, Paris, 1954, 595–602; H. Somers, *Image de Dieu et illumination divine*, ibid., 452–462; G.B. Ladner, *The Idea of Reform. Its Impact on Christian Thought and Action in the Age of the Fathers*, Cambridge, Mass., 1959; P. Hadot, "L'image de la Trinité dans l'âme chez Victorinus et chez S.Augustin," *St Patrist.*-TU, Berlin, 1962, 409–442; W.R. Jenkinson, "The Image and the Likeness of God in Man in the Eighteen Lectures on the Credo of Cyril of Jerusalem," *ETL.* 40 (1964), 48–71; B. Lonergan, *La notion de Verbe dans les écrits de S.Thomas*, Paris, 1966, 191–227; J. Cordero, "La imagen de la Trinidad en el justo segun Santo Tomas," *La Ciencia Tomista*, 93 (1966), 3–86; J.F. Sullivan, *The Image of God, The Doctrine of St.Augustine and its Influence*, Dubuque, Iowa, 1963; R. Javelet, *Image et ressemblance au XIIe siècle, De S.Anselme à Alain de Lille*, 2 vol., Paris, 1967; V. Lossky, *A l'image et à la ressemblance de Dieu*, Paris, 1967; additional bibliographies, *RAC* 4, *Ebendbildlichkeit*, (H. Merki) 461–479; *Eikon* (G.B. Ladner), 771–786; [2]*De Incarn.*, 54, 9, 3C 18, 312 Text from International Theological Commission *Doc. Cath.*, 1983, 119ff.; *ITQ* 49 (1982) 285ff; [3]*Strom.* II, 22, 131, 6; SC (C. Mondesert) 38, 133; [4]*Adv. haer.*, V, 16, 1–2, PG 7, 1167, 68; [5]*Contra Celsum*, VI, 63, tr. H. Chadwick, Cambridge, 1953, 378; [6]*De Incarn*, 12–13, PG 25, 116d–120b; [7]*Adv. Praxeam*, 12, 3, CCL 2, 1173; [8]*Libri adversus Arium*, I, 63, SC 68, 383; [9]*GS* 22; [10]L. Scheffczyk, *DSp*, 7, 1468; [11]*Ibid.*

INDWELLING OF THE TRINITY, THE

The review of scholastic teaching on "created" and "uncreated" grace has removed some encumbrance in the understanding of the divine indwelling in the souls of the just. Once the importance of uncreated grace is made clear, light is thrown on the reality and wonder of God's personal interest in us. We are not dealing with an abstruse "entitative" gift or endowment, but with the Father, Son and Holy Spirit. We are not obliged to investigate the nature and modalities of divine grace at length before we go on to study its effects, one of which is the divine indwelling. The grace which we receive as the root of our new life in God, "a kind of beginning" as St. Thomas said, "of eternal life," that is, created grace, demands at once and constantly thoughtful advertence to the divine persons, to uncreated grace. The terms are strictly correlative, if they have any validity.[1]

On the fact of the divine indwelling Scripture speaks abundantly (cf. Mt 23:9; Lk 10:22; Jn 14:23, 26; 1 Jn 1:3; 2:23; 3:24; Rom 8:9–16; 1 Cor 3:16; 6:19; 8:6; Gal 2:20; Phil 1:21; Eph 3:14–19). How it takes place is the further pertinent question. So is the relationship of the divine presence to the gift of grace: which comes first? So especially is the relationship set up between the soul and the separate divine persons: is the indwelling the effect of activity by all three and attributed by "appropriation" to one or the other, or is each person directly involved in the process and perpetually committed to its continuation?

Scripture does not speak of "God" taking up his abode in the soul, but of the Father and Son doing so (Jn 1:23) or the Holy Spirit, the Counsellor, being sent (ibid., 26). As is stated in the article on grace, these statements are "in possessione." Because of the thinking of writers like Karl Rahner, there has been a loosening in the rigid doctrine of appropriation (qv) as the key to the indwelling. The passage quoted from his important essay on uncreated grace in the article on grace is here also relevant. He adds in a note: "By this ('The Spirit dwells in us in a particular and proper way') it is not meant that the Spirit alone makes his dwelling-place in us. Each Person communicates himself and dwells in us in a way proper to him. And because the indwelling ascribed to the Holy Spirit in Scripture (as a Power who sanctifies, consecrates, moves, etc.) corresponds precisely to the personal particularity of the Spirit and of his going forth from the Father and the Son, there is absolutely no objection to saying that in this way only the Spirit dwells in man."[2]

Leo XIII had spoken of the indwelling being effected by the whole Trinity, but being in a peculiar way attributed to the Holy Spirit.[3] Pius XII laid down this principle: "And, besides, let them hold this with a firm mind as most certain, that all activities in these matters are to be held as common to the Most Holy Trinity, insofar as (quatenus) they depend upon God as the supreme efficient cause."[4]

Those who argue for a personalist meaning in the indwelling take the Pope's statement as referring to God's causal action. Union with the divine persons is a different aspect of the spiritual reality, which remains profound, mysterious, disclosing an intimate, sensitive domain wherein God, majestic and transcendent, meets the natural mystery of the human person.

Prayer practice in the Church assumes that communication with each of the divine persons is possible, since the Christian can, and is encouraged to, pray to each one by name. In liturgical prayer such personal forms of address are frequent. The Christian sentiment thus expressed surely is that the Trinitarian presence is personalist—though an apodictic argument can scarcely be based on liturgical practice alone.

As to how the presence of the Trinity is effected, opinions differ. The ancient view linking it with the divine action whereby God's universal presence is assured, his immensity, is generally discarded. Petavius thought that the Greek Fathers justified the notion of a divine seal on the soul; he attributed the action to the Holy Spirit. M.J. Scheeben (qv) thought of all three persons being involved in the presence: "When we receive grace, God becomes the object of our possession and enjoyment in his entire essence. Evidently, then, all three persons come to us and give themselves to us, inasmuch as they are one with the essence and in the essence with each other. Yet the individual persons, too, as distinct from one another and especially so far as one proceeds from another, can give themselves to us for our possession and enjoyment. The proceeding person is presented to us for our possession and enjoyment by the producing person, and by that very fact also presents his author to us for our possession and enjoyment."[5]

A particularly stimulating opinion was expressed by Fr. M. de la Taille, S.J., previously renowned for his great work, Mysterium Fidei. In two articles in RSR he proposed his theory of created actuation by uncreated act. De la Taille saw this actuation in the hypostatic union, in the beatific vision and in grace. God communicates himself by his act to the obediential potency. This is not information (in the technical philosophical sense of the word), though there is occasional talk of quasi-formal causality. The result of the divine self-giving, that is, the created actuation, is distinct both from the uncreated act and from the potency being actuated. In the natural order such a communication implies dependence of the act on the potency, that is, some imperfection; it can be otherwise in the supernatural order. In the process of divinization the soul is actuated by the uncreated, vital principle which gives it the radical power for the divine life; the ultimate phase of sanctifying grace, the intended fulfilment of this, is the beatific vision.

Karl Rahner, not aware of De la Taille's solution to the problem, proposed a somewhat similar theory. Arguing strongly from the proportion between sanctifying grace, created grace and the beatific vision he says: "In this question too we may surely have recourse to the concepts developed in scholastic theology in its treatment of the *visio beatifica*. Just as there the light of glory is seen as the *dispositio ultima quae est necessitas ad formam*, so here an analogous relationship may be assumed to hold between created and uncreated grace. In this regard created grace is seen as *causa materialis* (*dispositio ultima*) for the formal causality which God exercises by graciously communicating his own Being to the creature. In this way the material and formal causes possess a reciprocal priority: as *dispositio ultima* created grace is in such a way the presupposition of the formal cause that it can itself only exist by way of the actual realization of this formal causality."[6] So close is the relationship that "there does not exist even the beginning of a possibility of thinking of created grace apart from uncreated grace."

In the perspective of such views it is possible to hope for a renewal of interest in the Trinitarian, personalist presence in the souls of the just.

---

[1]Cf. bibliographies to Grace and Image of God; Petavius, *De Trinitate*, lib. VIII, cap. 4–6; T. de Regnon, *Etudes*, IV, 27, ch 4, 553–8; G. von Holtum, "Die heilmachende Gnade in ihrer Beziehung zu der Einwohnung des Heiligen Geistes in der Seele," *Divus Thomas*, 4 (1917), 435–63; P. Galtier, *De SS Trinitate in se et in nobis*, Paris, 1933; *id.*, *L'habitation en nous des trois personnes*, 2nd ed, Rome, 1950; H. Schauf, *Die Einwohnung des Heiligen Geistes*, Freiburg, 1941; M.J. Donnelly, "The Theory of the R.P. Maurice de la Taille on the Hypostatic Union," *ThSt* 2 (1941), 510–526; *id.*, "The Indwelling of the Holy Spirit according to M.J. Scheeben," *ibid.*, 7 (1946), 244–80; *id.* "The Inhabitation of the Holy Spirit; A Solution according to St.Thomas and de la Taille," *CathAssAmerica*, 4 (1949), 38–89; *id.*, "Sanctifying Grace and our Union with the Holy Trinity: A Reply," *ThSt*, 13 (1952), 190–204; M. de la Taille, *The*

Hypostatic Union and Created Actuation by Uncreated Act, West Baden, Inc., 1952 (tr. C. Vollert of "Actuation créed par Acte incrée," *RSR* 18 (1928), 253–268); J. Trutsch, *SS Trinitatis inhabitatio apud theologos recentiores*, Gregorian University, Trent, 1949 (bibliography); J.M. Gonzalez Ruiz, "La semejanza divina de la gracia Explicación de una inhabitación formalmente trinitaria," *Revista española de teología*, 8 (1948), 565–600; F. Bourassa, "Les missions divines et le surnaturel chez S.Thomas d'Aquin," *ScEccl*, 1 (1948), 41–94; *id.* "Adoptive sonship, Our Union with the Divine Persons," *ThSt*, 13 (1952), 309–335; *id.*, "Appropriation ou Propriété," *ScEccl* 7 (1955), 57–85; "L'inhabitation de la Trinité," *ibid.*, 8 (1956), 59–70; P. de Letter, "Sanctifying Grace and our Union with the Holy Trinity," *ThSt*, 13 (1952) 33–58; *id.*, "Created Actuation by the Uncreated Act, Difficulties and Answers," *ibid.*, 18 (1957), 60–92; "Sanctifying Grace and Divine Indwelling," *Greg* 41 (1960), 63–69; R. Verardo, "Polemiche recenti intorno all'inhabitazione della SS Trinità," *Sapienza*, 7 (1954), 29–44; Enrico de Santa Teresa, "Proprietà o appropriazione," *EphCarmelit*, 4 (1950), 239–290; V. Rodriguez, "Inhabitacion de la SS Trinidad en el alma en gracia," *Ciencia Tomista*, 86 (1959), 65–115; F.L.B. Cunningham, *The Indwelling of the Trinity. A historico-doctrinal Study of the Solution of St.Thomas Aquinas*, Dubuque, Iowa, 1955; E. Haible, "Die Einwohnung der dre göttlichen Personen im Christen nach den Ergebnissen der neuren Theologie," *TheolQuartal* 139 (1959), 1–27; P.F. Chirico, *The divine Indwelling and distinct Relations to the indwelling Persons in modern theological Discussion*, Rome, 1960; esp. K. Rahner, "Concerning the Relationship between Nature and Grace," *Theological Investigations*, I, London, 2nd ed., 1965, 297–318; "Some Implications of the Scholastic Concept of Uncreated Grace," *ibid.*, 319–346; A. Michel, *DTC*, 15.2, 1841–55; H. Schauf, *LTH*, 3, 769–772; R. Moretti, *DSp*, 7, 1735–1757; [2]*Op.cit.*, 345, n2; [3]*Divinum illud munus*, *AAS*, 29, 653; [4]*Mystici Corporis*, *AAS*, 35, 231 2; [5]*The Mysteries of Christianity*, tr. C. Vollert, 1946, 160; [6]*Op.cit.*, 341.

INTERNATIONAL THEOLOGICAL COMMISSION, THE

On 28 April, 1969, Paul VI established the ITC. He was acting in response to a wish expressed in the Episcopal Synod of 1967, and an idea current since Vatican II (*qv*).[1] The body, composed of thirty members, is to study doctrinal questions of major importance in order to offer advisory assistance to the Holy See and in particular to the Congregation for the Doctrine of the Faith. It is composed of thirty members, and may be renewed every five years. Of those named to the first commission besides Fr. Y. M.-J. Congar, O.P., two others were experts in Trinitarian doctrine, Fr. Bernard Lonergan (*qv*) and Fr. Karl Rahner (*qv*); Fr. Rahner had resigned before the quinquennium ended and Fr. Lonergan did not seek renomination. Fr. Hans Urs von Balthasar, still a member, is proficient in this area. Since 1979 the commission has been studying Christology; in the 1981 session it turned also to the theology of the Trinity. The conclusions published are used in the present work (see ANTHROPOLOGY, CHRIST-OLOGY, IMAGE OF GOD, PRE-EXISTENCE OF CHRIST).

---

[1] AAS 61 (1969), 431–432; 713–16.

IRENAEUS, ST. (c. 130–c. 200)

A bishop with pastoral care to safeguard his flock from danger, which, as the title of his principal work *Adversus Haereses* shows, meant one thing: heresy. The "father of Christian theology," I. was equally attentive to conveying convincingly the doctrine of salvation in Christ, which he elaborated in the "recapitulation."[1] Clear enunciation of the faith of the Church was his method: "The Church, though spread through the whole world to the extremities of the earth, has received from the apostles and from their disciples faith in one only God, the Father almighty who made heaven and earth and the seas, and all that they contain; and in one Christ Jesus the Son of God, incarnate for our salvation; and in the Holy Spirit who announced by the prophets the "economies" and the comings and the virginal birth and the Passion and the Resurrection from the dead and the bodily ascension into heaven of the beloved Christ Jesus, our Lord, and his "parousia" from the heavens above in the glory of his Father, to recapitulate all things, to raise all flesh of all the human race."[2] This passage at the beginning of the *Adversus haereses* is matched by another at the end: "Quite the contrary," he continues, "those who are of the Church follow a unique way which crosses the whole world; it is a firm tradition which comes from the apostles, which fixes our minds on one only faith, all confessing one only same Father, all believing in the same economy of the incarnation of the Son of God, all recognising the same gift of the Spirit."[3]

Likewise in the *Proof of the Apostolic Preaching*: "Now this is what faith does for us, as the elders, the disciples of the apostles, have handed down to us. First of all, it admonishes us to remember that we have received baptism for remission of sins in the name of God the Father, and in the name of Jesus Christ, the Son of God, who became incarnate and died and was raised, and in the Holy Spirit of God, and that this baptism is the seal of eternal life and is rebirth unto God, that we be no more children of mortal men, but of the eternal and everlasting God; and that the eternal and everlasting One is God, and is above all creatures, and that all things whatsoever are subject to him; and that what is subject to him was all made by him, so that God is not ruler and Lord of what is another's, but of his own, and that all things are God's; that God, therefore, is the Almighty, and all things whatsoever are from God."[4]

On the Trinity in creation (*qv*) I. wrote perceptively: "In this way, then, there is declared one God, the Father, uncreated, invisible, maker of all things, above whom is no other God whatever, and after whom there is no God. And God is rational, and therefore produced creatures by his Word, and God is a spirit, and so fashioned everything by his Spirit, as the prophet also says: *by the word of the Lord the heavens were established, and all the power of them by his Spirit*. Hence, since the Word 'establishes', that is, works bodily and consolidates being, while the Spirit disposes and shapes the various 'powers', so the Word is fitly and properly called the Son, but the Spirit the Wisdom of God. Hence too his apostle Paul well says: *one God, the Father, who is above all and with all and in us all*; for 'above all' is the Father, but 'with all' is the Word, since it is through him that everything was made by the Father, and 'in us all' is the Spirit, *who cries: Abba, Father*, and has formed man in the likeness of God. So the Spirit manifests the Word, and therefore the prophets announced the Son of God, but the Word articulates the Spirit, and therefore it is himself who gives their message to the prophets, and takes up man and brings him to the Father."[5]

To these long quotations one may add another, equally important, as it shows such astonishing clarity in formulation at such an early date in Church history: "And this is the drawing-up of our faith, the foundation of the building, and the consolidation of a way of life. God, the Father, uncreated, beyond grasp, invisible, one God the maker of all; this is the first and foremost article of our faith. But the second article is the Word of God, the Son of God, Christ Jesus our Lord, who was shown forth by the prophets according to the design of their prophecy and according to the manner in which the Father disposed; and through him were made all things whatsoever. He also, *in the end of times*, for the recapitulation of all things, is become a man among men, visible and tangible, in order to abolish death and bring to light life, and bring about the communion of God and man. And the third article is the Holy Spirit, through whom the prophets prophesied and the patriarchs were taught about God and the just were led in the path of justice, and who *in the end of times* has been poured forth in a new manner upon humanity over all the earth renewing men to God."

I. then emphasizes our initiation into Trinitarian life: "Therefore the baptism of our rebirth comes through these three articles, granting us rebirth unto God the Father, through his Son, by the Holy Spirit. For those who are bearers of the Spirit of God are led to the Word, that is, to the Son; but the Son takes them and presents them to the Father; and the Father confers incorruptibility. So without the Spirit there is no seeing the Word of God, and without the Son there is no approaching the Father; for the Son is knowledge of the Father, and knowledge of the Son is through the Holy Spirit. But the Son, according to the Father's good-pleasure, administers the Spirit charismatically as the Father will, to those to whom he will."[6]

In strict theology I. is insistent on the divinity of the *Logos* (qv). "If someone asks us: 'How then has the Son been uttered by the Father?' we shall answer him that this utterance, or generation, or speaking, or revelation, or finally this ineffable generation, by whatever name one wishes to call it, no one knows it, neither Valentinus, nor Marcion nor Saturninus nor Basilides, neither angels nor archangels, neither principalities nor powers, no one but the Father who has begotten and the Son who has been born. Since then his generation is ineffable, all those who claim to explain generations and utterances do not know what they are saying, when they promise to explain what is ineffable."[7]

The Son is God like the Father. He is equally eternal. "The Son, who always coexists with the Father from the beginning, reveals the Father to angels, archangels, powers, virtues, to all those to whom God wishes to reveal himself."[8] "The Word of God did not seek the friendship of Abraham through want, he who was perfect from the beginning: 'before Abraham was, I am' he says; but it was to give Abraham eternal life."

Like the Son, the Holy Spirit is eternal: "God always has with him his Word and his Wisdom, the Son and the Spirit."[9] "The Word, that is, the Son, has always been with the Father. As for Wisdom, who is the Spirit, she has also been with him before the creation of the world."[10] I. gives the Spirit many names—the divine seal, the unction with which Christ was anointed, Paraclete, Gift, living Water, dew of God, pledge of our salvation, especially and often, like St. Theophilus of Antioch, Wisdom. This does not mean that I. was binitarian, any more than he was subordinationist for using the image of the Son and the Spirit as the two hands of God. The Son reveals God, and the Spirit sanctifies.

[1]Works, crit. ed. SC, *Adversus Haereses*, 213, 214, 210, 211, 100, 151, 153; *The Proof of the Apostolic Preaching*, Eng. tr. J.P. Smith, *Ancient Christian Writers*; French tr. L.M. Froideveaux, SC 62; cf. A. Benoit, *Saint Irenée, Introduction à l'etude de sa théologie*, Paris, 1961; A. Orbe, *Hacia la primera teología de la procesion del Verbo*, Rome, 1958, 114ff; V. Grossi, in *Semanas de Estudios Trinitarios*, VIII, "La Trinidad en le Tradicion prenicena," 109–39; Altaner, 110–117; Quasten I, 287 313; F. Vernet, *DTC* VII, 1923, 2394–2533; L. Doutreleau, S.J.—L. Regnault, O.S.B., *DSp* VII, 1923–1969; [2]*Adv. Haer.*, I, 10, 1; [3]*Ibid.*, V, 20, 1; [4]3, ACW, 49, 50; [5]*Ibid.*, 5, ACW, 50; [6]*Ibid.*, 6, 7, ACW, 51, 52; [7]*Adv. Haer.*, II, 28, SC, 294, 282; [8]*Ibid.*, II, 30, SC, 294, 322; [9]*Ibid.*, IV, 20, 1 SC, 100, 626; [10]*Ibid.*, IV, 20, 3, SC, 100, 633; cf. esp. J. Lebreton (qv) *Le dogme de la Trinité*, II, 517–617.

J

JACOBITES, DECREE FOR

Issued by the Council of Florence (*qv*). On 4 February, 1442, the Bull *Cantate Domino* recalled the circumstances which led to the reunion and gave infallible teaching on truths of the faith.[1] It summarized the doctrine on the Trinity: "These three persons are one God and not three gods. The three have one substance, one essence, one nature, one divinity, one immensity, one eternity and all is one in them where the opposition based on the relations allows. 'Because of this unity the Father is entirely in the Son, entirely in the Holy Spirit; the Son is entirely in the Father, entirely in the Holy Spirit; the Holy Spirit is entirely in the Father, entirely in the Son. None precedes the other in eternity, outdoes the other in greatness, surpasses the other in power. From all eternity and without beginning the Son has his origin from the Father; from all eternity and without beginning the Holy Spirit proceeds from the Father and the Son.'[2] Whatever the Father is or has, he has it from no other; he is the beginning without beginning. Whatever the Holy Spirit is or has he has it, at the same time, from the Father and the Son. But the Father and the Son are not two points of origin of the Holy Spirit, but one point of origin. In the same way the Father and Son and Holy Spirit are not three points of origin but one of creatures."

---

[1]Msi 31B1735 D; *DS* 1330–1331; *Conciliorum Oecumenicorum Decreta*, Bologna, 546–548; [2]Words taken from St. Fulgentius (*qv*), *De fide ad Petrum*, PL 65, 674A.

JOACHIM OF FIORE (c. 1132–1202)

A controversial and to some extent a magic name.[1] His career was exciting; his posthumous legend the seed ground of many wild plants. A court lawyer, he turned his back on worldly prospects, went on pilgrimage to the Holy Land, lived for a while as a hermit, then became a Cistercian, abbot of the monastery of Santa Maria of Corazzo; he organised its full incorporation into the order. Soon he was personally sponsored as a writer and eventually a reformer by three Popes successively. He left the Cistercians and founded his own monastery at Fiore. Confirmed by an imperial letter from Henry VI, J. saw his foundation and religious Constitutions approved by a papal Bull from Celestine III, 25 August, 1196; he further enjoyed the patronage of the empress Constance and her son Frederick II, *Stupor Mundi*. Six monastic foundations were proof of his personal charisma. After his death he was the object of a local cult, and though not canonised he figures in the *Acta sanctorum* of the Bollandistes and in the 1965 *Bibliotheca sanctorum*. Though his ideas against Peter Lombard were condemned by the Fourth Lateran Council (*qv*), this same assembly acknowledged his wish, committed to writing, to have his works submitted to the judgment of the Apostolic See, and corrected if need be; Pope Honorius III, 16 December 1220, spoke of him as "a Catholic man, a follower of the holy, orthodox faith."

J's writings are mostly biblical commentaries. One, in which he clashed with Peter Lombard, *De unitate seu essentia Trinitatis*, concerns us directly; it has been lost. His principal legacy is in three works, *Concordia novi et veteris Testamenti*, *Expositio in Apocalipsim* and *Psalterium decem chordarum*. He wrote a number of other works and there is an apocryphal literature. The extensive complicated phenomenon of Joachimism, the Spirituals and the Fraticelli, which has a substantial bibliography, does not concern us.

The essence of J's thought is a reading of history in strict correlation with the three Persons of the Trinity. There are three stages (*status*) or phases in history, each with a beginning (*initiatio, exordium*), a period of growth to a peak (*fructificatio, claritas*), then decadence (*defectio*), towards an end (*consummatio, finis*).

The first phase began with Adam, reached its peak in Abraham, and had its consummation in Christ. It belonged to the Father, for "in many and different ways God the Father spoke to the fathers in the prophets." It was under the sign of the law and circumcision and was represented by the marriage or lay state, *ordo conjugatorum seu laicorum*.

The second phase was "*initiatus ab Ocia, fructificavit a Zacharia, accepturus consummationem in temporibus istis.*" It corresponds to the New Testament and belongs to the Son, for the Son was made manifest in it and by the teaching of his gospel converted to himself a multitude of peoples. It is represented by the *ordo clericorum*.

The third phase began, J. thought, with St. Benedict; it began to bear fruit from the twentieth generation after him and will have its consummation at the end of the world. It belongs to the Holy Spirit, and may be called the age of the *ordo monachorum*.

Not only does J. link each stage in history with a divine Person, but he characterizes each in relation to spirit and flesh. Men lived, in the first stage, according to the flesh, in the second between the spirit and the flesh; in the third they will live "*sub spirituali intellectu.*" The first age was marked by servile subjection, the second by filial obedience; the third will be an age of liberty. The sequence is of fear, faith and charity; of old people, young people and children. Each will have seven epochs. Despite upheavals, even persecutions, there is continuity. J. asserts that there will be two Anti-Christs and two second comings of Christ.

The theological basis of J's system is tritheism (*qv*) with more than a suspicion of inequality between the divine persons as J. sees them. No argument supported by valid theological method is set forth. It is a construction not always intrinsically coherent; analogies are forced, allegories arbitrary and fluctuating.

[1]Cf. esp. C. Baraut, *DSp* VIII, 1179–1201, ample bibl.; cf. E. Buonaiuti, *Gioacchino da Fiore, I tempi, la vita, il messagio*, Rome, 1931; "Joachim-Studien," *Zeitschrift für Kirchengeschichte*, 50 (1931), 24–111; "Creator Spiritus, Die Geistlehre des Joachim," *Eranos Jahrbuch* 25 (1956), 285–355; B. Hirsch-Reich, "Die Quellen der Trinitätskreise von Joachim . . . und Dante," *Sophia* 22 (1954), 170–178; A. Crocco, "La teologia trinitaria di Gioacchino," *Sophia*, 25 (1957), 218–32; *id.*, "L'Età dello Spirito Santo," *Humanitas* 9 (1954), 728–42; *id.*, *Gioacchino da Fiore*, Naples, 1960; H. Grundmann, *Neue Forschungen über Joachim von Fiore* (Münstersche Forschungen, Hft 1) 1950; St. Otto, "Die Denkform des Joachim . . . und das Caput 'Damnamus' des 4 Laterankonzils," *Münchener theologische Zeitschrift*, 13 (1962), 145–154; V. Ferrara, *La 'Madre della Chiesa' nel pensiero di Dante . . . e di Gioacchino*, Rome, 1966; G. Penco, "Maria modello della vita contemplativa secondo Gioacchino," *Benedictina*, 14 (1967), 51–56; H. Mottu, *La Manifestation de l'Esprit selon Joachim de Fiore*, Thesis, University of Geneva, Neuchâtel-Paris, 1977; M.W. Bloomfield, "Recent Scholarship on Joachim of Fiore and his Influence," *Prophecy and Millenarianism, Essays in Honour of Marjorie Reeves*, ed. Ann Williams (1980), 21–52; on Joachimism cf. M.E. Reeves, *The Influence of Prophecy in the Later Middle Ages. A Study in Joachimism*, Oxford, 1969; H. (Cardinal) de Lubac, S.J., *La posterité spirituelle de Joachim de Fiore*, Paris, 1979ff.

JOHN OF DAMASCUS, ST., DOCTOR OF THE CHURCH (c. 675–between 749–753)

Last and one of the greatest of the eastern Fathers of the Church, J.'s Trinitarian theology, contained in his best known work, *De fide orthodoxa*, is borrowed to the point of virtual repetition from a work, *De Sacrosancta Trinitate*, generally printed at the end of the works of St. Cyril of Alexandria (*qv*). The author, known for this reason as Pseudo-Cyril, wrote at the end of the seventh or beginning of the eighth century: the *De Fide orthodoxa* is the third part of a large work *Pege gnoseos*, the "Fount of Wisdom."[1] Translated into Latin in the twelfth century, it had considerable influence in the west.

J's Trinitarian theology has been summarised thus by a reliable scholar: "1. The Father is the only cause in the Trinity; this causality cannot be divided or shared. The category of 'secondary cause' is completely absent in the teaching of John Damascene; 2. John's theology of the Trinity is dominated by the ideas of *nous, logos* and *pneuma*. It expresses in a single movement the fact that the Spirit reveals the Word and the Word reveals the Father; 3. The procession is not begetting and the Spirit is not the son of the Son; 4. The Spirit rests in the Word and accompanies him, that is, he participates indissolubly in this activity by making him manifest. He is the revelation and the image of the Son; 5. The procession of the Spirit goes back to the begetting of the Son; at the level of the *perichoresis*, the Spirit comes from the Father through the Son and is poured out in him; 6. In the divine activity, the Son provides the basis of the work that is wanted by the Father and the Spirit perfects it."

In J's theology there is no separation between economy and theology; they are completely integrated into a single vision. Save against Arianism and Manicheism and possibly Islam, there is no polemical element in his writing. "He is not a filioquist because, in his teaching, the causal category does not and cannot apply to the eternal relationship between the Spirit and the Son. He is not a monopatrist because, in his theology, an essential presupposition for the procession is the begetting of the Word and the procession refers entirely to that begetting."[2]

The Bonn Conference (*qv*) accepted a summary of J's teaching about the Holy Spirit under the following heads:

"1. The Holy Spirit comes from the Father (*ek tou Patros*), as from the principle (*arche*), the cause (*aitia*) and the source (*pege*) of divinity (*De rect. sent. 1; Contra Man 4*); 2. The Holy Spirit does not come from the Son (*ek tou Huiou*), because there is only one principle (*arche*) and one cause (*aitia*) in the divinity through which everything that is in that divinity is produced (see *De Fide orthod.*: *ek tou Huiou de to Pneuma ou legomen, Pneuma di Huiou onomazomen*; 3. The Holy Spirit comes from the Father through the Son (*De fide orthod.* I, 12; *Contra Man 5; De hymno Trisag. 28; Hom. in Sabb. S. 4*; 4. The Holy Spirit is the image of the Son, who is himself the image of the Father (*De fide orthod.* I, 13) proceeding from the Father and dwelling in the Son as his radiating power (*De fide orthod.* I, 7, I, 12); 5. The Holy Spirit is the personal procession coming from the Father, who is of the Son, but not coming from the Son, because he is the Spirit from the mouth of the divinity, expressing the Word (*De hymno Trisag. 28*); 6. The Holy Spirit is the medium between the Father and the Son and he is connected to the Father through the Son (*De fide orthod.* I, 13). In reproducing this summary, the quotations from J. have been omitted.[3]

[1]Works PG 94–96; cf. J. Nasrallah, *Saint Jean de Damas, son époque, sa vie, son oeuvre*, Harissa, Lebanon, 1950, with bibl.; G.L. Prestige, *God in Patristic Thought*, 2nd., ed., London, 1952, 263, 64, 80; J. Bilz, *Die Trinitätslehre des Johannes von Damaskus*, Paderborn, 1909; esp. J. Gregoire, "La relation éternelle de l'Esprit au Fils d'apres les écrits de Jean de Damas," *RHE* 64 (1969), 713–755; B. Fraigneau-Julien, "Un Traité anonyme de la Sainte Trinité attribué à S.Cyrille d'Alexandrie," *RSR* 49 (1961), 188–211, 386–405; Congar, the Holy Spirit, III, 36–48; [2]Apud Congar, *The Holy Spirit*, III, 39–40, from J. Gregoire, *op. cit.*, 754, 755; [3]Apud Congar, *op.cit.*, 192, 93.

JOHN PAUL II (1920–   )

On May 18, his sixty-sixth birthday, John Paul II announced the publication, on May 30, of his fifth Encyclical, *Dominum et Vivificantem* (Lord and Giver of Life) on the Holy Spirit. It completes, he said, a "Trinitarian trilogy", with *Dives et Misericordia*[1] on the Father and *Redemptor Hominis*[2] on God the Son. The Pope also treated of the Holy Spirit in his letter to the world episcopate for the sixteenth centenary of the Council of Constantinople (*qv*)[3] and in the two addresses at the ceremony,[4] as in his address to the International Congress on Pneumatology held to commemorate the Council.[5] John Paul spoke on Trinitarian themes twice: December 4, 1985[6] on the distinction of relations (*qv*) within the Trinity, and March 5, 1986 on creation (*qv*) as a work of the Trinity.[7] The Pope is thus a Trinitarian theologian, declaring himself fully in the renewed current of thought on this central truth of Christianity, in the spirit of Blessed Elizabeth of the Trinity (*qv*) whom he beatified, November 25, 1984 and extolled.

John Paul's thinking, as seen in the addresses on relations and on creation, matches the subject in depth. The Blessed Three are consubstantial (*qv*). In the Encyclicals he interprets each Person in the light of his work, the Father source of mercy, the Son restoring creation by his redemption, the Spirit fountain of light in pagan lands and to distracted modern man. The subject awaits a doctoral thesis.

[1]AAAS, 72 (1980), 1172–1232; [2]AAS 71 (1979), 257–324; [3]AAS 73 (1981), 515–527; [4]AAS 73 (1981), 485–492; [5]AAS 74 (1982), 694–702; Acts of the Congress, II, 1515–21; [6]Osservat. Roman, December 5, 1959;[7]Osservat. Roman, March 6, 1986.

JOHN SCOTUS ERIUGENA (c. 810–877)

An Irishman who enjoyed the patronage of Charles the Bald, E. had a flair of originality in theology; his reading in philosophy and in the Fathers of the Church was astonishingly wide. He translated Dionysius the Ps.-Areopagite. His predilection was for Maximus the Confessor, whom he called his "venerable master"; he was known to have translated the *Ambigua*; his translation of the *Quaestiones ad Thalassum*, discovered in the present century, is the oldest textual witness and is printed alongside the Greek in the CCSG version.[1]

In the first part of the *De divisione naturae*, E. considers the doctrine of the Trinity, analysing the essence in three substances, giving an account of the different approach of the Greeks and Latins: "The Greeks say one *ousia* and three *hypostases*, that is, one essence and three substances. St. Augustine and the other Fathers writing in Latin formulate their faith in the holy Trinity thus: one substance and three persons. They designate the unity of the divine nature by the name of substance, and what properly belongs to each of the three substances by the expression three persons. Modern Greeks use the same language; they say one *hypostasis*, that is, one substance, and three *prosopa*, that is, three persons. It is the same faith with all, despite the diversity of formulas."[2] He prefers the Greek formulation.

On the *Filioque* E. knows that "Catholic faith obliges us to profess that the Holy Spirit proceeds from the Father and the Son, or from the Father through the Son."[3] He has a difficulty as to the Father and the Son acting as one cause; he turns around the problem, and finally, whatever the formula used, he thinks, "we believe and understand that the same Spirit proceeds substantially from one cause, that is, the Father."[4] Fr. Jugie takes him severely to task for this "Photian" opinion.[5]

On creation E. expounds a stimulating doctrine of the Trinitarian origin of things as he also sets forth a rich doctrine of the divine image in man. Some have thought that he claimed to prove the truth of the Trinity from reason. This is a misreading of his ideas. He is seeking "with all his might, the *image* (qv) of the creative Trinity," "certain traces and theophanies of the truth."[6] He has a cosmic conception of the mystery of the Trinity. He has an abiding sense of the mystery of the Trinity, well aware though he was of Augustine's "psychological" approach.

[1]Works PL 122, 125–1244; bibl., J.P. Sheldon Williams, "A Bibliography of the Works of Johannes Scotus Eriugena," *Journal of Ecclesiastical History*, 10 (1959), 198–224; cf. esp. M. Cappuyns, *Jean Scot Erigène Sa vie, son oeuvre, sa pensée*, Louvain, 1933; esp. R. Roques, *DSp*, 8, 735–761; bibl., J.M. Alonso, C.M.F., "Teofanía y visión beata en Escoto en Erigena," *Rev.española de teol.*, 10 (1950), 361–389; 11 (1951), 255–281; T. Gregory, "Note sulla dottrina delle 'Teofanie' in Giovanni Scoto Eriugena," *Studi medievali*, 4 (1963), 75–91; [2]*De divisione naturae*, 2, 34, 613B–C; [3]*Ibid.*, 2, 33, 611B; [4]*Ibid.*, 2, 34, 613A; [5]*Theol. Dogmatica Christianorum Orientalium ab Ecclesia Catholica Dissidentium*, I, Paris, 1926, 256–263; [6]*Op. cit.*, 2, 23, 567D; 2, 35, 614C.

JUGIE, MARTIN, A.A. (1878–1954)

A great Byzantine scholar of vast erudition and a prolific writer, J. served the cause of Trinitarian theology in his writings and in editing the remarkable work of Theophanes of Nicaea (qv).[1] In his *Theologia dogmatica Christianorum Orientalium ab Ecclesia catholica dissidentium* he expounds, as no other western writer had done, the Orthodox theology of the Trinity.[2] In two volumes of this work he had dealt at length with the *Filioque* (qv);[3] he had also published separate studies on the problem,[4] as on the Epiclesis (qv).[5] All this writing is a quarry for research by those seeking to advance the ecumenical movement in an enlightened way.

[1]D. Stiernon, A.A., *Catholicisme*, VI, 1190–93; *Mélanges Martin Jugie*, REB, 11 (1952), 19–32, bibl. of J. 19–32; [2]*Theologia dogmatica Orientalium ab Ecclesia catholica Dissidentium*, 1933, II, 224–534; [3]*Ibid.*, I, 1926, 286–311; II, 296–535; [4]*De Processione Spiritus Sancti ex Fontibus Revelationis et secundum Orientales Dissidentes*, Rome, 1936; "Origine de la controverse sur l'addition du Filioque au symbole," RSPT 28 (1939), 369–85; [5]*De Forma Eucharistiae, De Epiclesibus Eucharisticis*, Rome, 1943.

JULIUS I, ST., POPE (337–352)

With J. the Papacy emerged from the apparent "retirement" in which it had passed a quarter of a century, that is, since the council of 313 held under Pope Miltiades.[1] The Pope assumed a role in the Arian controversy and conflict; therein he would clarify the prerogative of his own office, or point the way to clarification. In the year of J's accession to office the first Caesaro-papist, Constantine the Great, died. The succession, divided, contested, eventually unified in a single heir, would complicate matters. At its best the sequence of events shows that the doctrine of the faith, the development of theology, is not a clerical preserve (see ARIANISM, SENTIMENT OF THE FAITHFUL). At its worst, it threw up intriguers, spawned factions, politicized bishops, nourished rivalries—all embarrassing to record because the dominant issue was the mystery of the Incarnate Word, the ultimate reference the Holy Trinity.

The theological *dramatis personae* were still the same: the hero, Athanasius (*qv*), often at bay, indomitable; his antagonist Eusebius of Nicomedia (*qv*), now installed in Constantinople, fortified by continuing patronage of the eastern emperor, Constantius II. Thus empowered Eusebius and the Arian sympathisers requested J. to ratify the acts of the synod of Tyre, to accept its condemnation of Athanasius and to install the Arian bishop Pistus in the see of Alexandria. Tyre was seen by the emperor as an ecclesiastical jury.

J., desirous to serve justice, sent the dossier to Athanasius: it was his first sight of it. He assembled a council of more than eighty bishops at Alexandria. They forwarded to Rome a lengthy detailed refutation of all the charges that had been made against Athanasius. When the bearers of this "Encyclical Letter of the Council of Egypt"—thus it was styled, for it was sent to all bishops—reached Rome, the Eusebian messenger, Macarius, departed, leaving two deacons in his place, Hesychius and Martyrius.

The underlings were ill fitted to cope with the Egyptian document as J. tells us: "For Martyrius and Hesychius had been publicly refuted by us, and the Presbyters of the Bishop Athanasius had withstood them with great confidence; indeed, if one must tell the truth, Martyrius and his fellows had been utterly overthrown; and this it was that led them to desire that a Council might be held."[2] J. agreed and, in writing, invited the Bishop of Alexandria and his accusers to a synod, its time and place to suit them. Constantius, not without violence, forced another bishop on the see of Alexandria, Gregory the Cappadocian; Athanasius was free in more senses than one to obey J's summons. His accusers demurred, whereon J. sent a second invitation, fixing a time limit at the end of 339. Only on its expiry did they release his envoys. These bore a letter which is one of the strange texts of the Arian upheaval. A summary of it is given by the historian Sozomen: "Having assembled at Antioch, they wrote to Julius an answer elaborately worded and rhetorically composed, full of irony and containing terrible threats. For in their letter they admitted that Rome was always honoured as the school of the Apostles and the metropolis of the Faith from the beginning, although the teachers had settled in it from the East. But they did not think that they ought to take a secondary place because they had less great and populous churches, since they were superior in virtue and intention. They reproached Julius with having communicated with Athanasius, and complained that their synod was 'insulted and their contrary decision made null,' and they accused this as unjust and contrary to ecclesiastical law. Having thus reproached Julius and complained of his ill-usage, they promised, if he would accept the deposition of those they had deposed and the appointment of those whom they had ordained, to give him peace and communion; but if he withstood their decrees, they would refuse this."[3]

This manifesto, as Mgr. Philip Hughes rightly comments, "strikes a new note in the history of the relation between Rome and the other sees. It is the first open denial of her primacy, the first occasion when the Bishop of Rome has been threatened with rebellion to coerce his jurisdiction."[4] Nonetheless the council was held and Athanasius and the other bishops were cleared of the false accusations. Then J. committed himself to writing. He composed a letter to be sent to the Eusebians which has been characterised by the great Tillemont as "one of the finest monuments of antiquity," a work of "great, exalted genius with at the same time strength, finesse and attractiveness."

J., in terms of serene character, unmasks the weakness of the Eusebian position in the light of church tradition, of recent history, and of elementary justice. On Athanasius for example: "Now although what has already been said were sufficient to show that we have not admitted to our communion our brothers Athanasius and Marcellus either too readily, or unjustly, yet it is but fair briefly to set the matter before you. Eusebius and his fellows wrote formerly against Athanasius and his fellows, as you also have written now; but a great number of bishops out of Egypt and other provinces wrote in his favour. Now in the first place, your letters against him are inconsistent with one another, and the second have no sort of agreement with the first, but in many instances the former are answered by the latter, and the latter are impeached by the former. Now where there is contradiction in letters, no credit whatever is due to the statements they contain. In the next place if you require us to believe what you have written, it is but consistent that we should not refuse credit to those who have written in his favour; especially considering that you write from a distance, while they are on the spot, are acquainted with the man, and the events which are occurring there, and testify in writing to his manner of life, and positively affirm that he has been the victim of a conspiracy throughout. Again, a certain Arsenius was said at one time to have been made away with by Athanasius, but we have learned that he is alive, nay, that he is on terms of friendship with him."[5]

Having gone through all the falsehood, all the irregularities, J. comes to a general conclusion: "And why was nothing said to us concerning the church of the Alexandrians in particular? Are you ignorant that the custom has been for word to be written first to us, and then for a just decision to be passed from this place? If then any such suspicion rested upon the bishop there, notice thereof ought to have been sent to the church of this place; whereas, after neglecting to inform us and proceeding on their own authority as they pleased, now they desire to obtain our concurrence in their decisions, though we never condemned him. Not so have the constitutions of Paul, not so have the traditions of the Fathers directed; this is another form of procedure, a novel practice. I beseech you readily bear with me: what I write is for the common good. For what we have received from the blessed Apostle Peter that I signify to you."[6]

The letter went unheeded. Later that year the Council *In Encaenis* was held at Antioch, adopting four different creeds, one of them drafted by St. Lucian of Antioch (*qv*).

J. still hoped for reconciliation between east and west. Through Constans, he made overtures to the eastern ruler and they both agreed to a council. It would meet in Sardica (now Sofia), a city with western territory but close to the eastern frontier. In the event, 343, one hundred and seventy bishops came, seventy-six from the jurisdiction of Constantius. Hosius of Cordova (*qv*), one of the most eminent bishops of the Church, presided, as he had done at Nicaea (*qv*). The easterns set an impossible condition to their participation: preliminary agreement to their condemnation of Athanasius and Marcellus, one of the questions

to be discussed. On refusal by Hosius, they drew up a lengthy protestation, excommunicated the Pope and Hosius, and departed at once. Once more Athanasius was pronounced innocent, as was Marcellus—though he was obliged to give an explanation of his ambiguous statements. The unlawfully appointed bishops and the leaders of the recent schism were excommunicated. The creed of Nicaea was once more published. A synodal letter was sent to J., acknowledging the Roman see as the head.

Another meeting took place at Milan, 345, with no favourable outcome. Constantius changed in his attitude towards Athanasius, allowing him to return to his see in 346—he had spent seven years in exile. The Alexandrine freed himself of any link with Marcellus, now an embarrassment whose disciple Photinus (*qv*) was objectionable to all parties: he was deposed in 351, after a formal debate with Basil of Ancyra (*qv*) arranged by the emperor in his palace in Sirmium. (Constantius was now emperor of the whole Roman world since the assassination of his brother Constans in 350.) Two years later J. died, having deserved well of the Church.

---

[1]Sources, Athanasius (*qv*), *Apologia c. Arianos*, 21–35, 52f; PL 8, 857–944, Supplement, A. Hamman, O.F.M., I (1958), 191f; H. Lietzmann, *Apollinarius von Laodicea und seine Schule*, 1904, *passim*; esp., J. Chapman, O.S.B., "St. Athanasius and Pope Julius I," in *Studies on the Early Papacy*, London, 1928, 51–71; church histories, e.g. Philip Hughes, I (1948), 198–207; J. Chapin, *NCE* VIII (1967), 51f; [2]Athanasius, *Apologia c. Arianos*, 22, LNPF, IV,112; [3]H.E., III, 8, apud Chapman, *op. cit.*, 55, 56; [4]*Op. cit.*, 200; [5]*Apologia* 27, *op. cit.*, 114; [6]*Ibid.*, 35, 118.

JUSTIN MARTYR, ST. (c. 100–c. 165)

Greatest of the "Apologists", J. was primarily interested in the transcendence of God and in the *Logos* (*qv*); his intention, as that of the Apologists generally, was to convince the Greeks that Christianity was the true philosophy.[1] Harnack summed up his Christology in a formula that has become classical: "Christ is the *Logos* and the *Nomos*." Challenged at his trial J. summed up his faith as follows: "That we pay reverence to the God of Christians, whom we hold to be the beginning, the Maker and Framer of all creation, both visible and invisible; and the Lord Jesus Christ the Son (or Servant) of God, who also has been proclaimed beforehand by the prophets as about to come to the human race as the herald of salvation, and the teacher of good disciples. And I, being a man, think that I can say but little with reference to his boundless Deity, and acknowledge that a kind of prophetic power is necessary for that, since it has been proclaimed beforehand of him whom I just now spoke of as being the Son of God. For I know that the prophets spoke of old concerning his appearance among men."[2]

Some of J's texts are a little disturbing on the question of subordinationism (qv) of which he has been accused: "His Son, the only one who is properly called Son, the Word who before all creatures was with him and had been begotten when, at the beginning, the Father made and ordered all things."[3] "What man of sound mind would not admit that in no sense are we atheists, we who worship the creator of this universe? But we are instructed that our teacher of these things, born to this task, Jesus Christ, and crucified under Pontius Pilate in the days of Tiberius Caesar, is Son of the true God; we have proved that not without reason do we worship him in second place, keeping the prophetic Spirit in the third rank."[4]

Thus in the *Apologies*. In the *Dialogue with Trypho* we read: "Yet another testimony from the Scriptures will I give you, my Friends, I said, namely that God has begotten as a beginning, before all his creatures a kind of reasonable Power from himself which is also called by the Holy Spirit the Glory of the Lord, and sometimes Son, and sometimes Wisdom, and sometimes Angel, and sometimes God, and sometimes Lord and Word. Sometimes also he speaks of himself as Chief Commander, as when he appeared in the form of a man to Joshua the son of Nun. For he can have all these names, from the fact that he ministers to the Father's purpose; and has been born of the Father of his own will." J. then applies the analogy of the human word and that of fire, which show no diminution. He goes on: "But the Word of wisdom will act as witness for me, being himself this God begotten of the Father of the universe, and being all the time the Word and Wisdom and Power and Glory of him who begat and spoke as follows by Solomon."[5] Then follows a lengthy extract from Proverbs 8: 22ff. Further on we read: "But this Offspring, which in reality was put forth from the Father before all his works, was with the Father, and with him the Father conversed as the word showed us plainly by means of Solomon, that this Itself which is called Wisdom by Solomon was begotten by God both as the beginning before all his works and as his offspring."[6]

In assessing these texts one should bear in mind the reservation made by B. Lonergan (qv) in regard to the Pre-Nicene writers and subordinationism. One must note the silence on the Holy Spirit where it would be expected.

---

[1]Works PG 6; Eng. tr. *Apologies* ANCL 1867, *Dialogue with Trypho*, A.L. Williams, London, 1930; cf. H. Chadwick, "Justin Martyr's Defence of Christianity," *Bulletin of the John Rylands Library*, 47 (1965), 275–297; Altaner, 65–71; Quasten, I, 196–219; G. Bardy, *DTC*, VIII, 2, 1919–25, 2228–77; id. *DTC* XV, P. Toschi, *EC* VI (1951), 841–45; [2]Repr. from J.C.T. Otto, Williams, *op. cit.*, xi; [3]*Apol.* II, 6; [4]*Apol.* I, 13; [5]*Dialogue*, 61, Williams, 126, 27; [6]*Ibid.*, 62, 130.

K/L

KELLY, J.N.D. (1909–   )
Oxford patristic scholar, committed as a member of the academic council of the Ecumenical Institute of Jerusalem to inter-faith dialogue, a quality that will be evident in his forthcoming book on the Papacy, K. has had a profound influence on Trinitarian studies through his two best-known works, *Early Christian Creeds*, 1958 and *Early Christian Doctrines*, 1958. Each has gone through several editions. They are marked by exhaustive scholarship, clear, felicitous presentation and, above all, a capacity to situate authors and movements of ideas in their proper context. K. has also produced the standard work on *The Athanasian Creed* (*qv*), the Paddock Lectures for 1962, 63, issued in 1964.

LANGUAGE OF TRINITARIAN THEOLOGY

Traditional language about the Trinity is challenged on more than one front. The dehellenizers (*qv*) think that it is time to shed the words, and consequently the concepts, of Hellenic culture. Students of psychology object to the words person and personality (*qv*). Existentialists may be put off by what they would think to be the whole abstract paraphernalia of scholastic theology, which takes such an effort to master and finally imprisons the mind; an esoteric set of linguistic symbols, when assimilated, may become an intellectual straight jacket. Others, like the process theologians (*qv*), come to the bare data of revelation with a ready-made set of mental categories which they impose at will. Certain radicals would distort the entire meaning of revelation. The feminist theologians one must mention with respect.

Pluralism is valid; it is also difficult to apply. What is ancient is not necessarily obsolete; what is new not automatically true. The problem of the theological communicator in this area is similar to that affecting the whole field of theology: how to translate a message which has come to him from above for the benefit of those around him, without betraying its meaning through weakness on his part or, by defective presentation, depriving them of its full content. Nor must he forget the indispensable channel of faith. He must be in full possession of the truth: an enormous prerequisite. He must assess exactly the medium he uses, first in its demands on his power of expression, second in its impact on the mind of others.[1]

---

[1]Cf. F. Ferré, *Le langage religieux a-t-il un sens? Logique et foi*, Paris, 1970; G. Ebeling, *Einführung in theologische Sprachlehre*, Tübingen, 1971; H. Fischer, *Glaubensaussage und Sprachstruktur*, Hamburg, 1972; D.M. High, *Sprachanalyse und religiöses Sprechen*, Düsseldorf, 1972; A. Grabner-Haider, *Glaubenssprache, Ihre Struktur und Anwendbarkeit in Verkündigung und Theologie*, Freiburg, Basel, Wien, 1975; J. Splet, *Reden aus Glauben, Zum christlichen Sprechen von Gott*, Frankfurt, 1973; B. Casper, *Sprache und Theologie, Ein philosophische Hinführung*, Freiburg, Basel, Wein, 1975; W.D. Just, *Religiöse Sprache und*

analytische Philosophie, Sinn und Unsinn religiöser Aussagen, Stuttgart, 1975; J. Track, *Sprachkritische Untersuchungen zum christlichen Reden von Gott* (Forschungen zur systematischen und ökumenischen Theologie 37), Göttingen, 1977; J. Meyer zu Schlochtern, *Glaube—Sprache—Erfahrung, Zur Begründungsfähigkeit der religiösen Überzeugung* (Regensburger Studien zur Theologie 15), Frankfurt a. M., 1978; T.W. Tiley, *Talking of God, An Introduction to Philosophical Analysis of Religious Language*, New York, 1978; E. Biser, *Religiöse Sprachbarrieren Aufbau einer Logaporetik*, Munich, 1980; I.U. Dalfert, *Religiöse Rede von Gott* (Beiträge zur evangelischen Theologie 87) Munich, 1981; R. Schaeffler, *Fähigkeit zur Erfahrung. Zur transzendentalen Hermeneutik des Sprechens von Gott* (Quaest. disp. 94); Freiburg, Basel, Wien, 1982.

LATERAN COUNCIL, IV (1215)

Greatest of the Lateran Councils, called by Innocent III at the peak of his powerful pontificate, attended by four hundred archbishops and bishops and a cohort of secular dignitaries, it proclaimed a succinct doctrine of the Trinity and in the context of the clash between Joachim of Fiore (*qv*) and Peter Lombard (*qv*) clarified the question of the essence and the Persons.[1]

"Firmly we believe and we confess simply that the true God is one alone, eternal, immense, and unchangeable, incomprehensible, omnipotent and ineffable, Father and Son and Holy Spirit: indeed three Persons but one essence, substance, or nature entirely simple. The Father from no one, the Son from the Father only, and the Holy Spirit equally from both: without beginning, always, and without end; the Father generating, the Son being born, and the Holy Spirit proceeding: consubstantial and coequal and omnipotent and coeternal; one beginning of all, creator of all visible and invisible things, of the spiritual and of the corporal; who by his own omnipotent power at once from the beginning of time created each creature from nothing, spiritual and corporal, namely, angelic, and mundane and finally the human, constituted as it were alike of spirit and the body. For the devil and other demons were created by God good in nature, but they themselves through themselves have become wicked. But man sinned at the suggestion of the devil. The Holy Trinity according to common essence undivided, and according to personal properties distinct, granted the doctrine of salvation to the human race, first through Moses and the holy prophets and his other servants according to the most methodical disposition of the time."[2]

After condemning Joachim's view of Peter Lombard, the Council proceeded to enunciate doctrine positively, making four points: there is identity between the Persons and the essence; there is real identity between the essence and the Father insofar as he begets the Son, with the Son as begotten by the Father and with the Holy Spirit proceeding from the two; the essence, in not being begotten or proceeding, has an absolute character; there is not a quaternity in God, which would be the case if there were a real distinction between the Person and Essence (Joachim accused Peter Lombard, and through him traditional doctrine, of affirming this quaternity). "We, however, with the approval of the sacred Council, believe and confess with Peter Lombard that there exists a most excellent reality, incomprehensible indeed and ineffable, which truly is the Father, and the Son, and the Holy Spirit, at the same time three Persons, and any one of the same individually; and so in God there is Trinity only, not a quaternity; because any one of the three Persons is that reality, namely substance, essence or divine nature, which alone is the beginning of all things, beyond which nothing else can be found, and that reality is not generating, nor generated, nor proceeding, but it is the Father who generates, the Son who is generated, and the Holy Spirit who proceeds, so that distinctions are in Persons and unity in nature."[3] There follows an explanation of the consubstantiality in the Trinity and of possible misunderstanding of it (see LYONS, COUNCIL OF, 1274).

[1]Mansi, XXII, 953–1086; HfL V, 2, 1316–98; F-M, X, 94–211; A. Lucharire, *Innocent III*, vol. VI; H. Tillmann, *Papst Innocenz III*, Bonn, 1954; A. Garcia y Garcia, "El Concilio IV de Letrán y sus comentarios," *Trad.*, 14 (1958), 484–502; S. Kuttner and A. Garcia y Garcia, "A new Eye-witness Account of the Fourth Lateran Council," *Trad.*, 20 (1964), 115–78; F. Vernet, DTC VIII, 2, 2652–67; [2]DS 800; [3]DS 804.

LEBRETON, JULES, S.J. (1873–1956)

L. taught dogmatic theology, then for a long period the history of Christian origins at the Institut Catholique in Paris. In 1910 with L. de Grandmaison, S.J., he founded *RSR*, to which for years he contributed a bulletin reviewing publications on the history of Christian origins.[1] In 1910, at the height of the Modernist crisis, he published his monumental work, *Les Origines du dogme de la*

Trinité, which he recast completely for the fourth edition in 1919. In that year also he brought out a shorter work, *Le Dieu vivant, la révélation de la Sainte Trinité dans le Nouveau Testament.* Somewhat more than a third of the main work dealt with the Hellenistic milieu and the Jewish preparation, the bulk of it with the New Testament; there were valuable appendices, two of which treated of the Logos (*qv*) in Philo and Hebrews and John respectively. In 1927, 28 the work appeared in two volumes with a slightly altered title, *Histoire du dogme de la Trinité des origines au Concile de Nicée*: I, *Les Origines*, II, *De S.Clément à S.Irenée.* It was the principal work on the subject since Th. de Regnon's (*qv*), scholarly and doctrinally sound. L. contributed to the great collections appearing or initiated in France, notably Fliche-Martin, entrusted especially with themes and figures in the pre-Nicene period.

---

[1]Cf. *DTC* Tables 2:2925–27; *Mélanges Jules Lebreton, RSR* 1951–52—bibliography 446–77; *LTK* 6 (1961), 869; R. D'Ouince, *Etudes* 1956, 274–78; *Catholicisme* 7, (1969); J. Lecler, 7 (1969), 188–91; *DSp*, 9, 456–57; *RSR* 44 (1956), 321–22.

LIBERIUS, POPE (352–366)

As Pope L. had to deal with Constantius II, now sole ruler of the empire and a man dedicated to the destruction of the Nicene doctrine and of the man who embodied it, Athanasius.[1] L's predecessor, St. Julius I (*qv*), had been solid for Nicaea and Athanasius; he was a man of strong nerves. L. was not so. The eastern bishops put pressure on L. as soon as he was Pope—he was to annul the approval given to Athanasius by Julius and the Council of Sardica L. did not cooperate and maintained the Bishop of Alexandria in his see; the Alexandrine had sent him a document signed by 80 of his Egyptian fellow bishops.

L. next sent legates to Constantius asking him to convene a council at Aquileia. The emperor preferred the advice of Ursacius of Singidunum and Valens of Mursa and held the council at Arles where he was in residence. All the bishops present, with one exception, confirmed the condemnation of Athanasius: the exception was Paulinus of Treves. The papal legates went along with the crowd.

L. was still worthy of his office, for he wrote to Constantius once more proposing a council: he put to the emperor other religious considerations besides the "affair of Athanasius"; he replied to false charges in regard to his handling of this affair, particularly over correspondence derogatory to the Alexandrine. This he had received, "read to the Church, read to the council and answered." He made a statement of personal Christian integrity: "You in your wisdom see that nothing has entered my mind which those serving God would unworthily think. God is my witness, the whole Church with its members is my witness, that I trample and have trampled earthly things as gospel and apostolic principle prescribes." He has not been led by rash feeling, "has not fulfilled what pertains to the law through boastfulness or the desire for glory." "And this office, as God is my witness, I accepted against my will; in it, as long as my life lasts, I desire to remain without offending God."[2]

The council was to have a sequel humiliating for L. It met in Milan and was attended by two papal legates. Frightened by Constantius, all the bishops save four—Paulinus of Treves, Lucifer of Cagliari (*qv*), Eusebius of Vercelli (*qv*) and Denis of Milan—signed against Athanasius; again the legates complied. The emperor's attempt to cow the dissidents is a notorious scene ending in the outburst: "My will is canon law! Bishops in Syria make no such objection when I address them. Obey or go into exile." They refused even when he brandished his sword and threatened execution. Exile followed.

An imperial eunuch was sent to bribe the Pope, but was rebuffed. He left the presents at the shrine of St. Peter, whence L. had them thrown out. Alexandria was soon reliving the persecution of Diocletian, with Catholic convicts, bishops, priests and laity condemned to the mines for their loyalty to Athanasius. On L. Constantius personally concentrated. He had the Pope kidnapped. After a sharp dialogue during which L. never flinched, Constantius sent him into exile. The Pope wrote a letter to the three bishops who had withstood Constantius, congratulating them and asking them to pray for him that he should "be able to bear the serious wounds of attacks threatening him daily."

Did he succeed in doing so, or did he collapse? From Beroea in Thrace he was brought to Sirmium where the court was in session and in 358 returned to Rome. He is thought to have paid a price for freedom, abandonment of Athanasius and signature of an objectionable formula. On the

debated question a completely satisfying monograph has not appeared. Ancient authorities
scarcely mince matters. Thus Athanasius wrote:
"But Liberius, after he had been in banishment
two years, gave way, and from fear of threatened
death subscribed." But magnanimously he continues: "Yet even this only shows their violent conduct, and the hatred of Liberius for the heresy,
and his support of Athanasius, so long as he was
suffered to exercise a free choice. For that which
men are forced by torture to do contrary to their
first judgment, ought not to be considered the
willing deed of those who are in fear, but rather
of their tormentors."[3] St. Jerome is acid: "*Liberius,
taedio victus exilii et in haeretica pravitate subscribens,
Romam quasi victor intraverat.*"[4]

The case against L. would be cast-iron if four
letters found among the fragments of St. Hilary
(*qv*) were proved genuine.[5] Historians divide on
the issue: K. Hefele, C. L. Saltet, P. Batiffol, D. di
Capua and P. Glorieux are against authenticity,
speaking of forgery or Arian interpolation, which
hypotheses are scarcely supported by contemporary evidence; L. Duchesne, A. Wilmart, A. Feder,
O. Bardenhewer, E. Caspar and E. Amann support authenticity. In the letters L. repudiates
Athanasius and in one admits that he suscribes to
the Sirmian formula. But which formula is not
clear: the first, though omitting the *homoousios*,
would bear a near-orthodox interpretation.

L's years after his return to Rome were worthy.
He was not represented at the Council of Rimini,
and when the occasion offered he was clear in his
repudiation of Arianism and in his support for
Nicaea. Like Vigilius and Honorius I, he was discussed at the time of the definition of papal infal-
libility by the First Vatican Council. His case does
not present a real difficulty as he acted under
duress, and the full truth is not known.

[1]Writings PL 8, 1349–1410; crit. ed. letters A. L. Feder, CSEL
65 1916 inter opera Hilary (*qv*); cf. J. Chapman, O.S.B., "The
Contested Letters of Pope Liberius," *R.Ben.* 27 (1910), 22–40,
172–203, 325–51; A.L. Feder, *Studien zu Hilarius von Poitiers,*
I, Vienna, 1910, 153–83; E. Caspar, *Geschichte de Papsttums,* I
(1930), 166–95; P. Glorieux, "Hilaire et Libere," *MSR* 1 (1944),
7–34; Bardenhewer, III, 585–88; H. Leclercq, *DACL* IX, 1,
(1930), 497–530; E. Amann, *DTC* IX, 1, (1926), 631–59; P.T.
Camelot, O.P., *NCE* VIII (1967), 714–716; [2]Epistula 'Obse-
cro', Hilarii fragm 5, Kirch, *Enchiridion,* 552, p. 337; [3]*Historia
Arianorum,* V, 41, LNPF, IV, 284; [4]*Chronicon,* apud Kirch,
Enchiridion, 630, p. 364; [5]Text of four letters Kirch, *Enchiridion,* 560–69, p. 541–45.

LITURGY, THE

Consultation of the indices in works on the Liturgy, for example the *Enchiridion Liturgicum* of P.
Rado, O.S.B., or any of Fr. Jungmann's basic
works, will show that the official prayers and cer-
emonies of the Church express belief in the mystery of the Trinity.[1] Some aspects of this influence
are dealt with in the articles on Baptism, Doxology
and the Epiclesis (*qqv*). Here suggestions for study
are offered while awaiting the monograph which
the subject deserves. Value judgments are not
expressed; nor does the author feel obliged to
assert that every recent change has been beneficial. The most evident change is the suppression
of the prayer, *Suscipe Sancta Trinitas* and its pendant *Placeat Sancta Trinitas* in the *Ordo Missae* promulgated by Paul VI.

The first text of a Mass in honour of the Trinity, a votive Mass for Sunday, is found in the works
of Alcuin (*qv*). Before long it was said on the Sunday after Pentecost. This was the culminating point
of the liturgical year; it marked a departure from
the general pattern since it did not celebrate an
event in the history of salvation, but an intrinsic
divine mystery, the central, dominant, determining mystery of all. This is a liturgical echo of the
debate on the "economic" and "immanent" Trinity.

The first feast of the Trinity was instituted by
Stephen, bishop of Liège (903–920), with full Mass
and Office.[2] The feast seems to have been
prompted by the Norse threat. It met resistance
at first in Rome. Pope Alexander II, consulted
about its suitability, said that "according to the
Roman ordinal no day should be especially
assigned to a solemnity of the Holy Trinity, any-
more than to the holy unity since every Sunday,
indeed daily, the memory of each is celebrated."[3]
His successor and namesake, Alexander III,
agreed, saying that every day the *Gloria* and similar pertinent words of praise met the need. But
from the thirteenth century the feast spread widely
and in 1334 John XXII, at Avignon, ordered it
for the whole Church. With slight alterations it is
found in the Missal of St. Pius V. The Preface of
the Trinity is in the Gelasian Sacramentary from
the seventh century: the words "*in substantia Trinitatis*" proclaim the consubstantiality (*qv*); "*sine differentia discretionis*" (in some MSS "*sine differentia
et discretione*") announce the equality.

The *Suscipe Sancta Trinitas,* before the *Orate
Fratres* in the preconciliar Roman Missal, has a
still more ancient origin. It is found in northern

France in the ninth century, and existed in some ordinals in as many as thirteen different formulations. The priest could pray for himself, for the congregation present, for the King and Christian people, and for the sick and the dead. In the form finally established the offering was made in memory of the mysteries of Christ and with advertence to the Communion of Saints:[4] "Receive, O Holy Trinity, this oblation which we make to thee, in memory of the Passion, Resurrection and Ascension of our Lord Jesus Christ, and in honour of Blessed Mary, ever Virgin, blessed John the Baptist, the holy Apostles Peter and Paul, and of all the saints, that it may avail unto their honour and our salvation, and may they vouchsafe to intercede for us in heaven, whose memory we celebrate on earth. Through the same Christ our Lord."

As a pendant to this prayer the priest before giving the final blessing quietly recited the *Placeat tibi, Sancta Trinitas*: "May the performance of my homage be pleasing to thee, O Holy Trinity; and grant that the sacrifice which I, though unworthy, have offered up in the sight of thy majesty, may be acceptable to thee, and through thy mercy, be a propitiation for me, and for all those for whom I have offered it. Through Christ our Lord."

The Mass, therefore, through the Middle Ages, one of the highest moments in Christian civilization, was, in its aspect as oblation, Trinitarian and explicitly so. Thus it remained down to the Second Vatican Council. This was the Mass which survived the crises of the Reformation, the Enlightenment and the French Revolution, which was carried throughout the world in the great missionary movement of the nineteenth and twentieth centuries.

Let us briefly note the changes. The Offertory prayers now do not have an explicit reference to the Trinity: "Blessed are you, Lord God of all creation," is the opening phrase of the prayer over the bread and wine. The God of creation (*qv*) is the Trinity, but this is left at the implicit level. The first Eucharistic Prayer, the Roman Canon, opens with an invocation of the "most merciful Father through Jesus Christ, thy Son, our Lord." The third Eucharistic Prayer, a post-conciliar addition, is addressed to the Father, with direct advertence to the Son and the Spirit: "Father, you are holy indeed and all creation rightly gives you praise. All life, all holiness comes from you through your Son Jesus Christ our Lord by the working of the Holy Spirit. From age to age you gather a

people to yourself so that from east to west a perfect offering may be made to the glory of your name." The theme is continued after the consecration in the words addressed to the Father, which recall the saving mysteries of Christ and the hope of his second coming. Then this prayer is said: "Look with favour on your Church's offering, and see the Victim whose death has reconciled us to yourself. Grant that we, who are nourished by his body and blood, may be filled with his Holy Spirit, and become one body, one spirit in Christ."

In contrast the second Eucharistic Prayer opens with the word "Lord," who is addressed as "holy, the fountain of all holiness" with these words which imply a Trinitarian idea: "Let your Spirit come upon these gifts to make them holy, so that they may become for us the body and blood of our Lord, Jesus Christ."

The fourth Eucharistic Prayer opens with the words "Father, we acknowledge your greatness," then evokes the creation of man in God's image, man's fall and God's repeated offer of salvation. This section ends with the words: "Father you so loved the world that in the fullness of time you sent your only Son to be our Saviour."

Then comes the Christological section, which summarizes Christ's life from his conception by the power of the Holy Spirit to his death and resurrection. Again there is an implied Trinitarian statement: "And that we might live no longer for ourselves but for him, he sent the Holy Spirit from you, Father, as his first gift to those who believe, to complete his work on earth and bring us the fullness of grace."

Finally let us note the retention of the Communion prayer which is in the same pattern, invocation not of the Trinity as such, but of Jesus Christ with allusion to the other Persons: "Lord Jesus Christ, Son of the living God, by the will of the Father and the work of the Holy Spirit your death brought life to the world. By your holy body and blood free me from all my sins and from every evil. Keep me faithful to your teaching, and never let me be parted from you."

The same separate naming marks the antiphons and prayers in the new Mass of the Holy Trinity. Whereas in the old Mass the Trinity is named in the Introit, the Collect and the Postcommunion prayer, only once does the name occur in the new Mass. The new entrance antiphon is: "Blessed be God the Father and his only-begotten Son and the Holy Spirit for he has shown that he loves us." The old Introit was: "Blessed be the Holy Trinity and undivided Unity: we will give glory to him, because he has shown his mercy to us—(Ps 8:2) O Lord, our Lord, how wonderful is thy name in all the earth . . . ." The old Collect had the words "who hast granted to thy servants, in confessing the true faith, to acknowledge the glory of the eternal Trinity, and in the power of Majesty to adore the Unity." There is, in the new Mass, a choice of two prayers: "(To the one God, Father, Son and Spirit, that our lives may bear witness to our faith) Father, you sent your Word to bring us truth and your Spirit to make us holy. Through them may we come to know the mystery of your life. Help us to worship you one God in three Persons by proclaiming and living our faith in you." "(To our God who is Father, Son and Holy Spirit) God we praise you: Father all-powerful, Christ, Lord and Saviour, Spirit of Love. You reveal yourself in the depths of our being, drawing us to share in your life and your love. One God, three Persons, be near to the people formed in your image, close to the world your love brings to life. We ask you this, Father, Son and Holy Spirit, one God, true and living, for ever and ever."

Of the two the second is more powerful theologically. There is a clear teaching on the divine indwelling (*qv*), on the divine image (*qv*), on the Trinitarian aspect to creation (*qv*). Even the conclusion is distinctive; in the first prayer the word Trinity does not occur. In the line of many references to the Trinity in the documents of Vatican II, it is the separate naming of the Persons that is adopted: and note the frequent use of the word Person (*qv*). However, just as Vatican II does occasionally use Trinity, it occurs in the prayer after Communion: "Lord God, we worship you, a Trinity of Persons, one eternal God. May our faith and the sacrament we receive bring us health of mind and body."[5]

The reference to the Persons singly is also found in the Apostolic Constitution, *Missale Romanum*, 3 April, 1969, by which Pope Paul VI officially promulgated the new Missal: "we now express a similar hope (to that of St. Pius V in his time) that this book will be received by the faithful as an aid whereby all can witness to each other and strengthen the one faith common to all, since it enables one and the same prayer, expressed in so many different languages, to ascend to the heavenly Father through our High Priest Jesus Christ in the Holy Spirit—a prayer more fragrant than any incense."[6]

There is a new set of readings for the Mass of the Trinity, three for each cycle, with separate responsorial psalms: the OT readings recall a theophany to Moses (Ex 34:4–6, 8–9), Moses' praise of God's fidelity to his covenant (Deut 4:32–34), and the well-known passage on Wisdom in Proverbs (8:22–31), often applied to Our Lady; the NT readings include St. Paul's tripartite formula "The grace of the Lord Jesus Christ and the love of God and the fellowship of the Holy Spirit be with you all" (2 Cor 11–13), and two passages from Romans, one ending in the words "God's love has been poured into our hearts through the Holy Spirit which has been given to us" (Rom 5:1–5), the other including the words "When we cry 'Abba! Father!' it is the Spirit himself bearing witness with our spirit that we are children of God, and if children then heirs of God and fellow-heirs with Christ, provided we suffer with him in order that we may also be glorified with him" (Rom 8:14–17).

The gospel readings are the end passage of Matthew which includes the baptismal formula, and from John a brief excerpt from the discourse with Nicodemus on the mission of the Son (3:16–18), and the well-known promise on the sending of the Spirit which ends with the words "All that the Father has is mine; therefore I said that he will take what is mine and declare it to you" (16:12–15).

The Sacraments often invoke the Trinity. In Baptism the profession of faith is made in each Person of the Trinity and the baptismal formula is in the name of the Father and of the Son and of the Holy Spirit.[7] In the Apostolic Constitution, *Divinae consortium naturae*, 15 August, 1971, Paul VI stated that in the formula for Confirmation found in the twelfth century Roman Pontifical "which later became the common one first occurs: 'I sign you with the sign of the cross and confirm you with the chrism of salvation. In the name of the Father and of the Son and of the Holy Spirit.'"[8]

The Pope changed this formula with the justification: "As regards the words which are pronounced in Confirmation, we have examined with due consideration the dignity of the venerable formula used in the Latin Church, but we judge preferable the very ancient formula belonging to the Byzantine rite, by which the Gift of the Holy Spirit himself is expressed and the outpouring of the Spirit which took place on the day of Pentecost is recalled (see Acts 2:1–4, 38). We therefore adopt this formula rendering it almost word for word."[9] By his supreme apostolic authority "in order that the revision of the rite of Confirmation may fittingly embrace also the essence of the sacramental rite," the Pope decreed "that the following should be observed for the future: 'The Sacrament of Confirmation is conferred through the anointing with chrism on the forehead, which is done by the laying on of the hand, and through the words: Accipe signaculum Doni Spiritus Sancti (Be sealed with the Gift of the Holy Spirit).'"[10] Here then we have a change from the traditional western Trinitarian formula. As has been said, no value judgment is entered.

Absolution in the sacrament of Penance is given with the words: "I absolve you from your sins in the name of the Father and of the Son, and of the Holy Spirit." In Matrimony the Trinity is invoked in the giving of the rings. "N., take this ring as a sign of my love and fidelity, In the name of the Father, and of the Son, and of the Holy Spirit."

In the Anointing of the Sick the prayer of thanksgiving over the blessed oil is as follows: "Praise to you, Almighty God and Father. You sent your Son to live among us and bring us salvation. R. Blessed be God./Praise to you, Lord Jesus Christ the Father's only Son. You humbled yourself to share in our humanity, and you desired to cure all our illnesses. R. Blessed be God./Praise to you, God the Holy Spirit, the Consoler, You heal our sickness with your mighty power. R. Blessed be God."

If the oil is to be blessed this prayer is said: "Lord God, loving Father, you bring healing for the sick through your son Jesus Christ. Hear us as we pray to you in faith, and send the Holy Spirit, man's Helper and Friend, upon this oil, which nature has provided to serve the needs of men. May your blessing come upon all who are anointed with this oil, that they may be freed from pain and illness, and made well again in body, mind and soul. Father, may this oil be blessed for our use in the name of our Lord Jesus Christ who lives and reigns with you for ever and ever."[11] In the Anointing these words are said: "Through this holy anointing, may the Lord in his love and mercy help you with the grace of the Holy Spirit. R.

Amen. May the Lord who frees you from sin save you and raise you up. Amen."

In the prayer over the ordinand in the ceremony of priestly ordination the bishop asks that the Spirit be especially stirred in him.[12]

Finally we turn to the Breviary, the Liturgy of the Hours according to the Roman rite. If the Apostolic Constitution of Paul VI, Canticum Laudis, 1 November, 1970, does not have a reference to the Trinity, the General Instruction, which is rightly admired, speaks not only of "The Son of God himself 'who is one with his Father' (cf Jn 6:38), who, entering the world said, 'Here I am! I am coming, O God, to obey your will' (Hebrews 10:9; cf Jn 6:38) deigned to show us how he prayed."[13] It also includes a passage like this, "Throughout their Letters, the apostles give us many prayers, especially of praise and thanksgiving. They enjoin us to offer prayer to God the Father through Christ in the Holy Spirit, with constancy and perseverance, pointing out its efficacy for our sanctification."[14]

The special Office of the feast of the Trinity deserves attention. The prayer through all the Hours is the first prayer of the Mass already quoted. The Invitatory Antiphon shows a tendency present throughout—to use the word Trinity: "The true God is one in Trinity and a Trinity in one; come let us adore him." Several of the antiphons to the psalms have "Holy Trinity," "Blessed Trinity." The short responsory after the Reading at Morning Prayer is "To you be praise and glory, O blessed Trinity"; the antiphon to the Benedictus is "Blessed be the creator and ruler of all things, the holy and undivided Trinity, both now and forever and for ages unending." Though the Persons are occasionally mentioned separately, the sense of the Trinity dominates. The first Reading in the Office of Readings is 1 Cor 2:1–16, in which the passage on the "Spirit who reaches the depths of everything, even the depths of God" occurs; the second Reading is fittingly from St. Athanasius (qv) on the Trinity, from the first epistle to Serapion. The Reading at Evening Prayer I is Rom 11:33–36, beginning "How rich are the depths of God"; that for Morning Prayer is 1 Cor 12:4–6 on the "variety of gifts but the same Spirit . . . the variety of services but the same Lord . . . the same God"; those for the Prayer during the day are 2 Cor 1:21–22, God's seal and the Spirit dwelling in our hearts, as "a pledge of what is to come"; Gal 4:4, 5–6 God sent his Son . . . "The proof that you are sons is that God sent the Spirit of his Son into our hearts, the Spirit that cries 'Abba, Father'!"; Rev. 7:12 "Praise and glory and wisdom and thanks and honour and power and might belong to our God for ever and ever. Amen." Finally the Reading for Evening Prayer II is Eph 4:3–6: on "the unity which the Spirit gives . . . one body and one Spirit, just as there is one hope to which God has called you. There is one Lord, one faith, one baptism; there is one God and Father of all men, who is Lord of all, works through all and is in all."[15]

Who composed the Mass and the Office we do not know. We cannot explain the change in emphasis by a conscious decision of the same people or by the fact that two different groups had somewhat different views. The corpus of biblical texts would repay study in the light of the general question of the biblical witness (see BIBLE) or of the so-called Trinitarian "problem" (*qv*).

As to the general content of the Divine Office each psalm, as is known, ends with the lesser Doxology (*qv*). So do many of the hymns. Noteworthy is the fact that the concluding stanza of some hymns, especially those used in the Prayer during the Day, is addressed directly to the Trinity: "O blessed, holy Trinity," "Most blessed Trinity of Love," "Blessed Trinity from age to age"; St. Patrick's Breastplate is occasionally used in the Divine Office said throughout the English-speaking world.

[1]*Enchiridion Liturgicum*, 2 vols, Rome, 2nd ed., 1966; J.A. Jungmann, S.J., *Missarum Sollemnia*, ed. 4, 1958; *The Mass of the Roman Rite*, 1959, Eng. tr. of earlier ed.; *id.*, *Public Worship*, London, 1957; *id.*, *The Place of Christ in Liturgical Prayer*, London, 1965; cf. F. Cabrol, O.S.B., "Le culte de la Trinité dans la Liturgie et l'institution de la fête de la Trinité," *EphLit*, 45, (1931), 270–78; A. Klaus, *Ursprung und Verbreitung der Dreifaltigheitsmesse*, Werl-in Westfalen, 1938; J.M. Sustaeta, "La doctrina trinitaria en la evolución liturgica y en la Constitución de Sagrada Liturgia," *EstTrin*, i (1967), 139–157; J. Lopez-Martin, "Función didascalica de la liturgia en el Misterio Trinitario segun el 'Missale Romanum' y el 'ordo poenitentiae'," *EstTrin*, XII 12 (1978), 3–52; *id.*, "La experiencia de la Trinidad en la liturgia romana restaurada," *EstTrin* 13 (1979), 151–206; *id.*, "Trinidad y Mision en el Missale Romanum," *EstTrin* 15 (1981) 211–288; [2]P. Rado, *op.cit.*, 1278–81; [3]PL 151, 1020; [4]J.A. Jungmann, *The Mass*, 337f; [5]Tr. *The Roman Missal*; [6]Tr. A. Flannery, O.P., Vatican II, *Conciliar and Postconciliar Documents*, Dublin, 1975, 141; [7]*The Rites of the Catholic Church as revised by the Second Council and published by authority of Pope Paul VI*, Eng. tr. New York, 1975, 143–47; [8]*Ibid.*, 295; [9]*Ibid.*, 295f; [10]*Ibid.*, 296; [11]*Ibid.*, 602; [12]*The Rites*, ed. 1977, 66; [13]*The Divine Office*, I, xx; [14]*Ibid.*, xxii f; and cp. *The Action of the Holy Spirit*, xxiv f; [15]*The Divine Office*, III, 3–20.

LOGOCENTRIC THEOLOGY

A theory which explains the Incarnation within the general context of the indwelling (*qv*) of the Holy Trinity in the soul of the just.[1] It begins with a concept of creation as the beginning of divinization—it has been remarked by Fr. Congar that Catholic theologians have unfortunately separated creation and redemption. The work of God sanctifying men, of the Trinity dwelling within them, constitutes a series of stages pointing by the force of their identical intrinsic spiritual reality to the peak of divine action which is the Hypostatic Union. The sanctification of the individual Christian is caused in the same way as the sanctification of the human nature of Christ.

But the uniqueness of Christ must be affirmed. So must the infinite distance between an incarnate divine Person and Trinitarian indwelling. Our Lady is the test case. Where does she, at the peak of human sanctification, stand vis-à-vis the Word her incarnate Son? Infinitely beneath him is the answer of Christian teaching.

With these reservations the L. theory should be developed, particularly in what it can say about the inter-relationship between creation and salvation.

[1]Cf. S. Beggiani, "A Case for Logocentric Theology," *ThSt* 32 (1971); *id.*, *NCE*, XVI, 263, 64; see articles on Grace and Indwelling of the Trinity.

LOGOS (WORD)

The meaning of the word Logos in Philo Judaeus and in Stoicism is of general interest,[1] but the judgment of J. McKenzie that it is unnecessary to invoke this history to explain the ancestry of the Johannine word and idea is acceptable. The word is found in Rev 19:13, 1 Jn 1:1, and esp. Jn 1:1; 1:14. The origin and genesis of these texts, of the word therein, can be located in the OT and NT milieu. The Revelation passage occurs in an eschatological context, described in the language characteristic of that book: conflict ensuing in defeat and condemnation of the malicious; the leader of the forces of righteousness, a rider on a white horse, has, among other names, that of the Word of God. "He is clad in a robe dipped in blood and the name by which he is called is the *Word* of God." The reference in 1 John is within the opening passage descriptive of God's revelation in Christ: "That which was from the beginning, which we have heard, which we have seen with our eyes, which we have looked upon and touched with our hands, concerning the *Word* of life—the life was made manifest, and we saw it, and testify to it, and proclaim to you the eternal life which was with the Father and was made manifest to us— that which we have seen and heard we proclaim also to you, so that you may have fellowship with us; and our fellowship is with the Father and with his Son Jesus Christ" (1 Jn 1:1–3).

The most important text, however, is Jn 1:14: "And the *Word* became flesh and dwelt among us, full of grace and truth; we have beheld his glory, glory as of the only Son from the Father." A. Grillmeier's comment is apposite: "The climax in the NT development of christological thought is reached in John. His prologue to the fourth Gospel is the most penetrating description of the career of Jesus Christ that has been written. It was not without reason that the christological formula of Jn 1:14 could increasingly become the most influential text in the history of Dogma."[2] As the same author says, "The first element which underlies the Johannine Logos-concept is the idea of 'revelation' and 'revealer.' Christ is the Word of God, already existing before the world, and spoken into the world. The office of 'revealer' is so closely bound up with the person of Jesus that Christ himself becomes the embodiment of revelation." There is another aspect to the *Logos* as John expounds it: "The personal presence of the revealer is a presence in the flesh. The Word of God has appeared *visibly* (1 Jn 1:1ff). The Logos of God *is* man. The peculiarly Johannine contribution lies in the sharpness of the *antithesis* and the depth of the *synthesis* of Logos and sarx."[3]

The prologue to the Gospel was a unique statement with the Logos idea at its core: it surpasses the Stoic concept by insistence on transendence, and the Philonic formulas—though resembling the Johannine terms—are totally devoid of the idea of incarnation. It was a unique statement destined, calculated doubtless, to echo profoundly in the Greek mind; in fact it may be taken as the starting-point of the prolonged and fruitful dialogue between the best of Hellenism and Christianity, not ending in the imprisonment of the latter as the dehellenizers may suggest.

In the long reflection engaged by theologians on the biblical data, beginning already in the post-apostolic age, again and again the content of the Johannine prologue was to be examined and debated: the transcendence of Jesus allied to his cosmic role of enlightenment and production, the dependence of the universe on him and his preexistence (*qv*), his functional role in life and his eternal equality with the Father. For Jesus was seen as Logos-Son, not temporally bound in his existence by the fact that he was uttered, but who came forth in time.

It is the work of historians of theology to show with what stuff the frame of *Logos* was filled from age to age, to look for continuity between the Semitic formulas of the Bible and the Hellenistic formulas of the fourth and fifth century Councils, between the concrete and historical terms of the Bible and the systematic categories of philosophers. As a study of continuity and coherence within the Gospel of John one may take C.H. Dodd's *The Interpretation of the Fourth Gospel*: "We might put it thus, that the Prologue is an account of the life of Jesus under the description of the eternal Logos in its relations with the world and with man, and the rest of the gospel an account of the Logos under the form of a record of the life of Jesus; and the proposition 'the Word became flesh' binds the two together, being at the same time the final expression of the relation of the Logos to man and his world, and a summary of the significance of the life of Jesus. We may regard the Prologue as giving, in the barest skeleton outline, a philosophy of life, a *Weltanschauung*, which is filled in with concrete detail out of the gospel as a whole."[4]

---

[1]Cf. biblical commentaries on Scripture passages, esp. Jn 1:14 and biblical dictionaries s.v. Word or *Logos*, esp. ed. G. Kittel, *TDNT* IV, 69ff. (G. Kittel, A. Debrunner, H. Kleinknecht, O. Procksch, G. Quell and G. Schrenk); J. Rendel Harris, *The Origin of the Prologue to St. John's Gospel*, London, 1917; *id.*, "Athena, Sophia and the Logos," *Bulletin of the John Rylands Library*, 7, 1922/23, 56ff; M.E. Boismard, O.P., "Dans le sein du Père," *RB*, (1952), 23–39; *Le Prologue de saint Jean*, Paris, 1953 (Eng.tr. Westminster, Maryland, 1957); esp. C.H. Dodd, *Interpretation of the Fourth Gospel*, Cambridge, 1953, 263–85; S. de Ansejo, "Es un himno a Christo el Prólogo de san Juan," *Est.Bibl.* 15 (1956), 223–277, 381–427; R. Schnackenburg, "Logoshymnus und johanneische Prolog," *Biblische Zeitschrift* N.F., 1 (1957), 69ff; O. Cullmann, *The Christology of the New Testament*, London, 1959, 249–269; A. Grillmeier, S.J., *Christ in Christian Tradition*, London, 1964, 29–35; *id.*, *Der Logos am Kreuz*, Munich, 1956; W. Pannenberg, *Jesus, God and Man*, London, 1968,

158–187, esp. for the Trinity, 179f; E. Haenchen, "Probleme des johanneischen Prologs," *Zeitschrift für Theol. und Kirche*, 60 (1963), 313ff; [2]A. Grillmeier, *op.cit.*, 27; [3]*Op.cit.*, 29; [4]C.H. Dodd, *op.cit.*, 285.

LONERGAN, BERNARD, S.J. (1904–1984)

One of the great minds of the century, L. was Canadian born and taught in higher institutes in his own country, eventually was professor of dogma in the Gregorian University in Rome for twelve years, alternating courses in *De Verbo Incarnato* and *De Deo Trino*.[1] Two high points mark his career: *Insight, A Study of Human Understanding*, 1957 and *Method in Theology*, 1972. The latter work expounds eight functional specialities: in phase one Research, Interpretation, History and Dialectic, and in phase two Foundations, Doctrines, Systematics and Communications.

Relevant to Trinitarian studies are the two volumes *De Deo Trino*, 1964 (with which, to understand his intellectual evolution, note *De Sanctissima Trinitate*, 7 March, 1955, notes for L.'s students in Rome, preparation for his first textbook), and *Divinarum personarum conceptio analogica*, 1957 (for the use of his students) which, much revised, became *De Deo Trino, II, Pars systematica* in the *De Deo Trino*. In 1961 he issued, also for students, *De Deo Trino, Pars analytica*. He had come to see the difference between the aim, proper object and method of dogmatic theology and those of positive theology in the strict sense, and this work was an example of dogmatic theology. Revised for the 1964 edition it bore the title "Dogmatic part." Important also in L's thought is *Verbum, Word and Idea in Aquinas*, and articles in the *Collections of Papers*.

L. illustrates how powerful genius can surmount apparently insuperable obstacles. He spoke thus about his work *De Deo Trino*: "Well—those things are practical chores, that you have to do if you're teaching a class of 650 people. They're not going to get it on the wing out of lectures. One of the techniques of getting them to come to the lectures and get something out of them is to provide them with a thick book so that they'll be glad to have some map as to what's important in it and what you can skip. It belongs to a period in which the situation I was in was hopelessly antiquated, but had not been demolished—it has since been demolished. But to be a professor of dogmatic theology was to be a specialist in the Old Testament—not just in the Pentateuch or something like that—the Old Testament, the New, the Apostolic Fathers, the Greek Fathers, the ante-Nicene, Greek and Latin, the post-Nicene, the medieval Scholastics, the Renaissance period, the Reformation, contemporary philosophy and so on. There's no one who is a specialist in all that; but that was the sort of thing you had to handle . . . . It was a matter of doing that and also of introducing what I could. For example my analysis of the ante-Nicene period on Trinitarian doctrine: I was developing there also what I consider something permanently valid, namely this type of interpretation that is concerned with things that the thinkers themselves didn't think about. Tertullian has a Stoic background, Origen has a middle Platonist background, Athanasius' account of Nicaea is something totally new that you can't reduce to anything Platonic, Aristotelian, Gnostic, or Stoic, and so on; a new situation is created. It's second-level thinking, the sort of thing that is possible within a Hellenistic culture. But that comparison of all three, revealing their different backgrounds—the different ways in which they conceived the Son to be divine, totally different ways—is an understanding of the process from the New Testament to Nicaea. That, I think, is something valid. But having to write the books at all was totally invalid—yet necessary concretely."[2]

The nine sections preceding five theses in *De Deo Trino I* have appeared in English translation Perusal of these pages and of the whole book, first entitled *Pars analytica*, then *Pars dogmatica* by L., does show him striking out originally, as does the whole of volume II, *De Deo Trino, Pars systematica*. His books are in marked contrast with the theological manuals up to his time. He achieved his synthesis on method within the context of Trinitarian theology. This is high commendation.

Facing the problem of personality (*qv*) in contemporary idiom L. advances this statement: "Father, Son and Holy Spirit are in virtue of one real consciousness three subjects conscious of themselves, of one another, and of their act (of being) both notional and essential."[3]

[1]The review *Method* coordinates studies on L.; centres of research on his work with abundant material exist in Regis College, Toronto, Milltown Park, Dublin, Canisius College, Sydney; cf. esp. Translator's (Conn O'Donovan) Introduction to *The Way to Nicea* (sic), London, 1976; David Tracy, *The Achievement of Bernard Lonergan*, New York, 1970; *Spirit as Inquiry. Studies in Honour of Bernard Lonergan, S.J.*, ed. F.C.

Crowe, S.J., *Continuum* 2 (1964); H. Meynell, "Bernard Lonergan," in *One God in Trinity*, ed. P. Toon, J.D. Spiceland, Westchester, 1980, 95–110; [2]*A Second Collection, Bernard Lonergan*, ed. W.F.J. Ryan, S.J., and B.J.T. Tyrrell, S.J., London, 1974, 211ff; [3]*De Deo Trino*, II, 186.

LOSSKY, VLADIMIR (1903–1958)

Expatriate Russian Orthodox (*qv*) theologian, L. was educated in Russia, Prague and Paris, was acquainted with the U.S. where he lived for a while, and was associated with the remarkable group of Russian Orthodox writers in France, though he opposed S. Bulgakov's sophiological theory and was instrumental in having it officially repudiated.[1] He was much drawn to the works of Eckhart (*qv*) in his last years; he remained throughout the champion of Orthodox theses, and was particularly insistent in rejecting the *Filioque*.

In the course of his theological career, L. had one important achievement: he was chiefly responsible for the revival of interest in St. Gregory Palamas. In all his works he is never far from thought about the Trinity. This is especially true in his *The Mystical Theology of the Eastern Church* and in the collected papers which appeared under the title *The Image and Likeness of God*. The first is a brilliant synthesis, unquestionably one of the most remarkable works by an Orthodox writer in the present century: it has a lesson for western theologians, a lesson of fidelity to the Fathers of the Church, as of the importance of doctrine on the Trinity. Regrettably the great Karl Rahner (*qv*) who was so desirous of making Trinitarian doctrine meaningful to the faithful, did not give sufficient attention to the Orthodox, especially to L. This is also true of other recent writers on the theme.

In the *Vision of God* L. speaks of the "Father unknown manifesting himself in the world by the Son and the Holy Spirit." In *Apophasis and Trinitarian Theology* he discusses the proper mode of theological investigation of the Trinity: "*Theologia*—which was for Origen a knowledge, a *gnosis* of God in the *Logos* (*qv*)—means, in the fourth century, everything which concerns Trinitarian doctrine, everything which can be said of God considered in himself outside of his creative and redemptive economy." "To the economy in which God reveals himself in creating the world and in becoming incarnate, we must respond by theology, confessing the transcendent nature of the Trinity in an ascent of thought which necessarily has an apophatic thrust. Now we cannot know God outside of the economy in which he reveals himself. The Father reveals himself through the Son in the Holy Spirit; and this revelation of the Trinity always remains 'economic' inasmuch as, outside of the grace received in the Holy Spirit, no one could recognize in Christ the Son of God and in this way be elevated to knowledge of the Father."[2]

L. thought that "it is an exclusive attachment to the economic aspect of the Trinity, with stress on the cosmological significance of the *Logos*, which renders Ante-Nicene Trinitarian theology suspect of subordinationism. To speak of God in himself outside of any cosmological link, outside of any engagement in the *oikonomia vis-à-vis* the created world, it is necessary for theology—the knowledge which one can have of the consubstantial Trinity—to be the result of a way of abstraction, of an apophatic decanting by negation of all the attributes (Goodness, Wisdom, Life, Love, etc.) which in the plane of economy can be attached to notions of the divine hypostases—of all the attributes which manifest the divine nature in creation." L. thinks that with this process what will remain will be "the notion of absolute hypostatic difference and the equally absolute essential identity of the Father, the Son, and the Holy Spirit."[3]

L. was much attracted, as has been seen, by the doctrine of St. Gregory Palamas; he particularly adopted the idea of divine energies, and he was convinced that when Palamas spoke of God he meant the Trinity. L. is also stimulating on the divine image (*qv*). But it is in his defence of the Orthodox position on the *Filioque* that he concentrated all the resources at his command.

L. places great emphasis on the Father as the principle of unity in the Trinity. He speaks of causality, but only as a "somewhat defective image, which tries to express the personal unity which determines the origins of the Son and the Holy Spirit." The unique cause is not prior to his effects nor is he superior to them. "He is the cause of their equality with himself. The causality ascribed to the Person of the Father, who eternally begets the Son and eternally causes the Holy Spirit to proceed, expresses the same idea as the monarchy of the Father: that the Father is the personal principle of unity of the Three, the source of their common possession of the same content, of the same essence."[4]

L. maintained that "all triadology depends on the question of the procession of the Holy Spirit." He rejected the findings of the Russian theologian, Boris Bolotov. He thought Roman Catholic theology guilty, "from the point of view of Orthodox theology, of an inadmissible error of confusion concerning the Trinity"; this harsh comment was in regard to "the relations of origin as notional acts and of two processions *per modum intellectus* and *per modum voluntatis*."[5] He was still more stringent: "By the dogma of the *Filioque*, the God of the philosophers and savants is introduced into the heart of the living God, taking the place of the *Deus absconditus, qui posuit tenebras latibulum suum*. The unknowable essence of the Father, Son and Holy Spirit receives positive qualifications. It becomes the object of natural theology: we get 'God in general', who could be the god of Descartes, or the god of Leibnitz, or even perhaps, to some extent, the god of Voltaire and of the dechristianized Deists of the eighteenth century."[6] Scarcely a fitting comment on the theology of M.J. Scheeben (*qv*), not to mention St. Thomas Aquinas (*qv*).

But L. ends on a happier note. He thinks that reconciliation will be possible. The West must not think of Byzantine theology as an absurd innovation. He does think that the *Filioque* is the greatest obstacle to reunion, as he is convinced that the divergent views explain the different spiritual outlooks. He is convinced that the modern Byzantine theologians preserve the theology of the Fathers of the first five centuries. "The Greeks have ceased to be Greeks in becoming sons of the Church. That is why they have been able to give to the Christian faith its imperishable theological armory. May the Latins in their turn cease to be solely Latins in their theology! Then together we shall confess our catholic faith in the Holy Trinity, who lives and reigns in the eternal light of his glory."[7]

Eastern spirituality, L. thought, was explicitly Trinitarian: "The goal of Orthodox spirituality, the blessedness of the Kingdom of Heaven, is not the vision of the essence but above all a participation in the divine life of the Holy Trinity, the deified state of the co-heirs of the divine nature, gods created after an uncreated God, possessing by grace all that the Holy Trinity possesses by nature." "The Trinity is for the Orthodox Church the unshakeable foundation of all religious thought, of all piety, of all spiritual life, of all

experience. It is the Trinity that we seek in seeking after God, when we search for the fullness of being, for the end and meaning of existence."[8]

[1]Cf. O. Clement, "Vladimir Lossky, un théologien de la personne et du Saint Esprit," *Messager de l'Exarchat du Patriarche russe en Europe occidentale*, 30–31 (1959), 137–206; B. Schultze, S.J., *DSp* IX, 1018–1019; B. Dupuy, *Catholicisme*, VII, 1091–92; [2]*In the Image and Likeness of God*, 1974, 15f; [3]*Ibid.*; [4]*The Procession of the Holy Spirit*, repr., *In the Image and Likeness of God*, 82; [5]*Ibid.*, 86; [6]*Ibid.*, 88; [7]*Ibid.*, 96; [8]*The Mystical Theology of the Eastern Church*, 1957, 63, 65.

LUCIAN OF ANTIOCH, ST. (d. 312)

One of the most influential figures in the history of the early Church, L. was probably born in Antioch, of which he became a presbyter.[1] He there founded a theological school, where he had among his pupils many of the leading figures in the history of Arianism (*qv*), including Arius himself. Though dead through a heroic endurance of martyrdom L. may well have been the dominant influence on Arius, as G. Bardy remarked.[2] A. Robertson had put the point forcibly some time before him: "We find a number of leading Churchmen in agreement with Arius, but in no way dependent on him. They are Eusebius of Nicomedia, Maris (of Chalcedon), Theognis (of Nicaea), Athanasius of Anazarba, Menophantes (of Ephesus); all Lucianists. The first Arian writer, Asterius, is a Lucianist . . . . It has been urged that, although Arius brought away heresy from the school of Lucian, yet he was not the only one that did so. True; but then the heresy was *all of the same kind* (cf. list of pupils of Lucian in Philostorgius, H.E., ii, 14; iii, 13). Aetius, the founder of logical ultra-Arianism and teacher of Eunomius, was taught the exegesis of the New Testament by the Lucianists Athanasius of Anazarba and Anthony of Tarsus, of the Old by the Lucianist Leontius. This fairly covers the area of Arianism proper."[3]

It is then tantalising to note that we have practically nothing directly from the hand of L. There is a long apologetic discourse of disputed authenticity, and some fragments and one statement of doctrine which was adopted as a creed at the Dedication Council of Antioch. Of the apologetic discourse Bardy says, "it does not tell us much about the personal thought of its supposed author." The same patrologist, along with Loofs, challenges any dependence of L. on Paul of Samosata (*qv*).

L. was excommunicated after the condemnation of Paul, but for an error opposed to that of the man from Samosata. His error was subordinationism, an idea of Origen (*qv*), "grown on the hard soil of Antioch" (Bardy). He must have been a remarkably gifted teacher, his prestige doubtless increased by his success in biblical linguistics—his corrected version of LXX and the gospels was widely accepted—ultimately hallowed by his heroic death, which crowned a singularly blameless life. The text of what Jerome calls the *Libelli de fide* might enlighten us as the creed reproduced by Athanasius[4] and Hilary[5] does—on what must have been powerful charisma: charisma unfortunately serving error.

Here is the text of the creed: "We believe, conformably to the evangelical and apostolical tradition, in one God, the Father Almighty, the Framer, and Maker and Provider of the Universe, from whom are all things. And in one Lord Jesus Christ, his Son, Only-begotten God (Jn 1:18), by whom are all things, who was begotten before all ages from the Father, God from God, whole from whole, sole from sole, perfect from perfect, King from King, Lord from Lord, Living Word, Living Wisdom, true Light, Way, Truth, Resurrection, Shepherd, Door, both unalterable and unchangeable; exact Image of the Godhead, Essence, Will, Power and Glory of the Father; the first born of every creature, who was in the beginning with God, God the Word, as it is written in the Gospel, 'and the Word was God' (Jn 1:1); by whom all things were made, and in whom all things consist; who in the last days descended from above, and was born of a Virgin according to the Scriptures, and was made Man, Mediator between God and man, and Apostle of our faith, and Prince of life, as he says, 'I came down from heaven, not to do mine own will, but the will of him that sent me' (Jn 6:38); who suffered for us and rose again on the third day, and ascended into heaven, and sat down on the right hand of the Father, and is coming again with glory and power, to judge quick and dead. And in the Holy Ghost, who is given to those who believe for comfort, and sanctification, and initiation, as also our Lord Jesus Christ enjoined his disciples, saying, 'Go ye, teach all nations, baptizing them in the Name of the Father, and the Son, and the Holy Ghost' (Mt 28:19); namely of a Father who is truly Father, and a Son who is truly Son, and of the Holy Ghost, who is truly Holy Ghost, the names not being given without meaning or effect, but denoting accurately the peculiar subsistence, rank and glory of each that is named, so that they are three in subsistence and in agreement one. Holding then this faith, and holding it in the presence of God and Christ, from beginning to end, we anathematize every heretical heterodoxy. And if any teaches, beside the sound and right faith of the Scriptures, that time, or season, or age, either is or has been before the generation of the Son, be he anathema. Or if anyone says, that the Son is a creature as one of the creatures, or an offspring as one of the offsprings, or a work as one of the works, and not the aforesaid articles one after another, as the divine Scriptures have delivered, or if he teaches or preaches beside what we received, be he anathema. For all that has been delivered in the divine Scriptures, whether by Prophets or Apostles, do we truly and reverentially both believe and follow."[6]

---

[1]Cf. esp., G. Bardy, (*qv*), *Recherches sur Lucien d'Antioche et son école*, Paris, 1936; *id.*, *DTC*, IX, 1, 1926, 1024–31; A. d'Alès, S.J., "Autour de Lucien d'Antioche," *Mélanges de l'Université de Beyrouth*, 21 (1936), 185–190; Altaner, 214f; Quasten, II, 142–44; A. Vaccari, S.J., *EC* VII (1951), 1625f; [2]*RHE* 22 (1926), 272; [3]*Prolegomena to LNPF* IV, Athanasius, xxviii; [4]*De synodis*, II, 23; [5]*De synodis*, 29; [6]*LNPF*, IV, 461.

LUCIFER OF CAGLIARI (d. c. 371)

Anti-Arian to the point of desiring martyrdom, L. was turbulent in his utterance, even in presence of the emperor, and in his writing.[1] At the Synod of Milan where he represented Pope Liberius (*qv*) he defended Athanasius with such vigour that, at the behest of the Arians, Constantius (*qv*) kept him in detention in the imperial palace for three days. His dialogue with the emperor, far from being muted by this ill-treatment, was vociferous, blunt and utterly intransigent. Exile followed, first to Palestine and then to the Thebaid; but not silence, for he despatched missives in the same style to the emperor: *De non conveniendo cum haereticis; De regibus apostaticis; De S. Athanasio; De non parcendo in Deum delinquentibus; Moriendum esse pro Dei Filio*. He benefitted by the general release after the accession of Julian, 362. He remained intransigent, refusing to attend the conciliatory synod of Alexandria in 362, though he did send two deacons, and consecrating Paulinus bishop of Antioch: the result was a schism.

[1]Works: PL 13, 767–1038; CSEL 14, CCL 8, cf. F. Piva, *Lucifero di Cagliari contro l'imperatore, Costanzo*, Trent, 1928; G. Thornell, *Studia Luciferiana*, Uppsala, 1934; C. Zedda, "La teologia trinitaria di Lucifero di Cagliari," *Divus Thomas*, Piacenza, (1949), 276–329; E. Amann, *DTC*, IX, 1, 1926, 1032–44; Altaner, 367.

LUTHER, MARTIN (1483–1546)—See Reformation, The

LYONS, COUNCIL OF, OECUMENICAL XIV (1274)

Called by Gregory X to achieve the liberation of the Holy Land and promote the reform of morals, but especially to further union with the Greek Church.[1] It was attended by five hundred bishops, sixty abbots and a thousand other prelates. Among its members were St. Philip Benizi, General of the Servites, St. Albert the Great, the Dominicans Humbert de Romanis and Peter of Tarentaise, the future Innocent V, and St. Bonaventure (*qv*) who preached at the High Mass when the legates of the Greek Emperor, Michael Paleologus, three times repeated the *Filioque*. The emperor sought Roman cooperation in restraining the ambition of Charles of Anjou, his design of a Latin empire of Constantinople. St. Thomas Aquinas died on his way to the Council.

The declaration regarding the Holy Spirit read as follows: "In faithful and devout profession we declare that the Holy Spirit proceeds eternally from the Father and the Son, not as from two beginnings, but from one beginning, not from two spirations but from one spiration. The most holy Roman Church, the mother and teacher of all the faithful, has up to this time professed, preached, and taught this: this she firmly holds, preaches, declares, and teaches; the unchangeable and true opinion of the orthodox Fathers and Doctors, Latin as well as Greek, holds this. But because some through ignorance of the irresistible aforesaid truth have slipped into various errors, we, in our desire to close the way to errors of this kind, with the approval of the sacred Council, condemn and reject (those) who presume to deny that the Holy Spirit proceeds eternally from the Father and the Son; as well as (those) who with rash boldness presume to declare that the Holy Spirit proceeds from the Father and the Son as from two beginnings, and not as from one."[2]

The Profession of Faith of Michael Palaeologus has passages relevant to our subject, one preceding, the other following the Christological section: "We believe that the Holy Trinity, the Father, and the Son, and the Holy Spirit, is one God omnipotent and entire Deity in the Trinity, coessential, and consubstantial, coeternal and co-omnipotent, of one will, power and majesty, the creator of all creatures, from whom are all things, in whom are all things, through whom are all things which are in the heavens and on the earth, visible, invisible, corporal and spiritual. We believe that each individual Person in the Trinity is one true God, complete and perfect . . . . We believe also that the Holy Spirit is complete and perfect and true God, proceeding from the Father and the Son, coequal and consubstantial, co-omnipotent, and coeternal through all things with the Father and the Son. We believe that this holy Trinity is not three Gods but one God, omnipotent, eternal, invisible, and unchangeable."[3]

[1]Cf. HfL V, 2, 1633–1679; VI, 1, 153–209; J. Geanakoplos, *Emperor Michael Palaeologus and the West*, Cambridge, Mass, 1959; H. Jedin, *Ecumenical Councils of the Catholic Church*, New York, 1960; F. Dvornik, *The Ecumenical Councils*, New York, 1961; F. Vernet, *DTC* IX, 1, 1361–91; V. Grumel, *ibid.*, 1391–1410; [2]DS 850; Msi XXIV 81B; [3]DS 851, 853; Msi XXIV 70Af.

M

MACEDONIUS (d. c. 362)

The heresy of the Macedonians was condemned at the Council of Constantinople I (*qv*): these were identified as "Those opposing the Spirit." It was from then on believed that the particular heretics, the *Pneumatomachi* (*qv*) owed their origin to Macedonius, who seems to have become Bishop of Constantinople in 342 after the death of Eusebius in the previous year and remained in this office until he was deposed by the Arian Council of Constantinople in 360. He defended the Semi-Arian position at the Council of Seleucia in 359. It is difficult to establish his connection with the heresy of the Pneumatomachi.

---

[1]Cf. F. Loofs, PRE, XII, 1903, 41–44; G. Bardy (*qv*), *DTC* IX, 1926, 1464–78.

MARY, MOTHER OF GOD

"Redeemed, in a more exalted fashion by reason of the merits of her Son and united to him by a close and indissoluble bond, she is endowed with the high office and dignity of the Mother of the Son of God, and therefore she is also the most loved daughter of the Father and the sanctuary of the Holy Spirit."[1] Thus Vatican II (*qv*) succinctly states the mystery of Mary's relationship with the Blessed Trinity. The approach is personalist, specifying how Mary's destiny involves each of the Three, suggesting how the mystery she embodies may open a path of revelation.[2] The key to all is the mystery of the Incarnation. That was the vital moment of her unique entry into Trinitarian life. Then there was a personal decision on her part of momentous, everlasting consequences. An eastern Father of the Church put it thus: "The incarnation of the Word was not only the work of the Father, of his power and of his Spirit, but was also the work of the will and the faith of the Virgin; without the consent of the Immaculate one, without the contribution of her faith, this plan was as unrealisable as without the intervention of the three divine persons themselves."[3]

There are different approaches possible to the mystery of Mary in the mystery of the Blessed Trinity. One is to analyse her relationship with the Father, Son and Holy Spirit separately. The theme of Mary and Jesus, symbolized in the prayer *O Jesu vivens in Maria*, was central to the doctrine of the French school of spirituality. The ideal of spirituality taught by De Berulle was interior assimilation to the states of Jesus, and herein Mary's role was capital as exemplar and advocate. Others like Jean Jacques Olier, founder of the influential Society of St. Sulpice, worked out this exalted programme in detail.

Since the Council there has been an immense intellectual activity and enthusiasm centered on the subject of Mary and the Holy Spirit. Sessions of Marian societies, in particular the prestigious French Society, have explored the many aspects of the subject, biblical, patristic, magisterial, liturgical, and doctrinal. High points in this widespread research and reflection have been the International Marian Congress in Rome, 1975 on Mary and the Spirit, marked by an important essay on the subject in the form of a papal letter by Paul VI to the Legate, Cardinal Suenens and, from the same Pope, in his Apostolic Exhortation *Marialis Cultus*, 2 February, 1974, a very suggestive passage on the relationship between Mary and the Spirit, instructive in that it is set in a Trinitarian context.

On Mary and the Father there is as yet little by way of theological speculation. Here we do come to another approach to the general theme, Mary and the Trinity: Mary as the Spouse of God. For some early eastern Fathers saw her as the Spouse of the Father, as did writers of the seventeenth century French school. Almost alone among them St. Louis Marie Grignion de Montfort saw her as Spouse of the Spirit, as did some medieval writers and two Popes, Leo XIII and Pius XII. Vatican II did not use the title, preferring "sanctuary of the Spirit" as we have seen. The influential M.J. Scheeben (*qv*) sought to establish the thesis that Mary's motherhood is bridal, thereby developing a thought assumed, not often elaborated, of the soul in grace as *sponsa Verbi*.

Has there been much thought given to Mary's attitude towards the Trinity without separate advertence to the Persons? We enter the area of her knowledge of divine reality while she still lived on earth. Some modern biblical scholars tend to be reductionist here. They would not speak as enthusiastically as did ancient writers of the Trinity manifesting itself in the moment of the Annunciation. Without discounting or minimizing the results of genuine biblical scholarship one may perhaps echo the word of Père Congar: "I study the science of exegetes; I reject their magisterium." On a vast challenging subject much still remains to be achieved.

---

[1]*Constitution on the Church*, 53; bibl. to articles "Father, God the," "Spirit, the Holy," "Spouse of God, Mary as," "Trinity, the Most Holy," in *Theotokos*, M. O'Carroll, C. S. Sp., Wilmington, 1982. [2]Cf. M. O'Carroll, C.S.Sp., "Mary as Revelation," *Marianus*, 44 (1982), 257–285; [3]Nicholas Cabasilas, *In Annunt*, 4, PO 19, 488.

MAXIMUS THE CONFESSOR, ST. (c. 580–662)

A Byzantine aristocrat, M. left the imperial administration to become a monk in the monastery of Chrysopolis; he was abbot of this monastery.[1] He fled to Africa from the Persians and, in doctrine, from 640, emerged as a resolute opponent of Monothelitism. He instigated its condemnation by several African synods and joined in the repudiation of it expressed by the Roman Synod, the Lateran Council, 649. Unyielding under the pressure of imprisonment, exile and torture, he died in utter loneliness in the fortress of Schemaris in 662; he was vindicated in personal holiness and doctrinal orthodoxy by the Third Council of Constantinople eighteen years later.

Principally studied for the favourite Greek theme, the divinisation of man and eastern monastic spirituality (see IMAGE), M. expresses remarkable insights on the theology of the Trinity, especially in his *Commentary on the Our Father* and the *Ambigua*, an elucidation of certain texts of Gregory of Nazianzus (*qv*). Interest by western theologians in M. is relatively recent; Hans Urs von Balthasar was something of a pioneer. Due probably to this writer's influence, M. is one of the few authorities named in reports by the ITC.

M. thinks that the Our Father leads us to honour the Trinity as creative cause of our being and author of the grace of our sonship: "It (the Our Father) teaches us to take to ourselves the good things of which alone God the Father, through the Son naturally mediator, in the Holy Spirit is the dispenser. Since in fact the Lord Jesus is, according to the divine apostle, 'mediator of God and men' (1 Tim 2:5), he makes manifest to men through his flesh the Father who is unknown to them; to the Father, through the Spirit, he leads men reconciled in him."[2] This is theology according to the Lord Jesus. "Theology," says M., "the Logos of God made flesh, teaches, in fact, insofar as he shows in himself the Father and the Holy Spirit. For wholly was the Father, wholly was the Holy Spirit essentially and perfectly in the Son, who was whole and entire, though incarnate—they not being incarnate."[3] M. mentions the hypostasis. The Logos realises the union of the flesh with the Logos according to his hypostasis, which is constantly penetrated by the Father and the Spirit. The hypostasis of the Son is the principle of union of the humanity to the divinity and, in this union also, the hypostasis of the Son is communion with the Father and the Spirit. There is perhaps a lesson here for modern reductionist Christologists, advocates of a Christology from below, that Jesus, the Logos, the Son of God, is, in every moment of his human existence, one of the sublime, transcendent, infinitely majestic triune God. M. goes on to comment on the words "hallowed be thy name, thy kingdom come": "The words of the prayer in fact show us the Father, the name of the Father and the Reign of the Father so that we should learn, from the very beginning, to honour the monadic Triad, to invoke and adore it. For the name of God and Father essentially subsisting is the Son and the Reign of God and Father essentially subsisting is the Holy Spirit."[4]

Influenced by Gregory of Nazianzus, M. saw the importance of relations in the distinction of Persons: "The Son and the Spirit have always subsisted essentially with the Father, being naturally from him and in him beyond cause and reason, but they are not after him as if they came from a later cause. For relation has the capacity to show one in the other at the same time those of which it is and is said to be relation, not allowing them to be considered one after another."[5]

M. thought that the Triad was *homoousion* (see CONSUBSTANTIAL). He was insistent on the unity of the divine *Monad* and *Triad*. We are taught by the sense of God in Christ "to know one only nature and power of the divinity, that is, one God contemplated in the Father and the Son and the Holy Spirit, as a unique Thought (*Nous*) subsisting essentially without cause, begetter of the unique Logos who is without beginning, subsisting according to the *ousia*, and origin (*pege*) of the eternal Life subsisting essentially in the Holy Spirit. Triad in Monad and Monad in Triad."[6] There follows an elaborate explanation of the final succinct statement culminating in an assurance that by maintaining both one escapes polytheism on one hand and atheism on the other.

M. pursues the analysis of this question, the Monad and the Triad. The hypostases are identical with the divine *ousia*. There is no relation of causality between the Monad and the Triad. If the hypostases are in relation between themselves, they are not in relation to the divine ousia, from which they would thus be naturally distinct. The Monad is the non-relative identity; the Triad is immediately the Monad, identically, non-relatively. M. takes up difficult texts of Gregory of Nazianzus, in this context, seeking to set forth the truth as he sees it.[7]

There are many references to the Spirit, some of which are explicitly Trinitarian.[8] In the vexed question of the *Filioque* (*qv*) M. thinks that the different Greek and Latin theories are due to linguistic misunderstanding, a question of how to translate exactly the verbs *proienai* and *ekporeuesthai*, though it must be added that the Latin insistence on the relation between the Spirit and the Father and the Son must be rendered in appropriate Greek. M. knew of the consensus of Latin Fathers and also of the views of Cyril of Alexandria.[9]

[1]Bibliographies in works of L. Thunberg, A. Riou and J.-Miguel Garrigues infra; also select I.-H. Dalmais, *DSp*, 10, 836–847; works PG 90, 91; cf. R. Devreesse, "La vie de saint Maxime le Confesseur et ses recensions," *AB* 46 (1928), 5–49; P. Sherwood, O.S.B., *An Annotated Date-List of the Works of Maximus the Confessor*, Rome, 1952; id., *The Earlier Ambigua of Saint Maximus the Confessor and his Refutation of Origenism*, Rome, 1955; Hans Urs von Balthasar, *Kosmische Liturgie, Maximus der Bekenner*, ed. 2, 1961, Einsiedeln, French tr., 1947; L. Thunberg, *Microcosm and Mediator, The Theological Anthropology of Maximus the Confessor*, Lund, 1965; W. Volker, *Maximus Confessor als Meister des geistlichen Lebens*, Wiesbaden, 1965; A. Riou, *Le Monde et l'Eglise selon Maxime le Confesseur*, Paris, 1973; J.-Miguel Garrigues, *Maxime le Confesseur, La charité avenir divin de l'homme*, Paris, 1976; id., "La personne composée du Christ d'après Maxime le Confesseur," *RT* 74 (1974), 181–204; *esp.*, P. Piret, *Le Christ et la Trinité selon Maxime le Confesseur*, Paris, 1983; V. Grumel, *DTC* 10, 1, 448–459; [2]*Pater* PG 90, 876 A-B; [3]*Ibid.*, 876C-D; [4]*Ibid.*, 884B; [5]*Ibid.*, 884C, [6]*Ibid.*, 892C; [7]*Ambigua, ibid.*, 1260C-D; 1036B; [8]Cf. References to the *Quaestiones ad Thalassium*, P. Piret, *op.cit.*, 97 n. 76; [9]Cf. P. Piret, 100f.

MISSIONS, THE DIVINE

The theology of the divine missions is closely related to that of the processions (*qv*).[1] The mission is a projection outside the godhead of the procession which is immanent in the divine life; a prolongation at a moment in time which leads to the existence of the eternal divine Person in a new manner in a rational creature. Since one divine Person proceeds from another, the mission, that is, the sending, is by the originating Person. Hence the Father may come—"If a man loves me, he will keep my word, and my Father will love him, and we will come to him and make our home with him" (Jn 14:23); but he is not sent. The Son, who proceeds from the Father, is sent. The mission or sending of the Son, in the Incarnation (*qv*) is the conspicuous instance of mission. The fourth gospel abounds in affirmation of this reality: "For God sent the Son into the world, not to condemn the world, but that the world might be saved through him" (Jn 3:17; cp. 5:23; 6:38, 39; 6:58; 12:44; 17:23; esp. 20:21). This explicit statement points to the visible character of the mission, which is also clear in St. Paul's words: "But when the time had fully come, God sent forth his Son, born of a woman, born under the law, to redeem those who were under the law, so that we might receive adoption as sons" (Gal 4:4).

In this passage of Galatians Paul continues with a reference to the mission of the Spirit: "And because you are sons, God sent the Spirit of his Son into our hearts, crying 'Abba! Father!'" (Gal 4:6). Here, however, we are instructed on an invisible mission (cp. Mt. 10:20). The visible mission of the Spirit took place at the baptism of Christ (Mt 3:13–17; Mk 1:9–11; Lk 3:21–22; Jn 1:31–34); the symbol was a dove. A second visible mission occurred at Pentecost, in fulfilment of the promise of Christ: "But the Counsellor, the Holy Spirit, whom the Father will send in my name, he will teach you all things, and bring to your remembrance all that I have said to you" (Jn 14:26); "And behold, I send the promise of my Father upon you; but stay in the city, until you are clothed with power from on high" (Lk 24:49); "And while staying with them he charged them not to depart from Jerusalem, but to wait for the promise of the Father, which he said 'you heard from me, for John baptized with water, but before many days you shall be baptized with the Holy Spirit'" (Acts 1:4–5).

Building on this plenary disclosure of divine intent, theologians, notably St. Thomas, have elaborated a theory of divine mission, visible and invisible. In regard to the latter the reader is referred to the article Indwelling, with this remark of St. Thomas: "By sanctifying grace the whole Trinity dwells in the soul."[2]

The invisible mission is never of one divine Person: the Son and the Holy Spirit are sent and the Father comes with them. One Person is sent in the visible mission: the Son in the Incarnation, which is the "mission of missions," the Holy Spirit at Pentecost. Three conditions are required: a visible sign, a new sign, a sanctifying effect. The first rules out the prophetic action of OT, the second the sanctifying effect of the Sacraments, the third the theophanies of OT: St. Thomas says that the visible mission of the Spirit came more suitably after the visible mission in the flesh of the Son.

Visible missions may be substantial or representative. In the first, of which the Incarnation is the sole example, God unites himself hypostatically to a chosen creature, humanity. The representative mission is effected by the whole Trinity, with angels cooperating. It is not in the name of an angel and the Trinity is not visibly manifested, but one Person: "As the Father, Son and Holy Spirit," says St. Thomas, "are expressed by different names, so they can be manifested by different signs, though there is never separation or diversity between them."[3]

Four representative missions, all proper to the Holy Spirit, are identified: at the baptism of Christ, under the sign of a dove (Mt 3:12 and parallels); in the mystery of the Transfiguration under the sign of a luminous cloud (Mt 17:5 and parallels); after the resurrection of Christ, under the sign of his breathing on the apostles, as he said "Receive the Holy Spirit" (Jn 20:22); at Pentecost under the sign of tongues of fire (Acts 2:3). In the substantial mission of the Son he comes as author of our sanctification; in the visible missions of the Spirit he comes as a sign of this sanctification which he operates as the Son's envoy, equal to him in all things. Let us remark in passing that missions imply no inequality, any more than does the order of processions (qv).

The visible missions on the Son are representative without being efficacious, for Christ was all-holy; those on the apostles were efficacious, for they signify the grace and charisms really produced in their souls.

The missions thought out exhaustively would lead us to a better understanding of the close relationship between creation and redemption; they would shed a new light on the truth that the creation is the work of the three divine Persons. God planned the world for the separate powerful manifestations of his Trinitarian life which are the essence of the missions. Thus his self-communication was intended; thus the setting for it prepared.

[1]St. Thomas I, q 43; M.J. Scheeben, *The Mysteries of Christianity*, ch VII; B. Lonergan, S.J., *De Deo Trino*, II, 216–260; E. Hugon, O.P., *Le Mystère de la Trinité*, Paris, 1921, 287–298; [2]I q. 43, 4 ad 2; [3]*Ibid.*, 7 ad 1.

MODALISM

A form of Monarchianism (qv) sometimes taken for Patripassianism (qv). The Godhead was not consistently Trinitarian; the persons succeeded each other in a passing way, as modes of God's expression and activity. It was defended as a theory by Noetus (*qv*) and Praxeas (*qv*).

MONARCHIANISM

The name taken by second and third century writers who fell into the heresy of denying separate persons in God.[1] Desirous of safeguarding monotheism, of effectively countering Gnostic theories of intermediate aeons between God and creation and to avoid subordinationist trends, they still have to cope with the biblical texts which spoke of a Person equal in power and glory to the Father (Jn 10:30; 14:9–11, 16ff; Rom 9:5; Phil 2:6ff; 2 Peter 1:1). They thought of the Son as God in a lesser sense than the Father; he was absorbed in the Father eventually.

Different names are used. The Adoptianists (*qv*) held that Jesus was a mere man, in whom God dwelt in a special way. Others denied the distinct personality of the Son. They were called Patripassians. They were the western Modalists: Father, Son and Holy Spirit are not the names of distinct persons, but of modes, energies, aspects, phases of one divine Person. Since God the Father appeared on earth as the Son, He must be said to die; hence the name Patripassians.

According to Hippolytus (*qv*), Theodotus of Byzantium acknowledged God as creator, but thought Jesus a mere man, born of a virgin by divine ordinance. When Jesus was baptized in the Jordan he did not become God but was endowed with miracle-working power: a certain spirit, the heavenly Christ, descended upon him in the form of a dove and dwelt within him. Some of the members of the sect launched by Theodotus thought that Jesus became God after his resurrection.

Eastern Modalists were called Sabellians, after Sabellius, who may, like Noetus and Praxeas, have been Roman, though St. Basil and Timothy of Constantinople say he was from Libya or the pentapolis. He took up the doctrine of Noetus and is said to have been excommunicated under Pope Callistus (c. 220).

---

[1] Cf. G. Bardy, *DTC* X, 2, 1929, 2193–2209.

MYSTICISM

The word has been gravely misused to denote freakish spiritual behaviour. It is a branch of scientific theology, difficult to expound and master, but valid.[1] The reality it studies is immediate awareness of the Deity. We are not here considering the mysticism of the great non-Christian religions, for in our subject belief in the Trinity is assumed. How did the great Christian mystics have knowledge of the Trinity?

One striking example in the present century is Blessed Elizabeth of the Trinity (*qv*). Her well-known prayer is evidence of mystical union with the Trinity. Her predecessors in this sublime adventure are not all known to us, for literary statement is not a necessary concomitant of mystical experience. Mary, the Mother of God, had the highest mystical experience possible and she has left us no record of this reality.

St. Gregory of Nazianzus (*qv*), sometimes called the "minstrel of the Trinity," tells us that he enjoyed a keen experience of the triune God from a particular moment of conversion in his life. He was "blinded by the light of the Trinity whose brightness surpasses all that the mind can conceive for from a throne high exalted the Trinity pours upon all the ineffable radiance common to all three."[2] With such a testimony one may perhaps link the beautiful prayers of St. Hilary of Poitiers (*qv*) and of St. Augustine (*qv*). If there is reservation on the subject and the prayers are taken more as the product of reason enlightened by faith rather than of immediate experience, it must surely be to the latter that St. Catherine of Siena's (*qv*) composition was due. In its terms and thought pattern it resembles the prayer of Blessed Elizabeth and the source must have been personal experience. For the saint, now a Doctor of the Church, did not elaborate a theological structure by way of support. This is fire and light struck from the flint.

Inevitably the mind turns to the two great Spanish Doctors, John of the Cross and Teresa of Avila. St. John, commenting on the line "the breathing of the air" in the *Spiritual Canticle*, sets forth a theory of union with the Blessed Three which is truly inspired and inspiring: "By his divine breath-like spiration the Holy Spirit elevates the soul sublimely and informs her and makes her capable of breathing in God, the same spiration of love that the Father breathes in the Son and the Son in the Father, which is the Holy Spirit himself, who in the Father and Son breathes out to her in this transformation in order to unite her to himself. There would not be a true and total transformation if the soul were not transformed in the three Persons of the Most Holy Trinity in an open and manifest degree. One should not think it impossible that the soul be capable of so sublime an activity as this breathing in God, through participation as God breathes in her. For granted that God favours her by union with the Most Blessed Trinity in which she becomes dei-form and God through participation, how could it be incredible that she also understand, know and love—or better that this be done in her—in the Trinity, together with it as does the Trinity itself? Yet God accomplishes this in the soul through communication and participation. This is transformation in the three Persons in power, wisdom and love, and thus the soul is like God through this transformation. He created her in his image and likeness that she might attain resemblance."[3]

This is John speaking as a "practicien de la contemplation," to recall Jacques Maritain's pithy description of him. Here we are at the peak of the spiritual perfection made possible by the divine indwelling (qv), man made in the divine image recovering the lost splendour of that divine imprint.

John, who did not lack formal training in theology, brought to his mystical doctrine a powerful intuitive sense, the ability also to transcribe accurately what he felt at the level of spiritual reality. St. Teresa is still more markedly in the category of the great intuitive theologians, yet utterly orthodox—in which she differs, say, from Ruysbroeck (qv)—practical, in complete control of empirical phenomena, while her soaring, supple intellect reaches to the heights of the divine.

It is in the *Interior Castle*, one of the supreme classics of mystical literature, begun on Trinity Sunday, 2 June, 1577, that the saint describes the revelation made by the Trinity to the soul advanced to the ultimate, the seventh, mansion: "But in this Mansion everything is different. Our good God now desires to remove the scales from the eyes of the soul, so that it may see and understand something of the favour which he is granting it, although he is doing this in a strange manner. It is brought into this Mansion by means of an intellectual vision, in which, by a representation of the truth in a particular way, the Most Holy Trinity reveals itself, in all three Persons. First of all the spirit becomes enkindled and is illumined, as it were, by a cloud of the greatest brightness. It sees these three Persons, individually, and yet by a

wonderful kind of knowledge which is given to it, the soul realizes that most certainly and truly all these three Persons are one Substance and one Power and one Knowledge and one God alone; so that what we hold by faith the soul may be said to grasp by sight, although nothing is seen by the eyes, either of the body or of the soul, but it is no imaginary vision. Here all three Persons communicate themselves to the soul and speak to the soul and explain to it those words which the Gospel attributes to the Lord—namely, that he and the Father and the Holy Spirit will come to dwell with the soul which loves him and keeps his commandments . . . . Each day this soul wonders more, for she feels that they have never left her, and perceives quite clearly, in the way I have described, that they are in the interior of her heart—in the most interior place of all and in its greatest depths."[4]

St. Teresa says that the presence is not always realized so fully as when it first comes. But always there is a certainty which she compares to that of a person in a dark room who knows there are others with him, though he does not see them. The soul is not so absorbed as to lose the sense of the realities of life. On the contrary it is more alert in the things that concern God and service of him.

Fray Luis de Leon, first editor of the *Interior Castle*, adds a note to the passage as follows: "Though man in this life, if so raised by God, may lose the use of his senses and have a fleeting glimpse of the Divine Essence, as was probably the case with St. Paul and Moses and certain others, which though fleeting, is intuitive and clear, but of a knowledge of this mystery which God gives to certain souls, through a most powerful light which he infuses into them, not without created species. But as the species is not corporeal, nor figured in the imagination, the Mother says that this vision is intellectual and not imaginary."[5]

St. Teresa's contemporary and fellow-countryman, St. Ignatius of Loyola, gives a concrete example of the truth which she enunciated. The *Spiritual Diary* for several days in 1544 has touching and revealing passages on the saint's experience of the Trinity. Thus on 19 February he records that before going to Mass he was "not without tears" and during Mass felt a wonderful sense of repose, and "understanding of the Most Holy Trinity which illumined my mind to the point where it seemed to me that in studying I would not know as much; after reflecting again on what I understood, felt and saw I had constantly the impression that this would be so even if I were to study all my life."[6] St. Ignatius noted that he had a special understanding of the appropriation of the prayers of the Mass to the divine Persons, of the operations of the Persons, their processions, "feeling and seeing rather than grasping." On the same day he felt "much interior gladness" and later was affected by triune patterns in the people and things he met.

On one experience he wrote vividly: "During this Mass, I knew, felt and saw, *Dominus scit*, that in speaking to the Father, in seeing that he was one Person of the Most Holy Trinity, I was inflamed with love for the whole Trinity, so much the more that the other Persons were in him essentially. I felt the same thing in prayer to the Son and the same in prayer to the Holy Spirit, rejoicing to feel indiscriminately the consolations of one or other Person referring them to all three, and finding my joy in the fact that they came from all three."[7] The allusion by the words *Dominus scit* to St. Paul's account of his mystical experience in 2 Cor 12:2 shows that St. Ignatius was conscious of an unusual, very exalted phenomenon. His feeling was accompanied by a sentiment that he was unworthy to invoke the Father, Son or Holy Spirit.

Another striking experience is recorded by one of the great mystics of the seventeenth century: Blessed Mary of the Incarnation, the "Teresa of the New World." In her case the direct sentiment of the Trinity was linked with the grace of spiritual marriage: "Having, as it were, sunk in the presence of this adorable Majesty, Father, Son and Holy Spirit, in the recognition and acknowledgement of my lowliness, offering them my adoration, the sacred Person of the divine Word made known to me that he was truly the Spouse of the faithful soul. I grasped this truth with certainty and the significance attaching to it led me to immediate preparation to see it realized in me. That more than adorable Person took possession of my soul, and embracing it with love ineffable, united it to himself and made it his spouse."[8]

St. Mary Magdalen de Pazzi felt that within her soul there was a divine interaction between the three Persons: she did not put the technical terms of theology in her account. St. Teresa of the Child Jesus and the Holy Face interpreted her love in regard to each of the Persons: "To live from love is to keep you uncreated Word (*Verbe*), Word (*Parole*) of my God. Indeed you, divine Jesus, know that I love you. The Spirit of love sets me aglow with his fire. It is in loving you that I draw the Father; my weak heart retains him. O Trinity! you are prisoner of my love."[9] A prayer which the saint composed for one of her priest brothers, which she asked him to recite daily for her, continues the theme: "Merciful Father, in the name of your sweet Jesus, of the Blessed Virgin and the saints, I ask you to set my sister on fire with the Spirit of love, to grant her the grace to make you much loved."[10]

This prayer represents the saint's mature experiential response to the Trinity dwelling within her; it was composed in the last year of her life, some seven months before she died. But already three years earlier she had entered on the way of Trinitarian mystical experience: she wrote thus to her sister Celine, still in the world, later to enter Carmel and take the name Geneviève of the Holy Face: "What a call (we have received). For look! We ourselves did not dare consider ourselves, our condition appeared horrible in our eyes and Jesus calls us to look upon us at length . . . . He wishes to see us, he comes and the other two adorable Persons of the Holy Trinity come with him to take possession of our soul. Our Lord had promised this formerly when he said with ineffable tenderness: '*If anyone loves me, he will keep my word; and my Father will love him and we will come to him, and we will make our abode with him*' (Jn 14:23). To keep the word of Jesus is the unique condition of our happiness, the proof of our love for him; and this word it seems to me that it is himself, since he is named the Verbum or uncreated Word of the Father. In the same gospel of St. John he utters this sublime prayer: *Sanctify them by your Word, your Word is truth* (Jn 17:17). In another place Jesus tells us that he is *the way, the truth and the life* (Jn 14:6). We then know what word we have to keep; we cannot say with Pilate, 'What is truth?' (Jn 18:38). We possess the Truth, since the Beloved dwells in our hearts."[11] The whole inspiring passage, redolent of personal experience, is by way of commentary on Song 6:13 "*Return, return, O Shulamite, return, return, that we may look upon you*."

All these are examples of mystical experience oriented directly to the Trinity, fortunately transcribed and open to study. Clearly there have been countless others who passed along the same way, who either did not have writing skill or the desire to communicate to others how the Trinity had worked within their souls.

[1]Cf., as well as general works on Mysticism, G.P. Widmer, *Gloire au Père, au Fils, au Saint-Esprit*, Neuchâtel-Paris, 1963; H. Cozin, *Du Christ à la Trinité d'après l'expérience de Marie de l'Incarnation*, Lyon, 1936; Symposium, *La communione con Dio secondo S.Giovanni della Croce*, Rome, 1968; E. Ancilli (ed.) *Il mistero del Dio vivente*, Rome, 1968; on the great Latin doctors, F. Bourassa, "Théologie trinitaire de saint Augustin," *Greg*, 58 (1977), 675–716; 59 (1978), 375–410; J.F. Dedek, *Experimental Knowledge of the Indwelling Trinity: an historical study of the doctrine of St. Thomas*, Mundelein, 1958; N. Molloy, O.P., "The Trinitarian Mysticism of St. Thomas," *Angelicum*, 1981, 373–388; see bibl. to Experience of the Trinity, Indwelling, the divine; I.V. Rodriguez, "Teologia y vida mística en S. Juan de Cruz," *EstTrin* XVI (1982), 217–239; M. Herraiz, *Vida mística en S. Teresa de Jesús, ibid.*, 241–60; C.A. Bernard, S.J., "L'Esperienza spirituale della Trinità" in *La Mistica*, ed. E. Ancilli, M. Paparozzi, Rome II, 1984, 295–316; [2]*Poemata de seipso*, PG 37, 984, 5; [3]*The Spiritual Canticle*, Stanza 39, Commentary 3, *Collected Works*, tr. K. Kavanaugh, O.C.D., O. Rodriguez, O.C.D., Washington, 1973, 558; [4]*Interior Castle*, VII, 1, *Collected Works*, tr. E. Allison Peers, II, London, 1946; 331, 32; [5]*Ibid.*, 331, n.5; [6]*Obras*, I, Madrid, 1947, 706, 07; [7]*Ibid.*, 709; [8]*Relation de 1654, Escrits spirituels et historiques*, II, Paris, 1930, 252; [9]*Poème, Vivre d'amour, Sainte Thérèse de l'Enfant Jésus*, ed. Carmel 381; [10]*Lettre IIIe*, a ses frères spirituels, *ibid.*, 367; [11]*Lettre VIIIe à Céline, ibid.*, 339.

N

NICAEA, COUNCIL OF (325)

The first General or Oecumenical Council of the Church. The occasion was the Arian heresy (see ARIUS and ARIANISM). Constantine (*qv*), failing in his efforts to achieve agreement between Arius and Alexander, possibly with some idea of the emperor as Pontifex Maximus taking a similar role now that Christianity was the state religion, summoned a meeting of all the bishops of the time. He invited them to assemble at Ankyra, but later changed the venue to Nicaea (modern Iznik) in Bithynia. It met according to tradition on 20 May, 325, and closed on 25 July, some modern scholars contend that this was but an adjournment, and that the final session took place in 327.

St. Ambrose (*qv*) and St. Hilary (*qv*) mention the figure of 318, symbolic, it is thought, from the number of Abraham's servants. (Gen 14:14); 220 signed and possibly 250 attended. The majority were from the east: 100 from Asia Minor, 30 Syro-Phenicians and less than 20 from Palestine and Egypt. Besides the two priests, Vitus and Vincentius, who represented Pope Sylvester, there were few from the west, six bishops in all. Among them, however, was the man with most influence on the emperor, Hosius of Cordova (*qv*). Others whose names are to recur in the subsequent history were there: Eustathius of Antioch, Eusebius of Caesarea (*qv*), Marcellus of Ancyra, and Eusebius of Nicomedia (*qv*). Alexander of Alexandria was there as was his powerful secretary, Athanasius (*qv*). Others of some note at the time were Leontius of Caesarea in Cappadocia, Caecilianus of Carthage and Macarius of Jerusalem.

The proceedings, which took place in the great hall of the imperial palace, were opened by Constantine in glittering apparel. Hosius of Cordova may have presided, but some think it was Eustathius of Antioch.

The minutes or *acta* of the Council have disappeared, if they ever existed. The Creed, the Synodal Letter and the collection of canons exist. For what happened in the Council we have sparse information in a fragment of Eustathius of Antioch, some chapters of Athanasius and the letter written by Eusebius of Caesarea to his subjects explaining his action during the Council.

Some informal discussions had apparently taken place before the formal opening by Constantine. The emperor in his address spoke of the evil of sedition within the Church; his overriding wish was unity among the bishops. Thereon a question: what part did he play in the crucial debates on the wording of the Creed? To which another is linked: what was the basis of the Creed, that is, what previous credal statement was used as a first text by the drafting committee?

There were three groups, it appears, among the assembled bishops: the small group, between 17 and 22, led by Eusebius of Nicomedia, who supported Arius; those on the opposite wing who sought a forthright affirmation of the divinity of the Son, preferring the word *Homoousios* once it had been suggested; and those who held the middle ground, who were not Arian but shrank from the use of the word *Homoousios* (see CONSUBSTANTIAL, *HOMOOUSION*).

It was once believed that Constantine suggested the key word; this has been supported by the witness of Eusebius of Caesarea. But Eusebius was rather free in praise of the emperor, whose role may have been to reassure those who feared the word on account of its previous history. He did intervene; but it was signatures he wanted. Commentators have then turned to Hosius as the proponent of the important word. He was the confidant and adviser of Constantine and, according to the historian Philostorgius, he had come to an agreement with St. Alexander before the council; they had met in Nicomedia.

The question of the primitive credal text used is dealt with in the article on the Nicene Creed.

All the bishops present save two signed the creed finally drafted and presented; signers included Eusebius of Nicomedia. Eusebius of Caesarea stated in his letter that he scrutinized every word carefully and heeded the assurances of Constantine before doing so. The two dissidents were Theonas of Marmarica and Secundus of Ptolemais; they were deposed and sent into exile.

The council also took decisions on the Melitian schism in Egypt and on the Paschal Controversy, and published twenty disciplinary canons.

---

[1] Cf. bibliographies to Arianism, Athanasius, Constantine.

NICENE CREED, THE

This article deals with the creed drawn up at the Council of Nicaea (*qv*); the article on the Constantinopolitan Creed deals with that used in the Eucharistic liturgy, which is sometimes given the name Nicene Creed.

The letter which Eusebius of Caesarea (*qv*) sent to the people of his diocese has been misunderstood. He wished them to know what he had said, the formula which he had submitted and the one which the Council promulgated. He says "which (the Fathers) put forth with some additions to our words," insinuating that the Council took his text as the basis of its creed. This opinion was backed by Hort and Harnack. Recent scholars, principally H. Lietzmann, contend that the creed used had a Jerusalem origin. The point of Eusebius' intervention would, on this view, have been to clear his own orthodoxy. His own words on the matter are: "On this faith being publicly put forth by us, no room for contradiction appeared; but our most pious Emperor, before anyone else, testified that it comprised most orthodox statements. He confessed moreover that such were his own sentiments, and he advised all present to agree to it, and to subscribe its articles and to assent to them, with the insertion of a single word, of one substance (*Homoousios*), which moreover he interpreted as not in the sense of the affections of bodies, nor as if the Son subsisted from the Father in the way of division, or any severance; for that the immaterial, and intellectual and incorporeal nature could not be the subject of any corporeal affection, but that it became us to conceive of such things in a divine and ineffable manner. And such were the theological remarks of our most wise and most religious Emperor; but they with a view to the addition of 'of one substance', drew up the following formula." He then gives the Nicene Creed.[1]

St. Basil (*qv*) thought that a Cappadocian priest named Hermogenes, who later became bishop of Caesarea in Cappadocia, was a dominant member of the group which drafted the final text, but his materials are not known to us. The creed of Eusebius is here given first, then the Nicene formula:

"We believe in one God, the Father almighty, the maker of all things visible and invisible; And in one Lord Jesus Christ, the Word of God, Light of Light, Life of Life, Son only-begotten, First-born of all creation, begotten of the Father before all the ages, through whom also all things were made; who was made flesh for our salvation and lived among men, and suffered, and rose again on the third day, and ascended up to the Father, and shall come again in glory to judge the living and dead; We believe also in one Holy Spirit."[2]

The Nicene formula: "We believe in one God, the Father almighty, maker of all things, visible and invisible;

"And in one Lord Jesus Christ, the Son of God, begotten from the Father, only-begotten, that is, from the substance of the Father, God from God, light from light, true God from true God, begotten not made, of one substance with the Father, through whom all things came into being, things in heaven and things on earth, who because of us men and because of our salvation came down and became incarnate, becoming man, suffered and rose again on the third day, ascended to the heavens, and will come to judge the living and the dead;

"And in the Holy Spirit,

"But as for those who say, 'There was when he was not,' and, 'Before being born he was not,' and that he came into existence out of nothing, or who assert that the Son of God is from a different hypostasis or substance, or is created, or is subject to alteration or change—these the Catholic Church anathematizes."[3]

[1]Cf. A.E. Burn, *An Introduction to the Creeds and to the Te Deum*, 1899; id., *The Nicene Creed*, Oxford, 1909; I. Ortiz de Urbina, S.J., *Il simbolo niceno*, Consejo Superior de Investigaciones Cientificas, 1947; J. Burnaby, *The Belief of Christendom, Commentary on the Nicene Creed*, 1959; G.L. Dossetti, *Il simbolo di Nicea e di Constantinopoli*, critical ed., 1967; Kelly, *Creeds*, 205–262; [2]Tr. H. Bettenson, *Documents of the Christian Church*, p.35; [3]Tr. Kelly, *op.cit.*

NOETUS (c. 200)

A shadowy figure known to us from the refutation of his heresy by Hippolytus in his *Refutation of All Heresies* and in another work generally attributed to Hippolytus, latterly questioned as to genuineness, *Contra haeresim Noeti*.[1] N. taught, apparently, that God the Father became man and suffered for us, he was possibly the first Patripassian. He interpreted the Johannine *Logos* (qv) allegorically. He was condemned by a meeting of elders at Smyrna, c. 200.

[1]B. Lonergan, S.J., *The Way to Nicaea*, 38, 50f, see article Hippolytus, St.; P. Nautin, *Hippolyte, Contre les Héresies, Fragment, Etude et ed. critique*, Paris, 1949.

NOVATIAN (3rd century)

Biographical details about N. are scarce. His life was set in the controversy about papal succession in third century Rome. He was the first western writer in Latin.[1] His treatise *De Trinitate* was the first work of this kind in Latin on the subject. It is apologetic in intention, against the Gnostics and against Marcion. He defended the true humanity of Christ against the Docetists and his godhead against the Adoptianists (qv); he defended his sonship against the Sabellians.

N. had an opinion that the power of the divinity transmitted from the Father to the Son is directed back again from the Son, into the Father. He considers the Father unbegotten, the source, and the Son, born and begotten, as coming from the source. The Father he thought invisible, the Son visible—yet the Son as God is also invisible. Speaking of the Son's relation with the Father N. implies that there was a dependence: "when he wished the Son the Word was born"; "he was with the Father before time, and when the Father willed, he proceeded from him."[2]

N. has a stimulating passage on Christ the Image: "Every man by believing in the Son, exercises himself in the contemplation of the Image, that he may advance and grow even to the perfect contemplation of God the Almighty Father after he had been accustomed to see the divinity in the Image."[3]

N. has a magnificent chapter, 29, on the Holy Spirit (qv), "who was in times past promised to the Church and duly bestowed at the appointed, favourable moment."[4] He is the same Spirit in OT and NT—against the Marcionites—but then he was given transiently, now forever. Different phases of his action are described. Did N. think him God? It does not appear so.

[1]Text of *De Trinitate*, PL 3, 911–82; crit. ed. G.F. Diercks, CCSL, 4; Eng. tr., H. Moore, 1919; R. J. de Simone, *Fathers of the Church*; Cf. A. d'Ales, *Novatien, Etude sur la théologie romaine au milieu du IIIe siècle*, Paris, 1925; W. Keilbach, *Divinitas Filii ejusque Patri subordinatio in Novatiani libro de Trinitate*, Zagreb, 1933; M. Simonetti, "Alcune osservazioni sul De Trinitate di Novaziano," *Studi in onore di Angelo Monteverdi*, II, Modena, 1959, 771–783; G. Miroux, *Novatien, théologien de la Trinité*, Paris, Dissertation, 1964; R.J. De Simone, *The Treatise of Novatian, the Roman Presbyter, on the Trinity. A Study of the Text and the Doctrine*, Rome (Eph. August. IV), 1970; [2]31, CCSL, 4, 75f; on N's subordinationism cf. G. Aeby, *Les missions divines de saint Justin à Origène*, Fribourg (Switzerland), 106; [3]*Fathers of the Church*, ch. 28, 98; [4]*Ibid.*, ch. 29, 99.

O

OLD CATHOLICS, THE

The Old Catholics, after breaking away from the Catholic Church in 1871, were ready and eager for a justifiable association with other churches.[1] They were represented at the Bonn Conference (*qv*), and when the Russian Holy Synod set up a commission to continue the work, they also appointed one. In 1931 and 1932 they promised to withdraw the *Filioque* from the creed, but they allowed it to be held as a private opinion. The Orthodox were dissatisfied; they wanted total denial of the idea and conveyed this wish to the Old Catholics at a meeting in Belgrade in September 1966.[2] The International Conference of Old Catholic Bishops, which comprises church rulers and members of the Union of Utrecht, officially suppressed the *Filioque* in its creed in 1969 on the grounds that it had not been added canonically, that it was not theologically founded and that it contributed to the disunity of the Churches. At Chambesy, in August 1975, the Old Catholics adopted the Orthodox position.[3]

---

[1]Congar, *The Holy Spirit*, III, 192f;   [2]*Ibid.*, 195;   [3]*Ibid.*, 196.

ORIGEN (c.185–254)

What the powerful genius of Alexandria, the author of the first systematic presentation of Cath-

olic doctrine, the *De Principiis* (*Peri Archon*), thought of the Trinity cannot be stated with total certainty, since so much of his writings have disappeared and of those extant the text in Latin translation may have suffered some alteration by the translator, Rufinus.[1] With such reservations we attempt a summary of his teaching.

O. based his rule of faith on the ecclesiastical tradition which he accepted entirely. He speaks of this as coming from the apostolic preaching: "The points clearly taught in the apostolic preaching are the following. First, there is but one God, creator and controller of all things, who has drawn the universe from nothing . . . . In the second place Jesus Christ, the same one who came into the world, was born of the Father before every creature. Having been the associate of the Father in the creation of things—for all things have been made by him—he emptied himself in the fullness of time, God that he was, becoming man, and remaining God . . . . Finally apostolic tradition associates the Holy Spirit with the Father and the Son, in honour and in dignity. Is he begotten or not? Must he or must he not be considered the Son of God? This does not appear clearly; it is a question that must be settled by attentive study of Sacred Scripture, and by the effort of theological reasoning. What the Church teaches without a shadow of doubt is that this same Spirit is the inspirer of all the hagiographers, prophets and apostles, before as after the coming of Christ."[2] The divine unity is in no way affected by the trinity: "We believe that there are three hypostases: the Father, the Son and the Holy Spirit."[3]

O. thought that God possesses three qualities which distinguishes him from creatures: he is immaterial, omniscient and substantially holy.[4]

There is no doubt in the works which have reached us about the strict distinction between the Son and the Father. The Son is the substantially subsisting wisdom of the Father, he is absolutely incorporeal, eternal, Son by nature and not by adoption; he is the invisible image of God. The idea of image is basic in the whole tradition of Alexandria. But with Origen it reached a summit.[5] We get some ideas from excerpts like these: "But again, the archetype of all images is the Logos, who is with God in the beginning, because he is with God and never ceases to be God; but he would by no means have remained God if he had not remained in perpetual contemplation of the Father's profundity."[6] "And perhaps this is the reason why he is the invisible image of God; for the image that is in him is the image of the first will; and the divinity that is in him is the image of the true divinity. However, being also the image of the Father's goodness, he says: 'Why do you call me good?' For indeed it is this will that is the Son's own food, and it is because of this food that he is what he is."[7]

Did O. consider the Son a creature? The first passage to be examined is this: "For we do not say, as the heretics think, that some part of the Father's substance became the Son; neither do we say that the Son came from outside of the Father's substance, being created by the Father, so that there was a time when he was not. But, excluding every corporeal interpretation, we do say that the Word and wisdom were born, without any bodily process, of the invisible and incorporeal God, in the manner in which an act of willing proceeds from the mind. And thus it will not seem absurd, since he is called 'the Son of his love' (cf. Col 1:13), if in the same way he is considered the Son of his will."[8]

This is the version of Rufinus. St. Jerome, on the other hand, speaks as follows: "Candidus says that the Son is of the Father's substance, erring in this, that he asserts a *probole*, that is, an extrusion from the Father's substance. Origen, on the other hand, according to Arius and Eunomius, rejects the notion of his being extruded, or born,

because this would suggest that the Father is divided into parts; what he says, rather, is that the Son is the highest and most excellent of creatures, and that he came into being through the Father's will, as did all other creatures."[9]

There is no doubt that O. held the Son to be eternal; he also stated that he was not made, being the first-born of everything that was made—note the argument being drawn against this view from John 1:4 (following the reading "What was made in him, was life"). He denied that the Son had a beginning, before which he was not: "As there could not be light without that which shines, so the Son cannot be understood without the Father, he who is called the expressed image of his substance, his Word and his wisdom. How then could one say that there was a time when he was not Son? This is to say that there was a time when truth did not exist, when wisdom did not exist, when life did not exist, since in all these things the substance of the Father is thought perfectly to be."[10]

Can we then say that for O. the Word is consubstantial with the Father? He does say that the Son, though distinct from the Father, is inseparable from him, that his sonship is through a participation in his essence, not through adoption or grace. The word *homoousios* is not found in any unquestionably genuine Greek text; it is found in a fragment on the epistle to the Hebrews, quoted by Pamphilus in his Apologia for Origen.[11] One authority contends that, all things considered, O. admits the consubstantial.

What of the Holy Spirit? O. thought that Christians alone had knowledge of him. "But as to the being of the Holy Spirit, no one could think of it, except those who study the Law and the Prophets, and those who profess their belief in Christ."[12]

The Holy Spirit is eternal. "Some, I know, misunderstanding the newness of the Spirit have concluded that the Holy Spirit is new, in the sense of not having existed beforehand, and as if he had not been known to the ancients; and they are not aware that they commit a serious blasphemy. For the Holy Spirit is in the Law as he is in the Gospel. He is with the Father and the Son, he is, he has been and he will always be with the Father and the Son. He is not then new, but he renews all who come to the faith."[13]

Apart from the subordinationist tendency to be considered separately, O.'s doctrine on the Holy Spirit is not as satisfactory as his doctrine of the

Logos. He did not doubt the divinity, but as to his relationship with the Father and the Son O. is hesitant. Important texts—stating that the Spirit of God and the Spirit of the Son are the same, that the Spirit of the Father and the Spirit of the Son and the Holy Spirit are the same, that the Son and the Spirit proceed from the paternal knowledge of the Father, that the properties of the Father, Son and Holy Spirit must be recognised, while confessing that there is no diversity of nature or substance—these texts are known only in the translation of Rufinus.

Elsewhere O. comes to grips with the problem of the procession of the Spirit: "Whoever admits that the Holy Spirit is produced, in presence of these words: 'Everything has been produced by the Word' must necessarily conclude that the Holy Spirit has been also produced by the Word, who is therefore anterior. If, on the contrary, one denies that the Holy Spirit has been produced by the Word, he would have to be called unproduced to safeguard the truth of the Gospel . . . . For us who confess three hypostases, the Father, Son and Holy Spirit, and who believe that nothing is unproduced outside the Father, we say in conformity to piety and truth, that all having been produced by the Word, the Holy Spirit is the worthiest and the first in rank of all beings produced by the Father by means of Christ. And perhaps this is the reason why he is not called Son of God, the Only-begotten being originally the only Son by nature and the Holy Spirit having need of him, it appears as of the one who communicates to him his hypostasis, and not only being but wisdom, intelligence, justice, in a word, all the attributes which he must possess to participate in the nature of Christ."[14]

Is this a subordinationist view? When taken with another passage it certainly does imply, even assert so much, though defenders of O. have sought to explain his whole thinking otherwise. "As for us who believe the Saviour when he said 'The Father is greater than I', and who for that reason did not allow that the word 'good' should be applied to himself in its full, true and perfect sense, but attributed it to the Father and gave him thanks, condemning him who would glorify the Son to excess—we say that the Saviour and the Holy Spirit are without comparison and are very much superior to all things that are made, but also that the Father is even more above them than they are themselves above creatures even the highest."[15] Did O. then see the Trinity as a hierarchy? Did

he still conceive this as allowing equality? He was, let it be remembered, the one who gave theology such meaningful words as *physis, hypostasis, ousia, theanthropos,* and possibly *homoousios.*

---

[1]Bibl. H. Crouzel, *Bibliographie critique d'Origène*, Instrumenta *Patristica*, 1971; works PG 11–17; GCS; some works in SC; cf. H. Crouzel, S.J., *Théologie de l'image de Dieu chez Origène*, 1956, Paris; *Origène et la connaissance mystique*, Louvain, 1961; M. Harl, *Origène et la fonction révélatrice du Verbe incarné*, Paris, 1958; P. Nemeshegyi, S.J., *Paternité de Dieu chez Origène*, Paris, 1960; De Regnon, *Etudes*, III; Quasten II, 37–101; Altaner, 197–209; G. Bardy (*qv*), DTC XI, 2, 1932, 1489–1565; *id.*, DTC, XV, 1639–1645; *id.*, "La règle de foi d'Origène," *RSR* 9 (1919), 162–196; J. Lebreton, *Les origines*, II; A. d'Ales, "La doctrine d'Origène," *RSR*, 20 (1930), 224–268; J.J. Maydieu, "La procession du Logos d'après le commentaire d'Origène sur l'évangile de saint Jean," *BLE*, 35 (1934), 3–16, 49–70; C.W. Lowry, "Origen as Trinitarian," *JTS* 37 (1936), 225–240; *id.*, "Did Origen style the Son a ctisma?," *JTS* 39 (1938), 39–42; A. Lieske, *Die Theologie der Logosmystik bei Origenes*, Munster, 1938; [2]*De principiis*, I, praef.; [3]*In Joann.*, II, 10, 75, GCS IV, 65; [4]*De principiis*, I, 1, 1; [5]Cf. H. Crouzel, *op.cit.*; [6]*In Joann.*, II, 2, Preuschen, 55, 4f; PG 14, 110B; [7]*Ibid.*, XIII, 36, Preuschen 261, 24ff; PG 14, 461C; [8]*De principiis*, IV, 4, 1 (28), Koetschau, 349, 3–10; [9]*Apol. adv. Ruf.*, 19, PL 23, 442f; [10]IV, 4, 1 *De principiis*; [11]Cf. G. Bardy, DTC XI, 1520 for references, quoting Tixeront in support; cf. Quasten, *op.cit.*, 78; [12]*De principiis*, I, 3, 1; [13]*In Rom. VI*, 7; cp. *De princip.*, I, 3, 4; [14]*In Joann.*, II, 6, PG, 14, 125f; [15]*In Joann.*, 13, 25.

ORTHODOX, THE

The Orthodox, fully seized by the mystery of the Trinity, have tended to continue the ideas of the eastern Fathers of the Church, the clarification of the consubstantial by St. Athanasius (*qv*) and of the distinction between *ousia* and *hypostasis* by the Cappadocians.[1] In general their approach is primarily to the Persons, then to the nature, whereas the western approach, largely influenced by St. Augustine, is first to the nature and then the Persons: one cannot harden this difference systematically.

Orthodox writing on the Trinity since the time of Photius (*qv*) has given a large place to the *Filioque* (*qv*). Fr. M. Jugie's (*qv*) treatment of the Trinity takes over 300 pages in volume two of his large work on the dogmatic theology of the separated eastern Christians; of these over 140 deal with the processions, mostly the *Filioque*. The influence of the great eastern theologian Gregory Palamas (*qv*) has been strong in recent times. An eastern writer from before the break in communion, St. Maximus Confessor (*qv*), well known to Orthodox writers, is being discovered in the west.

The efforts made to solve the *Filioque* problem are dealt with in the relevant article. Here the further contribution of the illustrious Catholic ecclesiologist and ecumenist, Fr. Y. M.-J. Congar, O.P., must be noted.[2] A notable contribution to Orthodox Trinitarian literature has been made by V. Lossky (*qv*); another expatriate Russian, Sergey Bulgakov, has concentrated on the Holy Spirit.[3] Lossky was instrumental in having his sophiological doctrine repudiated.

A recent summary of Orthodox Trinitarian theory, as well as emphasising traditional eastern concepts, such as the importance of the divine energies—"union with the Trinity means union with the divine energies, not with the divine essence"—draws attention to the influence of Trinitarian belief on the liturgy (*qv*). The author also develops an idea which must henceforth find a response in Catholic circles, the relationship between the Church (*qv*) and the Trinity: "Passing on now to the period of grace, we see that the first offspring of the Trinity is the Church. This is par excellence the Church of the Holy Trinity, 'filled by the Holy Trinity' as Origen clearly states.[4] The Trinity lives, remains and dwells within the Church, perfecting and leading it ever higher, to prepare it better for its final destiny, that is, participation in the eternal life and everlasting glory of God. One can say that the life of members of the Church ideally reflects the ineffable life of the Blessed Trinity . . . . The Church in fact has a Trinitarian character in its very nature and its activities . . . . Dwelling permanently in the Church, the Trinity animates the supreme economy and operation of its activities. John Chrysostom affirms categorically that in the life of the Church 'all is governed by the Father and the Son and the Holy Spirit.'"[5]

Much effort is still needed to bring together the two strands of thought, Orthodox and Latin or western. Where spiritual genius is called for is in the identification of those things which are complementary and may ultimately prove mutually enriching.

[1]Extensive bibl., *EstTrin*, XI, (1977), "Número extraordinario, Bibliografia trinitaria," Orthodox, 45–77; M. M. Garijo-Guembe, "La pneumatogia en la moderna teólogia Ortodoxa," *EstTrin* IX, 359–382; P N. Trembelas; *Dogmatique de l'Eglise Orthodoxe Catholique*, Chevetogne-Paris, 1966, vol. I, 266–361; "Orthodoxie et Catholicisme—du personnalisme en théologie," *Rev. Theol.* Louvain 6 (1975), 7ff; [2]*The Holy Spirit*, III; [3]*Le Paraclet*, Paris, tr. Andronikof, 1944; [4]*The Holy Trinity in Human Life*, Metropolitan Emilianos Timiadis, *One in Christ*, 21 (1985), 8; Origen, Comm in Ps 29, 1, PG 12, 1265; [5]*Ibid.*, 9, St John Chrysostom, Comm. in Johan. hom. 87, 4, PG 39, 472.

P

PALAMAS, ST. GREGORY (1296–1359)

It is only within the last half century that P. has been worthily studied in the west: T. de Regnon (*qv*) did not mention him in his four-volume work on the Trinity.[1] Things have changed considerably, at least in continental European theological literature. Of interest to the theme of this work is P's theory of the divine energies. God's aim is the deification of man (see article Image). In God there is a secret essence which cannot be known or shared and a radiation which once experienced ensures our deification. To organise his ideas into a system P. distinguishes the unknowable essence, the hypostases, that is, persons, and the uncreated energies, for these energies are the mode by which God exteriorises his existence while retaining his transcendence.

Some general principles may be recalled. For P. every manifestation of God *ad extra* is personal. He acts in the world as Father, Son and Spirit. The necessarily personal character of God's existence *ad extra* reflects the very Trinitarian existence. It is the hypostasis of the Father which is for P., as for Greek thought in its entirety, the personal origin of the divine being itself.[2] "God is one not only because his nature is one, but also because the Persons who proceed, the Son and the Spirit, go back to the unique person of the Father."[3] In God he says "the origin is hypostatic."[4] "When God conversed with Moses he did not say: 'I am the essence', but 'I am who am' (Ex 3:14). It is not then He who is who comes from the essence, but the essence comes from He who is for He who is comprises in himself the whole of being."[5]

The relationship between the divine essence and the energies takes much of P's attention. He calls the essence the "cause" or "origin" of the energies, which in a certain sense are inferior to it, because God remains transcendent to his own revelation. But this superiority does not break the simple and absolute unity of God: the fact that "the Father is greater than the Son" (Jn 14:28) does not contradict "I and the Father are one" (Jn 10:30). The fact that the essence is the cause of the energies does not exclude their personal character; the energies, without revealing the essence, show the circumincession (*qv*) of the divine hypostases: "God is the same in himself because the three hypostases possess one another naturally, totally, eternally and indivisibly, but also without mixture or confusion and also because they interpenetrate themselves naturally in such wise as to possess one sole energy."[6]

The divine energy is then one because every divine act *ad extra* is always a Trinitarian act; in fact the whole of creation was made by the "one, uncreated, coeternal energy of God".

On the question of the relationship between the energy and the hypostases, Sergey Bulgakov found P. unsatisfactory; treatment of the question was slight and imprecise. More thorough research does show that there is a personal mode whereby each divine hypostasis can exercise the common energy and thus there can be consideration of the manifestations or energies of the Son and the Spirit: "the movement of the divine will is begun by the primordial Principle, the Father, proceeds through the Son, and shows itself in the Holy Spirit."[7]

The divine energies are therefore "inhypostatized". Palamite theology implies a particular role for the Holy Spirit, with unusual contact between him and the pure of heart, and a theory of divine light, resembling that of Tabor. His role was revealed at Pentecost; but no incarnation of the hypostasis of the Spirit took place, nor was the divine essence communicated. The manifestation of his Person by the energies indicates a dependence with regard to the Son: "The grace is therefore uncreated and it is what the Son gives, sends and grants to his disciples; it is not the Spirit himself, but a deifying gift which is an energy that is not only uncreated, but also inseparable from the Holy Spirit."[8]

It is not always crystal clear how the energies and the Spirit are related. There is room for more exact analysis, as on the whole question of Palamism vis-à-vis the Fathers and vis-à-vis the Catholic faith. There has recently been no shortage of good will nor expertise in the pursuit of such studies.

[1]Works PG 150, 151; for bibliography (303 items), D. Stiernon, A. A., *REB* 30 (1972), 231–341; cf. D. Habra, "The Source of the Doctrine of Gregory Palamas on the Divine Energies," *ECQ*, 12 (1957–58), 244–252, 294–303, 338–347; G. (Cardinal) Journet, "Palamisme et thomisme, À propose d'un livre recent," *RThom*, 60 (1960), 429–452; J. Meyendorff, *A Study of Gregory Palamas*, London, 1964; id., *The Holy Trinity in Palamite Theology, Trinitarian Theology, East and West*, Brookline, Mass, 1977, 25–43; id., *DSp*, XII, 93ff; G. Florovsky, "Grégoire Palamas et la patristique," *Istina*, 8 (1961–62), 115–125; A. de Halleux, "Palamisme et Scolastique," *RTL* 4 (1973), 409–422; id., "Orthodoxie et Catholicisme: du personnalisme en pneumatologie," *ibid.*, 6 (1975), 3–30; id., "Palamisme et tradition," *Irenikon*, 48 (1975), 479–93; Amphilokios Radovic, "'Le Filioque' et l'énergie incrée de la Sainte Trinité selon la doctrine de S. Grégoire Palamas," *Messager de l'Exarchat du Patriarche russe en Europe occidentale*, 89–90 (1975), 11–44; Congar, *The Holy Spirit*, III, 61–71; M. Jugie, A.A., *DTC* 11 (1932), 1735–1818; id., *Theologia dogmatica Christianorum Orient. ab Ecclesia cath.diss.*, II, Paris, 1933, 47–183; [2]T. de Regnon, *Etudes sur la Trinité*, I, 337–339; [3]Apud J. Meyendorff, *DSp, l.cit.*, 98; [4]*Ibid.*; [5]*Ibid.*; [6]*Chapters* PG 150, 1197B; [7]*Ibid.*, 1197C; [8]*Triad* III, 8.

PATRICK, ST. (c. 390–c. 460)

Tradition associates the doctrine of the Trinity in a particularly close way with P. Widely diffused legend says that in his catechesis he used the shamrock as an explanatory symbol of the belief.[1] He refers in his principal work, the *Confession*, to the "rule of faith" (*mensura fidei*, cp. Rom 12:3) in the Trinity. He states his Trinitarian faith in a full creed in chapter four of the work. We have here the rule of faith of the British Church, from which P. came to Ireland as a missionary. This formulary is traceable to Victorinus of Pettau, with some additions which reflect the Arian debate.[2] It now is of interest to those who are seeking a solution of the Constantinopolitan problem of the Nicene (*qv*) creed: why is there no evidence of use and recognition of this formula between 381 when it was drawn up and 451 when it was authorized at the Council of Chalcedon? Here, perhaps, in the Confession of P., is the required evidence.

The text of P. is as follows: "Because there is no other God, nor was there ever any in times past, nor shall there be hereafter, except God the Father unbegotten, without beginning, from whom all things take their beginning, holding all things (i.e. Almighty), as we say, and his Son Jesus Christ, whom we affirm verily to have always existed with the Father before the creation of the world, with the Father after the manner of a spiritual existence, begotten ineffably before the beginning of anything. And by him were made things visible and invisible. He was made man, and having overcome death he was received up into heaven to the Father. And he gave to him all power above every name of things in heaven and things in earth and things under the earth; and let every tongue confess to him that Jesus Christ is Lord and God in whom we believe. And we look for his coming soon to be; he is the Judge of the living and the dead, who will render to every man according to his deeds. And he shed on us abundantly the Holy Spirit, the gift and pledge of immortality, who makes those who believe and obey to become children of God the Father and joint heirs with Christ whom we confess and adore as one God in the Trinity of the Holy Name."

A distant effect of P's Trinitarian commitment was the preamble of the Constitution of Ireland, enacted by the People on 1 July, 1937: "In the Name of the Most Holy Trinity, from whom is all authority and to whom, as our final end, all actions both of men and States must be referred."

[1]Text in *Saint Patrick, Confession et Lettre à Coroticus*, ed. R.P.C. Hanson and C. Blanc, SC 249; for bibliography cf. *Saint Patrick. His Origins and Career*, Oxford, 1968; M. O'Carroll, C.SS.Sp. *DSp*, s.v.; [2]Cf. R.P.C. Hanson, "The Rule of Faith of Patrick and of Victorinus," in *Latin Script and Letters*, (Festschrift Ludwig Bieler), edd. J. O'Meara and B. Neumann, 1976, p. 25–36; *id.*, "Witness from St. Patrick to the Creed of 381," *AB* 101 (1983), p. 297–299; J.N.D. Kelly (*qv*), *Creeds*, 296–320.

PATRIPASSIANISM

A third-century heresy, which held that the Father, like the Son, suffered. It was sometimes taken for Sabellianism (*qv*). On the very recent problem raised about suffering and the Godhead, that is, the Trinity, ITC have issued a notable statement exposing every aspect of the subject, pointing to "some of the greatest of all difficulties, such as anthropomorphism (*qv*)," Here human and theological reasoning "encounter the ineffable mystery of the living God and realise the limits of thought itself." The statement is comprehensive and honest.[1] It is, of course, relevant to Jürgen Moltmann's writings.

[1]Text in ITQ, 49(1982), 296–299.

PAUL VI, POPE (1963–1978)

Pope Paul VI's Trinitarian teaching is contained principally in the *Credo of the People of God*, which he pronounced officially on 30 June, 1968, on the concluding day of the year of faith proclaimed to commemorate the nineteenth centenary of the martyrdom of SS Peter and Paul.[1] In his introductory remarks he referred to "the disquiet in matters of faith which is unsettling some of the convictions of our contemporaries. These have not escaped the influence of a world in total change, a world in which many truths are either completely denied or called in doubt."[2]

The controversy following the appearance of the Dutch Catechism (see CATECHETICS) was possibly a factor in the Pope's decision to issue a formal *Credo*. It opens thus: "We believe in one God, the Father, the Son and the Holy Spirit, Creator of what is visible—such as the world where we live out our lives—and of the invisible—such as the pure spirits which are also called angels—and Creator in each man of his spiritual and immortal soul.

"We believe in this one God, who is as completely one in his most holy essence as in the rest of his perfections; in his omnipotence, in his infinite knowledge, in his providence, in his will and his love. *He is who is*, as he himself revealed to Moses. He is love, as John the Apostle taught us. These two names, therefore, Being and Love, express the same unattainable truth concerning him who manifested himself to us and who, *inhabiting light inaccessible*, is in himself above every name, above everything and every created intelligence. God only can grant us a true and perfect knowledge of himself, revealing himself as Father, Son and Holy Spirit in whose eternal life we are called by grace to share here on earth in the obscurity of faith and after death in everlasting light. The mutual bonds which eternally constitute the three Persons, each of whom is one and the same divine Being, are themselves the inmost and blessed life of the Most Holy God, which is infinitely beyond our possibilities of understanding. Wherefore we give thanks to the divine Goodness that so many believers can testify with us before men to the unity of God, even though they do not know the mystery of the Most Holy Trinity.

"We believe, therefore in God, who from all eternity begets the Son, we believe in the Son, the Word of God, who is eternally begotten, we believe in the Holy Spirit, the uncreated Person who proceeds from the Father and the Son as their eternal Love. And so in the three divine Persons who are co-eternal and co-equal with one another, the life and beatitude of God, who is uniquely One, is realized and fulfilled in overwhelming plenitude in the supreme excellence and glory which is proper to him who is the uncreated Being, in such wise that *unity in the Trinity and Trinity in the unity must be humbly acknowledged*.

"We believe in our Lord Jesus Christ, who is the Son of God. He is the eternal Word born of the Father before time began, one in substance with the Father, *homoousios to Patri*, through whom all things were made. He was incarnate of the Virgin Mary by the power of the Holy Spirit and was made Man. Equal, therefore, to the Father according to his divinity, less than the Father according to his humanity, his unity deriving not from some impossible confusion of substance but from his Person.

"He dwelt among us full of grace and truth. He announced and established the Kingdom of God, enabling us to know the Father."

There follows a summary of the lifework of Jesus Christ. Then comes the passage on the Holy Spirit:

"We believe in the Holy Spirit, the Lord and giver of life, who together with the Father and the Son is adored and glorified. He it is who spoke through the prophets. He it was who was sent to us by Christ after his resurrection and ascension to the Father. He enlightens, vivifies, guards and rules the Church whose members he purifies as long as they do not turn away from grace. His action, which reaches to the inmost centre of the soul, enables man, in the humility which he draws from Christ, to become perfect even as the Father in heaven is perfect."[3]

Pope Paul completed his views with a more fully developed doctrine on the Holy Spirit (see SPIRIT,HOLY). This he did in the Apostolic Exhortation *Marialis Cultus*—introducing his thought with an allusion to the Trinity, and in a number of other addresses or documents, notably on the occasion of the Rome International Marian Congress, which coincided with the world congress of the Charismatic Movement: the theme of the Marian Congress was Mary and the Holy Spirit. In *Marialis Cultus* the Pope wrote: "In the first place it is supremely fitting that exercises of piety directed towards the Virgin should clearly express the Trinitarian and Christological note that is intrinsic and essential to them. Christian worship in fact is of itself worship offered to the Father and to the Son and to the Holy Spirit, or, as the liturgy puts it, to the Father through Christ in the Spirit."[4]

In the address to the charismatic congress the Pope dealt with the problems of the Spirit's action in the personal life of the Christian; in the letter to Cardinal Suenens, Legate to the Marian congress, *E con sentimenti*, the question was, understandably, the principles and detail of the relationship between Mary and the Spirit.[5]

To Paul VI also we owe the establishment of the International Theological Commission (*qv*), which has illumined our theme notably.

---

[1]B. Margerie, S.J., *La Trinité chrétienne dans l'histoire*, Paris, 1974, 324–29; J.A. de Aldama, S.J., "La profession de fe de Pablo VI," *Estudios ecles.*, 43 (1968), 478–505; E. O'Connor, *Pope Paul and the Holy Spirit*, London, 1978; [2]AAS 60 (1968), tr. A. Flannery, Vatican II, 2, 389, 90; [3]*Ibid.*; [4]AAS 66 (1974); [5]Texts O'Connor, *op.cit*, 125ff.

PAUL OF SAMOSATA (3rd century)

Known from his birthplace—not from Antioch, where he held ecclesiastical office and published his heretical views.[1] As *Procurator Ducenarius* he was involved with the civil authority; he became bishop in 260. His wordliness caused comment; his teaching caused disquiet. Zenobia, Queen of Palmyra, was his patroness. In 264 a council attended, among others, by Firmilian of Caeserea and Helenus of Tarsus met at Antioch to judge his opinions. The result, due to his evasiveness and skill in self-defence, was inconclusive. The genuineness of a letter sent to him after the meeting by Hymenaeus and five other bishops—called the Hymenaeus epistle—has been disputed; it has been accepted by serious scholars.[2] He was invited in this letter to accept a formulary of faith. He apparently became more brazen in heresy, which may have occasioned three councils altogether. The important one met in 268; between seventy and eighty bishops were present.

P's doctrine was examined, and to help the bishops a priest named Malchion undertook a lengthy discussion with him; it was taken down in shorthand with results put thus by Eusebius of Caesarea (*qv*): " . . . and the leader of heresy in Antioch was detected, and his false doctrine clearly shown before all, and he was excommunicated from the Catholic Church under heaven. Malchion especially drew him out of his hiding-place and refuted him. He was a man learned in other respects, and principal of the sophist school of grecian learning in Antioch; yet on account of the superior nobility of his faith in Christ he had been made a presbyter of that parish. This man, having conducted a discussion which was taken down by stenographers and which we know is still extant, was alone able to detect the man who dissembled and deceived the others."[3]

Though deposed from his bishopric P. remained on in the episcopal residence while his patroness, Zenobia, was in power. He was ejected by Aurelian after the Roman had entered the city.

Eusebius goes on to relate that "The Pastors who had assembled about this matter prepared by common consent an epistle addressed to Dionysius bishop of Rome, and Maximus of Alexandria, and sent it to all the provinces. In this they make manifest to all their own zeal and the perverse error of Paul, and the arguments and discussions which they had with him, and show the entire life and conduct of the man." Having listed the bishops to whom they sent their letter, Eusebius continues with extracts: "We sent for and called many of the bishops from a distance to relieve us from this deadly doctrine; as Dionysius of Alexandria and Firmilianus of Cappadocia, those blessed men. The first of these, not considering the author of this delusion worthy to be addressed, sent a letter to Antioch, not written to him but to the entire parish. But Firmilian came twice, and condemned his innovations, as who were present know and testify, and many others understand. But as he promised to change his opinions, he believed him and hoped that without any reproach to the Word what was necessary would be done. So he delayed the matter, being deceived by him who denied even his own God and Lord and had not kept the faith which he formerly held." Eusebius quotes the letter which then tells that as Firmilian was on his way once more to Antioch, he died.

There follows in the letter a detailed description of P's scandalous life-style, his sudden accumulation of wealth by dubious means, his ostentation and self-glorification. Hints of P's doctrinal aberrations are in such phrases as "he stops the psalms to our Lord Jesus Christ, as being the modern productions of modern men"; "he is unwilling to acknowledge that the Son of God has come down from heaven. And this is not a mere assertion but is abundantly proved from the records which we have sent you; and not least where he says 'Jesus Christ is from below.' But those singing to him and extolling him among the people say that their impious teacher has come down an angel from heaven. And he does not forbid such things; but the arrogant man is even present when they are uttered."[4]

Eusebius gives no complete account of P's doctrine. In search of it the historian of theology is handicapped by the fact that P. disappeared from public knowledge until the fourth and fifth centuries. He was revived in the fourth century by Basil of Ancyra (qv),[5] since he and his fellow Homoeousians (qv) maintained that the condemnation of the *Homoousios* which was used by P. made any use of the word improper: hence the frequent references to P. in the writings of Athanasius (qv), and the specific allusion to his use of *homoousios* in Hilary of Poitiers (qv): "And with regard to the meaning of *homoousion* and *homoiousion* your proof has left no difficulty untouched. As to the latter which implies the similarity of substance, our opinions are the same. But in dealing with the *homoousion*, or the one substance, you declared that it ought to be rejected because the use of this word led to the idea that there was a prior substance which two Persons had divided between

themselves. I see the flaw in that way of taking it. Any such sense is profane, and must be rejected by the Church's common decision. The second reason that you added was that our fathers, when Paul of Samosata was pronounced a heretic, also rejected the word *homoousion*, on the ground that by attributing this title to God he had taught that he was single and undifferentiated, and at once Father and Son to himself . . . . Some misunderstand *homoousion*; does that prevent me from understanding it? The Samosatene was wrong in using the word *homoousion*; does that make the Arians right in denying it? Eighty bishops once rejected it; but three hundred and eighteen recently accepted it . . . . Holy brethren I understand by *homoousion* God of God, not of an essence that is unlike, not divided but born, of the substance of the unborn God, that he is begotten yet co-eternal and wholly like the Father . . . . Let us join in condemning the misunderstanding, but not deprive our faith of its security. Do you think we must subscribe to the Samosatene Council to prevent anyone from using *homoousion* in the sense of Paul of Samosata? Then let us also subscribe to the council of Nicaea, so that Arians may not impugn the word."[6]

Scholars have been reduced to a laborious search for fragments attributable to P. in the writers mentioned and in those of a later age; obliged also to allow for what polemical interest might do to quotations. For what concerns his Trinitarian theology, he was not Sabellian but very strongly Monarchian. In the *De Sectis* ascribed falsely to Leontius of Byzantium we read that he did not consider "the Father, Son and Holy Spirit the same, but he gave the name of Father to God who created all things, that of Son to the mere man, that of Spirit to the grace which dwelt in the Apostles."[7]

P. in the view of Eusebius, Pamphilus, Alexander of Alexandria (qv), Didymus (qv), Augustine (qv) and other later writers, was a disciple of Artemon (qv). Artemon was led to deny the divinity of Christ through fear of ditheism; in which opinion he was followed by P., for whom only the Father exists substantially and the *Logos* (qv)—which title he prefers to Son—was but a word uttered, a sound from his mouth. Hence St. Epiphanius quotes from the letter of Basil of Ancyra a passage justifying P's condemnation: "Such a claim compelled the Fathers who judged P. of Samosata, to apply to the Son also the word *ousia*, so as to show that the Son has a hypostasis, and that he is subsistent, that he exists and is not a mere word; they showed by this word *ousia* the difference between what does not exist of itself and what is subsistent."[8]

Another late testimony, however, attenuates somewhat the opinion of P. on the *Logos*: "The Father, at a given moment, begets him, and thus the *Logos* became subsistent."[9] The sense here remains vague, with no idea of the separation of Son from Father. P. is vague on the eternity of the *Logos* and makes no reference to his role in creation. He is so sparing in reference to the Holy Spirit that his doctrine on the theme is practically unknown; there is no satisfactory proof for Loofs' view that he identified the Spirit and divine Wisdom. He did speak of Wisdom united so closely with Jesus that it made him structurally different from us, making him superior to all men, the prophets, even Moses: but the theory is obscure. In later times P. was seen as the father of adoptianist (*qv*) and Nestorian heretical opinions.

---

[1] Cf. H.J. Lawlor, "Collection of fragments of P.," *JTS* 19 (1917–18), 20–45, 115–121; P. Galtier, S.J., "L'homoousios de Paul de Samosate," *RSR*, 12 (1922), 30–45; A. von Harnack, "Die Reden Pauls von Samosata an Sabinus (Zenobia?) und seine Christologie," *Sitzungsberichte etc.*, Berlin, 1924, 130–151; F. Loofs, *Paulus von Samosata*, TU 11, Hft 5, 1924; E. Schwartz, "Eine fingierte Korrespondenz mit Paulus dem Samosatener," *Sitzungsberichte* etc., Bayr., 1927 Hft 3; esp. G. Bardy, *Paul de Samosate, Étude historique*, new ed., Louvain, 1929; id., *DTC* 12, 1, 1933, 46–51; H. de Riedmatten, O.P., "Les Actes du procès de Paul de Samosate," Fribourg, *Paradosis* 6, 1952—collection of fragments 135–158; M. Richard, "Malchion et Paul de Samosate, Le témoignage d'Eusèbe de Césarée," *EIL* 35 (1959), 325–38; R.M. Grant, VigChr 3 (1949), 225–229; Altaner, 204; Quasten II, 140–42; M. Jugie, *EC*, 9, 742–43; [2] Text in Loofs, *op.cit.*, 324–330; Bardy, *op.cit.*, 13–19; [3] H.F., VII, 29, LNPF I, 313, *Ibid.*, 30, 313–315; [5] Cf. Epiphanius, *Haeres* LXXIII, PG 42, 428; [6] *De synodis*, 81, 86, 88, LNPF IX, 25–28; cp. St. Basil, Epist. 52; [7] PG 86, 1216; [8] Apud Epiphanius, *Haeres*, j. cit., LXXIII, PG 42, 428; [9] Apud Justinian, *Tractat. contra monoph.*, PG LXXXVI, 1117–1120.

PAULINUS OF AQUILEIA, ST. (c. 726–802)

Born near Friuli, P., a man of learning, was called to the Frankish court by Charlemagne (*qv*) and there was closely linked with Alcuin (*qv*). Appointed Bishop, Patriarch, of Aquileia by Charlemagne, he was active in church affairs, esp. in the relations between the Byzantine church and the West. His role in doctrinal history is principally in regard to Adoptianism (*qv*), particularly at the Council of Frankfort; he is commonly taken as author of the *Libellus Sacrosyllabus contra Elipandum* sent to the Spanish bishops in the name of their Italian colleagues; he was also the author of the *Libri III contra Felicem*.[1] He was a leading spirit at the Council of Friuli, where Adoptianism was again condemned. Here he defended the *Filioque* (*qv*), as at a local synod at Cividale he had imposed a form of creed, mostly like the Constantinopolitan, with the addition, urging his clergy to memorize it.

---

[1] Works, PL 99, 9–683; cf. C. Giannoni, *Paulinus II Patriarch von Aquileia*, Vienna, 1896; G. Ellero, *S. Paolino d'Aquil*, Cividale, 1901; J. Fleckenstein, *LTK* 8, 207, 8; J. Reviron, *DTC* XII, 1, 62–67.

PERSONALITY

One approach to the question of personality in God is to ask what is the meaning of "I" when God uses it. In OT the reference is to God in the monotheistic sense of the revelation of the Old Covenant, "I am the Lord your God who brought you out of the land of Egypt, out of the house of bondage. You shall have no other gods before me" (Exod 20:2–3). But NT gives us the divine "I" in a very different context: "Thou art my beloved Son, with thee I am well pleased" (Mk 1:11; and par. Mt 3:17; Lk 3:22; Jn 1:33). Here it is the Father who speaks. Next consider these quotations: "I and the Father are one" (Jn 10:30); "I glorified thee on earth, having accomplished the work which thou gavest me to do; and now, Father glorify thou me in thy own presence with the glory which I had with thee before the world was made. (Jn 17:4)"; "In that day you will know that I am in my Father, and you in me and I in you" (Jn 14:20). "I" statements with divine meaning are not frequent in regard to the Holy Spirit, but the first personal use with "I" is in this important passage, important because of the implied transcendence and authority: "Set apart for me Barnabas and Saul for the work to which I have called them" (Acts 13:2).

We are not involved here with the debate on the "I" of Christ. A prime datum in the scriptural witness is that each of the Blessed Three in the grammatical use of the first person pronoun asserts autonomy, separateness, self-sufficiency. The biblical language pattern also resembles so closely that of human discourse and dialogue that we dare not risk an imposed cleavage on our part in the common language. God the Father says "I am a Father"; the Son speaks similarly; the Holy Spirit uses "I" in a vital sense. The theologian's problem is to explain the transfer of human concepts to the divine, with total respect for the infinite mystery, majesty and transcendence of God.[1]

The growth of the terminology is of interest. *Prosopon*[2] in the east was first used to designate the separate person. This is an example of adaptation rather like the use made of the word *homoousios* (see Consubstantial), which originally meant "of the same stuff" and elevated to a theological level came to mean "of one substance." "*Prosopon*" first meant "face", then came to mean "person". But it was replaced in the east by *hypostasis*. Meanwhile in the west "persona" was similarly adapted from its meaning "face" to "an individual." Here Tertullian (*qv*) had a capital role, as in fixing the distinction between *hypostasis* and *ousia* the Cappadocians exerted decisive influence. Under the influence of St. Basil (*qv*) and St. Jerome, Pope Damasus gave his approval to the use of *persona* and *substantia* equivalently to *hypostasis* and *ousia*.

As to clearcut definition, the first important name is Boethius (*qv*). His definition lasted for centuries: *rationalis naturae individua substantia*. St. Thomas (*qv*) worked with it, though he also quotes Richard of St. Victor's definition of person in God, *divinae naturae incommunicabilis existentia*. Elsewhere he himself uses the phrase *distinctum subsistens in intellectuali natura*. The point in these slightly different formulae is how a particular nature becomes actually existing or subsisting. Duns Scotus (*qv*) did not insist on the distinction between nature and person. With time commentators on St. Thomas added a new idea to his conception: personality implied a *modus* or mode which completed the subsistence in each case. This may be metaphysics for the sake of metaphysics.

Thus things stood in Catholic theology until the present century, very recently therein. We live in an age overwhelmingly conscious of the human person. Psychologists and psychiatrists give attention to personality structure, personality disorders and ailments, or even diseases like schizoid states; they do so with reasonable certainty that their language is valid, that it will be understood. As a consequence of this intellectual explosion—which had as parallel the very vocal views of social scientists and jurists concerned with personality as a supreme value in their world—it was felt in certain circles that the word person no longer expressed accurately the idea of personality as it is applicable to the Holy Trinity. Karl Barth (*qv*) dropped it and substituted the concept of "modes"; Karl Rahner (*qv*) suggested "distinct manners or modes of subsisting." One obvious difficulty about this phrase, as about the idea suggested by Barth—who did not espouse ancient modalism—is precisely that of the language quoted from the NT. How can a "distinct mode of subsisting" say "I", without being taken for the godhead identical with every use of "I"? How can the distinction of persons evident in the use of "I" separately by each be maintained? How can the distinctive properties be understood? How can generation (*qv*) and spiration be predicated of "modes of subsistence"? How can words like "the only-begotten" and "the Paraclete" be applied to them?

B. Lonergan (*qv*) has proposed a different definition: "Father, Son and Holy Spirit are in virtue of one real consciousness three subjects conscious of themselves, of one another, and of their act (of being), both notional and essential."[3] This formulation has been subjected to a searching critique by J.A. Bracken, who maintains that as elaborated by Lonergan it seems to give the Father a decided pre-eminence over the Son and the Spirit in the matter of personal self-awareness and self-consciousness; this critic would contend that Lonergan's statement "does not seem upon closer examination really to establish the distinct self-hood or self-consciousness of all three Persons within the Trinity."[4]

The word "person" is certainly consecrated by the "sentiment of the faithful" (*qv*); it is used instinctively. This for more that 1500 years, a fact which for a while restrained Karl Rahner's desire to change, though he did later change it. We need to bear analogy (*qv*) in mind: "The very difference involves the consequence that the notion of hypostasis and person which we abstract from creatures is applicable to the divine hypostases and persons only in an analogous sense, hence with qualifications."[5]

Human personality has an element of mystery; human beings are not entirely known to us. Human personality is nonetheless limited, in its very origin, its existence and its destiny. We must rise above such things when thinking of personality in God. In human language the word father does not reveal anything about the one who is a father; the term is universally used. It relates to one aspect, essentially to one moment in a man's life: a man remains a father if he dies immediately after begetting his child. His relationship to this child is basically carnal; he cannot beget spiritually but only corporeally—of course because of the psycho-physical unity in his being he can and ought to establish a spiritual relationship with his offspring, who for a time remains his inferior, dependent.

In contrast fatherhood in God is spiritual, continuous, implies no superiority, is utterly independent, and is in no sense impaired by the eternal act of begetting. If we are to transfer the idea of personal fulfilment to the divine Persons, it is identical with their very existence, subsistence separate from one another while intimately one in the essence and bound to one another by the relations of origin.

Present-day thinkers may find it difficult to conceive a subsistent relation (qv) as constitutive of person in God. As Fr. Hill remarks, "the contemporary religious mind tends to be baffled by this unembarrassed 'metaphysics of faith.'"[6] He rightly defends it. Our embarrassment is caused by too rigid adherence to human categories of thought. Thus the word son in a human context in its essence is a genealogical reference; the son has his own existence apart from his father. He is not at all times equal to his father and may in many ways eclipse or be eclipsed by him. There is not that constant presence to the father which in the Trinity we call circumincession. There is not total identity with the essence of the father and the mother; there is not joint communication with the father out of which another exists—one cannot say "comes", for again it is eternal and again implies no dependence of inferiority.

With so many differences in the use of Father, Son and Spirit in a Trinitarian context from use in human contexts, it may well appear that the word "person" is totally inadequate: but we may have this feeling about all language in regard to God and especially the Trinity. With the requirements of analogy the term is valid. We may recall that in normal discourse the word personality is used in three different contexts: social, psychological and philosophical. The first refers to the effect of an individual on other human beings, the second to identity and continuity within a psycho-physical unit, what Pius XII called "the psychosomatic unity of man, in so far as this is determined and governed by the soul."[7]

When we speak of personality in philosophical terms we are thinking of an autonomous source of moral action, of independence in being, incommunicability. There is nothing to prevent us from raising this conceptual content to the divine level, by the proper use of analogy. Even when in ordinary discourse we speak of the rights of the human person, we have left the domain of social and psychic variables and are thinking of an intrinsic core of spiritual reality which is superior to and independent of them, while existing in them. The rights of the person inhere in one socially deprived or outcast, psychologically null. The word "person" may then, and in the opinion of this writer, should be retained.

[1]The literature on personality in a psychological context is extensive, available in bibl. to articles in encyclopaedias etc.; on the social and juridical context cf. Emmanuel Mounier, *Manifeste en faveur du personnalisme*, Paris, 1936; St. Thomas I, qq 29, 30; M. J. Scheeben, *The Mysteries of Christianity*, 73–86; B. Lonergan (qv), *De Deo Trino*, II, 153–208; C. Stead, *Divine Substance*, Oxford, 1977; A. de Halleux, "'Hypostase' et 'Personne' dans la formation du dogme trinitaire," *RHE* 79 (1984), 313–369; 625–670; [2]Cf. Arndt and Gingrich, *A Greek-English Lexicon of the New Testament and the Other Early Christian Literature*, Chicago, Cambridge, 1957, 728, 29; [3]*De Deo Trino*, II, 186; [4]*What are they Saying about the Trinity?*, New York, 1979, 7, 8; [5]M.J. Scheeben, *op.cit.*, 80; [6]*The Three-Personed God*, Washington, 1982, 71; [7]*Address of 10 April, 1958*; cf. *DCath.* 1958, 519f; cf Tome of Damasus, DS 173.

PETER LOMBARD (c.1100–1160)

The author's *Sententiarum libri quatuor* was the basic text book in theology, and commentary on it was obligatory for high academic status. It thus dominated the world of Scholasticism, not competing in speculative content with the works of St. Thomas and the other great thirteenth century Doctors—all of whom mounted on the steps fixed by P.L., using his texts as starting point—yet prevailing until the sixteenth century.[1] Of the four books the first is devoted to the Trinity, draws heavily on St. Augustine (qv) and much less on St. Hilary (qv): altogether he quotes Augustine 100 times, Hilary only 30 times.

P.L. figures in two church councils. At Rheims (qv) he was the adversary of Gilbert de la Porrée, and he was posthumously vindicated by name at the Fourth Lateran (qv) Council against the criticism of his Trinitarian doctrine by Joachim of Fiore.

P.L. like Augustine starts from the divine unity. In his exposition he draws on OT texts as was the custom of his time, in such a way as would not nowadays be accepted by biblical scholars.

---

[1] E. Amann, *DTC* XII, 1991–92.

PHOTINUS (4th century)

"Photinus was the scandal of Marcellus (of Ancyra), Marcellus of the Council of Nicaea."[1] So wrote A. Robertson, summarizing the career of a heretic who had been a pupil of Marcellus and later became Bishop of Sirmium, where his teaching gave offence to Arians and anti-Arians. He was deposed by the Arian party in 347 but without effect. In 351 he was deposed and exiled after his erroneous doctrine had been condemned at a council called in Sirmium by Constantius (*qv*). None of his writings is extant. He appears to have held a form of Sabellianism. St. Augustine (*qv*) thought that P. denied the pre-existence of Christ. The Photinians, his followers, were condemned by name at the Council of Constantinople, 381.

---

[1] D. Petavius, *De Photino Haeretico ejusque damnatione*, Paris, 1636; F. Loofs, *PRE* 3rd ed., XV (1904), 372–74; G. Bardy (*qv*), *DTC* XII, 2, (1935), 1532–36.

PHOTIUS (c. 810–c. 895)

P's ecclesiastical career was marked by striking vicissitudes.[1] His contribution to the history of Trinitarian theology was, on one point, to have enduring effects. He changed the attitude towards the *Filioque* from being one of theological speculation to controversy and polemics. He dealt with the subject principally in the *De Sancti Spiritus Mystagogia*, with occasional references elsewhere in his works. He proceeded from four assumptions: we must distinguish between properties which belong to the divine nature and those which belong to the hypostases; what is common in the Holy Trinity is so to all the hypostases, what is hypostatic is individual and belongs only to the hypostasis involved; hypostatic properties are incommunicable and singular; the Father is linked with the Son and Holy Spirit as unique cause of their existence, and by him they are caused.

According to P. the procession of the Holy Spirit comes from a property in the Father which is of his hypostasis, not from the common divine nature. It cannot therefore belong to another Person of the Holy Trinity, for participation by another Person would be contrary to the fact that properties of the hypostasis are incommunicable and singular. Since the Father begets the Son and makes the Spirit proceed, any participation by the Son in the procession of the Holy Spirit would imply that the Son shares the hypostasis of the Father, takes his place or is a part of the hypostasis of the Father, which, P. thinks, would reduce the Trinity to two Persons.

If, the argument goes on, the operation by which the Father makes the Spirit to proceed is not of his hypostasis, but springs from his nature, it would result that not only does the Son participate in the procession but the Spirit himself does so. The double procession reduces the Father to a mere appelation, deprived of sense; the property designated by the word Father would not belong exclusively to him and the two divine hypostases would be merged into one and the same person: worthy of Sabellius, or some semi-Sabellian monster, he thinks. From another standpoint he thinks that the double procession would lead to a plurality of hypostases: the divine Persons being equal, if the Son is begotten by the Father and the Spirit comes from the Father and the Son, then the Spirit must himself produce something: four or more hypostases.

P. insists that the Father must remain the unique cause of the mode of existence of the Son and of the Spirit. If the Son is with the Father the cause of existence of the Spirit, there are two principles in the Trinity, irreconcilable with the divine monarchy of the Father. He sees all kinds of strange consequences. He thinks that the procession of the Spirit from the Father and the Son would mean that it was imperfect from the Father.

P. is not beyond charges of a very polemical kind, references to polytheism, Greek mythology, Gnosticism, an allusion to the Spirit as "grandson" of the Father, to the heresy of Macedonius—on the *Filioque*. He was convinced too that the Bible and the Fathers were on his side. He argues from Jn 16:14 and Gal 4:4 to deprive them of any *Filioque* content. He dismisses the views of Ambrose, Jerome and Augustine as either based on falsified texts or explainable on grounds of human fallibility—noting too that they did not write dogmatically. He lists a number of Popes who were of a contrary opinion to Ambrose and Augustine and thinks that six of the seven ecumenical councils declared likewise.

He has been the quarry ever since for opponents of the *Filioque*, despite the fact that he did not really consider the essential Greek position "through the Son."[2]

[1]Cardinal Hergenrother, *Photius Patriarch von Konstantinopel*, 3 vols, Regensburg, 1867–1869; esp. F. Dvornik, *The Photian Schism*, Cambridge, 1948; on the Filioque cf. J. Slipyi, *Die Trinitätslehre des byzantinischen Patriarchen Photios*, Innsbruck, 1921; V. Grumel, "Le 'Filioque' au concile photien de 879–880 et le témoignage de Michel d'Anchialos," *Echos d'Orient*, 29 (1930), 257–264; L. Lohn, *Doctrina Graecorum et Russorum de Processione Spiritus Sancti a solo Patre*, I, *Photii temporibus*, Rome, 1934; M. Jugie, A.A., *Theologia Dogmatica Christianorum Orientalium ab Ecclesia Catholica Dissidentium*, I, Paris, 1926, 179–222; *id., De Processione Spiritus Sancti ex Fontibus Revelationis et secundum Orientales Dissidentes*, Rome, 1936, 282–386; *id.*, "Origine de la controverse sur l'addition du Filioque au Symbole," *RSPT* 28 (1939), 369–385; (against Jugie) V. Grumel, A.A., "Photius et l'addition du Filioque au Symbole de Nicée-Constantinople," *REB* 5 (1947), 218–234; R. Haugh, *Photius and the Carolingians, The Trinitarian Controversy*, Belmont, Mass., 1975; M.A. Orphanos, in "La Théologie du Saint Esprit," ed. L. Vischer, *Faith and Order*, 103, French tr., Paris, 1981, 29–33; De Regnon, *Etudes*, III, 241–383; [2]Summary of P's arguments in *Mystagogia*, PG 102, 309–380, also 285.

PNEUMATOMACHI (4th century)

Heretics who denied the divinity of the Holy Spirit. The historians Sozomen and Socrates as well as St. Jerome, Rufinus and others thought that Macedonius (*qv*) was their founder.[1] This is difficult to establish with certainty, chiefly because he was no longer Bishop of Constantinople when they became really active: the capital date is given as 373 when Eustathius of Sebaste, onetime pupil of Arius (*qv*) at Alexandria, a man who had been unreliable in adherence to the Creed of Nicaea, then an associate in monastic foundation of St. Basil the Great (*qv*), finally broke with Basil and took the leadership of the Pneumatomachi. At Ancyra and Lampsacus he took the homoiousian side. Yet it was he apparently who influenced Basil in the monastic movement.

The Pneumatomachi were not fortunate in their time. They met a determined Pope, St. Damasus, who condemned them in 374. They had to reckon with the genius and inspired writing of the three great Cappadocians, St. Basil, St. Gregory of Nazianzus and St. Gregory of Nyssa (*qqv*); Didymus of Alexandria also entered the fray against them.

[1]Cf. *Message of the Fathers*, ed. J.P. Burns, S.J., G.M. Fagin, S.J., Wilmington, 1984, *The Holy Spirit*.

PRAXEAS

Known as to his teaching from the sustained, brilliant, criticism in Tertullian's (*qv*) work, *Adversus Praxeam*, he is thought to have come to Rome from Asia, towards the end of the second century. He had suffered for his faith and was influential with the Pope against the Montanists. He assumed the leadership of the Patripassianists (*qv*): God, being one, suffered through total identification with Christ. P. recanted his heresy before death.[1]

[1]Cf. *Adversus Praxeam*, ed. E. Evans, London, 1948.

PRE-EXISTENCE OF CHRIST, THE

The problem has been excellently dealt with in the report issued after the 1981 plenary session of the International Theological Commission. The text merits full reproduction and examination:

"(1) Since classical Christology could always presuppose Trinitarian theology, the pre-existence of Jesus Christ did not present a great problem. But in modern Christological research, where the earthly life of Jesus has been subjected to considerable scrutiny, pre-existence has often been presented as something alien to biblical faith and religion and made to seem rather as something Greek—a form of speculation simply—in fact a myth which betrays the true human nature of Jesus. It is therefore said that the pre-existence of Jesus Christ is to be understood today not literally but in purely symbolic terms. It is simply a way of speaking of his uniqueness, his irreducible originality, and of the way in which Jesus transcends the world and history. Jesus Christ had a more than worldly origin. In these modern interpretations the idea of pre-existence seems to have exhausted its purpose and been surpassed.

"(2) Attempts to claim that the biblical statements about the pre-existence of Jesus Christ arose from mythical, hellenistic and gnostic sources do not hold water: today, in fact, relationships are detected with the intertestamental literature (cf. Eth. Enoch 48:3,6; 4 Ezra 13) and above all with Old Testament sources, especially in the Wisdom theology (Prov 8:22ff., Sir 24). In addition, much more is made of elements within biblical Christology itself: the unique relationship of Jesus on earth with God the Father ("Abba" on the lips of Jesus); the unique mission of the Son and his glorious resurrection. In the light of this exaltation the origin of Jesus Christ is openly and definitively understood; sitting at the right hand of God in his post-existence (i.e. after his earthly life) implies his pre-existence with God from the beginning before he came into the world. In other words, his eschatological state can be no different from his pre-incarnation state and vice versa. The unique mission of the son (cf. Mk 12:1–12) is inseparable from the person of Jesus Christ, who not only had a prophetic role, which was temporal and limited, to play on earth, but also has a co-eternal origin from the Father. The Son of God received everything in eternity from God the Father. In the light of this eschatological-soteriological perspective we must say that Jesus Christ cannot open the way to eternal life for us if he is not himself 'Eternal'. The eschatological message and the eschatological doctrine presuppose a divine pre-existence of Jesus Christ.

"Jesus Christ's origin from the Father is not a conclusion of subsequent reflection but is made clear by his words and the facts about him, namely, that Jesus took it for certain that he had been sent by the Father. Therefore, at least in an indirect fashion one finds manifested the consciousness of Jesus with regard to his eternal existence as Son of the Father, whose task it is to reconcile the whole world to God. (One can see as primary fundamental elements the 'I' of Jesus Christ in the Synoptic Gospels, the words 'I am' (ego eimi) in the Fourth Gospel, and the 'mission' of Jesus in many New Testament writings.)

"(3) Biblical studies have shown how the original datum has evolved through various stages and in different aspects within the limits of the New Testament as the full meaning of the pre-existence of Jesus becomes clear:

"the eternal election and predestination of Jesus Christ (cf. Eph 13:7, 10f; 1 P 1:20);

"the sending of the Son of God into the world and into the flesh (cf. Gal 4:4, Rom 8:38, 1 Tim 3:16, Jn 3:16f.);

"'kenosis', incarnation, death, and glorious resurrection of Jesus Christ on the cross, as steps on the way from the Father, all of which show the soteriological and salvific meaning of the event of Jesus Christ (cf. esp. Phil 2:6–11);

"Jesus Christ was already present and active in the history of the people of Israel in a hidden way, (cf. 1 Cor 10:1–4, Jn 1:30; 8:14, 58);

"Jesus Christ, as the intermediary in the creation of the world, now also keeps the world in being. He is head of the body of the Church and the reconciler of all things (cf. 1 Cor 8:6; Col 1:15f.; Jn 1:1–3, 17; Heb 1:2f.). All mediators, or acts of mediation which seemed to have significance for salvation, are taken away or must be understood in a subordinate fashion. Jesus Christ himself has an absolute pre-eminence over against all other acts of mediation, and in his work and in his person is God's final action and event;

"Jesus Christ obtains the lordship of the universe and gives redemption to all, a process which is understood as a new creation (cf. Col 1:15f.; 1 Cor 8:6; Heb 1:2f; Jn 1:2);

"in the exaltation of Jesus Christ the process of vanquishing evil powers has begun (cf. Phil 2:10; Col 1:16–20).

"(4) The post-biblical word 'pre-existence' includes many Christological elements. Even if this conception is in fact based on Scripture, at the same time pre-existence is not invoked there in an isolated fashion, and does not constitute the only reason for the statements of the New Testament. We are speaking of a systematic concept which synthesizes many theological meanings. In many statements it rather furnishes a background (l'arrière-plan, Hintergrund) or a presupposition of the reason for the other aims. Therefore, just as we cannot be satisfied with a purely formal use of the term, neither must we use it in an univocal fashion but rather analogically, carefully, and according to the content and the richness of the various doctrinal elements already mentioned. Although it is subject to multiple interpretations, the concept of pre-existence does not signify only an 'interpretation' which would in the end be purely subjective, but in fact the real ontological origin of Jesus Christ, his origin outside of time of which he is also consciously aware, as we have already said. Understood in the biblical sense, pre-existence does not signify only that Christ is co-eternal with God. This expression connotes the whole Christological movement and mystery, beginning from existence with the Father, including the 'kenosis' and the Incarnation, the infamous death on the cross, and the glorious exaltation. In the end it attests to the redemption of all men, to the primacy of Christ in the Church, and to universal and cosmic reconciliation. All this is presented in terms of redemptive suffering. Almost all of these formulations of the pre-existence of Jesus Christ are found in hymnic contexts. For this reason they take the form of testimony and praise, born of the Church's experience of the presence of the Lord. This soteriological and doxological character does not exclude a truly chronological meaning but it does impose clear limits on those forms of speculation about pre-existence which do not confirm these characteristics.

"(5) The concept of the pre-existence of Jesus Christ has acquired greater clarity as Christological reflection has evolved. In certain places the prefix 'pre' (e.g. 'before all things', 'before Abraham') has and keeps a temporal meaning, granted the historical character of Christian salvation; but in the last analysis it signifies absolute and timeless primacy over the whole of creation. In the Christological field, in the Nicene Creed (qv) (cf. DS 125), such a pre-existence acquires, after the Arian crisis, definite clarity. The Son of God generated from the Father is not created, but consubstantial with the Father.

"In this way the idea of the pre-existence of Jesus Christ is par excellence, as was said above, the point at which Christology and Trinitarian theology meet and come together (1, C and D). Between the Son in the eternal life of God, and the Son in the earthly life of Jesus Christ, there is a most strict correspondence or, better still, a real identity, nourished by the unity and the filial union of Jesus Christ with God the Father. The pre-existence of Jesus Christ should also be understood from the standpoint of the history of Jesus Christ and above all of his consummation in the event of Easter. From the beginning of Christological reflection, co-eternal with the Father—that is, if we consider it as a descending movement and, as it were, from above—was equally grasped in relation to the communication and gift of Jesus Christ for the life of the world. This relationship is rooted in the eternal Sonship through which Jesus Christ is generated by the Father. This relationship is constituted by means of 'mission', as this is conceived in biblical terms.

The gift of salvation is valid for us and for all men only if it is born in God, namely in the pre-existing Son of the Father. This shows anew the soteriological character of pre-existence."[1]

---

[1] Text *ITQ* 49 (1982), 293–96; *DCath* 1983, 123–24; cf. P. Benoit, O.P., "Pauline and Johannine Theology, A Contrast," *Cross Currents*, 16 (1965) 339–53; R.E. Brown, S.S., *Jesus, God and Man*, 1968, 1–38; O. Cullmann, *The Christology of the New Testament*, London, 1957, 270–305; A. Gelin, ed., *Son and Saviour*, London, 1962; W. Kramer, *Christ, Lord, Son of God*, SBT, 50, London, 1966; V. Taylor, *The Names of Jesus*, London, 1953, 52–65; Richards, *ITNT*, New York, 1958, 147–53; L. Sabourin, *The Names and Titles of Jesus*, New York, 1967; R.H. Fuller, *The Mission and Achievement of Jesus*, London, 1954; E. Schillebeeckx, O.P., *Jesus, An Experiment in Christology*, 1974, 652–669; *Jerome Commentary*, 810–11; *New Cath. Commentary*, 860–66, P. Grech, O.S.A.

PRISCILLIANISM

P. derived from Priscillian, a man with opinions not easily clarified or even attributable to him personally, since the capital document in the case is, at least, of doubtful authenticity.[1] His notoriety was enhanced by a series of condemnations; his rigorist ideas were condemned by St. Martin of Tours, St. Amrose and Pope Siricius. He was executed after trial in an imperial court on a charge of sorcery in 386. Bishop of Avila, he had from the outset found support in the hierarchy. The last of the condemnations, at the Council of Braga, 561, itemizes the errors as follows: "1. If anyone does not confess that the Father, and the Son, and the Holy Spirit (are) three persons of one substance, and virtue, and power, just as the Catholic and apostolic Church teaches, but says there is only one and a solitary person, so that he himself is the Father who is the Son, and also he himself is the Paraclete, the Spirit, just as Sabellius and Priscillian have asserted, let him be anathema. 2. If anyone introduces some other names of the Godhead in addition to the Holy Trinity, because, as he says, there is in the Godhead himself a Trinity of the Trinity, just as the Gnostics and Priscillians have stated, let him be anathema. 3. If anyone says that the Son of God our Lord did not exist before he was born of a Virgin, just as Paul of Samosata and Photinus and Priscillian have said, let him be anathema."[2]

---

[1] Cf. A. d'Ales, S.J., *Priscillien et l'Espagne chrétienne à la fin du IVe siècle*, Paris, 1936; J.M. Ramos y Loscertales, *Prisciliano, Gesta rerum* (Acta Salmaticensia, Filosofia y Letras, v, No.5),

1952; B. Vollmann, *Studien zum Priszillianismus, Die Forschung, die Quellen, der fünfzehnte Brief Papst Leos des Grossen* (Kirchengeschichtliche Quellen und Studien, vii 1965); R. Lopez Caneda, *Priscilliano, Su pensamiento y su problema histórico Compostela*, 1966, bibl; Altaner, 374; G. Bardy, *DTC*, XII, 1, 1936, 391–400; J.N. Hilgarth, *NCE*, XI, 1967, 790f; H. Chadwick, *Priscillian of Avila*, Oxford, 1970; [2]DS 451–464.

"PROBLEM," THE TRINITARIAN

The historian of theology must deal with the fact that *Triados*, approximately trinity, occurs first not in the Bible (*qv*), but in the second century, and *Trinitas* in the west is still later: St. Theophilus of Antioch (*qv*) was author of the first, Tertullian (*qv*) of the second. Close examination of the writings of Theophilus will show that his doctrine of the Holy Spirit (*qv*) was sketchy: chiefly he saw him as the author of prophecy. The entire doctrine, as an accepted synthesis with all its elements fully in place and fully justified, appears not to have been established until comparatively late in the Christian experience, in the last quarter of the fourth century. Trinitarianism as we know it, one God in three Persons, was then, and not fully until then, an integral part of Christian belief.

This constitutes a problem. But implicit in that problem and in time prior to it is the question: How does the Bible (*qv*) convey Trinitarian revelation? This second question is acutely put in recent times in consequence of the method and techniques of biblical exegesis now prevalent.[1]

There are some obvious difficulties. First is the relationship between Christ and the Father, brought to its sharpest point in the Johannine writings. Christ is called "Son" by preference and God "Father". In the gospel and the epistles "Father" occurs 137 times as against 123 times in the rest of the NT. "Son" occurs 52 times in the Johannine writings, 67 times in the rest of NT. The Johannine understanding of the Father-Son relationship is crucial. It is expressed with a sense of apparent paradox.

John emphasizes Christ's limitless superiority, ascending through such titles as Judge, Saviour, Resurrection, Life, Good Shepherd, Bread of Life, to the final proclamation from the lips of Thomas, "My Lord and my God." This language from the life of Christ reaches the level of John's opening words by way of introduction: "In the beginning was the Word, and the Word was with God, and the Word was God . . . . And the Word became flesh and dwelt among us, full of grace and truth; we have beheld his glory, glory as of the only Son from the Father" (1:1, 14).

With such an affirmation of the divinity of Christ, made with varying modalities, but essentially undeniable, John offers us a different set of statements: "the Son can do nothing of his own accord, but only what he sees the Father doing" (5:19). "For as the Father has life in himself so he has granted the Son also to have life in himself" (5:26). "My teaching is not mine but his who sent me" (7:16). "If you loved me, you would have rejoiced, because I go to the Father; for the Father is greater than I" (14:28).

Here we have two apparently conflicting lines of thought. The author shows us how they may be reconciled in such texts as these: "My Father, who has given them to me, is greater than all, and no one is able to snatch them out of the Father's hand. I and the Father are one" (10:29, 30). "If a man loves me, he will keep my word, and my Father will love him, and we will come to him and make our home with him" (14:23). "The glory which thou hast given me I have given to them, that they may be one even as we are one" (17:22). "Now Jesus did many other signs in the presence of his disciples, which are not written in this book; but these are written that you may believe that Jesus is the Christ, the Son of God, and that believing you may have life in his name" (20:30).

Did John personally reflect on the problem of reconciling the two sets of statements? The fact remains that the harmony is ultimately made clear: Jesus sometimes spoke as man, sometimes as God; sometimes as Godman: "As the Father has sent me, even so I send you" (20:21). The history of Arianism (*qv*) shows how arduous was the task of clarifying in acceptable language the relationship between the Father and the Son. The problem had been there from NT times, for Jesus had appeared among the Jews as a man.

Another aspect of the Trinitarian problem was the identity of the Spirit, his divinity and his relationship with the Father and with Christ. This could not arouse the same intellectual excitement and it was more strictly a question of theological discourse. The debate was closed with the Council of Constantinople (*qv*).

Finally we come to the core of the Trinitarian problem: how far were NT writers aware of a relationship between Father, Son and Spirit? How did their ideas emerge more clearly in the immediate post-apostolic generation? At this point in the debate consideration is generally given to the "bi-partite" and "tri-partite" formulae in NT. From 2 Thess, St. Paul in almost all his epistles uses a "bi-partite" formula as a salutation: "Grace to you and peace from God the Father and the Lord Jesus Christ" (2 Thess 1:2); "Grace to you and peace from God the Father and our Lord Jesus Christ" (Gal 1:3; 1 Cor 1:3; 2 Cor 1:3; Rom 1:7; Eph 1:2). Paul is at times more explicit, specifying number: "yet for us there is one God, the Father, from whom, are all things and for whom we exist, and one Lord, Jesus Christ, through whom are all things and through whom we exist" (1 Cor 8:6); "For there is one God and there is one Mediator between God and men, the man Christ Jesus, who gave himself as a ransom for all, the testimony to which was borne at the proper time" (1 Tim 2:5, 6); with which cp. "In the presence of God who gives life to all things, and of Christ Jesus who in his testimony before Pontius Pilate made the good confession" (ibid., 6:13), where number is not specified, but understood.

To these few "bi-partite" formulae we may oppose some 40 "tri-partite" expressions of faith, teaching, prayer or greeting found in the writings of St. Paul, together with other occasional mentions in NT. On the vocation to the faith Paul writes thus: "But we are bound to give thanks to God always for you, brethren beloved by the Lord, because God chose you from the beginning to be saved, through sanctification by the *Spirit* and belief in the truth. To this he called you through our gospel, so that you may obtain the glory of our Lord Jesus Christ" (2 Thess 2:13, 14); with this cp. "Peter, an apostle of Jesus Christ, to the exiles of the Dispersion in Pontus, Galatia, Cappadocia, Asia and Bithynia, chosen and destined by *God the Father* and sanctified by the *Spirit* for obedience to *Jesus Christ* and for sprinkling with his blood" (1 Pet 1:1, 2). Paul in Gal 4:4–7 points to filial adoption as the end of the divine missions: "But when the time had fully come, *God* sent forth his *Son*, born of a woman, born under the law, to redeem those who were under the law, so that we might receive adoption as sons. And because you are sons, *God* has sent the *Spirit of his Son* into our hearts, crying, 'Abba! Father!'. So through God you are no longer a slave but a son, and if a son then an heir."

In Rom 8:11 the idea is not very dissimilar: "If the *Spirit* of *him* who raised Christ Jesus from the dead dwells in you, *he* who raised *Christ Jesus* from the dead will give life to your mortal bodies." Further down we read "For all who are led by the *Spirit of God* are sons of *God*. For you did not receive the spirit of slavery to fall back into fear, but you have received the spirit of sonship. When we cry, 'Abba! Father!' it is the *Spirit himself* bearing witness with our spirit that we are children of *God*, and if children, then heirs, heirs of *God* and fellow heirs *with Christ*, provided we suffer with him in order that we may also be glorified with him" (ibid., 14). The hymn in Eph 1:3–14 which opens with reference to the eternal plan of the Father ends thus, maintaining a Trinitarian pattern: "In *him (Christ)* you also, who have heard the word of truth, the gospel of your salvation, and have believed in him, were sealed with the promised *Holy Spirit*, which is the guarantee of our inheritance until we acquire possession of it, to the praise of *his glory*" (ibid., 13, 14).

The economy of salvation originates in the will of the Father, is accomplished in the Christ event, attains fulfilment in the gift of the Spirit: "for through *him (Christ)* we both have access *in one Spirit to the Father* . . . . you are fellow citizens with the saints and members of the household *of God*, built upon the foundation of the apostles and prophets, *Christ Jesus himself* being the cornerstone in whom the whole structure is joined together and grows into a holy temple *of the Lord*; in whom you also are built into it for a dwelling place of *God* in *the Spirit*" (Eph 2:18–22).

Paul in his address to the elders of the church of Ephesus at Miletus spoke thus: "Take heed to yourselves and to all the flock, in which the *Holy Spirit* has made you overseers, to care for the *Church of God*, which he obtained with the blood of his own *Son*" (Acts 20:28). Cp. Rom 15:16 where he speaks of "the grace given me by God to be a minister of *Christ Jesus* to the Gentiles in the priestly service of the gospel *of God* so that the offering of the Gentiles may be acceptable, sanctified by the Holy Spirit."

St. Paul speaks thus of the justification received in baptism: "But you were washed, you were sanctified, you were justified in the name of the *Lord Jesus Christ* and in the *Spirit of our God*" (1 Cor 6:11). "But when the goodness and loving kindness of God our *Saviour* appeared, he saved us, not because of deeds done by us in righteousness, but in virtue of his own mercy, by the washing of regeneration and renewal in the *Holy Spirit*, which he poured out upon us richly through *Jesus Christ our Saviour* so that we might be justified by his grace and become heirs in hope of eternal life" (Tit 3:4–7).

The sacred names are set down in the great passage, 1 Cor 12 on the varieties of gifts, the varieties of services and the varieties of working: "the same Spirit," "the same Lord," "the same God." Similarly in Eph 4:4–5: "There is one body and *one Spirit*, just as you were called to the one hope that belongs to your call, *one Lord*, one faith, one baptism, *one God and Father* of us all, who is above all and through all and in all." Finally there is the farewell formula in 2 Cor 13:13: "The grace of the Lord Jesus Christ and the love of God and the fellowship of the Holy Spirit be with you all." The origin may be liturgical.

It is clear from this survey that we cannot take the view that in NT times there was an evolution from a single member profession, that is, of faith in Christ, to a dual member formula in Christ and the Father, to the final triadic phrasing. All were contemporary. Faith in Christ implied the Trinity, as faith in the Trinity was in the God revealed to us in Christ. By "Trinity" a completely logical doctrinal synthesis is not implied; it was not to be expected, but the materials were there (see BIBLE). Fr. Pierre Benoit, O.P. sums it up: "The whole message of the NT is based on the cooperation of the three divine Persons in the achievement of salvation. If it is true that the Father and the Spirit are generally considered in the context of the Son's work, it would be false to conclude therefrom that he is first in faith. O. Cullmann's judgment is unacceptable: 'Because the first-century Christian believes in Christ as Lord, he believes in God and in the Holy Spirit.' One should put it in the opposite sense: it is because the Christian believes in the Father who raised him and in the Spirit whose outpouring manifests his triumph, that he believes in Jesus the Lord."[2]

A further aspect of the Trinitarian "problem" is the evolution of the idea through the generation immediately after the Apostles. Their ideas persist in the writings coming after them. Thus St. Clement of Rome, about 90 A.D.: "Or have we not one *God*, and one *Christ*, and one *Spirit of grace* poured out upon us? And is there not one calling in Christ?"[3] And again "Receive our counsel, and there shall be nothing for you to regret, for as *God* lives and as the *Lord Jesus Christ* lives and the *Holy Spirit*, the faith and hope of the elect . . . ."[4]

Typical texts from St. Ignatius of Antioch are quoted in the article on him. Polycarp has a bi-partite formula inspired by 1 Pet 1:21.[5] Justin Martyr (*qv*) speaks of the Father, the Son and the Spirit of prophecy, as he does of the "Son of the true God whom we put in second place and the Spirit of prophecy in third place."[6] The *Epistula Apostolorum* (between 140 and 170) has this formula: "I believe in the *Father all-powerful*, in *Jesus Christ*, our Saviour and in the *Holy Spirit* (Paraclete), the holy Church, the remission of sins."[7]

Bi-partite formulae are found in the writings of the Apostolic Fathers, but the tri-partite formulae continue to recur and have the support of giants like St. Irenaeus (*qv*). He as well as Justin and later Hippolytus (*qv*) and Tertullian (*qv*) testify to the Trinitarian rite in baptism (*qv*).

What we have then in these first post-apostolic generations is something which is beginning to appear again in Christian literature: attention to each of the divine Persons. As has been made clear the idea and concept of Trinity appeared before very long. Henceforth the two trends would be maintained: attention to each Person, and assent to the dominant mystery of the triune God. Out of the truth expressed in each would come the long Trinitarian battles of the third and fourth centuries. The Trinitarian "problem" was solved, as all fundamental questions of the kind were solved, by the Church docile to the Holy Spirit. Elemental Trinitarianism, as it is sometimes called, evolved into developed theology. It would be regrettable if now the solution of the "problem" as stated were to result in a retreat to elemental Trinitarianism. There is much to be done at the scholarly and pastoral levels, much of which will mean discovering in their purity the riches of the past.

[1]Extensive bibl., *EstTrin*, XI (1977), "Número extraordinario, Bibliografia trinitaria," X. Pikaza, "Bibliografia trinitaria del Nuevo Testamento," 138–305; see bibl. to articles on The Bible, Creeds, Doxology; A.W. Wainwright, *The Trinity in the New Testament*, London, 1962, esp. 248ff; R.L. Richard, *NCE* XIV, 294–306; G.A.F. Knight, *A Biblical Approach to the Doctrine of the Trinity*, Edinburgh, 1953; *Lumière et Vie, Le Mystere de la Sainte Trinité, Données bibliques*, 29 (1956), 1–142; E. Yarnold, *The Trinitarian Implications of Luke and Acts*, HeyJ, 7 (1966), 18–32; B. Rey, *De la fe en Jahweh a la fe en la Trinidad*, FAX, 1973; Symposium, *La Trinidad en la Biblia, Semanas de Estudios Trinitarios*, 1973, Secretaria Trinitaria, Salamanca, 1973; P. Benoit, O.P., "Les origines du symbole des Apôtres dans le Nouveau Testament," *Exégèse et Théologie*, II, Paris, 1961, 193–211; H. Neufeld, *The Earliest Christian Confessions*, New Testament Tools

and Studies, V, Grand Rapids, 1963; H. Geisser, "Der Beitrag der Trinitätslehre zur Problematik des Redens von Gott," *ZTK* 65 (1968), 231–255; J. Courtney Murray, *The Problem of God*, New Haven, 1964, 31–76; C.H. Dodd, *The Apostolic Preaching and its Developments*, London, 1963; [2]*Lumière et Vie*, II, 57; [3]*To the Corinthians*, 46, 6, *Apostolic Fathers*, tr. K. Lake, London, 1912, I, 89; [4]*Ibid.*, 58, 2, *op.cit.*, 109; [5]*To the Philippians*, 2, 1, *op.cit.*, 285; [6]*Apol.* 1, 6; 1, 13; [7]D. 1, 1.

PROCESS THEOLOGY

The ferment of thinking on Process Theology inevitably had an influence inside the Catholic Church in the post-conciliar age. Traditional categories of thought were being reviewed. What may be ultimately assimilated to the basic enduring synthesis cannot yet be foreseen. The meaning which Whitehead attaches to divine omnipotence, creative power and causality would need to be considerably refined, altered some would say, to be acceptable. So would Hartshorne's theory on God and the world. He considers that God's essential attributes are abstractly necessary, but their manifestation in concrete cases is contingent; likewise he thinks that the existence of the world is abstractly necessary, but what character it assumes in the concrete is contingent.

When Hartshorne enters into the problem of interaction between God and the world, the area known to Christians as divine Providence, he meets with opposition which is understandable. He abandons the ideas of God as absolute and immutable, thinking him most relative, assimilating to himself all the changes that take place in the world. Our actions enlarge God's experience and in this acceptance by him lies their full meaning. How to safeguard divine transcendence on this view is for some impossible. Process theologians resort to their intricate theory of causality to provide the solution.

The language of some of the mystics would, doubtless, be similar to this kind of suggestion. When Schubert Ogden thinks that the divine experience is enriched by human life, which thereby acquires meaning, he may be thought to echo St. Paul's claim that he was filling up in his body what was lacking in the passion of Christ. But the mystics and St. Paul thought in a Christian *Weltanschauung* in which many constituent elements would not belong to the categories of process theism.

Process theism asserts that God is abstract and concrete, necessary and contingent, unchanging and changing, independent and dependent on the world: it is maintained that these contrasts can be explained by looking at God from different aspects: abstract, necessary, unchanging if viewed metaphysically, concrete, contingent, changing in his experience and specific responses to the world. God becomes the centre of countless prehensions, which achieve unity because of the divine unity or simplicity. Process theists maintain that analogy, which is necessary to our knowledge of God and God's infinity, can be safeguarded in their system—if system is the word. They think that the emphasis on becoming which is intrinsic to process theology, the distrust of static concepts, the almost excessive preoccupation with man's contribution to divine experience, does not minimize our idea of the life of God.[1]

Can there be a process Trinitarianism? Is the Trinity a process? Does not a theologian like Karl Rahner (*qv*) tell us that the economic Trinity is the immanent Trinity and vice versa? But Rahner is attentive to the primordial assumption of Catholic theology: divine revelation is its indispensable support, and this revelation is absolutely free in its initiative, its historical moment, its content. Its total content is the Son of God incarnate.

The initiative in regard to revelation was in a world made by the revealer. The reality of creation, with all that it entails, is overlooked by process theists. So is the rigorous exigence of revelation. They risk taking from revelation elements necessary to their reflection, such as the very fact of God's existence, and then reverting to the level of natural theology. Analogy cannot be put in a secondary place in the theological discourse—it is central to knowledge about God. On the basis of what analogy can the Trinity be said to be a process? Can the notion of becoming be applied to the divine Persons? How then can they be equal, eternal? How can process theists explain that it was the Logos, the Son, who became man? Christians take it from revelation. Is the language of process theology capable of expressing all the aspects of Trinitarian life, the processions, the properties, the missions? What does Pentecost mean in process theism? Again Christians have this from revelation. Is the "Christian Trinity reduced to a linguistic symbol for expressing the transcendence-immanence of a di-polar God"?[2] Are we led to "an interpretation which asserts itself finally as unitarian rather than Trinitarian in disallowing any real distinction in God of a personal kind?"[3]

It is increasingly clear that Christology (*qv*) is closely linked with Trinitarian theology. It is difficult to see how Process theology can provide an appropriate methodology in this task of interpreting the data of revelation as conveyed to us in Scripture and Tradition with due attention to the Teaching Authority.

---

[1]On Process Theology in general cf. A.N. Whitehead, *Religion in the Making*, Cambridge, 1926; *id., Adventures of Ideas, ib.,* 1933; C. Hartshorne, *Man's Vision of God and the Logic of Theism*, New York, 1941; *id., The Divine Relativity*, New Haven, 1948; *id., A Natural Theology for our Time*, La Salle, Ill., 1967; B.E. Meland, *The Realities of Faith*, New York, 1962; J.B. Cobb, Jr., *A Christian Natural Theology*, based on the thought of A.N. Whitehead, 1966; S.M. Ogden, *The Reality of God and Other Essays*, 1967; P. Hamilton, *The Living God and the Modern World*, London, 1967; N. Pittenger, *God in Process*, New York, 1967; *id., Process-Thought and Christian Faith*, New York, 1968; *id., Christology Reconsidered*, New York, 1968; D.D. Williams, *The Spirit and the Forms of Love*, New York, 1968; J.Cobb, *God and the World*, Philadelphia, 1969; E.H. Cousins, *ed., Process Theology*, New York, 1971; D. Brown, R.E. James, and G. Reeves, eds., *Process Philosophy and Christian Thought*, Indianapolis, 1971; on process Trinitarianism cf. A. Kelly, "Trinity and Process, Relevance of the Basic Christian Confession of God," *ThS*, 31 (1970), 393–414; W.J. Hill, *The Three-Personed God*, 208–216; D.D. Williams, "Process Trinitarianism," *Journal of the American Academy of Religion*, 43 (1975); N. Pittenger, "Trinity and Process: Some Comments and a Reply," *ThSt* 32 (1971) 290–296; P. Schoonenberg, "Process or History in God," *Theol.Digest*, 23 (1975) 38–44; [2]W.J. Hill, *op.cit.*, 216; [3]W.J. Hill, *ibid*.

PROCESSIONS, DIVINE

The word traditionally used to signify that one divine Person takes his origin in another.[1] The idea is thus expressed in Jn 8:42: "Jesus said to them, "If God were your Father, you would love me, for I proceeded and came forth from God; I came not of my own accord, but he sent me" (see article Missions); and again, "But when the Counsellor comes, whom I shall send to you from the Father, even the Spirit of truth, who proceeds from the Father, he will bear witness to me" (Jn 15:26). This procession must not be understood as departure or cleavage, rather as emanation. The analogical character (see ANALOGY) of the idea of procession must be borne in mind. The Father does not proceed from any other Person; the Son proceeds from the Father, and the Holy Spirit proceeds from the Father and the Son

(see FILIOQUE). These processions are immanent to the life of the Trinity; they are not external such as the procession of creatures from the creative hand of God. The divine missions (*qv*) are distinct from them, though related or corresponding with them. The Johannine texts quoted, though implying procession directly, speak of mission. (For Church teaching see LATERAN, FOURTH COUNCIL.)

---

[1]Most treatises from early times and modern manuals, L. Billot, S.J., *De Deo Trino*, B. Lonergan (*qv*), *De Deo Trino*, deal with the subject, as do works popularizing theology, e.g. E. Hugon, O.P., *Le Mystère de la Sainte Trinité*, Paris, 1921, 141–171; V.-M. Breton, O.F.M., *The Blessed Trinity*, London, 1934, 120f; cf. esp. St.Thomas (*qv*), I, q. 27; M.J. Scheeben (*qv*), *The Mysteries of Christianity*, St.Louis, London, 1946, 87–117; B. de Margerie, S.J., *La Trinité chrétienne dans l'histoire*, Paris, 1974, 205f; W.J. Hill, O.P., *The Three-Personed God*, Washington, 1982, 262ff.

PROPERTIES, DIVINE

These are distinguishing marks of the divine persons: a property in this sense belongs to one divine Person only.[1] For the Father (*qv*) the proper, exclusive, differentiating attribute indicates his act of generation (*qv*). The Greeks thought of him as the source, the principle of the other divine persons. Fatherhood is therefore his property; his is fatherhood primordially, originally, eternally. In him fatherhood is subsistent, independent, absolute, the model and source of every lesser paternity "in heaven and on earth."

The property of the second person is sonship, filiation. But it is sonship of a unique kind, for he is "the image of the invisible God" (Col 1:15); "He reflects the glory of God and bears the very stamp of his nature" (Heb 1:3) and he is consubstantial with the Father, for his generation is from the entire substance of the Father in its total profundity. To see him is to see the Father (Jn 14:9).

For the Greeks the personal property of the Spirit is sanctity, sanctity which is self-diffusive, as, in a different context, fatherhood is a unique kind of self-communication. "In the same manner, in the matter in question," says St. Basil, (who has been talking of *ousia* or *essence* as distinguished from individual properties in human beings), "the term *ousia* is common, like goodness or Godhead, or any similar attribute; while *hypostasis* is contemplated in the special property of fatherhood or sonship or the power to sanctify."[2]

For the Latins the property of the Spirit is passive spiration (*qv*). Common spiritation as a mark of Father and Son is not a property, for it is not distinctive of a single person only. "Common spiration is not a property," says St. Thomas, "for it belongs to two persons."[3]

---

[1]Cf. St. Thomas (*qv*), I, q. 40; M. Schmaus, *LTK* 8:805; [2]Letter 214, LNPF VIII, 254; cp. esp. Letter 38, *ibid.*, 137–141; [3]I, q. 32, 3.

R

RAHNER, KARL (1904–1984)

Unquestionably one of the giants of contemporary theology, R. has made a notable contribution to Trinitarian studies.[1] He has rendered the service of stimulating interest, almost of rehabilitating the subject. His remarks that Christians are "in their practical life almost mere 'monotheists,'" and that if, *per impossibile*, the doctrine were to be eliminated as false, "the major part of religious literature could well remain virtually unchanged"[2] may well verge on hyperbole, for different reasons, one being the concentration of interest in Jesus Christ over the last two lifetimes, which interest stirs attention to the Father and the Spirit. Yet the point had to be made. What was verbally proclaimed the most important mystery of our faith did not seem to have the most important place in our lives.

R's Trinitarian theory has to be seen against the background of his general theology and philosophy, as expressed in *Spirit in the World*[3] and *Hearers of the Word*.[4] Despite what has been said his original theses remain controversial. One concerns the assertion that "the economic Trinity is the immanent Trinity and vice versa" (see ECONOMIC TRINITY); the other is his wish to abandon the word "person" (see PERSONALITY).

His theory on the "economic" and "immanent" Trinity is dealt with in the article on the Economic Trinity. His attempt to find a substitute for the word "person" has not been generally welcomed. His objection to continuing use of the word is that "person" in its modern meaning and connotation means an autonomous centre of consciousness. Three such centres would, R. thinks, verge on tritheism (*qv*). He proposes the use of "ways of existing"; it must be admitted that he changed his opinion because in *The Trinity* he thought that the word "person" was in use, it had a history of more than 1500 years, and he could not see that a better word would be found, one which would be understood by all "and give rise to fewer understandings".[5] Yet he later changed his mind and spoke of "ways of being" as well as "ways of existing," and "distinct manners of subsisting."

Since R. is so insistent on the importance of the Trinity in the "economy," the obvious remark must be made. In the history of the "economy" as it is found in the Bible, the names, Father, Son and Spirit occur; they analogically refer to what in the Trinity corresponds to personality in a human context. When terms like "generation," "only-begotten," "indwelling," and "procession" are used it is not easy to adapt their meaning to what is conveyed by the new terms urged by R. He repudiates anything like classic Modalism (*qv*); but on his premise is it avoidable without dialetics beyond even the most intelligent?

R. has also pertinent things to say about the place of the Trinity in dogmatic theology. It is not a mere question of arrangement, whether the treatise *De Deo Trino* should come first or last, but of grasping a truth which he enunciates thus: "If the *Oikonomia* is really the whole of theology and likewise contains and reveals the immanent Trinity itself, the whole of dogmatic theology is Trinitarian theology, which means that the theology of the Trinity is only really articulated by theology as a whole."[6]

---

[1] See bibl. to article Economic Trinity; works of R., "Remarks on the Dogmatic Treatise 'De Trinitate,'" *Theological Investigations*, 4, 77–102; *The Trinity*, Eng. tr. from *Mysterium Salutis*, Einsiedeln, 1967, London, 1970; Preface to '*O Misterio de Deus em nossa vida*' by Mario de Franca Miranda, Sao Paolo, 1975, 7–13—the book is a study of R's thesis on the "Economic Trinity"; *Foundations of Christian Faith*, 1978; articles on Trinity in *Encyclopaedia of Theology: The Concise Sacramentum Mundi*, 1975; "Theos in the New Testament," *Theological Investigations*, I, 79–148; "Some Implications of the Scholastic Concept of Uncreated Grace," *Th.Invest.*, I, 319–46; "On the Theology of the Incarnation," IV, 105–20; on R's Trinitarian theology, besides work cited, cf. G. Lafont, *Peut-on connaître Dieu en Jesus-Christ?*, Paris, 1969, 220, 226f; E. Hill, "Karl Rahner's 'Remarks on the Dogmatic Treatise de Trinitate' and St.Augustine," *Augustinian Studies*, II, Villanova University, 1971, 67–80; Congar, The Holy Spirit, III, 11–18; J. Moltmann, *The Trinity and the Kingdom of God*, London, 1980, 144–48; F.X. Bautle, "Person und Personbegriff in der Trinitätslehre Karl Rahner's," *Münchener Theol. Zeitsch.*, 30 (1979), 11–24; W.J. Hill, O.P., *The Three-Personed God*, Washington, 1982; 130–145; id., "Uncreated Grace: A Critique of Karl Rahner," *The Thomist* 26 (1963), 333–356; [2] *The Trinity*, 10–11; [3] Tr. *Geist in Welt*, London, 1968; 2nd German ed. by J.B. Metz, 1957; [4] Eng. tr *Hörer des Wortes*, rev. ed. J.B. Metz, Munich 1963; London 1969; [5] *The Trinity*, 44; [6] *Encyclopaedia of Theology*, 1767.

RECENT WRITERS

The comment that the Trinity is a neglected subject in contemporary theological writing may have been true twenty years ago, even ten years ago.[1] The great awakening has come. Special articles in this work deal with giants of present-day theology like Karl Rahner or Bernard Lonergan, or with patristic scholars of a not too distant generation like Jules Lebreton, Gustave Bardy, and J.N.D. Kelly, still living, or a great Orientalist, Martin Jugie. Karl Barth is also of our time, and Basil Bolotov, historian of the *Filioque* controversy in Russia is not too remote. Certain themes emerging in contemporary religious literature—Process Theology and Logocentric Theology—deserved attention.

There are still many currents of thought, many writers who should command notice, whose

reflection and research will surely further theological awareness and development. Many of the insights validated by Vatican II need to be more fully developed.

The contribution of Heribert Muhlen and of Fr. Yves M.-J. Congar has been mentioned in the context of the Holy Spirit. Jürgen Moltmann demands attention, if not unqualified agreement, for his thesis on the Crucified God, on the attempt to focus Trinitarian revelation on the Crucifixion. In his work on *The Trinity and the Kingdom*[2] he comes to grips with the theories of Karl Rahner and Karl Barth. He has a summary of his thought on the Trinity in the published dialogue which he undertook on *Jewish Monotheism and Christian Trinitarian Doctrine*[3] with the Jewish scholar, Pinchas Lapide on 22 May, 1978, in a German village Niefern bei Pforzheim.

One large problem to be faced is the evangelization of the great non-Christian religions, with particular reference to the doctrine of the Trinity. Vatican II opened the way for dialogue with them. How is this used on the subject of the Triune God?

Meanwhile other stimulating approaches are noticeable in writing which continues to flow on the renewed subject. Joseph Bracken, S.J., taking as his starting point Josiah Royce's *The Problem of Christianity*, has sought to explore the idea of community as a dialectical technique to expound Trinitarian doctrine. Paul Tillich concentrated on the aspect of symbolism, as did Cyril Richardson with different emphasis and results. No claim is made here to deal in any way but by indicating general characteristics with the intellectual ferment which increases about the central mystery of the Christian faith.

It is not a question of advocating any and every kind of pluralism, but of welcoming and sifting the results of hard thinking and sincere expression of opinion. The whole thrust of this present work is to enlighten students of Trinitarian theology on the search in age after age for satisfying valid formulas of knowing and speaking in this most challenging and ultimately most rewarding area of Christian thought.

We need not only to use the intellectual tools fashioned in western centres of thought, but to take serious note of the great Orthodox tradition represented by the school of theologians centred on the St. Serge Institute in Paris. A cluster of great names is led by Sergius Bulgakov, author of a penetrating work on the Holy Spirit, *Le Paraclet*, writers staunchly faithful as in the case of

Vladimir Lossky, (*qv*) truly ecumenical as Paul Evdokimov, and so many others. The author of the present work, it is clear, accepts the teaching of the Catholic Church; he is bound by the directives of the Second Vatican Council to seek a fuller understanding of all other traditions. (See articles *Filioque* and *Epiclesis* as examples of acute problem areas between Latin and Orthodox.)

Very recent contributions to note and welcome are *The Divine Trinity* by David Brown (1985), a serious analysis of the problem of reconciling authentic philosophy and scientific biblical study; and *The Mystery of the Trinity* by Edmund Hill (1985), which has highly suggestive models for catechetical presentation (see CATECHETICS).

---

[1]Surveys of recent literature in W.J. Hill, *The Three-Personed God*; J.A. Bracken, *What are they saying about the Trinity?*, New York, 1979; C. Welch, *The Trinity in Contemporary Theology*, London, 1952; *One God in Trinity*, ed. P. Toon, J.D. Spiceland, Westchester, 1980, on contemporary writers or problems; cf. also J.A. Bracken, *The Triune Symbol, Persons, Process*, University of America Press, as well as his articles in his work *j.cit*; [2]San Francisco, 1981; [3]Philadelphia, 1981.

REFORMATION, THE

The Trinity was not in the area of doctrinal controversy at the time of the Reformation: the rule of faith—*Scriptura sola*, authority in the Church, the sacrifice of the Mass, the meaning of justification, devotion to Mary and the saints, the sacramental system absorbed intellectual energy and left the essential dogmas of the Trinity and the Incarnation practically untouched.[1] The Reformers followed some ideas, held some assumptions of the time, such as that the doctrine of the Trinity is contained not only in NT but in OT (see Bible, The; Problem, the Trinitarian). When, after statements of belief by the leaders, George Calixtus (1614–58), published in 1649 at Helmstadt his work which queried, though not too aggressively, this assumption, *Num mysterium S. Trinitatis e solius V.T. libris demonstrari possit*, a storm erupted. Replies were :Calov, *Scriptura V.T. Trinitatis revelatrix*, Wittenberg, 1680; Pfeiffer, *Dissertatio Trinitatem personarum in unitate Dei exoraculis V.T. V.T. probans*, Erlangen, 1743.

Luther (1483–1546): L's belief in the Trinity is clearly stated in the Schmalkaldic Articles, I,1. In the *Short Catechism* three articles spelled out the reality of the Trinity: the first which speaks of God the Father and the work of creation, the second of God the Son and the work of redemption, the third of God the Holy Spirit and the work of sanctification. Though there is here reference to the economy, it would be unfair to Luther to think that his interest in the Trinity was solely practical. The large catechism extends this whole argumentation.

Luther was explicit: "Thus there are three Persons and one God clearly proved in Scripture. Nor would I believe the writings of Augustine or the Master (i.e. Peter Lombard) if the Old and New Testament did not show this most clearly." Each Person, he thought, is the whole Godhead, and yet no Person is for himself without the other two, the Godhead. He accepted the faith of Nicaea with the exception perhaps of *Deum de Deo*.

But Luther did not accept what he thought to be the "subtleties" of scholastic theology. He dismissed the distinction between person and nature in God as a "useless and frivolous philosophical invention." His language was risky as he developed this idea; it is clear that he did not see the risk. He also had an opinion on the Holy Spirit as Mediator of the real presence of Christ in faith, which is potentially luminous, needing scrutiny.[2]

Zwingli (1484–1531): Zwingli is in the broad Christian tradition about the Holy Trinity. Melanchton (1497–1560) still more explicitly so, using fully the psychological analogy.

Calvin (1509–1564): Calvin is author of the fullest, most evidently traditional and orthodox Trinitarian theology. His teaching is contained in Bk III, ch. 13 of the *Institutes*.[3] He amplified it after the appearance of Michael Servetus' work attacking the doctrine of the Trinity: *De Trinitatis Erroribus Libri VII* (1531); this author was ultimately, after the appearance of his second work, *Christianismi Restitutio*, arrested in Geneva, where he had fled, on Calvin's orders and burned as a heretic (27 October, 1553).[4]

The title of ch 13, *op. cit.* reads: "It is handed down in Scriptures that there is one essence of God (known from) creation, and this contains in itself three Persons." One pithy excerpt will give an idea of the doctrine: "The distinction which allows us to prove that the Son is one God with the Father, because with him he abides in the Spirit, and that the Spirit is not different from the Father and the Son, because he is the Spirit of the Father and the Son, does not affect the utter unity of God. The whole (divine) nature is comprised in each hypostasis, with the fact that each has his special property. The Father is wholly in the Son and the Son wholly in the Father, as he himself states: 'I am in the Father and the Father in me' (Jn 14:11); nor do church writers think that one can be separated from the other by any difference of essence." Here in outline is the whole Trinitarian doctrine, unity of nature, distinction of persons, properties, even circumincession and the Filioque by implication. (qqv)

---

[1]Cf. for Luther A. Michel, DTC XV, 2, 1767; B. de Margerie, S. J., *La Trinité chrétienne dans l'histoire*, Paris, 1974, 272–77; P. Vignaux, *Luther, commentateur des Sentences*, Paris, 1935; R. Prenter, *Spiritus Orator*, Philadelphia, 1953; P. Althaus, *Die Theologie Martin Luthers*, Gutersloher Verlagshaus Gerd Mohn, 1962, *Die Trinität*, 175–77; for Calvin, A. Michel, *op. cit.*, 1768–74; B. Werfields, *Calvin's Doctrine of the Trinity, The Princeton Theological Review*, October, 1909, 553–652; for Zwingli and Melanchton, A. Michel, *op. cit.*; [2]Cf. P. Vignaux, *op. cit.*; [3]*Calvini Opera*, ed. P. Barth, G. Niesel, vol. III, 108ff; [4]Cf. also Calvin's work: *Defensionem orthodoxae fidei de sacra Trinitate contra prodigiosos errores M. Serveti per Johannem Calvinium*, 1554; *Corpus Reformatorum ed.* of writings, VIII 457ff; [5]*Calvini Opera, j. cit.*, 152.

RELATIONS IN THE TRINITY

A modern student, even one acquainted with theology, may find it difficult to understand a proposition like: persons in the Trinity are constituted by subsistent relations.[1] This is the abstract language, not of all theology, but of the scholastic theologians. It seems foreign to the Bible and some may think that it is partly responsible for the cleavage between theology and the religious practice of the faithful—if such a cleavage exists. Yet a little reflection will show that to say "father" (qv) as Our Lord so often did implies a relationship; so does Son of God (qv).

What the pedagogy of the Holy Trinity demands is therefore explanation of these relationships at two levels, one accessible to the ordinary mind, the other to the sophisticated or more cultured. The mistake has been the presentation of the truth always at the deepest level.

If there is a relationship at all in God clearly it must be one that accords with divine transcendence, divine infinity, with the coeternity and equality of the divine Three. Since, moreover, everything in God is identical with his essence, we must discard not only all that denotes the created, the transient, but also the accidental when we apply the concept to God.

We are dealing with a high point in the Trinitarian theology of St. Thomas, for though the concept existed before him he worked it out to its logical conclusion. He did so with the aid of Aristotelian metaphysics, with the creative power of analogy (qv) which is the binding force in all his thinking, and with the overruling sense of faith which prevented his theology from hardening into a system. If the language were permissible one could say that the finished product has an inherent elasticity which will meet every problem and leave the mind satisfied but aware of its own inadequacy, its fragility before the absolute. The hard systems came later.

"The analogical projection of such a notion upon God means (i) on the one hand, an absolute identity of the relation with the divine substance since it is unthinkable that anything could accidentally accrue to divine being as an acquisition previously lacking, yet (ii) on the other hand, a pure reference of a relating subject to some other as term to which it is related. It is logically coherent then to speak of subsistent relations within the Godhead, for there is something interior to divine being that is at once *subsistent* (nowise distinct from divinity, save in thought) and *relative* (positing therefore another in real opposition). In brief, there is real distinction within God enabling one to speak in plural terms, yet a distinctness that is purely relative in kind (that is, operative only between the correlates) such that each instance of distinction and all of them together are indistinguishable from divinity."[2]

Relation is the order of an entity towards another: of a subject to its term, on some particular basis. Analogy enters with maximum meaning to raise this theory to the Godhead. Where St. Thomas's predecessors, Gregory of Nazianzus[3] (qv) and John of Damascus[4] (qv) were content to acknowledge the fact—it is a prime datum of Scripture, which uses words Father, Son and Spirit implying relation—he explored it and, though the achievement is not often marked, in doing so proved the harmony between faith at its purest and reason at its most powerful.

In human reality father and son are related. But part of human development is to lessen the relationship. If the father dies the son remains an independent being. Father and Son in the divinity are necessarily and intrinsically and unchangeably one, with each united wholly to the divinity, each God, each having all the other has, save to be other. In basing the theory of divine personality (qv) on the relations there is a twofold danger, anthropomorphism on the one hand, quaternity on the other. "In the relation of persons number appears, but in the substance of divinity, what might be enumerated is not understood. Therefore, in this alone they imply number, that they are related to each other; and in this, that they are to themselves, they lack number"[5]

"The sacrosanct Roman Church, founded by the voice of our Lord and Saviour, firmly believes, professes, and preaches one true God omnipotent, unchangeable, and eternal, Father, Son and Holy Spirit . . . . These three persons are one God and not three gods, because the three have one substance, one essence, one nature, one divinity, one immensity, one eternity, where no opposition of relationship interferes."[6]

---

[1]St. Thomas I, q. 28; M.J. Scheeben, *The Mysteries of Christianity*, 52f; B. Lonergan, *De Deo Trino*, II, 115–151; W.J. Hill, *The Three-Personed God*, 69f; [2]W.J. Hill, *op.cit.*, 71; [3]*Orat. Theol.*, V, 9, PG 36, 141; Orat. XXIX, 16, PG 36, 96; [4]*De Fide Orthodoxa*, Bk I, ch X, PG 94, 837; [5]*Council of Toledo, XI*, DS 530; [6]*Council of Florence, A decree in behalf of the Jacobites*, DS 1330; for the opinions of John, theologian of the Latins, and Cardinal Bessarion for the Greeks cf. Hrd IX, 203, 339.

RELIGIOUS ORDERS AND CONGREGATIONS

The principal religious order in honour of the Trinity is the Trinitarians (Order of the Most Holy Trinity) founded by St. John of Matha (d. 1213) and possibly St. Felix of Valois, a shadowy figure. Innocent III gave his approval in 1198; thirty-five houses existed at the time of the death of the founder. The rule, also approved by Innocent III, was strict; it bore the mark of that of the Abbey of St. Victor in Paris. The members were to combine the contemplative life with works of charity. For a long time the work undertaken was the ransom of those held in slavery by Moslems, in Spain, North Africa and the Near East: to this end one third of the order's financial resources were assigned. When the phase of active rescue of this kind had ended, a figure of 140,000 was mentioned for the beneficiaries. Other works of education and charity were then undertaken. As with many religious orders decline set in towards the sixteenth century. Two reform movements sought to effect the needed restoration, in France from 1578 and in Spain from 1597. The leading spirit in the Spanish revival was Blessed John Baptist of the Conception (1561–1613); influenced probably by his early education from the Discalced Carmelites, he instituted this change in the discipline of the Trinitarians, making them also discalced. By 1580 there were nineteen houses of his observance.

An objective of the order has been to spread devotion (*qv*) to the Trinity. An Archconfraternity of the Most Holy Trinity has been founded, and members wear a scapular; the mother house in Rome is the centre of the Perpetual Adoration of the Most Holy Trinity.

Sisterhoods affiliated to the order have existed from the beginning. Other congregations of sisters have sought inspiration also in the Holy Trinity as formal patron of their religious life.[1]

---

[1]A. Velez de la Conceptión, *EstTrin*, IX (1975), 125–154.

RHEIMS, COUNCIL OF (1148)

This council issued a statement of Trinitarian doctrine in the historical context of controversy surrounding Gilbert de la Porrée. Its teaching was as follows: "1. We believe and confess that God is the simple nature of divinity, and that it cannot be denied in any Catholic sense that God is divinity and divinity is God. Moreover, if it is said that God is wise by wisdom, great by magnitude, eternal by eternity, one by oneness, God by divinity, and other such things, we believe that he is wise only by that wisdom which is God himself; that he is great by that magnitude which is God himself; that he is eternal only by that eternity which is God himself; that he is one only by that oneness which is God himself; that is, that he is wise, great, eternal, one God of himself.

"2. When we speak of three persons: Father, Son, and Holy Spirit, we confess that they are one God, one divine substance. And contrariwise, when we speak of one God, one divine substance, we confess that the one God himself, the one divine substance, is three divine persons. 3. We believe (and we confess) that only God the Father and Son and Holy Spirit are eternal, and not by any means other things, whether they be called relations or peculiarities or singularities or onenesses, and that other such things belong to God, which are from eternity, which are God. 4. We believe (and confess) that divinity itself, whether you call it divine substance or nature, is incarnate only in the Son."[1]

---

[1]Mansi, 712 Ef; PL 185, 617; cf. A. Hayen, S.J., "Le Concile de Reims et l'erreur théologique de Gilbert de la Porrée," *AHDLMA*, X, 1930, 29–102.

RICHARD OF ST. VICTOR (d.1173)

Of Scottish origin, R. entered the famous Abbey of St. Victor in Paris, and eventually became its prior. Among his many works the treatise *De Trinitate* with certain opuscula, *Quomodo Spiritus Sanctus est amor Patris et Filii* and *De tribus Personis appropriatis in Trinitate* interest us in the present work.[1] In his doctrine he was indebted to his abbot Achard (*qv*) and also to Augustine (*qv*) and Anselm (*qv*).

R. elaborates his doctrine of plurality or trinity in the one divine substance by arguments which he directs to reason. "In God, the supreme and absolutely perfect good, there is total goodness in its fullness and perfection. Where there is a fullness of total goodness, however, there is necessarily true and supreme charity . . . . It is never said of anyone that he possesses charity because of the exclusively personal love that he has for himself for there to be charity, there must be a love that is directed towards another. Consequently where there is an absence of a plurality of persons, there cannot be charity."[2] This divine sovereign charity, to be perfect and perfectly ordered, must be expressed towards a person of equal dignity, that is, to a divine person. In God too there is fullness of happiness. but what is more enjoyable than mutual love demanding one who loves, one who answers love. Again in God there is fullness of glory. But true glory is to communicate all one possesses, which assumes an associate in glory. R. thinks the threefold argument unanswerable.

The two persons, R. thinks, are coeternal, coequal, possess the same perfection, one only substance, one only God. He goes on to argue for the trinity: supreme and perfect charity wills to share the happiness savoured in love and thus wills that another be loved as one is oneself loved. Each of the two persons must then wish to have an object of common love. This desire must be harmonious and equal in the two; otherwise there would be failure in charity, loss of happiness, damage to glory. Without a duality of persons, there is no communication of greatness, no true love, which would be contrary to the fullness of goodness, of happiness, of glory. Without a trinity of persons there would be no communication of the delights of charity, which would be contrary to the love in each one of the two persons. In this way supreme goodness demands a third person. All three persons are equal, coeternal; all possess in common the supremely simple being, the unique divine essence.

Genuine love is self-transcending, infinite love infinitely so. Where there is only one person charity cannot exist. This self-transcending character of genuine love demands also a third person. Thus R. appears satisfied that he has provided a "necessary reason" for the Trinity, wherein he differs from almost unanimous orthodox opinion: here St. Thomas (*qv*) is principal spokesman.[3] Yet a certain value has been seen in his synthesis. This also includes, in the subsequent books of his treatise, pertinent remarks on the persons, processions, and names. R. is dissatisfied with the classic definition of person given by Boethius (*qv* and see article Personality). The divine person he defines as *divinae naturae incommunicabilis existentia*. Though his fundamental approach is highly distinctive he can comprehend the traditional belief of the Church. His theory a rounded view of the Trinity as community in love, as sublime society— evokes admiration, even assent down to modern times.[4]

In regard to the relation between divine essence and plurality of persons R. is not easily classified as either Latin or Greek—the simplistic view of T. de Regnon—but his view of the person brings him nearer to the Greeks. Without confronting these he asserts the *Filioque* (*qv*): "If the two (the Father and the Son) possess the same power in common, it must be concluded that it is from both that the third Person of the Trinity received his being and has his existence."[5] In the Trinity the third Person proceeds both from the one who was born and from the one who cannot be born (*innascibilis*). This is not Augustine's idea of the Spirit as the love of the Father and Son for each other. "The Spirit is, according to R. "the particular and incommunicable mode of the divine substance, which is Love. This special way of existing which characterizes the divine Persons consists in a manner of living and realizing Love. That Love is either pure grace, or it is received and giving, or it is purely received and due. This can then be expressed equally well in terms of procession and therefore also in terms of origin. Beginning with the one who is *innascibilis*, there is an immediate procession, that of the Love-Son, and one that is simultaneously immediate (from the Father) and mediate (from the Son), that of the *Condilectus* or Spirit."[6]

No other Person proceeds from the Spirit. But through him God as Love is bestowed on the believer and grows in him: hence the appropriate name of Gift for the Spirit: "Insofar as we enable the love that is due to our creator to go back to him, we are quite certainly configured into the property of the Holy Spirit . . . . For the rest, this gift is sent to us, this mission is given to us at the same time and in the same way by the Father and the Son. It is, after all, from the one and from the other that the Spirit has everything that he possesses. And because it is from the one and from the other that he has his being, power and will, it is right to say that it is they who send and give him, who has received from them the power and the will to come from them into us and to dwell in us."[7]

---

[1]Text PL 196, 887–902, defective; J. Ribaillier, *Richard de Saint-Victor, De Trinitate. Texte critique*, Paris, 1958; id., critical ed. *Richard de Saint Victor, Opuscules theologiques*, Paris, 1967—for *Quomodo Spiritus Sanctus est amor Patris et Filii* and *De tribus Personis appropriatis in Trinitate*, partly found in *De Trin.*, VI, 15; esp. G. Salet, *Richard de Saint Victor, La Trinité*, Latin text, French tr., notes, SC 63 1959; cf. T. de Regnon, *Etudes de théologie positive sur la Sainte Trinité*, II, Paris, 1892, 233–335; G. Buonamici, *Riccardo da S.Vittore*, 1898; J. Ebner, *Die Erkenntnisse Richards von St.Viktor* BGPM 19, Hft 4, 1917; C. Ottaviano, "Riccardo di S.Vittore, La vita, le opere, il pensiero," in *Memorie della R. Accademia Nazionale dei Lincei, Classe di scienz morali, storiche e filologiche* Ser. 6, iv (1933), 411–541; A.-M. Ethier, *Le 'De Trinitate' de Richard de Saint-Victor (Publ. de l'Inst. d'Etudes med. d'Ottawa, IX)*, Paris, Ottawa, 1939; F. Guimet, "Notes en marge d'un texte de Richard de Saint-Victor," *Arch. hist. doctr. litt. M.A.* 14 (1943–1945), 361–394; id., "'Caritas ordinata' et 'amor discretus' dans la théologie trinitaire de Richard de Saint-Victor," *Rev. M.A.latin*, 4 (1948), 225–236; G. Dumeige, *Richard de Saint-Victor et l'idée chrétienne de l'amour*, Paris, 1952; J. Bligh, Richard of St. Victor's De Trinitate: Augustinian or Abelardian?, *Heythrop J.*, 1 (1960) 118–139; Congar, *The Holy Spirit*, III, 103–108; W.J. Hill, *The Three-Personed God*, Washington, 1982, 225–232; X. Pikaza, "Notas sobre la Trinidad en Ricardo de San Victor," *EstTrin*, 83–101; [2]*De Trin.*, I, 20; [3]Cf. S. T., I, q. 32, a. 1, ad 2um for the answer to R.; [4]Cf. E. Cousins, "A Theology of Interpersonal Relations," *Thought* 45 (1970), 56–82; W. Pannenberg, *Jesus God and Man*, English tr. 1968, 181; [5]De Trin. V, 13, SC 321; [6]Congar, *The Holy Spirit*, III, 105; [7]*De Trin.*, VI, 14 SC 413, 417.

ROSCELLINUS (d. c.1125)

R's life is not completely known and his philosophical and theological opinions must be almost entirely constructed from the writings of his opponents: there is one exception, a letter to Abelard (*qv*); his other adversaries were Anselm (*qv*), and John of Salisbury.[1] He was a Nominalist, and had much to do with starting the theory. He was denounced and condemned at the synod of Soissons, 1092, for holding tritheism (*qv*).[2] He repudiated the accusation, but made a retraction. True to his nominalist position he could not conceive anything but individual, concrete substances, which led him into tritheism, at least implicitly. "If the three persons are one thing, *una res*, and not three things, *tres res*—each existing separately for himself, as three angels or three souls, but in such fashion that they are identical as power and will—it would follow that the Father and the Holy Spirit were incarnate with the Son."[3] Abelard had refuted the tritheism of R. in his *De Unitate et trinitate divina*. R. sent him a letter in which he protests abusively against the decrees of the synod of Soissons.[4]

---

[1]Cf. A. Wilmart, O.S.B., "Le premier ouvrage de S.Anselme contre le tritheisme de Roscelin," *RTAM*, 3 (1931), 20–36; F. Picavet, *Roscelin, Philosophe et théologien, d'après la légende et d'après l'histoire* (Ecole pratique des Hautes Etudes. Section des Sciences Religieuses, Rapports annuels), 1896; enlarged ed. 1911; M.M. Gorce, O.P., *DTC* XIII, 2, 1937; A. Michel, *DTC* XV, 1713; [2]Hefele-Leclercq, V, 365–67; [3]Apud Anselm, *De fide Trinitatis*; [4]PL 178, 357–72; crit. ed., J. Reiners, *Der Nominalismus in der Frühscholastik*, BGPM, VIII, Hft. 5; 1910; cf. also "Letter from Walter of Honnecourt to Roscellinus," *RevBen* 22 (1905), 172–5.

ROSMINI-SERBATI, ANTONIO (1797–1855)

Best known outside Italy as a religious founder, R. undertook, with papal encouragement, the revival of philosophy in Italy. In 1849 two of his works, wherein he dealt with needed reforms in the Church, were placed on the Index; to this decision he submitted at once. His writings were finally cleared. But when his posthumous work, *La Teosofia* (1859–1874), five volumes, appeared, he was once again delated to Rome. Forty propositions extracted from his writings were condemned in a decree of the Holy Office (14 December, 1887) which was approved by the Pope. R. had tried to assimilate the opinions of modern philosophers. Of indirect or direct relevance to our subject are the following: "(4) Indeterminate being, which without doubt is known to all intelligences, is that divine thing which is manifest to man in nature. (5) Being which man observes, must be something of the necessary and eternal being, the creating cause, the determining and final cause of all contingent beings; and this is God. (6) In the being, which prescinds from creatures and from God, which is indeterminate being, and in God, not indeterminate but absolute being, the essence is the same. (7) The indeterminate being of intuition, initial being, is something of the Word, which the mind of the Father distinguishes, not really, but according to reason, from the Word. (25) When the mystery of the Most Blessed Trinity has been revealed, its existence can be demonstrated by merely speculative arguments, negative indeed, and indirect; yet such that through them the truth is brought to philosophic studies, and the proposition becomes scientific like the rest; for if it were denied, the theosophic doctrine of *pure reason* would not only remain incomplete, but would also be annihilated, teeming with absurdities on every side. (26) If the three highest forms of *being*, namely subjectivity, objectivity, sanctity; or, reality, ideality, and morality, are transferred to absolute being, they cannot be conceived otherwise than as subsisting and living persons. The Word, insofar as it is the loved object, and insofar as it is the Word, that is, the object subsisting in itself, known by itself, is the person of the Holy Spirit. (27) In the humanity of Christ the human will was so taken up by the Holy Spirit in order to cling to objective Being, that is, to the Word, that it (the will) gave over the rule of man wholly to him, and assumed the Word personally, thus uniting with itself human nature. Hence, the human will ceased to be personal in man, and although person is in other men, it remained nature in Christ. (28) In Christian doctrine, the Word, the sign and configuration of God, is impressed on the souls of those who receive the baptism of Christ with faith. The Word, that is,

the sign, impressed on the soul in Christian doctrine, is real Being (infinite) manifest by itself, which we thereupon recognize to be the second person of the Most Blessed Trinity."[2] M. Flick argues that this condemnation—which was without censure—was not based on total consideration of R's works and thought.[3]

[1]Bibliography ed. C. Bergamaschi, 2 vols, Milan, 1967; *Theodicy*, 3 vols tr. F. Segnini, London, 1912; Works, *Opere edite e inedite*, Rome 1934f; 30 vols thus far; 13 vols (700 pp) letters; C. Caviglione, *Enciclopedia italiana*, XXX (1936), 123–26; G. Bozzetti, *EC* X, (1953), 1359–71; A. Michel, *DTC* 13, 2, 2917–52; A. Hilckmann, *LTK* 9, 53–55; *RGG*[5] V 1188–89; D. Cleary, *NCE*, XII, 677–79; C. Leetham, *Rosmini, Priest, Patriot, Philosopher*, New York, 1957; [2]DS 3204–3210; [3]*Gregorianum*, 40 (1959), 564f.

RUYSBROECK, JAN VAN (1293–1381)

The Flemish mystic whose doctrine was criticised by John Gerson and whose language Bossuet found "strange" and "exorbitant," has been nonetheless beatified by the Church.[1] But the Church did not adopt his language; it did accept that of Tertullian (*qv*), though he died outside its communion. The problem with R. is that some of his expressions give the notion of instability in the divine Persons: they seem, in his view, to constitute a phase—dialectical according to his exposition—between an initial impersonal existence and a final depersonalization—this to emphasize the essence and the abiding unity. Does he sacrifice the eternity of the Persons? Not, it would appear, in his own personal belief, but in the minds of some readers: an effect not unconnected with his obscure style. Unlike Eckhart he has not come under ecclesiastical censure. The general quality of his principal work, *The Spiritual Espousals*, which did not impress Gerson, has won great praise from others.

[1]Cf. P. Henry, "La Mystique trinitaire du Bienheureux J. Ruysbroeck," *RSR* 40 (1952), 335–368; 41 (1953), 51–75; B. de Margerie, S.J., *La Trinité dans l'histoire*, 339–345.

S

SABELLIANISM

Little is known of Sabellius. He may have been Roman, though St. Basil, who refers frequently to him, thought him Libyan—he was active in Rome, his views popular in the Pentapolis of about the third century. He espoused Monarchianism of a Modalist kind (see MODALISM). In the literature the word Sabellianism, often used, encapusulated denial of separate Persons in the Trinity.

SCHEEBEN, MATTHIAS JOSEPH (1835–1888)

The great German theologian dealt with the Trinity in the course of his *Handbuch der katholischen Dogmatik*, dealing with the NT witness and the history; he treated of the dogma and offered some theological considerations, stressing by way of conclusion that the external temporal mission was based on the eternal origin, without prejudice to their unity and their equality; he also saw the intrinsic value of analogy (*qv*) in Trinitarian theology.[1] S., in his book *Natur und Gnade*, (its ideas popularized in *Die Herrlichkeiten der gottlichen Gnade*) propounded the thesis of the indwelling of the Trinity in the soul possessed of divine grace.[2] Such ideas would not make S. singular. This his *Mysterien des Christentums* does (esp. read in the second edition, which he had prepared but which was only fully written from his notes by Joseph Huber in 1941). His treatment of the nine mysteries puts such emphasis on the Trinity that it may be said to be central to his theological reflection as here expressed. Adding to the part which deals with the Trinity the section in part four (The Mystery of the Godman and his Economy) on the Godman in his relations with the Trinity and as Mediator between the Trinitarian God and the world, and some pages on the Eucharist and the Trinity in the part dealing with the Sacrament, it emerges that the theme takes up much more than one quarter of the whole work.

But it is not the quantity of what S. writes on the subject that bears notice. It is the intuition he has of the relevance of the Trinity to the world and to human life, possibly we should now say his reading of the problem of the "economic" and the immanent Trinity: "The Trinity of divine persons proves to be the root of the order of grace in this sense, too. It thrusts the branches of its interior organism into the organism which is modeled upon it; that is, it exhibits itself in the order of grace as a prolongation of the eternal productions and processions, and really introduces their eternal products into the creature that is endowed with grace. As has to some extent been indicated, we find many expressions in Holy Scripture and the Fathers which certainly imply more than a mere imitation of the eternal productions and products in the creature. They speak of a real sojourn of the Son of God in us, whereby he is reborn in us, and especially of an interior light he confers upon us, in which he manifests the Father to us. But above all we are confronted throughout the entire New Testament with the idea of an outpouring of the Holy Spirit into creatures, whereby he dwells in creatures and unites them with the divine persons from whom he proceeds. Viewed thus, the relation of the Trinity to the outer world is clearly perceived to be much closer and more intimate, and its significance for that world far greater and richer in consequences."[3]

S. concludes a profound series of reflections on the Godman in his relation with the Trinity with this remark: "Therefore the incarnation of the Son most magnificently and impressively extends and reveals to the outer world God's glorification of himself in the Trinity".[4] He continues this theme in dealing with the Eucharist: "And, as the mysteries of grace and glory are inextricably interwoven with the mysteries of the Trinity and the Incarnation, the same is necessarily true of the Eucharist. As concerns the Trinity, we have already remarked that the oneness of substance and life existing between the Father and the Son is transmitted to us and reproduced in us most perfectly by the Eucharist. In particular the Eucharist is the agency that effects the real and perfect mission of the divine persons to the outer world. Above all it crowns the Son's mission to us on earth. For in the Eucharist the Son unites himself to us in the most perfect way, to give us in general the power to become sons of God, and also to make us one Son of God by incorporating us in himself. In the Eucharist we likewise perceive the real and intimate mission of the Holy Spirit. For, since the Holy Spirit, the Spirit of the Son, is really united to the Son's body, in which he reposes and dwells, he also comes to us in this same body, to unite himself to us as our own. In the body of the Logos, which is filled with the Holy Spirit, we receive the Holy Spirit himself, as it were, from the breast and heart of the Logos whence he proceeds."[5]

S. also attempted a synthesis between Trinitarian theology and his singular concept of the bridal motherhood of Mary (qv): "Further, the bringing into prominence of the person of the Holy Spirit in the principle and term of the marriage causes the union of Mary with God to appear, not as specifically limited to the person of her Son, and still less to that of the Father, but as extending to the entire Trinity."[6] The idea is developed and applied with all the author's speculative power. His *Mariology*, given to a wide public in the forties of the present century, found a ready response; so did the *Mysteries of Christianity*, a unique achievement for a nineteenth century work of this scope, on such a theme.

[1]*Gesammelte Schriften*, ed. J. Hofer, 8 vols, Freiburg i. Brisg.; K. Feckes et al., *M.J. Scheeben*, Mainz, 1935; F.S. Pancheri, O.F.M., *Il pensiero teologico di M.J. Scheeben e S.Tommasso*, 1956, with bibl.; E. Paul, *Denkweg und Denkform der Theologie von Matthias Joseph Scheeben*, Munich, 1970; G. Fritz, *DTC* XIV, 1 (1939), 1270–74; A. Piolanti, *EC* XI (1953), 33f; J. Hofer, *LTK* IX (1964), 376–9; [2]*Nature and Grace*, Tr. C. Vollert, S.J., St. Louis, London, 1954; [3]*The Mysteries of Christianity*, tr. C. Vollert, St. Louis, London, 1954, VI, 26, p. 147; [4]*Ibid.*, 361; [5]*Ibid.*, 528; [6]*Mariology*, Eng. tr., I, St. Louis, London, 1946, 177.

SCHLEIERMACHER, FRIEDRICH D.E. (1768–1834)

In the line of Kant and Hegel (qv) S. found it impossible to deal with the Trinity save as a second-level construct made of elements in the feeling of religion; but feeling had for him a profound sense, something akin to intuition. He relegated the subject to an appendix at the end of his book, *The Christian Faith*; he did not think that it had a place in a Christian Dogmatic, as he understood this. S. sees Christology as the centre of his theological system, a Christology without a Trinity. He does offer suggestions, tending towards symbolism, of how the traditional Trinitarian language may be used, but without entering the depth of the mystery of the inner godhead.[1]

[1]*The Christian Faith*, ed. H.R. Mackintosh and J.S. Stewart, Edinburgh, 1928, 2 vols; "On the Discrepancy between the Sabellian and Athanasian Method of Representing the Doctrine of the Trinity," *The Biblical Repository and Quarterly Observer* 5 (1835) 265–353, 6 (1835) 1–116; cf. W.J. Hill, *The Three-Personed God*, 84–91.

SENTIMENT OF THE FAITHFUL, THE

If the Trinity is to enter into the consciousness of the faithful as a dynamic ideal it will help very considerably to clarify the role which the faithful themselves have in the transmission of divine revelation about the Trinity (see DEVOTION). The faithful, which means the laity, participate in the prophetic or teaching role of the Church. There has been a different approach to a somewhat complex phenomenon through the centuries: in the Middle Ages the emphasis was on the sense of the faith; in the sixteenth century thought was of the sentiment of the faithful or of the Church, whereas recently it is given to the faith of the Christian people, the common faith of the Church. The general truth that the faithful join with the teaching authority in maintaining the faith of the Church is of biblical and patristic origin. The faithful are not mere passive recipients, nor, at the other extreme, an autonomous source. The Church teaching and the Church that is taught complement each other; at times the weight of the latter has been salutary and corrective. Newman maintained that it was the faithful who saved the day in the Arian crisis (see ARIANISM).[1]

---

[1]for bibliography cf. art. Sentiment of the Faithful in *Theotokos*, by M. O'Carroll, C.S.Sp., 322–23.

SON OF GOD

Jesus Christ, known and fully accepted for centuries by his followers as the eternal Son of God, the inspiration of countless lives, the theme of artistic and literary masterpieces of surpassing power, the subject of contemplation by the noblest spirits in history, the ideal for whom men and women have lived and died even to the shedding of their blood in agony as varied as the ingenuity of malice could invent, loved to the limit of heroism by the untutored and the giants of learning, equally cherished by those with the unspoiled innocence of youth and the mature wisdom of old age, the Lord of history and the physician of souls broken or wounded by sin, the shining exemplar of virtue, the inexhaustible source of compassion, the plenitude of divine revelation—one may continue without exhausting the imponderable mystery, in mere terms of human history, of this man who began life as a village tradesman and finally stamped his image and ideas on the intimate mind of all mankind. We are, in recent times, faced with a vast literature on him, so much so that at times he seems to disappear behind the accumulation of books, articles, memoranda. If one speaks or writes of Jesus Christ, the Son of God, one is supposed to seek a way through this mass of print—

let that be said with deep respect for genuine scholarship.[1]

We begin with the biblical witness. Jesus does not in the synoptic gospels call himself the Son of God; he does call himself the Son of Man. Others do call him the Son of God (9 times in Mt, 5 in Mk, 6 in Lk). It is clear that his own conviction on the subject was the source of this belief: this conviction is insinuated strongly in the contrast between the servants and the son, the heir in the parable of the vinedressers (Mk 12:1–12), in the use of "my Father" to point to the different relationship he enjoyed with God from that of the disciples, marked by use of "your Father" (Mt 7:21; 10:32,33; 11:27; 12:50; Lk 2:49; 10:22). He never refers to God as "our Father", though the disciples are to address him thus. An important passage is Mt 11:27, which runs thus: "All things have been delivered to me by my Father; and no one knows the Son except the Father; nor does anyone know the Father except the Son, and him to whom the Son chooses to reveal him."

R.E. Brown asks "What right has the exegete to assume that 'my Father' implies a more intimate relationship to God than 'your Father' implies?"[2] The same writer also points out that 'my Father' in frequent occurrence is characteristic of Matthew, with no parallels for any of Matthaean usages; Mark never uses "my Father", Luke only four times.

Brown does not see any help to a solution in Jesus' use of *Abba* (qv). J. Jeremias drew attention to this "fact of fundamental importance. *We do not have a single example* of God being addressed as *Abba* in Judaism, but Jesus *always* addressed God in this way in his prayers. The only exception is the cry from the cross (Mk 15:34, Mt 27:46) and the reason for that is its character as a quotation."[3] Brown does, however, concede that "one may suspect that if Jesus presented himself as the first of many to stand in a new and special relationship to God as Father, that very claim implies that his sonship was in some way superior to the sonship of all who would follow him."[4]

There are other passages in the synoptics. There is the confession of Peter in Mt 16:16, which O. Cullmann, against a number of modern commentators, accepts as genuine, though he would place it elsewhere. Cullmann, following J. Bieneck, thinks that the words of praise addressed to Peter—"Blessed are you, Simon Bar-Jona! For flesh and blood has not revealed this to you, but my Father who is in heaven"—are related to the confession of faith in Jesus' divine sonship: an echo of "no one knows the Son only the Father" previously quoted.

The title was proclaimed in most solemn manner in the Baptism of Christ and again in the Transfiguration—this one may state without agreeing with those who think that it was at Baptism that Jesus learned that he was the Son of God—how then explain his reply to his Mother when he was twelve years old: "Did you not know that I must be in my Father's house" (Lk 2:49).

Still staying with the Synoptics one must offer for discussion the texts from the narratives of the trial: "Again the high priest questioned him. He said, 'Are you the Christ, the Son of the Blessed?' Jesus said, 'I am. And you will see the Son of Man seated at the right hand of the Almighty, and coming on the clouds of heaven.' Then the high priest, tearing his clothes, said, 'What further need do we have of witnesses? You have heard the blasphemy; how does it seem to you?'" (Mk 14:61–64); "They (the Sanhedrin) said, 'If you are the Christ, tell us.' But he said to them, 'You will not believe me if I tell you; neither will you answer if I question you. But from now on the Son of Man will be seated at the right hand of God Almighty.' They all said, 'Are you then the Son of God?' He said to them, 'You say that I am.' They said, 'What need do we still have of testimony? We have personally heard it from his own lips.'" (Lk 22:67–71). "Son of God" for the Sanhedrin implied a unique relationship, far beyond any messianic claim.

"The Holy One of God" (Mk 1:24) belongs to the same category as "Son of God." Interestingly Mk uses it as he opens his gospel with the words "The beginning of the gospel of Jesus Christ, the Son of God" (1:1); as he recalls towards the end the centurion's confession: "Truly this man was the Son of God" (15:39). Are we then justified, despite the rarity of the title in Mark, in assenting to the judgment: "As scholars have often observed, the intention of the whole gospel is apparently to show in all the events it reports that Jesus is the (first of all hidden) Son of God. In opposition to Wrede's thesis, we have shown that this hiddenness can be explained by Jesus' own reserve."[6]

When we turn to the gospel of John and to the epistles of Paul we have more subtle problems of exegesis, but with a result that is massively positive. In John from chapter 5 Jesus asserts in many ways his oneness with the Father. He repeatedly says that the Father sent him, or that he came from the Father. "I and the Father are one" (10:30); "The Father is in me and I am in the Father" (10:38). His sonship thus links up with the *Logos* (*qv*) of the prologue: "before Abraham was, I am" he says to make the point more explicit. He and the Jews put the matter beyond all doubt: "do you say of him whom the Father consecrated and sent into the world, 'You are blaspheming' because I said, 'I am the Son of God'?" (10:36). With which compare, "The Jews answered him (Pilate), 'We have a law and by that law he ought to die, because he has made himself the Son of God'" (10:36).

Why the need for subtlety in face of these utterances? Out of respect for Johannine scholars who seek to discern the hard core of logia deriving directly from Jesus.

With Paul we have also need to respect scholarly reticence or diverging opinions. *Kyrios* is the characteristic word used by the Apostle of the Gentiles to convey the unique status of the risen Christ. "Therefore God has highly exalted him and bestowed on him the name which is above every name (that is, Yahweh), that at the name of Jesus every knee should bow, in heaven and on earth and under the earth, and every tongue confess that Jesus Christ is Lord (*Kyrios*) to the glory of God the Father" (Phil: 2:9–11).

How is this lordship to be understood? Like Yahweh's in OT it is associated with creative power (1 Cor 8:16; Col 1:13–17); he is the "first-born of all creation" (Col 1:15). The important text in Gal 4·4 speaks of the preexistence and the sonship: "But when the time had fully come, God sent forth his Son, born of a woman, born under the law." Paul tells us that Christ was in the form of God from the beginning (Phil 2:6). He puts the Son on the same level as the Father in the Trinitarian texts (Eph 4:4–6; 1 Cor 12:4–6; 2 Cor 13:14).

The Son of God concept is dominant in the epistle to the Hebrews. One text is typical: "Since then we have a great high priest who has passed through the heavens, Jesus, the Son of God, let us hold fast our confession" (4:14). As the *Logos* and Son of God coincide in John, the Christology of the High Priest is in Hebrews united fruitfully with that of the Son of God.

With this starting-point in biblical revelation it is not surprising that the whole relationship of

Father and Son was in subsequent centuries the object of much reflection. The syntheses elaborated by Athanasius and the Cappadocians in the east, by Hilary and Augustine in the west, with the final classic doctrine of St. Thomas Aquinas, could all constantly appeal to the NT elements which would be their irreplaceable guarantee, the undeniable constituents of Trinitarian doctrine.

[1]Besides bibl. of articles "Logos" and "Pre-existence of Christ" cf. L. Cerfaux, *Christ in the Theology of St. Paul*, London, 1959; X. Léon-Dufour, S.J., *Les evangiles et l'histoire de Jésus*, Paris, 1963 (Eng. tr. *The Gospels and the Jesus of History*, 1971); E. Schillebeeckx, O.P., *Christ the Sacrament*, London, 1963; W. Marxsen, *Anfangsprobleme der Christologie*, Gütersloh, 1960; H. Ristow/K.Matthiae, *Der historische Jesus und der kerygmatische Christus*, Berlin, 1960; R. Bultmann, *Jesus*, Tübingen, 1961; F. Hahn, *Christologische Hoheitstitel. Ihre Geschichte im frühen Christentum*, Göttingen, 1963; R.H. Fuller, *The Foundations of New Testament Christology*, London, 1965; M. Hengel, *Der Sohn Gottes, Die Entstehung der Christologie und die jüdisch-hellenistische Religionsgeschichte*, Tübingen, 1975; W.G. Kummel, "Jesusforschung seit 1950," *Theol.Rundschau* N.F. 31 (1965/66), 15–46; W. Trilling, *Fragen zur Geschichtlichkeit Jesu*, Düsseldorf, 1966; H.R. Balz, *Methodische Probleme der neutestamentlischen Christologie*, Neukirchen-Vluyn, 1967; E. Schweizer, *Jesus Christus im vielfältigen Zeugnis des Neuen Testaments*, Munich, 1968; J. Gnilka, *Jesus Christus nach den frühen Zeugnissen des Glaubens*, Munich, 1970; J. Jeremias, *New Testament Theology*, I, London, 1971; G. Schneider, *Die Frage nach Jesus Christ—Aussagen des Neuen Testaments*, Essen, 1971; H. Schürmann, *Das Geheimnis Jesu. Versuche zur Jesusfrage*, Leipzig, 1972; C. Duquoc, *Christologie, essai dogmatique* I, *L'Homme Jésus*, Paris, 1968; II, *Le Messie*, 1972; id., *Jesus, homme libre esquisse d'une christologie*, Paris, 1972; C.H. Dodd, *The Founder of Christianity*, London, 1975; symposium, *Les Quatre fleuves*, IV, Paris, 1975, 13 contributors, *Le Christ, Visage de Dieu*; J. Sobrino, S.J., *Christology at the Crossroads*, London, 1976; W. Kasper, *Jesus der Christus*, Mainz, 1978 (Engl. tr.) W. Thusing, *Die neutestamentlichen Theologien und Jesus Christus*, I, Düsseldorf, 1981; P. Benoît, O.P., "La divinite dé Jésus," *Exégèse et Théologie* I, Paris, 1961, 117–142; [2]*Jesus God and Man*, 88; [3]*Op.cit.*, 66; [4]*Op.cit.*, 90; [5]O. Cullmann, *The Christology of the New Testament*, 294.

SPIRIT, THE HOLY

The third person of the Trinity. If the doctrine of the Spirit has long been a cinderella of theology, a gigantic effort has been made in very recent times to effect the needed change.[1] Especially within the Catholic Church since Vatican II (qv), intellectual interest has been concentrated on the theme, with an ample literature as one evident effect. Marian theologians were attracted to the theme of Mary (qv) and the Spirit as a logical consequence of ideas which emerged in the final session. In the interval between the third and fourth sessions of the Council, Orthodox dissatisfaction with the conciliar doctrine on the Spirit was firmly stated.[2] In the rewriting of two important texts—"On the ministry and life of priests" and "On the missionary activity of the Church," some elements of doctrine on the Spirit were included, partly in a Marian context, within which there had, in the promulgated text on the Church, also been some references to the Spirit.[3] One may discuss the question of the Council's teaching on the theme. Altogether there are 258 references to the Spirit in the sixteen documents promulgated; but, leaving out those issued during the fourth session, what synthesis could one fashion from these scattered allusions? How many were nominal?

Nonetheless the stimulus was given to research and reflection, and the rapid expansion of the charismatic movement was a further incentive. We have every reason to welcome such things. Study is pursued with strict attention to scientific method. This means beginning with the Old Testament. Here the spirit, *ruah*, originally the wind and the breath, is the dynamic force by which Yahweh works. Especially he works by his spirit in the prophets, inspiring them: "The Spirit of the Lord God is upon me, because the Lord has anointed me to bring good tidings to the afflicted; he has sent me to bind up the broken-hearted, to proclaim liberty to the captives, and the opening of the prison to those who are bound; to proclaim the year of the Lord's favour, and the day of vengeance of our God . . ." (Is 61:1–2). The Spirit of Yahweh is a charismatic Spirit given to those who hold office, judges, kings, eventually to be poured out on the whole messianic people: but especially on the messianic king (Is 11:2) and on the servant of the Lord (Is 42:1).

There is a wealth of material on the Spirit in NT: at decisive moments such as the conception of the Saviour (Mt 1:18–20), his baptism (Mt 3:13–17; Mk 1:9–11), his identification as the Messiah (Lk 4:16–21; Is 11:1ff); especially in the Lucan works, the gospel and Acts, the Spirit has manifold functions. Mgr. G. Philips, draftsman of the Marian chapter of the Constitution on Church with Fr. K. Balič, O.F.M., admitted that much more could have been made in the text of the Spirit in the mysteries of Jesus' infancy. In the final satisfactory synthesis which we await on the Spirit in NT, attention will no doubt be given to the relationship between certain personalities and the Spirit: John the Baptist (Lk 1:15), Zechariah

(1:67), Simeon (Lk 2:26, 27), Peter and the other apostles at and after Pentecost (Acts passim), Paul, and especially Mary (Lk 1:35; Acts 1:14). Mary presents the unique case of: a) a double reception of the Spirit; and b) an apparent assumption that after the initial outpouring promised in Lk 1:35 she is his inseparable associate. Lk states explicitly that others, in the infancy mysteries, are moved by the Spirit, e.g. Zechariah and Simeon, but he does not find it necessary to say this about Mary—in regard to the Visitation of Elizabeth, the Magnificat, the birth of Jesus, the Finding in the Temple, the perpetual custody of the word of God (Lk 2:19, 51).

The Russian expatriate theologian, Sergius Bulgakov, went so far as to say, in this context, that "the Annunciation was a complete and therefore hypostatic descent of the Holy Spirit and his entry to the Virgin Mary. By his coming into the Virgin Mary the Holy Spirit identifies himself in a way with her through her God-motherhood . . . . He does not at all leave her after the birth of Christ, but remains forever with her in the full force of the Annunciation."[4] "He abides, however, in the ever-Virgin Mary as in a holy temple while her human personality seems to become transparent to him and to provide him with a human personality."[5]

A french theologian, H M Manteau-Bonamy, O.P., commenting on the doctrine of Vatican II, contended that for the first time in the Latin Church, the Council taught a visible mission of the Holy Spirit on the Blessed Virgin Mary at the Annunciation. He had in mind especially the passage in the Decree on the Missionary Activity of the Church where Pentecost, the Baptism of Christ and the Annunciation are placed on the same theological level: "The 'Acts of the Apostles' began with Pentecost, just as Christ was conceived in the Virgin Mary with the coming of the Holy Spirit and was moved to begin his ministry by the descent of the same Holy Spirit, who came down upon him while he was praying."[6] The present writer supports this view, as he does that of Sergius Bulgakov, the uniqueness of Christ's hypostatic union being safeguarded.

This is a long way from the biblical exegesis of those who, with the possible exception of Mt 28:19, deny that NT speaks of the Spirit as a person; they would not agree that he is revealed as a person in the Annunciation. Yet here, because there was a unique recipient, a woman becoming a virgin mother, which had never been seen in OT narratives, there was in her womb the visible sign of a divine mission, a new human being without the cooperation of a man, an effect proclaiming personal action and therefore a divine personality (qv). This is not the prophetic impulse of OT; this is a divine agent fashioning a new creation, which centres on the divine personality incarnate.

The many references to the Spirit in John 14 through 16 prompt J.L. McKenzie, to write: "Here perhaps a distinct personal reality is more explicitly asserted than elsewhere in the NT."[7] Of the 62 references to the Spirit in Acts, 18 describe him in personal terms: he speaks, forbids, thinks good, appoints, sends, bears witness, snatches, prevents, is deceived, tempted and resisted.[8] If the other references mostly have to do with the influence of the Spirit, with people filled with him, acting through or in him, they do not contradict the sense of the passages where he is anthropomorphically, but really, described as a person. Likewise in the First Epistle of Peter the Spirit "testifies" (1:11); several times in the Apocalypse he is said to "speak." In the epistles of St. Paul the Spirit is spoken of as a person: he is grieved, teaches, conducts as a guide, bears witness, cries, leads, makes intercession, as he speaks, is given personal titles like "Comforter" and "Advocate".[9]

Elaboration of a theology of the Spirit occurs in Church history when, with the Arian (qv) debate resolved, an attack was made on the divine personality of the Spirit by the Pneumatomachians. The Cappadocians reacted strongly, though the precise force of Basil's (qv) contribution, in the De Spiritu Sancto (see article on Doxology) is controverted. He would not call the Spirit God. The issue was settled by the Constantinopolitan (qv) Creed. With some of the Apologists, notably Theophilus of Antioch (qv), to whom we owe the first use of the word Triados, there is a tendency to think of the Spirit as the source of prophecy and not to explore his relationship with the Father and the Logos (qv). Hilary of Poitiers (qv) did not publish a full theory of the Spirit. Augustine (qv), under the influence of Ambrose, himself indebted to Didymus the Blind (a plagiariser according to Jerome), possessed a firm doctrine, and among the medieval theologians there are either formal treatises, independent as with Anselm (qv) or plenary statements inset in larger theological syntheses, as with St. Thomas (qv).

The great spiritual writers, two Frenchmen among them, Lallemand and St. Louis Marie Grignion de Montfort, saw the need for a living theology of the Spirit. A great theologian such as Scheeben (qv) relieves a certain obscurity on the subject through the nineteenth century, though he also could lapse when it came to formulating the essentials of the Church's position.[10] Cardinal Manning's book, *The Internal Mission of the Holy Ghost*, was a solitary contribution in its age; in the present century Mgr. Landrieux could entitle his book on the same subject, *The Forgotten Paraclete* (*Le divin Méconnu*), as Dom Columba Marmion was accustomed to apply to the contemporary spiritual world the word of Acts, "No, we have never even heard that there is a Holy Spirit" (19:2).

Two Popes had made pronouncements on the Holy Spirit, Leo XIII in the Encyclical *Divinum Illud*, 9 May, 1897, and Pius XII in an important section of *Mystici Corporis Christi*, 29 June, 1943. But one cannot speak of a widespread concerted exercise of the teaching authority on the subject. As has been made clear it was Vatican II that triggered the revival, so long overdue, under the influence of an Orthodox theologian. Again it is a case of bringing forth from the treasure "*nova et vetera*,"; a return to the sources will discover immense riches which were neglected.

The bibliography to this article makes it clear that much labour has already been expended on this task. Two contributions may be singled out. Heribert Mühlen in two works of undeniable power has suggested a new approach to the problem of the Spirit's identity.[11] In one book he offers a theory which seeks to prove "one divine consciousness in three distinct but related ways." He suggests a phenomenology of discourse wherein each divine person answers to "I", "Thou" and "We". He substitutes for Richard of St. Victor's preoccupation with love an analysis of discourse based on Dietrich von Hildebrand's phenomenology: the very opposition of "I" and "Thou" releases a new dynamism wherein the two combine into one. There are problems here of safeguarding full distinction of persons, of rightly founding the distinction. While unity is clearly safeguarded, the danger is of one single consciousness emerging as the result of the argument, which critics have pointed out to H. Mühlen. In his other work, again with a laudable intention—of showing the plenary role of the Spirit in the Church—Mühlen relates the indwelling of the Spirit in each of the faithful to his presence in Christ: thus "One Person in many persons" makes *Una Mystica Persona*. Again the unicity of the

Incarnate Word must be safeguarded. As with the other work Mühlen has stirred new reflection, opened new horizons, even if his syntheses need adjustment.

The second notable contribution to our subject has been made by one of the greatest theologians of the age, Fr. Y.M.-J.Congar.[12] Towards the end of a long career as a professional theologian and writer, within sight of his eightieth birthday, he undertook the assembly of a comprehensive, practically exhaustive treasure-house of theological lore from the Bible to our own time on the Holy Spirit: every aspect is considered, every author of any significance presented. It is all marked by the serenity of judgment and the impeccable scholarship which are characteristic of this theologian. No one wishing to further scientific knowledge about the Holy Spirit can ignore this vast corpus.

All study of the Spirit is henceforth enriched by the proceedings of the symposium held in Rome under the patronage of John Paul II, who addressed the participants, to commemorate the sixteenth centenary of the Council of Constantinople (qv), 381–1981. The papers, read by over one hundred speakers, taking 1520 pages, cover every aspect of the subject: scriptural, theological, historical, conciliar, liturgical, patristic, relevance to the world today, with consideration of the non-Christian religions. Many of the themes and theologians, Fathers of the Church and Doctors through the ages, dealt with in the present work, figure in the contents: *Credo in Spirituam Sanctum, Atti del Congréso Internazionale di Pneumatologia*, Vatican City, 1983, 2 vols.

[1]Articles in biblical dictionaries on the Holy Spirit, esp. G. Kittel, *TDNT*, IV, *Pneuma*; esp. *Esprit Saint, DSp*. IV, 1960, 1246–1333 (J. Guillet, S.J., J.Gribomont, O.S.B.,P.Smulders, F.Vandenbrouche, S.Tromp, J.L.Witte); H.B. Swete, *The Holy Spirit in the New Testament*, 1909; id., *The Holy Spirit in the Ancient Church*, 1912; H. Watkin-Jones, *The Holy Spirit in the Mediaeval Church*, 1922; id., *The Holy Spirit from Ariminius to Wesley*, 1929; W.H.G. Thomas, *The Holy Spirit of God*, 1913; T. Rees, *The Holy Spirit in Thought and Experience*, 1915; B.H. Streeter, *The Spirit, God and his Relation to Man considered from the standpoint of Philosophy, Psychology and Art*, 1919; F. Buchsel, *Der Geist Gottes im Neuen Testament*, 1926; H.W. Robinson, *The Christian Experience of the Holy Spirit*, 1928; C.K. Barrett, *The Holy Spirit and the Gospel Tradition*, 1947; J. Guillet, "La révélation progressive du Saint Esprit dans l'Ecriture," *LumV* 8 (1953), 18–32; P. van Imschoot (author of several articles on Spirit in OT), *La théologie de l'Ancien Testament*, 2 vols., Tournai, 1954, 56; F.J. Crump, *Pneuma in the Gospels*, Washington, 1954; J. de Baiocchi, "Comment reconnaître la personnalité du Saint

Esprit?", *NRT* 77 (1955), 1025–49; M.A. Chevalier, *L'Esprit et le Messie dans le bas-judaisme et le Nouveau Testament*, Paris, 1958; id., *Esprit de Dieu, paroles d'hommes*, Neuchâtel, 1966; bibl., Th. Ruesch, *Die Entstehung der Lehre vom Heiligen Geist*, Zurich, 1953; T. Maertens, *Le Soûffle de l'Esprit de Dieu*, Paris, 1959; A.-M. Henry, *L'Esprit Saint*, Paris, 1959; J. Isaac, *La révélation progressive des Personnes divines*, Paris, 1960; H. Opitz, *Ursprünge frühchristlicher Pneumatologie*, Berlin, 1960; A. Orbe, *La teología del Espiritu Sancto*, Rome, 1960; G. Kretchmar, "Le développement de la doctrine du Saint Esprit du Nouveau Testament à Nicée," *Verbum caro*, 88 (1962), 5–55; E. Haulotte, "L'Esprit de Yahvé dans l'Ancien Testament," *L'Homme devant Dieu, Mélanges H.de Lubac*, I, Paris, 1963, 25–36; H. U. von Balthasar, *Spiritus Creator, Skizzen zur Theologie*, III, Einsiedeln, 1968; H. Berkhof, *Theologie des Heiligen Geistes*, Neukirchen, 1968; J.P. Martin, *El Espiritu Santo en los Origenes de Cristianismo. Estudio sobre I Clemente, Ignacio, II Clemente y Justino Martir*, Zurich, 1971; D. Mollat, *L'expérience de l'Esprit Saint selon le Nouveau Testament* 2nd ed. Paris, 1973; J. Moltmann, *Kirche in der Kraft des Geistes. Ein Beitrag zur messianischen Ekklesiologie*, Munich, 1975; W. Kasper/G. Sauter, *Kirche—Ort des Geistes*, Freiburg, Basel, Vienna, 1976; K. Blaser, *Vorstofs zur Pneumatologie*, Zurich, 1977; Joseph (Cardinal) Suenens, *A New Pentecost*, 1975; E. Schweizer, *Heiliger Geist*, Stuttgart, 1978; O.A. Dillschneider, *Geist als Vollender des Glaubens*, Gütersloh, 1978; G.T. Montague, *The Holy Spirit: Growth of a Biblical Tradition*, New York, 1976; W. Harrington, *Spirit of the Living God*, Wilmington, 1977; X. Pikaza, "Maria y el Espiritu Santo," *EstTrin*, XV (1981), 3–81; [2]Especially by N. Nissiotis, "The Main Ecclesiological Problems in the Second Vatican Council and the Position of the Non-Roman Churches Facing It," *The Ecumenical Review*, 2 (1965), 31–62, esp. 48; 3. Cf. art. "Spirit, the Holy," in *Theotokos*, M. O'Carroll, C.S.Sp., 329–332; bibl.; [4]*Le Paraclet*, Paris, 1946, 238–239; [5]*The Wisdom of God*, London, 1937, 176; [6]*Decree on the Missionary Activity of the Church*, 4; [7]*Dictionary of the Bible*, 845; [8]A.W. Wainright, *The Trinity in the New Testament*, 200, 201; [9]*Ibid.*; [10]On Scheeben's view that the Eucharist, Mary and the Holy See are the binding links of the true Church, cf. Congar, *The Holy Spirit*, I, 160ff; [11]*Der Heilige Geist als Person*, 2nd ed, Münster, 1966; *Una Mystica Persona. Eine Person in vielen Personen*, Paderborn, 1964; cf. J. Bracken, "The Holy Trinity as a Community of Divine Persons," *Heythrop Journal*, 15 (1974), 166–82; 257–70; W.J. Hill, *The Three-Personed God, The Trinity as a Single Shared Consciousness*: H. Mühlen, 232–237; Congar, *The Holy Spirit*, I; [12]*Je crois en l'Esprit Saint*, I, *L'expérience de l'Esprit*; II *Il est Seigneur et Il donne la vie*; III *Le Fleuve de Vie coule en orient et en occident*; Paris, 1979, '80; *Eng. tr.*, New York, London, 1983.

SUBORDINATIONISM

A theory about the Trinity which sees the Son as in some way less than or inferior to the Father, or the Holy Spirit as subordinate to both.[1] In the second and third centuries Christian thinkers at grips with the intellectual problems raised by the Scriptures, especially by the *Logos* (*qv*) and other Johannine texts, seeking for solutions without the clearly defined mental categories needed, spoke or wrote a language which betrays this want, which can easily be used to justify the charge of subordinationism. One recent writer has taxed practically all the ante-Nicene authors with a degree of the error—if one can speak of degrees of error:[2] Justin (*qv*), Tatian, Athenagoras (*qv*), Theophilus of Antioch, Tertullian (*qv*), Hippolytus (*qv*), Novatian (*qv*), Clement of Alexandria (*qv*). Beginning from the subordinationism of Lucian of Antioch (*qv*), Arius (*qv*) eventually developed his own system of which it is a determining component.

A facile, superficial reading of biblical texts which show that the Father is the one from whom all things come (1 Cor 8:6; Col 1:17; Heb 1:3; Jn 1:3), whereas the Son is the one through whom they come, or again of those which say the Son is the Word (Jn 1:1, 18), the wisdom of God (1 Cor 1:24), the image of God (2 Cor 4:4; Col 1:15—harking back also to OT texts such as Prov 8:22f; Ps 32:6; Gen 1) could be gravely misleading. A conclusion that the Son came of a voluntary decision of the Father to help him in creating and ruling the universe would be heresy. The substance of the Father and the substance of the Son, the Council of Nicaea would affirm, are one. This identity precludes any possibility of the Son depending on an act of the Father's will.

As to dismissal of the ante-Nicene authors as tained with subordinationism, we do well to heed the wise words of Bernard Lonergan (*qv*); "If the term, subordinationism, is used to describe a certain fact, namely that the ante-Nicene authors were not well up in the theology of a later age, then of course its use is both legitimate and useful. For before anything can be understood and explained, one must know precisely what is to be understood and explained. On the other hand, if we consider the proper goal of scientific inquiry, which is understanding, then the term, subordinationism, becomes a source of the greatest obscurity and confusion. For it is anachronistic to conceive the doctrine of the ante-Nicene authors according to the criteria of a later theology; and anachronism precludes correct historical understanding."[3]

---

[1]Cf. G. Aeby, *Les missions divines de Justin à Origéne*, Fribourg (Switzerland), 1958; A. Orbe, *Hacia la primera teología de la procesion del Verbo*, Rome, 1958; B. Lonergan, S.J., *The Way to Nicaea*, London, 1976, 40–42; W.J. Hill, *The Three-personed God*, Washington, 1982, 37–41 (Origen); esp. W. Marcus, *Der Subordinationismus*, Munich, 1963; [2]G. Aeby, *op.cit.*, 14, 15, 23, 68, 97, 106, 130; [3]B. Lonergan, *op.cit.*, 41.

T

TERTULLIAN (d. after 200)

The great African fashioned the Latin language of the Trinity, and many of his words and phrases remained permanently in use: the words *Trinitas* and *persona*, the formulas "one substance in three persons," "God from God, Light from Light."[1] He uses the word *substantia* 400 times, as he uses *consubstantialis* and *consubstantivus*, but hasty conclusions cannot be drawn from usage, for he does not apply the words to Trinitarian theology. He had a Stoic background, not the decided forensic ideas Harnack thought.

In the *Apologeticum*, written before T. joined the Montanists, he gives an idea of his position on the relationship of Father and Son: "We say that God has brought forth this spirit and in bringing him forth he begot him, and that, for this reason, he is called the Son of God and God, because of the unity of the substance; for God also is spirit . . . . Thus what came forth from God is God, the Son of God and the two are but one."[2]

It was, however, in the *Adversus Praxean* that T. came to grips with the problems of Trinitarian theology. In his thinking the "economy" has a very important place: "We believe in one only God, yet subject to this dispensation, which is our word for economy, that the one only God has also a Son, his Word, who has issued (*processerit*) out of himself, through whom all things were made and without whom nothing was made (cf. Jn 1:3). He

was sent from the Father into the virgin and born of her, man and God, son of man and Son of God, and named Jesus Christ . . . as if thus also the one could not be all, since all are from the one, namely, through the unity of substance; while at the same time the mystery of the divine economy should be safeguarded, which of the unity makes a trinity, placing the three in order not of quality but of sequence, different not in substance but in aspect, not in power but in manifestation; all of one substance, however, of one quality and of one power, because the phases, the aspects, the manifestations, are all of the one God, in the name of the Father and the Son and the Holy Spirit."[3]

Was T. a binitarian in theology before he joined the Montanists? In *De Praescriptione*, 36, and in *De Virginibus Velandis*, 1, formulae are used which on first reading seem to allow this interpretation. His best commentator exonerates him.[4] He clarifies things also in regard to the meaning of *persona*, not with T. a fully elaborated concept, as in later thinking. T. has been accused of tritheism (*qv*) by Harnack,[5] whereas J. Tixeront, a historian of dogma, thought that he was already expounding the consubstantial (*qv*)[6].

There is little doubt about the meaning of these assertions: "Two we specify the Father and the Son, and then three with the Holy Spirit, from the principle of the economy which gives the number"[7] "And the Father is God, the Son is God and the Holy Spirit is God, and each is God."[8] "The second person is his Word (*sermo*) and the third the Spirit in the Word."[9] T. used *per Filium* in regard to the procession of the Spirit (see FILIOQUE).

T. uses imagery to express his ideas: "For God brought forth the Word, as the Paraclete also teaches, as the root brings forth the shoot, as the spring brings forth the stream, as the sun brings the beam. And these manifestations are emissions of those substances from which they proceed. And I would not hesitate to say that the shoot is the son of the root, the stream the son of the spring, the beam the son of the sun; because every source is a parent and everything that is brought forth from a source is its offspring. Much more is true of the Word of God, who received the name of the Son in the proper sense."[10]

It would be unfair to ask from a second century writer the development of ideas which the clash of minds a century and a quarter later would effect. Thus he writes: "Because God is Father and God is judge, nevertheless not that he was always father and judge because he was always God. For he could not be father before there was a son, nor judge before there was a crime. There was a time when there was neither sin to make God a judge nor a son to make God a father."[11]

Not everyone has reacted against this phrasing as strongly as Petavius.[12] Though the phrasing is defective T's idea seems to have been that there was a time when the Word had not been manifested outside God. How does one explain T's use of the word "*portio*" to describe the character of the Son? "This does not properly mean 'part' (*pars*). The Son is not a 'part' of the divine substance, but has a 'share' in it. The Father possesses the *substantiae plenitudo*, the Son is a *portio* and as such has a share in this fullness. The divine substance is essentially one; the Son is, as it were, an effluence of this one substance: *Pater enim tota substantia est, filius vero derivatio totius et portio*."[13] "With regard to him (the *Logos*), we are taught that he is derived (*prolatum*) from God and begotten by derivation (*prolatione*) so that he is the Son of God and called God because of the unity of the substance."[14]

Was T. then a subordinationist? The view has been held from time to time and latterly by a competent scholar.[15] Some of his sentences are less than clear, as when he says of the Father and Son "the one commanding what is to be done the other doing what has been commanded."[16] In such statements he seems to contradict his own basic thesis. He also used the word *monarchia* without incurring heretical monarchianism. For him the will of God towards salvation is the guarantee of the *monarchia*, the norm of the Son's work, the ground of the existence of the Son and the Spirit.

[1]Works CCL, I–II; CSEL 20, 47, 70, 76 etc.; cf. A. d'Ales, *La théologie de Tertullian*, Paris, 1905, 67–103; M. Kriebel, *Studien zur älteren Entwicklung der abendländischen Trinitätslehre bei Tertullian und Novatian*, Ohlau i. Schl, 1932, 95ff., J.M. Restrepo-Jaramillo, "Tertullián y la doble fórmula en el símbolo apostólico," *Greg* 15 (1934), 3–58; J.F. Bethune-Baker, *The Meaning of Homoousios in the 'Constantinopolitan' Creed, Texts and Studies*, VII, 1, Cambridge, 1901; G. Aeby, *Les missions divines de saint Justin à Origène*, Fribourg (Switzerland), 1958, 68ff; Th. L. Verhoeuven, *Studien over Tertullianus' Adversus Praxean*, Amsterdam, 1948; R. Braun, *'Deus Christianorum', Recherches sur le vocabulaire doctrinal de Tertullien*, Paris, 1962; G.C. Stead, "Divine Substance in Tertullian," *JTS*, 14 (1963), 46–66; B. Piault, "Tertullian a-t-il été subordinatien?", *RSPT*, 47 (1963), 181–204; S. Otto, *'Natura' und 'dispositio'. Untersuchung zum Naturbegriff und zur Denkform Tertullians*, Munich, 1960; K. Wolfl, *Das Heilswirken Gottes durch den Sohn nach Tertullian*, Rome, 1960, 35–117; *esp*, J. Moingt, *Théologie trinitaire de Tertullien*, 3 vols, Paris, 1966; *idem*, "Théologie trinitaire de Tertullien," *RSR* 54 (1960), 337–369; B. de Margerie, S.J., *La Trinité chrétienne*, 121–27; B. Lonergan, S.J., *Nicaea*, 43–47; W.J. Hill, *The Three-Personed God*, Washington, 1982, 34–37; G. Bardy, *DTC*, 15, 1, 147–151; *ibid.*, 2, 1633ff.; Quasten, II, 266–340; Altaner, 148–63; M. Pellegrino, *E.C.*, 11, 2025–33; Kelly, *Doctrines*, 111–115; Fliche-Martin, III, 680–683 (J. Lebreton); A. Qulquarelli in *Semanas de Estudios Trinitarios*, VII, Salamanca, Secretaria Trinitaria, 141–187; [2]*Apol.*, 21; [3]*Adv. Prax.*, 2; [4]J. Moingt, *op.cit.*, I, 81ff; [5]*Dogmengeschichte*, I, 577, n. 2; II, 298, n. 1; [6]*Histoire des Dogmes* I (1915), 401–402; [7]*Adv. Prax*, 13; [8]*Ibid.*; [9]*Adv. Prax.*, 12; [10]*Ibid.*, 8; [11]*Adv Hermonegem*, 3; [12]*Theol. dog. de Trinitate*, I, 5, 2; [13]*Adv. Prax.*, 9; [14]*Apol.*, 21; [15]G. Aeby, *op.cit.*; [16]*Adv. Prax.*, 12.

THEOPHANES OF NICAEA (d. 1381)

T.'s work *Sermo in Sanctissimam Deiparam*, first published in 1935 by M. Jugie, A.A. (*qv*), contains one of the most daring syntheses ever composed on Mary, the Blessed Trinity and the created universe.[1] Fr. Jugie thought T. the greatest writer on Mary's universal mediation. It is the section wherein Mary's relations with each of the divine Persons is considered that interests us in the present work. Mary is united with the Father through the Son common to each.[2] Through this union there is one and the same divine grace and energy of the Son and Mother which through her reaches us—an idea borrowed indirectly from St. Maximus the Confessor (qv). Mary has become the place of the new sacrifice, to the High Priest alone accessible. The living tabernacle of the Mother of God is the Holy of Holies, whence light reaches those outside. In regard to the Son, T. thinks that Mary stands towards him, but analogously, as the Son to the Father. He enters into a profound analysis of the union of Mother and Son which, while safeguarding the difference between creature and Creator, establishes the truth of a unique relationship. With the Holy Spirit (qv) her relationship is seen from the very first moment of her life, when she was conceived of sterile parents—a frequent idea among the early Byzantines—as very close. Her conception was a type of the conception of Jesus; the Holy Spirit was her guardian, leader, judge, beautifier, as it were, a sponsal leader. Mary has all perfection possible to a creature, with the Spirit prepurifying and sanctifying her: Gabriel found the Spirit more present in Mary than in heaven. Through this total presence, wherein T. sees a form of circumincession (perichoresis) (qv), Mary is the image of the Spirit, "by participation and grace so that alone among all creatures she should embody his exemplar and the graces of the Son should shine in her. She is thus the fountain and distributor of all graces. She cares for all as she is our mother."

---

[1]Sermo in Sanctissimam Deiparam, nova series, Lateranum, Rome, 1935; cf. B. Schultze, S.J., "Theologi palamitae saec. XIV de mediatione Mariae," in De Mariologia et Oecumenismo, ed. C. Balić, O.F.M., Rome 1962, esp. 398–403; M. Candal, S.J., "El 'Sermo in Deiparam' de Teofano Niceno," Marianum, 26 (1964), 72–103; M. Jugie, A.A., L'Immaculée Conception dans l'Ecriture sainte et dans la tradition orientale, Rome, 1952, 240–46; M. O'Carroll, C.S.Sp., Theotokos, Wilmington, 1981, s.v. Theophanes of Nicaea, 341;   [2]Page references in detail apud Schultze, op.cit.

which he made all things, as it is his power and wisdom, taking on the person of the Father and Lord of all things, came to paradise in the person of God and conversed with Adam. For divine Scripture itself teaches us that Adam said that this voice was heard by him; but what else is that voice but the Word of God, which is also his Son, not as poets and mythologists imagine sons of the gods begotten from intercourse, but, as truth relates, the Word ever existing and set in the heart of God (Logon endiatheton en cardia Theou)? Before anything was made, he used him as his counsellor; for he is his mind and his prudence. When God wished to make those things which he had decreed, he begot this Word (ton Logon egenesse prophorikon) externally, the first-born of every creature; not, however, as if he was empty of the Word, but bringing forth the Word and always united with the Word. These things the Sacred Scriptures teach us, and as many as they are inspired by the Holy Spirit, among whom John says, 'In the beginning was the Word and the Word was with God,' teaching that at the beginning was God alone and the Word with him. Then he adds, And the Word was God; all things were made by him and without him nothing was made.' The Word then, since he is God and begotten of God, the Father of all, sends in any place he wishes, and when he comes there, he is heard and seen, sent by him and found in place."[2] T. thinks of the Spirit principally in terms of prophetic action.

---

[1]Ad Autolycum with Eng. tr. R.M. Grant, Oxford Early Christian Texts, 1970; PG 6, 1023–1168; Trois Livres à Autolycus, tr. J. Sender, ed. G. Bardy (qv) SC 20, 1948; F. Loofs, Theophilus von Antioch und die anderen theologischen Quellen bei Irenäus, TU 46.2, 1930; R.M. Grant, HTR 40 (1947), Altaner, 75–77; Quasten, I, 236–42; E. Rapisarda, EC XI (1953) 1952f;   [2]Ad Autolycum 2, 22; PG 6, 1088; SC 20, 105.

THEOPHILUS OF ANTIOCH (later 2nd century)

T., one of the Apologists, has a place in the history of Trinitarian doctrine as he first used the word Triados, Trinity: "The three days which preceded the lights, were an image of the Trinity, of God, his Word and his Wisdom."[1] Like all the writers of his time T. directed his attention to the Logos; he furthered theological development thereon. His distinction between the Logos endiathetos and the Logos prophorikos was original: "But his Word, by

THOMAS AQUINAS, ST., DOCTOR OF THE CHURCH (1225–1274)

T. brought all the elements of the Trinitarian theologies of his predecessors into a metaphysical synthesis consonant with his Aristotelian philosophy.[1] With him we have an ontological basis for the dogma. His doctrine is principally found in: In I Sent., d. 3 to 31; Contra Gent. IV, 1–28; Contra Err. Graec.; De Pot., q. 8 to 10; and Summa Theologiae, 1a q. 27–43. Fr. B. de Margerie, in his work on the Trinity, lists references to over 100 passages in the writings of T.[2] The essence of his teaching is, unquestionably, contained in the *Summa*. To read these pages is to understand how this theological system, wherein reason joins with and is enriched by divine revelation, has had such enduring impact on subsequent ages. T. considers successively processions in the godhead, relations, and persons, showing how relations as subsistent are constitutive of persons.

T. also considers each person separately, not without discussing our way of knowing them, coming down with a firm negative on the possibility of rational knowledge. Dealing with the Son he gives, among other themes, a valuable treatment of the "Image" (qv). He shows at length how the Spirit comes "from the Son" and "through the Son" (see FILIOQUE), and explains the names given to the Spirit, "Love" and "Gift."

T. then considers the persons in relation to the essence, to the properties, and to notional acts. He turns finally to the question of equality in divine persons and the divine missions.

T. is indebted to his predecessors in Trinitarian theology, especially Augustine (qv); he also quotes Hilary (qv) and Boethius. When he quotes the Athanasian Creed (qv) he takes it as the work of St. Athanasius (qv). Some references to Pseudo-Dionysius and John of Damascus (qv) and two to "*Doctores Graecorum*"[4] are the total of his evident debt to the Greek Fathers; he inherited much more, not least the orthodox teaching forged at the eastern councils.

The view expressed about "personality" in God is worked out in considerable detail; he does prefer the word person: "*Person* signifies that which is most perfect in the whole of nature, namely that which is subsistent in rational nature. Then since all that is of perfection must be attributed to God, because his essence contains in it all perfection, it is appropriate that this word should be applied to (spoken of) God; not, nevertheless, in the same way as it is applied to (spoken of) creatures, but in a more excellent way (*excellentiori modo*); as are other names applied to God which we give to creatures; which was shown already when we were speaking of divine names."[5]

T. generally follows the definition of person given by Boethius (qv) "*substantia individua rationalis naturae*," the individual substance of rational nature. But he concedes that in divine realities it may need to be improved, and he quotes Richard

of St. Victor's (qv) substitute, *divinae naturae incommunicabilis existentia*, the incommunicable existence of divine nature. On subsistent relation as the basis of divine personality he writes: "Person in any nature signifies what is distinctive in that nature; as in human nature it signifies this flesh, these bones, this soul, the individuating principles of man; which though they are not intrinsic to the meaning of person in general, are so to the meaning of person in man. But in divine realities distinction only occurs by the relations of origin as has already been said. But relation in divine realities is not as an accident inhering in a subject, but is the very divine essence. Therefore it is subsisting as the divine essence subsists. Just then as the godhead is God, so the divine fatherhood is God the Father, who is a divine person. Therefore a divine person signifies relation as subsistent; and this is to signify a relation in the manner (*per modum*) of substance, which is a hypostasis subsisting in divine nature; though the one subsisting in the divine nature is not anything other than the divine nature."[6] From this general statement T. draws a number of conclusions as to consideration of hypostasis and substance. The metaphysical basis he thought solid. When people recommend dropping the word person they should attend to his qualifying phrase "in more excellent manner."

A point which was to influence the passing agreement of east and west on the *Filioque* (qv) at Florence was T's defence of the thesis that the Spirit proceeds from the Father through the Son: "Because therefore the Son holds from the Father that by which the Holy Spirit proceeds from him, it can be said that the Father through the Son breathes the Holy Spirit, or that the Holy Spirit proceeds from the Father through the Son; which is the same thing."[7]

But the Angelic Doctor is emphatic and comprehensive on the essential meaning of the *Filioque*: the Spirit proceeds from the Son. "If he were not from him, in no way could he be personally distinguished from him. "He then argues this proposition very closely on the basis of his doctrine of the persons as subsistent relations. He is equally lucid and strong on the thesis that the Father and Son are one principle of the Holy Spirit, as with the doctrine of missions, showing the difference between visible and invisible missions, the relationship between processions and missions.

All these concepts have been part of the fabric of scholastic theology since the thirteenth century, the object of study by the great commentators, formalised and at times possibly dessicated in the manuals, still inspiring great dogmatic treatises in the twentieth century writers, Louis Billot and Bernard Lonergan (qv), acclaimed by Scheeben as supreme.

---

[1]Besides the great commentators cf. H.D. Simonin, "Autour de la solution thomiste du problème de l'amour", *Archives d'Histoire doctr. et litt. du Moyen Age*, 6 (1931) 174–276; M.T.L. Penido, "Gloses sur la procession d'amour dans la Trinité," *ETL* 14 (1937), 33–68 and 15 (1938) 318–344; *id.*, "Cur non Spiritus Sanctus a Patre Deo genitus: S.Augustin et S. Thomas," *RThom* 1930, 508–527; A. Krapiec, "Inquisitio circa Divi Thomae doctrinam de Spiritu Sancto prout amore," *Divus Thomas* (Piacenza), 53 (1950), 474–495; S.J. Dockx, "Note sur la procession de terme dans la volonté," *Angelicum* 15 (1938), 419–428; H.-F. Dondaine, O.P., *La Trinité*, ed of S. T. with French tr., notes, 2 vols, Paris, 1943; H. Barre, C.S.Sp., *Trinité que j'adore*, Paris, 1964, 94–100; A. Malet, "La synthèse de la personne et de la nature dans la théologie trinitaire de S. Thomas," *RThom* 54 (1954), 483–522, 55 (1955), 43–84; *id.*, *Personne et amour dans la théologie trinitaire de S.Thomas*, 1956; P. Vanier, S.J., *Théologie trinitaire chez saint Thomas d'Aquin*, Paris, Institut d'Etudes Medievales, Montreal, 1953; E. Bailleux, "Le personnalisme de S.Thomas en théologie trinitaire," *RThom* 61 (1961), 25–42; *id.*, "La creation oeuvre de la Trinité selon S.Thomas," *ibid.*, 62 (1962), 27–60; G. Hibbert, Mystery and Metaphysics in the Trinitarian theology of St. Thomas, *ITQ* 31 (1964), 187–213; C. Strater, S.J., "Le point de départ du traité thomiste de la Trinité," *Sciences Eccl.*, 14 (1962), 71–89; F. Bourassa, S.J., *Questions de théologie trinitaire*, Rome, 1970, *passim*; Congar, *The Holy Spirit*, III, 116–127; J. Pelikan, "The Doctrine of the Filioque in Thomas Aquinas and its Patristic Antecedents," *St.Thomas Aquinas Commemorative Studies* 1, Toronto, 1974, 315–336; W.J. Hill, *The Three-Personed God*, 62–78; [2]*La Trinité chrétienne dans l'histoire*, 486–88; [3]q. 35; [4]Ia, q 35, a.2, and ad 4; cf. G. Bardy, "Sur les sources patristiques grecques de S.Thomas dans la Ie partie de la Somme théologique," *RSPT* 12 (1923), 493–502; [5]q. XXIX, a. 3; [6]*ibid.*, a. 4; [7]q. XXXVI, a.3.

TOLEDO, COUNCIL OF, XI (675)

Important among the eighteen national councils held in the city between 400 and 700 because of the lengthy profession of faith which was adopted.[1] It was called by King Wamba and the Metropolitan, Quiricius, presided; it was attended by seventeen bishops, two representatives of absent bishops and six abbots. Considerably more than half the text deals with the Trinity; the rest with the Incarnation and Redemption. On the Trinity it brings together the teaching of the previous councils and Fathers; it is explicit on the *Filioque* (qv). A central passage is typical: "This is the account of the Holy Trinity that has been handed down. We must call and believe it to be not triple but triune. Neither can we rightly say that in one God is the Trinity, but that one God is the Trinity. In the relative names of Persons, however, the Father refers to the Son, the Son to the Father, and the Holy Spirit to both, in that while relatively three Persons are asserted, yet we believe they are one nature or substance. Neither as three Persons, so do we predicate three substances, but one substance, however three Persons. For as he is Father not to himself, but to the Son; and as he is Son not to himself but to the Father, similarly also the Holy Spirit refers in a relative sense not to himself but to the Father and to the Son, in that he is proclaimed the Spirit of the Father and the Son."[2]

There are no anathemas. It has been suggested that residual elements of Priscillianism (qv) were thought of; there is a statement that the "Son is Son of God by nature, not by adoption" but nothing further on that subject. The creed may have been composed by an unknown fifth-century theologian and received by the council. It cannot be proved that Innocent III approved it.

---

[1]Cf. R. d'Abadal, *Els Concils de Toledo, Homenaje a Johannes Vinke*, 1962, 63, 21–45; J. Madoz, S.J., *Le symbole du XIe concile de Tolède*, 1938; A. Michel, *DTC* XV, 1, (1946), 1176–1208; I. E. Alberca, *NCE*, XIV (1967), 189–91; [2]DS 528.

TRITHEISM

A fundamental error which does not take the crude form of affirming three gods, but which undermines the unity of substance, identifying it exclusively and separately with each person,[1] denying therefore the consubstantiality, the unicity of the nature with the three separate persons. The heresy, for such it is, has a varied history. It was supported by some Monophysites in the sixth century, John Philiponus (d. after 600) best known of them: just as Peter, Paul and John are three individuals of the species "man," so there are three individuals of the species "God": three component substances in one joint substance. All of this was largely theory; John Philiponus was faithful to the Church. Later the views of Roscellinus (qv) and Gilbert de la Porrée (qv) led to some misunderstanding, and they too were arraigned on grounds of tritheistic heresy: the Councils of Soissons and of Rheims (*qv*) dealt with them. Influenced possibly by Gilbert, Joachim of Fiore (*qv*) propounded a theory which left him open to the charge of tritheism: the result was the pronouncement of the Fourth Lateran Council (*qv*). In the nineteenth century Anton Günther (*qv*) lapsed in the same direction, and there is another instance in the present century, Grutzmacher, who wrote of the three-one God, our God. The Mormons have also been suspect, as they only accept a reduced form of belief in the Trinity.

[1] J. Brinktine, *Die Lehre von Gott*, 2 Band, *Von der göttlichen Trinität*, 1954, 21ff; M. Schmaus, *LTK*, X, 365, 66; J. Lebreton, *DTC* XV, 1860.

U

UNITARIANISM

Monarchianism (*qv*) in the early Church was a form of U., for this theory declares that there is but one person in God, and denies also, as a logical consequence of this view, that Jesus Christ was God. Modern U. dates from the age of the Reformation. It has taken life in different areas, principally Poland, Hungary, England and the United States. In the sixteenth century the names which made history were Juan de Valdes (c. 1500–1541), Bernardino Ochino (1487–1564) and Michael Servetus (1511–1553).

In Poland the life-span of U. was relatively short. A division in the Reformed Church was accentuated by the arrival of Italian evangelical rationalists, foremost among them a Piedmontese physician, George Blandrata. As the division continued those excluded because of their anti-trinitarian views formed the Minor Reformed Church of Poland, 1565. An Italian immigrant, Faustus Socinus, led the movement until his death, 1604. The following year the Racovian Catechism summarised Socinian teaching: the Scriptures were the sole ground of truth; the way of salvation was knowledge and a holy life; the knowledge of God, with rejection of the Trinity; the person of Christ, a wonderful man divinised by his resurrection; his prophetic role; his kingship; his priesthood and the Church. Pressure was on the U. in Poland from 1638: their college at Racow was suppressed in 1638; twenty years later they were expelled.

Initially support was available to the Hungarian U. from the king, John Sigismund; the movement here too had been furthered by Blandrata. It encountered persecution, even after recognition as a legitimate religion, but survived.

John Biddle is considered the founder of U. in England, with *XII Arguments drawn out of the Scripture* (1647) and *A Twofold Catechism* (1654). Unitarians were excluded from benefit by the Toleration Act (1689); they were legally penalised until 1813. T. Lindsey in the eighteenth century and J. Priestly, T. Belsham and especially J. Martineau in the nineteenth furthered the spread of U., which had legal difficulties over transfer of chapels; it penetrated a section of the educated classes. It had a journal of liberal theology, the *Hibbert Journal*. A strain of radical U. showed itself early in the present century. Despite simplification of the organisational structure, by the amalgamation in 1925 of the century-old British and Foreign Unitarian Association with the National Conference to form the General Assembly of Unitarian and Free Churches, membership continues to decline.

U. in the United States arose within New England Congregationalism. The first Unitarian group had been in King's Chapel, Boston: after some time Unitarians were accepted in Congregationalist churches. The American Unitarian Association was founded in 1825, and in 1865 the first National Conference of Unitarian Churches was formed. William Ellery Channing, by his "Baltimore Sermon" in 1819 and Ralph Waldo Emerson by his Divinity School address in 1825, had given noted prestige to American U., which in 1852 already was able to organise outside New England.

Religious humanism has affected U. It declined but showed some revival capacity when F.M. Eliot and D. McLean Greeley were presidents of the American Unitarian Association; there was support from Harvard Divinity School. A "Council of Liberal Churches (Unitarian Universalist)" was set up in 1953 to foster cooperation between Unitarians and Universalists. In 1961 the Unitarian Universalist Association was established.

[1] Cf. E.M. Wilbur, *A History of Unitarianism, Socinianism and its Antecedents*, Cambridge, Mass, 1946; *id., A History of Unitarianism in Transylvania, England and America, ibid.* 1952; C. Wright, *The Beginnings of Unitarianism in America*, Boston, 1955; *id., The Liberal Christians, Essays on American Unitarian History*, Boston, 1970; H.B. Scholfield, *Unitarian History: A Brief. An Information Manual for the Use of Unitarian and Universalist Churches, Societies and Fellowships*, Wellesley Hills, Massachusetts, 1958; D.B. Parke, *The Epic of Unitarianism*, Boston, 1951; H.H. Cheetham, *Unitarianism and Universalism*, Boston, 1962.

V

VATICAN II

There is no single document of Vatican II which has the Trinity as its theme.[1] But throughout many of the principal documents there is a recurrence of teaching on each of the persons, in close association with the other two. Thus to many of the of the conciliar themes there is given a Trinitarian enrichment: the role of the divine persons is explicitly stated, or the thought content is given a Trinitarian structure, or set in a Trinitarian background. The word "Trinity" is not often used; the language is biblical; the orientation is towards the "economy," not the immanent life of the triune godhead.

We begin with the basic conciliar text, *Lumen Gentium*. In ch.I the role of the Father, Son and Holy Spirit is, in each case, described as to the origin of the Church (see THE CHURCH): "He (the Father) planned to assemble in the holy Church all those who would believe in Christ. Already from the beginning of the world the foreshadowing of the Church took place. She was prepared for in a remarkable way throughout the history of the people of Israel and by means of the Old Covenant . . . . The Son therefore came on mission from his Father. It was in him, before the foundation of the world, that the Father chose us and predestined us to become adopted sons, for in him it has pleased the Father to re-establish all things (cf. Eph 1:4–5 and 10). To carry out the will of the Father, Christ inaugurated the kingdom of heaven on earth and revealed to us the mystery of the Father . . . . When the work which the Father had given the Son to do on earth (cf. Jn 17:4) was accomplished, the Holy Spirit was sent on the day of Pentecost in order that he might forever sanctify the Church, and thus all believers would have access to the Father through Christ in the one Spirit (cf. Eph 2:18) . . . . Thus the Church shines forth as 'a people made one with the unity of the Father, the Son, and the Holy Spirit.'"[2]

Before taking some applications of this general doctrine, we should study the passage in *Ad Gentes* which complements it. It is known that considerable rewriting took place on this text between the third and last council sessions, some of it prompted by an article which expressed the dissatisfaction of the Orthodox with the scant treatment in council ecclesiology of the Holy Spirit.[3] That request was met; the Trinitarian dimension was also stated: "The pilgrim Church is missionary by her very nature. For it is from the mission of the Son and the mission of the Holy Spirit that she takes her origin, in accordance with the decree of God the Father. This decree flows from 'that fountain of love' or charity within God the Father. From him, who is the 'origin without origin', the Son is begotten and the Holy Spirit proceeds through the Son."

The Council next considers "God's universal design for the salvation of the human race." To this end he sent his Son "clothed in human flesh" in order that through this son he might snatch men from the power of darkness and of Satan (cf. Col 1:13; Acts 10:38) and that in this Son he might reconcile the world to himself (cf. 2 Cor 5:19). Through him, God made all orders of existence." There follows a brief summary of the lifework of Christ, concluding thus: "But what was once preached by the Lord or what was once wrought in him for the saving of the human race, must be proclaimed and spread abroad to the ends of the earth (Acts 1:8), starting from Jerusalem (cf. Lk 24:27), so that what was accomplished for the salvation of all men may, in the course of time, achieve its universal effect." "Christ sent the Holy Spirit from the Father to exercise inwardly his saving influence, and to promote the spread of the Church. Without doubt the Holy Spirit was at work in the world before Christ was glorified. On the day of Pentecost, however, he came down on the disciples that he might remain with them forever (cf. Jn 14:16); on that day the Church was openly displayed to the crowds and the spread of the gospel among the nations, through preaching, was begun. Finally, on that day was foreshadowed the union of all people in the catholicity of the faith by means of the Church of the New Alliance, a Church which speaks every language, understands and embraces all tongues in charity, and thus overcomes the dispersion of Babel. The "acts of the apostles" began with Pentecost, just as Christ was conceived in the Virgin Mary with the coming of the Holy Spirit and was moved to begin his ministry by the descent of the same Holy Spirit, who came down upon him while he was praying."[4]

We have in these texts a Trinitarian soteriology, with the Trinity involved in the work of salvation more than has been stated in any previous pronouncements of the Teaching Authority. There is an echo, if not an application, of the general principles in the Constitution on the Liturgy: "God who 'wills all men to be saved and come to the knowledge of his the truth' (1 Tim 2:4), 'who in many times and various ways spoke of old to the fathers through the prophets' (Heb 1:1), when the fullness of time had come sent his Son, the Word made flesh, anointed by the Holy spirit, to preach the Gospel to the poor, to heal the contrite of heart, to be a bodily and spiritual medicine: the Mediator between God and man."[5]

Related also to the Trinitarian outlook is this succinct statement about Our Lady: "Redeemed, in a more exalted fashion by reason of the merits of her Son and united to him by a close and indissoluble bond, she is endowed with the high office and dignity of the Mother of the Son of God, and therefore she is also the beloved daughter of the Father and the sanctuary of the Holy Spirit." The sentence occurs at the beginning of the Marian chapter of *Lumen Gentium,* which ends with a prayer that "All families of peoples, whether they are honoured with the title of Christian or whether they still do not know the Saviour, may be happily gathered together in peace and harmony into one People of God, for the glory of the Most Holy and Undivided Trinity."[6]

Nor is it any wonder that when the Council faced the problem of opening out the Church to those with whom it wished to achieve unity, it should still turn its attention to the "Son of God sent by the Father" and recall that "the Lord Jesus poured forth the Spirit whom he had promised." The climax of its theological reflections is: "This is the sacred mystery of the unity of the Church, in Christ and through Christ, with the Holy Spirit energizing its various functions. The highest exemplar and source of this mystery is the unity, in the Trinity of Persons, of one God, the Father, and the Son and in the Holy Spirit."[7]

On the fundamental subject of divine revelation, central to all theological speculation, Vatican II, as is well known, changed the approach from propositional to personalist, in effect to Christocentrism: "The most intimate truth which this revelation gives us about God and the salvation of man shines forth in Christ, who is himself both the Mediator and the fullness of revelation."[8] Preliminary to that affirmation there is an overall view given thus: "It pleased God, in his goodness and wisdom, to reveal himself and to make known the mystery of his will (cf. Eph 1:9). His will was that men should have access to the Father, through Christ, the Word made flesh, in the Holy Spirit, and thus become sharers in the divine nature (cf. Eph 2:18; 2 Pet 1:4)."[9] If Christ is the centre of revelation it has been rightly said that its structure, in the teaching of Vatican II, is Trinitarian. But the structure is in outline, not developed.

All these texts do not amount to a close-knit body of doctrine on the Trinity. The Council Fathers were, possibly unconsciously, in these and some parallel passages noted, answering Karl Rahner's query: Why, if the Trinity is the fundamental mystery of our religion, knowledge of it the most important truth of revealed religion, is there so little said or written and apparently thought about it? A passage in the *Decree on Ecumenism* could have been more fully developed: "The faithful should remember that they promote union among Christians better, that indeed they live it better, when they try to live holier lives according to the Gospel. For the closer their union with the Father, the Word, and the Spirit, the more deeply and easily they will be able to grow in mutual brotherly love."[10] If some such thought had not been expressed it might, unjustly no doubt, be said that a young Carmelite nun had something to teach the combined brains and authority of the twentieth century Church (see ELIZABETH OF THE TRINITY).

Noteworthy too is the fact that it was a Council given a pastoral orientation which did have insights of this kind. This will no doubt be taken into account by students of the "economic–immanent" Trinity debate.

---

[1]Cf. N. Silvanes, O.SS.T., "Panoramica Trinitaria del Concilio," *Est. Trinit.*, I, 1967, 7–44; B. de Margerie, S.J., "La Doctrine trinitaire de Vatican II," in *La Trinité chrétienne dans l'histoire*, 303–331; N. Silanes, "Trinidad y Revelación en la Constitución Dei Verbum," *EstTrin*, XVII (1983), 143–214;   [2]Art. 2–4;   [3]N. Nissiotis, "The main ecclesiological problems in the Second Vatican Council and the position of the Non-Roman Churches facing it," *The Ecumenical Review*, 1964, 31–62;   [4]*Decree on the Missionary Activity of the Church*, 2–4;   [5]Art. 5;   [6]Art. 53, 69;   [7]*Decree on Ecumenism*, 3;   [8]*Constitution on Divine Revelation*, 2;   [9]*Ibid.*;   [10]Art. 7.

VICTORINUS AFER CAIUS MARIUS (4th century)

African born, V., after his conversion to Christianity, resigned his post as rhetor in Rome and devoted himself to refutation of Arianism.[1] His work *De Trinitate* comprises a reply to a series of objections against the orthodox doctrine by one Candidus, and three books against Arius. V's aim is to use philosophical argument as much as possible; in this he occasionally becomes difficult to follow.

In the reply to Candidus V. deals with the objections that generation would offend the immutability of God and that if the *Logos* (qv) is begotten he must come from nothingness. He deals at length with the *Logos* idea. Taking Nicaea as his starting-point in the second book, he first analyses many Pauline texts to reach a favourable conclusion on the consubstantial (qv), dismissing

homoiousion and the Photinians on the way. He returns to the *homoiousion* to expose its paltry history and then expounds at great length his idea of the consubstantial: the Logos is the act, the image, the reflection, the Son of God: consubstantial because all things are in him, through him, for him: image of God as Son of Mary, Logos as Son of God; consubstantial because he is the power and wisdom of God, Son of God because he is the life. On then to the triumphant conclusion: the generation of the Son implies no change in God. V. winds up with swift rebuttal of the Patripassians, the Arians, the moderate Arians, Marcel of Ancyra, and Photinus with Basil of Ancyra and his coterie.

In the second book he goes over some of the same ground, is at pains to convey his idea of *substantia*, and discusses the problem of translating *homoousion* while answering objections. In the third book he first summarizes the previous books, attempting a synthesis which brings into prominence his idea of the Logos, light of light, the image of light consubstantial with the light.

V. too elaborates his theology of the Trinity on his theory of mutual implication and personal predominance. He draws on Neoplatonic triad, being, living, and thought; being, living, and thought mutually imply each other and are distinguished by the predominance of one over the other according to its proper mode. V. also links this schema with his—an opposition between being and form, substance and movement. V. has mostly spoken of the Father and the Son, but he hopes to establish the hypostatic distinction between Christ and the Holy Spirit, though he knows nothing of the procession of the Spirit: in fact he speaks of the Son as double, Christ and the Holy Spirit, for there is only one generation, one movement in God. To safeguard the Trinity V. resorts to a double dyad. All his theological ideas he applies to the working of the Trinity in the "economy."

It would be too much to say that V. was the first of the Scholastics, but he made a notable attempt to unite philosophy with the truths of the faith as contained in Sacred Scripture and interpreted by the Teaching Authority. He also wrote three poems to the Trinity.

---

[1]Works PL 8, 993–1310; CSEL 83, 1971 ff, ed. P. Henry, S.J., P. Hadot; SC 68, 69 *De Trinitate*, tr. P. Hadot, ed. P. Henry, S.J.; cf. P. Hadot, *Marius Victorinus, Recherches sur sa vie et ses oeuvres*, Paris, 1971; P. Sejourne, *DTC* XV, 2, 1950, 2887–2954; *ibid.*, G. Bardy; Altaner, 368ff.

W—Z

WILLIAM OF ST. THIERRY (c.1085–1148)
A friend of St. Bernard of Clairvaux, W. was first a Benedictine, then a Cistercian[1] and a worthy representative of the powerful current of sound mystical writing which rose in the twelfth century. His theology of the Trinity, formulated a century before St. Thomas Aquinas, was a reply to Abelard (qv) but stands on its own as an exposition of the western tradition, dominated by his master, St. Augustine. superior in some sensitive points to St. Anselm (qv), he was influenced even to the extent of literal borrowing of St. Maximus the Confessor (qv). W.'s basic work here is the *Enigma fidei*; ideas are found elsewhere in his extensive writings.

W. aimed to give back to the Augustinian analogies their true theological meaning, this by replacing them in the revealed perspective of the Trinitarian missions: "'Go baptize all nations in the name of the Father, and of the Son and of the Holy Spirit' (Mt 28:19) said the eternal Truth. He would certainly not have said it if the reality did not exist. Nor would he have said 'in the name' but 'in the names', if the Father, the Son and the Spirit were not one and the same God. What further proof do we need? If God the Father were not distinguished from the Word his own Son, we should not read in the book of Truth, 'He sent his Son'. And if he was his own gift or the gift of his own Son, we would no more read, 'He whom the Father will send in my name' and 'He whom I will send from the Father'. Thus the Father is not the Son and the Son is not the Spirit."[2]

W. avoids, like St. Anselm, reducing the person to the essential act which is at its origin. "The Son and the Spirit are as much in their 'principle' (point of beginning) as in themselves, and that from all eternity, for the three divine Persons possess themselves, one in the other, and exist one for the other."[3]

The persons are relative, even in their very names: "I can never name a person in the singular without referring to another by the very name which I give the first. Impossible to evoke one without implying the other two . . . . Doubtless I cannot pronounce at one and the same time the three divine Persons, but I am no more allowed to grasp them separately than to confuse them together in my language and thought."

W. sees in the order of processions the manifestation of consubstantial communion of the Father and the Son, and of the Son and the Holy Spirit: "Principle of the divinity, God the Father is said to be the principle in regard to the Son whom he begets and in regard to the Holy Spirit who proceeds from them. The Father and the Son are in reality one only principle of the Holy Spirit, but the Father principally because it is from the Father that the Son receives, in birth, that by which he is with him the principle of the Holy Spirit.

This 'principally' must not be understood as precedence in time, nor as priority, as of a degree of dignity, of greatness or majesty. It simply indicates the *quid de quo*, the *quid ad quem* or the *quid ad quid* in the nature of the consubstantial Trinity. The Father taking his origin from none other is in reality the origin of the divinity. It is from him that the Son possesses what he receives from him in birth. From the Father and the Son likewise, but 'principally' from the Father is the Holy Spirit, who proceeding from one and the other, has in common with with one and the other, to be what they are."[4]

Here, as elsewhere W. shows his understanding of the Augustinian *"principaliter"*. He has enlightening passages on the Spirit as the Gift of God, source of all divine gifts to man,[5] artisan of our adoptive sonship, of our divinisation. He worked out a truly Trinitarian spirituality: memory corresponding to the Father, reason to the Son, love to the Holy Spirit.

[1]Works PL 180, 201–726 and inter opera St. Bernard; cf. J.M. Dechanet, O.S.B., *Guillaume de St.Thierry, L'homme et son oeuvre*, Paris 1942; *id.*, in *DSp*, s.v. VI (1967), 1241–63, with bibl.; O. Brooke, "The Trinitarian Aspect of the Soul's Ascent to God in the Theology of William of St.Thierry," *RTAM* 26 (1959) 85–127; *id.*, "The Speculative Development of the Trinitarian Theology of William of St. Thierry," *RTAM* 27 (1960), 193–211; M.-J. Le Guillou, O.P., "Guillaume de S.Thierry, l'equilibre catholique," *Istina*, 1972, 367–74; *History of Christian Spirituality* ed. J. Leclercq, L. Bouyer.; [2]*Enigma fidei*, PL 184, 408A–C; [3]*Ibid.*, 427A; [3]*Ibid.*, 429B–D; [5]*Ibid.*, 430D–431A.

WORLD COUNCIL OF CHURCHES

In 1946 the provisional committee organising the first meeting of WCC sent invitations to 95 churches to join on the basis of this formula: "The World Council of Churches is a fellowship of churches which accept the Lord Jesus Christ as God and Saviour."[1] At the first assembly in Amsterdam, 1948, 144 churches accepted membership on this basis—Unitarians (*qv*) are not members. From 1961 the Roman Catholic Church appoints observers to assemblies; since 1968 it has accepted full membership of the Faith and Order Commission; from that year too a joint secretariat exists linking WCC work in social and international justice with the Vatican Secretariat for Justice and Peace.

Dissatisfaction was felt among member churches at the first basic formula: queries and requests mostly turned on the need for a more explicit Christocentrism, a reference to the Sacred Scriptures and especially an affirmation of Trinitarian belief. The matter came to a head at the third assembly in New Delhi, 1961. On 2 December, by 386 votes to 37 with 7 abstentions, 426 participating out of a total of 577 electors, the following formula was adopted: "The World Council of Churches is a fellowship of churches which confess the Lord Jesus Christ as God and Saviour, according to the Scriptures and which seek to fulfil together their common calling to the glory of the One God, Father, Son and Holy Spirit."

The statement is bare and in its Trinitarian phrasing mostly oriented to worship. The word "confess" is stronger than "accept" in the previous formula. In the course of a lively debate which preceded the vote, to the objection made by Baptists, as to what Scripture text justified the imposition of belief in the Trinity, Archbishop Nicodim, Orthodox Metropolitan of Leningrad, replied: "The new basis is linked with the Baptism which makes us Christians: Go, teach all nations, baptize them in the name of the Father and of the Son and of the Holy Spirit."

One of the Greek Orthodox present, Alivizatos, expressed the joy of the Orthodox generally. Since 1948 the Greek Church had been asking for the addition, for belief in the Trinity is distinctive of the Christian faith, and is in harmony with revelation and with the early tradition. There is no other Christian faith than that in God the Father, Son and Holy Spirit. At the end of the debate Mr. H. E. Fry, president of the New Delhi assembly, asked for all delegates present to join in thanksgiving to the Trinity for having allowed the churches to make this step which would lead them to the unity willed by Christ.

[1]A.A. Wenger, *NRT* 84 (1962), 63–71; B. de Margerie, S.J., *La Trinité*, 300–301; Oxford Dictionary, s.v., 1499.

ZWINGLI, ULRICH (1484–1531)—See Reformation, The